Dec. 2024

To Geoffrey
with grateful memories
of fine visits to St Helen's
and much more!

The History of Easter Laughter

Benny Grey Schuster

The History of Easter Laughter

Johannes Oecolampadius' *De risu paschali* from 1518 with an Introduction, Annotated Translation, and an Account of the Cultural, Ecclesiastical, and Theological Transformation of Laughter

Berlin · Bruxelles · Chennai · Lausanne · New York · Oxford

Library of Congress Cataloging-in-Publication Data
A CIP catalog record for this book has been applied for at the Library of Congress.

Bibliographic information published by the Deutsche Nationalbibliothek.
The German National Library lists this publication in the German National Bibliography; detailed bibliographic data is available online at http://dnb.d-nb.de.

Cover Illustration: 1490s fresco in Vrangstrup church, Diocese of Roskilde © Benny Grey Schuster

ISBN 978-3-631-91483-0 (Print)
E-ISBN 978-3-631-91484-7 (E-PDF)
E-ISBN 978-3-631-91485-4 (EPUB)
DOI 10.3726/b22285

© 2024 Peter Lang Group AG, Lausanne
Published by Peter Lang GmbH, Berlin, Deutschland

info@peterlang.com - www.peterlang.com

All rights reserved.
All parts of this publication are protected by copyright.
Any utilization outside the strict limits of the copyright law, without the permission of the publisher, is forbidden and liable to prosecution. This applies in particular to reproductions, translations, microfilming, and storage and processing in electronic retrieval systems.

When the Son of God came to the gates of hell and touched them with his cross,
Two devils stretched forth their long noses to serve as bars for the gate.
When Christ pounded, however, then the door and its hinges burst open,
breaking off the two devils' noses.
The scholars of that time called such stories risus paschalis.
Johann Mathesius: *[History of ... Dr Martin Luther in 17 Sermons],* 1566

When you preach on the doctrine of justification
people fall asleep and cough,
but when you begin to tell stories and give examples
they are fully attentive and listen carefully.
I believe that many speakers among us
preach so that I fall off the bench and up again.
Martin Luther: *Table Talk,* 1532 *(WA TR 1, no. 2408)*

Et factum est dum fabularentur et secum quaererent
et ipse Iesus adpropinquans ibat cum illis.

Luke 24:15 *(Vulgate)*

In memory of Martin Sander Harbsmeier (1976-2013),
whose work on the Danish translation of Johannes Oecolampadius'
De risu paschali was pivotal for this book.

Table of Contents

Introduction 11
   1. Easter Laughter as a Denominational Point of Contention 17
   2. (Easter) Laughter as a Historical Point of Contention 20
   3. A Note on the Outline of this Book 25

Chapter I: What *Was* Easter Laughter? 27
   1. Distinguishing Characteristics of Easter Laughter 27
      A Brief Excursus on Bakhtin and 'the Culture of Laughter' 30
   2. The Means Used to Stimulate Easter Laughter 34
   3. How Old Is Easter Laughter? 44
   4. The Geographical Spread of Easter Laughter 55

Chapter II: The History of the Effects of Easter Laughter 57
   1. Continuation of the Practice of Easter Laughter 58
   2. Easter Laughter as a Denominational Point of Contention until the Baroque Period 61
      i. The Beginning of Its Critique 61
      ii. Lutheran Critique 69
      iii. Oecolampadius' Legacy 71
   3. Brief Characterisation of the Critique of Easter Laughter After the Baroque Period 78
   4. Re-evaluation I: Nuances in Luther's and Mathesius' Critique 80
   5. Re-evaluation II: Theological Motives Behind the Protestant Critique of Easter Laughter 86
   6. The Scholarly Rediscovery of Easter Laughter in the First Half of the 20th Century 95
   7. The Scholarly Study of Easter Laughter during the Second Half of the 20th Century 98

8. General Classification of the Way Easter Laughter Has Been Treated as a Literary Topos in Scholarly and Popular Literature of the 20th Century 100

9. Easter Laughter in the Scholarly Literature since 1990 104

Chapter III: Arguments For and Against Easter Laughter 107

1. Pragmatic Arguments 108
2. Pedagogical Arguments 111
3. Tradition as an Argument 115
4. Anthropological Arguments 117
5. Joy as an Argument 120
    i. The Easter Hymn 120
       Intermezzo: The Concept of Dignity in Child-Rearing 125
    ii. Laughter of the Heart 129
    iii. Scholasticism: 136
        a. Silence – Humility 136
        b. Aristotle and Aquinas 138
        c. The Four Temperaments 145
        d. Sin and Purgatory 147
    iv. A Couple of Female Mystics – and a Male 151
    v. Summary 154
6. The Resurrection as an Argument 155
    i. Spring in Nature and Myth 156
       A Brief Excursus on Abraham, Sarah, Isaac, and Laughter 159
    ii. Sexuality and Fertility 161
    iii. The Uroboric Powers of Laughter 165

Chapter IV: Did Jesus Laugh? An Essay on the Cultural, Ecclesiastical, and Theological Transformation of Laughter 169

1. Did Jesus Laugh? Yes, *Naturally!* (He Could Easily Have Done So) 169
    i. How Literally Should We Understand the Incarnation? 175

  ii. Can We Even Imagine a Human Being Not
   Laughing? 182

 2. Did Jesus Laugh? Maybe! (Depending on What Is Meant by
  'Laughter') 189

  i. Different Forms of Modern Research Into Laughter 191
  ii. The Historical Break in the Concept of Laughter 193
  iii. The (Bodily) Context of Laughter 195
  iv. Laughter as an Educational or Liberating Force 197
  v. And Then There Was Humour! 201
  vi. Humour and the Conception of the Human Being 204
  vii. Humour in the Service of Critique of Religion 206
  viii. Humour as a Substitute for Religion 211
  ix. Do Structural Similarities Between Christianity and
   Humour also Imply a Causal Relationship? 217
  x. Why Does Jesus Have No Sense of Humour? 220

 3. Did Jesus Laugh? Probably Not! (But He Began Doing So
  150 Years Ago) 222

  i. What Enabled Us to Start Hearing the Laughter of Jesus? 227
  ii. Will the Right Jesus be so Kind as to Step Forward? 231

 4. Did Jesus Laugh? No! (And Is That Why We Can?) 237

Chapter V: Johannes Oecolampadius: *De Risu Paschali* 247

 Wolfgang Capito's Preface, April 1518 247

 Johannes Oecolampadius' Letter, March 1518 252

Afterword and Acknowledgements 307

Bibliography 311

Index of Names 369

Index of Bible Texts 381

A Note on the Author 385

Introduction

Easter Laughter! The expression alone is so alluring that we cannot help but react and let our imagination soar. It is quite amusing, albeit unintentionally, that these reactions are not only spontaneous and typically strong but also the diametrical opposite of each other. Strikingly, neither those of us who are attracted nor those who are repelled seem particularly interested in what the expression actually means. In its historical setting that is. For even when the expression – and (to a lesser extent?!) the practice behind it – has gained such widespread popularity in recent times that it is tempting to consider it a timeless and borderless phenomenon, it is nevertheless possible, with only a slight exaggeration, to pinpoint the hour when, and the house where, the concept of 'Easter Laughter' was born.

Insofar as there is some truth to this exaggeration, the expression 'Easter Laughter' celebrated its half millennium anniversary on 18 March 2018. For on this day in 1518 the priest Johannes Oecolampadius (1482–1531) sat in the parsonage of Weinsberg in Southern Germany finishing a lengthy letter which he then mailed to the cathedral chaplain and dean of the theological faculty in Basel, Wolfgang Capito (1476–1541). A month later the letter, together with a foreword by Capito, was published as a small booklet by Johann Froben's (*c.* 1460–1527) famous humanist publishing house under the title *De risu paschali Oecolampadii, ad V. Capitonem Theologum epistola apologetica*. Here, for the first time in world history, Easter Laughter is named, described, and evaluated in detail.

This is not to claim that Oecolampadius invented the practice. Even if this seems occasionally suggested when reading about Easter Laughter (perhaps due to misconstruing the appearance of the word 'apologetica' in the title?),[1] Oecolampadius is so very far from defending the practice, he is vehemently *denouncing* it. The letter was provoked by one or more of Oecolampadius' fellow preachers complaining to Capito that Oecolampadius was 'all too serious', and in his letter he is actually making an 'apology' for himself, in the sense that he explains in detail why he will not demean either himself or the pulpit by making use of this contemptible laughing at Easter. What does remain, however, is that from all available accounts Oecolampadius is the one who invents the very 'catchphrase' which, ironically, contributes decisively to preserving the memory

---

[1] Most surprisingly, even an authority like Vladimir Yakovlevich Propp (1895–1970) seems to make this mistake, Propp 1984, 138.

of the custom into modernity. That irony is all the stronger for the fact that it almost seems a *coincidence* that Oecolampadius actually coins the phrase, for only once during the book's twenty-five pages does he use the suggestive expression *risus paschalis*.

Despite the fact that even Oecolampadius notes that his opponents defend Easter Laughter by referring to it as a *custom*, a search in the electronic edition of the 221 massive volumes of Jacques-Paul Migne's (1800–75) collection of more than a thousand years' worth of theological and ecclesiastical documents yields not a single occurrence of 'risus' and 'paschalis' (including truncated forms) in close proximity of each other.[2] This, on the other hand, is in stark contrast to a different kind of search which documents our current fascination with this phenomenon: google searches conducted in late November 2012, mid May 2017, and early March 2024 revealed the following drastic rise in the number of hits: 'risus paschalis' went from 12,700 via 15,300 to 58,800, 'Osterlachen' from 603 (*sic*) and 13,000 to 15,800, while 'Easter Laughter' leaps from 503 (yet again: *sic*) to 13,600 to 375,000.[3]

---

[2] Even though each of these is also rare, it is worth drawing attention to other medieval expressions in which 'laughter' is part of a notable connection, such as A) 'the laughter of love' (*risus caritatis*), B) 'the laughter of Easter grace' (*risus paschalis gratiae*) and C) 'the image of our laughter' (*nostri forma risus*):

A) 'Love is a laughter, because it is cheerful, indeed, merry, but not hilarious' (*Caritas enim risus est, quia hilaris est. Laeta quidem, non tamen dissoluta*), Bernard of Clairvaux (1090–1153), Sermo 93 (1862, col. 716).

B) 'Grant us, Lord, so to suffer with you / that we may become sharers in your glory, / to spend these three days in grief / that you may allow us the laughter of Easter grace' (*Tu tibi compati sic fac nos Domine / Tuae participes ut simus gloriae, / Sic praesens triduum in lucture ducere, / Ut risum tribuas paschalis gratiae*), Peter Abelard's (1079–1142) Good Friday hymn 'Solus ad victimam', *Hymnarius Paraclitensis*, quoted from O'Connell 2002, 50.

C) 'The boy, the pattern of our laughter, / for whom the ram was slain, / signifies the joy of life' (*Puer, nostri forma risus, / pro quo vervex est occisus / vitae signat gaudium*), Adam of St Victor's (d. 1146) Easter hymn *Zyma vetus expurgetur* (1880, col. 1438), quoted from O'Connell 2002, 50.

The most remarkable expression seems to be the last one, considering that the boy we are talking about is the patriarch Isaac (and the ram in Gen 22:13), whom the song typologically interprets as an image of laughter, thus making laughter a paraphrase for Christ!

[3] As users of Google will know, the algorithms used by the search engine are guarded with secrecy. Since the number of hits may vary from one search to the next during the

Despite the thousands of hits, we have to acknowledge a rather curious historical state of affairs, since we can make the paradoxical, yet reasonable claim that Easter Laughter has never before been so popular and at the same time unknown as it is today. Our generally positive assessment shows a striking difference to the first three or four hundred years of discussing Easter Laughter: at that time the knowledge of the actual historical practice was possibly as weak as now, but whenever people wrote about it, it was largely only with utter contempt. Although coming from diametrically opposed viewpoints, there seems both then and now to exist an inverse proportional ratio between actual knowledge about the historical sources and more or less justified speculation about the practice and meaning of laughing on Easter Sunday.[4]

In the age of electronics we have learned that knowledge disseminated on the internet can be of dubious validity, in particular when it is documented by references to other sites on the internet in an ever-expanding but all the same closed circuit. The thousands and thousands of online posts about Easter Laughter reveal inordinate amounts of redundancy, and they are likely of more use to a folklorist researching how stories arise and develop through inbreeding than to anyone interested in learning about the historical reality which those definitions purport to describe.

Thus, it may prove opportune in advance to put to bed one of the most frequently repeated explanations which would have us believe that Easter Laughter was a legacy of the liturgy of the Greek Orthodox Church, thus making the custom up to a thousand years older than the Reformation period. Even if at this early stage of the book there is a serious risk of appearing pedantic it is worth the effort to dig a bit deeper into this theory of the genesis of Easter Laughter, because this kind of claim seems symptomatic for much of the discussion about the topic. In countless cases it is casually claimed that Easter Laughter originated in the liturgy of the Greek Orthodox tradition, and this is apparently so obvious that with remarkably few exceptions the writers do not offer any form of documentation. Sometimes a reference will be given to a modern author, who in turn refers to another author, who either states it as a simple fact ... or refers us on to yet another. As far as it is possible to trace these strings of references they quite

---

same day these figures must be taken with a grain of salt – yet they give a clear picture of the *relative* increase in interest.

4   Cf. the concise wording of Volker Wendland (1939–2019): 'Thus a minimum knowledge of the sources caused people to invest a maximum of speculation in its evaluation, derivation, and interpretation.' 1980, 59.

possibly converge on a lone source. If that is indeed the case, this source turns out to be a highly-learned article containing a more or less casual observation which to all appearances has been short-circuited by its later interpreters.

The earliest example that I have been able to trace of the alleged connection between the Greek Orthodox Easter liturgy and a congregational laughter is to be found in a 1912-article on 'Le rire rituel' by the French historian of religion Salomon Reinach (1858–1932). It does not require much detective work to track down Reinach, as celebrities such as Propp and Mikhail Bakhtin (1895–1975), and after them a large number of scholars in general, refer to Reinach's article as a pioneering work in research on the *history* of laughter. In particular, it is his name that is often cited as a reference if and when the Greek Orthodox origins of Easter Laughter are to be documented. However, the nature of Reinach's 'documentation' is rarely reproduced.

Reinach juxtaposes and comments on Egyptian and Oriental but especially Hellenistic myths about the power of laughter, which not only gives life but also overcomes death. As a closing remark to the article Reinach makes a suggestion on how to find a kind of parallel to these ideas within Christianity:

> However, the Greek Orthodox Church has preserved a trace of the exuberant joy that in ancient cults greeted the return of a dead god or hero to life: this is the noisy manifestation of Easter Sunday, which, like a Dionysian jubilation in the Greek cities, unleashes the cry repeated a thousand times: Christ has risen![5]

Thus, Reinach writes only about 'a *trace* of the exuberant joy', and although he dares to compare the cry of resurrection with 'a Dionysian jubilation', he does not really mention anything about laughter during the mass.[6]

In a final footnote consisting of a few lines, Reinach adds that he has recently been made aware of another phenomenon that could count as a Christian parallel to the ancient myths: Easter Laughter. Posterity has clearly allowed Reinach's tentative considerations to merge and solidify into a fixed theory; but even though this claim has been repeated endlessly in academic literature of the 20th century

---

5   Reinach 1912, 127.
6   Neither does James George Frazer (1854–1941), who otherwise never shies away from mentioning the smallest detail, see any reason to mention laughter. Rather, like Reinach, he emphasises the joy and jubilation in connection with the cry of resurrection: '[…] and immediately the whole city bursts into a cry of joy, which makes itself air in screams and shouts, in endless firing of firecrackers and muskets and in the explosion of fireworks of all kinds. In the same hour, out of the plight of fasting, people immediately pounce on the enjoyment of Easter lamb and pure wine.' 1961, 170.

on Easter Laughter (and thus not only on the internet), I have never been able to find the phenomenon documented in generic works on Greek Orthodox theology and liturgy. Likewise practising Orthodox priests have assured me that there is no tradition of combining the admittedly loud joy of Easter Morning with ritual, liturgical, homiletical, or spontaneous outbursts of laughter.[7]

However, not least the intense nature of both the negative and positive attitudes suggests that the phenomenon is attracting interest on several diverse levels. The juxtaposition of Christianity and laughter seems to trigger some reactions, the ferocity of which reveals such a great discrepancy between cause and effect that it is easy to get the idea that there must be something more behind it. In that sense, Easter Laughter can serve as a mental-historical prism, wherein we are confronted, *en miniature,* with some of our perennial questions, such as the relationship between soul and body, religion and sexuality, God and humans. Not least it says something about our understanding of the God-Man from Nazareth. It is no coincidence that in the broader context the most frequently asked question has been 'Did Jesus laugh?'. This has been the case since John Chrysostom (349–407) first formulated it in some sermons from the 390s[8] – a

---

[7] It seems advisable here also in advance to mention a widespread tendency to mix phenomena which may indeed be more or less related or comparable, but where there are nevertheless good reasons for trying to maintain a factual distinction. We can only speculate on this, but it is tempting to imagine how it may have helped to promote the 'theory' of Easter Laughter originating in the Eastern Churches that from them the West received texts in the early Middle Ages that actually dared to mix Christianity and laughter. They did this in the form of parodic Bible tales, a kind of edifying jokes and riddles known as *Ioca monachorum* (and slightly more distant *Cena [/Coena] Cypriani*). It can also be attractive to think of the Eastern tradition of the so-called Holy Fools, which of course draws on St Paul's speech about the folly of the cross (1 Cor 1:18–31), but which, for instance, also point forward to the figure of the fool in the dramas of William Shakespeare (1564–1616) and *The Idiot* by Fyodor Dostoyevski (1821–81). On Holy Fools cf. Benz 1938, Hauptmann 1959, Balthasar 1965, Fedotov 1966, Saward 1980, and Grebe 2005.

To be fair, it should be added that such theories are not a new phenomenon, because academic papers of the 18th century indulged in bold speculations about Easter Laughter as a more or less direct heir to Greco-Roman, Jewish, Old Norse, or Germanic laughter rituals, cf. Wendland 1980, 79 ff. and below III,6,i-ii.

[8] In several places Chrysostom uses the contrast between the two explicit statements about Jesus' weeping (Lk 19:41 and Jn 11:35) and the *e silentio*-argument of the meaningful, i.e. non-coincidental, lack of corresponding statements about Jesus laughing in order to banish laughter from the Church. Most often, in scholarly treatments, reference is made to his '6th Homily on Matthew 8' (1862b, col. 69), but he also uses

then purely rhetorical question whose contemporary, often favourable, answer is in stark contrast to the self-evident rejection of the preceding well over one and a half millennia.

If we were to give a few graphic images of how big the difference is between then and now, we can point out that while the Christian tradition is filled with moving examples of statues that unexplainably begin to weep, we are still waiting for a church to report on one of its statues having miraculously begun to laugh heartily. The same basic assumption – that since the core of Christianity is the crucified one, it can come as no surprise that weeping seems more appropriate than laughter – will undoubtedly influence our answer to another simple question: what does a Bible look like? Until a few decades ago, that question was almost pointless, was the answer not clear from the outset? A Bible has a black or suitably dark cover, and the title is printed with gold letters; but if we visit the online shops of various Bible Societies today, we have to look hard to find an edition where the cover is not in the brightest, most cheerful colours.[9] Many of them are marketed as suitable for confirmands and young people; but does that kind of a gaily colourful cover fit the Bible that is supposed to lie on the altar of

---

the same rhetoric in the '17th Homily on Ephesians' (1862a, col. 119): 'Christ was crucified for your sins, and you laugh?' (*Christus in crucem actus est propter tua mala: tu autem rides?*), and in the '15th Homily on Hebrews' (1863, col. 121 f.). In the first context, Chrysostom expands the biblical foundation for the negative view of laughter by pointing to the reproach against Sarah (Gen 18:12–15) and the condemnation of Ham (Gen 9:25), who, according to Jewish narrative tradition, laughed at the drunkenness of his father Noah, although this is not evident in modern translations.

For the record, it should be added that this is a bit like 'the first lark of spring'. Tradition has permanently linked Chrysostom's name to the question of Jesus' laughter; but it is a convenient fabrication to appoint him 'the first'. Similar considerations can be found in Basil of Caesarea (330–79) when, in his rule for monks (probably from around the year 366 [according to the publisher's foreword, 2013, 8]), he argues for the monks' abstinence from laughter, citing the role model of Jesus ('The Longer Rule', 'Question 8'; 2013, 96). For a compact overview of the writers who repeated this Jesus-did-not-laugh trope a thousand years from Basil and Chrysostom to the High Middle Ages see note 23 in Kemper 2005, 19 f.

9 An utterly unscientific study, based on a review of the many versions of the Bible that are on the shelves in the library of my own former institution – as well as on those of the Danish Bible Society – indicates that the first Danish edition with brightly coloured covers is a New Testament from 1952. My thanks to the Society's secretary general for corroborating this information.

the church on Sundays? If we detect the slightest hesitancy in giving an answer the question may still be relevant: what does a *real* Bible look like?

1. Easter Laughter as a Denominational Point of Contention

On another level – and in light of the proximity between Oecolampadius' letter and Martin Luther's (1483–1546) early writings – it is no less interesting that this topic also says something about the relationship between Catholicism and Protestantism. This was not the case from the very beginning of the Reformation movement, as we find condemnations of Easter Laughter from many camps; but surprisingly quickly it became a point of contention between the denominations, almost on the same level with the disputes over the trade in indulgences. This already happened in the course of Luther's generation and reached its peak in the time of Orthodoxy.

One way to illustrate the long-term effects of both these denominational differences as well as the radical change across the denominations within just the last 75 years or so is by making a quick survey of the leading encyclopaedias within this field and noting the discrete yet significant differences between them. The Catholic *Lexikon für Theologie und Kirche* (*LThK*) was published in its 2nd edition in 1957–68 and in its most recent 1993–2001. The former does not contain an entry for Osterlachen/Ostergelächter/Risus paschalis (the German and Latin expressions for Easter Laughter), but in volume 7 from 1962 the article about 'Ostern' finishes with a paragraph on 'Osterbräuche' ('Easter customs') containing this short notice: 'In the Middle Ages and even more recent times, the Easter sermon brought the faithful to Easter Laughter (risus paschalis) by its human joyful nature.' A generation later in the 3rd edition's volume 8 (1999) 'risus paschalis' appears as a separate entry of ten lines which happens to mention Oecolampadius and some of the major works of contemporary scholarship.

This is matched by the Protestant *Die Religion in Geschichte und Gegenwart* (*RGG*), whose 3rd and 4th editions were published in 1957–65 and 1998–2007 respectively. Neither of these has an entry for Easter Laughter, but volume 4 from 1960 does have a relatively comprehensive and decidedly religio-historical article on 'Lachen und Weinen' ('laughter and weeping'), which mentions ancient ideas of the life-creating power of laughter in, for example, the Hymn to Demeter. The passage is rounded off as follows: 'The Greeks also created the term "serious-ridiculous" (*spoudogéleion*), but the matter as such is known in all cultures and times (cf. for example risus paschalis in the church).' A generation later, in the 4th edition (2002), this parenthesis is allowed to swell into a full sentence:

Annual rituals sometimes include extraordinary grief over the death or disappearance of a deity, followed by regenerative laughter. Such rituals can be found in the mystery religions of the Greco-Roman world. In the Christian Middle Ages, the celebration of Christ's resurrection on Easter Sunday was sometimes accompanied by Easter Laughter (risus paschalis).[10]

The 'discreet yet significant' differences, especially with regard to the epochal shift, become even more evident when turning to the *Theologische Realenzyklopädie* from 1977–2004. It is considered a successor to the *Realencyklopädie für protestantische Theologie und Kirche*, whose 3rd edition (1896–1909) had neither entries for Easter Laughter nor laughter in general, nor did it touch on the subject in connection with 'Easter.'[11] A little more than a hundred years later the 'successor', which is admittedly both far more voluminous and also strives to be ecumenical, continues to have no separate articles about laughter or Easter Laughter; but in the 1995 article on 'Osterpredigt' ('Easter Sermon') space has been given to a substantial and nuanced section on 'Ostergelächter' which concludes: 'In the last twenty years the old homiletic-liturgical custom of Easter Laughter (risus paschalis / Easter Laughter) has aroused new interest.'[12]

---

10 In addition, the expression '[Easter-] laughter' is paralleled in a list of customs such as 'Easter egg', 'Easter bunny', etc. in the section: 'Easter, IV History of Customs'. Quotes from *LThK*: Dörrer 1962 and Eybl 1999, and from *RGG*: Grant 1960 and Gilhus 2002.

11 To be fair it should be added that the extraordinarily extensive article about Oecolampadius covering more than fourteen pages of folio size does include eight lines about his *De risu paschali*, Hadorn 1904, 288. Just as we can observe a kind of parallelism in the publication of *LThK* and *RGG*, something similar can be seen regarding the *Realencyklopädie für protestantische Theologie und Kirche* and the *Kirchenlexicon, oder Encyclopädie der katholischen Theologie und ihrer Hülfswissenschaften*, which appeared in its 2nd edition between 1882–1903. In this case, the contrast is all the stronger because not only has the latter lexicon the most comprehensive article on 'Easter-tales [*Ostermärchen*] and Easter Laughter' in any theological lexicon before or since, but also the three-column long article can be regarded as the first attempt at a modern scientific treatment of the phenomenon, H. Weber 1885.

12 The author of the article is Harald Schroeter (b. 1961), 1995, 532.

As will transpire, there are good historical reasons for using German literature for information about Easter Laughter. However, when we dispense with the narrow focus on Easter Laughter and broaden the scope just a little, the comparative overview of the Catholic and Protestant encyclopaedias can be complemented, and, furthermore, a glimpse can be given of the equally important dividing line between a Continental and an Anglo-Saxon tradition. At the same time, we can get an impression of the change in the general cultural (intellectual-historical) environment that has fostered the 'new interest' that Schroeter identified.

A relevant cue to this was provided by the Lutheran church historian, Hans von Campenhausen (1903–89), when by the early 1960s he registered how, over the past decade, a whole wave of literature had emerged highlighting the value of 'merriment' (*Heiterkeit*) in Christianity. While Campenhausen, on the one hand, welcomed such a perspective, he disapproved of the inadequate argumentation and the trivial repetitions of this literature on the other. In passing, he observes that the then current publication of the third edition of the *RGG* does not include an entry for 'humour'. For Campenhausen, this signifies that theological reflection on this topic was not at the same level as the interest in it in church and in society, and that therefore the well-intentioned, popular, and edifying literature is below academic standard and often exceeds the limits of good taste. 1963a, 318.

Just as *Realencyklopädie für Protestantische Theologie und Kirche* from the previous turn of the century was cleansed of material about Easter Laughter, it had unsurprisingly no interest in humour either. In contrast to this there are once again good historical reasons why the situation is quite different in an Anglo-Saxon context (see below IV,2,v-viii). At this stage of our presentation this can be illustrated by means of the almost concurrent *Encyclopedia of Religion and Ethics* (1908–27), which has a full article on 'Humour' – and, by the way, also one on 'Laughter' (Reid 1913 and Morgan 1914 respectively).

The differences between *LThK* and *RGG* are also noticeable regarding 'humour' and are here even more revealing than when it comes to the rarer term 'Easter Laughter'. The second volume of the *RGG* from 1959 covers the words starting with 'H', but it has nothing about 'humour' (the word itself appears only in the articles about Søren Kierkegaard [1813–55] and the term 'realism'). On the other hand the fifth volume of the *LThK* from 1960 has not only a comprehensive article about humour but in that article even a special section on 'Christian humour' (Braun 1960). In the next generation of both encyclopaedias, this imbalance is evened out and in a certain way turned around. *LThK* still has an article but now without a special section on Christian humour, whereas the *RGG* makes room for an article on 'humour', half of which is on humour in theology and pastoral care (Köhler 2000).

This new way of prioritising in the *RGG* seems to be symptomatic of the Protestant encyclopaedias at the end of the 20th century, as illustrated by elaborate entries for humour in *Theologische Realenzyklopädie* (Steiger 1986), *Praktisches Lexicon der Spiritualität* (Thiede 1988), *Evangelische Kirchenlexicon. Internationale theologische Enzyklopädie* (Winkler 1989) and *Evangelisches Lexikon für Theologie und Gemeinde* (Eber 1993). As far as encyclopaedias are concerned *Reallexicon für Antike und Christentum. Sachwörterbuch zur Auseinandersetzung des Christentums mit die antiken Welt* must be considered in a league of its own, as it considers the concept of 'humour' worthy of a minor dissertation covering more than twenty densely-written columns, including considerable information about Easter Laughter (Luck 1994).

2. (Easter) Laughter as a Historical Point of Contention

Already at this point it has transpired how important it is to approach the subject with a sense of historical awareness. This, however, points to a not insignificant challenge, as an obvious reaction to this alleged need would be to meet it with an overbearing smile – and a shrug of one's shoulders. While it may be entirely valid out of pure historical interest to delve into the quarrels of the past over the legitimacy of laughter in connection with the Church and Christianity, it is tempting to think that the historical distance is so great that both the phenomenon of Easter Laughter and, in particular, the opposition to it can only be understood as an anachronism, as a historical oddity with no appreciable contemporary relevance.

At this introductory stage we must ask a counterweight question as to how great that distance actually is. Qualitatively, so to speak, we can maintain that even if and when most sermons today have no problem at all with including a joke or two, this does not necessarily mean that we have overcome the legacy *theologically*. Our attitude may simply have changed without any real arguments for such a change (including counterarguments against the condemnations of the past). Maybe we are just servile to an age that calls for entertainment, and where 'it-must-be-fun' is a parameter that is by no means restricted to the entertainment industry but has spread to almost all areas of society. There is a lot of canned laughter on TV, but how many Greek Choruses of 'professional mourners' are employed in the media? To avoid being misunderstood I hasten to add that, conversely, the point is not that sermons necessarily have to be boring, that it may not be 'entertaining' to go to church, nor that the church hasn't earlier in history been faced with such demands (and that Easter Laughter may possibly be a testimony to that effect). Rather it is the presumed weight and imperialist spread of the parameter that is so striking. Why is it that it has suddenly become an argument – and a weighty one – that it must be fun to go to church – along with the expectations that it should be fun to go to school, to be at work, to go to bed with one's partner? Should it also be fun to be in jail, undergo heart surgery, or lie in a hospice?[13]

---

13 If Richard Sennett (b. 1943) is right in his analysis, when in *The Fall of Public Man* he claims that we have made intimacy and warm feelings our god, we could add that we have simultaneously made laughter the prophet of that god. Sennett argues that 'the reigning belief today is that closeness between persons is a moral good. The reigning aspiration today is to develop individual personality through experiences of closeness and warmth with others. The reigning myth today is that the evils of society can all be understood as evils of impersonality, alienation, and coldness. The sum of these three

Furthermore, it may also be worth considering 'quantitatively', so to speak, that even though in our current cultural climate there may be a wide gap in attitude between then and now, it is chronologically surprisingly narrower. To mention only one well-publicised case from the mid-1990s, it aroused equal parts curiosity and indignation, when the so-called Toronto revival made the congregation's loud laughter a hallmark of the Holy Spirit's presence during the service. The reactions of that time just a few decades ago may be a warning against exaggerating the distance between Oecolampadius and our time. Perhaps ecclesiastically and theologically we have not abandoned or overcome a mistrust of laughter entirely. The limitations to our acceptance of laughter in church may not have been lifted but simply shifted – more or less according to denomination, nationality, region … or perhaps rather according to individual mood and taste? An easy litmus test is to ask ourselves: is it permissible/desirable to smile during an (Easter) service? Is it permissible/desirable to laugh? To laugh loudly? To slap our thighs in a fit of laughter? If just one of the questions triggers a pause, it may be worth the trouble to read Oecolampadius and the subsequent discussion of his concern.

Just as faith in the resurrection is not restricted to Easter Sunday, neither can Easter Laughter be confined to such a narrow framework,[14] so if it is illegitimate in that context, laughter is probably problematic in general. Conversely, if the condemnations of Easter Laughter in the past are overcome, does both it and any other form of laughter have the same legitimate place in church and theology as all other human emotions, reactions, and expressions?[15] When many in our time have not only relaxed their resistance to laughter but are attempting to develop a theology of laughter, we must try not to lose sight of what the challenge is. It may indeed be a symbolically important step to allow laughter into the church, but this is not necessarily the same as having developed a theology to support it,

---

  is an ideology of intimacy: social relationships of all kinds are real, believable, and authentic the closer they approach the inner psychological concerns of each person. This ideology transmutes political categories into psychological categories. This ideology of intimacy defines the humanitarian spirit of a society without gods: warmth is our god. The history of the rise and fall of public culture at the very least calls this humanitarian spirit into question.' 1978, 259.

14 Cf. Thiede 2011, 118.
15 In Karl-Josef Kuschel's (b. 1948) opening chapter, 'A Short Theology of Laughter', he suggests that if it is possible to demonstrate that laughter has a legitimate place in the church, this must mean that it should not only be leniently or strategically allowed, but that it is rather a deficiency if and when it is absent. Kuschel 1994, xv-xxi.

certainly not if access to the church is mainly due to the fact that we have given up resisting the omnipresence of laughter in the surrounding society.

It is not likely that any theologians of laughter will use this as a justification; but it is with laughter as with so many other modern cultural phenomena that are invited inside the church: it will always turn out whether the motive was basically one of accomodation, since the result will soon be either involuntarily comic imitations or we sense an ulterior motive and do not really feel like laughing. By extension, it is also not enough to use laughter in the church for strategic reasons, as it is particularly customary in homiletics to argue. Humour is *recommended*, as it is demonstrably good at catching the congregation's attention; but as soon as we get to the point of our sermon, we have to leave it behind! Arguably humour and laughter are used to serve the gospel, but apparently they have nothing to do with the gospel itself. Nor is it adequate to aim for laughing *in* the church *at* the church,[16] although this can be interpreted as a display of an otherwise admirable self-critical consciousness, a kind of safety valve against an inflated sense of self-importance. That valve function certainly has an illustrious place in the theory of laughter, but quite frankly it is a kind of a negative defence, which could be reformulated thus: we legitimise laughter for the sake of our sinfulness; it is needed as protection against our penchant for pharisaism, pride and lust for power. All this is part of it; but does laughter also have anything to do with salvation?

Insisting on such questions is not only in respect for the Church and theology but certainly also out of awe of laughter. It is relevant and respectable to examine the many possible functions of laughter and decide which of them we will try to apply – and expose ourselves to. The crucial thing, however, must be to combine this with reflections on what the *meaning* can be behind the many types of laughter, and what significance this can have in a theological and ecclesiastical context. The addition of 'exposing ourselves to laughter' refers to the dialectic nature of laughter, that it is naïve to think that laughter can be used as a pure means. Precisely because laughter can seize control and make itself a goal, it is all the more necessary to clarify laughter theologically as a phenomenon and carrier of meaning, before making it a programme to bid it welcome within the church service.

This, of course, is ultimately related to the complication in the relationship between gospel and laughter that it does not directly and unambiguously work both ways. If joy is included as the link between the two, we can say that from a

---

16 Cf. Kuschel 1994, xviif.

theological point of view joy belongs constitutively to the gospel, and anthropologically/psychologically we can observe that joy often finds expression in laughter. In that sense laughter cannot be completely foreign to the gospel. However, the order cannot be reversed; partly because laughter has many sources other than joy, partly because joy has other expressions than laughter – not to mention the fact that not even joy is able to circumscribe the gospel. Just as we may think it narrow-minded and prudish to want to exclude laughter from the gospel, it can be just as naive and dangerous to let laughter be evidence of the gospel being received, or to try to arouse laughter in order to let it be the entrance door to the service. Oecolampadius would probably have agreed with these reservations.

It can be a great stimulus to reflect on Richard G. Cote's (1934–2005) call to 'imagine what might happen if God's laughter became a living religious symbol in the church, just as God's remorse or God's omnipotence or God's providence once were'.[17] Likewise, it should not be dismissed in advance that Merritt Conrad Hyers (1933–2013) may be onto something worth serious reflection when he suggests that the inclusion of humour and laughter in 20th-century theological and ecclesiastical considerations may be an expression of 'a special virtue of modern spirituality'.[18] The present book presupposes that Cote's and Hyers' deliberations are legitimate and that it is not a major problem if the present were to stand alone in finding such thoughts relevant, even without being able to refer to substantial precedents in our tradition. We could argue that the world, humanity and/or the Church have changed so much that new conditions and possibilities appear. However, if we think that it is going too far to work with such ontological implications, we could settle for a more cautious, yet perhaps more polemical consideration: 'modern spirituality' is not necessarily an expression of a whole new relationship with God, but it may be a release of the aspects of that relationship which tradition has under-exposed, suppressed or condemned.

How do we strike the best balance between tradition and the present? How can tradition be considered an inexhaustible source of inspiration without giving it the power to veto change? How can we champion the latest answers to today's issues without ignoring the ideas of the past simply because they are old? A benchmark could be the wisdom behind the canonical principle (at least in the Danish Lutheran Church) that we can introduce new rituals without thereby nullifying the validity of the old ones. As such this principle is the opposite of a cancel-culture that would want to tear down statues of people because they are

---

17   Cote 1986, 56.
18   Hyers 1969b, 12.

an uncomfortable reminder of who we were one or more generations earlier. On the one hand, this benchmark is a sign of the churches' attempt to preserve their identity in the face of change, and on the other hand, it testifies to a self-confident openness that we are able to accommodate a certain diversity. It is legitimate for a living faith to introduce something new, while at the same time it is an awareness of continuity that we do not thereby invalidate the tradition. Let this serve as a model that finds it fully justified to invent new ways of talking about God and Jesus, but which at the same time is a warning against treating the newfound openness of recent generations to speak of the laughter of God and Jesus almost as an expression of a crypto-philosophical belief in historical progress! For when we study the cornucopia of contemporary theologies of laughter, an unmistakable tendency becomes clear: in the attempt to rehabilitate themselves in relation to the traditional critique, these theologies often come recklessly close to turning the laughter-sceptical worship and forms of faith of the past into heresy.

It is not the concern of this book to promote the viewpoint that God meets us especially in the power of laughter to break down barriers, or that humour should be particularly consistent with a Christian view of life. Even if it has been scientifically proven endless times in the 20th century that laughter is healthy and can have a healing effect, this does not *eo ipso* make it blissful or redemptive. For laughter can be just as much an expression of avoiding life as of embracing it, of hiding in a shell as of self-disclosure, of isolating oneself as of reaching out for a community. Conversely, it is indeed our concern – at least as a counterweight and supplement to the historical one-sidedness – to plead the case of laughter not being the opposite of seriousness, that God *can* also meet us in the laughter of joy as well as in the tears of repentance and sorrow, and finally that laughter as a natural bodily expression lies beyond, or *before* a good-bad dichotomy – and even more so a good-evil antinomy. The phenomenon of laughter is neither diabolical, as many of the Church Fathers *et alii* feared, nor – as it is now widely taken for granted – in itself heavenly.

As for the latter, it might be sobering with a Kantian-Protestant relation to laughter! We could try to distinguish the laughter of faith (and of humour) from a natural laughter. Not in order yet again to introduce false distinctions but to emphasise that to the extent that laughter is assigned a special ethical and religious role – whether we believe it leads to salvation or perdition – we must be wary of turning a natural inclination (the Kantian *Neigung*), such as a sunny disposition and being quick to laugh, into something particularly pleasing to God or stemming from the Devil. If not directly a Kantian 'duty' (*Pflicht*), the laughter of faith is not (only) rooted in a bubbling joy of life (*joie de vivre*) and a cheerful mood, but it contains pain and sorrow and springs from the fact that death did not have the last word about the Word ... at the first Easter, and every day since.

3. A Note on the Outline of this Book

If the diagnosis is correct that the exponentially growing number of hits when googling 'Easter Laughter' testifies to a remarkably high interest in this phenomenon while at the same time factual knowledge about its historical roots is very low, then a number of obvious questions arise which can serve as an outline for this book.

Firstly (Chapter 1) there is the historical question of *what*. What was Easter Laughter, where did it take place, who practised it, when did it originate, and how widespread was it – and equally interesting: can anything at all be said about how the laughter was triggered?

Secondly (Chapter 2) some historical questions arise of a slightly different kind, concerning the history of the effects (*Wirkungsgeschichte*) of Easter Laughter: how long did Easter Laughter stay alive, who criticised it so harshly ... and why – and were there none at all who defended it? As we shall see when we come to discuss the invention of the technical term *risus paschalis*, it turns out to be quite an ironical twist of fate that Easter Laughter seems especially to have survived thanks to its critics. Rather than a continued ecclesiastical practice, Easter Laughter was for several centuries a literary *topos* in scholarly feuds. Thus, it was carried forward from the implacable rejection in the period of the Baroque and Enlightenment via the historicising curiosity of Romanticism to an age, namely modernity, which suddenly welcomed the phenomenon as the return of a deeply missed Prodigal Son.

Thirdly (Chapter 3), by focusing on the question of *why*, Easter Laughter can be approached through systematic theology. Here the perspectives from dogmatics and practical theology come into view when we examine the contemporary attempts to argue for (and later to theorise about) why it is precisely in connection with Easter that such a practice could arise and in some ecclesiastical circles be considered legitimate. Other theological perspectives, of course, appear in the resistance to this custom.

Finally (Chapter 4) this leads to an examination of the history of ideas. The guiding question in this context will be whether some explanations can be given for the significant difference in the assessments of laughter through the ages. This paves the way for some suggestions as to why modernity has generally been far more positive about phenomena such as Easter Laughter. Where the other chapters relate narrowly to Easter Laughter, the concluding chapter deals more broadly with laughter in general. Yet in order to keep focus on the theological relevance of laughter the discussions will be concentrated around the classic question of whether Jesus laughed. It should be noted, however, that the primary aim of this book is not to present yet another answer to that question. Such answers have been given so abundantly over the past 50–75 years. Instead, the ambition here is to present some historical material that partly documents the astonishing distance between the understanding of laughter in the past and today, and partly illustrates the astonishing speed and radicalism of this turnaround. When dealing with topics that different eras have been intensely interested in, but in vastly diverse ways, a historical awareness is invaluable.

Chapter I: What *Was* Easter Laughter?

In all its ostensible simplicity the phenomenon of Easter Laughter was that a preacher with the help from a cheerful tale (and/or a 'performative' element) sought to make the congregation burst into laughter on Easter morning. To a modern mind it can be difficult to understand this as anything other than just plain banal, and must it not also have been perceived that way back in a time when the church calendar was teeming with the kind of celebrations that Bakhtin has referred to as the medieval 'culture of laughter'?[19] Although Bakhtin lists Easter Laughter along with many other seemingly similar phenomena, it is precisely when compared to, for instance, carnivals or the various forms of religious pageants (morality, mystery, and miracle plays) that it is easiest to see how Easter Laughter distinguishes itself in at least three significant ways.

1. Distinguishing Characteristics of Easter Laughter

Firstly, it is unique that laughter takes place inside the church and during a 'normal' service. Admittedly, there is no full consensus among scholars about the nature of the medieval liturgical plays; but even when, on the one hand, dramatic performances have certainly been staged inside the churches,[20] there is, on the other hand, much to suggest that the more exuberant ones of this kind (later on during the Middle Ages) have been reserved for a very limited circle (typically monks and clerics of the lowest ranks). In addition, the folk festivals never came closer to the church than the square in front of the building. More often these were staged around the city in squares or suitable places in the vicinity – and therefore they could more appropriately be referred to as a kind of religious local theatre acted by amateurs and supported primarily by the guild system.[21]

---

19 Bakhtin 1984.
20 The oldest known 'liturgical drama' was even developed precisely in connection with Easter morning, the so-called *Quem quaeritis* dialogue between the angel and the women at the tomb, found in a manuscript from St Gallen which can be dated as far back as the middle of the 10th century.
21 The classic collections of source material are the monographs by Edmund K. Chambers (1866–1954) *The Medieval Stage* (1903¹) and Karl Young (1879–1943) *The Drama of the Mediaeval Church* (1933¹). Shorter surveys can be found in works by Allardyce Nicoll (1894–1976) *Masks, Mimes, and Miracles. Studies in Popular Theatre* (1931¹) and Oscar G. Brockett (1923–2010) *History of the Theatre* (1968¹).

Secondly, the agent is neither one from the lowest clergy nor people in general who are allowed to break the world order and turn clerical rankings upside down by, for example, acting as a bishop or an abbot ... *for a day*, but it is the celebrating priest. Just as importantly the audience is the congregation celebrating their regular Easter service. In this way Easter Laughter differs categorically from the so-called *sermon joyeux*, an otherwise on the surface closely related and more or less contemporaneous phenomenon known from the Gallic church. Most certainly the purpose of the *sermon joyeux* was also to provoke laughter and it could very well do that by exposing clerical clichés; but this was a distinctly theatrical undertaking performed by an actor outside the church building and intended precisely as a parody of the preaching in the church.[22]

This implicitly points to two important things: Easter Laughter did not stem, at least not directly, from a popular demand. It is not something that the people of the church reluctantly give in to and/or try to control, channel, or domesticate, in the same way as appears to be the case with the popular activities around Christmas, Lent and the Feast of the Body and Blood of Christ (*Corpus Christi*). Next, it surely is one of the oldest commonplaces (not just in Christianity but arguably in all religions) that when laughter and priests have something do with each other, the priest is most often the *object* of laughter – not least as a way of exposing his hypocrisy in relation to the norms and ideals he represents and expresses. What is special about Easter Laughter is that laughter is the priest's *ally*.[23]

---

22 Cf. the chapter 'The "joyful sermons" as dramatic monologues and their development into farces' in Jacobsen 1903, 67–76. In a broader perspective, Sander L. Gilman (b. 1944) has tried to identify 'the parodic sermon' as a distinct literary genre, which, as the subtitle indicates, he reviews in a true *tour de force* 'from the Middle Ages to the Twentieth Century', Gilman 1974.

23 However important this point is, it should not be misunderstood as a claim that it was only in connection with Easter Laughter that preachers managed to become the master of laughter and not just its butt. Rather, Easter Laughter can be seen as an heir to the ecclesiastical renewal that has been called 'the pastoral reformation' of the 12th and 13th centuries. It consisted not least in the spreading of the gospel, both geographically and socially, by means of preaching in the vernacular – especially thanks to the new orders known as the 'Preaching Friars' (*fratres predicatores*), i.e. primarily the Dominicans and Franciscans, but also the Carmelites and the Order of the Hermits of St Augustine. If Christianity was not something that only the learned scholastics debated in Latin, and if the gospel was to be preached not only in the churches but also in the streets, it was surely not only a question of using the local languages and dialects but also of exploiting all available rhetorical devices.

At the same time this points to the third and, from a historical perspective, culturally most auspicious difference, as Easter Laughter is thus not a tolerated intrusion into the service but an integrated goal. This means that where in other contexts laughter served at best as a kind of safety valve, and where we have to look with a microscope to find church representatives who speak positively or even just neutrally about it, there Easter Laughter was instead given a place of honour at the very celebration of the Lord's resurrection.

This characteristic in itself contains two significant perspectives. It implies that laughter as such cannot be considered to be utterly evil, and, NB, here we are not only dealing with the controlled (i.e. polite, civilised) smile or soft laughter, but also the untamed giggle and raucous laughter. In a theological context this is indeed revolutionary! The radicalism of this different view of laughter is evidenced not least in how far preachers were apparently willing to go in order to achieve the desired effect. Means were resorted to which it is difficult to imagine even the most ardent supporters of the custom would consider appropriate in any other liturgical context (despite whatever kind of merriment the church calendar had to offer in connection with Christmas or Lent). Moreover, as a direct extension of this, we can plausibly consider this – at least implicitly – qualitatively different assessment of laughter to be one of the decisive prerequisites for

---

> Another way of pleading for the presence of a basically changed attitude to laughter during the High Middle Ages can be found in Francis of Assisi's (1182–1230) own rules, not only in the form of the methodologically questionable *e silentio*-argument but also in explicit statements. To be sure, in the so-called 'Admonitions' (which are believed to have been created over a long period of time and which perhaps consist of his own written and/or dictated admonitions) in the section 'The happy and the silly religious' this warning is also found in Francis: 'Woe to the religious who amuses himself with silly gossip, trying to make people laugh' (section 21; 1964, 85). What is striking, however, is that this is an isolated occurrence in the various Franciscan collections of rules. Especially compared to the other contemporary monastic rules, which often copy or are close to Benedict's Rules on this point, Francis is surprisingly reluctant to repeat these frequently recurring condemnations of laughter among the brothers (regarding Benedict of Nursia [*c.* 480–547] see ch. 4 ('The instruments for doing good works'), vv. 51–4, ch. 6 ('On silence'), v. 8, and ch. 7 ('On humility'), vv. 59–61). On the other hand, in the Rule from 1221 there is this significant exhortation: 'They should let it be seen that they are happy in God, cheerful and courteous, as is expected of them, and be careful not to appear gloomy or depressed like hypocrites' (ch. 7; 1964, 38). According to the Danish editors of Francis' texts it is claimed in Thomas Celano's (*c.* 1200-*c.* 1270) biography of Francis from 1246 that exactly this sentence was personally inserted by Francis (2 Cel 128) 1999, 43.

the transformative development over the following centuries, when laughter ceased to be a sure sign of perdition. Admittedly, no one yet dreamed of formulating it so sharply, but in principle a line was thus opened to the kind of outright theologies of laughter that first appeared more commonly after World War Two, and where laughter was not only recognised as contributing to a person's health[24] but also to their salvation.

A Brief Excursus on Bakhtin and 'the Culture of Laughter'

Although the focus here is on the distinctive features of Easter Laughter, it is worthwhile with a short digression into the heated discussion in recent decades of Bakhtin's interpretation of other parts of the medieval 'culture of laughter'. For this discussion will prove to be relevant for the assessment of Easter Laughter, not only because there are obvious overlaps, but also because the very discussion provides a good sketch of changes in the *Zeitgeist*. In all fairness it ought from the beginning to be stressed that rather than Bakhtin himself, whose views are actually more nuanced than often portrayed, the following remarks are concerned

---

24   In addition to a recognition of the possible educational significance of laughter, which can also be found in the philosophers and political thinkers of antiquity, some of the first not only neutral but outright positive assessments of laughter were based on quasi-medical and psychological considerations. These can already be found among the scholastics of the High Middle Ages, who recognised laughter as re-creative. The major breakthrough for this kind of recognition of the biology of laughter came with a French doctor who was born two years before the death of Oecolampadius. In 1560, Laurent Joubert (1529–82) published a groundbreaking treatise on the causes of laughter; but his major work appeared in 1579 with the sweepingly ambitious title: 'Treatise on Laughter, Containing Its Essence, Its Causes and Its Marvellous Effects, Curiously Researched, Reasoned, and Observed by Mr. Laur[ent] Joubert' (cf. Prütting 2013, ch. 2.9).

   In passing, it should be noted that over the last 40 to 50 years the Anglo-Saxon world in particular has been intensely involved in scientific studies of the positive effects of laughter, effects both in the social interaction between people, and, above all, within psychology and medicine. Here they try to demonstrate that not only is it good to laugh because of 'internal' causes (humour, comedy), but that even 'mechanically' triggered laughter is beneficial for both health and psyche. Suffice it here to point to the popular spread of hospital clowns (cf. Matthiae 2023 for a short historical overview and a testimony of her own practice) or Norman Cousins' (1915–90) international bestseller *Anatomy of an Illness as Perceived by the Patient* (1979), which the publishers of the Danish translation chose to give the very telling title: 'I laughed myself healthy'.

with the history of his influence, his epigones, and like-minded people during the 1960s-70s.

In order to recall the mood from just half a century ago, we can for example refer to Harvey Gallagher Cox's (b. 1929) immensely popular *The Feast of Fools* from 1969 with its telling subtitle: *A Theological Essay on Festivity and Fantasy*. The rapid translation of the book into all the major languages illustrates the receptivity of that period to Cox's Bakhtin-esque celebration of the essence of festivities and their potential for effecting social change. What Cox emphasises as a characteristic of a social institution such as a feast or a carnival can, roughly speaking, also be said – and has often been said – about the phenomenon of laughter.

Cox defines a feast (or more broadly: festivity) as 'a socially approved occasion for the expression of feelings that are normally repressed or neglected'. It is characterised by being both a 'conscious excess' and a 'celebratory affirmation', and it achieves its special status by being a clear contrast to everyday life (Cox uses the term 'juxtaposition' to signify the holding together of two very different worlds). In addition to these analytical definitions, Cox adds the religious-sounding interpretation that part of the 'excess' of the feast is to suspend the ordinary life's reduction of the present to serve the future, so that participants in the feast can devote themselves fully to the moment (*nunc stans*). In other words, the potential of a feast is to become a counterweight to the kind of longing for the future which despises the past and hates the present, i.e. a gnostic hatred of that which precisely ties us to these circumstances, namely the body and the earth.[25]

Two important cues have already been given for this fundamental discussion about the understanding of medieval feasts. One was signalled when 'for a day' was put in italics, while the remark about the priest's traditional position in relation to laughter constituted the second cue. Roughly speaking, the disagreement revolves around whether these feasts really can support the claim that they constitute a kind of independent lifestyle and world view. Did they actually establish a counterculture with a potentially destructive threat to society, or did they, with their regulated content and as fixed parts of the church calendar, rather serve a socially stabilising function?[26]

On the one hand, it sometimes seems as if descriptions of the medieval festivals have fallen for an obviously tempting anachronism in almost confusing them with the infamous happening during the French Revolution, where God was

---

25   Cox 1969, 22–4 and 40.
26   Cf. Moser 1990, 93 and Teuber's article from 1988 titled 'Carnival as radical Dissent'.

deposed by placing a statue of Reason in the place of the altar in Paris' Notre Dame Cathedral. Such a projection leads astray, for as Max Harris (b. 1949) has shown in his brilliant post-Bakhtinian monograph: when a choir boy or a subdeacon was elevated to bishop during the Feast of the Innocents (28 December) or the Feast of the Circumcision (1 January) the point was not to stage a rebellion against God, not even against the ecclesiastical hierarchy. By letting 'one of the least' appear as a representative of the kind of Lord who Christ is, this has to be understood in the light of Mary's Canticle ('he has brought down the mighty from their thrones and exalted those of humble estate', Lk 1:52 *ESV*) and thus becomes a lesson in the heavenly hierarchy and a reminder to the earthly rulers of proper humility.[27]

On the other hand, we can appreciate Peter von Möllendorff's (b. 1963) scepticism towards reducing the carnival events completely to an ecclesiastical educational project.[28] Even if we sense yet another anachronistic ideologisation of the political dimension of the feasts, Zucker's philosophical reflection can give some support to Möllendorff's point of view: although the upside-down world of the feasts definitely took place within fixed frameworks, 'yet the phenomenon of tolerance of disorderliness, for even the shortest period, provides us with some insight into the ontological ambiguity of all order.'[29]

Despite the fact that Marcel Marc Gutwirth (b. 1923) is not referring specifically to the Middle Ages nor the Feast of the Ass/Child Bishop, but is more generally concerned with laughter and comedy (epitomised in the figure of the jester), he very aptly pinpoints the problem when basing political visions on the 'revaluation of all values' of the feast and the jester: first because – apropos 'for a day' – 'I rejoice in the defeat of reason in laughter solely because it is brief and unenduring';[30] secondly, because politicisation overburdens amusement by underestimating both its ephemerality and (one might say) its 'faithlessness':

> In a culture of rebellion laughter finds itself invested with a mission that goes well beyond its charter: that of a transvaluation of values, bringing down what is now high,

---

27 M. Harris 2011, 68. For some of the other festivals cf. Wolfgang Max Zucker's (1905–83) point that though Shrovetide could be exuberant it still 'ended on the minute' on Ash Wednesday (1967, 314). Likewise Erik Thorstensen (b. 1972) criticises the one-sided focus of previous research on the donkey (in the Feast of the Ass, most often celebrated on 14 January) as a symbol of sexual appetite or lack of intelligence, thereby underestimating its use as a typology of low status and humility (1999, 46). Here and througout the book three capital italicised letters identify the particular English Bible translation from which a quotation is taken. A key to unlock the abbreviations can be found on biblehub.com.
28 Möllendorff 1995, 87–90.
29 Zucker 1967, 314.
30 Gutwirth 1993, 28.

setting up what was deemed low. The Lord of Misrule, however, is king only for a day. Laughter does briefly institute a world that is topsy-turvy; it does not erect inverted towers. Revolutionary fervour is as fair a target as establishment piety.[31]

The same point, but now as a painful observation, is reached by Stefan Zweig (1881–1943), when on the one hand he observes that Desiderius Erasmus of Rotterdam (1466–1536) in his *In Praise of Folly* (1511) had put forward a criticism of the popes and the Roman Church which was completely in line with Luther's, but on the other hand had to acknowledge 'that it is not reproof of a wrong, but the form the reproof takes, which is of historical importance'. This is because 'derision and laughter exist only as negative forces, they are not capable of assembling energies for a creative impact'.[32]

However, the argument can be taken one step further by making Gutwirth's general 'culture of rebellion' more specific. This is done by Keith Vivian Thomas (b. 1933) who deals with a period 'of rebellion' closely related to Oecolampadius' lifetime, namely the Reformation in England in the 16th century. His subject is not exactly the church festivals but a kind of written counterpart to these in the form of the so-called Jest Books. These were used for political as well as ecclesiastical and theological satire – and often in a very crude style. Thomas, too, has an eye for dialectics and sees that in the midst of its biting criticism, the distortion of the comic is in its own way quite conventional, i.e. 'it reinforced accepted morality by mocking superiors by standards which they themselves uphold'. At the same time, Thomas also recognises that while 'most laughter may have been conservative in effect, [...] there was also a current of radical, critical laughter which, instead of reinforcing accepted norms, sought to give the world a nudge in a new direction'. The additional perspective comes with Thomas' emphasis on this crucial difference: whether the humourist's criticism is exercised within a monoculture or in a schismatic culture. In a Catholic medieval setting the Church can tolerate a lot of ridiculous turning-things-on-their-head, safe in the knowledge that at the end of the feast things will figuratively return to their feet; but in a time of intensely warring denominations, laughter becomes far more dangerous – which is one of Thomas' explanations for the intensification of censorship under the Tudor and Stuart monarchs.[33]

---

31 *Ibid.*, 72.
32 Zweig 1937, 145.
33 Thomas 1977, 77 ff. For a brief and well-documented account of both Bachtin's own project as well as the arguments from later scholars supporting or opposing his historical claims see Lühl 2019, 106–27.

2. The Means Used to Stimulate Easter Laughter

In Chapter III, the theological but certainly also very mundane arguments for linking Easter and laughter will be reviewed more systematically. Here we turn instead to the more immediate question of how laughter was evoked – and the perspectives therein. Judging by the few contemporary examples of Easter Laughter, there are some which – liberally! – could be interpreted as attempts to maintain some kind of genuine connection, i.e. in the sense that especially the depiction of the Devil's defeat Easter Morning seems to have been the subject of great enjoyment (cf. the epigram from Johannes Mathesius [1504–65]).[34]

Unfortunately for us, Oecolampadius subjects himself to self-censorship: 'I am ashamed to defile my writings with such jokes, so as not to offend pious ears'

---

34 To anticipate our later discussion, it should be noted that there is a considerable risk of distorting the historical description of Easter Laughter even further by writing 'especially'. For it is not at all improbable that the story of Jesus' victorious and laughter-provoking descent into hell on Easter Saturday may have been told only once in a sermon, maybe twice, and then retold by historians *ad infinitum* – and now also in this book! Cf. note 74.

Be that as it may, it is still quite fascinating to discover how a folktale and an apocryphal motif can overlap despite a thousand-year separation. Among the texts from Nag-Hammadi a story attributed to the apostle Bartholomew was found in which Jesus' dwelling in hell ('Amente') after his crucifixion is described in surprising detail. Death notices that something has disturbed the order in hell, and when he discovers that Jesus has been put to rest he figures that his body is the cause of the disturbance. He goes to seek out the body, but when he stands before it asking it a lot of questions, Jesus does not answer any of them; instead he does something so remarkable that apparently Death has never before seen it, for it certainly has a drastic effect on him: 'Then Jesus removed the napkin which was on His face, and He looked in the face of Death, and laughed at him. Now as Death gazed on the Saviour as He was laughing at him, he became greatly disturbed; and he fled away back, and fell down upon the earth.' However, Death returns, and when Jesus once more laughs him in the face, this very laughter gives Death a clue about his identity: 'Who art Thou? Shew me. Is it possible that Thou art the first-born of the Father, the Holy Lamb?' Budge 1913, 181–2. The text is not included in Edgar Hennecke (1865–1951) and Wilhelm Schneemelcher's (1914–2003) first German editions of the Apocrypha; but in the later editions (both the German and the English translation) it is mentioned briefly at the end of volume 1. Schneemelcher estimates the text to date from the 5th-7th centuries, but possibly with roots in a tradition reaching back to the 3rd-4th centuries, 1991, vol. 1, 557.

(|14|);³⁵ but even so, we are not completely at a loss when it comes to getting an idea of the character of laughter. There are at least two places where we can plausibly look for comparable material. This assumption is supported by the fact that the short list of examples which Oecolampadius does offer are strikingly reminiscent of the tone and content found in these two other sources (cf. |16|).

Although it was claimed earlier that Easter Laughter differs from the religious plays that flourished especially in England, France, and Germany in the late Middle Ages and Early Modern Period, that distinction is more about the 'setting' than the subject matter. If we therefore take a look at these kinds of religious drama, we will discover a perhaps quite unexpected fact: while the mystery plays not surprisingly derive the majority of their material more or less directly from the Bible, the added material, according to a couple of leading scholars, is characterised by being mainly of a comic nature.³⁶ These scholars also confirm that in their material it is the Devil in particular who is the target of laughter (and probably constitutes a source for the development of the Harlequin figure and the jester³⁷). Other figures than the Devil also become the butt of laughter. According to these scholars, a manifestly popular scene, since it occurs in several versions, is about how the women on their way to the tomb on Easter

---

35   While not using the expression *risus paschalis* Oecolampadius most definitely refers to it in his sermon 'Of true joy on the day of Easter' (1927b, cf. note 241), but here too there is not much help to be had for the historically curious. Standing in the pulpit he is obviously even more restrained in that he does not give a single example of what it is that he is condemning. Numbers in vertical bars refer to the sections in ch. 5.

36   Nicoll 1963, 179; cf. ch. 6 ('Religious Laughter') and ch. 7 ('The Invention of Comic Action') in Kolve 1966, 124–74; Wehrli 1984, 171–3, and Diller 1999, 181 ff. Interestingly, Detlef Metz (b. 1964) shows in his doctoral dissertation on Protestant drama and theatre, which emerged as early as 1523, that although serious biblical and church historical figures and themes could be depicted at length, this was often combined with a comic subplot: 'These are often scenes characterised by crude comedy, in which the authors like to have farmers appear. These *interludi* have a purely entertaining function and are obviously intended to satisfy the audience's need to keep their attention focused on the action, which is sometimes considered too serious.' Metz 2013, 27.

A church historian provides a crude, indeed outrageous example of the slapstick comedy involved in this kind of drama (unfortunately without citing his source): 'In an Easter play, during the high priest's interrogation, Malkus pulls the chair away from Christ, so that he falls to the floor.' Bergmann 1944, 189, note 1.

37   With regard to the sermons, cf. Wendland 1980, 44 and Linsenmayer 1969, 180, note 2.

morning are late for the resurrection because they have to buy ointments and are delayed by an endlessly haggling merchant (Mk 16:1 provides the biblical fig leaf for this comical effect). The male disciples were perhaps better at avoiding such cheap sales tricks, but instead their competition to be the first to reach the grave became another popular motif for amusement (cf. Jn 20:3–10). We can also easily imagine the comedy of confusion which John exposes Mary Magdalene to in the following verses of his gospel, for is it really Jesus or just a gardener?[38]

Another source of indirect knowledge about Easter Laughter also happens to be preserved in writing, for in the years just before and after Oecolampadius' book two popular collections of stories were published by Heinrich Bebel (1472–1518) (*Libri facetiarum iucundissimi* ['Books of the Most Delightful Tales'], 3-volume work 1508–12) and Johannes Pauli (*c.* 1455–1530/33) (*Schwank und Ernst* ['Amusing and Earnest Tales'], 1522).[39] That it is acceptable to use these

---

[38] It should be noted that Christmas is also capable of providing opportunities for comedy, such as Joseph musing about being a trusting husband or a gullible cuckold, or the shepherds in the field who pass the time complaining about the weather and quarrelling among themselves about who is best suited to tend the sheep. Perhaps the theologically weightiest joke of them all is the stunned reaction of the midwife who checks Mary after having given birth only to discover that she is still a virgin, cf. Nicoll 1963, 179–87. Not only his conception but also his birth was immaculate?!

[39] From a broad historical perspective, such collections can be considered part of a tradition reaching back to literary masterpieces such as *The Decameron* by Giovanni Boccaccio (1313–75) and Geoffrey Chaucer's (*c.* 1343–1400) *Canterbury Tales*, both of which are 'anthologies' of independent stories tied more or less together by a framing narrative. Nor should we forget the great forerunner to Bebel and Pauli, namely the famous Gian Francesco Poggio Bracciolini (1380–1459), who from the middle of the 15th century was the first to publish collections of very diverse stories under a title which from then on became the name of a specific literary genre: 'Facetiae'. Before Poggio's books were placed on the Index Expurgatorius in 1559 by the Council of Trent they had been reprinted all over Europe in close to 200 editions; cf. Oecolampadius' reference to Poggio in |38| and the notes there.

While this kind of literature was primarily intended for a secular public, it had an ecclesiastical counterpart in collections of tales and riddles (e.g. 'who is dead without being born?' 'Adam!', Suchier 1955, 83) with biblical material, but with a decidedly comical or satirical twist. These flourished in the monasteries in the early Middle Ages under names such as *Ioca monachorum* or the even older work *Cena Cypriani* (both of which were mentioned by Umberto Eco [1932-2016] in *The Name of the Rose*, 1984, 436–8; cf. Lehmann 1922, 22 f. and 25–30, and Modesto 1992). As such, these collections of cheerful stories fit into the slipstream of the homiletical handbooks that were very common in the Middle Ages and which helped the preachers with suitable

books to infer something about the means used to arouse the congregation's Easter Laughter should be apparent from Pauli's own preface. He not only specifically designates three target groups, but at the same time uses some of the arguments that appear most frequently in defence of Easter Laughter over the following centuries. On the one hand, Pauli has those in mind who 'live in castles and citadels and are lascivious' (*vff den schlössern und bergen wonen vnd geil sein*), for they can reform themselves after reading the book's 'frightening and stern cases' (*erschrockenliche vnd ernstliche ding*). On the other hand, his book is also suitable for 'the spiritual children' (*die geistlichen Kinder*) in the monasteries so that from time to time they can invigorate their spirits, because, Pauli argues, it is not good to be serious all the time. Finally, the book ensures that 'the preachers can have examples that can wake up the sleepy and make them want to listen, and that they can have an *osterspil* at Easter'.[40] Pauli adds the assurance that 'nothing is included here that cannot be preached honourably'; but as a precaution – if something 'punishable' (*sträflichs*) should have crept into his book – Pauli ends the preface with asking for mercy and forgiveness not only from Our Lord, but also from His mother, a few saints, the whole heavenly host, and all people.[41]

A morally reassuring attempt at an overall description of this kind of literature is provided in a French introduction to the subject from 1786:

> Under the name *Faceties* are nowadays included all stories of a free and common character, neat tales, witty answers, short bold satires, paradoxes, which amuse by their contrast to the generally accepted ideas, all kinds of amusements, which do not always agree with an exquisite tone, and finally all kinds of pranks which, so as not to alarm modesty, are clever enough to make themselves unintelligible to innocence.[42]

---

narrative material (the so-called 'examples'). According to Herbert Wolf (1930–2017), some of the most used were *Speculum exemplorum* by Jacques de Vetry (d. 1240), *Moralizationes historiarum* by Robert Holkot (d. 1349), *Dialogus miraculorum* by Caesarius von Heisterbach (d. *c.* 1240), *Disciplina clericalis* by Petrus Alphonsi (d. *c.* 1110), and *Alphabetum narrationum* by Arnoldus Leodiensis (d. *c.* 1309) – to name just a few from Wolf's long list. Although emphasis here was not placed especially on the comic, Wolf nevertheless emphasises the entertaining character of the material, which their publishers clearly attempted to domesticate by means of a drastic, pasted-on allegorical moral, Wolf 1962, 79 ff.

40   Pauli 1866, 14. 'Osterspil' seems to have had several meanings ranging, broadly speaking, from an equivalent to the British mystery plays and similar kinds of religious drama to the telling of a good story, including jokes.
41   Ibid.
42   *Bibliotèque universelle des romans*, 3–4.

With the methodological caveat that Elfriede Moser-Rath's (1926–93) material is much younger than that to which Oecolampadius refers, an observation from a third source can be inserted to expand the French description. For in this context it does not seem unreasonable to assume an essential relationship between the preachers of the late 16th and 17th centuries and those from around 1500.[43] The benefit from studying the baroque material is that it is extracted from printed sermons and thus not culled from special collections of stories whose representativeness and influence it can be difficult to determine anything about with certainty (even if the number of reprints is a good indicator). In other words, it gives an insight into the actual preaching, and as such it is a great help in forming an impression of the breadth of the narrative material used in terms of its formal and literary character. In this way, the misunderstanding is averted that it consisted purely of vulgar jokes, which is otherwise the impression left by Oecolampadius and a long line of critics during the following period.[44] Indeed, Moser-Rath admits that scholars are not sure how to appropriately define the non-biblical narrative material in the sermons. She then goes on to emphasise that:

---

43 That assumption is supported by comparing Moser-Rath's examples with the many medieval 'Easter tales' (*Ostermärchen*) presented by Wendland, 1980, 117–61.

44 'In the confessional polemics, however, the Protestant side soon began to condemn both the sermon tale [*Predigtmärlein*] and, as a prime example, Easter Laughter in the same breath as untrue legends, visions, fake relics, and dubious reports of miracles as one single web of lies on the Catholic side.' Wendland 1980, 52.

   It is either an expression of brutal irony or a sensible warning against lumping all non-biblical narratives together that one of Oecolampadius' most devoted 'disciples', Johannes Gast (d. 1552), is known not only for having recorded and published Oecolampadius' sermons and lectures but also for having published *Convivales sermones* in 1541–51, a highly popular collection of anecdotes in three volumes. The fact that Gast's collection is said to have provided the template for the Faust story as well as the *Lalebuch* (somewhat similar to English chapbooks with low-comedy stories) at first points us in the direction of irony, but perhaps we could also think of the collection as a very stubborn attempt to distinguish between entertainment and edification. As such, Gast could be a forerunner of the publications of lighthearted tales during the subsequent century, which publishers struggled to make morally palatable by emphasising that they did not serve for imitation but for deterrence. At least this kind of defence is what the German translator of Otto Melander's (1571–1640) *Ioco-Seria* uses in his preface signed 1605, Melander 1617, vol. 1, 3–4. In all fairness it should also be noted that Gast does not apparently imagine his collected stories to be used in the pulpit, but rather, as is clear from the 'subtitle', as something with which to spice up the conversation in the company of pleasant friends.

> [...] basically, any story, be it a religiously instructive example or a legend, an ancient anecdote, a historical report, a chronicle, a fable or a tall tale [*Schwank*], sometimes even a novella or fairy tale, can become a sermon tale [*Predigtmärlein*], as long as there is some spiritual or moral pedagogical instruction to be derived from it.

Moser-Rath rounds off these genre considerations with a particularly enlightening conclusion: 'The word [i.e. *Predigtmärlein*] does not characterise the type, but rather the function of a story as part of the sermon.'[45]

Despite Pauli's declaration that nothing dishonourable could be found in his book, both he and Bebel include, to put it euphemistically, a lot of *very* non-biblical narrative material in their collections. Where the first edition of Pauli only has titles for the individual stories, the later editions add thematic headings to the chapters which the stories are divided into. Even a first glance at these headings gives a sense of the content:

> 1) About emperors and secular authority; 2) about rulings, judges, and notaries; 3) about doctors and students; 4) about household and business; 5) about art and artists; 6) about fools and idiots; 7) about vices, in general; 8) about the pope and papal authority; 9) about monks and priests; 10) about nuns and monastic women; 11) about penitence and confessions; 12) about devils and evil spirits; 13) about death and dying.

Behind this wide-ranging gallery of persons and motifs, we can, broadly speaking, identify as the most frequent characters: hypocritical clerics, stupid (and uncouth) peasants, and, above all, the *lusty* youngsters, followed closely by the quarrel between spouses (in other words, an almost straight line can be drawn to characters known from Shakespeare, Molière [1622–73], and many other writers of comedy).[46] Based on Oecolampadius' short list of examples (|16|), it can be

---

45 Moser-Rath 1964, 3; cf. Wolf 1962, 78. In this sense *mährlein* is an equally wide-ranging and thus difficult to define genre as *facetiae*, about which Barbara Cherry Bowen (1937–2019) similarly writes: 'To call them [e.g. Poggio's collections] "joke-books" or "jestbooks" is actually misleading, since alongside jokes we can still laugh at today, they contain classical anecdotes, maxims and apophthegms, medieval *exempla*, fables, proverbs, fragments of autobiography, epigrams, and even riddles.' Bowen 1988, xiv.

46 A charming and oft-quoted example of how Bebel strives for fairness in describing the battle of the sexes (even if the men's victory is achieved by the narrowest of margins) is given in his double anecdote about two alleged incidents in the same year: 'On the day of the Lord's resurrection, a preacher in Waiblingen commanded, as it is customary everywhere on this day to perform plays and pranks, that any man present, if it is he and not the woman who is master of the house, should begin singing "Christ arose from the dead". When the preacher had waited in vain for a long time, he cried

assumed with some degree of certainty that the stories used by preachers were in line with those of Bebel and Pauli. If so, this suggests that it was more the scatological than the eschatological stories that stimulated laughter, even though there is considerable disagreement among scholars about the extent to which an erotic element figured as a means to trigger Easter Laughter.[47]

As a starting point, we should take note of what Oecolampadius has experienced: 'I have seen the most venerable men, dutiful and faithful listeners to the word of God, rushing home at this point, lest they should have their worship defiled by such jokes' (|14|). Though the question then is: what made the respectable men take offence? The few examples given by Oecolampadius are undeniably silly but hardly vile. Far more suggestive is a passage in Capito's short preface where he defends Oecolampadius with this statement: 'He does not make his listeners burst into raucous laughter when proclaiming Christ. He neither entertains with obscene remarks nor behaves like an actor who, by means of lewd imitations, evokes before their eyes what spouses tend to delight themselves

---

out: "Alas, almighty God, has the manly courage among you completely disappeared, that no one rules like a man?" At last there was one who would no longer bear that shame, and he began to sing. The other men praised him as a defender of manly honour and saluted him because he had been an ornament and honour to all men. In the same year, namely 1506, a brother from the Order of Preachers did likewise in the monastery of Marchtal, which is located on the Danube. But when no man wanted to start, he asked those women who ruled at home to start. Then they all immediately broke out into a struggle for power.' Bebel 1907, 13 (no. 21). A third variant of the joke has the preacher, when none of the men in church dares to show with his singing that he rules at home, burst into song himself, and supposedly that incident should have taken place a good hundred years earlier in 1399, although Hanns Fluck (b. 1908, fl. 1931-4) admits that he has no reliable documentation for the dating, Fluck 1934, 189.

47 We are well advised to keep Bowen's sober and nuanced admonition in mind: only with great caution can we draw general conclusions about taste and the sense of humour in the Early Modern Period. Bowen's warning is based on much more extensive material than Bebel and Pauli, i.e. from Petrarch (1304–74) to a French publication in 1559, but her two arguments are powerful and simple: there is a big difference between the various collections, where some indulge in obscene jokes, while others are completely free of erotic innuendo. Furthermore, according to Bowen's estimation, up to 90 % of the material is copied from sources ranging from antiquity to the present, so how are we to draw any firm conclusion about what was typical of the material that amused people in this particular period? Bowen also warns against the temptation to talk about national characteristics and uses an example that is highly relevant in this context: 'Does the scatology in Bebel prove that Germans are

with in the bedroom, when they are alone and without witnesses' (|2|, cf. |27–28| where Oecolampadius suggests something similar).

On the one hand, Moser-Rath argues that posterity's treatment of the topic exaggerates the erotic nature of the stories. For one thing she claims that such material is absent in the many hundreds of sermons (admittedly from the 17th century) which are presented in her book; moreover, she points out that the question of misplaced eroticism is not raised by the many critics who otherwise did not excel in distinguishing between factual and unsubstantiated accusations.[48]

On the other hand, Wendland prefers to explain the absence of obscenities in the *written* sources as due to the same kind of modesty that makes Oecolampadius refrain from describing the obscenities in detail.[49] Not surprisingly, Maria Caterina Jacobelli (b. 1928) goes the furthest, both because her overall perspective is to view laughter and sexuality as two sides of the same, ecclesiastically repressed, coin,[50] and because she also analyses the material from a religio-historical theory that is very similar to that of Reinach.[51] Moser-Rath offers a truly thoughtful observation when she remarks that in an age that otherwise had a robust relationship with the sexual,[52] it would indeed have had to be extremely crude pranks used by the preachers if precisely that element caused people to flee from church.[53]

---

partial to scatology (an often-heard opinion)? But there is almost none in Bebel's disciple Adelphus, or in Luscinius, also Germans.' Bowen 1988, xvi-xvii. Bowen refers to Johann Adelphus (Müling) (1445–1515/1522) and Otmar Luscinius (Nachtigall) (1487–1536).

48   Moser-Rath 1964, 31–5.
49   Wendland 1980, 179.
50   Cf. note 482 with Jacobelli's suggestion for an even more explicitly sexual translation of an obscure passage in Capito's text.
51   Cf. the intermezzo in chapter III,6 and p. 14 f.
52   This can be found, for example, in the popular stories about Till Eulenspiegel, which first appeared in print in 1510, in the plays of Hans Sachs (1494–1576) from the mid-16th century, and not least in the many almost lascivious figures with which medieval churches were decorated both outside and inside. Jacobelli draws heavily on this kind of material in her analyses, cf. the subtitle of her book: 'Sexuality and Desire in the Space of the Sacred' (see e.g. 35 ff. and 44 ff.), cf. furthermore the articles in the 2012 anthology on smiles and laughter in medieval art edited by Wilhelmy. Another source for gaining an impression of the Middle Ages' brash use of nudity and sexuality can be found in the marginal illustrations to many texts, where especially jester figures appeared scantily dressed, cf. J. Palmer 1994, 45.
53   Moser-Rath 1964, 31 f. A similar disagreement can be found between Fluck and Jacobelli. Interestingly, while they broadly agree on the presentation of the material

What matters in this context, to return to Pauli's statement, is not the question of whether we in general agree with him in finding the stories acceptable in church, or whether we can always follow him in particular cases in his attempt to draw firm didactic moral lessons from the jokes (throughout the book he alternates between the 'jest' and 'seriousness' of the title, *Schimpf und Ernst*). Instead the decisive impression we are left with after reading Oecolampadius' few examples combined with the more than a thousand stories from Bebel and Pauli is a desire to raise laughter at any cost! Does that signal the arrival of an understanding of laughter beyond morality?

This, to be clear, is not intended as a claim that preachers in the time of Oecolampadius had already invented the sympathetic and conciliatory kind of laughter which is popularly called laugh-with as opposed to laugh-at laughter.[54] Historically speaking it would be more reasonable to credit the British

---

they are in diametrical disagreement about the interpretation of the development of Easter Laughter. Fluck's thesis is that it is a story of decline, where an original evangelical laughter of joy undergoes a profanation and vulgarisation. Jacobelli, on the other hand, believes – and her interpretation does seem more convincing – that the decidedly sexual and scatological allusions were at the core of the original practice, whereas the means to make people laugh are cleaned up and stylised over the course of the 16th and especially the 17th centuries. This is done by largely narrativising the phenomenon, which is to say that the various physical expressions and actions are replaced by laughter-inducing anecdotes. These could very well be quite risqué in themselves, but over the course of a few generations these too were transformed into standardised and edifying narratives that were more likely to invite a good-natured smile than provoke a raw and lecherous guffaw. For the record, it should be added that Fluck seems theoretically to presuppose an 'original' Easter Laughter, the decline of which had already occurred by the time of Oecolampadius. Fluck 1934, 209–11 and Jacobelli 1992, 63 respectively.

54 This distinction is pregnant with historical meaning and we shall be returning to it in subsequent chapters, but in order already at this point to give a fuller impression of what the distinction entails it is helpful to borrow from Terri Bednarz' (b. 1962) figure of a broad understanding of humour. Even though Bednarz' main focus is on humour, her distinction between non-tendentious and tendentious humour throws light on what we mean by laugh-with vs. laugh-at, or as she prefers: sympathetic vs. derisive laughter. Under non-tendentious forms of humour she lists bantering, paradox, incongruity, comic exaggeration, absurd images, scatological jokes, irony, witty dicta, befuddling stories, and paronomasia. On the other side she places derogatory epithets, ridicule, invective, disarming wit, sarcasm, satire, cutting irony, trenchant rejoinders, raillery, derisive caricatures, and acerbic rhetoric. 2015, 4.

humourists with a decisive role in having developed that kind of laughter some centuries later.[55] However, what can reasonably be argued as the theological and cultural-historical potential of Easter Laughter is this: while the examples of Oecolampadius, Bebel, Pauli, and the religious plays probably most often do appeal to a superior laugh-at laughter, i.e. ridiculing sin (and sinners), they also open up for a laughter that is not only laughter for the *sake* of laughter. In other words, they clear the way for a kind of laughter that has detached itself from being domesticated by morality, a laughter that not only puts us in our place, but is also liberating, a jubilant laughter beyond morality.

Can laughter in itself be a good thing? If the preachers were willing to go as far as the historical documents indicate in order to release laughter, is that then a sign of them having allowed themselves to reverse the order of the factors: just as joy *can* express itself in laughter, can laughter in itself create joy? If so: even a joy commensurable with the overcoming of death and the return of life in the resurrection of Jesus?[56]

---

55 Throughout the 20th century there seems to have been a conscious effort among scholars in various fields of the humanities to rehabilitate the Middle Ages and shake off their reputation for being 'dark'. Thus many have argued that the Middle Ages were also full of fun in the broadest sense, see for example pioneers such as Curtius 1939, Tatlock 1946, and Adolf 1947; more recent articles and monographs by White 1960, Kremer 1961, Blaicher 1970, Billman 1980, Resnick 1987, Haug 1989, Lindgren 1995, Le Goff 1997 and 2008, Röcke 1998, Ferm 2002 and 2008, Coxon 2008, and Trokhimenko 2014; as well as the anthologies from recent decades, typically with contributions from international interdisciplinary conferences: Röcke & Neumann 1999, Halsall 2002, Braet, Latré & Verbeke 2003, Grebe & Staubach 2005, Röcke & Velten 2005, Gvozdeva & Röcke 2009, Classen 2010, Biessenecker 2012, Biessenecker & C. Kuhn 2012, and Wilhelmy 2012a. It goes without saying that significant contributions about the Middle Ages are also included in anthologies about the history of laughter in general, such as S. Jäkel & Timonen 1994–5, S. Jäkel, Timonen & Rissanen 1997, Bremmer & Roodenburg 1997a, Pfister 2002, and Richert 2009.

 The subject can easily turn into a fruitless dispute about words, but without necessarily wanting to give the 18th-century British novelists a *copyright* on humour something special does happen in that era that at least urges caution against presuming that words like 'laughter', 'the comic', 'humour', etc. have exactly the same meaning before and after that time. Cf. IV,2,v.

56 At this point, let it serve as a testimony to the complex relationship between laughter and joy that Pope Paul VI's (1897–1978) apostolic letter on Christian joy (*Gaudete in domino*, 9 May 1975) manages to write close to thirty pages about this topic, yet mentions laughter only once. This one use of the word appears when the document quotes the verse from the Beatitudes of Jesus about weeping and laughter (Lk 6:21).

3. How Old Is Easter Laughter?

The quote from Pauli contains two modest, yet significant keywords that can lead us to the most contentious questions among historians: when and where did Easter Laughter originate? As mentioned in the introduction, Oecolampadius has only *coined* the technical and scholarly expression *risus paschalis*, and determining both its age and geography is to a considerable extent a matter of *definition*. In short, the tighter the definition, the narrower the localisation in both time and space. Some of the important characteristics of Easter Laughter have been highlighted above, and it is precisely because of the groundbreaking nature of these characteristics that a relatively strict definition is preferable.

The first of Pauli's keywords is 'also'! For this indicates that his humorous stories were intended for use throughout the year, including but not restricted to Easter. This points to a methodological dilemma that should be kept in mind: while on one hand it speaks to an obvious kinship between different kinds of laughter, there is, on the other hand, a risk of overlooking the crucial *differences* which the initial description of Easter Laughter highlighted. It is obviously relevant to consider the narrow discussion of Easter Laughter in the light of the broader discussion about the ambivalent relationship of laughter to faith and the Church, which, as already indicated, stretches back to the earliest Christianity. However, if and when this is done, we should be aware of those differences, especially if we assume that Easter Laughter in particular has helped theologically and ecclesiastically to pave the way for a changed view of laughter in general.

Even if we narrow the topic down to a specific concern with the interaction of priests with laughter in the Church, the debate is almost as old. For Chrysostom not only poses the rhetorical question about Jesus' own laughter, but also elaborates his criticism of laughter in connection with a discussion of the inappropriateness of laughing in Church in the same way as people do in the theatre.[57] In this broad perspective, it is possible within canon law from as early as the High Middle Ages and throughout the following centuries to find prohibitions against priests causing excessive (read: audible!) laughter in the church as well as strict rules for their own laughter.[58] To contextualise and to put

---

57 Cf. Chrysostom's 'Against games and theatre. A sermon against those who leave the church to go to the games and the theatre' (1862c); cf. Oecolampadius' use of Chrysostom in |47|.
58 As Heinz-Günter Schmitz (1938–2021) thought-provokingly points out, it even applies to the otherwise 'cosmopolitan' (*weltfreudige*) and 'culture-affirming' (*kulturbejahende*) 12th century that the great theologians of the period warn priests against

this kind of legislation into perspective, reference can be made to the two literary giants, Dante (1265–1321) and Boccaccio. Although they have quite different agendas the very fact that both of them allude to this homiletic laughter gives us a sense of how noteworthy and how problematic the approach to, and use of, laughter by the new monastic orders seemed to their contemporaries.

---

behaving like buffoons (German: *Possenreisser*, or the Latin terms *histrio* and *iocolator*) in the pulpit with inappropriate narratives (referred to in the sources with various terms with overlapping meaning for sharp, worldly, or silly jokes such as *sales, facetiae, urbanitas,* or *otiositas*). As referenced in H.G. Schmitz 1972, 196 this applies, among others, to Peter Damian (*c.* 1006–72) (1853, col. 258) and Bernard of Clairvaux (1859, col. 736). The latter makes sure that he does not refer to the harmless meaning of *otiositas* ('leisure', 'idleness') by succinctly defining it as 'the mother of jokes, the stepmother of virtues' (*mater nugarum, noverca virtutum*).

Jacobelli has written the only monograph to date dealing exclusively with Easter Laughter. As the earliest example she has been able to find she cites from a collection of rules for the proper conduct of priests from 852 by Hinkmar (800/10–882), Archbishop of Rheims: '[the priest] must not bring about applause or unbridled laughter [*risus inconditos*], or tell frivolous stories [*fabulas inanes*] or sing'. Though it is off-topic it is too tempting not to quote the end of the instruction as well: 'nor shall he permit indecent acts to be performed before him with bears and dancers, nor tolerate that demon masks, popularly called animal masks, are presented', Hinkmar 1852, col. 776; cf. Jacobelli 1992, 31 f. However, it appears that Jacobelli does not quite hit the mark, because Hinkmar's teaching is hardly about church ceremonies but about the (social) gatherings of priests (*kalendae*) and their participation in other festivities ... with or without bears. Therefore it must be emphasised that Jacobelli places Hinkmar in a section on the '*prehistory*' of Easter Laughter, but evidently not everyone cares to appreciate this point and so feels free to state as a matter of fact without even referencing Jacobelli that 'the practice of Easter Laughter is documented in Rheims in 852', F. Lienhard 2023, 251; cf. p. 13 f. about attempts to trace Easter Laughter back to the Greek Orthodox tradition.

Joachim Suchomski (fl. 1975–9) has compiled a whole list of similar canon law prohibitions from the time after Hinkmar, i.e. throughout the 10th-14th centuries (1975, 24 ff.); he has also found a section in the much older collection of canonical rules known as *Hibernensis* (*c.* 710), which regulates against the participation of priests in festivities where 'scurrilous' and 'shamelessly joking' words will damage their reputation (*clericus scurrilis et verbis turpibus jocularis degradetur*). In fact, Suchomski argues that this rule itself is based on a provision in the even older collection that goes by the name *Statuta ecclesiae antiqua* (formerly attributed to a Fourth Lateran Council in 398, but according to later research the *Statuta* is rather collected and edited by the end of the 5th century). In this statute from late antiquity the threat is palpable and drastic, because if a priest uses those kinds of words he is to

In *The Divine Comedy* (c. 1320) Dante writes tartly:

> Such fables, shouted through the year from pulpits – / some here, some there – outnumber even all / the Lapos and the Bindos Florence has; // so that the wretched sheep, in ignorance, / return from pasture, having fed on wind – / but to be blind to harm does not excuse them. // Christ did not say to his first company: / 'Go, and preach idle stories to the world'; / but he gave them the teaching that is truth, // and truth alone was sounded when they spoke; / and thus, to battle to enkindle faith, / the Gospels served them as both shield and lance. // But now men go to preach with jests and jeers, / and just as long as they can raise a laugh, / the cowl puffs up, and nothing more is asked.[59]

Conversely, in *The Decameron* (c. 1353) Boccaccio uses the comparison with the friars to construct a defence behind which he himself can hide:

> I affirm that I am not of gravity; on the contrary I am so light that I float on the surface of the water; and considering that the sermons which the friars make, when they would chide folk for their sins, are to-day, for the most part, full of jests and merry conceits, and drolleries, I deemed that the like stuff would not ill beseem my stories, written, as they were, to banish women's dumps. However, if thereby they should laugh too much, they may be readily cured thereof by the Lament of Jeremiah, the Passion of the Saviour, or the Complaint of the Magdalen.[60]

Although these examples from official regulations and men of letters are more relevant than a global reference to Feasts of the Ass, Feasts of Fools, Boy Bishops, Shrove Tuesday parades, masquerades, conventions for priests (*kalendae*), etc., we ought to consider the presence of the following elements as *constitutive* of Easter Laughter (and thus potentially a qualitatively different theological assessment of the nature of laughter as such): an Easter worship service, a preacher, a narrative,[61]

---

be disrobed (*clericum scurrilem et verbis turpibus jocularem ab officio retrahendum*), 1783, 469, no. 56 (in Munier 1960, 92 it is number 73); cf. Suchomski 1975, 261. Both *Hibernensis* and *Statuta* predate Hinkmar by a considerable margin; but although it does not seem unreasonable to imply the involvement of laughter this is admittedly not mentioned *expressis verbis*.

59 'Paradise', Song 29, ll. 103–17; 1980–4, vol. 3, 258.
60 *The Decameron*, 'The Author's Epilogue', 1903, vol. 2, 403.
61 Possibly, the narrative may be accompanied by gestures or a performative element (cf. |27|) – which is of course difficult to document or to get a real impression of from written sources, cf. the attempts at interpretation in Röcke 2002.

Although they risk contributing to the anachronistic conflation of Oecolampadius' contemporaries and its much later history of effects (*Wirkungsgeschichte*), two alleged eyewitness accounts can be mentioned, because, despite everything, they both give an impression of a scene which we could well imagine being played out also in the beginning

and laughter (and joy). However, and here we come to Pauli's other important keyword, a given historical record does not necessarily have to mention the term 'Easter Laughter' itself. While it would be almost limitless to talk in general about the problem of laughter in Church, it would limit the field unnecessarily to make the occurrence of '*risus paschalis*' in the sources an indispensable criterion, as Pauli mentions precisely all the constitutive elements and then adds a final keyword: not 'Easter Laughter' but 'Easter Play' (German: *Osterspil*).

At the risk of once again opening up too broad a field (since by no means all of the diverse narratives that the preachers used had laughter as their purpose) we should note a number of more or less technical terms for the nonbiblical narrative material which were used to spice up the Easter sermons. The terms certainly overlap but are not necessarily identical to what is meant by *risus paschalis* (or, for that matter, the later German equivalents: *Osterlachen* or *Ostergelächter*[62]): *ostermärlin*, *ostermärchen*, *osterneu* (= 'Easter tale') as well as

---

of the 16th century. One report dates from 1643 and concerns the priest Abraham Widmann of Röhrmoos near Dachau, who made the congregation laugh by having an assistant crow like a rooster and cluck like a flock of hens throughout the Easter service.

A dramatic, but even more distant example, both in relation to 1518 and to the theme of Easter, dates from as late as 1802. A letter to the editor of the *Münchner Tagblatt* wants to testify to the continued existence of the evil tradition (*böse Sitte*) in the countryside. During the previous Easter Sunday the writer had experienced a 74-year-old priest telling and performing one of those stories which according to the letter was both against reason and the good of the fatherland. In the course of his barbaric narrative the priest used words that a decent newspaper cannot print, allegedly in order to warn youth against speaking just like that. To show what would happen to them if they did, he wrapped the *pallium* around his neck and 'hung' himself with the tongue lashing out of his mouth and with a violent shaking of both hands and feet, before he fell to the bottom of the pulpit. There he lay for several minutes so that the congregation thought something had really happened to him, before he got up and continued joking until he left the pulpit, thus bringing the Easter story to an end. Cf. Wendland 1980, 291–3, where the entire letter is reprinted, and 203 f. about Widmann.

62 Wendland (1980, 300) nominates Veit Ludwig von Seckendorff's (1626–92) history of the Reformation *Commentarius Historicus Et Apologeticus de Lutheranismo* (1688) as the book in which for the first time we see the direct German translation 'Ostergelächter' in print (vol. 1, 22); but at the risk of seeming to be nitpicking we actually find the term – albeit with a hyphen: 'Oster-Gelächter' – a few years earlier in Georg Samuel Dörffel's (1643–88) aggressively titled 'The Dismal Papacy's Worst Poison of the Soul' (*Das ärgste Seelengifft des trostlosen Pabstthums*), 1682, 200 (in the 1683 edition available online, 201).

Regarding 'Osterlachen', see note 119.

many differently spelled variants as the German orthography was far from being determined at this point in time.[63] In addition, there is an even longer series of relevant terms, partly the more general ones ('Sermon tale' [*Predigtmärlein*] as a superordinate category to 'Easter tale' [*Ostermärlin*], etc.), partly the derogatory Latin and German descriptions which naturally only the critics use. Latin terms and idioms: 'ludicrous tales' (*ludicrae fabellae, nugae*), 'made-up tales' (*fabulae confictae*), 'common even obscene tales' (*plerumque etiam obscoenae fabellae*), 'scurrilous sayings' (*scurrilia dicta*), 'Satanic toys' (*Satanae ludibria*), 'demons' food' (*cibus daemonorum*), and 'seeds of most grave abuses' (*semina graviorum abusuum*). German terms and idioms: 'witticisms' (*Schwänke*), 'foolish talk' (*Narrenteiding*), 'insulting speech' (*schimpfliche Red*), 'foolish tales' (*närrische Gedicht, närrische Fabuln, närrische Mährlein*), 'unreasonable and loose chatter' (*ungereumbte und lose Geschwetz*), 'studied antics and jokes' (*gestudierte Possen und Zotten*)[64] – or as it is called with a slight variation in an epistle sermon by Luther from 1525 (3rd Sunday in Lent): 'fools' talk and foolish ridiculous chatter' (*Narrenteydinge und nerrisch lecherlich geschwetz*). As can be seen from the expressions alone, they can all stimulate bursts of laughter, even if only the words *ludicrae* and *lecherlich* ('ridiculous') signal this explicitly. Compared to all of these, *risus paschalis* sounds both more scholarly and dry, but right up to the age of Romanticism those who use the term do so pretty much interchangeably with any of the expressions above.

Thus if we bypass the term *risus paschalis*, Oecolampadius is suddenly not the only source, as we find several testimonies almost contemporary with his which apparently do not know of a precise term for the phenomenon but which nevertheless undoubtedly refer to Easter Laughter, as they all list the constitutive elements in continuous passages. This already applies to Bebel in 1508, closely surrounded by Jakob Wimpfeling's (1450–1528) *Apologia* (1506)[65] and Johann(es)

---

63 *Ostermärl, Ostermäll, Osterm'ahrlein, Ostermayrl*, and *Ostermärchen*.
64 The list is compiled from the lists made by Fluck (1934, 209) and Nickel (1945, 103). In Latin literature, the derogatory terms are matched by more soberly descriptive ones such as 'tale for the day of resurrection' (*fabula in die resurrectionis*), 'Easter tale' (*in die pascae fabula, fabula paschalis*), 'Easter day tiding' (*in die pascae rumor*), 'Easter illustration' (*exemplum paschale*), and, in texts after the year 1500, 'Easter mystery' (*aenigma paschale*), Wendland 1980, 299–300. The English translations of both the Latin and German expressions are only meant as helpful approximations.
65 Strictly speaking, neither Wimpfeling nor Bebel fully meet the criteria described. Wimpfeling is interesting, however, because he had been the teacher of Oecolampadius while he was studying in Heidelberg; but although Wimpfeling has a passage in *Apologia pro Republica Christiana* strongly admonishing laughable preaching, he

Geiler from Kaysersberg (1445-1510) in a posthumous collection of sermons from 1512.⁶⁶ After Oecolampadius' book, a short series of testimonies followed within remarkably few years: the already mentioned Pauli in 1522,⁶⁷ J. Kessler (*c.* 1502-74) in his chronicle *Sabbata* about St Gallen, probably from 1524,⁶⁸ and

---

does not expressly mention Easter. Quoted in Wendland 1980, 60 (the quote is on scan image 32 in the online edition given in the bibliography).

Similarly, Bebel does not mention the element of 'laughter' directly; but he can reasonably still be included because of the obviously ludicrous nature of his facetia no. 21 and the context in which Bebel himself gives it: 'On the day of the Lord's resurrection, a preacher in Waiblingen commanded, as is customary on this day, to engage in witticisms and foolery [*Schwänk und Narrenteiding*], [...]', (cf. note 46).

66 The relevant passage from one of Geiler's sermons is quoted by Oecolampadius himself: '[...] has corruption grown so much during Easter, since people are provoked to laughter and levity by certain ridiculous preachers with too many excesses?' (see |63| and the notes to that section). Wendland has found another passage in a collection of Geiler's sermons also from 1512, which in Low German is very similar to the one in Latin just quoted, although this too does not explicitly mention laughter, 1980, 60.

67 It truly was a 'small world'! In addition to his collection of anecdotes Pauli is known for having published several volumes of Geiler's sermons (1515 ff.), including, in 1520, his translation of Geiler's sermons from 1498 on Sebastian Brant's (1457-1521) *The Ship of Fools*, Lappenberg 1854, 363 ff. and Österley 1866, 2. Indeed, Pauli drew many of his short stories from Geiler's colourful preaching.

68 J. Kessler studied theology in Basel and Wittenberg, from where he returned to St Gallen in 1523 and pursued a civil career while also serving as an occasional preacher. As a dutiful Protestant J. Kessler did not (ab)use (!) working hours to write down his observations of life in the city, for he claims to have written only on Sundays and holidays ('while others sleep at night or amuse themselves in the evening'). Hence the name of his manuscript, *Sabbata*, covering the years 1523 to 1539, but first published as late as 1866 (p. 22; 1902, 13). Before J. Kessler begins the actual chronicle his introduction makes sharp contrasts between Jesus and the Pope, and between the Evangelical Movement and the Roman Church; and in order to document the decline of the Church he lists all the many ceremonies that people have either invented (that is, without biblical foundation) or have taken over from paganism. J. Kessler follows the Church year and thus eventually reaches Easter morning: 'Easter Sunday [*urstendtag*] is celebrated in the most glorious and splendid way with organs, pipes, and singing, with dresses [liturgical vestments] and the display of all sorts of church ornaments. And since throughout Lent, and especially during the last week, we have tempered and weakened our bodies in abstinence and mourning, the preachers are in the habit of telling a ridiculous coarse joke and a cheerful story in their sermons (that is what we call the Easter Play [*osterspil*]), which would also be fairly indecent in the lads' taverns, so that the sorrowful hearts might be moved to laugh and lay off their melancholy. From there the old habits are revived again, which for a time

Luther in the sermon just quoted from 1525.[69] Johannes Bugenhagen's (1485–1558) slightly later reference we defer to the next chapter because of its particular perspectives; but at this point the contributions of Erasmus and Mathesius should be highlighted separately, just as Pauli's preface deserves further comment.

---

had been suppressed with forced piety, but not so openly and shamelessly, and only after the feast of the Ascension of Christ, when Christ has left the earth and is no longer present and looking at our evil, but has ascended to heaven. As if there was no opportunity for Christ to look down from heaven on the wicked nature of men. That is why one should not speak in this way.' 1902, 53–54 (with a slightly different orthography: 1866, 100 f.).

According to Ernst Götzinger (1837–96), publisher of the 1866 edition, J. Kessler probably began the actual writing down of his observations and reflections in 1524 and then continued in a diary-like manner with continuous notes until he made a fair copy in 1533. The manuscript was not intended for publication but was written for his children and descendants (1866, vii-viii). Since the remark about 'urstendtag' appears outside the chronicle proper in an introductory, more systematic and principled chapter, it can hardly be determined with certainty when J. Kessler wrote this part. That it is placed as the first chapter in the otherwise chronologically structured book may have been a decision made in connection with the fair copy, so in principle the entire decade of 1524–33 must be in play for a possible dating.

69 The words can be found in a passage where Luther, as one of several targets for his criticism of the extravagances during the church calendar, unmistakably refers to Easter Laughter: 'Particularly unchristian is every kind of such buffoonery in the church when men are gathered to hear and learn the Word of God. But the practice is common where many come together. Even where at first things of a serious nature are discussed, men soon pass to frivolous, wanton, foolish talk, resulting in a waste of time and the neglect of better things. For instance, on the festival of Easter, foolish, ridiculous stories have been introduced into the sermon to arouse the drowsy. And at the Christmas services, the absurd pantomime of rocking a babe, and silly declamations in rhyme, have found vogue. Similarly the festivals commemorating the three holy kings, the passion of Christ, Dorothy and other saints were characterised.' 1525, 205 f.; 1997b, 131.

Although it was rare, this was not the only reference, since a few years later Luther brought the topic from the pulpit to the lectern when in his lectures on the Epistle of Titus he once again touches on Easter Laughter. This happens in connection with his interpretation of Paul's admonition: 'in your teaching show integrity, seriousness and soundness of speech' (Tit 2:7 *NIV*). Luther exemplifies this with the argument that preaching must be according to the spirit and not the flesh. Therefore, 'do not be frivolous in your teaching, as are those who with their eloquence and rhetoric only tickle their hearers to laughter, to serve their itching ears, as on Easter'. 1527, 47; 1968, 59.

First of all, though a minor detail it is still worth noticing that Pauli himself dates his preface three years before the publication of the book, namely 1519, thus practically coinciding with Oecolampadius' letter; even more interesting is the further fate of the preface. Pauli specified that he had different audiences in mind, but the close to fifty reprints of *Schimpf und Ernst* (1522) before the century was over[70] bear witness to the fact that appetite for such a book extended well beyond penitent townspeople, monastic brothers seeking encouragement, and preachers with a passion for stories. These were not reprints in the usual sense, as the material was rearranged; the thematic headings already mentioned as well as new stories were added, and the books were aesthetically enhanced with illustrations; but in this context it is the preface that attracts attention. It is not surprising that the editions after Pauli's death (date unknown, probably 1533 at the latest) gradually replaced his preface with completely rewritten ones by the respective publishers. It is striking that while the editions from 1525 until the end of the 1540s reprint Pauli's own preface, this is done in an abbreviated form and precisely with the passage about the target audiences omitted. An educated guess would be that this was not due to the cessation of 'Easter plays' (*osterspil*), but rather that the market for the book was much larger than the people of the Church.

As for Erasmus and Mathesius, they do not stand out because of the chronology which plausibly coincides with that of the others.[71] Rather, they both distinguish themselves by not only mentioning the custom in very general terms (*that laughable tales were told at Easter*), but by both giving concrete examples and especially by not reporting second hand but based on their own experiences.[72]

---

70   Lappenberg 1854, 363–80, Hermann Österley's (1834–91) introduction to Pauli 1866, 1–12, and Johannes Bolte's (fl. 1858–1937) bibliography in Pauli 1924, vol. 2, 141–54.
71   To be sure, the book in which Erasmus talks about the tradition did not appear until 1535, but he probably began work on it already around 1520 although the exact year is not known, cf. Frederick J. McGinness' (b. 1944) introduction to the English translation, Erasmus 2015b, vol. 67, 82. Similarly Mathesius' biography of Luther is published posthumously in the form of a series of sermons as late as 1566, but he dates the incident with Easter Laughter to his youth. Wendland argues that this may likely have happened during his time studying in Ingolstadt in 1523–4, 1980, 186.
72   'As a boy I heard a certain Dominican [...]' (*Puer audiui quendam Dominicanum* [...]), Erasmus 1535, 125; 2015b, vol. 68, 508. 'In my youth I heard some Easter tales of this sort' (*wie ich solcher Ostermehrlein inn meiner jugent etliche gehöret*), Mathesius 1566, 77r; 2018, 286.

Among other things Erasmus remembers hearing a priest tell a not half bad joke about a nun who had got herself pregnant. When the prioress blames her for not raising the alarm when the young man had entered her bed, she defends herself in the most pious manner by referring to the commandment to maintain silence in the dormitory. Furthermore, Erasmus even gives us a hint of the sound effects that priests were willing to use (although he does not explicitly limit this rhetorical trick to Easter): some preachers make some noise or shout to wake up a sleepy congregation, while others – almost like a precursor to Victor Borge's (1909–2000) famous 'phonetic punctuation' – have the entire congregation clear their throats simultaneously between each section of the sermon.[73]

With regard to Mathesius two things are worth noting. Firstly, his recollection of the two devils that lose their noses in connection with Jesus' descent into hell is by far the most frequently cited example of Easter Laughter.[74] Secondly, in this

---

[73] Erasmus 1535, 125 f., cf. 2015b, vol. 68, 508. It is tempting to believe that this was recognised in the homiletics of the time as a tip straight from the horse's mouth, when we come across the information about the preacher Olivier Maillard (c. 1500) that in the margin of his sermons he carefully marked when to cough, Schindler 1992, 157; cf. Burke 1978, 101. Another sample of laughable sound effects deserves to be mentioned with the caveat that it is from a Christmas sermon and thus not an Easter Laughter. In his book on 'German Folk Humour' Moritz Busch (1821–99) includes a chapter on 'Humour in the Pulpit' in which he describes how a monk from Dijon let the animals speak in a sermon about the birth of Jesus: ' "The rooster crowed: Christus natus est", while the preacher imitated the rooster's crowing. "The bull asked: ubi, ubi?" he continued, bellowing Ubi. "The sheep answered: in Bethlehem, in Bethlehem!" – Finally the donkey with a "Jamus! Jamus!" encouraged all to come to the divine child.' Busch adds the comment: 'the Middle Ages will probably have heard something similar in all churches. But much later, at least here and there, such oddities were woven into the speeches from the pulpit'. Unfortunately, M. Busch does not provide a specific date or source for the story, nor does his book contain a bibliography. 1877, 307.

[74] Not least in the light of how often this story has been retold or referred to in the 17th and 18th centuries as well as in modern times and that it always happens with a reference – if one is given – to Mathesius, it is rather interesting that yet another source exists for it. The story is recounted in Philipp Julius Rehtmeyer's (1678–1742) work on the church history of Braunschweig. Admittedly this was first published in 1707, but according to its title page it deals with matters 'as they were shortly before the Reformation up to the year 1521' and announces as its basis the 'Archives, rare manuscripts and other proven historical materials, including the associated documents and writings'.

context he is perhaps even more interesting because he is one of the first not only to describe the phenomenon but explicitly to use the actual term '*risus paschalis*' – though seemingly independent of Oecolampadius.[75]

As it appears, all of these sources belong to a decade surrounding Oecolampadius' book and are therefore not providing a decisive clue to the age of the tradition. The only significantly older piece of evidence[76] that has been found

---

It is quite a thrilling fact that while it is undoubtedly the same story as in Mathesius, there are, both in terms of terminology and details, such significant mutual differences that it points more in the direction of two independent sources than a copy (although Wendland is not entirely convinced of its authenticity, 1980, 187). If so, there seem to be three possibilities: a) Mathesius' and Rehtmeyer's informant(s) must have participated in the one Easter service where it happened; b) the story of Jesus' descent into hell was so popular that it was (re)used perhaps over several years and in various churches (and now perhaps even all the way up north in Braunschweig); or c) the account of the Catholic priest who told the story of the descent had become a Protestant cliché taking on a life of its own.

If the last-mentioned is the case, most of the 'thrill' disappears, because then we are just dealing with another case of a more or less trumped-up Protestant speculation about the *alien* Catholic phenomenon. If, however, Rehtmeyer's source, as it professes, is based on an eyewitness account, the small differences from Mathesius contain at least two that are worth pointing out. One concerns the 'technique' used, as more than the narrative itself it seems to have been the volume of the preacher's voice ('a fellow […] who could scream terribly') with which he finally startled the congregation with a loud roar. Although shock effects are a well-known means of triggering (nervous) laughter, it is, secondly, equally striking that the effect mentioned here is not laughter, but that the sleepy congregation 'wakes up, shakes and trembles', Rehtmeyer 1707, 308.

75   Because Mathesius, in his discussion of the laughable stories at Easter, uses a terminology that is different from the words used by Oecolampadius, Wendland thinks it safe to conclude that Mathesius did not know about Oecolampadius' book, 1980, 74.

If so, two possibilities open up when Mathesius writes that 'the scholars of that time called such stories *risus paschalis*' (1566, 77r; 2018, 286): either it was not Oecolampadius who invented the expression after all, or else his Latin expression had indeed won acclaim among scholars in the period between 1518 and 1566 (or, to be more precise, 11 April 1562 when that particular sermon was preached) without Mathesius himself necessarily knowing about its origin. Bugenhagen's testimony suggests that the latter is the case, cf. II,2,ii.

76   We hereby ignore an alleged example from 1399 mentioned by Fluck, but for which he himself regrets not having been able to find any documentation (1943, 189), as well as Lenz Prütting's (b. 1940) attempt to find an *implied* position on Easter Laughter in a text from 1250, see below p. 149.

is a sermon by Johannes Geus (*c.* 1370–1440) from Vienna, which is unpublished and undated but must be from before the year of his death in 1440.[77] All of these sources agree in referring to it as a *custom*; however, since this is obviously an elastic indication of time, and since Oecolampadius intriguingly labels it as 'modern' or 'recent' (*mos recens*, |7|), it would be tempting to date the emergence of Easter Laughter almost exactly to the last quarter of the 15th century. Although the term 'old' is also elastic, it points in the opposite direction that Geiler blames 'the preachers of old'[78] for the custom of cheerful jokes.[79] Likewise, we can speculate that it must have taken a considerable period of time before Easter Laughter became such a widespread and well-established custom that Oecolampadius'

---

77 Hans Niedermeier (fl. 1963–70) studied Geus' surviving manuscripts in order to bring out their information about everyday life in 15th century Vienna. In this connection he quotes from a sermon, 'Sermo bonus de praedicatoribus nec non auditoribus verbi dei' (*Codex latinus monacensis* 11751, fol. 220–224), where Geus seems to present a kind of homiletics, or in any case clearly wants to protect the art of preaching from abuse. The passage that is particularly interesting in our context is reproduced by Niedermeier in his article: 'Therefore, the words of God are not vain fables, as some people recite in their sermons to make the people laugh and thereby destroy devotion. Of such sermons the Prophet says: "Narraverunt mihi iniqui fabulationes, sed non ut lex tua" (Ps 118:85 [= 119.85 in *KJV*]), and of those preachers and their listeners who like to hear fables and not useful sermons, says the apostle, "The time will come when they will not endure sound doctrine, etc." (2 Tim 4:3). [...] Some people are in the habit of preaching fables about the fox and the rooster, especially at Easter, and such preaching is not only fabulous, but also harmful.' 1970, 227 f.

Please also note that the *KJV* translation follows the Hebrew text and makes Psalm 119:85 speak of 'digging pits', whereas Geus quotes from the *Vulgate* and focuses on the occurrence of 'fables' which the psalmist puts in opposition to God's law: 'The wicked have told me fables: but not as thy law' (*DRB*).

78 It is admittedly possible to interpret Geiler's expression, *die alten prediger*, as having nothing to do with locating them on a timeline but only telling us that the preachers themselves were old.

79 To be sure, Geiler does not explicitly mention laughter, but he connects the impropriety to *Ostertag*, he lists several of the terms for inappropriate sermon material which we have met in other sources (*märle, fablen, schwenck*), and he asserts that the old preachers *Osterspil machen*. ('does an Easter Play', or: 'tells Easter jokes'). He does so in a sermon for the 21st Sunday after Trinity in a collection of his sermons published posthumously in 1512. The Strassburg edition from 1522 is available online and the quote is on scan image no. 566.

colleagues – whether as good-natured banter or a serious complaint – turned to their superior, Capito, and thereby provoked Oecolampadius to write his defence. In considering these arguments the most important thing to take into account is the discovery of Geus' testimony. While an exact dating remains impossible, a qualified guess that neither makes Easter Laughter an exclusively Renaissance phenomenon nor places its roots in the Early Church can instead point to the 14th century as the period between Geus (*terminus ante quem*) and the late medieval, more nuanced, reflections on laughter, which will be discussed below (*terminus post quem*) (p. 137). Plausibly this was a century in which popular preachers sought to appropriate the power of laughter that had flourished in the religious festivities of the 12th and 13th centuries, especially during Christmas and Lent but also during the Corpus Christi festival in the Trinity season.

4. The Geographical Spread of Easter Laughter

Almost completely parallel to this, a discussion about the dissemination of Easter Laughter must decide how broadly or narrowly the phenomenon is to be perceived. As should have become clear by now, when we have the history of ideas in mind there are promising perspectives in attempting to maintain a distinction between Easter Laughter and laughter in general. Accordingly it is advantageous to strive for as narrow a definition as historically possible and thereby distance ourselves from those who think they can hear echoes of Easter Laughter throughout Europe during the late Middle Ages and the Early Modern Period. The most serious stumbling block to a radical narrowing of the geography is actually Erasmus' example, because, if he remembers correctly, it stems from his childhood in the Netherlands. Similarly, though to a lesser extent, Mathesius' personal experience may widen the geography. With him, too, it is impossible to know for certain what he means by dating the incident with *risus paschalis* in his 'youth' (*jugent*), for if that refers to an age before he at 17 moved to Nürnberg in 1521, then the Easter Laughter tradition had at least spread as far north as Saxony, where he attended elementary school in Rochlitz and Mittweida, i.e. level with Dresden and just about a hundred kilometers south of Wittenberg.[80] However, as Wendland has documented, all other testimonies (assessed both from the identified areas of activity of the preachers and the location of the printing houses that published stories and sermons with humorous material) are concentrated along

---

80 Wendland opts for identifying 'youth' even later, to when Mathesius had transfered to the University of Ingolstadt in 1523 thus placing him *c.* 300 kilometer south of his childhood hometown and right between Nuremberg and Munich.

an axis from Salzburg via Munich to Augsburg and with Innsbruck as one of the southernmost areas.[81]

In relation to the ideas that circulate about the geographical spread of Easter Laughter this may seem like an unnecessarily drastic limitation; but we should rather be surprised that the phenomenon was able to spread itself at all over the majority of the southern German and northeastern Austrian regions. The spread alone is remarkable, considering that it was primarily a purely oral tradition and that it was limited to only one or two days (some sources mention Easter Monday) per year.[82]

---

81 Wendland 1980, 297. Earlier in his book, Wendland distinguishes between two areas where Easter Laughter was practised: partly in the 'Swabian-Alemannic south', where it died out with the advance of Protestantism in the course of the 16th century, and partly in the 'purely Catholic Austro-Bavarian language area up to Frankonian Augsburg', where the custom was allowed to live on undisturbed, 77 and 200.
82 Ibid., 164.

Chapter II: The History of the Effects of Easter Laughter

A few methodological difficulties and reservations regarding the material over the following three centuries should be mentioned right from the beginning. Hopefully the least serious of these is that the present author, apart from a few 'samples' prompted by the secondary literature, has not himself carried out studies in this part of the primary literature, neither in archival manuscripts nor in the published books of the period, whether in Latin or German. Therefore, knowledge of the sources is predominantly second-hand, relying on the later academic literature continuously referenced in the footnotes. More mischievous is the fundamental difficulty which to some extent also affects the linguistic and historical experts: that laughter is such an ethereal and elusive phenomenon.

Here we are specifically thinking of the fact that while laughter may very well be universal and common to all humankind, the social framework for laughter and the accepted means to arouse it are not. In this particular sense, tears and grief seem to be more independent of time and place. To illustrate this point: many a theatre company has experienced how much more 'updating' is needed to make an older comedy arouse laughter than is required to grip the audience with an ancient tragedy. Every comedian soon learns the cruel and banal fact that even a completely topical joke can raise a laugh one night and bomb the next, that a particular audience does not catch the punchline. The relationship between the preacher's story and/or antics to induce Easter Laughter and the actual congregation's reaction must certainly have been equally fragile. Moreover, when dealing with historical material it becomes extremely difficult, if not impossible, to know anything with certainty about the connection between intention and effect. Was what the modern reader perceives as funny also meant that way by the historical author – and vice versa?[83] The methodological problem is therefore not only whether a given preacher's preserved manuscript or published sermon succeeded in triggering the congregation's laughter. Nor is the problem limited to the uncertainty of whether what a modern sensibility considers amusing was actually intended and perceived as such. In addition, there may in principle have

---

83 Anachronistic examples of 'innocent' amusement and displays of a total lack of feeling for the (often rude) comedy of the past are particularly evident in the modern search for humour and smiles on every other page of the Bible, cf. p. 232 on Leviathan.

been given – and for that matter published – many more laughable sermons than those that explicitly state it as the preacher's concern. In other words, this means that the potential source material can be even greater than the publications and texts that themselves acknowledge being part of that tradition, or that make direct use of one or more of the aforementioned more or less technical terms, be it 'Easter Laughter', 'Easter Plays', 'Easter Tales', etc.[84]

1. Continuation of the Practice of Easter Laughter

The obvious price for following Wendland in his delimitation of the historical Easter Laughter to Southern Germany, Northern Switzerland and Western Austria is that we must then ask ourselves how a relatively local tradition was apparently allowed to spread first to the rest of North-West Europe and then, as recently witnessed by the Internet, beyond *all* borders. As already suggested in the introduction, we can surely question whether it was the custom itself that spread, or whether it was rather the polemic against it that made it known in wider circles.

Nevertheless, there are undeniably *later* examples, particularly through the Baroque period, of preachers publishing books with cheerful narrative material. Noteworthy as a *primus inter pares* is Andreas Strobl's (1642–1706) three-volume *Ovum paschale novum* (1694, 1698, and 1708), because the sermons in this 'new Easter egg' are explicitly intended for Easter; although Strobl in his opening address ('To the Friendly Reader') does not directly mention laughter, the book has a self-declared desire to arouse amusement because, as he clarifies in this preface, the 'Christian Catholic church' allows 'the preachers [...] to cheer up their listeners with a joyful or entertaining poem and Easter tale'.[85]

If, perhaps, it was initially only *implied* that the 'cheering up' might result in laughter, it is revealed in volume 2 four years later. It opens the collection with Easter Sunday, declared in the title 'a joyful day on which one can undertake honest recreation or enjoyment'. Validated by the Bible's 'a merry heart doeth

---

84 Regarding the medieval material, cf. Riising: 'It must always be remembered that the Danish sermon material, like most of the foreign material, represents the average and respectable sermon. There is a lack of polemical sermons, there is a lack of church political sermons, and there is a lack of dubious sermons by indulgence mongers. Finally, the humorous sermons, which often in parodic form express the baroque humour of the time, are also missing.' 1969, 448.
85 Strobl 1694, scan image 15.

good like a medicine: but a broken spirit drieth the bones' (Prov 17:22 *KJV*), Strobl declares that it is:

> not entirely wrong, but rather commendable at times to amuse the mind, to go into a clearing in the forest, engage in entertainment, tell something funny or ridiculous, as long as it does not go against the honour and good name of our neighbour or involve coarse jokes and pranks.[86]

To legitimise this claim, a select line of men are listed who were deeply serious but nevertheless allowed themselves relaxation and merriment: Pythagoras (*c.* 580–*c.* 500 BCE), Socrates (469–399 BCE), and Pharaoh Amasis (d. 525 BCE). Strobl also draws on the classic illustration used by such theological giants as Augustine (354–430): if we keep a bowstring taut all the time it will become slack. Via Ecclesiastes' 'a time to weep, a time to laugh' (3:4) Strobl even includes Chrysostom, whom he does not quote for his usual criticism of laughter. Instead, Strobl makes use of the passage in the Greek Church Father's 5th Homily on Hebrews, where Chrysostom acknowledged that laughter as such is not evil, but is only so when misplaced and uncontrolled.[87] Strobl believes he is able to draw from this the following conclusion:

> Laughing is innate in us so that the mood can sometimes be relieved or relaxed, but not to be excessively exuberant. Since the Christian Catholic Church itself encourages us to be happy with the cheerful Alleluia, I am thinking today of telling an entertaining Easter tale [*Oster-Märlein*] for spiritual encouragement, and then extract some useful lessons from it afterwards, etc.[88]

The author was clearly not alone in this view, for the books are not only provided with the necessary *imprimatur* but in the colophon to volume 1, diocesan provost Johann Baptist Caspar Pockh (*c.* 1659–1709) on behalf of the Salzburg bishop assures readers that the book contains nothing 'contra Orthodoxam Fidem, & bonos mores'.

While the '*primus inter pares*' should not overshadow how unique Strobl's book is in its scope and focus,[89] the research done by Moser-Rath and Wendland, among others, has demonstrated an unbroken chain of entertaining (Easter) tales embedded in published sermons spanning close to 200 years. Indeed, even

---

86 *Ibid.*, scan image 1 & 2.
87 *Ibid.*, scan image 3.
88 *Ibid.*, scan image 40–2.
89 'A counterpart to Strobl's collection of a hundred Easter sermons with as many highly enjoyable Easter fairy tales [*Ostermärlein*] (63 stories [*Schwänken*], 36 fables and a legend called "vera historia") has not yet been found.' Moser-Rath 1964, 30.

special collections of this kind continue right up to the 456 pages of Johann Jacob Zeller's (fl. 1767–73) 'The Shameful Vice of the Modern World. Through so-called Easter tales, each accompanied by moving morals, along with a content or instruction on how to create sermons from them' (1771). Zeller's work apparently became the last of its kind.[90] The title alone suggests a built-in apology, and the sense of having arrived at a new age is reinforced by Zeller's preface, where, invoking both Aristotle (384–22 BCE) and Augustine, he vigorously defends his undertaking. With an irresistible comparison, Zeller points out that just as health is one and diseases are many, so are the virtues few and the vices countless and still increasing in 'today's world'. Rather than combatting vices one by one with a direct admonition, laughter is better suited to having an indirect effect on a much broader scale because nature itself has arranged it in such a way that a 'book of teasing jokes' (*Scherzschrift*) works better than anything else that reason has at its disposal.[91]

Despite both the *imprimatur* and Zeller's enlightened defence, the tradition subsequently dies out even in purely Catholic areas. The fact that this happens is certainly also due to strict episcopal prohibitions; but more than the opposition from supervising authorities the spiritual death blow comes from the spirit of the times. It has become the Age of Enlightenment.[92] Throughout the 19th century and into the 20th century, reports of priests practising Easter Laughter keep appearing, but now only as isolated and 'anachronistic' exceptions.[93]

---

90 Wendland 1980, 290.
91 Zeller 1771, 3v-4r.
92 A few years before the Reformed theologian Friedrich Schleiermacher (1768–1834) in *On Religion* (1799) apologetically addressed its 'cultured despisers', we sense the same tactfulness so typical of this period in a Catholic cleric: 'Clemens Wenzeslaus [1739–1812], the last Prince-Bishop of Augsburg, justified a decree issued in 1774 against abuses solely on the external grounds of "appropriate decency", the reputation of the Church, and its resonance in the face of the "spirit of contempt for religion" of the time.' Wendland 1980, 289. Wendland is paraphrasing the decree 'Guidance and Instruction for Candidates of the Priestly State', *Acta Selecta Ecclesiae Augustanae*, 1785, 349 f.
93 Cf. note 61 about the letter in *Münchner Tagblatt*.

2. Easter Laughter as a Denominational Point of Contention until the Baroque Period

i. The Beginning of Its Critique

As we turn towards the criticism of Easter Laughter, two remarkable observations by Wendland provide a smooth transition. One confirms the 'artificiality' of the term '*risus paschalis*', no matter how fitting it seemed for many later generations, for among the many Catholic preachers from the 17th and the 18th century who like to tell 'Easter stories' Wendland has not found a single one who himself uses the expression 'Easter Laughter' (whether in Latin or German).[94] This is countered by the equally striking silence among the many North German Protestant critics in the same period, who always treat Easter Laughter as a historical phenomenon from the time of the Reformation without ever mentioning it as still being practised. Despite the survival of contemporary Catholic books this could at first glance lead to the conclusion that Easter Laughter had died out as a church practice. However, Wendland has a perhaps even more thought-provoking interpretation, as he attributes the silence about current Easter Laughter to the spiritual iron curtain that existed between the denominations in their almost hermetic isolation from one another.[95]

As already illustrated by the samples from Strobl and Zeller, there is a somewhat two-sided justification for the claim that Easter Laughter actually survives through the criticism of it. On the one hand it is, indirectly, documented by the fact that many publications with humorous sermons begin with an apology for doing so. Even when this kind of preaching was openly practised and when self-conscious examples of amusement were published, the opening reservations expressed by the preachers and authors documented that they were clearly not unaware of the problematic and somewhat controversial nature of doing so.

On the other hand, it is equally apparent that the kind of literature which unmistakably deals not only with amusing sermons in general but specifically pertains to Easter and uses the term 'Easter Laughter', belongs to another level. It does so in the sense that it is predominantly written within genres other than

---

94 Wendland 1980, 93 (note 2) and 299.
95 *Ibid.*, 288 and 90 respectively. A correlate to this is Johanna Nickel's (1916–84) discovery that when the many treatises in the 18th century seek to illustrate what an Easter story (*Ostermärlein*) is, Strobl and his *Ovum paschale novum* are ostensibly unknown to them in so far as he is never ever mentioned nor are examples given from his book, 1945, 106.

homiletics and collections of sermons, namely in various forms of historical overviews and, in particular, accounts of the Reformation and its background. In this way, Easter Laughter was given artificial respiration by being incorporated into the spiritual warfare between the denominations.

Not least from this perspective it is interesting to return to Oecolampadius, since he can also be interpreted as a symptomatic figure that in a way contains, if not all, then several dimensions of the protests against phenomena like Easter Laughter. For at the time when he wrote his letter about laughter, he had undergone a thorough humanistic education and had worked closely with Erasmus for a few years.[96] However, he had also known Philip Melanchthon (1497–1560), since they both studied in Tübingen in 1513, while in 1518 Oecolampadius was considered a candidate for the professorship of Hebrew at the University of Wittenberg. Moreover, during the same period, he studied and wrote about Luther intensively (e.g. as early as 1519 on the disputation in Leipzig between Andreas Karlstadt [1486–1541] and Johann Eck [1486–1543] on Luther's 95 theses). For these reasons, among others, several of his biographers believe that when Oecolampadius eventually moved away from Reform Catholicism, he might very well have ended up as a Lutheran, if it had not been for the close connection that developed with Ulrich Zwingli (1484–1531) instead. This relationship began after Oecolampadius had asked Zwingli to become a pen pal around the turn of the year 1522–3.[97] Luther himself seems to share the view of Oecolampadius as the promising theologian who slipped through the fingers of the Wittenbergers, as he referred to Oecolampadius as Icarus and Zwingli as his Daidalos in one of his table talks.[98] In later church historiography Oecolampadius is probably best

---

96   Cf. note 539.
97   '[Oecolampadius] asked Zwingli for friendship by mail [*Brieffreundschaft*]', Christ-von Wedel 2017, 108.
98   The statement is made after Zwingli's death on the battlefield at Kappel, a fate that Luther interprets in light of Jesus' words in Gethsemane about drawing and dying by the sword (Mt 26:52); but then he adds that the two Swiss sought to master Scripture and interpret it as they pleased, but fell. Luther 1531–3, 95, no. 220. (Oecolampadius is mentioned nine times in the American edition of *Table Talks*, but this particular reference is not included). The reference is from Fudge 1997, 269, which also brings a number of quotations from Luther's letters where Oecolampadius is mentioned with strong praise; however, later on Luther does not hesitate to label him an enthusiast [*Schwärmer*], which in Luther's vocabulary is not a positive category but puts him in the company of Zwingli and Karlstadt.

known for having been the reformer of Basel[99] and for having participated in the great dispute over the Lord's Supper in 1529. This happened at the meeting in Marburg where Philip of Hesse (1504–67) tried to get the German and Swiss reformers to unite, and where Oecolampadius assisted Zwingli in the negotiations with Luther and Melanchthon.

In the spring of 1518, Oecolampadius can therefore be regarded as a prism for his time, and his biography can remind us that Easter Laughter met with strong criticism from various quarters. Not only the admittedly far more enduring and intransigent criticism from the Protestants, but also from both the church hierarchy and the humanist Reform Catholicism – and if we were to place Oecolampadius at the time of writing *De risu paschali*, it must likely be in the latter camp.[100] That criticism of Easter Laughter came from several camps is in

---

99 However, some 'reduce' Oecolampadius' role to being one among several important agents in the city's reformation, since it is apparently not conclusively proven that he had been the actual author of Basel's *Reformationsordnung* which was presented on 1 April 1529, thus Schäufele 2013, 190 f.

100 In line with several others, Olaf Kuhr (b. 1962) convincingly argues for 1522 as the year when Oecolampadius became a Protestant, symbolised by his decision to leave the monastery in Altomünster in January of that year after only about a year and a half of residence. Kuhr 1999, 22 and 39. Seen in this light, it is a fine characterisation of Oecolampadius' somewhat meandering position at this moment of his life which Wilhelm Hadorn (1869–1929) gives in his assessment of *De risu paschali*: 'This first attempt of his was only "reformist" in the sense of Savonarola [1452–98], as he left the church doctrine untouched and only aimed at eliminating abuses. He was still far from a Reformation in the sense of Luther at that time.' Hadorn 1904, 288. What Hadorn writes about the booklet on laughter in particular agrees closely with McNeill's general characterisation of its author and his like-minded colleagues: 'None of these men, it appears, passed through anything like the throes of Luther's inner struggle, or felt a "sudden conversion" after stubborn resistance such as Calvin was to experience. They did not, like Luther, publicly quarrel with Erasmus or other humanists. They graduated from Christian humanism to Zwinglian Protestantism, extending rather than basically revising their theology, and translating thought into action. The Bible, studiously consulted, often in the light of the Church Fathers, in whom they delighted, rather than the frame of any theological system, shaped their message.' McNeill 1967, 54. Finally, let us add a theological nuance to this assessment by way of a quote from Ernst Staehelin (1889–1980), who may very well have been the scholar most familiar with Oecolampadius' work ever. On the occasion of the 450th anniversary of the Reformation he delivered a lecture in Weinsberg about the town's famous son in which he sums up the two men's different road to reform: 'The Wittenberg monk starts from his own crisis of conscience, from the despair of man as a sinner, and he seeks to find an answer from the Gospel that will free him from

itself a testimony to the fact that, despite the highlighted characteristics of Easter Laughter, we are still far from the historical development where Catholics more unreservedly could exploit it (if not exactly always with the blessing of the hierarchy as in the case of Strobl and Zeller). Furthermore, the differences hidden in the apparently shared criticism are probably equally interesting.

The proximity to the Reform Catholics can be inferred from the fact that out of the approximately two dozen authors that Oecolampadius either quotes or alludes to in his book, only two are contemporaries: the Reform Catholics Geiler and Erasmus (|63| and |37| respectively). Bearing in mind that the older Oecolampadius, in his role as Basel's reformer, is notorious for introducing a very strict church discipline,[101] it could be tempting to make a possibly too harsh interpretation of the passage where he goes on the counterattack against the priests who had complained to Capito about his dull preaching, and where Oecolampadius proclaims them to be heretics (|57|). In this choice of words, we can see an affinity to the attempts by the Catholic authorities to curb Easter Laughter with the help of legislation and threats of severe sanctions. In any case, it is generally accepted that while the Protestants counter Easter Laughter with the help of polemics, the Catholic Church also resorts to canon law. In reality,

---

this crisis; this is justification by faith. Oecolampadius has not been led into this crisis of conscience. He does not ask, "How do I obtain a merciful God?", but he searches for the truth, for the true essence of the biblical message, seemingly independent of his own crisis. And so he discovers what could be called the "regnum Christi", the kingship of Jesus Christ. This is the true centre of the biblical message for him: Christ has risen, Christ has become King, and we now want to help establish the kingship of Christ in the world.' Staehelin 1967, 67.

This detail regarding the discussion of when to consider Oecolampadius as belonging to one or the other side of what eventually became conflicting confessions is coincidently an important reminder of how fluid the positions were in a time when everything was in turmoil. Christine Christ-von Wedel (b. 1948) masterfully captures this situation with the sobering opening of her preface to a monograph on Basel's period of reformation upheaval: 'Anyone publishing on the Reformation era today must first clarify some terms. Since the mid-19th century, the word "Reformation" has been used to refer to a movement that began with Luther and Zwingli and divided Western Christianity into various denominations. In the 16th century, the term *"reformatio"*, encountered in many Latin sources, had a different connotation. It was not only used by what are now called the Reformers, but also by all Latin-writing authors who were dissatisfied with the relationship between the Church and the State and wanted to change, or rather, reform something.' 2017, 10.

101 Cf. Demura 1964 and Kuhr 1999.

there is nothing surprising or sinister in this, because there is only reason to take a position on a practice officially if it actually takes place within one's own ranks, whereas the Protestants could content themselves with scorn and ridicule against something practised by *the others*.

However, from a methodological point of view, extreme caution is required here, for although the secondary literature is teeming with such *apparent* references and documentation, to my knowledge no one either in Catholic or Protestant sources has yet succeeded in bringing a single prohibition to light that is incontrovertibly directed against Easter Laughter as such.[102] It is indisputable, however, that completely parallel, albeit on a smaller scale, to the ecclesiastical legislation that throughout the Middle Ages limits, condemns, or prohibits the various festivities (*kalendae*, Feast of the Ass, etc.), there is in the 16th and 17th centuries a steady flow of restrictions against *either* preachers' use of 'stories' *or* making the congregation laugh.[103] It may seem pedantic to italicise 'either/or'; but I have not come across a source in which the two are directly linked – and even more importantly, no official sources in which the admonitions against stories or laughter are linked to Easter. It must thus be open for discussion whether we are willing to imply 'laughter' when storytelling is banned (and vice versa), or to imply 'Easter' when storytelling or laughter is mentioned; but, of course, there can hardly be any doubt that *if* cases of 'Easter Laughter' had been submitted to the authorities who authored the many letters and regulations, they would have included it among the customs from which they wished to distance themselves.[104]

---

102 Cf. Prütting 2013, 556. Very promisingly one anonymous author seems very assured in claiming that Easter Laughter 'was prohibited by Clement (1670–76) and in the eighteenth century by Maximillian III and the Bishops of Bavaria', but most frustratingly no details, quotes, or references are given, and neither Pope Clement X (1590–1676) nor the Elector of Bavaria (1727–77) are mentioned anywhere else among scholars, Anonymous 1914, 482.

103 Moser-Rath provides a long list from which a select few will be mentioned in what follows, 1964, 20.

104 In addition, it ought to serve as a supporting argument for limiting the practice of Easter Laughter narrowly both geographically and temporally, because if it had been such a long-lasting and widespread phenomenon, as some scholars have claimed, it is very strange indeed that so far no one has been able to find it mentioned in the archives with countless letters and documents from popes, bishops, and councils.

   Just as Jacobelli's reference to Hinkmar has already been questioned in note 58, there is every reason to doubt the value of Fluck's reference to the *Prager*

If we allow ourselves to assume that the whole debacle between Oecolampadius and his colleagues arose in connection with his failure to use cheerful stories when he preached in Weinsberg on Easter Sunday in 1517,[105] which that year was 12 April, then with the wisdom of hindsight it appears deeply ironic that just a few months earlier, during the 11th session of the Fifth Lateran Council (11-19 December 1516), it had been decided to issue a *Bulla de modo predicandi*. The intention of this 'sermon guide' was to clean up the priests' dissolute ways of preaching, and under the threat of excommunication the preachers were enjoined to refrain from making use of 'fabricated miracles, new and false predictions, and other frivolities scarcely distinguishable from old wives' tales' (*conficta miracula & nova ac falsa vaticinia, aliaque levia & ab anilibus fabulis parum distantia*).[106] Although the council's condemnations of *aniles fabulas* harks back to St Paul (1 Tim 4:7) and to the terminology used by Luther in his rejection of Easter Laughter,[107] it should not be overlooked that at no point does the *Bulla* mention either Easter or laughter.[108]

The council apparently did not have the power it would have liked, evidently not in the vicinity of Weinsberg; nevertheless it is worth noting that a preoccupation with the improvement of the quality of preaching was an ongoing matter. These efforts only intensified after the Reformation, where 'the reform of preaching [...] was an important item on the agenda of the Council of Trent'.[109] In the documents from that council, however, only very general words are used for the

---

Poenitentialcodex from 1353–1415, which admittedly Fluck himself only does with reservations, 1934, 203 f., cf. Wendland 1980, 115.

105 We can only speculate whether it was his sermon 'Of true joy on the day of Easter' which provoked his colleagues to react with a counter-attack, or a previous disagreement between them caused Oecolampadius to address the problem of laughter already in the sermon. The sermon is undated, but while Staehelin suggests that it was delivered in 1518 (in that case 4 April) he adds in a note that 1516 and 1517 are both possible, 1927/34, vol. 1, 60.

106 Labbé & Cossart 1732, col. 945.

107 Cf. note 477.

108 The emphasis seems rather to be on *miracula* and *vaticinia*, as the assembled clerical primates are especially concerned with curbing a kind of doomsday preaching that frightens the congregations with lurid signs in sun and moon: 'They are in no way to presume to preach or declare a fixed time for future evils, the coming of Antichrist or the precise day of judgment; for Truth says, it is not for us to know times or seasons which the Father has fixed by his own authority.' English translation from the online version of 'On how to preach'.

109 Moser-Rath 1964, 5.

dangers that the preacher must avoid, such as *errores, scandala,* or *heresis*.[110] Only three years after the conclusion of the council Pius V (1504–72) took office as the new pope in 1566 and in the very same year he issued as one of his first official acts the bull *Cum primum apostolatus*, which, among other things, addressed the state of worship and the question of holy days as public holidays (*Ordinationes circa observantiam divini cultus in Ecclesiis, & venerationem Festivitatum*). In this bull, laughter of the immoderate kind, suddenly appears in a series of phenomena that need to be countered; but despite the length of the document, it does not specifically mention Easter, nor does the text come closer to 'tales' other than 'empty, hideous, and worldly speeches'.[111]

The Austrian Jesuit and Viennese court preacher, Georg Scherer (1540–1605), can serve to round off both the century and the Catholic 'self-criticism' (which, admittedly, is a mischievous choice of words considering Scherer's reputation as a staunch counter-reformer). In his collection of sermons from 1603, Scherer

---

110   5. session, ch. 2, *Sacrosanctum Concilium Tridentinum* 1781, 45; 1848, 29; and Tanner 1990, 670.

111   The full text is as follows: 'No one should incite rebellion with words in the churches, provoke unrest, provoke shouts or attacks; empty, obscene, and profane conversations, unrestrained laughter and noise from all expressions of opinion, and anything else that can disturb the sacred task should cease.' Pius V in 1947, 198.

Midway between these two councils, in a collection of liturgical regulations by Verona's bishop, Giovanni Matteo Giberti (1495–1543), there is a section where the bishop, amidst a swarm of rhetorical bombast, apparently attempts to suppress laughter through the establishment of a network of ecclesiastical snitches – and we sense the bishop's urgency in his style which evidently has no time to waste on full stops: '*On the need for reporting on scandalous preachers*. As we desire that preachers, who have been sent by us to address the people, return with abundant harvests to the Lord's field and not come back empty-handed, and knowing that a preacher whose conduct is looked down upon is superfluous, as his preaching is also despised, resulting in the gathering of weeds instead of figs and thorns instead of grapes, we impose upon all priests and chaplains under our authority, who have the care of souls, that if they become aware of any preachers, regardless of rank and order, who present themselves with scandalous conduct or incite the people to ridicule and laughter in the manner of the lowest jesters, while reciting ridiculous and vulgar tales, either disparaging the highest prelates and priests of the churches or spreading false teachings or extorting money by listening to confessions, they should diligently inform and report to us or our vicar, for if our priests and chaplains are found negligent in this matter, they should know that they will not escape the same arbitrary punishment that they themselves, as offenders, would have received

opens with a lengthy section spanning ten pages titled 'Several Christian Rules for Preachers', where he lists thirteen rules for the right way to preach. Quite sensibly the first rule declares that the ministry of preaching must not be despised, for it is to be considered 'a great, noble, and honourable office'. Furthermore, Scherer writes, the Council of Trent has 'recently' emphasised that every preacher acts on behalf of the bishop to whom the office truly belongs. Indeed, ultimately, preaching is an 'English Werck', meaning, *pardon the pun!*, not the work of the Angles but of the Angels. In the following rules, Scherer stresses the importance of 2) preparing oneself properly (the sermon is compared to a meal: if it is not cooked sufficiently, it is tasteless and unhealthy); 3) supporting the preaching by 'living exemplary and edifying lives'; and 5) refraining from the use of insults and direct criticism of opponents from the pulpit (it is better to do this with arguments in a different context). Towards the end, 8) he warns both against the priest's vanity (that he appropriates the praise that belongs to the Word) 'so that the praise does not devour him', and 9) against the tendency to shout like a quack (*Triacks Krämer*). It is precisely in direct continuation of these warnings against the temptations for popular preachers that Scherer declares in his tenth rule:

> Preachers must not be jesters, story tellers, or joke peddlers [*Possenreisser, Mährleinsager und FabelHansen*], but they should serve the Word of God with appropriate dignity and majesty. It is not forbidden occasionally to delight and encourage the weary hearers with stories or witty words related to the matter at hand. However, to enthusiastically engage in ridiculous and vile obscenities and foolishness in order to attract people and gain a large audience should not take place at all, and such filth does not belong in the pulpit but elsewhere.[112]

When both condemnations and admonishments from individuals as well as bans from the authorities so clearly had to be repeated again and again, two obvious interpretations emerge which are probably not incompatible yet differ significantly. Either we are dealing with a popular phenomenon that irresistibly bubbles up from below (be it from 'the people' or the local priests), and as such it represents an undercurrent, a counter-tradition in the history of the church (this will be an attractive conclusion for those who are enthusiastic about the revolutionary potential of the culture of laughter). Or the denunciations from synods and bishops served as a kind of official cover for an unofficial tolerance or, perhaps more likely, they masked a clerical disagreement, for even back

---

according to the nature and magnitude of the offense, if they could have been apprehended.' 1542, 22v.
112 Scherer 1603, scan image 24 f.

then there were strong opposite sides within the same denominations. Put into a simplified formula, we repeatedly observe a development in the position of the Roman Church on this or that phenomenon, *in casu* Easter Laughter and the colourful narrative material, which ranges from sheer condemnation via nuanced distinctions to practical regulation. If it does not always end with an explicit permission then often there is a tacit acceptance – but only in the second half of the 20th century outright encouragement to make use of it begin to see the light of day.

ii. Lutheran Critique

When Oecolampadius wrote his letter, he was still a Catholic priest, so strictly speaking his book cannot be claimed to represent a Protestant position on Easter Laughter, either of the Lutheran or of the Reformed kind. The roles as pioneers in the confessional critique of Easter Laughter can instead be given to Luther (1525) and J. Kessler (1524).[113]

While both Luther and J. Kessler undoubtedly addressed the phenomenon, neither used the term 'Easter Laughter'. In J. Kessler's case it is a downright tease, since he found occasion in his chronicle to mention Oecolampadius more than twenty times, including an obituary and a mini-portrait.[114] When at one point in the portrait he even referred to Oecolampadius as 'a strict preacher' (*an ernshafter prediger*), it is frustratingly easy to blame the well-read J. Kessler for not having included a comment on the *De Risu Paschali* book.

In the Protestant struggle with the old church's relationship to the many folk customs, a tradition developed of letting the technical term *risus paschalis* serve as a kind of *pars pro toto* for everything that the Protestants believed deserved to be either abolished or cleansed. It is customary to designate Mathesius from the following generation as the originator of this (in the sermon on Luther published in 1566); but there is actually another testimony which makes it possible with an even smaller margin to pinpoint when this custom (and Oecolampadius' 'casual' name for it[115]) came to be included as a *shibboleth* in Lutheran polemics.

---

113 However, it is debatable whether J. Kessler, only one year after his studies in Wittenberg with Luther, Melanchthon, Karlstadt, and Bugenhagen, which he himself describes enthusiastically, can yet be considered as Reformed, if by this term is meant something significantly different from Lutheran. Cf. note 68.
114 J. Kessler 1902, 384 and 91 respectively.
115 Cf. p. 11 f. and |18|.

In 1524, Bugenhagen published a Latin compilation of the New Testament accounts of Easter, which two years later was issued in German. Both included a short preface in which Bugenhagen polemicised against previous gospel harmonies for causing ambiguity rather than harmony in conveying the biblical message. The German version was an immediate success, and from 1530 until Bugenhagen's death in 1558 it appeared in fifteen more editions. Initially, these were mostly 'reprints' (although with a few major additions); but in 1543 Bugenhagen subjected the book to a final revision,[116] which was then published the following year in Wittenberg: 'The Passion and Resurrection of Our LORD Jhesu CHrist diligently brought together by D. Johan Bugenhagen Pomerania from the four evangelists. Newly diligently emended. Also a brief account of the destruction of Jerusalem and of the Jews'.

One of the modifications is that the previously single page preface has swelled to ten pages, and that a new piece of polemic is inserted:

> But the story of the resurrection of Our Lord Jesus Christ, which is so loving and joyful, was not respected in such a way that you bring it together from the four evangelists and preach it entirely as the passion or suffering of Christ, just as some preachers only look for ways to make people happy at the Easter feast and cause *risus paschalis*, that is Easter Laughter, with their fables.[117]

If only there had been ongoing revisions by Bugenhagen every time the passion harmony was published, it would have been possible to date with an accuracy of a couple of years when Bugenhagen had come to experience Easter Laughter. Or rather: since it seems almost unthinkable that the custom should have spread so fast since Oecolampadius' book – and certainly not as far north as Saxony – we get instead reliable testimony to the fact that Easter Laughter was already developing into a polemical platitude in the period between 1526 and 1544.[118] The fact that

---

116   Geisenhof 1963, 105.
117   Bugenhagen 1544, scan image 8–9. The same applies to the two Latin editions: in 1524, there is no mention of Easter Laughter, but a corresponding passage to the one in the German edition has been included in the preface to the 1546 edition: 'But some preachers had rather this one desire, that when one returns to eating meat, they could entertain the crowd with their uneducated and deceitful stories instead of a proper sermon and thus provoke *risus paschalis*, as they called it, among the people. How can these idiocies contribute to the majesty of the honourable resurrection?' Bugenhagen 1546, 3.
118   Wendland, who otherwise in his dissertation has been incredibly thorough in his search for sources, has surprisingly not been aware of Bugenhagen. It is downright unlikely that Mathesius, who knew Bugenhagen personally and had a close

Bugenhagen thinks it worthwhile to mention both the Latin and the German term points us in the direction of two exciting interpretive possibilities: either it shows that *risus paschalis* is indeed a neologism which he translates literally into an equally new German word, *Osterlachen*; or he explains the new Latin designation by referring to an already known German word. Since scholars have not found the German terms (*Osterlachen* or *Ostergelächter*) in older sources, it points to the 'translation'-interpretation as the most likely.[119]

iii. Oecolampadius' Legacy

If Bugenhagen and Mathesius can serve as evidence of it being, if not exclusively, then predominantly, Lutheran theologians who commented on Easter Laughter in the following centuries, it is nevertheless due to a Reformed theologian, even an aggressively anti-Lutheran one named Rudolph Hospinian (1547–1626), that not only the name of Oecolampadius became inextricably associated with *risus paschalis*, but arguably also that this custom acquired a status where it was 'described and blamed as a representative for similar things'.[120] As mentioned,

---

relationship with Wittenberg (both Bugenhagen, i.e. 'Dr Pommer', and his time studying in the city are frequently mentioned by Mathesius in his Luther sermons), would not be familiar with the Passional. So it would not be unthinkable that Mathesius may have picked up the expression '*risus paschalis*' from Bugenhagen, which he (Mathesius) could then connect to his own experiences of amusing Easter stories from his youth. We do not hereby claim that Bugenhagen's book constitutes 'the missing link' that definitively gives Oecolampadius copyright to the technical term, as it could potentially be Bugenhagen himself (independently, parallel to his colleague in Basel) who invents the term ... or he may have obtained it from another as yet unidentified oral or written source.

In addition, it should be mentioned that throughout the rest of the century, the German version, according to Georg Geisenhof's (fl. 1900–08) Bugenhagen bibliography, was published in fifteen additional editions, all based on the 1544 edition, including the new preface with the lines about *risus paschalis*. It was not until 1618 that an edition was printed without the preface, and then nearly a hundred years passed before the next edition (1706) ... but once again with Bugenhagen's preface including *risus paschalis*. The Latin version, on the other hand, only saw the light of day again in 1600 and with a completely new preface written by the publisher Salomon Gesner (1559–1605), who did not find any reason to mention the Easter custom.

119   Anyhow, Bugenhagen's use of 'ein Osterlachen' trumps Wendland's identification of the first German translation of *risus paschalis* by c. 150 years, cf. note 62.
120   Wendland 1980, 70.

both Bugenhagen's and Mathesius' books became extremely popular with many reprints over the next 200 to 300 years (including translations into other languages, such as Danish editions in 1539 and 1844 respectively); but both of them only mention Easter Laughter completely *en passant* and as a catchword. So if these two gentlemen had stood alone, it must be considered doubtful whether exactly that particular custom would have attracted more attention than so many others, and far more widespread, linked to Easter (Easter eggs! Easter bunny! etc.), and Oecolampadius' booklet would have been buried in dust in a few archives.

Thus, it must be symptomatic that the book was never reprinted or translated,[121] and before the age of the Internet and the blessings of electronic scanning the work was very difficult to access. Nor did it exactly cause much of a stir when, 400 years later, it was included in Staehelin's scholarly edition of a large number of texts by and about Oecolampadius. On the other hand, thanks to Staehelin's colossal work in gathering data on everything Oecolampadius had written, it has become possible to claim that Oecolampadius himself was apparently quick to put the book behind him. For in addition to the books by Oecolampadius, Staehelin also took the trouble to procure not only the author's own correspondence, but also other contemporary documents (letters, printed matter) that mention him all the way up to 1593, more than half a century after Oecolampadius' death. This makes it possible to determine that during the rest of his life Oecolampadius – at least in writing – only twice touched on the booklet about laughter. This he does half a year after its publication in a letter to his old teacher in Hebrew, Johannes Reuchlin (1455–1522), and subsequently in a letter the following year to another Hebraist of the time, Kaspar Amman (*c*. 1450–1524). Although authors may not be the most reliable sources when it comes to assessing the reception of their work, the latter letter, in the absence of other and better testimony, does contain something of a scoop. Oecolampadius informs Amman that *De risu paschali* has brought joy among not so few (*non paucus gratus fuit*), and he regrets not being able to send Amman the book as he does not have more copies lying around. We do not know the circulation figures at the time, so do we get the impression that the book had been in high demand and

---

121 Salomon Hess (1763–1837) does state in his bibliography, *Chronologisches Verzeichniss der Schriften D. Johann Oekolampads*, that *De Risu Paschali* is supposed to have also been published in 1540 in octavo format (1793, 413); however, neither a worldwide search in library databases nor Staehelin's definitive catalogue from 1963 supports this information.

sold out?[122] Hardly, because in that case it stands to reason that an enterprising merchant like Froben would have reprinted it, but this never happened.

At the time of his death, Oecolampadius was such a celebrity that Staehelin was able to find large amounts of material relating to the life and work of the Basel reformer, both in the form of the immediate obituaries (and elegies) and various writings from the subsequent five decades. In the many praises of Oecolampadius' significance and listings of his works, there is no mention of *De risu paschali* except for a single tantalising reference that could potentially have meant an international breakthrough for the Oecolampadius-cum-Easter-Laughter cocktail … if only there had been some receptiveness to it in Europe at large.

The book on laughter was originally written as a letter to the friend and colleague Capito, so it is only fitting that he is the exception. In 1534, he published a 700-page work with Oecolampadius' commentary on the prophet Ezekiel, and for the introduction Capito wrote a ten-page biography, *De vita Oecolampadii*. Apparently, even Capito was no longer entirely clear about it ('I think it was 19 years ago' – did he not even have the book on the shelf anymore so he could have checked the year?), but despite the distance of these years he still recalls the essential details: that at the time when Capito himself had arrived at Basel, Oecolampadius was preaching in his homeland; that he was accused there of being a serious preacher because he would not scream like a madman in the pulpit or arouse laughter with vulgar antics; and that all of this prompted him to send Capito a small treatise on Easter Laughter, after which Capito arranged for him to be called to Basel as soon as possible.[123]

---

122 'I am sending my small talk, a book "On Easter Laughter", and also "Drakhmer from Greek literature", which the encouragement from my friends has compelled me to publish.' 'Oekolampad to Johann Reuchlin. Basel, [Early September 1518]', in: Staehelin 1927/34, vol. 1, 71.

   'I am sending and presenting to you "Guidelines on Repentance", which I have translated from Greek to Latin before I moved here from Basel. There are also other writings of lesser value that have been published by me, and of which I do not have a copy myself. Otherwise, I would have also shared them with you, especially the little book "On Easter Laughter", which many have been pleased with.' 'Oekolampad to Kaspar Amman. Augsburg, 22 February 1519', in: *ibid.*, 85.

123 The passage in its entirety is as follows: 'But this man has preached Christ for his country and garnered admiration from all truly spiritual and learned people, although there was still much of the old unbelief mixed in. But he heard that he was too strict a preacher because he would not shock people's ears with insane

When Theodor Bibliander (1504/09–64) edited a publication of the correspondence between Oecolampadius and Zwingli two years later in 1536, Capito's biography was included unchanged alongside a corresponding biography of Zwingli written by Oswald Myconius (1488–1552). Curiously enough, Simon Grynäus' (1493–1541) eyewitness account of Oecolampadius' death (as well as a vivid description of the preceding medical history), which had originally been a letter to Capito, was also added.[124] This oddity was motivated by the desire to dispel an ugly rumour that Oecolampadius had committed suicide.[125] When it is mentioned here, it is not out of fear of the old rumour resurfacing, but rather because those very three texts by Myconius, Capito, and Grynäus, supplemented by texts by Melanchthon on Luther's life and teachings, were allowed to venture out together into the wide world. This happened first with a translation into French published in Geneva in 1555 under the flowery title: 'History of the Lives and Deeds of Three Excellent Figures, First Restorers of the Gospel in Recent Times: Namely, Martin Luther, by Philip Melanchthon. Of John Oecolampadius, by Wolfgang Faber Capito and Simon Grynäus. Of Huldrych Zwingli, by Oswald Myconius. The whole newly translated from Latin into French and brought to light'. This publication also included the passage about Capito's recollection of the letter about Easter Laughter.[126] In itself, it is a reminder of Oecolampadius'

---

shouting and also would not liven up the holy ceremony through crude jokes, as these beggarly monks used to do back then. For he has always loved moderation and naturalness in speech. This unjust judgment prompted him to write a small book to me about Easter Laughter, which happily expressed his state of mind as it was then. It is, I believe, nineteen years ago.' Capito 1534, scan image 20 f.; reprinted in Staehelin 1927–34, vol. 2, 745 f.

124 Capito 1536, scan image 72-6 (the quote about laughter, 74). Grynäus' contribution is reprinted in Staehelin: 'Des Simon Grynaeus' Bericht an Wolfgang Fabricius Capito über Oekolampads Tod', 1927/34, vol. 2, 730–6.

125 Cf. Irena D. Backus' (1950–2019) imaginative heading to the relevant section of her chapter on the biographies of the Swiss reformers: 'Zwingli, a Christian Hero Complete with Miracles, and Oecolampadius, a Man too Saintly for Suicide', 2008, 47.

126 '[…] lors qu'il preschoit Christ en son pais, auec grand etonnement de tous spirituels & sçauans: iaçoit qu'il meslast encores maintes choses de l'ancienne superstitition. Neantmoins, on disoit qu'il estoit trop feuere prescheur, pource qu'en chaire, il ne crioit comme vn enragé, & ne sçauoit faire rire par plaisanteries mal-plaisantes, qui estoyent les manieres dont lors vsoyent ces belistres de moines. Luy au contraire aimoit tousiours garder modestie & saine grauité en son dire. Ceste corruption & peruersité de iugement luy donna occasion de m'ecrire vn petit liure du ris ou passe-tems de Pasque, où appertement il declaroit son esprit & courage, il y a ia, comme

status in his time, that he was made part of such a triumvirate, even if the other two gained a far greater and more lasting reputation in posterity.

Granted, Geneva is not exactly on the other side of the world from Basel, but its Swiss sister city was still outside the primary area of influence of the Easter Laughter practice. Furthermore, the book apparently provided direct inspiration for the Latin texts to be 'Englished' and published in London in 1561, this time also with an impressive marketing title: *A famous and godly history contaynyng the lyues a[nd] actes of three renowmed reformers of the Christia[n] Church, Martine Luther, Iohn Ecolampadius, and Huldericke Zuinglius. [...] newly Englished by Henry Bennet Callesian.*[127]

What appears to be the only surviving copy of the book is so badly damaged by the ravages of time that it is often difficult to read the faint text. While the University of Oxford Text Archive simply leaves quite a few lacunae, it is nevertheless possible to decipher most of these in the relevant passage from the scan available on Early English Books Online. It is a major frustration that the translator Henry Bennet (fl. 1561) apparently relied more on the French translation than on the Latin original when he reached the crucial point in our context. Instead of translating 'de risu paschali ... libellum' he reproduces the French paraphrase 'vn petit liure du ris ou passe-tems de Pasque': 'one litle treatise intituled, the Pastinze of passeouer'. Not only does Bennet ignore 'risu'/'ris', but it seems that he simply gave up when he came to 'passe-tems' which he tries to tackle with a neologism: 'Pastinze'. According to the Oxford English Dictionary, that word does not exist in the English vocabulary, so the typographical error has

---

ie pense, dixneuf ans passez.' Capito 1555, scan image 98. For an English translation see the following footnote.

In Staehelin's notes on Capito's life, he points out that 'a separate publication with the reports of Simon Grynaeus and Wolfgang Fabricius Capito, along with the poetic obituaries by Johann Sapidus ["Epigram by Johannes Sapidus on Oekolampadius. Between November 1531 and March 1532"], Theodor Beza ["Epigram by Theodor Beza on Oekolampadius. 1580"], etc., and the preface by an anonymous author from February 1617 can be found under the title: "De morte et vita Joannis Oecolampadii" at the Bibliothèque Mazarme in Paris'. 1927/34, vol. 2, 749. According to the Karlsruhe Virtual Catalog, the full title of the publication is 'De morte et vita Joannis Oecolampadii, Weinspergensis, Suevi' and besides France, only three other copies are preserved in Switzerland and Munich.

127 Here the lines about Easter Laughter are rendered as follows: '[...] and then he preached Christ in his Country, to the great admiracion of al faythful & learned people, albeit then he entermedled many thinges of the auncient supersticion, yet some affirmed he was a very seuere Preacher, because he rored not out in the Pulpit,

clearly punished Bennet for omitting the laughter. All the same, the expressions 'ris ou passe-tems de Pasque' and 'the Pasti[m]e of passeouer' had now at least been introduced to a wider audience.

As mentioned, Staehelin chose to conclude in 1593 with a lecture on Oecolampadius delivered by Amandus Polanus (1561–1610) on 15 May. It is a bit odd that Staehelin makes his cut precisely there, as it is in 1593 that Hospinian's work is published, which, to a far greater extent than Bugenhagen and Mathesius, definitively associates Oecolampadius' name with the phenomenon of Easter Laughter, that is: the *historical* phenomenon of Easter Laughter. Hospinian's book may not initially appear to have been a bestseller. It is published in an expanded edition in 1612, both this and the first edition in Zurich, where Hospinian worked. The work appeared again in Geneva in 1674 and finally as volume 2 of a seven-volume edition of his collected works in 1681. What ensured the survival of the work is indicated by its title: 'Christian Festivities, This Is: On the Origin and Development of Ceremonies and Rites of Christian Festivities' (*Festa Christianorvm, Hoc Est: De Origine, Progressv, Ceremoniis Et Ritibvs Festorvm Diervm Christianorum*). It offered a kind of encyclopaedic overview of the festivals and rituals during the entire church year, including all the liturgical 'branches' of the Roman Church that Protestants wished to prune. Along with a companion volume that similarly described the origins and development of Jewish, Roman, Greek, and Turkish rituals and ceremonies, the book gained the status of a standard reference work that was apparently indispensable in many a well-stocked learned home or scholarly library.

It is precisely as an example of this kind of archaeology of rituals that Hospinian not only mentions Easter Laughter in passing, but brings a very long quote from Oecolampadius' book.[128] The significance of this can only be underestimated, for over the following *c.* 150 years, i.e. when the majority of the literature is written which is (confessionally) critical of Easter Laughter, it is in all probability Hospinian's book rather than Oecolampadius' own that is used as the source. This

---

    & with pleasaunt gesture could not move laughter among hys gloming Auditors, as was the bestial Monkes custome, for he euer obserued modestye & grauitye in his urteraunce. This their corrupt & peruerse judgement gaue hym occasion to write unto me one litle treatise intituled, the Pastinze of passeouer, wherein he expressed hys mynde verye learnedly, and (as I collect not xix yeares past[)].' Capito 1561. The book is without page numbers or other markings, but the quote is on the tenth of the pages with Oecolampadius' life.

128   Hospinian 1593, 73v-74r; cf. notes 499, 509, and 58.

claim seems reasonable when we observe that, insofar as the authors bother at all to provide source references, one of two is applicable. Either Oecolampadius is not mentioned at all, only Hospinian, or they are both mentioned. However, in both cases as well as the many cases where neither of them is mentioned it seems a safe guess that Hospinian is the actual source, because it is always either a verbatim quote or paraphrase of the section he brought from Oecolampadius that is used. It must be admitted that Hospinian had a good nose for lifting the pages in *De risu paschali* that contain the juiciest and most provocative details; but it remains unlikely that almost all later authors would have made their cuts around exactly the same lines without having snipped them from him.

Although Wendland found examples of Lutheran preachers who continued to rail against Easter tales and laughter,[129] we can summarise the Baroque period by saying that Easter Laughter moves from the church and the pulpit to the study and the lectern. As mentioned at the beginning of this chapter, the present study has relied heavily on secondary literature, especially the research done by Moser-Rath and Wendland. However, a somewhat uncanny aid in forming an overview of the period, and in documenting Hospinian's role in disseminating knowledge about Oecolampadius and his book, can be found in a slightly older dissertation by Nickel.[130] Nickel has in fact closely studied 241 academic texts from the period 1590-*c.* 1750 in order to collect folkloric testimonies about the celebration and customs of Easter, and she devotes a special chapter to those mentioning Easter Laughter. It should perhaps be noted that according to Nickel's introduction, what she can ascertain about the relationship between 'Easter Laughter', 'Hospinian', and 'Oecolampadius' in particular, applies to the scientific treatises of the Baroque period generally: firstly, that they often quote from previous treatises on the same subject (in this case, Hospinian) rather than consulting the sources themselves (so much for the humanistic and Protestant call *ad fontes*), and secondly, these borrowings from other academics agree to

---

129 Wendland 1980, 91 ff.
130 Why call Nickel's dissertation 'uncanny'? That assessment is absolutely subjective! It is because of the *timing*. Not so much because Nickel happens to defend the thesis precisely in the week after Easter that year, but because of the promotion taking place on 20 April 1945. Thus, the scholarly defence of past peculiarities at Easter takes place at Friedrich Wilhelm University ... right in the middle of Berlin. Granted, the Russians had by then ceased their most intense bombardments, but how was it even possible to make oneself heard and keep one's concentration considering what else was happening around the city in those days?

such a degree with one another that 'today' (i.e. in 1945) they would be labelled plagiarism.[131] In the case of Easter Laughter, this kind of redundancy is particularly pronounced, both in the actual monographs on the custom as well as in the many other findings Nickel has made in broader presentations where Easter Laughter is only dealt with in a chapter or a shorter passage.[132]

3. Brief Characterisation of the Critique of Easter Laughter After the Baroque Period

While Easter Laughter appears to have completely faded away along with the Baroque period, criticism of it still survived, albeit not with the same intensity as before. The period after the mid-18th century will therefore not be examined in detail here either. Instead, at the risk of reducing the writers of the next 150 years to a caricature, we will declare that the interest in Easter Laughter can roughly be boiled down to three types.

First, there is the church-historical approach where Easter Laughter is treated relatively soberly. This applies, for example, to Johann Konrad Füssli (1704–75) when in his 'Contributions to the Explanation of the Church Reformation Histories of Switzerland' (1753) he naturally cannot avoid dealing with Basel's reformer. It is indeed noteworthy that Füssli (unlike Oecolampadius' contemporaries[133]) does not overlook the treatise on Easter Laughter, which, compared

---

131 Nickel 1945, 3 (general) and 104 (Easter Laughter).
132 It is beyond the scope of the current book to delve into this material; however, to provide a sense of it, a selection of the many and often revealing titles will be listed in chronological order (for brevity's sake the titles are not included here but can be found in the bibliography). For this occasion, the listed publications from Nickel (and a few from Wendland) have been checked via the Karlsruhe Virtual Catalog, which in some cases has led to minor corrections of dates and titles. Here, too, the baroque custom is followed, as explained by Nickel, where a work is not always catalogued under the author's name, since dissertations were listed under the name of the supervising professor, which is indicated here by adding information about the doctoral candidate. Monographs: Thomasius 1661, Wegner (candidate: Kesselring) 1705, Anonymous [Schramm] 1725, Beil 1746, and J.P. Schmidt 1747. Chapters and extended passages: Thumm (candidate: Capeller) 1624, Hildebrand (candidate: Hantelmann) 1655, Homborg 1683, Seckendorf 1688, Wildvogel (candidate: Heberlin) 1691, J.A. Schmidt (candidate: Tentzel) 1693, Hildebrand 1701, Krause (candidate: Starcke) 1710, Nettelbladt 1734, and Wernsdorf 1763.
133 Cf. the section on Oecolampadius' legacy, II,2,iii.

to the enormity of Oecolampadius' overall production, is so minuscule that it would seem excusable to ignore it in a general context. The historian, however, opens with this statement: 'I do not intend to make a list of all the writings of this great reformer here, but only to mention some rare ones [...]'. Thus, Füssli allows for a detailed description of Easter Laughter and does so by referring back to Oecolampadius' own book, paraphrasing its main points and including lengthy quotes from it. In fact, the quotes are so long that *De risu paschali* occupies about four out of the ten pages dedicated to the reformer.[134]

Next, Easter Laughter appears, not surprisingly, in the emerging and increasingly popular study of folklore in the broadest sense. Here, a famous work with an admittedly unique and sharply defined perspective on the subject can be allowed to represent the genre, namely Karl Friedrich Flögel's (1729–88) *Geschichte des Grotesk-Komischen* (1st ed. 1862), where Easter Laughter, among *many* other curiosities of the past, is given a brief mention – curiously enough without even mentioning Oecolampadius, but instead Mathesius and Bebel.[135]

Finally, as a third group, we could gather, across various fields of study, the kind of references to Easter Laughter where the custom is definitively reduced to a caricature. Somewhat maliciously, we may allow ourselves to wonder whether these types of authors had perhaps finally become so tired of repeating over and over again Mathesius' devilish noses and Oecolampadius' clucking cuckoo, hissing cow, and hooded peasant (cf. |16|), that in order to tell something new about the custom they had to invent it themselves. Georg Christoph Lichtenberg (1742–99) invents something that could easily pass for the South German Championship in Easter Laughter when he explains: 'Whoever was most skilled at this and could make the entire Christian community laugh as if with one voice, in the treble and continuo, was the best Easter preacher.' Apparently Lichtenberg had had access to a source equipped with a stopwatch, as he also claims to know: 'Even if such a person did not always give a laughter-sermon [*Lachpredigt*] from beginning to end, usually half or a third of it had this intention.'[136] That discipline is surely trumped by Peter Rosegger (1843–1918)

---

134 Füssli 1753, the quote: 446, exposition of *De risu paschali*: 447–51.
135 Flögel 1887, 217.
136 Lichtenberg 1787, 382 f. Without necessarily strengthening his credibility, Lichtenberg is not entirely alone in this fantasy of a pastoral competition, for it also seems to haunt the chronicler mentioned by Moser-Rath (1964, 33): 'Whoever could bring forth the most foolish chatter on Easter Sunday from the pulpit, causing people to laugh greatly, received the highest praise. But there was no mention of the resurrection of Christ, its benefits, and how we should find comfort in it.' This is a

when he manufactures The Heavenly Games where much more is at stake than the mere competition between preachers: 'In earlier times, it was common to celebrate the joy of Easter with Easter Laughter, when Mr. Priest would tell stories in the pulpit, [...] and anyone who laughed so much that tears came to his eyes had redeemed a poor soul.'[137]

4. Re-evaluation I: Nuances in Luther's and Mathesius' Critique

At this point it may be opportune to borrow from M. Harris' illustrative summary of later generations' descriptions of the loosely related church festivals during Christmas. Admittedly, the Feast of Fools or Feast of the Ass were most likely far more widespread phenomena in terms of period and geography, and undoubtedly also much more well-known and discussed in succeeding ages. However, the voluminous historiography's mythologising recycling of astonishingly few original sources is very similar, albeit on a smaller scale, to what has happened to Easter Laughter. Just as Oecolampadius (and Mathesius' and Erasmus' glimpses of memory) serve as a basis for most of what is actually

---

    quote from Tobias Schmidt's (d. 1659) *Chronica Cygnea or Description of the very Ancient, Praiseworthy, and Electoral City of Zwickau* [...], 1656, vol. 1, 375.

    If we were to take Lichtenberg's 'measurements' more seriously, Moser-Rath can be helpful in summarising the complexity of the relationship between narratives and preaching in the preserved sermons: 'Regarding the place of short stories [*Märlein*] in sermons, one cannot make any definite statements, as the structure of sermons, despite certain basic rules, is quite variable. Sometimes, a sermon takes its cue from a narrative presented at the beginning, while other times, the stories serve as a little extra feature at the end, as seen in Lucianus' sermons for children. Strobl dedicates a separate section to his little Easter story, usually as the third or fourth paragraph in the sermon, followed by a separate moral application. However, usually the stories are seamlessly woven into the discourse and connected to the preceding explanations in such a way that it is difficult to distinguish the beginning from the text. Finally, the narrative could also be used as a distinct constructive element in the sermon. It then serves as the framework for spiritual reflections or moralising digressions, as seen in examples from Lent or, for instance, in Pastor Helbig's fable contaminations.' Moser-Rath 1964, 35 f. She is here referring to Lucianus Montifontanus (1630–1716) and Johann Lorenz Helbig (1662–1721).

137 Rosegger 1875, 48. We sense a twinkle in Rosegger's eye from his comment on this notion of the redemption of souls: 'This source of help has dried up for the poor inhabitants of purgatory nowadays, but in return, the Masses have become cheaper.'

known about Easter Laughter, there are likewise some famous sources for the Feast of Fools that almost all subsequent research has based its presentation on: the first statements in Johannes Beleth's (fl. 1135–82) *Summa de ecclesiasticis officiis* (probably between 1160 and 1164), Pope Innocent III's (1160/61–1216) admonishing letter to the Polish Church's Archbishop in 1207, and, last but not least, the Paris Faculty's condemnations in a letter to the French dioceses dated 12 March 1445.[138]

Having studied in this field for almost his entire career, M. Harris opens his book, not least self-critically, with a summary of his conclusions in four main points, which it is helpful to further divide into two pairs. The first pair emphasises the need for source criticism, as 1) the original polemic is not always entirely credible when compared to other sources, and 2) local customs cannot necessarily be generalised. The next pair exposes the (involuntary) distortion of history when 3) historians selectively focus on certain elements from a larger (liturgical or, in the context of Easter Laughter, homiletic) context, and, perhaps worst of all, when 4) they combine such elements that were originally widely dispersed in time and place, creating the impression of one continuous sequence of excesses. It should certainly not be denied that excesses did occur, but precisely as deviations rather than as a recurring *tour de force* in scandals.[139]

With this warning in mind, before we trace the history of the impact of Easter Laughter up to our own time, it may be appropriate to provide some much-needed nuances regarding both the tradition itself as well as its *afterlife* in criticism. At the same time this will also give us the opportunity to make some attempts at an overarching characterisation of the treatment of Easter Laughter from the 17th to the 19th centuries.

Anne Riising (1926–2017) was cited in another context for her reminder of a particular bias in the preserved medieval sermons, namely that they probably represent a kind of golden mean, or perhaps not so 'golden' after all, as Riising has the slightly more boring run-of-the-mill in mind.[140] That reminder can also be turned on its head: when scholars have managed to find exceptional examples, it is only fair to remember how preachers willing to provoke laughter were indeed an exception whose material stood out from the overwhelming

---

138   Due to the use of a different calendar then, the letter is dated 1444 and is therefore referred to in older research literature, and nowadays often on the internet, as 'the letter from 1444'.
139   M. Harris 2011, 3–5.
140   Cf. note 34.

majority of serious, long-winded, and dry sermons to be found in the archives.[141] Furthermore, there is also every reason to remember the significant differences within the material: among the Catholic preachers we can observe how the various clerical orders had a preference for (and aversion against) different forms of material to be used in sermons, where it was no coincidence that primarily the mendicant friars were most open to the use of even very colourful subject matters.[142] To a large extent, the telling difference can rather be drawn *across* confessions, so that the dividing lines ran between the inadequately educated rough(er) preachers (both Catholic and Protestant) and those with a learned humanistic background.[143]

The cues from M. Harris provoke a potentially even more important nuance. For if we return to two of the quotes that have had a defining impact on making Protestants distance themselves from Easter Laughter, it turns out that earlier in this chapter a dubious practice of selective citation has been repeated, which entails a considerable risk of perpetuating a tradition of drawing unnecessarily simplifying and thereby potentially distorting conclusions. The most famous and frequently cited statement about Easter Laughter turns out, upon closer examination, to be only a half-baked quote, as immediately after the sentence, 'this was called by the scholars at that time risus paschalis' (which is where everyone breaks off!), Mathesius himself continues in the same breath:

> In past years at this time, we, too, followed the example of great people and dealt with allegories and amusing subjects – such as the cave of Machpela, which Abraham bought for the burial of his wife, Sarah, and Joseph's dungeon, in which we portrayed for you the resurrection of the Lord Christ and of the faithful and the godless; or again, Ezekiel's bones and Daniel's pit and den, in which we explained and depicted articles of Christian comfort – but this time we will continue in the history of Doctor Luther [...].[144]

---

141 Wendland 1980, 46. Cf. Moser-Rath 1964, 45.
142 Cf. Wolf 1962, 83 and note 23 above. In the same place, Wolf – almost teasingly – presents the claim that 'the reform preachers at the end of the Middle Ages almost completely [abstain] from inserted narratives (especially folk traditions), with the exception of Johann Geiler von Kaysersberg'. 1962, 83. The teasing aspect lies in the fact that this is the period just before Oecolampadius' polemical writing, and that Geiler is one of his sources, cf. |63|.
143 Cf. Wendland 1980, 57 and 288.
144 1566, 77r-78v; 2018, 286 f. Wolf lists several other places in Mathesius' sermons where, on the one hand, he expresses the same criticism of loose narratives from the pulpit, while on the other hand, he himself makes use of, for example, Aesop's fables and similar storytelling material, 1962, 85–9. Cf. Fluck, who expresses astonishment at the harsh criticism of narratives from a man like Mathesius, who otherwise

Mathesius apparently considers himself able to distinguish between two types of narrative: 'absurd and idle talk' (*mehrlein and nerrische gedicht*) and 'allegories and amusing subjects' (*allegorien und lustige materien*) respectively; and concerning the latter he devotes an entire sermon on Luther's fondness for and use of fables in general and Aesop in particular (which Luther also happened to work on a complete translation of, though unfinished).[145]

Already here, by way of Mathesius' example, it is signalled that when the Reformation battle cry of 'Scripture Alone' becomes combined with Luther's well-known criticism of medieval theologians' excessive allegorisations, this runs the risk of being used as an argument for an exclusive preference for *sensus literalis* as well as at the same time a complete mistrust of any *sensus spiritualis*. If and when this happens, we soon end up with reductionist interpretations that would be not only aesthetically but also intellectually ruinous.

We can get help from Luther himself to elaborate on Mathesius' implicit distinction by returning to his sermon on Ephesians 5. In the fourth verse, St Paul's text gives Luther an opportunity to explain what is meant by the apostle's strong condemnations of 'shamelessness' (αἰσχρότης), 'foolish talk' (μωρολογία), and 'levity' (εὐτραπελία). At first glance it may not seem promising to turn to Luther for help, as in 1523, when he published 'Concerning the Ordering of Divine Worship in the Congregation', he begins that treatise by listing those three abuses that have caused the decline of worship and necessitated reform. Right up in second place Luther places the accusation: 'When God's Word had been silenced, there entered in its stead such a host of unchristian fables and lies, both in legends, songs, and sermons, that it is a thing horrible to behold.'[146] That assessment seems as harsh and uncompromising as St Paul's admonition to the Ephesians. However, in the sermon two years later it can be observed that Luther, as already quoted earlier, does not settle for the mere condemnation of 'foolishness' (*narrenteyding*).[147]

Although it is difficult to make precise comparisons across languages, it is worth noting, solely on the level of vocabulary, how Luther positions himself in

---

tells stories that are far more elaborate than the one about Jesus' descent into hell, 1934, 195.
145   In the 1566 edition this sermon is number 7, thus placed immediately before the one opening with *risus paschalis*, but in all later editions of Mathesius' Luther sermons it is moved to number 9, cf. 2018, lxxxvii.
146   Luther 1523a, 35; 1997a, 47.
147   Cf. notes 477 and 69.

relation to the Latin translations made by the *Vulgate* and Erasmus, particularly concerning the concept of *eutrapelía*. While the *Vulgate* uses the word *scurrilitas*, which predominantly carries negative connotations, Erasmus opts for *urbanitas*, a term with mostly positive associations. Does Luther, then, position himself somewhere in between with his use of *schertz*? In terms of content, something interesting certainly occurs, as immediately after the remark that at Easter 'ridiculous stories have been introduced into the sermon to arouse the drowsy', Luther goes on in the next paragraph to introduce a theological distinction between dogmatics and ethics, thus allowing him to nuance his position. 'The legends of the saints and the confused mass of lies concerning miracles, pilgrimages, masses, worship of saints, indulgences, and so on, which once dominated the pulpit' are dangerous if and when people base their faith on them. This, however, should be contrasted with 'mere human tales […] serving as mere occasion of merriment', which, Luther adds, 'nobody believes, which no one will place reliance on'. And as Luther transitions from *mōrología* to the interpretation of *eutrapelía*, he seems to continue along the same path: ' "Jesting" has reference to those conversational expedients which pander to gaiety in the form of scandal; they are called among us banter and badinage. Laughter, mirth, and gaiety are their purpose, and we meet with them generally in society and high life.' Essentially, Luther aligns himself closely with a definition that Aristotle, for whom *eutrapelía* was one of the most important social virtues, would likely have approved of.

The sole purpose of returning to Mathesius and Luther has been to document the presence in them of a more nuanced view on the non-biblical narrative material, which preachers of that time used. This is intended as a challenge to the one-sided impression we often get of the Protestant tradition, especially in the Baroque period. To make this point, we have perhaps moved so close to the opposite extreme that it may even be insinuated that Luther could have been a closet supporter of Easter Laughter. So, for the record, it must be admitted that the extended quotations above from Luther's sermons are still shortened (and somewhat 'adjusted') and thus do not fully reflect his position. For actually Luther continues after 'more occasion of merriment' to describe the risk of such stories if they are used in a different context, such as from the pulpit, as they can become 'a source of general moral corruption, an obstacle to improvement, and a cause of cold, indolent Christianity'. Likewise, Luther acknowledges that St Paul simply does not agree with Aristotle but condemns *eutrapelía* along with *mōrología*, which is why he advocates for a completely different form of eloquence when in church and talking from the pulpit 'among Christians, who certainly may find conversational expedients of a different kind, such as will inspire a cheerful and joyous spirit in Christ'. Alluding to Jesus' proclamation about being accountable for 'every idle word' on Judgment Day (Mt 12:36), Luther summarises his thoughts with a most complex declaration: 'Christians should be a very firm, though courteous, people. Courtesy should be coupled with seriousness, and seriousness with courtesy [*ernste freundlichkeit und eyn freundlicher ernst*] according to the pattern of the life of Christ supplied in the gospel.'[148]

Wendland agrees that Luther, unlike Oecolampadius, tries to find an attitude towards life that mediates between seriousness and frivolity. However, especially in light of the last remarks mentioned, Wendland believes that he must still conclude that Luther 'allows as little room for a natural sense of life as Oecolampadius does. He formulates [his idea] about consciousness of the mind and mastery of temperament in a postulate of the highest rhetorical artificiality, combining paradox and chiasmus: "serious friendliness and a friendly seriousness".'[149]

To some extent we would dispute this interpretation by arguing that while it is quite possible that Luther himself could not or did not want to draw any further consequences from the fundamental distinction between entertaining diversions and legends that can support faith, he has nonetheless opened the possibility for a later interpretation to further differentiate between harmful and harmless entertainment. This could perhaps be a good opportunity to bring the invaluable concept of *adiaphora* into play when it comes to evaluating the material with which preachers can spice up their sermon. If the stories directly harm faith, they should be avoided; if they 'only' distract the congregation's attention for a while, we could perhaps approach them pragmatically, based on the criterion that Mark (9:40) seems to adopt in contrast to Matthew (12:30).[150]

---

148   Luther 1525, 209; 1997b, 132.
149   Wendland 1980, 72.
150   Without necessarily having aspirations to document a similar approach in Luther himself, reference can, however, be made to a table talk where he apparently believes he is capable of making an even more intricate distinction between all of four (actually five!) types of lies: *mendacium iocosum, -officiosum, -perniciosum*, and *-impius*, of which he even believes that the first two can and should be praised: 'There are four kinds of lies: the first is the joke, *ein guter, lecherlicher bosse*, which encourages people or brings joy to the sorrowful. The second is the helpful lie, *ein gute, nützliche lugen*, and arises out of love, so that the neighbour is saved by it. Such a lie was Abraham's when he said that his wife Sarah was his sister [Gen 12:10 ff.], Michal saved David [1 Sam 19:13 ff.], and likewise Elisha in 2 Kings 6: this is not the way, nor is this the city [2 Kings 6:19].'

5. Re-evaluation II: Theological Motives Behind the Protestant Critique of Easter Laughter

Can we allow ourselves to give an overall characterisation of every author from Hospinian to the end of the 19th century who has dealt seriously with Easter Laughter? With due caution we could dare to crystallise some overarching motifs among those authors who not only in passing spice up a given presentation by

> The third is the harmful lie, *nach weltlichem lauff liegen*, that is to say, deceiving and causing harm. The fourth is the impious lie, which mocks God. The first two should be praised because they do no harm; the last two should not be accepted because they offend both humans and God. There is also another kind of lie, namely the necessary one, although it does not differ much from the second kind, the helpful one; and it can also be used without sin if no oath has been taken beforehand: *warlich, trawen, bey Gott* etc.' Luther 1531–3, 527, no. 1044 (not included in the *Table Talk* volume in the American edition of *Luther's Works*).
>
> Based on quotes like this, H.-G. Schmitz assesses Luther's attitude towards amusement: 'Pranks [*Scherzlüge*] can indeed become sinful when they degenerate into mischief, into shameful speech, but in general, Luther has no objection to playful pranks, that is, *ridicula, iocosa*, "naughty little jokes".' H.-G. Schmitz 1972, 210–2.
>
> This point can be supported and clarified by comparing the table talk with quotes from the sermon on Ephesians, as it would then emphasise that the 'praise' of 'playful pranks' in the dinner conversation needs to be nuanced in relation to whether the prank is used in a religious context or in everyday life. On the one hand, this means recognising that Luther fundamentally maintained a greater homiletic restraint than many modern Lutheran preachers probably adhere to. On the other hand, it does not necessarily mean that this kind of strictness can be applied to either civil life or other forms of church activities. The first (civil life) is abundantly attested to by the rich conversations at his dinner table, while the second, such as pastoral care, can be found documented in a striking letter that Luther wrote to his children's tutor, Hieronymus Weller (1499–1572), when Luther learned that Weller was threatened by depression (or, in the language of the time, 'spiritual sadness'). Here, Luther provides no-nonsense pastoral care in the form of an encouragement for equal parts conversation and sociability, while identifying the Devil as the source of melancholy.
>
> He begins the letter by declaring: 'In this sort of temptation and battle contempt is the easiest road to victory; laugh your enemy to scorn and ask to whom you are talking.' Before finishing the letter, Luther gives Weller some robust advice: 'Whenever the devil harasses you thus, seek the company of men or drink more, or joke and talk nonsense, or do some other merry thing. Sometimes we must drink more, sport, recreate ourselves, aye, and even sin a little to spite the devil, so that we leave him no place for troubling our consciences with trifles. We are conquered if we try too conscientiously not to sin at all.' 1530a, 518 f.; 1911, 323.

off-handedly mentioning the curious custom but who also demonstrate that they have a point in doing so – be it long or short.

As for the first general motif, already Hospinian, on the page just before his section on Easter Laughter, lists a number of other specific customs associated with Easter Sunday which he does not hesitate to characterise as *abusus & superstitiones*. In addition to mentioning customs from the Early Church, condemned by various synods, popes, or learned theologians, he also refers to some locally practised curiosities, among others a custom from Ireland.[151] According to both Nickel and Wendland, we see here the beginning of a recurring practice in literature about Easter Laughter, namely the quest for its roots in ancient customs.[152] In a way this motif can be said to have had an even longer history of impact than the confessional struggle and denominational legitimisation. For while a generally more ecumenical mindset has minimised interest in writing about Easter Laughter in order to point a finger at a medieval or Catholic decay, theorising about the origins of Easter Laughter still thrive in many other contexts. It should be pointed out that this does not refer to a phenomenological comparison, where scholars look for common features in comparable but mutually independent customs across the boundaries of epochs and cultures, but rather to the search for direct historical influences.

What Luther wrote in confidence to a friend, he could also openly say in the company of others, where collections of anecdotes (the stories of the mischievous yet clever characters Markolfo and Till Eulenspiegel) are recommended on par with the gospel itself as a remedy against melancholy: 'The best medicine against temptation is that you turn your thoughts away from it, that is, talk about other things, about Markolfo, Eulenspiegel, and similar ridiculous pranks, which have nothing to do with such matters, neither pure nor useful, so that you may forget those heavy thoughts or immediately turn to prayer and simply focus on the text of the gospel.' Luther 1531–3, 548, no. 1089 (this one, as well, is not included in *Luther's Works*).

151 The reason for specifically mentioning the Irish custom is that later scholars in the Baroque period used, among other things, Hospinian's mention of it to launch a theory about the origin of Easter Laughter in pagan customs. It is difficult to see from Hospinian's brief description what the Irish custom has to do with Easter Laughter unless he simply wants to show how things that have absolutely nothing to do with the Christian Easter are still connected to it in strange traditions: 'Some people from Ireland believed that they showed obedience to God if, throughout the year, they gathered booty through theft and robbery, which they could consume during the Easter season in lavish meals, as a tribute to the risen Lord. And there was a fierce dispute among them so that one would not be outdone by the other in the immoderate preparations of the dishes.' Hospinian 1593, 73r-v.

152 Nickel 1945, 106 and Wendland 1980, 77 ff.

It is profitable to distinguish between two forms of – or perhaps rather two phases in – conducting this kind of intellectual archaeology. Initially, there is what we today would call a religio-historical interest in demonstrating a continuity that reaches back to ancient customs, whether pagan (Greek, Roman) or biblical, and thus making it an almost boundless phenomenon in both time and place.[153] While this kind of research was almost exclusively carried out by theologians and Protestant historians, a new phase emerges with a completely different approach to Easter Laughter, as the study in the period of Romanticism is taken over by folklorists and Germanists. To start with, it leads to a kind of 'revaluation of all values', for whereas the search for the ancestors of Easter Laughter previously uncovered distant pagan, barbaric, and morally disreputable 'relatives', instead we are now met with a longing for originality and that which is rustic and folksy.[154] With both the proverbial 'necessary changes' and 'grain of salt' these modified ways of approaching Easter Laughter may very well be said to extend right up to our own time. Therefore, we hasten to add that we can hardly blame this new form of preoccupation with the origins of Easter Laughter for later being incorporated into the cultural program of National Socialism with its strong focus on Aryan roots and the transformation of vitalism into its cult of power and will. It remains thought-provoking, however, that during the 19th century and into the first decades of the 20th we can observe how interest in popular customs in general and Easter Laughter in particular in an ideologically conscious way increasingly turned its gaze away from Athens and Rome towards Nordic mythology and Germanic cult in search of the roots of Easter Laughter. It is also noteworthy how it was even possible to detach it from the connection to the biblical accounts of Easter and resurrection and instead find inspiration in ideas about the power of the life force to overcome death.[155]

---

153 'The legend of a deep antiquity and widespread dissemination of Easter Laughter increasingly solidifies into a doctrine, supported by historical speculation.' Wendland 1980, 83.
154 Cf. *ibid.*, 103–12.
155 A notorious example of this viewpoint is presented by Eugen Fehrle (1880–1957) in an article about laughter in the religious beliefs of different peoples, where he also touches upon Easter Laughter, and where his concern is to show how laughter is a phenomenon that is, so to speak, 'older' than the association with individual gods or figures, in this case, Christ: 'Customs of this kind are initially not tied to individual gods but exist on their own based on the belief that laughter brings and sustains life. However, over time, they are justified by myth and associated with some deity to whom growth is attributed.' Fehrle 1930, 2. It is perhaps worth noting that Fehrle joined the

Another recurring motif has been circumscribed by Wendland with this sharp observation:

> The focus of Protestant men of the church on the Easter tradition gained a new perspective with the turn of the 17th century: the necessity of the Reformation needed to be historically justified. [...] While Oecolampadius aimed to juxtapose authoritative norms and abusive practices, the polemic also raises questions about origin and development. In addition to criticism, it involves historical evaluation and explanation.[156]

What Wendland initially writes about the appetite of the academics of the Baroque period for providing historical legitimisation also applies to the following centuries and perhaps becomes even more evident when a serious historian allows the polemic to slip out between the lines ... or in an inserted parenthesis. At the young age of 30, Heinrich Ernst Ferdinand Guerike (1803–78) published his 'Handbook of General Church History' which begins with a section on the 'Church's Need for Reformation'. The section is a roller-coaster ride of abominations, and to top it off it concludes with a remark about Easter Laughter. This is supposed to illustrate how the congregations had become victims of a Church whose monopoly had become so great, 'that the poor people patiently allowed it when their preachers, on the joyous festival of Easter, just to ensure the customary Easter Laughter the most, [had to put up with ...]' – whereupon Guerike, without mentioning Oecolampadius by name, presents all of his examples of animal sounds and the tale of St Peter and the innkeeper (cf. |16|). Five years later, Guerike's church history can be published in a 'third, expanded, and improved edition', and as for the passage just quoted, the expansion and improvement is limited to the fact that in an otherwise 'photographic' reprint, after the word 'Easter Laughter', this explanatory parenthesis is inserted to avoid any misunderstanding: '(the caricature of the missing holy Easter joy)'.[157]

NSDAP the year after the article and during his career under Nazism worked to find the pure Germanic roots of German customs. Thus, in 1936 he wrote an article about 'The Essence of the People' which was included in a series of pamphlets about the 'Foundations, Structure and Economic System of the National Socialist State', where he tried to show how throughout its history Germany had been threatened by alien cultural forces coming from the Mediterranean south (in particular the Latin-speaking church) as well as from the east and west (but not the north!). Neither Otto von Bismarck (1815–98) nor Kaiser Wilhelm II (1859–1941) had been able to cleanse the nation and its people from these influences, that task was left for the Führer to fulfil.

156 Wendland 1980, 77.
157 Guerike 1833, vol. 2, 578 and 1838, vol. 2, 714; cf. Wendland 1980, 94. The third edition from 1838 has also been supplemented with a footnote that reproduces Mathesius' memory of Christ's descent.

People like Guerike ineluctably reinforce the impression that certain Protestants almost turned the attitude towards Easter Laughter into a kind of *status confessionis*, a denominational marker of the divide between 'us' and 'them'. When emotions ran high, some could even go so far as to make Easter Laughter one of the motives behind the Reformation, as when the church historian Johann Jacob Herzog (1805–82) in his work on Oecolampadius' life and the Reformation in Basel believes he can draw this kind of conclusion:

> For the further down in the Middle Ages, the more such distortions of the sacred accumulate, the more something worldly, burlesque, often even obscene elements were mixed into the service, through which the clergy and the worship lost the respect of the people and paved the way for the Reformation.[158]

This observation makes us wonder why Protestants, judging by the sources, were more successful in keeping Easter Laughter out of their churches than Catholics, just as we might ask why they considered resistance to it to be so important. Help in answering such questions can be found by incorporating Peter Burke's (b. 1937) frequently reprinted and reedited attempts to provide a comprehensive picture across the entire continent in *The Popular Culture in Early Modern Europe* (latest edition 2009; references below are to the first edition from 1978). While Burke may not mention Easter Laughter in his otherwise encyclopaedic enumeration of phenomena, it clearly falls within his definition of 'popular culture'.

While Burke argues that quite generally he can demonstrate a wide range of similarities between Catholics and Protestants in their increasingly critical attitude towards popular culture, there are also some interesting differences, of which the time gap is not the least important. The Protestant movement, as the term suggests, arises as a protest not only against specific dogmatic tenets but particularly against the many customs developed by the practised faith, whereas the Catholic Church waited a couple of generations before intervening. This means that up until the Council of Trent, sporadic Catholic resistance against certain local or regional customs (such as Easter Laughter) can be found, but by the end of the 16th century, the opposition to certain aspects of popular culture becomes consolidated into a movement.[159]

The next stratagem in Burke's exposition is that he distinguishes between a negative and a positive reaction, where the negative consists of attempts to

---

158   Herzog 1843, vol. 1, 125.
159   Burke 1978, 218.

abolish, suppress, or alter ('purify'). As mentioned above, the Catholic Church did this with varying degrees of success through ecclesiastical legislation (cf. p. 64 f.), so this form of purification is common to the various denominations. Yet, there is a clear indication that it was particularly among the Reformed that this 'puritanism' could turn rampant.[160] More interesting is the fact that Burke does not content himself with listing prohibitions in various church ordinances and synod documents, or condemnations in tracts and sermons preserved in writing, for he also writes about a positive resistance.

Why did the Protestants succeed in their implementation of this 'purge'? A significant reason was that their criticism was not allowed to stand alone. In the efforts to disseminate evangelical theology as far and wide as possible, a counter-culture was established as a sort of side benefit to these efforts which could replace and mitigate the absence of past festivals and customs. A 'Culture of the Word' was promoted through the distribution of the Bible in vernacular languages, books with hymns set to familiar melodies and/or Christian reinterpretations of popular love songs, catechisms with a pedagogical question-answer structure, devotional books, pamphlets, and, last but not least, sermons that were so long that a new piece of furniture was generally introduced in churches: seats for the listening congregation.[161] Inside the church this received its illustrative counterpart in the replacement of altarpieces so that the congregations could feast their eyes on edifying words from the Bible or the catechism instead of opulently painted images.[162]

Although Burke argues that there were mainly differences in degree rather than in kind between the reform initiatives of Catholics and Protestants, he also maintains that there was a significant difference. In order to round off our attempt

---

160 Besides the festivals and plays, which especially roused their ire, 'a comprehensive list [of the things they wanted to weed out] would reach formidable proportions, and even a short list would have to include actors, ballads, bear-baiting, bull-fights, cards, chap-books, charivaris, charlatans, dancing, dicing, divining, fairs, folktales, fortune-telling, magic, masks, minstrels, puppets, taverns and witchcraft'. *Ibid.*, 208.
161 *Ibid.*, 223–33.
162 The strategy of also moving the Word from the church to the home was not exclusive to Protestants. One example of this could be the long, descriptive title of Strobl's collection of cheerful Easter sermons, *Ovum Paschale Novum*, which on the book's cover concludes the presentation of its merits and possible uses with this recommendation: '[These stories] can be useful not only for the gentlemen preachers in the pulpit, but also for other private individuals for conversation or to pass the long while and time, and they can be used with spiritual benefit.'

to summarise the theological motives behind the criticism of Easter Laughter, we could highlight two doctrines that may explain some of this 'significant difference': the concept of *simul justus et peccator* and the theology of the cross. Indirectly Burke himself provides a cue to combining the *simul*-anthropology with this topic when he reflects on the differences between the criticism of the festivals by Reform Catholicism and the Counter-Reformation on the one hand, and the Protestants on the other. For his conclusion is that while the Catholic reforms tended towards moderation, the Protestant reforms more often led to abolition. In this context he remarks that even though there are examples of Protestants attempting to adjust the celebration of a particular feast or holiday, they were fundamentally opposed to the very idea that some days should be holier than others.[163]

Just as the *simul*-idea opposes a fragmented view of humanity – where some aspects are good and others are bad – by insisting on a theological anthropology where human beings are totally determined by original sin yet in God's eyes and by virtue of Christ's atoning work are totally justified, so could we apply this principle to the relationship between holidays and weekdays. In the Catholic Church the categorical distinction between sacred and profane had developed into an often pragmatic dualistic thinking, where there were perpetual negotiations about where to draw the dividing line and how to observe the boundaries in practice. Late in the High Middle Ages this administrative practice had been accompanied by a theological sense of thinking in degrees on a continuum (most clearly seen in the developed distinction between mortal sins and venial sins that could be forgiven ... and for which time in purgatory could be shortened through the trade of indulgences, see below III,5,iii,d). In contrast to this the Protestants, in a certain sense, returned to an either-or thinking like the one practised by the ascetic Desert Fathers, though with a search for a different theological solution to the possibility of conforming to such sharp distinctions without having to abandon ordinary earthly daily life in a radical renunciation. An illustrative example could be Luther's interpretation of the Lord's Prayer, which describes how a Christian manages to 'pray without ceasing' (referring, among others, to Lk 21:36 and 1 Thess 5:17) without necessarily having to be woken up for all the canonical hours – and still remain vigilant in the intervals.[164]

---

163   *Ibid.*, 215.
164   To put it bluntly, the 'solution' is to rate quality over quantity: 'It would be better for you to pray one Lord's Prayer with a devout heart and with thought given to the words, resulting in a better life, than for you to acquire absolution through reciting all other prayers.' The commandment to 'pray at all times' (Lk 18:1) gives Luther the

From an impact-historical perspective, we have to consider whether this rejection of dualistic thinking in certain Protestant circles led to a kind of secularisation of all days of the week, while in others it led to a sacralisation of everyday life as well.[165] Applied to Easter Laughter: while Oecolampadius, at least at the time of writing his letter against Easter Laughter,[166] fully understands that there are situations outside of Sunday and in private settings where people can legitimately enjoy themselves (see |23|), there have been some, especially within those parts of church life dominated by a Puritan and Pietist inclination, who preferred to see laughter suppressed in daily life as well.

---

opportunity to expand on this difference both polemically and devotionally: 'There have been heretics, called Euchit – that is, people who prayed, who wanted to abide by the word of Christ and to pray (that is, they prattled with their mouth) day and night. This they did to the exclusion of everything else, entirely unaware of their folly, for while eating, drinking, or sleeping, they had to discontinue their prayers. Therefore Christ spoke of spiritual prayer, which may be carried on without interruption, even during physical labours, though, to be sure, no one ever accomplishes this perfectly either. Who is able to lift up his heart to God continuously? These words set a goal toward which we must strive. And when we see that we fall short of it, we must acknowledge that we are weak and frail human beings, be humbled, and plead for mercy because of our frailty.' Luther 1519, 83 & 84 f.; 1969, 22 & 24 f.

165 John Gordon Davies (1919–90) demonstrated in *The Secular Use of Church Buildings* a historical development that can serve as a material concretization of such a discrepancy between clear dogmas and a more diverse history of effects. In the Roman Church, there has always been a declared perception of the church space as sacred and thus sharply separated from the world; however, there has been a constant negotiation about what could then be allowed in this place. In contrast to this, particularly in a more reformed context, which is the perspective Davies writes from, there generally seems to be a very low-church attitude towards the church building, which should in principle pave the way for making the space accessible for almost any secular use outside of worship. Nevertheless, Davies believes he can observe that until the post-World War Two era Protestant church communities were far more restrictive than Catholics when it came to opening the church space for non-worship activities, resulting in buildings being left empty on weekdays rather than risking secular contamination of the space. Davies' polemical aim with this point was to argue that such a radical functional separation was based on a weak theology that did not take the incarnation seriously enough. Davies 1968, 217 ff. and 230 ff.

166 We may have our doubts about the older Oecolampadius, who left a reputation behind him for having given the citizens of Basel one of the strictest forms of church discipline of the century, and where we have to bear in mind that this kind of discipline had ramifications for civil life as well.

With the caveat that we admittedly run the risk of becoming overly speculative if we leave out too many nuances, the theology of the cross can also be brought into the discussion. To be sure, it should be taken with more than a grain of salt when we sharply distinguish the roles and assign them to Catholic and Protestant theology respectively. Just as the history of religions can observe that the wisdom traditions of antiquity have generally been highly sceptical of laughter, as in their worship of reason and balanced self-control it was considered a phenomenon too unruly, we could in a very broad sense argue that while Catholic theology has never been afraid to appeal to the emotions, Protestantism has spoken more to reason.[167]

In this respect regarding laughter, it is inspirational to follow Gerald A. Arbuckle (b. 1934) in making a fundamental distinction between creation and salvation theologies. Although such a distinction obviously cuts across denominations, it must be relatively uncontroversial to place the theologians of the Reformation primarily in the latter paradigm. The crucial point in this context is the clear tendency for a creation or salvation theology to perceive laughter diametrically opposite of each other. According to Arbuckle, a theology of creation is open to an exploration of the theological, pastoral, and liturgical potentials of laughter, while salvation theology typically proves far more restrictive. A theology concerned with humanity's need for reconciliation will typically view nature and humanity in light of the Fall, which is why it is sceptical about the possibility of finding traces of divine revelation even in the most positive phenomena from a human perspective, such as laughter in its most positive form (excluding *schadenfreude*, for example). Or, to put it slightly differently: a theology focused on reconciliation in the death on a cross will tend towards a form of seriousness, where laughter and merriment is suspected of being oblivious of the reality of sin.[168]

---

167   Cf. Gilhus 1997, 61 and 100.
168   Cf. Thomas' succinct summary of the development: the Reformation century resulted in various areas of life being exempted from laughter. When it primarily came to religion, this was due to the Protestant spirit making the connection between faith and seriousness (gravity, sobriety, etc.) an integral part of the matter itself. For Thomas, this ultimately relates to another change, as post-Reformation theology shifted the focus from Christianity being about a mode of behaviour to a matter of creed and belief, with the effect that 'it also gave expression to a narrower range of sentiments and emotions', Thomas 1977, 79.

In contrast to this, a theology of creation is based on the conviction that while humans are indeed sinners and that there is evil in the world, humans, through God's grace and their being created in the divine image, can yet strive for just and charitable actions and encounter glimpses of the promised life everywhere, such as when two individuals – or a congregation on Easter morning – come together in shared laughter.[169]

6. The Scholarly Rediscovery of Easter Laughter in the First Half of the 20th Century

If the sketch above and the remark about criticism persisting while the practice died out suggest a large volume of sources or their individual richness, it would be misleading. Rather, we could summarise the period as follows: between the considerable academic interest of the Baroque and, to some extent, the Enlightenment and our own time, Easter Laughter mostly gathered moss. Compared to the numerous treatises of the 17th and 18th centuries focused on Easter Laughter, it is reduced in the 19th century to an incident only mentioned in passing or as one exotic example among many others from the past, typically in general accounts of the Reformation or the history of preaching, in discussions of the church year and its popular customs, or, occasionally, in lexical entries.[170] Around the turn of the previous century, Easter Laughter just about appeared in isolated remarks in various works within the field of history of religions, which at that time was experiencing its heyday. There can hardly be a more striking testimony to how diminished the overall awareness of this custom had become than the fact that the otherwise encyclopaedically knowledgeable Reinach could

---

169 This is a liberal paraphrase of Arbuckle 2008, 112. In his doctoral thesis, Wendland also ventures to provide a theological explanation for the confessional difference, which can complement Arbuckle's analysis of the consequences of having a creation or salvation theology as our starting point: 'The emphasis placed on this Easter custom seems to be less a result of a fundamentally different understanding of preaching, but rather a consequence of a divergent understanding of the Easter event. For Protestant theology the essence of Easter lay in God's historical acceptance of Jesus' sacrifice, while Catholic doctrine emphasised the miracle of resurrection and the associated redemption of believers through the sacraments of the Church. Accordingly the solemn Good Friday was considered the highest festival in Protestantism, whereas for the Catholic Church it was the joyful Easter Sunday celebration.' Wendland 1980, 288.
170 E.g. Lutz 1814, Augusti 1818, E.T. Jäkel 1840, Alt 1846, Hagenbach 1859, H. Holland 1862, M. Busch 1877, Lippert 1882, and Linsenmayer 1886 (= 1969); cf. Introduction, 1.

write a 20-page article on 'ritual laughter' in 1911 without mentioning Easter Laughter at all. When the article was reprinted the following year in a book, Reinach added a new afterword explaining that in the meantime a German newspaper review of his article had made him aware of the phenomenon of *rire pascal*, wherefore he now included it in his global overview of laughter phenomena by way of Hospinian's lengthy quote from Oecolampadius.[171]

The fact that Easter Laughter not only escaped definitive oblivion but resurfaced with unprecedented appeal and growth in the latter half of the 20th century and accelerating exponentially into the 21st is likely thanks to two scholars who, independently of each other, took up the subject in the 1930s: Fluck and Bakhtin (cf. the next section). The actual work of systematically unearthing the sources was carried out by Fluck in a groundbreaking article from 1934, where he quite tellingly writes that to his great surprise he has discovered that both the phenomenon and Oecolampadius himself had almost disappeared from the attention of even supposed experts. Fluck's work not only provides the most comprehensive study up to that point but also fulfils Heinrich Weber's (1834–98) attempt not only to deal with the phenomenon anecdotally but to elevate it to a historiographical treatment in the modern sense.[172]

In addition to establishing an overview of the sources, Fluck also ventures to reconstruct the historical course, and he should certainly be credited for putting forward three overarching theories – even though he has been surpassed by later research in several aspects. We can hardly blame Fluck for his enthusiasm in finding sources scattered over such a long period and vast area, leading him to deduce that Easter Laughter has been widely and continuously practised from the Middle Ages until the transition to the 19th century.[173] Several times Fluck

---

171 Reinach 1912, 127–9; cf. above p. 14 f. about the 'fateful' effects of Reinach adding his remark about Easter Laughter to his article.
172 Fluck himself points to H. Weber (cf. note 11) as the one who had so far provided the best overview, and it says a lot about the state of research that as other descriptions of the phenomenon he can only mention Steger 1871 and Lichtenberg 1787, as well as a newspaper article that I have not been able to access: A. Dreyer: 'Ostermärchen', in: *Der Sammler. Belletristische Unterhaltungsbeilage zur München-Augsburger Abendzeitung* 1923, no. 26. Fluck 1934, 188, note 2. It deserves to be mentioned that neither H. Weber, Friedrich Steger (1811–94), nor Lichtenberg mention Oecolampadius by name despite including one or more of his examples. This must be a testimony to the fact that by this time these examples had become an anonymous part of the tradition.
173 *Ibid.*, 208.

himself cautions against reading too much into the many sources that do not explicitly mention Easter Laughter but merely something similar, and he also acknowledges that the overwhelming majority of sources point narrowly to Bavaria. Nevertheless, he succumbs to temptation and assumes its spread not only up to the Rhineland and northern Germany but also into Italy and France.[174] In this regard, the present exposition, in line with Wendland, allows itself to express disagreement.

Fluck's second theory, on the other hand, remains open to discussion, as he consistently distances himself from the 'modern' theories of his time that insist on finding pagan roots behind all kinds of church celebrations and popular customs. According to Fluck, it is unnecessary, even 'absurd', to search for a pagan heritage when the church tradition is already filled with festivities where pranks and mockery thrived (referring to the Christmas and Carnival seasons). Furthermore, Fluck argues that Easter Laughter in particular is liturgically embedded in a framework that invites joy both in the prescribed sermon text and the corresponding Psalm of David.[175] We will revisit this form of argument in the next chapter.

Finally, as his most speculative thesis, Fluck constructs a history of the decline of Easter Laughter. In a way, we could say that precisely where Fluck literally ends, the real interest of this present study begins! Fluck's last sentence reads as follows: '[…] the Risus paschalis, which initially for the preacher was merely a means to the desired end, soon became an end in itself, thereby immediately opening up the possibility of misuse and degeneration'.[176] The uncertainty about the historical course of events has already been mentioned (see note 53), but whether the Easter Laughter tradition *began* or *ended* with making laughter an end in itself to be striven for is not crucial in this context, for in both cases it is an important step towards the transformation of the status and reputation of laughter.

Whether Fluck's own interpretations are considered tenable or not, the foundation for further work on the subject had at least been established. However, if this collection of historical testimonies had been all that there was to it, it would be plausible to assume that Easter Laughter would for ever after have sounded like a dying echo buried in footnotes in scholarly research.

---

174   *Ibid.*, 205 ff.
175   *Ibid.*, 206 f.
176   *Ibid.*, 211.

To back up this assumption we can turn to two of the foremost figures in the humanities in the first half of the 20th century. In 1939, Ernst Robert Curtius (1886–1956) published an article titled 'Jest and Earnest in Medieval Literature', which includes a very short section on 'The Church and Laughter'. In the last sentence of the article, Curtius confesses that he has only scratched the surface of a rich, unexplored material on medieval laughter, and in a note he refers to Fluck, if anyone wishes to know more about ecclesiastical humour.[177] In the same year, 1939, Fluck also appears in the work of Propp, the Russian founder of formalist analysis of folktales. In an article on 'Ritual Laughter in Folklore', Propp not only refers to Fluck's pioneering work but also devotes a few remarks to both Oecolampadius and Easter Laughter. As a notable example of the bold claim made earlier about even the experts' deficient knowledge, it should be reiterated that Propp himself apparently gets the title of Oecolampadius' book completely wrong and attributes to him an apology for Easter Laughter.[178]

7. The Scholarly Study of Easter Laughter during the Second Half of the 20th Century

As already suggested, it is probably not as a result of Fluck's work that Easter Laughter truly emerged from obscurity. The claim here is that the decisive contribution to the breakthrough came when Easter Laughter was inserted into a comprehensive theory. That is what Propp's compatriot Bakhtin did in a doctoral thesis he submitted in 1940. It was indeed a protracted birth, as World War Two intervened, making it more important to defend the nation than academic dissertations, and the postponed university defence in 1947 did not give Bakhtin a doctorate but only resulted in him obtaining a candidate degree for his thesis on 'Rabelais in the History of Realism'. However, in our context this course of events appears to be almost providential, for when Bakhtin's revised study could finally be published in 1965 under the title *Rabelais and His World*, the times had indeed been *a-changin'* and were evidently far more receptive to its theses. The

---

177 Curtius 1939, 25.
178 Propp 1984, 138. In that article Propp seeks to develop a historically grounded understanding of laughter (which includes a polemic against, for example, Henri Bergson's [1859–1941] acclaimed but, according to Propp, speculative theory of laughter's timeless essence), and among the very few pioneers in this endeavour, he refers not only to Fluck but also to Reinach and Fehrle.

book arrived in the midst of what would become known as the '60s', and before the end of the decade, the book (or parts thereof) had been translated into all the major languages. The argument here is that *timing* made all the difference. Just as difficult as it may be to imagine a carnival in the streets of Aalborg in the 1940s and 50s,[179] it became equally conducive to the widespread knowledge of Bakhtin's ideas that the book's arrival in the West coincided with the so-called youth rebellion, where its ideas were seamlessly integrated as an important part of the *Zeitgeist* for those who had an appetite for historical and theoretical inspiration.

Regarding Easter Laughter, the inclusion in Bakhtin's book meant that it was placed in a broader context, not as a unique and bizarre exception, but as one among many similar and widely practised phenomena. While Bakhtin was primarily focused on rehabilitating François Rabelais (1494–1553) in all his sexual and scatological detail, he did so by reading him in light of popular carnivals and the Church's Feasts of Fools, which he lumped together into what he labelled 'the medieval culture of laughter'. Without referencing Fluck, who is not mentioned in the footnotes nor appears in the bibliography where only Johannes Petrus Schmidt (1708–90) 1747 and Reinach 1912 are named, Bakhtin also included Easter Laughter in that culture, and he clearly knew enough about this rare phenomenon to provide a brief and precise description in a single passage and continuously refer to it throughout the book.[180] It is certainly a bold claim to attribute to Bakhtin the credit for not only preserving Easter Laughter in scholarly works but also for it finding its way into popular and ecclesiastical culture,

---

179 Aalborg is a port city in the northern parts of Denmark that used to be known for its heavy industry, but since 1983 has hosted a carnival in May that has since grown into the biggest in Northern Europe.

180 Bakhtin mentions Easter Laughter a handful of times in passing; but if he truly relies only on the two people he mentions in a footnote, Reinach (who does not write anything independently about it but only brings the important quote from Oecolampadius through Hospinian) and J.P. Schmidt's baroque treatise, it is, indeed, astonishing how succinct an interpretation Bakhtin presents when he for once pauses and explains: 'During the Easter season laughter and jokes were permitted even in church. The priest could tell amusing stories and jokes from the pulpit. Following the days of Lenten sadness he could incite his congregation's gay laughter as a joyous regeneration. This is why it was called "Easter laughter". The jokes and stories concerned especially material bodily life, and were of a carnival type. Permission to laugh was granted simultaneously with the permission to eat meat and to resume sexual intercourse (forbidden during Lent). The tradition of *risus paschalis* was still alive in the sixteenth century, at the time of Rabelais.' 1984, 78 f.

gaining a popularity and geographical spread that it had never enjoyed before. To make it more plausible, it may not be enough to consider the spirit of the times; another factor must be added in the form of a semiotic professor exploding onto the scene as a novelist.

In the 20th century, the contributors to the substantial, scholarly treatment of Easter Laughter can be counted on exactly one hand: Fluck, Moser-Rath, Rainer Warning (1936–2024), Wendland, and Jacobelli.[181] With a pedagogically sharpened simplification it can be argued that while Fluck can be seen as a sufficient foundation and inspiration for the type of research continued by Moser-Rath, Wendland, and Warning, and while in Jacobelli's case it will be helpful to draw on Propp and Reinach to understand her theorising about Easter Laughter, Bakhtin appears to be an invaluable stepping stone on the path to Eco's novel. Despite the fact that Bakhtin, in total, devotes less than a page to writing about or referring to Easter Laughter, and although Eco does not even mention it in the course of *The Name of the Rose* (which would have been anachronistic in a story set in 1327!), the two together have likely had a greater impact on the international fame of Easter Laughter than any of the actual research done on the subject.

8. General Classification of the Way Easter Laughter Has Been Treated as a Literary Topos in Scholarly and Popular Literature of the 20th Century

Let it be a forewarning that it takes some daring, not to say presumptuousness, to attempt to trace and classify the impact history of Easter Laughter all the way up to the present day by providing a comprehensive characterisation of all (!) the articles and books published after Fluck's 1934 article in which Easter Laughter appears in the text. If we were to undertake a genuine scientific documentation, it would in itself not only fill an entire book, a very long one at that, but it would also quickly become both unreadably tedious, largely due to the sheer amount of redundancy, while at the same time missing the mark.

Even giving an estimate of the number of publications is fraught with uncertainty, but is partly based on extensive studies over many years, partly through searches for terms related to Easter Laughter in Latin, German, English, and Danish in Karlsruhe Virtual Catalog, books.google.com, and the ATLA Religion

---

181 From the present century one article and two books with valuable contributions to the discussion of Easter Laughter deserves to be added to this list of names: O'Connell 2002, Prütting 2013, and Lühl 2019.

Database.¹⁸² It would be easy to fall into the trap of adding up the absolute numbers from such searches, which would point towards approximately seven thousand publications. However, Easter Laughter has not become *that* dominant in the market of printed media. An estimate of the total number must take into consideration that on the one hand the number is significantly smaller since many texts mention two or more of the search-terms and therefore appear in multiple searches, while on the other hand there will be texts that are not captured by the electronic queries, as these require the search terms either to appear in the title or for the text itself to have been digitised. Given this, a qualified estimate would be around 350–400 articles and books. This is a conspicuously smaller number than the thousands of hits mentioned in the introduction; but this difference perhaps speaks more to the distinction between the completely unrestricted freedom of expression and publishing on the World Wide Web and, to a greater or lesser degree, the qualitative filtering involved in getting a text through a journal or publisher's editorial process.

Although 'only' in the hundreds, there will naturally still be some interpretative approximations involved when attempting to characterise them collectively. However, when it comes to the content, it is actually possible to offer a more qualified estimation. For this characterisation is based upon the roughly 175 titles in the bibliography (including older literature from before Fluck) which the author of this book has either read or found descriptions of in research literature.¹⁸³ Engaging with these titles has given a familiarity with the ways in which Easter Laughter is incorporated. Insofar as a taxonomy of these ways can be established without seeming entirely unreasonable, such a taxonomy, by virtue of the representativeness of the 175 titles, can reasonably be extended to the equivalent number of unread texts that have been discovered solely by electronic means.¹⁸⁴ For the sake of clarity, the material is limited in two respects: firstly, the focus here is on texts where Easter Laughter is involved for 'its own sake'. This means that texts where Easter Laughter only appears, so to speak, obligatorily, such as in

---

182   The database introduces itself with these numbers: 'The ATLA Religion Database includes more than 620,000 article citations from more than 1,746 journals (575 currently indexed).' These were the numbers as of July 2017 when research for this chapter was finished; by December of 2023 the numbers of citations and indexed journals had more than doubled.

183   Cf. the opening of this chapter where reliance on research done by others was mentioned, not least that of Wendland and Moser-Rath.

184   Actually, 'unread texts' is not entirely accurate because even though the texts have not been read from beginning to end (and thus nuances hidden in these skipped parts

articles and books about Oecolampadius' biography, Swiss Reformation history, historical overviews of homiletics, or encyclopaedia entries, are disregarded. Secondly, the starting point is the 75 texts from the past 100 years that meet this criterion.[185]

The first characteristic is quite uncontroversial as it is both purely formal and easily verifiable: the number of publications is increasing in a steep curve. Without being able to offer a deeper explanation for this, the number of publications clearly shows that 1990 represents a sort of turning point,[186] as in the 90s, 00s, and up until 2015, more texts have been published than in the rest of the 20th century – and as for the theological/ecclesiastical field, we can include all of the 19th century without reaching the same amount.[187]

Secondly, we can divide all these publications into three groups, which also tends to be entirely objective, as this division, roughly speaking, can be made by a simple count of printed lines. While nothing has been published that can compare to the handful of scholars mentioned above, there is a group (a) that, without being monographs on Easter Laughter, has significantly contributed to its interpretation (and the dissemination of knowledge about it) by organically incorporating a discussion of it in the various contexts that the texts themselves are otherwise about. From an 'objective' standpoint, this is reflected in the ample space dedicated to exploring the topic, typically in the form of separate chapters or longer sections. This may not at first hand sound terribly impressive, but it becomes all the more evident in contrast to the other two groups. In the first

---

may have been overlooked), approximately 25 % of the texts have been skimmed, while the rest can often be assessed reliably, albeit tentatively, on the basis of the 3–4 lines of context in which the keyword hits are presented.

185   In addition to the five main works by Fluck, Moser-Rath, Wendland, Warning, and Jacobelli, the just mentioned works by Reinach, Propp, and Bakhtin are also disregarded.

186   From a theological and ecclesiological point of view we could imagine that it took a gestation period for *The Name of the Rose* to turn its general popularity into scholarly research, but the surge in articles that mention Easter Laughter are probably just a special case in the same *Zeitgeist* that in 1988 have the first issue of *Humor* come into existence, a journal published by the International Society for Humor Studies which also since 1989 have organised annual interdisciplinary conferences.

187   In principle, we have to take a methodological weakness into account: the predominance of newer titles may simply be due to the fact that they were 'born' digital; but in practice this is probably offset by the extensive international projects involving scanning and digitising the libraries' collections of journals and older books.

of these (b), the mention of Easter Laughter takes up less than a page, typically even smaller; however, it can still be said that Easter Laughter has a contextually relevant place in the overall discussion. When we reach the last group (c), we are also close to the threshold where the quantitative aspect can shift into a qualitative assessment, as we are dealing with texts where Easter Laughter has become a sort of epochal buzzword. In practice, this means that the term 'Easter Laughter' is more or less arbitrarily inserted into the text and, at most, receives an explanatory parenthesis or a couple of lines along the way. If nothing else this seems indicative of a discourse where the phenomenon is either presumed to be familiar or can be considered a quite uncontroversial subject in no need of further explanation.

This tripartite division may prove more telling when held up against the year 1990. In the first group, there are 4 titles before 1990 and 8 after. For the middle group, there are 9 titles before and 6 after; while the general popularity of Easter Laughter shows itself in the last group of printed articles and books with 11 before and 37 after 1990. The significance of this is further reinforced by the fact that it can be claimed with reasonable certainty that among the 150–200 unread titles from the electronic searches, only a minimal number would upon closer inspection qualify for inclusion in the group with a substantial treatment of Easter Laughter. Therefore, the vast majority will be found in the remaining two groups, most likely with an even greater preponderance of those with a post-1990 publication date.

Finally, we can make a third classification of all publications since the year 1900 based on their academic field. On the one side there are those that can be aligned with Fluck *et alii*, which roughly means a 'cultural' side consisting of, among others, folklorists, literary scholars, and theatre historians. On the other side there are (practical) theological and ecclesiastical contributions whether in articles or as chapters in books. Something interesting emerges when bifurcating the titles in this way, solely from a statistical perspective, considering both the distribution in the groups from point two (a, b, and c) and the distribution before and after 1990. Before coming to that, it is worth noting that even though there are significant contributions from a theological/ecclesiastical standpoint, it is on the cultural side that the only two substantial studies since Jacobelli's work from 1991 can be found. One of these may only represent itself (more than a trend in the humanities), as there is an elaborate treatment of Easter Laughter in Prütting's unique and nearly 2,000-page 'phenomenological study on the nature, forms, and functions of laughter', as is the subtitle to his *Homo ridens* from 2013. If Prütting stands alone, there is something symptomatic and representative about Werner Röcke's (1944–2022) 2002 article on Easter Laughter, both in the sense that it is included in an anthology of papers from a seminar on related topics, and that his subtitle indicates the renewal of Bakhtin's legacy, i.e. attacking old literary and theatrical subjects from the perspective of a specific methodological focus on the body: 'Body language and ritual comedy in stagings of "risus paschalis".

In the group of cultural articles and books there are 27 titles that can be said to be relatively evenly distributed both chronologically (12 before 1990, 15 after) and in terms of the amount of space Easter Laughter is allowed to occupy in the contributions (7 a, 7 b, and 13 c).[188] There is a striking difference compared to the group of theological and pastoral titles, which show a significant increase on both counts: 12 publications before 1990 compared to 36 after, while the substantial treatments are very few in relation to those that 'name-drop' Easter Laughter: 6 a, 8 b, and 35 c.[189]

9. Easter Laughter in the Scholarly Literature since 1990

A conclusion to this bird's eye view of the bibliography could be that it can be observed that the engagement with Easter Laughter survived its burial at the turn of the previous century, and that it is especially in the sphere of church and

---

188 In addition to Röcke and Prütting we can add the following to the A-group: Gugitz 1949, Wolf 1962, H.-G. Schmitz 1972, O'Connell 2002, and Wolff 2009. The B-group consists of Fehrle 1930, Stumpfl 1936, Lohmeier 1972, Haug 1982 (= 1989), Schindler 1984 (= 1992), Le Goff 2008, and Schörle 2007. As for the C-group, there is no need to list such titles where Easter Laughter only appears in passing; but to emphasise that this naturally does not imply anything at all about the other qualities of these titles, a couple of books of the highest scholarly quality can be mentioned, where the author has simply chosen to mention the phenomenon of Easter Laughter without using it for anything else: Coxon 2008 and Halliwell 2008.

For the sake of completeness, it should be added that out of the five we have identified as constituting the actual research on Easter Laughter, at least four belong to this category, while it can be debated whether Jacobelli should be placed in the group that is primarily concerned with theological and ecclesiastical questions.

189 A-group: Thiede 1986, Kuschel 1994, Vinçon 1997, Paul Werner's (fl. 1979–2005) two overlapping articles from 2001 and 2005, and Ferm 2008. B-group: Heinz-Mohr 1957, Haebler 1957–8, Thielicke 1974, Wehrli 1982, Screech 1997, Suter 2005, Grün 2009, and Richert 2009. Nor again here would it make much sense to list the swarm of C-titles except to note that out of the 35, only 7 were published before 1990. It may be of interest to mention that the later Pope Benedict XVI (1927–2022), in his previous career as a cardinal, thought it relevant to speak favourably about Easter Laughter – but he was, let us remind ourselves, born, raised, and, before moving to the Vatican, served as archbishop in Bavaria. Ratzinger 1986, 119 f.

theology, which otherwise in previous centuries had shown a tolerant, strained, or hostile relationship with (Easter) laughter, that interest has intensified. Regardless of the validity of the assumption made above regarding the extent of Bakhtin's and Eco's influence (although *The Name of the Rose* does appear in many of the works), there seem to be two additional factors, particularly in recent decades, that have contributed to Easter Laughter capturing the attention and imagination of pastors and academics. Judging by the frequency of their names being cited, it has apparently had a significant impact that two respected theological professors, not only a Catholic but also a Lutheran (admittedly from Bavaria), wrote monographs on laughter only a few years apart, in which Easter Laughter fitted naturally into the context: Kuschel's *Laughter: A Theological Reflection* (the subtitle of the German original was even more suggestive: 'The Art of God and Humans', both 1994) and Werner Thiede's (b. 1955) 'The Promised Laughter. Humour from a Theological Perspective' (1986).

The same criterion of Easter Laughter being mentioned in the same breath as a person's name can also be used to pinpoint the second factor, and in passing it is very much worth noticing that the name is no longer necessarily that of Oecolampadius, for by now the term itself apparently does not require any actual (historical) grounding or elaboration, but can merely be used in a concise (new) way for the concept to come alive and circulate in journal articles and be picked up in popular culture. This is something that the even better-known theologian, Jürgen Moltmann (1926–2024), has clearly managed to achieve. Admittedly, Moltmann mentions *risus paschalis* as far back as 1971 in his essay 'The First Freed of Creation',[190] but by formulating the following sentence to end his eschatology – or rather, the American version of eschatology – 'The laughter of the universe is God's delight. It is the universal Easter Laughter in heaven and on earth', Moltmann has created an expression that elevates laughter from Bavarian village churches to heaven. In doing so, he struck a chord that has been allowed to resonate in both articles and, according to Google hits on www, in countless American sermons.[191]

---

190 Referring to Flögel for documentation, Moltmann even surprisingly designates the time of the Lutheran orthodoxy as the pinnacle of its practice, 1971, 36 and note 26 on page 78.

191 The German edition also included laughter, but not specified as Easter Laughter. The very last lines of the book in the original state that: 'Wird Schöpfung verklärt und verherrlicht, wie gezeigt, dann ist Schöpfung weder eine nur freie Setzung seines Willens, noch ein Resultat seiner Selbstverwirklichung, sondern sie ist wie ein grosser Gesang oder ein reiches Gedicht oder ein wunderbarer Tanz seiner

Finally, while it would have been only fitting for the 500th anniversary of Oecolampadius' book to have been an occasion for renewed interest, it was more likely the almost concurrent Reformation jubilee that has given Easter Laughter yet another boost in connection with the heightened attention to laughter and humour in our culture in general. Needless to say, it is nothing new for the sciences to turn their gaze towards previously overlooked or deliberately ignored dimensions of texts and individuals, in this case, for example, Luther's humour. The Swedish archbishop Nathan Söderblom (1866–1931) already did so back in 1919.[192] However, it seems that in the decade leading up to 2017, intense work was done to rebrand the Germanic image in general and the Lutheran/Protestant image in particular, images which otherwise tend to suggest that 'they' are only good at one thing, not only the proverbial *Ordnung muss sein*, but a humourless order at that – an impression that the internet is more than willing to buttress when simply googling 'Luther' in combination with 'laughter', 'humour', 'joke', and similar terms. As a finishing touch to making this point let us end by directing attention to Fritz Schmidt-Clausing's (1902–84) book from 1968 about another of the great protestant reformers, *Zwingli's Humor*. When it was reissued in an English translation in 2007 some smart marketing people added a telling subtitle: *The Lighter Side of the Protestant Reformation*. This edition leaves us with an eerie feeling of having come full circle when the newly written preface offers the bizarre piece of information that Capito, being convinced that otherwise the preacher would be speaking to empty churches, had been a defender of Easter Laughter.[193]

Phantasie, um seine göttliche Fülle mitzuteilen. Das Lachen des Universum ist Gottes Entzücken.' Moltmann 1995, 367. The American edition from the following year has a close translation into English but amends the final laughter: 'If creation is transfigured and glorified, as we have shown, then creation is not just the free decision of God's will; nor is it an outcome of his self-realisation. It is like a great song or a splendid poem or a wonderful dance of his fantasy, for the communication of his divine plenitude. The laughter of the universe is God's delight. It is the universal Easter Laughter in heaven and on earth.' 1996, 338 f.

192 In major articles on 'Luther's humour' and 'The meaning of humour for Luther' that are included as chapters in Söderblom's collection of Lutheran studies *Humor och melankoli*; cf. much later Gritsch 1983, Thiede 2010, and most recently Dober 2017b.

193 It is the author of the foreword, Matthias Freudenberg (b. 1962), who must take full responsibility for this interpretation, Schmidt-Clausing 2007, iv.

Chapter III: Arguments For and Against Easter Laughter

It may be true that nothing is exempt from the passage of time, not even systematic theology. However, as in logic and philosophy, the ambition is to make arguments timeless, independent of the whims of a particular era. Faced with phenomena from the past, we are well advised to recall what was already mentioned in the introduction, namely, that we should be cautious about issuing anachronistic condemnations or, for that matter, embracing them with untimely sympathy. When reading documents from past centuries, we can admittedly get a sense of an unbridgeable gap between then and now, both in life in general and specifically in church life. But before making this 'gap' even wider than it may initially appear, we should also remind ourselves firstly that the gap is often smaller and certainly shorter in time; secondly, that often we only gain knowledge about these different phenomena thanks to the criticism from colleagues or prohibitions from authorities of the time. So even back then there were apparently some who shared the attitudes of later generations, whether in approval or rejection.

As has become evident, there is by no means a consensus on how Easter Laughter was practised. There may have been significant differences over time (as seen in the disagreement about the theory of decay by Fluck and Jacobelli, note 53) or within the same period from region to region, so that Easter Laughter in a specific case would appear as strange (and perhaps even offensive) to a modern reader as prohibitions on ball games or keeping livestock in churches.[194] Most likely, however, the vast majority of examples of Easter Laughter would not

---

194 The Danish edition of this book contained a chapter about the possible spread of Easter Laughter as far north as Denmark. Although the chapter concluded that it had not, the research uncovered some curious coincidental details. One of these was a so-called open letter by King Christian IV (1577–1648) published in 1638 in which he condemns the appearance in church of the very book recommended by Luther (cf. note 150) as a remedy against melancholy, *Till Eulenspiegel*, alongside erotic songs, poems, fables, and indecent books about love, 'Åbent brev [...], 1 Oktober 1638, Glykstad', in: Secher 1897, vol. 4, no. 644, 735 f. Why 'appearance'? Because the king was not concerned about the preachers' use of literature, he just did not want it sold any longer in churches. In other words, book trade in churches by various approved printers was accepted, but after 1638 the books had to be of a certain quality.

However, it was not only high culture that was allowed on the premises. In a royal decree dated 29 May 1744 churches in Iceland were reminded that they were

cause a stir today considering how as individuals, congregations, and cultures we engage with laughter on a daily basis both within and outside the walls of the church. Yet even this last point can be misleading if and when it happens that laughter has changed its character, not only transitioning from being predominantly antipathetic to more sympathetic, but also shifting its location in the body over the centuries from the stomach and genitalia to the heart and eventually to the head (more on this later, IV,2,iii).

The historical arguments for and against Easter Laughter can in any case contribute to a more nuanced picture of the past. However, since Easter Laughter is no longer just a historical curiosity but, according to the numerous google-hits, a revived practice, and since this fact must undoubtedly be seen in light of the Western (?) world's relationship to entertainment and laughter in general, it may even in a contemporary and more liberal context also be worth the effort to provide a systematic overview of the various forms of arguments. They range from the very pragmatic to practical theology, biblical theology, and dogmatics – and a contemporary identification and relevance cuts across these categories.

1. Pragmatic Arguments

To begin with one of those pragmatic arguments that might initially seem to bridge the epochs, as such reasoning is frequently seen in the printed and electronic media when debating the legitimacy of this pastor's or that church's latest initiative to promote church attendance: it is actually striking how rarely, if at

---

allowed to store goods in the church (in 'closed lofts'), as long as they 'do not emit a bad smell or in any other way are indecent for the same place: but no extraneous trade may be conducted in the church, as anyone who does so shall pay one ounce of silver for each occurrence'. On 8 March 1757 churches in Norway were reminded that while beverages could be sold and strong drinks could be given to the sick inside the churches, spirits could no longer be sold. Such regulations undoubtedly relate to the fact that tithes were often paid in kind, which were then resold – and, we gather, often directly from the churches. Fogtmann, Hurtigkarl & Kollerup-Rosenvinge 1838–40, vol. 3, 378 f.

It was not only the Danish kings who had to keep an eye on the widely dispersed churches of the kingdom, as something similar applied throughout the rest of Europe, where authorities at times felt compelled to intervene against the practice of bringing hounds and hunting falcons to church – or attempting to exploit the right of asylum by housing livestock in the church to evade the bailiff. For these and many other examples see Davies 1968, 34, 74 f., 139, and 186.

all, we come across the concept of attracting those people to church who would otherwise not have come (although Capito actually mentions it, see |2|). As we have seen in the sources dating back to Chrysostom quite the opposite argument is frequently put forward, namely that pagan or 'merely' secular entertainment (circus, theatre, popular literature, etc.) keeps people from attending worship; but neither Oecolampadius' interlocutors nor later advocates of Easter Laughter recommend it for its appeal.[195] Indirectly, this supports the description of Easter Laughter's characteristics in that it does not in that sense pander to an external taste or demand.

All the more frequent is the second pragmatic argument about keeping the congregation awake, and judging from the sources, not in a figurative sense, but quite literally (cf. the epigram from Luther's *Table Talks*). Oecolampadius has also been confronted with this argument but responds tongue-in-cheek that if St Paul was not afraid to preach Eutychus to sleep (Acts 20:9) then preachers nowadays should not be bothered by it either (see |39|). However, this point is made so many times by Protestant critics that Moser-Rath cannot resist playfully counterattacking with another historical piece of information: 'In Protestant houses of worship, "church-sleep" [*Kirchenschlaf*] had apparently become so prevalent that a verger had to be appointed to wake up the sleepers. This did not exactly speak to the effectiveness of the sermons.'[196]

To this kind of sneak attack, a Protestant would have to respond by pointing out, however pedestrian it may sound, that it is only reasonable to assume that some of the congregations have followed the Orthodox tradition and prepared

---

195 Some four hundred years later American churches were hardly aware of this old German Easter tradition, but by then they had developed an interest in the very human aspects of the life of Jesus as well as the amusing aspects of Bible stories and would like to announce all of this to their potential flocks. Bednarz has dug up newspapers from the early years of the 20th century where churches ran ads in the local press promising sermons and lectures on these topics. Like Oecolampadius and Capito before them not everybody approved of this, and Bednarz gives the following summary of one columnist who let off steam in the Virginian *Lexington Gazette*: 'In one 1905 newspaper, there appeared a short piece, "Church Advertising – Sensational Topics Announced to Attract a Crowd", in which an anonymous writer strongly objected to the use of titles such as "Seeking Grass for Mules and Finding Elijah" or "The Humor of Jesus". Such titles, the author argues, are merely gimmicks for attracting churchgoers. In effect, the author equates humor or anything "entertaining" in the Bible with sensationalism, and argues that it is not fit for any solemn service to God.' Bednarz 2015, 61, note 2.
196 Moser-Rath 1964, 5.

for the resurrection with a vigil or devotion at dawn, and therefore it was to be expected that a few of the parishioners might have been a bit bleary-eyed come 10 o'clock. Having made that retort, it must be acknowledged that a general 'issue' became more acute in the Protestant part of the church. For even though there is hopefully no longer anyone who makes the mistake of polemically claiming that ordinary people had to suffer the torment of listening to sermons in Latin in the late Middle Ages,[197] there is little doubt that preaching took up more time among the Reformed and Lutheran communities. If nothing else, this is evidenced by the ever-increasing spread of new church furnishings by way of benches and chairs. A few centuries later, in Copenhagen in 1737 (and repeated in 1739 for Zealand and 1740 for the market towns), it became necessary, under royal threat of fines, to enjoin the pastors not to preach for more than an hour, so that there would also be room for a maximum of half an hour of catechism. Likewise, when organists are instructed not to play such long preludes that the part of the service leading up to the sermon lasts over an hour, we can recognise a distinct Protestant need for a verger to be on the lookout for anyone slumping in the pews.[198] However, we must insist that this challenge for preachers is greater than the confessional differences, as medieval homileticians intensely discuss the permissibility of using examples (of which *Ostermärlein* is just a special case), and if and when it is accepted, these pre-Reformation handbooks also recommend the

---

197 The fact that the majority of published sermons were in Latin is not a reflection of what was preached during the service; Latin ensured a wider dissemination among a reading public across Europe than if printed in the vernacular. Truth be told the problem was rather the reverse, namely that in the great majority of churches no sermons were heard at all because priests – certainly in villages but also in most towns and cities – as well as even many bishops were so poorly educated that it was all for the best that they devoted their time to liturgy and left out preaching. Leading up to 1500 a reform movement arose particularly in the southern parts of Germany for the establishment of so-called *Prädikaturen* or *Predigtpfründen*, that is, positions where the ones appointed should concentrate on preaching and teaching their colleagues in theology. This initiative came about in order to elevate preaching to its former status, when bishops like Chrysostom *et alii* had been renowned as much as preachers as for their theological writings. As it happened, Oecolampadius' first employment was his appointment to a brand new *Predigtpfründe* in his home town of Weinsberg in 1510. Staehelin 1967, 65.

198 Fogtmann, Hurtigkarl & Kolderup-Rosenvinge 1838–40, vol. 1, 107 (re organists) and 135–7.

use of examples because of their ability to keep the listeners from getting bored or falling asleep.[199]

2. Pedagogical Arguments

The deliberations of homileticians regarding the resourcefulness of good examples lead us to the next level of arguments, those focusing on pedagogy. Examples not only capture attention and keep people awake through their entertainment value, but even for an attentive and concentrated congregation they serve a communicative purpose better than so many other rhetorical tools: they can illustrate the points that a preacher wants to make. Once again this may sound strange to a modern ear, for is it not completely uncontroversial and certainly common to preachers regardless of their denominational affiliation to make use of illustrations? Yet, the examples presented in the context of Easter Laughter reveal a difference, at least in principle, even if we can discuss how these principles were handled in practice.

It is Röcke who puts us on the trail by combining a medieval cliché with a keen observation.[200] It goes without saying that speakers communicate not only with words and intonation but also through facial expressions and gestures. The rhetoricians of antiquity knew this, and the scholastic homileticians approved it with only one reservation: these non-verbal techniques should not be exaggerated. Röcke then reflects on the striking difference between Easter Laughter and the medieval manuscripts for dramatic performances inside and outside the church, particularly the Easter plays. Regarding the dramas, it is noteworthy that the dialogue often implies strong violent action, although the texts do not provide us with any explicit mention of gestures (such as stage directions), nor have any descriptions of outraged reactions to the violence from audiences after performances survived. In the case of Easter Laughter, the situation is quite the opposite. While the texts (judging from the *Schwank*-literature, etc.) may appear crude, they are otherwise too harmless to actually cause scandal. However, Capito and Oecolampadius particularly emphasise the preachers' gestural escapades, noting that it is precisely this bodily performance that makes them resemble the actors (*histriones*) whom the church has had a long tradition of condemning (see |2| and |27|). When Easter Laughter preachers unabashedly use loud speech, animal sounds, obscene gestures, and bodily mimicry, they make

---

199 Cf. Riising 1969, 115 f.
200 Röcke 2002, 344–5.

themselves more of a mockery than the laughter they seek to evoke. They place themselves in the company of, for example, market jesters, who, like haughty dandies and makeup-loving women, are criticised for cultivating the body at the expense of the heart or mind. Or the Word! Scholars, across denominations, and ecclesiastical authorities expressed their displeasure at any suspicion of the separation of the body from the spirit. However, with yet another clarification, Röcke opens up to the further perspective that needs to be pursued here: 'Undoubtedly, among Protestant theologians, the aversion to the bodily arts of the *risus paschalis* increases. This is to be expected, given the emphasis on word-based theology in Protestantism and the rejection of any form of visualisation or even embodiment of the gospel.'[201]

As suggested, it can be difficult in practice to explain the strongly divergent views on Easter Laughter solely or primarily by referring to a Catholic or Protestant background, without resorting to caricature or exaggerating the confessional differences. However, in a certain sense, the particular resistance to Easter Laughter highlighted by Röcke aligns with a general Protestant scepticism towards liturgy, albeit perhaps more pronounced in a Reformed context than in a Lutheran one. The theatre historian Jonas Barish (1922–98) has provided a superb historical overview in *The Antitheatrical Prejudice* of a couple of millennia of discomfort with and resistance towards the world of theatre. A recurring theme in the book is the notion that sees acting as deceit and pretence, and as the antithesis of authenticity and artlessness, which is an interpretation often made by lawmakers, philosophers, and even people from the theatre itself (modernists), as well as the great thinkers of the church from Quintus Septimius Florens Tertullian (160–220) and Augustine and onwards. Barish adds to this a keen analysis of how this anti-theatrical impulse in a religious context can manifest itself as an anti-liturgical scepticism, and why this is particularly the case among Protestants.[202] In a crucial passage for our use, Barish ties all these elements together:

> In this connection it is pertinent that many of the fiercer foes of the stage were also anti-liturgical, showing little interest in sacramentalism. What concerns them are actions, not enactments, even in worship itself – hence no doubt the developing stress on preaching. Those who espouse an ecclesiology of action tend to be deeply suspicious of mimesis.[203]

---

201 *Ibid.*, 346.
202 Cf. note 526.
203 Barish 1981, 76.

Seen from this perspective, at least some of the fierce criticism of Easter Laughter stems from a discomfort with the fact that the examples' alleged illustration of the proclaimed joy of the Easter gospel is physically externalised by way of a performance (primarily the preacher's gestures, but also the loud reaction from the congregation). If we should attempt to illustrate Barish's concise, yet seemingly sophisticated, distinction between 'action' and 'enactment/mimesis', and how this manifests itself in the conviction that the Word's proclamation is viewed as an *act* as opposed to the sacrament's risk of turning into a ritualised *performance*, we can compare Luther's two rituals for baptism from 1523 and three years later.[204] As is well known, the first ritual closely resembles the Catholic baptismal ritual that Luther grew up with, while the one from 1526 was significantly shorter. There are indeed adjustments and abbreviations in the wording of the prayers. However, in this context, it is primarily noticeable that Luther achieves his abbreviation by retaining the *words* (or perhaps more accurately: word-actions) but (apart from the sign of the cross, laying on of hands, and immersion in water) by removing a whole series of small mimetic elements, where the priest *does* what he *says*: blowing under the child's eyes, placing salt in the child's mouth, touching the child's ears and nose with saliva (*Effata*), anointing with oil between the shoulder blades, putting on a cap, and handing over the baptismal candle.

To the extent that this analysis is apt, it is a significant twist in the reception history that at least by the time of the Baroque period when Lutheran criticism of Easter Laughter was at its strongest, the very nature of the custom had shifted from being a kind of *enactment* to more of an *action*, indeed a pure word-action. Thus, Wendland wonders why Pauli chose to use the by then equally new technical term *osterspil* to describe the use of *Ostermährlein*, and he imagines that this can be interpreted as evidence that people were no longer aware of continuing a living tradition of storytelling, but rather that they were *replacing* the dramatically liturgical elements that had been pushed out of the church.[205] This interpretation would in a way harmonise well with Capito's and Oecolampadius' descriptions of preachers who were not only fond of storytelling but also of acting, hence of being theatrical. However, the custom had been transformed by the time we reach the 17th century, where *Ostermährlein* had been morally 'functionalised' to provide educational, terrifying, and edifying examples. As Röcke expresses it: in Strobl's time, these stories had clearly lost their dependence on the preacher's bodily performance and could freely be published as reading material

---

204 *Taufbüchlein* 1523 (1523b, 42–6) and *Taufbüchlein* 1526 (1526, 537–41).
205 Wendland 1980, 180.

sanctioned by the bishop. By now the aim of *Ostermährlein* both in the pulpit and in the parlour is more to cheer up people than to provoke their laughter. The change that we have here tried to capture with the help of Barish's distinction between 'action' and 'enactment' is referred to by Röcke as the narrativisation of Easter Laughter, and for him the result is that:

> [...] the original functional context of the 'Easter play' and 'Easter Laughter' [has] fundamentally changed. It is no longer the fascination with the body and its staging that takes centre stage, but rather the patient attention to the teachings of the example; not the grotesque comedy of deformation, violence, and sexual desire, but rather the didactic comedy that arises from moral insight based on the mistakes of others; not the joy of gestures, body language, and dramatic acting, but the willing insight into the rational order of the world.[206]

In passing, it can be added that when Easter Laughter is sporadically revived in later centuries, it is mostly done by reverting to the *performative* version – at least if it is to be mentioned in the newspaper, as in the case from 1802 with the priest who hanged himself in his *pallium* (cf. note 61).

Among other arguments predominantly motivated by their educational potential, there are some that border on the consideration that laughter acts as a kind of mnemonic amplifier. What we have laughed at together with others is better remembered. A variant of this can connect Easter Laughter with a communication strategy known from both the prophets of the Old Testament and the masters of Roman rhetoric, namely that when we need to convey truths to a superior power, the indirect form of communication – either by speaking in parables or speaking the truth with laughter (*ridendo dicere verum*[207]) – can be not only the healthiest (for the prophet's well-being) but also the most direct way to reach the recipient. This is not to insinuate that Nathan made David burst into laughter when he had to tell the king that he himself was the culprit (2 Sam 12:7), nor that the Easter Laughter preachers had congregations of royalty; but rather that all speakers in a sense always find themselves facing a superior power in the form of a resistance to understanding which they must try to overcome through language and other means of communication. This applies, even when it concerns a joyful (yet still incomprehensible) gospel, but certainly even more so if the medicine needs a little sugar to be consumed. Thus, Wendland offers a refreshingly alternative *raison d'être* for the preachers' documented great

---

206 Röcke 2002, 348–9.
207 Cf. note 550.

fondness for Aesop, specifically, and animal fables in general.[208] According to this perspective, it is not only about the possibilities of supplementing the fables with laughable animal sounds or movements. Nor is it merely about proclaiming the resurrection in a subtle or endearing way. More importantly, it was about being able to deliver a call to repentance to the many in the church who undoubtedly had transgressed the strict rules of the preceding period of fasting, by projecting the lust, gluttony, and greed of the congregation onto extravagant animals … but then leaving people with laughter stuck in their throats when finishing with Nathan's line: 'You are that "animal"!'.

3. Tradition as an Argument

The argument that is probably most frequently put forward in defence of Easter Laughter is, in a systematic theological context, more or less 'beyond category', as it sidesteps the need for further justification by referring to the antiquity of the custom (see introduction and chapter I). However, when viewed from the perspective of denominational differences, this can be seen as an example of the disputes about the value of invoking tradition versus questioning tradition by going back to the sources themselves. Without making further comparisons, Protestants were able to reject this particular custom based on the same principle used to sort through many other inherited customs and dogmas, including the number of sacraments on the premise: is there any biblical evidence for this?

It is plausible to imagine that it was precisely this issue that inspired another argument which, if it had not appeared so many times, would otherwise have been very tempting due to its artifice to attribute to a single village priest's unsuccesful attempt to find a basis in Scripture for his practice. The scriptural evidence is, so to speak, found in two versions: one based on an extremely literal reading of the text and a more literary one. The preacher's amusing stories, *fables*, are simply to be understood as a continuation of the disciples' own practice, for does it not say in the last chapter of the Gospel of Luke (24:15) that as two of them were walking towards Emmaus 'entertaining' each other, they were suddenly accompanied by the Lord himself? Only if we take the text literally. For in the *Vulgate* translation of the Greek word ὁμιλέω, the word *fabulo* (/*fabulari*) is chosen, which has both the more neutral meaning of 'conversing' and at the same time carries connotations of 'chatting', 'making up stories', and, indeed, 'entertaining'.

---

208   Wendland 1980, 167.

Judging from the distance of many years, it seems baffling how much effort was made to exploit the layers of meaning in a verb that in Luke's context appears to be of little relevance to draw upon. However, if nothing else, it probably shows that even back then some people sensed the dubiousness of this enterprise, as others apparently resorted to using a concordance to find more suitable examples of the Bible's use of the word-stem. For example, in 1667 the Bavarian preacher Geminianus Monacensis (1606–72) published a 'Guide to Heaven', which according to the title page has the ambitious quadruple purpose of providing 'help for preachers', 'encouragement for laypeople', 'instruction for the misguided', and 'comfort for all devout Christians'. To that end Geminianus allowed himself to spice up his collection of sermons with 'tales' (*Mährlein*), but hastens to add in his preface certainly not in order to arouse laughter or make jokes, but because for many years parables and 'tales' have been used in preaching. Indeed, he continues, this has been done when it comes both to chastising and to teaching the divine mysteries; he then reveals with a specific reference what he understands by 'many years', namely the prophet Baruch, who 'two thousand years ago' called such teachers *fabulatores*.[209] No matter how sympathetic we may find Geminianus' cause, we must once again question the biblical fig leaf. Baruch does indeed mention *fabulatores* (rendered as 'tellers of fables' in *KJV*); but from the context it is clear that even though 'fable tellers' are equated with 'those who seek wisdom', they are completely and utterly astray (Baruch 3:20–3).

Equally little help is to be found in the word's other nominal form, *fabula* ('story'), for when the *Vulgate* uses it in both an Old Testament and a New Testament context, it always has a strongly negative connotation. For example, in the previously cited passage from First Timothy, it is linked with *aniles* ('older women') and thus has its meaning transformed into 'gossip' (4:7; cf. 2 Tim 4:4 and 2 Pet 1:16). Instead of trying to hide behind occurrences of 'fable'-related words in the Book of Books, we might have done as Geminianus' English contemporary did, the poet John Bunyan (1628–88), who looked the difficulty of St Paul's paraenesis straight in the eye – yet found a literary loophole: 'Sound words, I know, Timothy is to use, / And old wives' fables he is to refuse; / But yet grave Paul him nowhere did forbid / The use of parables; in which lay hid / That gold, those pearls, and precious stones that were / Worth digging for, and that with greatest care.'[210] And on the title page of *The Pilgrim's Progress*, Bunyan has placed a far more fitting fig leaf from Hosea 12:10: 'I have used Similitudes'.

---

209   Geminianus 1667, scan image 18; cf. Moser-Rath 1964, 21.
210   Bunyan 1678, A5b (= scan image 5). Cf. Wolf 1962, 76.

We may seem to be moving away from the subject of laughter; however, not only in the late Baroque period but also in Oecolampadius' time, the most significant source of laughter in church was the stories told from the pulpit, so the disagreements about the legitimacy of Easter Laughter led via homiletics directly into the dispute about the proper way to interpret the Bible (see below note 510 on *sensus literalis* and *-spiritualis*). Thus we gain a little more understanding of the otherwise self-destructive attempts to find a biblical justification for preaching with the help of fables insofar as preachers were met with a critique from the ecclesiastical authorities which basically was grounded in a Platonic-idealist view that considered all made-up stories as lies and fiction as evil. Against this background it suddenly makes good sense to follow Bunyan and rely on the fact that Jesus himself used parables as one of his most important pedagogical and rhetorical tools. In passing, it is worth noting a kind of epochal difference in the way Jesus' parables are referred to. While countless modern authors can easily imagine the crowds bursting into understanding laughter when Jesus told them a parable, there seems to be none of the preachers of the Baroque period who can discern more than the faintest smile on the lips of the listeners in Galilee and Jerusalem. In our context the reference to the use of parables in the gospels is only intended as a validation of the use of 'figurative speech'. Additionally, as Wolfgang Rauscher (1641–1709) points out in a sermon for the second day of Easter, it is not only the pagan Aesop who employs the particular form of parable where the animal and plant kingdom have a voice, but the Bible itself contains a pure example of this in the fable of the trees choosing a king in the Book of Judges (9:8–15).[211]

4. Anthropological Arguments

If exegesis of the Book was not the most promising method for finding arguments in the tradition, we could instead turn to life itself and make more or less commonsensical anthropological and psychological deliberations. This line of defence of Easter Laughter was already known in the earliest sources but can also be found in a much later variant. In Oecolampadius' conversations, first with one opponent and the next day with a group of people who had participated in Easter Laughter services, this kind of reflection is touched upon with the statement

---

211 Cf. Moser-Rath 1964, 22–4, where she quotes a long passage from Rauscher's programmatic defence of the use of fables and *Mährlein* published in a collection of his sermons from 1690, which he chose to give an indeed fabulous title: 'Oil and Wine from the Good Samaritan for the Sinner's Wounds […]'.

that the purpose of the preachers, rather than explaining the resurrection, was simply to 'cheer up the audience if they were not amused and merry'. However, the underlying logic is not unfolded (cf. |16–17|). Mathesius, on the other hand, conveys it when he opens his sermon by explaining why there was a need to be encouraged at all: it was because people 'had been so afflicted by their penitence during Lent and had suffered along with the Lord Christ during Holy Week'.[212]

In a sense this argument contains a double regard for both soul and body. The immersion into the horrors of Christ's suffering during Holy Week required a spiritual counterbalance, and after the long, grey period of Lent leading up to Holy Week, a little relaxed amusement was permissible, which was also, as we saw above, an opportunity for preachers to admonish those members of the congregation who had not suffered overly much from the physical deprivation of fasting, using the animal fable as a means to get that particular message across. The type of laughter that arises from negative physical and psychological experiences, will later be described as stemming from a release of excess pressure, popularly referred to as the relief theory, whether in a sociological/political sense, as in the case of Bakhtin, or psychological, as in the case of Sigmund Freud (1856–1939). Without such concepts yet being available, the reasoning can be perceived as a pastoral acceptance of the physical and psychological conditions inherent to human beings, conditions that, if the Jesuit Franz Borgia Götzenberger (1709–53) is to be believed, also applied at the time of Jesus. In any case, Götzenberger opens a self-proclaimed *Mährlein*-sermon with what must undoubtedly be the most far-reaching backdating of contemporary customs (not to mention the structure of the liturgical year!), as he imagines that exactly the same needs lie behind the two disciples' storytelling on the road to Emmaus.

> It is not unlikely that among other reasons which led the two disciples to go to the small town of Emmaus there may also have been the following: namely that they needed to recover and ease their minds from the many sorrowful things that have befallen their dearest master Jesus Christ in his most sacred suffering and death in Jerusalem: these sorrowful things have also affected all the disciples and filled their hearts with sadness, distress, and bitterness.[213]

---

212   Mathesius 1566, 77r; 2018, 286.
213   Although laughter is not explicitly mentioned, Götzenberger himself in a breathtakingly long sentence establishes a connection to the context in which Easter Laughter later thrived: 'This sought-after relief of the mind among these disciples has surely also given rise, many years ago, to the practice of many preachers seeking to encourage their listeners during Easter after the long period of sadness they

During Götzenberger's time, which is to say the Enlightenment period, a related but independent defence emerged interpreting Easter Laughter historically as a typical expression of the more immediate and simplistic faith of the Middle Ages. This kind of interpretation anticipates the Romantic era's fascination with folk authenticity (as seen in the Grimm brothers and other collectors of folklore). If 'simplicity' at first hand suggests something childlike or innocent, we should not forget that it encompasses not only a blunt approach to eroticism and sexuality but also to religious subjects. So perhaps we could more accurately speak of the Middle Ages' coarse or sturdy spirituality. As an illustration of this, Bebel tells a joke about the inner Trinitarian conversation, where the Son is tricked by the other two into taking on the task of incarnation, as the Father hides behind his old age, while the Holy Spirit's excuse is that it would look ridiculous with a dove nailed to the cross.[214] Bowen is probably not entirely wrong in her assessment that this kind of fun 'may be too robust for modern tastes'.[215]

In more or less convoluted ways, the Romantic Movement's appreciation of those folkloric layers, which had previously been socially marginalised and academically ignored, became intertwined with nationalist interests and the attention from historians of religion. Specifically, aspects of phenomena such as Easter Laughter, which in the preceding centuries had been regarded as 'heathen, crude, or bizarre and therefore immoral customs',[216] were, during the 19th century – whether idealised or not – considered authentic. This 'authentic' quality referred to the perception that they could be seen as a kind of archaeological evidence of layers beneath (and before) Christian influences. Such interpretations partly leaned towards searching for something originally Germanic, as evidenced around the turn of the previous century and up until the 1930s (cf. note 155), when attempts were made to trace the origins of Easter Laughter in Norse and Germanic mythology (e.g. the laughter between Skadi and Loki, cf. below p. 156) and customs (for example as celebrations for the alleged spring goddess Ostara).[217] Furthermore, this reassessment of folkloric roots also paved the way

---

have felt in their hearts during the forty-day-long fast and especially during the sorrowful Easter week, where they have contemplated the suffering of Christ. Thus, it seems that the custom gradually emerged to present a pleasant and at the same time useful fable or Easter tale from the pulpits as a means to encourage their hearts.' Götzenberger 1752, 3–4.

214 Bebel 2005, 81 (= no. 97 in vol. 1).
215 Bowen 1988, 44, note 6.
216 Wendland 1980, 103 ff.
217 Cf. H. Holland 1862, 610; Fehrle 1930; Stumpfl 1936, and Gugitz 1949, 180–6. For a brief description of the possible, albeit quite speculative, connections between

for the cross-cultural and cross-epochal studies of the history of religions, where Easter Laughter could now be connected with various ancient or 'overseas' narratives and rituals related to the transformative power of laughter (see previous references to Reinach and further below, IV,6,i).

5. Joy as an Argument

Upon closer examination it must be concluded that all the arguments mentioned so far are entirely general and in principle could have been discussed in any homiletic context. They would only be specific to Easter Laughter if Easter were the only time in the church year when the congregation was sleepy. The use or non-use of *exempla* was precisely a general point of contention, and is it likely that there was only one day a year when some of the more colourful storytelling could evoke smiles and laughter? If there had not been other considerations that came into play, out of all the Sundays and festive seasons throughout the church year we could, instead of believing that Easter Sunday and its occasional laughter was a totally unique and solitary phenomenon, nominate it as a kind of *primus inter pares* (with Christmas as an obvious contender); but as such, it also became a scapegoat for the general dissatisfaction from the authorities and theological opponents with all the customs and rhetorical devices that deviated from a fixed order.

i. The Easter Hymn

A genuinely theological argument for linking laughter and Easter Sunday so that Easter Laughter's 'setting in life' (*Sitz im Leben*) is not a mere coincidence or has more to do with a sensitivity to the seasonal forces of nature than the narrative of the church year, is, oddly enough, touched upon by Oecolampadius himself. In his account of his heated dispute with one of the supporters of the tradition, he hints at the argument by posing the question to his adversary whether laughter can be an appropriate expression of Easter joy (see |15|). There is a clear liturgical basis for asking this question, as the prescribed Old Testament reading (or rather, gradual psalm) for Easter Sunday is taken from the Book of Psalms and contains the line: 'This is the day that the LORD has made; let us rejoice and be glad in it' (118:24 *ESV*). For Oecolampadius the question is merely polemical,

---

various Indo-European words for 'Easter' and an ancient Indian word 'Usra' that designates the dawn of day (*Morgenröte*) and a further possible connection to the name of the Roman goddess Aurora, see Zelger 1993, 128–9.

but actually he touches upon a topic that points us both forward yet also very much backward in the history of theology.

As previously mentioned, Oecolampadius began his academic career as an assistant to Erasmus in Basel while working on the publication of his critical edition of the New Testament in 1516. As also mentioned earlier, Erasmus recalled a personal experience of Easter Laughter from his childhood in his textbook on homiletics (*Ecclesiastes: sive de ratione concionandi*, 1535). It is tempting to conjecture that Oecolampadius and Erasmus themselves had some 'table talks' exchanging experiences and opinions, as Erasmus also addresses the relationship between Easter Laughter and joy. Unlike Oecolampadius' implied rejection, Erasmus leaves no doubt when he passes judgment: 'This is hardly the sort of joy to which the Easter Psalm invited' (*Nequaquam ad hoc lætitiæ genus inuitauit psalmus paschalis*).[218]

Nonetheless, this opens up a field of genuine theological relevance, and there is reason to hope that a scholar will one day undertake the task contained in Tobias A. Kemper's (b. 1973) observation that a systematic study of medieval sermons on Psalm 118:24 might provide a key to unravelling the mystery of the origin of Easter Laughter.[219] Although it goes without saying that there is no simple or direct relationship between joy and laughter, they *can* still influence and affect each other. Joy can express itself through laughter, and laughter can bring about joy, but neither is necessarily the case. This is true both psychologically and phenomenologically, and at the time of Oecolampadius and Erasmus theologians had had a tradition of more than a thousand years of contemplating these interrelationships.[220] Joy can certainly be associated with laughter, and the Easter joy of the Psalm of David may hold the key to Easter Laughter, but this

---

218   Erasmus 1535, 126; 2015b, vol. 68, 508.
219   Kemper 2005, 31.
220   To mention just one example of an early thinker, who was not in doubt about the close relationship, witness his 'ode to joy' which took the most positive of views: 'Laughter is the outward and bodily sign of the unseen joy in the mind, and joy is in fact the best and noblest of the higher emotions. By it the soul is filled through and through with cheerfulness, rejoicing in the Father and Maker of all.' These words were actually written by a contemporary of Jesus and St Paul, and it is intriguing to speculate what would have happened to the history of laughter and the Church if his thoughts had been taken as a starting-point for the later discussions. Theoretically, at least, it could have been a possibility, for although he was a Jewish philosopher living in Egypt it was mainly Christian Church Fathers who studied and treasured Philo of Alexandria's (*c.* 10 BCE- *c.* 45 CE) books. His remarks about laughter appear in the treatise on 'Rewards and Punishments', where he interprets Abraham, Isaac, and

was far from obvious to everyone, and while there was a wide range of attitudes, there was an overwhelming majority in favour of a particular viewpoint. The extremes, as well as a kind of middle position, can be briefly outlined here. The Church Fathers of the Early Church had, with very few exceptions, all distanced themselves from laughter (and for some, not only in the church but also in everyday life[221]) because first and last it was perceived as a humiliating case of the body's power over the soul.[222] A cautionary example of this is Ephrem the Syrian's (*c*. 306–73) particularly drastic admonition to those who would follow him into the hermit's life devoted to God: 'The beginning of the destruction (καταστροφῆς) of the monk's soul is laughter and loose talk (παρρησία).'[223] This indirectly points to two crucial factors.

Firstly, monasticism became the most important carrier of culture regarding the Christian understanding of laughter in late antiquity and the Middle Ages. Strict rules for containment and preferably eradication of laughter run as a common thread through all the major collections of rules for the monastic life, from

---

      Jacob allegorically to represent the religious virtues worth rewarding. He is very aware of the interplay between laughter and Isaac's name, and that Isaac's particular reward is joy. 1960, 330–1. To prove that these thoughts were not expressed on the spur of the moment we only have to look to another of Philo's books where the same kind of meditation on the interconnection between joy, laughter, and the blessed forefather finds an, if possible, even grander expression: 'For God is the Creator of laughter that is good, and of joy, so that we must hold Isaac to be not a product of created beings, but a work of the uncreated One. For if "Isaac" means "laughter", and according to Sarah's unerring witness God is the maker of laughter, God may with perfect truth be said to be Isaac's father.' *Quod det.* 123; 1994, 284–5.

221 The oldest testimonies are indeed known from collections of rules for monastic life and from sermons condemning laughter in the church; however, Suchomski argues that the long, persistent, and extensive cultural struggle against *mimi*, *histriones*, *scurrae*, and *joculatores* indicates a desire to make this attitude towards laughter binding for all believers. Suchomski 1975, 26.

222 It would be wise, however, to heed the warning of Indira Ghose (b. 1962) when she reminds us of how easily we fall prey to imposing an anachronistic separation of soul and body into the discussions in the Middle Ages and especially in the Renaissance about the forces that laughter unleashes. Strictly speaking, it would be more appropriate to speak of different forces within the soul, such as reason and appetite, which struggle for dominance with the help of the will. Ghose 2008, 68–70. Perhaps the distinction is captured most clearly by Helmuth Plessner's (1892–1985) aphorism that 'when we laugh, we do not *have* a body, but we *are* our body', cited from Ferm 2008, 23.

223 Heffening 1927, 107 and 1936, 62; cf. Steidle 1938a, 277.

Pachomius (*c.* 290–345) to Bernard of Clairvaux and their far-reaching historical impact.[224] Regarding the role as a 'carrier of culture', it can of course be argued that, as with all other 'legislation', there is a dynamic relationship between laws and transgressions. The claim is not that laughter was never heard in the monasteries, for if strict prohibitions against laughter had to be repeated for a thousand years, it is evidence in itself of recurring violations of those very same rules. However, these violations do not alter the implicit anthropology of the rules, that it was part of the ideal image of a true monk or nun to be able to control laughter. Likewise, we can certainly question the general impact of the monastic rules on society at large, but again, it must be emphasised both that the injunctions of the monastic rules resonated in the sermons of the preachers, and, even though a greater degree of resignation could be expected regarding the adherence of parishioners to the priests' exhortations, it does not alter the ideal that even the layperson could and should strive for the same self-control as the recluse.[225]

Secondly, the quote from Ephrem signifies that in the thousand-year long discussion among theologians, it became very much a triangular drama with joy split between laughter and dignity. The story of Christian theologians favouring dignity at the expense of laughter has often been told and has itself almost become a caricature in *modern* litanies about how past church figures do not share the very different views of today on these issues. Without disputing the accuracy of these portrayals in any way, the focus here should instead be on the small cracks in the historical wall of resistance which, regardless of an actual impact or not, can be said to constitute the condition of possibility, at least dogmatically, for a phenomenon like Easter Laughter.

As far as the undeniable and overwhelming opposition is concerned, we shall for now limit ourselves to acknowledging that on the one hand there is a very strong and representative common thread that can be traced from Ephrem to

---

224 Recently, Prütting has provided a superior overview of the entire period, 2013, 390–470.
225 Albeit an extreme case, in a letter from 385 Jerome (347–420) defended the young woman Blaesilla's way of showing her recent conversion to Christianity by not only giving up make-up, jewellery, and her former fine clothes but also topping it all with the severest scheme of fasting. Indeed, a change of life so radical that she, and he as her mentor, were publicly criticised for it, to which Jerome replied that this kind of ridicule was only to be expected, for 'we are called sour and severe if we keep sober and refrain from excessive laughter' – or to follow his Latin even closer: because 'we do not laugh with an open mouth' (*quia ebrii non sumus, nec cachinno ora dissolvimus, continentes vocamur et tristes*). 1845c, col. 465; 1893b, 47–8 (general description of her asceticism), 49 (laughter).

Hugh of St Victor (*c.* 1096–1141), who has an equally terse assessment of joy and laughter: 'It should be noted that joy is only criticised, while laughter is completely condemned because laughter is evil in every way. Joy is not always evil, [the exception being] when it is joy over something evil.'[226]

On the other hand, it may be worth remembering – without needing to serve as an apology – that Christianity was far from alone in harbouring suspicion of the impact of laughter on human dignity. In fact the Early Church and its theologians were not particularly original at all, but simply adopted and continued some basic attitudes from both the Greek and Roman ancient world, as known especially from the Pythagoreans and Stoic circles. Even the alleged testimony that Jesus never laughed, which we might initially consider as an almost inhuman characteristic, was far from unique but rather a common characterisation of great personalities, if not a standard, then certainly not a rarity. This applied, for example, to Plato (*c.* 427–348 BCE), about whom his student Heraclides Ponticus (*c.* 390-*c.* 10 BCE) could state that he had never seen him laugh uncontrollably, not even as a child.[227] Similarly, it was not a Christian invention when the first colonies of hermits emerged in the early 4th century and sought to regulate laughter. According to the historian Claudius Aelian (*c.* 175-*c.* 235), it was actually forbidden for students at Plato's Academy to laugh.[228] Another example, closer to Pachomius and his desert companions, is the Jewish sect in Qumran, which also had strict methods for dealing with laughter. In 'The Manual of Discipline' (7,14), it is stated: 'If a man indulges in raucous, inane laughter, he

---

226 To make sense of the statement the final sentence has been slightly amended: *Notandum quod gaudium tantum arguitur, risus vero omnino reporbatur, quia risus omnimodo malus est; gaudium non semper malum est, nisis quando de malo est*, Hugh of St Victor 1984, col. 163B.

227 'Heraclides declares that in his youth he [Plato] was so modest and orderly that he was never seen to laugh outright.' Laertius 1925, vol. 1, 301 (= book 3, section 26). According to Aelian, this also applied to Aristotle's student Aristoxenus (360–300 BCE), though he was yet to be surpassed by Anaxagoras (*c.* 500–428 BCE) about whom it was said that he never laughed nor even smiled. Aelian 1665, book 8, ch. 13.

228 '[…] for they endeavoured to preserve that place free from contumely and levity', *ibid.*, book 3, ch. 35. However, rumour has it that the prohibition only applied while teaching and not during break time in the colonnade. Rumours are good, but Stephen Halliwell (b. 1953) cautions against fully relying on them, as he suspects that Aelian is not merely picking up an oral tradition but rather initiating it himself by making a 'fictive "extrapolation" from Rep. 3.388e'. Halliwell 2008, 277.

In the relevant passage in the third book of Plato's *Republic* (3.388e-9a), a lengthy conversation takes place between Socrates and Adeimantus about the objectionable

shall be mulcted for thirty days.'²²⁹ Regarding the more general philosophical scepticism as well as the ascetic and disciplinary struggle against laughter, it can be concluded that while Christianity did not originate these ideas and attitudes, it was the Christian adaptation of them that was passed down through Western culture. This allowed figures like George Vasey (1822–93) to adopt the pedagogical programme nearly two thousand years later, stating: 'It is very questionable that children would ever begin to laugh if they were not stimulated or prompted, but were let alone, and treated naturally and rationally.'²³⁰

Intermezzo: The Concept of Dignity in Child-Rearing

If the ideals of ancient Greek philosophers or hermits in the desert may seem completely foreign to a modern self-understanding, and perhaps even far removed from daily life in Oecolampadius' neighbourhood, it may help make the ancient notions of human dignity somewhat more recognisable by taking a quick look at their impact on child-rearing. Such a brief excursion is also fitting because, while working on the aforementioned textbook on the art of preaching, Erasmus took the time as well to write a small guide on how to teach children to behave with dignity, indeed to be civil: *De Civilitas Morum Puerilium* (1530). It was republished many times and spread throughout Europe. The following year it was published in a German translation with a somewhat more elaborate title: 'Chaste manners of graceful conduct and polite gestures of youth: in every

---

    nature of Homer depicting the gods being subject to emotions, including laughter, and how it can have a harmful effect on young people to read about it. It is there that the remark about not being a 'friend of laughter' is made: ' "Again, they [the young] must not be prone to laughter (φιλογέλωτάς). For ordinarily when one abandons himself to violent laughter his condition provokes a violent reaction". "I think so", he said. "Then if someone represents men of worth as overpowered by laughter we must not accept it, much less if gods do". Plato 1937, 211 f.

229 Gaster 1964, 62. Irven Michael Resnick (b. 1952) has compiled a lengthy list from Christian monastic rules where violations of the prohibition on laughter are also addressed with various punishments. Two of the more striking examples are Isidore of Seville's (550–636) provision of excommunication (though limited to three days), 1850, col. 885. The other example is taken from the anonymous 'The Rule of the Holy Fathers Serapion, Macarius, Pasnutius, and the other Macarius' (*Regula SS. Patrum Serapionis, Macharii, Pasnutii et alterius Macharii*) where the brothers are spared exclusion from the community but instead are to be chastised with the 'whip of humility' (*flagello humilitatis*) for two weeks (Migne: *SL*, vol. 103, col. 943). Resnick 1987, 94–6.

230 Vasey 1877, 30.

way and according to the order of the whole body; for the young to practice in it; for the old to educate their children in such a manner' (later in a bilingual edition with an updated translation divided into sections provided with headings and the reformulated title: 'Gallant Politeness, through which especially the flourishing youth can behave in such a way in the political eyes of the present world that they become popular and pleasing everywhere', 1695).

The later edition includes a chapter titled '*De Gestibus Corporis* / On Body Gestures', which covers a wide range of good advice on posture and personal hygiene, such as on how best to remove mucus from the nose and a truly fascinating biblical typology: if the child puffs up its cheeks, it appears arrogant, like Thraso (a boastful soldier in Terence's [*c.* 190–60 BCE] plays, somewhat comparable to a figure like Shakespeare's Falstaff). Conversely, if the child sucks in its cheeks, it gives the impression of despair, like 'Judas the Betrayer'.[231] Naturally, we also find a detailed passage on laughter, which opens with a direct paraphrase of Aristotle's reflections on *eutrapelía* (cf. note 504), just as Erasmus does not mind borrowing the comparison with the neighing of horses from one of the Greek Church Fathers (cf. note 261):

> [Is it permissible to laugh at someone as well?] To laugh at every word or deed is the sign of a fool; to laugh at none the sign of a blockhead. It is quite wrong to laugh at improper words or actions.
>
> [Which laughter is not fine?] Loud laughter and the immoderate mirth that shakes the whole body and is for that reason called συγκρούσιον 'discord' by the Greeks, are unbecoming to any age but much more so to youth. The neighing sound that some people make when they laugh is also unseemly. And the person who opens his mouth wide in a rictus, with wrinkled cheeks and exposed teeth, is also impolite. This is a canine habit and is called a sardonic smile.
>
> [Is it not allowed to have a cheerful face?] The face should express mirth in such a way that it neither distorts the appearance of the mouth nor evinces a dissolute mind.
>
> [But what if excessive joy leads to laughter?] Only fools use expressions like: 'I am dying with laughter'. If something so funny should occur that it produces uncontrolled laughter of this sort, the face should be covered with a napkin or with the hand. To laugh when alone or for no obvious reason is put down to either stupidity or insanity. If, however, something of that sort happens, it is good manners to explain the reason for your laughter to others, or if you do not believe that a true reason should be offered, fabricate something lest someone suspect that he is being laughed at.[232]

---

231   Erasmus 1695, 23; 1985, vol. 25, 274 f. (mucus) and 275, where, however, Thraso is exchanged with Cain!

232   1695, 25/27; 1985, vol. 25, 275 f. The English translation is from 1985, but the square brackets and the division of the text into paragraphs are inserted from 1695.

But what on earth did Erasmus, the perpetually traveling bachelor, know about children? As this passage about laughter attests, he derived his 'experience' with children from literature rather than from the households of various host families. Throughout the pamphlet he draws on examples from ancient art and science, and several details about laughter are, as already suggested, directly taken from the Church Fathers and monastic rules – but then again that is quite in harmony with his famous belief in 'the philosophy of Christ' which was not so much acquired by revelation as by study of the Bible and other 'good books that make good men'. As the quote shows, he does prove himself a true humanist by adding the very practical and considerate advice about sparing other people from thinking that they are being laughed at behind their backs.

In contrast, the fourth Earl of Chesterfield, Philip Dormer Stanhope (1694–1773), cannot be accused of having learned his lesson through reading, for his famous letters (often published with the subtitle 'on the Fine Art of Becoming a Man of the World and a Gentleman') were, after all, not written to just anybody but to his own son. (We can of course question whether 400 letters testify to a high degree of physical presence and involvement in the child's daily life.) As his son approached his 16th birthday, around the same age as we can imagine many of the students at Plato's Academy, the Earl apparently deemed it was time to instruct him in the fine, yet challenging, art of laughter:

> Having mentioned laughing, I must particularly warn you against it: and I could heartily wish that you may often be seen to smile, but never heard to laugh, while you live. Frequent and loud laughter is the characteristic of folly and ill manners: it is the manner in which the mobs express their silly joy at silly things; and they call it being merry. In my mind, there is nothing so illiberal, and so ill bred, as audible laughter. True wit, or sense, never yet made anybody laugh; they are above it: they please the mind, and give a cheerfulness to the countenance. But it is low buffoonery, or silly accidents, that always excite laughter; and that is what people of sense and breeding should show themselves above. A man's going to sit down, in the supposition that he has a chair behind him, and falling down upon his breech for want of one, sets a whole company a laughing, when all the wit in the world would not do it; a plain proof, in my mind, how low and unbecoming a thing laughter is: not to mention the disagreeable noise that it makes, and the shocking distortion of the face that it occasions. Laughter is easily restrained by a very little reflection; but as it is generally connected with the idea of gaiety, people do not enough attend to its absurdity. I am neither of a melancholy nor a cynical disposition; and am as willing and as apt to be pleased as anybody; but I am sure that since I have had the full use of my reason, nobody has ever heard me laugh.[233]

---

233 Letter no. 144, 9 March 1748; Chesterfield 1927, vol. 1, 212–13. For a contextual article on Chesterfield and the tradition he is part of, see Heltzel 1928.

As becomes clear in the end, laughter has nothing to do with mood – or for that matter, joy. Control over laughter is solely a matter of willpower aided by reason, and once we have reached that stage, we can say about ourselves what the Church Fathers claimed about Jesus: 'I was never seen laughing!' If not earlier, from here on the empire's ideal and surest characteristic of a gentleman had been formulated: the ability to maintain a stiff upper lip, not only in a crisis but certainly also in lighthearted moments.

To conclude this digression on dignity as a barrier to laughter as an expression of joy, in a Danish context we cannot ignore the female response to Erasmus and Stanhope. If the two gentlemen did not quite succeed in bridging the gap between our times and antiquity, we can proudly observe that Emma Gad (1852–1921)[234], in her book 'Etiquette: About Dealing with People' (*Takt og tone: Om omgang med mennesker*), proves herself to be almost a modern successor to Aristotle and his emphasis on *eutrapelia* as a virtue, and at least she comes much closer to a contemporary sensibility. Admittedly, Gad only touches upon laughter twice, and upon first impression she may seem in line with her predecessors when she clearly warns against 'loud speech and laughter'. However, in both cases, the context conveys a different second impression, for her advice about quiet behaviour actually concerns visits to sanatoriums, where people come with 'a broken nervous system or an even more serious illness' to find peace, or when one is in a train compartment, possibly being seated next to 'lonely and subdued fellow travellers'. As for child-rearing, Gad does not explicitly mention restrictions on their laughter; instead, she elevates herself to a paean about a very special gift of grace:

> Teach your growing children the art of understanding and perceiving fun in the same spirit and form in which it is presented. Not everyone can by their own effort possess humour and wit – it is a gift of nature. However, anyone can receive a jest with kindness and certainly respond to it with good humour.
>
> Remember that the most deadly and boring person of all is the Apostle of Seriousness, who becomes offended as soon as someone jokes with him and considers any playful expression or lighthearted remark as a grinning mockery, simply because he has not in time learned to wield such light weapons and therefore stands powerless against the unexpected thrusts of wit's rapier.

---

234   Gad may well have been a female pioneer for writing drama in the latter part of the 19th century in Copenhagen, but by far she is remembered for her book on etiquette written shortly before her death. Already at the time of its publication it was probably quaintly old-fashioned, and certainly for a later generation in the 1960s and onwards her name and book were considered a somewhat ridiculous relict – yet continuously used as a stepping stone when one was obliged to give a speech on formal occasions

> Let a bright tone prevail in your home – a housewife is in charge of that – and your children will, without even knowing how it happens, come to possess the gift of humour.²³⁵

It cannot be completely dismissed that Stanhope could have endorsed these lines, as Gad does not explicitly say anything about whether the jest can and should evoke laughter; in her polemic against the Apostle of Seriousness, she does distinguish between joking and grinning which possibly reflects a slight difference in decibels. However, as a minimum, she delivers a beautiful plea for 'the Danish smile' as a complement to the stiff upper lip.

ii. Laughter of the Heart

When Erasmus declares it permissible for the face to show 'a cheerful countenance' (*vultus hilaritatem / Fröhlichkeit*), and when Stanhope allows for a 'cheerfulness to the countenance', they lead us back to the question of possible nuances in the condemnation of laughter in the Early and Medieval Church. Here, joy serves as a battering ram! Even though the history of effects in all likelihood became consolidated and aligned with the main concern of Church Fathers, abbots, and canon law, it was also oversimplified in relation to the sources, if, that is, they are to be taken at their word. We can in principle doubt the sincerity of more nuanced formulations when holding them up against other practices, such as the fierce and sometimes even brutal suppression of people from the 'entertainment industry',²³⁶ but, as already suggested by Curtius, we could also hypothesise that behind the incessantly repeated condemnations of 'excessive laughter' there may have been a tacit acceptance of a moderate one.²³⁷

The name of Chrysostom has become almost synonymous with an uncompromising condemnation of laughter, and he has even been ascribed a statement as concise as it is likely apocryphal: 'if there is laughter in the church, it is the work of the Devil' (*si risus in ecclesia diaboli opus est*).²³⁸ Nevertheless, caution should be exercised when even in his writings we can find statements

---

      like weddings etc. Fortunately feminist scholars have rescued her reputation in this new millennium not least by allowing her to be read with exactly that degree of humour which she extends to others in the quote below.
235 Gad 1918, 176 (asylums), 194 (train compartments), and 82 f. (humour).
236 Cf. note 221.
237 Curtius 1939, 6.
238 I have not been able to locate such a statement myself, even with the help of electronic search tools; nor have I found passages that could reasonably be 'combined' in such a way as to make the statement authentic. This is not to say that Chrysostom would not have agreed with the content of the sentence, as can be seen, for example,

about laughter that are quite different from those about Jesus' lack of it. One of these passages is all the more remarkable because here it is not just a matter of a modern reader detecting between the lines a possibly implied acceptance of non-loud laughter. For Chrysostom explicitly states that laughter is not evil (*non malum est risus*), and he further expands on this declaration with considerations about several legitimate occasions for laughter, such as when reuniting with a long-lost friend or lifting oneself or another person when feeling down.[239] So if we bracket Chrysostom's possibly simplistic posthumous reputation and historical impact and instead take his words at face value, we essentially find the same relatively clear stance as previously demonstrated in Luther's case: they both draw a sharp distinction between laughter inside and outside the church, in the former case primarily during worship (and thus an objection to Easter Laughter). On the other hand both recognise the spiritual and pastoral potential of laughter and both tolerate and even encourage laughter, at least certain forms of it, in civil life. One difference may be that judging from Luther's table talks it is difficult to imagine that there were only subdued bursts of laughter at the tables in Wittenberg.

However, in the long run and with an effect lasting at least a thousand years until Stanhope, the Gordian knot of laughter's relationship to joy was cut by making it silent ... and, to a large extent, also 'faceless' (recalling the lip and its stiffness). The foundation for this solution was already provided by Chrysostom's slightly older contemporary, Basil of Caesarea, who in the extended version of his monastic rules ('Question 17') actually presents a loophole for joy and thus

---

    in his 6th Homily on Matthew, where he speaks of the world not being a 'theatre of laughter' (*hoc quippe theatrum non risum admittit*) and concludes: 'It is not God who gives us [cause] to play, but the Devil' (*Non enim Deus id dat ut ludamus, sed diabolus*), 1862b, col. 70.

    One of those who quotes (but without a source reference) Chrysostom's statement is the Englishman William Perkins (1558–1602), who in a treatise from 1595 shows that though he has clearly read Chrysostom nevertheless allows himself – even as one of the Puritans known for being the strictest upholders of the moral heritage of the Church Fathers – to moderate the attitude based on an argument from creation theology: 'As for laughter, it may be used: otherwise God would never have given that power and faculty to man: but the use of it must be both moderate and seldom, as sorrow for our sins is to be plentiful and often. This we may learn from Christ's example, of whom we read that he wept three times at the destruction of Jerusalem, at the raising of Lazarus, and in his agony: but we never read that he laughed. And especially remember the saying of Chrysostom, *Si risus in Ecclesia diaboli opus est*, that is, to move laughter in the church is the work of the devil.' Perkins 2013, 61.

239 Cf. the quote from Chrysostom's '15th Homily on Hebrews' in note 586.

an alternative to the reviled 'immoderate laughter': '[a quiet] smile is appropriate to indicate the joy of the mind/spirit' (*subridendo tantummodo laetitiam mentis oporteat indicari*).[240]

When Basil did not pursue the matter further beyond his brief interjection, it was instead another 'Great' who came to set the precedent, Gregory (*c.* 540–604). It is somewhat droll to note that the very pope who is associated with giving *sound* to the church, i.e. the harmony of chanting, also almost *ex cathedra* found a formula that preserved laughter as a genuine expression of joy while at the same time silencing it and thus undeniably diminishing some of its vitality. Gregory the Great upheld his predecessor's distinction between a noisy sinful laughter and the spiritual smile, yet did not content himself with merely repeating it. If something is to be remembered and disseminated, it is never a bad idea to connect dogma with a metaphor, a vivid image, and that is precisely what Gregory added to Basil's distinction when he dared to transform the latter's 'smile' (*subridendo*) into a genuine 'laughter' (*risus*), but then added a specific localisation: it was a 'laughter of the heart' (*risus cordis*).[241] If this could be misinterpreted as just a neat paraphrase of the occasional special source for the mouth's audible laughter, thus distinguishing between the coarse laughter of the lustful lower body, the cynical laughter of the mind, or the chuckling laughter of the heart, Gregory used an image to stop such a misunderstanding in its track: the laughter of the heart comes from the 'mouth of the mind' (*ore mentis*), that is, the kind of

---

240 Here quoted from the new critical version of the Latin text established in the 2013 edition (page 96); in Migne, the wording is slightly more reserved: 'Indeed, it is not improper to reveal a gentle and cheerful relaxation of the soul with a smile' (*Risu quidem leni et hilari effusionem animi detegere indecorum non est*), 1857, col. 962.

241 As a testimony to the long-term effect of Gregory's solution it is interesting to note that Oecolampadius had evidently grasped its potential for solving the challenge of preaching about joy without any need whatsoever for the joy to be accompanied by laughter. In a sermon for Easter morning (undated, but Staehelin guesses it was held in 1518 or possibly in one of the two previous years, 1927/34, vol. 1, 63) Oecolampadius preaches glowingly about joy while condemning those who seek to arouse laughter in church. As one of his chief witnesses he refers to Gregory for having described the true joy as invisible and silent, that it is 'ineffable' because it is in the mind and cannot be verbalised: *Divus autem Gregorius iubilum vocat, quoniam ineffabile gaudium mente concipitur, quod nec abscondi potest nec sermonibus aperiri*. Nevertheless, there is an acceptable manner in which to reveal this inner joy: through song, which Oecolampadius supports with a reference to Psalm 89:16. He then coins a unique phrase to catch the true kind of joy inside a church (and perhaps a Christian?): 'Let it be true that gaiety is presented with the sauce of gravity' (*Verum sit illa hilaritas condimento gravitatis exhibita*). 1927b, 60–1.

visible, spiritual image known from later emblem art, where internal organs are depicted with external body parts.[242]

The elegance of Gregory's treatment of the matter lies in the fact that he at the same time paved the way for a solution to a major problem in the study of laughter, for what are we to do with the undeniable fact that the Bible's negative statements about laughter are by far the most frequent? Whereas in an oral culture we might get away with only highlighting sharply truncated biblical references, it more easily becomes embarrassing when it can be plainly seen in black and white how often theologians and preachers supported their interpretations with 'half-quoted' verses. As a modern reader, we may be astounded by the countless times texts refer to Ecclesiastes' 'A time to weep' without bothering to mention the end of the very same verse: 'a time to laugh' (3:4); or even more frequently, the supposedly definitive Scriptural proof in the form of Jesus' lamentation: 'Woe to you who laugh now, for you shall mourn and weep' (Lk 6:25), without feeling obliged to also mention the beatitude that precedes it: 'Blessed are you who weep now, for you shall laugh' (Lk 6:21). Does this not border on manipulating quotes in the service of a presumed good cause?[243]

---

[242] Considering how vivid and suggestive *risus cordis* appears as an expression, it is quite surprising that it seems impossible to find a renaissance or baroque artist who succumbed to the temptation of depicting this figure of speech. My own searches in books and on the internet have been in vain, and when even Erik Aksel Nielsen (b. 1941) and Carsten Bach-Nielsen (b. 1955) (arguably the two Danish scholars who know most about this peculiar art form) throw in the towel, it perhaps raises more questions about the prevalence of the expression than about the imagination of the artists who otherwise excelled in adorning body parts with various attributes in their emblems. However, Bach-Nielsen points to the title copperplate of bishop and poet Thomas Kingo's (1634–1703) *Aandelige Siunge-Koors Anden Part* (1681), where the struggle between damnation and salvation is illustrated by a body on the verge of being swallowed by the Devil's jaws at the bottom of the image, while a swarm of winged hearts ascends to the Trinity at the top. The hearts are undeniably smiling, and with a magnifying glass and a snippet of goodwill, some of them can even be seen laughing.

[243] Jacques Le Goff (1924–2014) confirms that early on a more or less fixed catalogue of Bible quotations was developed, even though several of the individual verses barely seem to touch on the subject, while others take a neutral or even positive stance towards smiles, laughter, and joy. However, when combined with the clearly negative condemnations, they must evidently have been influenced by them. The core of biblical references is already provided by Basil of Caesarea, referring to (those in italics have already been or will be mentioned later in the main text; all Bible quotations in this footnote are from *ESV*): *Gen 21:6*; *Job 8:21*; Prov 15:13 ('A glad heart makes a cheerful face, / but by sorrow of heart the spirit is crushed'); Eccles

It was perhaps less glaring to overlook the relatively few verses where the Bible unmistakably speaks positively about laughter without providing a negative counterpart in the immediate context. It was, however, precisely in his interpretation of one of these verses that Gregor, in his analysis of the Book of Job, went a step further and not only commented on the localisation of laughter in the body but also on its 'time'. 'He will yet fill your mouth with laughter and your lips with

---

2:2 ('I said of laughter, "It is mad", and of pleasure, "What use is it?"'); 7:6 ('for as the crackling of thorns under a pot, so is the laughter of fools; this also is vanity'), and *Lk 6:21.25*. While these biblical references are at least relevant, it looks quite different in Benedict's Rule where the entire criticism of laughter is based on three quotations of which only one is immediately relevant: Prov 10:19 ('When words are many, transgression is not lacking, / but whoever restrains his lips is prudent'); Ps 140:12 ('I know that the LORD will maintain the cause of the afflicted, / and will execute justice for the needy'), and Sir 21:20 ('A fool raises his voice in laughter, / but a wise man smiles quietly'). As a case in point, Sirach is usually quoted without the second half of the verse.

The most 'complete' medieval collection that Le Goff has found is from a chapter titled 'On Laughter and Crying' (*De risu et de fletu*) in the book *Liber scintillarum* (probably written around the year 700, at the earliest 636, at the latest 750) by Defensor of Ligugé (unknown except for one mention of himself in the book's preface). In this chapter, Defensor combines quotes from a handful of Church Fathers with a list of a dozen Bible verses: Mt 5:5 ('Blessed are the meek, for they shall inherit the earth'); *Lk 6:25*; 2 Cor 13:11 ('Finally, brothers, rejoice! Aim for restoration, comfort one another, agree with one another, live in peace; and the God of love and peace will be with you'); James 4:9 ('Be wretched and mourn and weep. Let your laughter be turned to mourning and your joy to gloom'); *Prov 15:13*; 15:30 ('The light of the eyes rejoices the heart, and good news refreshes the bones'); 17:22 ('A joyful heart is good medicine, but a crushed spirit dries up the bones'); 14:13 ('Even in laughter the heart may ache, and the end of joy may be grief'); 10:23 ('Doing wrong is like a joke to a fool, but wisdom is pleasure to a man of understanding'); 14:6 ('A scoffer seeks wisdom in vain, but knowledge is easy for a man of understanding'); 19:29 ('Condemnation is ready for scoffers, and beating for the backs of fools'), and Sir 21:26 ('The heart of fools is in their mouth, but the mouth of the wise is in their heart'). Le Goff 2008, 59–62.

Out of courtesy to Defensor, I have tacitly allowed myself to assume that Le Goff must have made a typo when, instead of Sir 21:26, he writes 21:23, which does seem a bit too difficult to make relevant in this context: 'The fool looks in through the door of the house, / but the person of understanding remains outside'. Le Goff uses the *Sources chrétiennes* edition; in Migne's edition the chapter is titled 'On Laughter and Sadness' (*De risu et tristitia*) and has number 54, where Defensor refers to Sir 21:20. Defensor 1862, col. 685–6.

shouts of joy', it says in Job 8:21. Instead of rushing ahead, Gregory pauses and gathers a small potpourri of more or less similar Bible verses. First and foremost, Jesus' promise to the disciples in his farewell speeches about 'the joy of the heart' (Jn 16:20.22), as well as King Solomon's characterisation of the 'noble woman' as one who 'laughs at the days to come' (Prov 31:25). Seemingly out of place since the verse does not mention laughter, he also includes verse 13 from the opening chapter of the Book of Sirach. However, the seemingly misplaced verse actually puts the interpretation in its right place: 'The one who fears the Lord will have a happy end; on the day of his death, he will be blessed', for Gregory postpones the bubbly laughter (*risu jubilant*) of the heart and mouth in harmony to heaven.[244]

It would undoubtedly be a gross simplification to give Gregory all the credit for this, but for the sake of pedagogical clarity we could suggest that the Pope had achieved a Pyrrhic victory, for what he gained in the short term, he lost in the long term, i.e. the truly long term. Time is a relative concept, as the 'short term' probably lasted 5–600 years, a period during which, at least in theory (meaning in the influential ecclesiastical discourse), laughter was successfully silenced within the domain of the Church. Nevertheless, Gregory's distinction marked

---

244 'For the "mouth" of the righteous will then be "filled with laughing" when the tears of their pilgrimage being done, their hearts shall be filled to the full with exulting in eternal joy. Concerning this laughing "Truth" saith to His disciples, Verily, verily, I say unto you, that ye shall weep and lament, but the world shall rejoice; and ye shall be sorrowful, but your sorrow shall be turned into joy (Jn 16:20). And again, But I will see you again, and your heart shall rejoice, and your joy no man taketh from you (ver. 23). Concerning this laughing of Holy Church, Solomon saith, And she shall laugh in the last day (Prov 31:25). Of this it is said again, Whoso feareth the Lord, it shall go well with him at the last (Sir 1:13). Not that there shall be laughter of the body, but laughter of the heart. For now from rioting in dissipation there springs a laughter of the body, but then from joy in security there will arise a laughter of the heart. Therefore when all the Elect are replenished with the delight of open vision, they spring forth into the joyousness of laughter in the mouth of the interior. But we call it shouting, when we conceive such joy in the heart, as we cannot give vent to by the force of words, and yet the triumph of the heart vents with the voice what it cannot give forth by speech. Now the mouth is rightly said to be filled with laughter, the lips with shouting, since in that eternal land, when the mind of the righteous is borne away in transport, the tongue is lifted up in the song of praise. And they, because they see so much as they are unable to express, shout in laughter, because without compassing it they resound all the love that they feel.' Gregory the Great: *Moralium* VIII,lii,88; 1862, col. 855–6; 1844, vol. 1, 489.

a crucial shift, one of the most important doctrinal prerequisites for the emergence of phenomena such as Easter Laughter, probably in the 14th century, as well as, after yet another half a millennium, for a growing appreciation of the compatibility of laughter with evangelical, earthly joy.

It may only seem like a flat joke giving the ultimate twist to the proverbial 'he who laughs last …', but from a theological perspective it can hardly be overestimated what Gregory has accomplished, for if laughter is to be heard in heaven, laughter cannot (solely) be part of the order of the Fall[245] but must also belong to the order of creation. In other words, not all laughter can have the Devil as its origin or be exclusively an expression of desire and blasphemy.[246]

---

245   To remind us of this more common viewpoint let one example suffice: 'For if Adam had neuer fallen, there should neuer haue beene laughter, nor weeping, but a heart possest with heauenly ioy, euen ioyfull sobriety.' This pithy statement is made by the puritan Thomas Granger (1578–1627) in his *A familiar exposition or commentarie on Ecclesiastes VVherein the worlds vanity, and the true felicitie are plainely deciphered* (1621, 50), quoted from Pfister 2006, 48.

246   When we advocate that we must go all the way up to modernity to have these potentials fully realised, this refers to the fundamentally changed attitude towards laughter among people in the church as well as in society in general. This does not mean, however, that we cannot encounter impressive and famous, albeit isolated, testimonies pointing in the same direction much earlier.

Some of the angel figures on the cathedral in Reims are unmistakably smiling, and their blissful and heavenly smiles were allowed to spread to other cathedrals of the 13th century (perhaps most notably the Prince's Portal in Bamberg where they most surely are laughing out loud), but it is still their relative rarity that warrants their fame, see for example Wilhelmy 2012b and Svanberg 1994. Without compromising the emphasis on 'isolated' and 'rarity', we can certainly acknowledge Kemper's point when he convincingly argues, with a series of specific quotations, that in the High and late Middle Ages a *nuanced* understanding of laughter thrived, and that in their ideas about heaven there were not only smiles to be seen but also laughter to be heard. Particularly striking among Kemper's quotes is his reference to the *un riso dell'universo*, which Dante lets his travellers hear near the goal, Kemper 2005, 26–9.

Mandelbaum, alas, contents himself with a smile in his translation: '"Unto the Father, Son, and Holy Ghost, / glory!" – all Paradise began, so that / the sweetness of the singing held me rapt. // What I saw seemed to me to be a smile [*riso*] / the universe had smiled; my rapture had / entered by way of hearing and of sight. // O joy! [*gioia*]. O gladness [*allegrezza*] words can never speak!' *The Divine Comedy*, 'Paradise', Song 27,1–7; 1980–4, vol. 3, 236.

iii. Scholasticism:

a. Silence – Humility

The use of subjunctives in the previous passage should be sufficient indication that Gregory represented just one, albeit an important, step along the way, and the parentheses could appropriately signal that the next equally important step is hidden in the ability, or rather the willingness, to discern and attribute value to the distinctions. An initial distinction has previously been touched upon, namely the very general one between theory and practice, that every rule, so to speak, presupposes (and entails?) a violation of the rule's content. For the sake of clarity it should be reiterated that when describing such a fleeting phenomenon as laughter, we are dealing primarily with what has been written *about* it, which for the most part means principled considerations of a philosophical or theological nature as well as various authorities' provisions. Indirectly, we may infer a practice from such sources, as the texts with their censures and codes are assumed to address how citizens and the church's own people have amused themselves. Furthermore, the existence of written material with humorous content, of which the previously mentioned *Ioca monachorum* and *Cena Cypriani* are the most famous, testifies to a secret or tolerated practice that the authorities chose to turn a blind eye to for one reason or another.

However, towards the High and late Middle Ages, a development takes place that challenges the simplistic official opposition to laughter; if not initially in the form of a significant theological reassessment of laughter, then at least as a practical theological reflection prompted by pastoral concerns. Therefore, it is not always necessary to label it as hypocrisy if and when we may detect a discrepancy between a dogmatic rejection of laughter co-existing alongside a more tolerant, therapeutically motivated *modus vivendi*. Such discrepancies were provoked by a sobering human discovery, for it turned out that monks and nuns were exposed to a far greater danger to their spiritual well-being than the threat of succumbing to the temptation to laugh. Actually the 'opposite' was worse: falling away from faith due to despondency and melancholy, the collective threat to recluses referred to in contemporary sources as *acedia* (melancholia) or *tristitia*. This is not the place to diagnose the causal relationship between monastic life and this ailment, instead we observe a growing recognition that laughter is not only something negative, or something solely to be tolerated due to its uncontrollable nature, but that it also has a positive value as mental therapy against despondency.[247]

---

[247] Cf. the chapter on 'Devilish sadness – divine fun' (*Teuflische Traurigkeit – göttlicher Scherz*) in H.-G. Schmitz 1972, 227–61.

However, it was not only therapeutic considerations that compelled theologians to make compromises. There were primarily three intellectual developments that made it unsatisfactory to continue condemning laughter categorically. Instead, the need arose to make qualitative distinctions between one sort of laughter and another. These were, firstly, the transition from silence to humility as a paradigm, secondly, the influence of Aristotle, and finally, the re-emergence of humoral pathology.

The magisterial medieval historian, Le Goff, has proposed a threefold division of the prevailing assessment of laughter: the first period extends from the earliest collections of monastic rules from late antiquity to the 10th century and is characterised by efforts to eliminate laughter through restrictions and threats. The next two periods both flourish under the auspices of scholasticism: in the 11th century, attempts were made to control laughter through definitions, that is, by distinguishing between different forms of acceptable or reprehensible laughter often based on a scale of good and evil. Finally, a third phase in the 12th century, where the will and desire to make distinctions developed into a downright casuistry of laughter with arguments for and against who, where, when, and how one may laugh. In order to illustrate the extent of such meticulous control, Le Goff offers an example from the court of Louis IX, the Holy (1220–74), where courtly laughter was esteemed except on Fridays, when it was not allowed to laugh.[248] The pious logic is, of course, that every Friday took on the character of Good Friday and required special abstinence, where not only such prohibitions arose but also injunctions, for example, to eat fish.

One of the intellectual breakthroughs that was a driving force in this development is hidden in Le Goff's analyses, as he observes a paradigm shift in the criteria by which laughter is measured.[249] In the oldest rules, laughter is perceived as a violation of silence which tends towards a pure either-or logic, where even a soft chuckle is as much a breach as a resounding burst of laughter. In later rules, exemplified by Benedict of Nursia, laughter is ranked on a scale of the virtue of humility. In principle, Benedict's Rule is just as strict in its opposition to laughter as the earlier rules, but by introducing a 'scale' where either-or mutates into more-or-less, the former tightly-closed door was left ajar.

---

248   Le Goff 2008, 38–40 and 20 (Louis).
249   Ibid., 24.

b. Aristotle and Aquinas

The second of the intellectual developments that allowed a later period to exploit this opening can be boiled down to the return of a single man, which was of invaluable importance not only for this particular subject but for the entire cultural history of the Western world. Aristotle's texts returned after several hundred years of European absence, preserved by Arabic and Roman scholars (though also in Greek manuscripts). By the time of Thomas Aquinas (1225–74), and thanks not least to him, Aristotle had attained a status akin to that of a fifth evangelist, whose thoughts, if at all possible, should be brought into harmony with the Bible.

In retrospect, or in the words of a Danish idiom: in the clear light of hindsight, it does seem deeply comical how a seemingly casual remark by Aristotle in his textbook on anatomy, 'On the Parts of Animals' (*De partibus animalium*), gained such a decisive significance for the ancient Roman commentators, then for the scholastics, and subsequently for virtually all thinkers who have pondered laughter. In the course of discussing various organs and body parts, Aristotle reaches the abdomen and notes that when one tickles humans there, they will, unlike animals, start to laugh ... due to the sensitivity of their skin! As if to preempt the question of why tickling, for example, an ape does not elicit laughter, Aristotle dryly adds that 'man is the only animal that laughs'.[250] The most peculiar thing is that Aristotle writes not a single word about the human's refined sense of humour or intelligent appreciation of comedy. Laughter is clearly assessed in this context as a purely physical, almost mechanical phenomenon.

Twice in the section on the abdomen, on facing pages in a modern edition of the text, Aristotle makes this laconic statement, and he does so without any further argumentation or illustration. Apart from these two occurrences, it is mentioned nowhere else in his many other works, and based on this thin foundation tradition has since developed the most significant expression ever formulated on this matter: *homo ridens*, 'the human is a laughing being'. The incongruity between its origin and its history of influence becomes even greater due to Aristotle's abrupt introduction of the statement and the fact that there is no further explanatory assistance to be found elsewhere in his works. This has left room for an endless discussion about the significance we should ultimately attribute to the definition, not to mention the basic uncertainty about whether Aristotle even intended the remark as a 'definition'. In this sense it is in

---

250 Aristotle: *Part.An.* III.10,673a; Ogle's translation in the 1912 edition is without page numbers.

the starkest contrast to Pliny the Younger's (60-c. 113) inclusion of laughter into a hall of fame of human characteristics and his self-conscious declaration that these are what make him who he is, perhaps as an individual but more importantly as simply being a human: *homo sum*.[251]

Nevertheless, already in late antiquity and the early Middle Ages, and thus before general access to Aristotle's own books, *homo ridens* was elevated by Roman philosophers and rhetoricians to a central anthropological dictum.[252] Although particularly over the past 150–200 years it has been considered as *the* characteristic of humans, as something essential to human nature (its *proprium*), several scholars, including none other than Halliwell in his majestic monograph on *Greek Laughter* (2008), argue that in a strict Aristotelian sense the connection between laughter and humans is accidental rather than a judgment about the defining nature of humans.[253] Additionally, there is the banal but often overlooked point that just because something may be a *proprium*, it does not inherently make that *proprium* morally good or socially desirable. Thus humans are arguably the only creatures that behave maliciously (for does it make much sense to describe predatory animals or a falling rock as evil?), but that does not make malevolence as a *proprium* of humans either good or desirable. Even if laughter is the *proprium* of humans, does it necessarily imply that every form of laughter is acceptable?

It ought to be a warning against overburdening the importance of *homo ridens* in Aristotle, that he would have had ample opportunity to bring this dictum into play if it had been as important to him as it became in the Western tradition. For as Halliwell also emphasises, there is no thinker in antiquity who treats laughter as comprehensively and in such an interdisciplinary way as Aristotle, as he

---

251   Pliny the Younger had neither the reputation of an Aristotle nor happened to formulate the captivatingly short expression of 'the laughing being', but in just a few lines he managed to put laughter into a context which it would take many hundreds of years for others to dare to emulate so self-confidently: 'I confess that I sometimes write verses of no very strait-laced kind; I furthermore listen to comedies, witness broad farces, read love-poetry, and enter into the spirit of the most wanton Muse. Besides all this, I not seldom indulge in mirth, wit and gaiety; and to sum up every kind of innocent amusement in one word, I am a man' (*aliquando praeterea rideo, iocor, ludo, utque omnia innoxiae remissionis genera breviter amplectar, Homo sum*). 1952, vol. 1, 366–7; cf. Figueroa-Dorrego & Lakin-Galiñanes 2009, 46–7.
252   Among others, Suchomski has traced it to Martianus Capella (fl. *c.* 410–20), Anicius Manlius Severinus Boëthius (*c.* 480–524/525), and Flavius Magnus Aurelius Cassiodor (*c.* 485-*c.* 585), 1975, 10 f.
253   Halliwell 2008, 1 and 315 f.

revisits it in his various books, not only, as in *De partibus animalium*, from a physiological and anthropological perspective, but also psychologically, ethically, sociologically, and in relation to comedy and drama theory.[254] Since the concept of *eutrapelia* has been touched upon repeatedly before, it should be noted that although laughter is not explicitly mentioned in that context (or rather, it is only mentioned in connection with someone who exaggerates mirth and stops at nothing to provoke laughter), Aristotle's considerations on eloquence in *The Nicomachean Ethics* are closely related to this. When Aristotle highlights the person who masters the cheerful *eutrapelía* as the art of balancing between presumptuous coarseness (βωμολοχία) and the dryness of the sluggard (ἀγροικία), he comes very close to elevating *eutrapelía* to a virtue, but nevertheless stops short of doing so.[255] Consequently, if we can assume that eloquence sometimes has laughter as its effect (whether of the same or of a different kind than what the *bōmólokhos* produces), then it follows indirectly that laughter itself, when serving as a social lubricant, becomes a desirable virtue.[256]

None of the scholastics were prepared to go that far. However, Aristotle has another important consideration, in which at least Aquinas dared to follow him almost all the way. In doing so, Aquinas consistently refers to Aristotle as 'The Philosopher', in the definite singular. Aristotle's view of laughter is conditioned by his overall view of play, namely play as a necessary good, a kind of medicine or therapy in relation to work. Aristotle's position is therefore not that play itself can be the goal of life, but it is a necessary supplement or even corrective to the exertion and stress of work.[257]

Such a view of laughter and play is adopted by Aquinas in his bold reassessment of the attitudes that had been dominant since Tertullian's broadside against multiple forms of entertainment in 'The Shows' (*De spectaculis*, c. 200).

---

254 *Ibid.*, 307 f.
255 Aristotle: *Eth.Nic.* IV.8,1127b34–1128b4; 1934, 243–9; cf. note 504, where another passage from *Eth.Nic.* is referenced, and *Eudemian Ethics*, where Aristotle stresses that wittiness, along with other kinds of 'middle states', are very praiseworthy without actually being virtues in themselves, *Eth.Eud.* III.7,1234a4–26; 1967, 353–5. For a convenient overview of all relevant passages in Aristotle (and other ancient writers), see Horst 1978.
256 For the Roman rhetoricians, like Marcus Tullius Cicero (106–43 BCE) and Marcus Fabius Quintilian (*c.* 35–*c.* 98), it was seen as a significant social virtue to be able to master, if not laughter itself, then certainly the art of wit, which naturally included a sense of timing, of place, and of individuals, cf. Suchomski 1975, 33–5.
257 To document this, Halliwell refers to 'Politics' (*Politika* V.3,1337b-38b; 1959, 637–47), 2008, 308–10. We could also add a significant passage from *Nicomachean*

Confronted with the diametrical disagreement between Aristotle and St Paul in their understanding of *eutrapelia*, Aquinas finds a way to argue for giving greater weight to The Philosopher than The Apostle.[258] In his defence of the recreational power and necessity of pleasure, Aquinas employs a particularly vivid image by referring to a bow: to maintain its elasticity, a bow must not be constantly kept taut, for then it becomes limp and ultimately useless.[259] In doing so, Aquinas not only follows in Aristotle's footsteps but also travels a well-trodden path among the pagan thinkers of antiquity. When considering the human need for relaxation and venting of feelings they tempered their critique with a sensible

---

Ethics: 'For amusement is a form of rest; but we need rest because we are not able to go on working without a break, and therefore it is not an end, since we take it as a means to further activity.' *Eth.Nic.* X.6,1176b6; 1934, 611.

Incidentally, it may be interesting to note that other interpreters apparently have used passages like these from Aristotle to argue for a hierarchy, and, quite remarkably, have used them as a supplementary argument to support the view that tragedies, for example, should be considered superior to comedies. However, Barry Sanders (b. 1938) points out that Aristotle does not value seriousness more than mirth, 'but in fact Aristotle implies that the former cannot exist without the latter. They complement each other. They function as two sides of one experience: the Good Life', after which he adds in a footnote: 'This misreading has had far-reaching implications. The classicist Paul Lejay [1861–1920] claims that out of this confusion arises the idea of the hierarchy of the genres, by which types of literature are ranked according to their degree of seriousness.' Sanders 1995, 104.

258 Aquinas addresses play (*ludus*), *eutrapelia*, and laughter in a focused manner in *Summa Theologica* II,ii,168,1–4; 1872, vol. 4, 407–12; 1920 online: newadvent.org/summa/3168.htm. He also discusses pleasure more generally, for example, in II,i,34; 1872, vol. 2, 259–63; 1920 online: newadvent.org/summa/2034.htm.

259 If we can trust John Cassian's (360–435) conversation with Abbot Abraham, this image and its use to defend the necessity and legitimacy of relaxation can be traced all the way back to John the Evangelist. This transpires from the 24th and final of Cassian's records of his conversations with the fathers in the Scetic Desert (*Collationes patrum*): 'It is said that the blessed John, while he was gently stroking a partridge with his hands suddenly saw a philosopher approaching him in the garb of a hunter, who was astonished that a man of so great fame and reputation should demean himself to such paltry and trivial amusements, and said: can you be that John, whose great and famous reputation attracted me also with the greatest desire for your acquaintance? Why then do you occupy yourself with such poor amusements? To whom the blessed John: what is it, said he, that you are carrying in your hand? The other replied: a bow. And why, said he, do you not always carry it everywhere bent? To whom the other replied: it would not do, for the force of its stiffness would be relaxed by its being continually bent, and it would be lessened

acceptance, if for no other reason than the cool realisation that the individual could return to everyday duties if better rested and encouraged.[260] As Aquinas also emphasises in the same breath, an acceptance is provided that the pleasure of play and laughter does not have indecent or harmful actions or words as its source. Furthermore, that we never surrender so completely to pleasure that we lose a sensible equilibrium, which, for example, can be gauged by not losing the sense of what is appropriate in any given situation.

To a modern reader it may at first seem like a somewhat meagre defence, since strictly speaking neither laughter nor play is acknowledged as having an independent value (aside from Albert the Great's *ludus liberalis* mentioned in the footnote), but they rather need to be legitimised by serving seriousness and work (is all laughter and play really that reasonable?). However, in relation to the ecclesiastical and theological past, present, and not least future with the Reformation, Counter-Reformation, orthodoxy, puritanism, and pietism, we must go well into the 19th century before we find more widespread voices in harmony with Aquinas' (and various other scholastics') nuanced considerations, while it is only after World War Two that those singing to the tune of Aquinas become a

---

260 and destroyed, and when the time came for it to send stouter arrows after some beast, its stiffness would be lost by the excessive and continuous strain and it would be impossible for the more powerful bolts to be shot. And, my lad, said the blessed John, do not let this slight and short relaxation of my mind disturb you, as unless it sometimes relieved and relaxed the rigour of its purpose by some recreation, the spirit would lose its spring owing to the unbroken strain, and would be unable when need required, implicitly to follow what was right.' 1846, col. 1312–15; 1894, 540 f. For a brief overview of the tradition, which includes Cicero and Lucius Annaeus Seneca (4 BCE-65 CE), see Suchomski 1975, 30 ff.

In addition to the philosophers' rational and pragmatic defence, Aquinas could also have listened to a theological praise of play, even from none other than his own direct teacher, Albert the Great (*c*. 1193–1280). In his commentary on Luke (*Enarrationes*), Albert distinguishes between different types of play and highlights the characteristic of true, free play (*ludus liberalis*) in that it is purposeless, that it is its own justification: 'That play is free in which we desire nothing other than play' (*Ludus liberalis est in quo praeter ludum nihil alius volumus*). Unfortunately for laughter, Albert does not include it in his considerations of which kinds of free play are capable of bringing gentleness and meekness to the participants, for it turns out that he is referring to the specific type of play mentioned by Jesus (Lk 7:32). This type, Albert believes, can only be found in activities such as music, singing, and playing the organ – and these are exceptions compared to the many others that can be useful at best (in the service of another matter, such as a soldier's training

full-fledged chorus. In passing, it can also be noted that while Oecolampadius in his small book on Easter Laughter makes room for about a dozen quotes from Greek and Latin Church Fathers, a dozen and a half allusions and quotes from ancient philosophers and authors, as well as borrowing points from several of his contemporaries, such as Erasmus, he does not mention a single scholastic, let alone quote them.

When we paint with such a broad brush, it is important to emphasise that it is precisely and 'only' the very general picture that is meant to be captured. For any historical period this means that if we search long and hard enough, there would be a reasonable possibility of discovering a person who has touched upon or perhaps even unfolded almost any position regarding laughter. It is therefore advisable to distinguish between main currents and undercurrents as well as keeping in mind that such a distinction works both ways: when our gaze is fixed on the main current, we should not become blind to the fact that there may be sources that flow in other or directly opposite directions. Conversely, encountering a source that flows against the current does not change the direction of the main current – and if it does, we are dealing with an epoch-making thinker.

In the overall picture the description is not undermined by the fact that we can find more balanced statements about laughter from Chrysostom (see note 586), or that even earlier, in the contemporary of Tertullian, Clement of Alexandria (150–215), we get a clear impression that when he makes room for some nuanced considerations, these are indeed more than just careless interjections made on the spur of the moment.[261] Despite these examples to the contrary, it was the unequivocal condemnations of laughter that exerted their dominance on history. Similarly, Le Goff's tripartite division of the Middle Ages does not become useless just because already in his first period – and notably before access to Aristotle's own writings – we can come across a theologian like Agobard of Lyon

---

    in horsemanship), but often are 'disgusting and indecent' (*ludus obscenus et turpis*). 1894, 492 f., cf. Ferm 2008, 82 f.

261 One of the most fascinating aspects of Clement's 'Christ the Educator' is that he undertakes the formidable task of measuring Christianity against the finest culture of his time, including its greatest philosophers. Clement believes he can demonstrate that Christianity meets and even surpasses the highest standards of the ancient world. The book is a kind of handbook for Christians, instructing them in proper behaviour and thinking in almost every area of life. Thus, there is a separate chapter that guides us in dealing with laughter, just as in the chapters immediately before and after Clement discusses an appropriate participation in the festivities (*Quomodo in conviviis se recreare oporteat*) and how to speak properly (or rather, avoid foul

(*c.* 779–840), who fully reaches the same level of sophisticated casuistry that Le Goff otherwise reserves for his third period.[262]

---

language, *De turpiloquio*). Furthermore, there is sound advice for Christians on furniture, sleep, reproduction, footwear, jewellery, cosmetics, and much, much more.

The small chapter on laughter is characteristic of the book's structure, as Clement includes quotes and allusions from the Bible as well as from Homer, Plato, and Aristotle. At first glance, we get the impression that Clement leans more towards Aristotle, but with great pedagogical insight he illustrates the perspective and limitations of *homo ridens*: just because it is inherent to a horse to neigh, it does not mean that it should neigh incessantly. Clement's main viewpoint seems to be that laughter should be adapted to time and place, and he emphasises that laughter should especially be restrained when in the company of elders and people who deserve respect. He warns that laughter can particularly lead to misunderstandings among children and women. Such an 'Aristotelian' interpretation of Clement would thus focus on the first half of his statement that 'we need not take away from people any of the things that are natural to them, but only set a limit and due proportion to them', Clement 1954, 134–6, quote 135.

Halliwell focuses, so to speak, more on the second half of that statement and argues that Clement not only leans towards a Platonic position but also adopts Plato's ideas of the ideal society in *The Republic* and applies them to the Christian community. 'Clement's position on laughter is actually more radical than any of those adopted in Plato's texts. He argues, with some manipulation of the nuances of the adjective *geloios*, that because comic or amusing speech can only come from a "risible" (and, by implication, flawed) character, not only must professional comic performers be "expelled", but even more so, "we ourselves" must eliminate laughter-making or joking (*gelotopoiein*) from our lives.' Naturally, Halliwell acknowledges the nuances mentioned above, but overall he believes that in the end Clement could only accept a Christian smile. Halliwell 2008, 484–95, quote 487.

[262] In Agobard's *De spe et timore*, Kemper has dug out a subtle interpretation made by the Archbishop of Lyon of Jesus' warning against laughter (Lk 6:25), which was otherwise usually taken as one of the definitive arguments against any tolerance. However, Agobard incorporates the understanding that 'laughter is natural for humans' into his considerations and concludes that if Jesus' statement referred to any and all kinds of laughter, no person would be exempt. Therefore, Agobard concludes, Jesus only refers to misplaced laughter, that is, laughing when one should have cried, or 'empty laughter over transient things'. 1981, 439; cited from Kemper 2005, 22 f.

Kemper concedes that Agobard stands out because of his differentiated view of laughter, and that he therefore does not necessarily contradict Le Goff's overall characterisation. Yet it is also important to him to plead the following conclusion to apply to the Middle Ages in general: 'Mostly, a differentiated attitude prevails, which is directed only against certain types of laughter, against mocking laughter, empty

c. The Four Temperaments

If we have engaged with the history of theology in general or with the topic of laughter in particular, we soon know that it does not require any special expertise to recognise the kinship between Aristotle and – as the scholastics' first among equals – Aquinas. There is nothing particularly new about this, except that it is still worth noting that not even such a prominent and influential figure as Aquinas succeeded in truly reversing the tide. On the other hand, Aquinas did become a stepping stone that theologians and church figures of a much later age could use if and when, in their modern interest in laughter, they found it relevant to seek support from tradition.

All the more reason to thank Prütting for bringing something new to laughter research by drawing our attention to other scholastics in the time just before and around Aquinas. Like him these thinkers do not alter the overall picture, but what is intriguing about them is that they enrich the discussion with the revival of ancient humoural pathology. This is the third of what was announced above as significant intellectual developments. As documented by H.-G. Schmitz and others, it was far from a mere mechanical adoption of the Hippocratic or Galenic humoural theory in the Middle Ages. Instead, it was further developed in the most imaginative ways, allowing the system to grow beyond anthropology and relate blood, yellow and black bile, and phlegm to colours, seasons, elements, planets, and almost anything else between heaven and earth that could be categorised into four groups.[263] Prütting's particular merit is to have discovered William of Conches (c. 1080/1090-after 1154), who in his work *De philosophia mundi* (1124) managed to also connect the bodily fluids with laughter. However,

---

laughter, and laughter at jokes, laughter in the church, and during prayer, because the knowledge of the ability to laugh as a fundamentally human characteristic implies that laughter could be considered appropriate or at least acceptable under certain conditions.' 2005, 26.

263 H.-G. Schmitz 1972, 93–115. Although it is both a late extension of the tradition and the reference is incomplete, it is irresistible to mention the theory that temperaments can be identified based on the vowel used in laughter: sanguine hoho, choleric hehe, melancholic hihi, and phlegmatic haha. Gisbert Kranz (1921–2009) mentions this as something that Johannes Damascenus Schaller (1620–69) is said to have presented in a text from 1662. Unfortunately, Kranz only refers to a German dictionary of proverbs, which in turn only provides Damascenus' name without any specific work. Kranz 1970, 86, n. 11. If the year is correct, it appears that the prolific Schaller only published one work in 1662, *Logici paradisi custos*, which unfortunately has not been made electronically available by the one Swiss library that seems to be the only in the world to possess a copy.

the path to this discovery is more convoluted than that, as the radical theological significance of the humours for laughter only emerges as a kind of byproduct of the difficult calculation of dividing seven by four, for how can we distribute the deadly sins among the temperaments?

Similar to the transition from 'silence' to 'humility', the crucial change lies in the fact that the theory of different human temperaments opens up for a differentiated anthropology. For a logically thinking scholastic, this necessarily leads to the question of how to reconcile such a view of a diversified human nature with a uniform doctrine of sin. When William of Conches attempted to distribute the cardinal sins (in the version of Gregory the Great) pride, envy, greed, wrath, sloth, gluttony, and lust, among the sanguine, choleric, melancholic, and phlegmatic temperaments, Prütting sums up his calculation in this way:

> However, since two of these cardinal sins correspond to three of the temperaments, namely wrath (more precisely, rage [*ira*]) with the choleric temperament, and sloth [*acedia*] with the phlegmatic and melancholic temperaments, then the sanguine temperament remained and fell outside the system of the seven cardinal sins. For it could neither be considered as greed [*avaritia*] nor accused of gluttony [*gula*] or lust [*luxuria*]. The only option left was to genetically connect laughter with the cardinal sins of pride [*superbia*] and envy [*invidia*], which would also have aligned with the traditional way of arguing, [...].[264]

At first glance, this does not seem to do laughter any service, because if any of the seven sins were to lay claim to being the worst, it would precisely be the one which Lucifer had succumbed to: pride. The next step in the considerations is therefore the decisive precondition for developing a fundamentally different view of laughter.

In the Middle Ages, when they discussed the innermost nature of humanity, it was tantamount to determining how Adam was in paradise prior to the fall, and when this question was mirrored in the doctrine of temperaments, the sanguine temperament was once again somewhat 'left over'. It was difficult to imagine the sinless Adam as choleric, melancholic, or phlegmatic ... so he must have been sanguine. However, William does not settle for the method of exclusion. By utilising one of the classical 'extensions' of the theory of humours, where the sanguine temperament is associated with warmth and moisture,[265] he dares to go against the traditional point that the ideal is the mutual equilibrium of the four humours. Moreover, he designates the sanguine temperament as the most authentic human temperament. In doing so, William redefines 'equilibrium' to

---

264   Prütting 2013, 478.
265   A schematic representation of some of the connections looks like this, cf. H.-G. Schmitz 1972, 95 and 104:

be synonymous with being warm and moist, but only as far as human beings are concerned, as all other animal species can be categorised into the other three temperaments, while only humans can be truly sanguine. This determination of the prelapsarian temperament of humans implies that the laughing human is the 'optimal form of humanity'.[266]

d. Sin and Purgatory

In Prütting's reconstruction of the connection, the utilisation of the doctrine of humours is closely linked to two other theological breakthroughs, which, on the other hand, may be difficult for a Protestant theologian to appreciate wholeheartedly: the invention of gradations in sin (Prütting credits Anselm of Canterbury [1033–1109] for contributing the lion's share to this development) and, more or less as a consequence of this, the invention of purgatory.[267] Purgatory made

blood	sanguine	air	warm-moist	spring	childhood
yellow bile	choleric	fire	warm-dry	summer	youth
black bile	melancholic	earth	cold-dry	autumn	maturity
phlegm	phlegmatic	water	cold-moist	winter	old age

266 Prütting 2013, 479–80. No matter how exciting it is to follow Prütting's interpretation of William of Conches, we cannot overlook the fact that he lacks a clear quotation from him as evidence that it is indeed William, and not just Prütting, who makes the decisive bridge between the considerations of Adam as sanguine and him being *homo ridens* in Paradise.
  The same applies to Prütting's even bolder interpretation of Genesis' second account of the creation of man and woman, where he must carry full responsibility for connecting 'a mist was going up from the land and was watering the whole face of the ground' (2:6 *ESV*) and 'the LORD God [...] breathed the breath of life into his nostrils, and the man became a living being' (2:7 *BSB*) to the moisture and warmth of the theory of temperaments, suggesting that God creates man by 'laughing into' him (German: *Anlachen*). However, it should be noted that Prütting is not caught concealing the risk of overinterpretation, as, firstly, he presents this interpretation in the form of a series of subjunctive phrases: 'what stops us from ...' (German: *was hindert uns ...*), and, secondly, he concludes by stating that William of Conches never went that far himself (but does Prütting leave himself a loophole when he adds: 'explicitly'?). *Ibid.*, 481 f.
267 Prütting is referring to Le Goff's *The Birth of Purgatory* (1984).

it possible to take into account, so to speak, the difference between venial and mortal sins also in the afterlife, so that not each and every sin led to hell and so that the venial sins were not left completely unpunished.

In short, the reasoning is that once it was acknowledged that we are not limited to evaluating a phenomenon like laughter according to a binary logic of either-or, but can analyse it on a scale of more-or-less, it suddenly became relevant to engage in serious and systematic consideration of the different types of laughter. It is important to note that this is not just speculation about the potential (left for later generations to explore) in the new doctrine of sin, as Prütting has succeeded in finding a theologian who ventures a step further than William of Conches and establishes a systematic theology of laughter – or at least lays the groundwork for it.

This concerns the English Franciscan, Alexander of Hales (*c.* 1185–1245), active at the University of Paris, whose texts were collected by his students in a posthumous *Summa theologica* (*c.* 1250). Alexander's approach is precisely to subject laughter to an analysis based on Anselm's distinction between venial and mortal sin, thus analysing laughter as not just simply laughter since it is motivated by various *intentions*. Prütting has no doubt about the implied perspective: 'Methodologically, this is a progress so significant that it is hard to praise it enough because it prohibits any form of intentional reductionism.'[268] In terms of content, what is remarkable is not that Alexander, like Aquinas a few years later, closely follows Aristotle's distinction between the elegant *eutrapelía* and crude *bōmólokhos*. What is unique is that Alexander does not adopt The Philosopher's 'aesthetic-sociological' evaluation uncritically, but through an independent moral-theological reasoning manages to incorporate this distinction between types of laughter into a gradation of sinfulness based on purpose, means employed, and the circumstance.[269]

As a case in point and in light of the theme of the relationship between laughter and joy, it is interesting that Alexander argues that jesting (*iocularitas*) is not a mortal but only a venial sin because it arouses the kind of joy and laughter that stem from a lightheartedness (*ex levitate mentis*). A little later, Alexander varies the argument by stating that laughter is as natural for humans as crying, and just as crying can express sorrow, so can laughter express joy. Thus, since we can cry without sinning, we can also laugh without sinning.[270] Perhaps most strikingly,

---

268   *Ibid.*, 496.
269   *Ibid.*, 501.
270   *Ibid.*, 502 and 509.

Alexander effectively undermines a thousand-year-old tradition of using the *e silentio*-argument with regard to the absence of statements in the gospels about Jesus laughing. This he does by appropriating the argument for his own purpose and turning it on its head: if laughter were truly such a great sin, would there not have been something about it in the Ten Commandments, as with the other mortal sins? However, the Bible lacks a direct divine prohibition against laughter![271]

Even if it is not entirely unproblematic it is still very refreshing that Prütting has brought some other voices into the historical debate about theologians' understanding of laughter. Though first it should be emphasised that it is a sobering reminder of the importance of historical awareness when Prütting warns a modern reader against being confused by (or taking offence at) the fact that Alexander exclusively discusses the types of laughter (similar to his treatment of dance and play) as various degrees of sinfulness, for anything else would be a pure anachronism.[272] In relation to the topic of this present book, it is also deeply stimulating that Prütting, in his extensive chapter on scholasticism (which, with its 130 pages, is in itself the length of a 'normal' monograph), continuously prepares for and lets the exposition culminate in the thesis that Easter Laughter is the ecclesiastical and practical consequence of the academic theologians' opening of cracks in the Church Fathers' and the monastic system's brick wall against laughter. As part of this thesis, Prütting even dares to push the earliest written evidence of Easter Laughter back nearly three hundred years before Oecolampadius and nearly two hundred years earlier than Geus' sermon: 'If this were to be the case, then Alexander's Summa from 1250 would be the earliest direct statement on this seemingly strange custom of Easter Laughter.'[273]

The problematic aspect of Prütting's innovation is not really the flight of fancy that we as critics expose him for committing, as he clearly signals it himself through his use of subjunctives. The problem remains that in the crucial places, particularly regarding our specific topic, it is often the case that Prütting can only make the sources say something 'new' by interpreting them in a way that runs the risk of becoming idiosyncratic. It is not necessarily a divisive disagreement

---

271 *Ibid.*, 512.
272 *Ibid.*, 513.
273 *Ibid.*, 505, cf. 437, 475, 520. At 485, Prütting highlights the significant temporal coincidence between William of Conches' texts and the emergence of the new literary genre, *Facetiae*. Prütting makes a focused examination of Easter Laughter in a separate section, 556–81.

when, in a passage at the end of chapter I, we made the argument for the emergence of Easter Laughter in the 14th century, while Prütting has to assume it was practised in the first half of the 13th century. For only that enables him to make the following claim about a passage from Alexander: 'It is very likely that he had the custom of Easter Laughter in mind with this entire chapter, which was probably already practised around this time [...].'[274] On the other hand, it appears more problematic that Prütting simultaneously has to assume a much broader geographical spread of Easter Laughter if an Englishman residing in Paris is supposed to have been interested in the phenomenon. When Prütting quotes Alexander considering the conditions that must be present to make it legitimate for preachers to tell *nugae* during the worship service,[275] it does not seem convincing to see this as 'the earliest direct stance' on Easter Laughter (which is not mentioned at all in the *Summa*). It is much more plausible that Alexander is addressing the preachers' use of *exempla* in general, a practice that had recently been promoted in the preaching of the Franciscans (Alexander's fellow friars), especially when one of Alexander's most important conditions for the preacher not committing a mortal sin by telling funny stories is that the 'offensive effect' happens unintentionally, inadvertently, for this cannot be claimed at all about Easter Laughter.

Having said this, there is all the more reason to go along with Prütting wholeheartedly at the point where he most soberly summarises the result of his studies of these somewhat lesser-known scholastics:

> However paradoxical it may sound: it was the discovery of venial sins around the year 1100 and the invention of purgatory around 1200 that made laughter acceptable to Christianity. Together they could have reconciled [laughter and faith] and justified an explicit theology of laughter, as we find glimpses of it in William of Conches, Alexander of Hales, and Thomas Aquinas, and as we find it realised in the custom of Easter Laughter (*risus paschalis*).
>
> All the same, an explicit theology of laughter, especially one officially endorsed *ex cathedra*, did not emerge at that time, although, as far as I can see, there has never been a greater opportunity for it in the history of theology than at this point.[276]

---

274   Ibid., 505; on the following page, Prütting acknowledges that it is equally possible that Alexander is simply referring to the type of plays in churches performed by travelling clergy.
275   Ibid., 503 ff.
276   Ibid., 471 f.

iv. A Couple of Female Mystics – and a Male

To both round off this section on joy and laughter and to illustrate Prütting's point about the epoch's unique 'opportunity', the exposition can be supplemented with two very special cases. The first is a beautiful example of how, in a rare case, a woman received a revelation on how to reconcile the two apparent contradictions. In a vision she could both uphold the tradition of Jesus' lack of laughter and simultaneously experience the legitimacy of a joyous and, according to the literal wording of the text, resounding (and Christian!) laughter. This is Julian of Norwich (1342–1416), to whom God has revealed that while the Devil is just as evil and constantly seeking to harm humanity as he has always been, the power of Jesus' suffering keeps him at bay, and that God does not allow the Devil to prevail. Julian then understands that 'in God may be no wreth, [...]. For our gode Lord endlesly hath regarde to His owne worshippe and to the profite of al that shall be savid'. This comforting insight elicits a uniqely moving reaction from her:

> For this sigte I lauhyd migtily, and that made them to lauhyn that were about me, and ther lauhyng was a likeing to me. I thowte that I wold that al myn evyn Christen had seen as I saw and than should thei al lauhyn with me. But I saw not Criste lawhyn; for I understode that we may lauhyn in comforting of ourselfe and joying in God, for the devil is overcome.[277]

Another female voice deserves to be included in the medieval polyphonic choir on the laughter of joy, and here, too, there is a very special reason to listen, because we can learn something new about three important details: in a truly unique way, Hildegard of Bingen (1098–1179) reprises the insinuations of past generations that the underlying basis for suspicion against laughter lies in the libidinous, in the instincts, and thus in the kinship between the pleasure of laughter and sexuality. Furthermore, she illustrates why not even joy always suffices as justification for laughter; and finally, as a pure bonus, she provides a recipe for a simple cure against the destructive form of laughter. All of this is presented in three short passages in her 'Causes and Cures' (*Causae et curae*, after 1150), where she delves into an account of the anatomy and biology of laughter.[278]

---

277 Julian of Norwich 1994, chapter 13 (= 5th vision), line 516–20, online version; see also her 16th vision in chapter 77, where the sight of the enemy's defeat once again makes her surrender herself 'mytyly to lauhen' (line 3145).
278 Cf. Prütting 2013, 485–91, who incorporates other passages from the book into his presentation.

In a section titled 'On Joy and Laughter' (*De laetitia et risu*), Hildegard offers a compelling image of the almost creative and certainly life-sustaining significance of joy: 'When a person's consciousness is not aware of anything sad, unpleasant, or bad in himself, this person's heart also opens itself to joy, just as blossoms open themselves to the sun's warmth.' The unique aspect of Hildegard's theological medicine (or medical theology?) is that this seemingly metaphorical concept is literally embodied: 'For the liver receives this joy and preserves it in itself just as the stomach retains nourishment in itself.' The rest of the section describes the journey of joy through the body's organs, and we are led to understand that once it reaches the liver and fills it up, it 'brings the person thus to laughter, and causes his voice, similar to the sound of an animal, to break out in laughter [*cachinnus*] like a neighing horse'. Likewise, excessive amounts of the otherwise milder laughter (*risus*) can harm the spleen and tire the stomach.[279]

In the preceding section titled 'On Cachinnation and Laughter' (*De cachinno et risu*),[280] laughter is depicted with an image as beautiful and evocative as that of joy, as laughter is said to have its roots in the sound of prelapsarian Adam's highest delight (*vox superiorum gaudiorum*). However, with the transition from paradise to earth, both joy and laughter, like sexuality, were transformed into an ambiguous phenomenon: 'Just as at Adam's fall the pure, holy form of begetting offspring was transformed into carnal desire, so also the voice full of heavenly joy that Adam possessed changed into the opposite sound of hilarity and resounding laughter.' Once again, Hildegard takes a further step and physically embodies the dogmatics of hamartiology by way of a phenomenological comparison between explosive laughter and orgasm:

> Inappropriate rowdiness and laughter have a certain commonality with carnal desire, and the same wind that sets loose laughter, emerges from a person's marrow and disturbs his abdomen and his bowels. Once in a while as a result of excessive disturbance, laughter drives as much tear water out of the eyes from the blood in the vessels as foam of the man's seed is driven out from the blood in the vessels by the heat of his passionate desire.[281]

In light of Hildegard's practical approach to major theological questions, we should perhaps not be surprised that she does not settle for the traditional attempts to curb laughter with admonitions, threats, and condemnations. Instead, she offers a very different effective remedy to her fellow nuns in the

---

279 Hildegard 1903, 149; 1994, 132.
280 Which Madigan chooses to translate as 'Echoing Laughter and Hilarity', *ibid*.
281 Hildegard 1903, 148 f.; 1994, 132.

monastery and to any reader of her book in the section titled 'On Excessive Laughter' (*De risu immoderato*):

> A person who is seized and shaken by excessive laughter should grind up some muscat nut, add half as much sugar, shake this in some heated wine, and drink it both on an empty stomach and after having eaten something. For immoderate laughter dries out the lungs and shakes up the liver. But the heat of the muscat nut has a healing effect on the liver, and the heat of the sugar that has become liquid restores the lungs. If these two agents are regulated with the heightened heat of the wine and then consumed, they restore the good humors to their proper order which, through immoderate laughing, have become unbalanced.[282]

In the name of gender equality, it should be added that men could also express such thoughts; but perhaps one would need to be a mystic for that to happen. Meister Eckhart (*c.* 1260-*c.* 1328) certainly has some sentences in one of his texts that point in the same direction as Julian and Hildegard when, on the second of the six stages that belong to the inner rebirth of the individual, he writes that it 'crawls out of the mother's womb and laughs towards the heavenly father'.[283]

Elsewhere, in a couple of sermons, Eckhart concludes one with a lengthy passage in which he even elevates laughter to an inner Trinitarian phenomenon, where the Father and the Son laugh at each other, thus – eventually – generating the Holy Spirit. Admittedly, the mysterious master adds that this is merely a parable.[284] But still! In the other sermon, Eckhart envisions the direct opposite of the laughter that God makes heard in Psalm 2:4, as he (Eckhart), based on his chosen Bible verse (Isa 49:13: 'Sing for joy, O heavens, and exult, O earth' *ESV*),

---

282 *Ibid.*, 199; 1994, 176; cf. Trokhimenko 2014, 84–5.
283 To give a bit more context, the quote is taken from the treatise 'The Nobleman': 'The second stage is when he not merely regards the outward examples and good people, but runs and hastens to the teaching and counsel of God and divine wisdom, turns his back on mankind and his face toward God, crawling forth from his mother's lap to smile up at his heavenly Father.' 2009, 559. This translation by Walshe deviates from the one given above in two places: while it is open for discussion how best to translate the Middle High German word 'schôz' (our 'womb' indicates a spiritual birth, whereas 'lap' perhaps more leans in the direction of upbringing), we find it curious that he opts for 'smile' instead of 'laughs' for German 'lachet'. In Middle High German the crucial sentence runs like this: 'kriuchet der muoter ûz der schôz und lachet den himelschen vater ane', Eckhart 1963, 112.
284 'To speak in parable, the Father laughs into the Son and the Son laughs back to the Father; and this laughter breeds liking, and liking breeds joy, and joy begets love, and love begets Person, and Person begets the Holy Ghost.' 1924, 59. Cf. Wehrli 1984, 320, note 21.

affirms that there is indeed joy and gladness in Heaven, and that God's joy and gladness surpass those of humans and angels to such an extent that in comparison to His theirs can only be compared to a lentil (*sic*): 'For God makes merry and laughs at good deeds'.[285]

v. Summary

The search for statements about joy and laughter has taken us far and wide, but even though the invitation in the Easter Mass hymn to 'let us rejoice and be glad' ensures some kind of connection to Easter Laughter, we are left somewhat in the same way as after examining the other types of arguments: they can be quite well thought out and even pertinent, yet they still do not provide a completely satisfying answer as to why it was specifically in connection with Easter rather than any other holiday that laughter should enter the church.

Firstly, we must once again question whether joy is reserved for Easter. Indeed, if it is allowable to generalise Riising's interpretation of the Danish sources (including her extensive use of German research) and apply it to other parts of Europe, it would, on the contrary, suggest that joy had a difficult time in the medieval devotion to the Man of Sorrows:

> This concentration on suffering as physical pain, moral guidance, etc., has inevitably left its mark on Easter sermons as well. It is as if the preachers do not really know what to do with the Easter Gospel, and in Easter sermons there are no shouts of victory, no overwhelming message of joy.[286]

Could it really have been completely different in Southern Germany, or was Easter Laughter perhaps a deliberate reaction against this?

Secondly, if we disregard the singular example of Julian of Norwich, it is a long and perhaps futile search to find a positive evaluation of other types of laughter than the single one that seems to have much more in common with a smile than with the hearty and boisterous laughter associated with Easter Laughter, certainly by its critics.

This leads us directly to the third and crucial observation: so far, no historical source has been found that can provide a plausible theological explanation for the origin of Easter Laughter. The closest is Prütting's diligent and well-argued

---

285 Truth be told, Eckhart also recognises that God reacts completely differently – as in Ps 2:4 – to the other kinds of deeds performed by humans: 'whereas all other works which are not done to God's glory are like ashes in God's sight', 2009, 445.

286 Riising 1969, 166; in note 46 she refers to Dreher 1951, 19–35 and concludes: 'This is characteristic of the entire medieval Easter preaching'.

attempt to link the most liberal scholastics with the emergence of *facetiae*-literature and Easter Laughter. The objections raised earlier against Prütting's theory can be nuanced by conceding that it is not necessarily required that a direct causal relationship between, for example, Aquinas and a particular village priest in Bavaria has to be documented in writing. Instead, we can settle for the assumption that they both, on their respective levels, are influenced by and reflect a new spirit more tolerant of laughter. However, the most problematic aspect remains, as Prütting also admits, in that the furthest the sources go is to *tolerate* laughter, often by resigning to the impossibility of eradicating it, but occasionally by granting it some positive value. Even when this occurs, we can question whether it is an intrinsic value, as evidenced by the numerous conditions for the legitimacy of laughter and its constant need to serve a utilitarian purpose. Throughout that period in history, the furthest they were prepared to go was to accept the permissibility of laughter in specific cases, never its desirability, let alone its necessity.

It is difficult to ignore the conclusion which has to be drawn from these observations: regardless of whether it occurred in one century or another during the High and late Middle Ages, and regardless of whether it was a local South German custom or widespread in broader areas of Europe, the emergence of Easter Laughter remains a mystery.

6. The Resurrection as an Argument

The mystery entails that if there is to be a convincing example of a theological justification for laughter's presence in the church and its connection to Easter, we most likely have to turn our attention away from Easter Laughter's historical sources. Instead we may have to settle for theories developed by much later generations. This applies to the ultimate argument for linking laughter specifically to Easter rather than any other part of the liturgical year, namely that there must be some intrinsic connection between laughter and resurrection. In a way, here we must methodically move backwards: if we start from the theoretically best dogmatic answer we can then search the historical sources, not with an ambition of finding pieces of irrefutable evidence but rather clues that may make any given theory plausible – or at least not impossible.

These archaeological expeditions have ventured even further than attempts to connect joy and laughter, as there does not appear to be any obvious connection between resurrection and laughter – at least not if we stick to the Bible or texts from the Early Church and medieval theologians. It should therefore come as no great surprise that in their search scholars have gone in widely different directions, or that there is significant disagreement among scholars from different eras about where the root is to be found. The alleged identification of the origin of Easter Laughter in paganism also contributed to making the disagreement pronounced, as it became entangled in confessional and ideological disputes. In fact, Hospinian indirectly suggested such a connection between Easter Laughter and paganism, when, in the section immediately before his lengthy quote from Oecolampadius, he listed 'various forms of abuse and superstitions' with which the Easter celebration had been associated over time.[287] However, according to Wendland, it was not until Ernst Friedrich Kesselring's (1685–1763) dissertation in 1705 that it was formulated for the first time as a definite thesis that Easter Laughter derived from specific pagan customs.[288]

Let it be noted in advance that here we want to argue that no one has succeeded in substantiating a direct causal relationship or the existence of any unbroken traditions, and, yet, it may still be worthwhile to explore the detour through pagan sources and traditions. The crux of the matter is whether we can accept that not everything that resembles each other needs to be the same, and, furthermore, that even if two traditions may be indistinguishable, it does not necessarily mean that one phenomenon is the genesis of the other. If we can come to terms with this, we can instead appreciate that the more or less corresponding phenomena and beliefs can, at the very least, serve as illustrative parallels and, at most, serve as a kind of hermeneutical key to uncover dimensions – or untapped potentials – in both the Bible and tradition.

i. Spring in Nature and Myth

Kesselring (and Hospinian) initially pointed towards Ireland, but two hundred years later there was a growing interest in the Germanic and Nordic cultures.[289] Consequently the focus shifted towards what was by some considered a clear connection to the scene with Loki reconciling Skadi, where his slapstick antics cause him to land in her lap and make her burst into laughter.[290] The majority,

---

287   Hospinian 1593, 73r-v, cf. note 151.
288   Wendland 1980, 82 f.
289   To mention a few examples, Fehrle 1930; Dölger 1939, 85; Propp [1939] 1984, 139, and Franz Rolf Schröder's (1893–1979) monograph *Skadi und die götter Skandinaviens* (1941).
290   The incident is mentioned in the chapter on the language of poetry in the *Edda* by Snorri (1179–1241): 'It was also in [Skadi's] terms of settlement that the Æsir were to do something that she thought they would not be able to, that was to make her laugh. Then Loki did as follows: he tied a cord round the beard of a certain nanny-goat and

however, turned their gaze in the opposite direction, looking towards the south, primarily Greece and Rome, while others have wandered the entire horizon and drawn examples from almost every continent. The further one explores, the further one naturally moves away from searching for empirically provable influences and instead becomes interested in phenomenological kinships. In almost all cases, the connection between (Easter) laughter and paganism, and subsequently Christianity, is found in the forces of nature during springtime.

Based solely on common experience, it would be relatively trivial to associate laughter (or at least certain types of laughter) with vitality and zest for life. Nevertheless, Propp has a sharp rebuttal to those scholars (including Fluck) who believe that the power of Easter Laughter can be explained solely based on everyday experiences, as this leads to shallow rationalism and speculative philosophy.[291] Instead, we must look towards rituals and mythologies (and the world of folktales), which take us a step further and connect zest for life with a creative life force of such strength that it can overcome death. By exploring such sources, we can learn about the relationship between laughter, death, and life among both humans and gods.

In the case of humans, the power of laughter manifests itself in two seemingly opposite ways: by laughing (aloud) and by not laughing at all. On the one hand, there is a prohibition against laughter of an entirely different kind than those previously mentioned. Here we are dealing with the well-known motif of people who in one way or another are allowed, or manage by themselves, to enter the realm of the dead. Such intruders must avoid laughter at all costs in order not to reveal their presence, arouse the envy and anger of the dead, and thereby risk being trapped for ever in the realm of the dead. From this, Propp argues that laughter is perceived as a sign of life, and that the dead do not laugh.[292]

---

the other end round his testicles, and they drew each other back and forth and both squealed loudly. Then Loki let himself drop into Skadi's lap, and she laughed. Then the atonement with her on the part of the Æsir was complete.' Snorri 1995, 61.

291   Propp 1984, 127.
292   *Ibid.*, 128 f. A glimpse of this notion of laughter as a sign of life can also appear in Christian, apocryphal texts, such as 'The Infancy Story of Thomas' (17.1): 'And after these things in the neighbourhood of Joseph a little sick child died, and his mother wept bitterly. And Jesus heard that great mourning and tumult arose, and he ran quickly, and finding the child dead, he touched his breast and said: "I say to you, do not die but live and be with your mother." And immediately he looked up and laughed. And he said to the woman: "Take him and give him milk and remember me"'. 1991, 448.

This folklore motif is also found in certain transitional rites, where laughter can disrupt the process of the old dying (the child) and the new emerging (the adult).[293]

Apart from such relatively rare stories, it is the connection between birth and laughter that is more widespread, though still something quite special. Aristotle allegedly empirically observed that human children only begin to laugh 40 days after birth;[294] but according to Pliny the Elder's (23–79) account of Zoroaster (/ Zarathustra), he laughed at birth (which is also one of several signs of his supernatural abilities),[295] and something similar is suggested about the birth of the promised Prince of Peace in Vergil's (70–19 BCE) *Fourth Eclogue*.[296] Based on examples of laughter accompanying the transition from life to death and vice versa, Propp considers whether we ought to have another look at the famously infamous *sardonic* laughter. Its reputation for being synonymous with brutality and cynicism stems from the legend that among the people of Sardinia, it was customary to kill old people amidst loud laughter; but perhaps this custom is not

---

293 Propp 1984, 130.
294 'After children are born, for forty days they neither laugh nor weep when awake, but sometimes do both in their sleep; nor do they usually feel when they are tickled, but they sleep the greater part of their time.' (*Historia animalium* VII.9,3) Aristotle 1883, 191 f.
295 'We find it stated that Zoroaster was the only human being who ever laughed on the same day on which he was born. We hear, too, that his brain pulsated so strongly that it repelled the hand when laid upon it, a presage of his future wisdom.' (*Naturalis Historia* 7,26 = *Natural History* 7,15) Pliny the Elder 1855, 155. It is a testimony to the rarity of this phenomenon that there are also examples of quite the reverse interpretation, when according to medieval folklore known from South Germany this 'premature' laughter anticipates the child's death or reveals it being a demon. Lühl 2019, 171 (quoting from Hanns Bächtold-Stäubli (ed.): *Handwörterbuch des deutschen Aberglaubens*, vol. 5. Berlin & Leipzig: de Gruyter, 1987, col. 877).
296 Towards the end of the poem Vergil refers to laughter (*risu* and *risere*, here translated with 'smile') as the point of contact between child and parents, and shortly before that the whole universe of the new age is overjoyed by the child's birth (*laeto*, translated by Greenough as 'enraptured'): 'Begin to greet thy mother with a smile, / o baby-boy! ten months of weariness / for thee she bore: O baby-boy, begin! / For him, on whom his parents have not smiled, / gods deem not worthy of their board or bed.' 4. Eclogue 60–3. 'See how it totters—the world's orbed might, / earth, and wide ocean, and the vault profound, / all, see, enraptured of the coming time!' (*Aspice convexo nutantem pondere mundum, / terrasque tractusque maris caelumque profundum! / Aspice, venturo laetentur ut omnia saeclo!*), 4. Eclogue 50–2. Cf. Haug 1989, 263 and Luck 1994, 764.

about the insensitivity of those people, as laughter serves a completely different function than being an expression of powerful derision. '[…] laughter accompanying killing transforms death into a new birth, nullifies murder as such, and is an act of piety that transforms death into a new birth. […] Laughter is one of the means for the creation and recreation of life.'[297]

The examples from the history of religions and ethnography can be very colourful, but strictly speaking, they hardly reveal anything that common sense could not already tell us: of course the dead cannot laugh, and of course laughter can disrupt any solemnity. However, this was only the first step, and the bridge to understanding laughter as more than a trivial sign of life, but rather as life-*giving*, is laughter at a person's entry into life, at birth. Propp brings up an example from Yakut folklore where laughter even contributes to fertilisation (and for Propp, it remains an open question whether laughter actually causes it). In passing, he suggests that such a belief could be interesting to consider in the exegesis of the scene at Mamre, where the prediction of Sarah giving birth to the promised son is so deeply connected to laughter that the child is given a name derived from the Hebrew word for laughter: Isaac.[298]

A Brief Excursus on Abraham, Sarah, Isaac, and Laughter

Jacobelli is one of the scholars who in this context most consistently follows up on Propp's connection of laughter to sexuality. Jacobelli believes that in antiquity she can observe this transition from laughter being associated with a divine creative power to also being related to human reproduction and sexual desire. Similar to Propp, she believes she can find traces of this in the biblical texts, which the tradition of translation has otherwise obscured. Jacobelli focuses on the somewhat peculiar scene in Genesis 21, which leads to the expulsion of Hagar and Ishmael. What is it that Ishmael does to Isaac that triggers Sarah's intense anger? The authorised Danish translation from 1992 only makes the scene even more peculiar, for why be angry that Ishmael is 'playing' with Isaac (21:9)? The 'play' can be interpreted in two seemingly different directions, but the point here is their deep, even intimate connection, because the Hebrew word translated as 'play' is also found in the scene with King Abimelech, who through the window sees Isaac 'playing' with his wife Rebekah; there it is translated as 'caressing',

---

297 Propp 1984, 134 and 135. Cf. Reinach 1912, 124 and Usener 1913, 469–470, where customs are mentioned that bear some resemblance to Propp's interpretation of sardonic laughter by closely associating death, burial, and laughter.
298 Propp 1984, 133.

meaning they had sexual intercourse (26:8) (*NIV* agrees with the Danish version, whereas *KJV* used 'sporting' and *ESV* goes for 'laughing'). The same word also appears in the scene where Sarah eavesdrops on the conversation between God and Abraham and hears about her impending pregnancy. As we know, she reacts not by 'playing' (nor, indeed, by 'sporting' or 'caressing' herself) but by 'laughing'. Why does Sarah laugh? Could the answer lie in her initial thought: 'Shall I have pleasure?' (18:12)? What pleasure, indeed? The pleasure of giving birth? Or the pleasure of conceiving? The other part of her thought indicates the latter: 'My lord being old'. These overtones and undertones in the Hebrew word lead Jacobelli to suggest that the beginning of both the expulsion from paradise and the history of salvation are marked by desire and laughter.[299]

However, we can also choose to utilise the many layers of the Hebrew term in a slightly different way, as we have previously seen that both Adam of St Victor (see note 2) and Oecolampadius (see |64|) perceive a form of connection between Isaac, laughter, and Christ. Hyers is one of the pioneers in late 20th century efforts to develop a 'theology of laughter', and he has repeatedly put forth the thesis that an explanation for the controversial status of laughter in our tradition may be attributed to the fact that Judaism and Christianity, unlike many other religions, lack a mythical foundation to legitimise laughter. In the absence of a better alternative, Hyers has pointed to the role of laughter in these crucial passages in the narratives of primeval history and the patriarchs as a possible quasi-mythical grounding for a theology of laughter.[300]

We do not need to be feminists to perceive it as discrimination against Sarah when Abraham's laughter in the preceding chapter goes unnoticed. Such an interpretation is certainly possible; however, we could also argue that the Book of Genesis, specifically chapters 17 to 21, presents a series of scenes involving laughter. Not just laughter 'as such', but rather archetypes of a range of types of laughter, which also explains why they elicit different reactions. Abraham's laughter stems from the joy of wonder (17:17), which even St Paul does not reproach him for as he discreetly overlooks Abraham's laughter in his otherwise detailed retelling in Romans 4, whereas Sarah's laughter arises from sceptical mistrust (18:12). Already Augustine, followed by countless others, distinguishes thus between the spouses' types of laughter in *The City of God* 16,26 and 16,31.[301]

---

299   Jacobelli 1992, 61–3.
300   Hyers 1981, 13 ff.
301   Augutstine 1948, vol. 2, 146 f.; cf. Kremer 1961, 198.

Instead of hearing undertones of paedophilia, rape, or the sexual games typical of childhood in the scene with Ishmael and Isaac, Sarah may have reacted because she heard Ishmael's laughter as mockery (21:9). This is the unpleasant version of laughter that becomes even more frightening when God expresses his sovereignty by responding to human ambitions for power with mocking laughter as He does in Psalm 2:4. There the word is translated as 'laughs', but the parallelism of the verse equates the term with the other Hebrew word, which can also mean 'laughs', but is usually translated as 'mocks' (or, in various English Bible translations, as 'scoffs', 'taunts', or 'holds them in derision'), as He does most chillingly in Job 9:23, where the Lord 'laughs at' or 'mocks' human suffering.

The type of laughter appears most complex in connection with the naming of Isaac, for why should he have that name (21:6)? Is it because Sarah has become a laughing-stock, so that both God and people ('everyone who hears it') laugh at her? The kind of laughter where we laugh at someone is usually perceived as something negative, and we can hardly avoid the possibility that Sarah is indeed the target of derisive laughter, in which case the option exists that the Hebrew term could also be translated as 'mocks'. However, there is also another kind of laughter where one still laughs *at* someone ('the butt'), but without malice, and if that is how the laughter is to be heard in this context, it could be seen as the birth of comedy (and benign humour) in a biblical sense.

For the sake of clarity, it should be added that when it is mentioned above that the 'same' Hebrew word is translated differently, it is not unusual, but rather the rule, that Hebrew word-stems have widely different meanings in their various inflected forms.

ii. Sexuality and Fertility

Thus, the step is taken towards the relatively many cases where laughter and life, sexuality and fertility are combined and incorporated into myths and rituals that celebrate the (re)emergence of vegetation gods during springtime. Naturally, there are stories and customs all the world over that revolve around the life-determining rhythm of the seasons, but perhaps surprisingly, laughter is often included as a constitutive element in these.[302] In a Western cultural context alone, figures such as Hathor, Osiris, and Tammuz can be noted in Egyptian

---

302 In a lengthy and detailed chapter on 'ritual laughter and the renewal of life', Halliwell identifies thirteen classical Greek and Hellenistic festivals that included processions with scurrilous laughter. This is documented in a wide range of contemporary descriptions, spanning from Plato and Aristotle to Iamblichus (*c.* 245-*c.* 325), and

mythology,[303] but it is especially the Greek and Roman material that has attracted attention. Rome allegedly even had festivals dedicated to 'The God of Laughter' (*deus Risus*), at least if Apuleius' (125–170) descriptions in *The Golden Ass* are to be believed,[304] which they not necessarily are, as such a festival has never been historically documented. Perhaps Apuleius should rather be understood as giving a poetic interpretation of, for example, the spring festival Hilaria (25 March, associated with the fertility goddess Cybele) or the shepherd festival Lupercalia (15 February), which included processions with laughter as a prominent element, as described by Plutarch (46–120) and others.[305] In a Greek context, the figures of Adonis and Dionysus are obvious candidates, but the fertility motif is most evident in the myths and festivals associated with Demeter and her daughter Persephone (/Kore). In Homer's (8th cent. BCE) 'Hymn to Demeter', it is told how Persephone, with Zeus' acquiescence, is lured down to Hades and how Demeter leaves the gods and wanders the earth looking for her daughter before reluctantly giving up the search completely distraught:

> A long time she sat upon the stool without speaking because of her sorrow, and greeted no one by word or by sign, but rested, never smiling, and tasting neither food nor drink, because she pined with longing for her deep-bosomed daughter, until careful Iambe – who pleased her moods in aftertime also – moved the holy lady with many a quip and jest to smile and laugh and cheer her heart.[306]

Later in the hymn, it is revealed how Demeter's grief has caused hunger and poor harvest on Earth, but when Zeus regrets and orders Persephone to be brought up

---

therefore, even without considering Homer, covers more than 600 years of practice. Halliwell 2008, 155–214.
303 Cf. Luck 1994, 757.
304 'As soon as Thelyphron had told his tale they who sat at the table, replenished with wine, laughed heartily: and while they cried for a toast after their fashion to Laughter, Byrrhaena spoke to me and said: "From the first foundation of this city, we alone of all men have had a custom to celebrate with joyful and pleasant rites the festival day of the god Laughter, […]"'. *Met.* 2,31; cf. 3,11; Apuleius 1924, 96–7; cf. 116–17.
305 'It was, namely, the festival of the Lupercalia, of which many write that it was anciently celebrated by shepherds, and has also some connection with the Arcadian Lycaea. At this time many of the noble youths and of the magistrates run up and down through the city naked, for sport and laughter striking those they meet with shaggy thongs. And many women of rank also purposely get in their way, and like children at school present their hands to be struck, believing that the pregnant will thus be helped to an easy delivery, and the barren to pregnancy'. Plutarch (*Plut. Cae.* 61,1–2) 1967, vol. 7, 585.
306 Homer 1914, 303, line 198–204.

from Hades, life returns to the fields – although they must henceforth live with the fact that Persephone must return to Hades for one third of the year.

The salient point is how Iambe, a human, manages to make Demeter, a goddess, come out of her state of 'un-laughing' (ἀγέλαστος). The boldness in the 'pleasing' apparently lies in the type of 'quip and jest' that makes Demeter laugh, and judging from the Greek word used, *paraskōptō*, whose root σκώπτω normally means 'mock', 'ridicule', 'deride', and the like, the answer seems to be that the human makes the goddess smile and laugh by means of blasphemy. It sounds strange at first, but the explanation may lie in qualifying the kind of 'blasphemy'. Only indirectly does Homer's poem provide help by virtue of the maid's name. For 'Iambe' also happens to be the term for the poetic meter that some scholars believe characterised the erotic satirical songs that were part of the Eleusinian Mysteries, while others see the coincidence between the proper name and the metre as just that, a mere coincidence. On the other hand, there is more reliable assistance to be found in a later (Orphic) version of the myth, as relayed by Clement of Alexandria, where Iambe is instead named Baubo, and where her 'quip and jest' is accompanied by a very specific gesture: she lifts up her garments and exposes her genitals to the goddess.[307] Does this point us in the direction of a possible interpretation of the woman's blasphemous act? Does she show the goddess of grain, who threatens the land with barrenness, the source of human fertility?[308]

---

[307] 'Yet how can we wonder if Tuscans, who are barbarians, are thus consecrated to base passions when Athenians and the rest of Greece – I blush even to speak of it – possess that shameful tale about Demeter? It tells how Demeter, wandering through Eleusis, which is a part of Attica, in search of her daughter the Maiden, becomes exhausted and sits down at a well in deep distress. This display of grief is forbidden, up to the present day, to those who are initiated, lest the worshippers should seem to imitate the goddess in her sorrow. [...] But to continue; for I will not forfear to tell the rest of the story. Baubo, having received Demeter as a guest, offers her a draught of wine and meal. She declines to take it, being unwilling to drink on account of her mourning. Baubo is deeply hurt, thinking she has been slighted, and thereupon uncovers her secret parts and exhibits them to the goddess. Demeter is pleased at the sight, and now at last receives the draught, – delighted by the spectacle! These are the secret mysteries of the Athenians! These are also the subjects of Orpheus' poems. I will quote you the very lines of Orpheus, in order that you may have the originator of the mysteries as witness of their shamelessness: "This said, she drew aside her robes, / and showed / A sight of shame; child Iacchus was there, / And laughing, plunged his hand below her breasts. / Then smiled the goddess, in her heart she smiled, / And drank the draught from out the glancing cup."' Clement 1857a, col. 82–3; 1919, 41–3.

[308] Cf. note 317 with Claudio Balzaretti's (b. 1956) alternative interpretation.

The strength of Propp's polemic against the proposal that Easter Laughter's *raison d'etre* is the cheering up of the congregation after the deprivations during Lent is that he does not ignore the fact that both Capito and Oecolampadius highlight the sexual element in the preachers' techniques. Instead of labelling this as an expression of the two critics' prudishness or the preachers' lack of education and vulgarity, it is actually the connection between sexuality and laughter that links Easter Laughter not only to this or that medieval or ancient custom but to timeless primal forces.

To be sure, Christ is not a vegetation god; but no one who has joined in singing Easter hymns will fail to sense that the celebration of Jesus' resurrection is nourished and supported by vivid images of nature – to name but one example we can think of Adam of St Victor's famous *Mundi renovatio nova parit gaudia*.[309] Ultimately, such a close connection between the resurrection and the awakening of nature goes back to Jesus himself when in the same breath he speaks of the glorification of the Son of Man and the grain of wheat that must be put into the ground and die in order to yield a bountiful harvest (Jn 12:23–4). Can we even begin to imagine how we would have interpreted, understood, and preached the resurrection of Jesus had he been crucified in the middle of November? No matter what, such a thought experiment should not obscure the crucial difference that regardless of how much the Christian (and Jewish) Easter may benefit, at least pedagogically, from the archetypal images of fertility cults, Christ's resurrection does not mark the phases of changing seasons, but rather the transition from one aeon to another, from mythical meteorology to eschatology (and soteriology).[310]

---

309 Literally 'The renewal of the world gives birth to new joys'; in Wrangham's poetic rendering of the first stanza it comes out as: 'Spring's renewal of earth's plain / Newborn joys to man supplies; / When the Lord doth rise again, / With Him also all things rise: / Elements upon Him wait, / Feeling, as their source, how great / Should be His solemnities.' Adam of St Victor 1881, 77.

310 Cf. Ingvild Sælid Gilhus' (b. 1951) commentary on the apparent similarity between the contrast of weeping and laughter, as seen, for example, in the Demeter cult and the Christian Easter: 'What is new is that this contrast is no longer part of an opposition between two phases in a ritual or two seasons of the year as in earlier times. It has become a contrast between this world and the next. What is at stake is no longer the seasonal renewal of life, but the salvation of human beings. Laughter has moved out of the present world and has become a subject of eschatology and apocalypticism, a sign of the joy which will be released at the end of time.' 1997, 60.

iii. The Uroboric Powers of Laughter

As a conclusion to the examination of attempts to connect laughter with resurrection we arrive at not only the newest but also the most original and daring proposal. This can be found in Prütting's interpretation of laughter as uroboric, as he employs an image from antiquity and the Renaissance of a snake eating its own tail, which, among other things, has been interpreted as a symbol of nature's cyclical (re)creation. Although Prütting's thesis is unique and may initially appear idiosyncratic and subtle, it aligns with the very phenomenological characteristics of laughter, which previous scholars have also used to connect it with other natural yet religiously powerful and ambiguous phenomena. The advantage of these approaches is that they precisely start from and exploit that particular characteristic of laughter which for many other interpreters has often caused difficulties and which has tempted them to come up with various strategies for domesticating it: that laughter takes control and in its expression is noisy, violent, and explosively sudden. As Gilhus accurately formulates it, it is precisely the ambivalence of laughter that 'makes it an apt expression for religious experience as well as a powerful religious symbol. Like religion, laughter is situated at the intersection between body and mind, individual and society, the rational and the irrational.'[311] It is precisely the powerful and eruptive nature of laughter that also leads Propp to compare it to another bodily activity in religious contexts because both are supposed to have magical powers which rituals try to harness:

> Laughter can be compared with the dance. If people dance before a hunt, war, sowing, etc., they do it not for aesthetic gratification, but so as to influence nature, which they cannot yet influence by rational means. The dance is merely a convulsive effort. Convulsive fits are often the tool of a shaman, and at this stage laughter is just such a convulsive effort. In this sense laughter is a 'magic', non-rational means for creating life.[312]

At the very least, these observations in the history of religions provide an important clue to Prütting's analysis. In his highly nuanced and differentiated descriptions of the various types of laughter, he nevertheless makes the 'convulsive' aspect one of his most central keys to unlocking the relevance of laughter in relation to the resurrection of Easter. The crucial novelty of Prütting's interpretation lies in the fact that he does not stop at the 'cramp-like contraction' element but maintains focus on the fact that laughter follows a certain course.

---

311 *Ibid.*, 2, cf. 4.
312 Propp 1984, 136.

The very loss of self-control triggered by ecstatic laughter, which has caused the greatest moral and theological discomfort since the time of Plato and the Church Fathers, is a characteristic it shares with the much more accepted and explicitly religiously cultivated act of weeping. Furthermore, for both weeping and laughter, this is only one 'half' of their sequence. Already the Teacher knew that there is a time to weep and a time to laugh (Eccles 3:4), but Prütting goes a step further and organically connects these two 'times' with each other. Or more precisely: both weeping and laughter would be destructive to life, even in a literal physical sense, if we were to remain in them; however, both are characterised by consuming themselves and can thus serve a cathartic function. Prütting refers to this self-consuming quality as their 'uroboric impulse': we break down in tears but at some point rise comforted after having cried out; we curl up in laughter but stretch out refreshed afterwards.[313] To emphasise this interpretation of laughter, Prütting does not shy away from presenting a polemical piece of motif research that insinuates that the ecclesiastical resistance was rooted in a battle for market share: 'However, in this cathartic potential lies also the scandalous aspect that laughter represents for all redemption religions because cathartic laughter can make the redemption offerings of these religions appear unnecessary, even if this type of redemption is "only" of an immanent nature.'[314]

When Prütting reaches the section on Easter Laughter, he adds yet another metaphor and compares the uroboric with the wax candle, which, by consuming itself when lit, serves its purpose and emits light. Based on this, he can summarise his interpretation in this concise and potent passage:

> Naturally, it is the symbolism of the consuming and self-consuming candle, which spreads radiant light while burning itself, that makes visible the uroboric impulse of 'die and become' in the mythological scenario of death and resurrection, and, mythologically speaking, aligns the resurrected and radiant laughing Christ of Christianity with the phoenix bird of ancient paganism. This very uroboric impulse also shapes laughter as its inherent teleological tendency, and thus it should be clear what the relationship between Easter Laughter and the Easter resurrection feast is, and that Easter Laughter is the appropriate performative mimesis of the Easter event.[315]

One strength of Prütting's bold proposal is that he is not only able to encompass the otherwise scorned *cachinnus* but also to limit himself methodically to laughter as such. This means that Prütting's theory, in a sense, manages to bracket the

---

313   Prütting 2013, 50.
314   *Ibid.*, 55.
315   *Ibid.*, 562.

object and purpose of laughter, even though, as mentioned, in other contexts of his work he establishes complex schemes and taxonomies of the subtle differences in the various types of laughter.[316] In this specific context, the benefit is that Prütting does not fall into the trap where many modern advocates of bringing laughter into theology and the church tend to find themselves, that is, accepting only a sanitised and toothless version. Nor does he swing to the opposite extreme and subscribe exclusively to the kind of laughter that particularly in an ecclesiastical or theological context only aims to be mischievous or provocative.

Thus, on the one hand we can acknowledge Jacobelli's concern when she brings up the fertility cults mentioned above and focuses on eroticism and sexuality as the 'shocking' secret behind Easter Laughter, as she herself puts it.[317] Yet, on the other hand we must agree with Prütting when he dryly states that after all it was not sexual orgies that were organised in the South German churches during Easter Mass. Capito, Oecolampadius, and Erasmus do indeed lament the frivolity of Easter Laughter, and contemporary collections of *Schwänke* do provide many examples of eroticism and sexuality as sources of a good laugh, but by no means does this apply to all their jokes. Prütting, therefore, opines that Jacobelli actually confuses the means with the end. The 'end' is not to liberate the church from a narrow-minded view or a distorted attitude to human sexuality and pleasure. However, as long as sexuality remains taboo in a cultural context, it remains an unparalleled means for triggering liberating laughter.[318]

If laughter in itself is the goal, then the triggering factor is essentially irrelevant, and therein lies the truly unsettling aspect of laughter: not that it reveals this or that specific hypocrisy or taboo, but that laughter, as the goal, sanctifies almost any means to elicit it. This is the radical price that Prütting is willing

---

316   Already in the introduction (52–61), Prütting presents in a brief overview his campaign against reductionist theories of laughter, which is then elaborated in great detail in the concluding systematic section of the work, spanning approximately 200 pages, on the 'Essence, Forms, and Functions of Laughter'.
317   Jacobelli 1992, 66. Her countryman, Balzaretti, has written an article questioning Jacobelli's methodology in focusing so strongly and exclusively on the sexual interpretations of the ritual laughter in connection with the Demeter and Baubo story. When it comes to such fertility rites, Balzaretti suggests an alternative path in order to understand what is going on as he observes: 'why not interpret agricultural fertility rituals taking into account that reproductive systems are also excretory systems? [...] Taking this first observation into account, Baubo's gesture ceases to have a sexual implication and refers to the insulting meaning of this exhibition: perhaps a threat to cover the recipient of the gesture with excrement'. 2016, 391.
318   Prütting 2013, 570.

to pay, as he believes it is the prerequisite for laughter to fulfil the pattern of tension-buildup-breakthrough-ecstasy that underlies the 'uroboric impulse'.[319]

As a sort of apotheosis of the conceivable arguments in defence of Easter Laughter, Prütting draws the full consequence of his interpretation of the essence of laughter and not only makes laughter permissible but also a genuine form of *imitatio Christi*:

> From this perspective, Easter Laughter is actually a form of following Christ, as strange as this may sound and as foreign as this form of imitation may appear to modern Christians, because in the form of laughter it participates in and experiences Christ's death and resurrection, thus making it, indeed, [...] something 'distinctly Christian' or, more precisely, *also* 'something distinctly Christian'.[320]

There may very well be those that wish to argue that Prütting is simply going much too far, but even though it is far from an infallible defence, his form of creative speculation is preferable to the scientific theories from the turn of the previous century that, for example, sought to explain the vigorous movements of laughter in an evolutionary manner. According to such theories, this supposedly dates back to the time when we were still living up in the trees, and where the muscle contractions helped us hold onto branches and not fall into the waiting jaws of predators on the ground while laughing.[321]

---

319   *Ibid.*, 571.
320   *Ibid.*, 573.
321   Richard Keller Simon (1945–2005) concludes his chapter, 'Survival of the Wittiest', on the scientific study of laughter, which gained momentum in the latter half of the 19th century, with this gem of a proposal that was put forth by the American surgeon, George Washington Crile (1864–1943), in his book *Man. An Adaptive Mechanism* (1916), as cited in Simon 1985, 209 f.

Chapter IV: Did Jesus Laugh? An Essay on the Cultural, Ecclesiastical, and Theological Transformation of Laughter

As mentioned in the introduction, the purpose of this chapter is to broaden our perspective on Easter Laughter, placing it in the context of the more general question of the relationship between laughter, church, and theology. For this purpose it is appropriate to revisit the Early Church Fathers' inquiries into Jesus' laughter. Even if the question was purely rhetorical at the time, we will engage with it historically and systematically. For what do we really mean when we ask whether Jesus *laughed*? What kind of answer are we expecting? Looking for? Hoping for? Begging for?

To this, the short and simple answer is: no, and we can consider ourselves fortunate for that! However, the slightly longer answer would be: yes, *naturally*, he could have done so, but the Good News is that Matthew, Mark, Luke, and John omitted to mention it. According to tradition, Jesus did not laugh, but he began to do so 150 years ago – give and take a few decades. This belief arose because people became more aware that the answer to the question of Jesus' laughter depends on how we understand laughter. The crucial question, therefore, may not be whether Jesus laughed, but rather how he laughed or could laugh. Did he laugh like his father in the Old Testament? Or did he not do that at all and therefore could we, as humans, come to laugh in a new way – even if it took us X amount of centuries to realise it?

1. Did Jesus Laugh? Yes, *Naturally*! (He Could Easily Have Done So)

In essence, there should be no discussion at all if only we were capable of thinking in logical syllogisms. According to Aristotle, humans are laughing beings. According to the Epistle to the Romans, God 'sent his own Son in the likeness of sinful flesh' (8:3b). Ergo, Jesus laughed. So why does the New Testament not mention it? As we know, the strength of syllogisms depends on the validity of their premises. If this particular syllogism does not hold, is it because Aristotle's definition is incorrect, or is it because there are limitations to Jesus' humanity? Was he not fully incarnate? If the limitation lies in the clarification in the Epistle to the Hebrews that Jesus 'has been tempted in every way, just as we are – yet he did not sin' (4:15 *NIV*), does it imply that if Jesus did not laugh, it is because laughter is sinful?

It is possible to form a historical and systematic overview of the responses based on which aspect of the syllogism is questioned. Amidst the overwhelming historical consensus to the contrary, it should not be overlooked that there are written sources that are just as old, if not older, than Chrysostom's sermons from the end of the 4th century, where the syllogism does not seem to be problematised at all. In fact, there are explicit and emphatic accounts of Jesus' loud laughter. Or rather: the laughter of Christ. In the version of the 'Apocalypse of Peter', which comes from the discoveries in Nag Hammadi, the apostle receives a vision of the impending crucifixion and simultaneously receives an interpretation of the scene from Christ himself. The disturbing focal point of the vision is that next to the one hanging on the cross, there stands a cheerful figure laughing:

> When he [Christ, 'the living Jesus'] said this, I saw him apparently being arrested by them. I said, 'What do I see, Lord? Is it really you they are seizing, and are you holding on to me? And who is the one smiling and laughing above the cross? Is it someone else whose feet and hands they are hammering?'
>
> The Savior said to me, 'The one you see smiling and laughing above the cross is the living Jesus. The one into whose hands and feet they are driving nails is his fleshly part, the substitute for him. They are putting to shame the one who came into being in the likeness of the living Jesus. Look at him and look at me.'
>
> When I looked, I said, 'Lord, no one sees you. Let's get out of here.'
>
> He answered me, 'I told you they are blind. Forget about them. Look at how they do not know what they are saying. For they have put to shame the son of their own glory instead of the one who serves me.'
>
> Then I saw someone about to approach us who looked like the one laughing above the cross, but this one was intertwined with holy spirit, and he was the Savior. And there was an unspeakably bright light surrounding them and a multitude of ineffable and invisible angels praising them. When the one who glories was revealed, I myself saw him.

To dispel any doubt about the nature of the Saviour's laughter, it is firmly established at the end of the text: 'he is laughing at their lack of perception, knowing that they were born blind.'[322] It is the condescending mockery of the one in the

---

322 Meyer 2007, 495 f. This particular form of non-heartfelt (mocking) laughter is found as a recurring theme in the *Gospel of Judas*, where Jesus both instructs the disciples, rebukes Judas, and combats the cosmic powers ('the wandering stars') through frequent outbursts of laughter at the ignorance surrounding him, 2006, 21, 24, 31, and 42. For a couple of fine articles full of perspectives and with additional relevant quotes from gnostic texts, see Bröker 1979 and Stroumsa 2004.

know towards the ignorant, and when a crucified person can overcome pain with a laugh, it is not an expression of the gallows humour that stoically accepts defeat or transcends the moment with a sovereign view of the bigger picture (nor is it part of the script for *Life of Brian*, 1979!). The explanation, instead, is that the pierced body is essentially an empty shell, the *earthly* Jesus, while the one speaking to Peter is Christ ('the living Jesus'), an untouched spiritual being. Indeed, in every way, it is a gnostic laughter, and as such it is able to follow the syllogism through a radical (heretical) reinterpretation of the incarnation.[323]

A less drastic method to adhere to the syllogism consists of expanding the field of relevant terms. Just as we can make a major point out of the minor difference between 'he who is not with me is against me' (Mt 12:30) vs. 'he who is not against us is for us' (Mk 9:40), we can approach the problem of the New Testament reticence about Jesus' laughter in two fundamentally different ways. 'If laughter is not explicitly associated with Jesus, it should be avoided' vs. 'if laughter is not explicitly prohibited by Jesus, it is allowed' – or more cautiously formulated: '*can* laughter be permitted'. *E silentio* arguments are not sufficient in themselves, as they can point in multiple directions. If we happen to lean towards the latter option, we cannot let our opinion be dependent upon an authoritative prohibition nor an explicit permission, but are left to interpret, evaluate, and take responsibility ourselves. At the same time as it cannot be denied that the New Testament does not contain a single direct statement about Jesus laughing, the gospels nevertheless describe him with other nouns and verbs that in every other context we would associate with an internal or even external form of laughter.

---

323 If we can trust Willis Barnstone's (b. 1927) audacious attempt to reconstruct a passage in another text from the Nag Hammadi discoveries, laughter is not only connected with Jesus at his crucifixion but already seems to be a crucial part of his own baptism: 'As soon as Christ went down into the water / he came out laughing'. Here, too, it is the same distinct type of laughter as in the 'Apocalypse of Peter', for 'he came out laughing at everything in this world / not because he thought it a trifle, but out of contempt'. Barnstone's courage is not that he dares to present a poetical version of 'The Gospel of Philip's coptic text, but that he so persuasively fills in the many blanks in the heavily damaged text. Whether or not the reconstruction is reliable, the text deserves to be included here because of its striking opening lines that fortunately have come down to us intact: 'The lord [Christ] said it perfectly: "Some have entered the kingdom of heaven laughing."' Barnstone's version appears in 'The Gospel of Philip' 2009, 306, whereas the fragmented text can be seen in 1988, 154.

One way to 'prepare the ground' for associating Jesus with such a degree of what some might perceive as an overly human sensitivity could be to pose this question: if it had not been explicitly stated twice that Jesus wept (Lk 19:41 and Jn 11:35; cf. Heb 5:7), would it not have been an equally open question whether we could expect such human (sentimental?) reactions from the Lord? The point of this thought experiment is not to claim that it was only Jesus' reaction to encountering Jerusalem and Lazarus with sorrow that became the foundation for the emergence of the long tradition of 'tear theology'.[324] Even without Jesus' example,[325] there are sufficient good reasons why a theology of tears developed among the Desert Fathers and in the monasteries, such as contemplative devotion to the crucifixion, meditation on our own sinfulness, fear of tempting demons, and dread of the Judgment on the last day.[326]

Among the other terms attributed to Jesus by the evangelists, there are probably none that unambiguously imply laughter; but once the presence of his tears has paved the way for attributing ordinary emotions to him, it is not entirely unreasonable to apply the same measure of human recognisability to the other

---

324   Cf. Steidle 1938b; Lot-Borodine 1939, and Schreiner 2002. In the second of Heinrich Innichenhöferus' (b. 1602, fl. 1623–42) published sermons, where he promises on the title page to discuss nineteen types of laughter, he also takes the time to develop an eightfold taxonomy of tears in the Bible. He not only focuses on genuine tears of repentance (*lacrymæ veræ poenitentiæ*, Mt 26:75) and crocodile tears (*lacrymæ fraudulentiæ*, Jer 41:6), but also tears of anger (*lacrymæ privatæ iracundiæ*, Gen 27:38) and tears of temptation and mental distress (*lacrymæ tentationis & mentis angustiæ*, Ps 32:3). Tears in and by themselves are not enough to move God, as He does not like all kinds. Innichenhöferus 1629, 26–7.

325   Cf. St Paul's self-testimony, 'I have served the Lord [...] with tears' (Acts 20:19), and the figure of 'the Lord's Suffering Servant' from the prophet Isaiah (53:3). In English this figure is often translated as 'Man of Sorrows', which more clearly emphasises the emotional dimension of suffering than 'Man of Pain' (German: *Schmerzensmann*).

326   Cf. Gilhus 1995, 64. To avoid discriminating against laughter more than necessary, it should be noted that it was not only loud *laughter* that was frowned upon, as there could also be a need to distinguish between quiet and audible *weeping*. The latter could be perceived as a somewhat overly demonstrative display of the monk's awareness of sin, and in the close community of the monastery, it could lead to complaints from the brethren if they were constantly subjected to loud weeping and streams of tears mixing with their food. However, if anyone were to argue that it went too far when Abbot Arsenius (350/354–445) was known to have cried his eyelids away, his contemporary, Abbot Poimen (340–450), defended him by saying that if we do not willingly mourn ourselves in this life, we may end up crying even more out of necessity in eternity. Steidle 1938b, 182–4.

emotional expressions. Even without being able to make audible laughter plausible, paying attention to these details can at least contribute to a more nuanced picture of Jesus. While the Suffering Servant may be the most important image of Christ from a soteriological perspective, did he also appear that way when he attended the wedding at Cana or sat at the table with tax collectors and sinners?

The two most interesting terms are 'joy' (χαρά) and 'rejoice' (ἀγαλλιάω), both of which appear relatively frequently and are used to describe listeners, disciples, and characters in various parables, as well as Jesus himself on a few occasions. It may not seem particularly significant that Jesus speaks of 'my joy', since the focus in both instances clearly lies on the disciples' reception of this joy (Jn 15:11; 17:13). However, highlighting the usage of these terms in John is due to the same Gospel's indirect indication that joy in this context is not merely an internal, inaudible, and perhaps even invisible sentiment. For it resembles an intriguingly Johannine 'realised eschatological' reinterpretation of the Beatitude on laughter in the Gospel of Luke ('Blessed are you who weep now, for you shall laugh', Lk 6:21b), when Jesus prepares his disciples for his imminent departure ('A little while, and you will see me no longer', Jn 16:16) with this consolation: 'Truly, truly, I say to you, you will weep and lament, but the world will rejoice. You will be sorrowful, but your sorrow will turn into joy' (Jn 16:20 *ESV*). (Of course, it is also possible to interpret those words so that instead of adding sound to joy, John rather silences the laughter of Luke!).

In Luke, the even more emotionally powerful word 'rejoice' is connected with Jesus in one particular instance. Although it is not articulated as triumphantly as in the 'Apocalypse of Peter', there is a certain thematic kinship between the spiritual laughter of Christ in the Nag Hammadi text, mocking the ignorance of the unenlightened, and the exultation of Jesus in the Gospel of Luke (10:21 *ESV*): 'In that same hour he rejoiced in the Holy Spirit and said: "I thank you, Father, […] that you have hidden these things from the wise and understanding and revealed them to little children".'

If the aforementioned difference between Matthew and Mark seems too subtle to be exploited in this way, we can instead ask whether the silence about Jesus' laughter is a deliberate punchline or a careless oversight, a blunder. Expressed in this manner, the question becomes closely related to the tension between St Paul and the Evangelists in their way of proclaiming the Message, and here we are primarily thinking of genre. Put bluntly, the question of Jesus' laughter feels far from urgent, not to say outright irrelevant, if all we need to nourish our faith is St Paul's declaration that 'even though we have known Christ according to the flesh, yet now we know Him thus no longer' (2 Cor 5:16 *NKJ*). This seems to have been the guiding principle for the Early Church confessions, which only concern themselves with the fact that Jesus was 'born of the Virgin Mary, suffered under Pontius Pilate, was crucified, died, and was buried'. A New Critic would knowingly and approvingly give the nod, as here there is no risk of committing the 'biographical fallacy', that is, using a person's (the author's) life and actions as evidence for the 'work'. However, if the Evangelists pry open the door to this 'fallacy' with their stories about Jesus' birth and early childhood, the apocryphal narratives then fling the door wide open by providing all those graphic details that the medieval church plays and the naturalistic art of the Renaissance sought to capture, and which subsequent 'Life of Jesus'-research in every era attempted to harvest scientifically. And here, laughter reappears as something relevant to consider.

It is important to remind ourselves that despite the many details about Jesus' life and teachings in the gospels, they should not be regarded as exhaustive biographies. There are many additional details about Jesus that posterity might have a great interest in but that none of the four Evangelists remembered, or wanted to inform us about. These might include something as mundane as his appearance, even more details about his behaviour and attitudes, or some general information about all the years between his birth and his first appearance in Galilee (except for the brief glimpse of a tweener visiting Jerusalem). If it were not for the fact that later generations have sought to base their own – and others' – way of life on Jesus' example in as much detail as possible, the absence of such material would have been harmless, at most regrettable, but hardly a catastrophe. This helps to explain the great fascination and perpetual disagreement about the authenticity of alternative sources such as the alleged eyewitness report of the Lentulus letter, King Abgar's Mandylion, Veronica's Veil, or the Shroud of Turin. As Kranz soberly points out: just because the gospels do not mention anything about Jesus' hair, it does not necessarily mean that he was bald; but between the lines it is implied that if such information had been provided, Jesus' hairstyle would surely have been elevated as the norm for true Christians (and in that case, Lentulus would come to the rescue with his unique information about both hairstyle and hair colour).[327] The question at hand is: if we do not turn silence about hair into

---

327 According to Pilate's apocryphal predecessor, Jesus was said to have shoulder-length wavy hair with a middle parting and coloured like a ripe hazelnut (*coloris nucis avellane premature*). The supposed governor also confirms that Jesus 'occasionally wept but never laughed' (*aliquando flevit, sed nunquam risit*), Lentulus 1913, 37, line 6 f. and 17 f.; 1984, 66–7.

a requirement for combating hair growth as a condition for discipleship, why impose other demands on laughter?[328]

It can quickly become absurd if we continue pursuing paths like these, and to avoid that we can do one of two things. We can either try to bring such speculations under control by seeking more credible historical testimonies than those found in the many apocryphal texts (and images) that are more than willing to fill the gaps opened by our insatiable curiosity; or we can block the entire project by simply adopting a historical-philosophical and theological distinction: what can be known vs. what is worth knowing? To make a judgment about the colour and style of hair or the tone and volume of Jesus' laughter we do not need to rely on an exotic text fragment waiting to be found, or jump to a conclusion based on a shrewd interpretation of, for example, the reported gossip about Jesus being a 'glutton and drunkard' (Mt 11:19) or his lax attitude towards alcohol at Cana (Jn 2:1-10). Instead, we can assess the syllogism based on a holistic consideration, an overarching Christological and anthropological evaluation: how literally should the Incarnation be understood, and can we imagine a human being who does not laugh without thereby becoming a monster?

i. How Literally Should We Understand the Incarnation?

Does the question of Jesus' laughter really have any significant relevance to the understanding of the Incarnation? Is it not a pseudo-problem that has arisen by blowing the silence of the Evangelists and other New Testament writers out of proportion? Perhaps we are not even reaching these anthropological and Christological heights, for is it not conceivable that the silence about Jesus' laughter is neither a sign of being inattentive nor a trivial matter (like the colour of his hair), nor by any means intended as a theological point, but simply a matter of modesty and common decency?

The problem with understanding the scope of this final consideration is that our time has almost completely lost the sense that laughter as such can be offensive and something that a polite writer should avoid mentioning. To get a sense of what was historically at stake, we can – at the risk of revealing more about this author's own limits than those of our culture – rephrase 'did Jesus laugh?' into the question 'did Jesus shit?'. If it is difficult not to be offended by the directness of that question, it is worth reflecting on what is at play in such a reaction. There is a comedic point in posing the question so vulgarly, in the most literal sense of the word: lavatorial. Substantively (that is, theologically), the problem remains

---

328 Kranz 1970, 60.

the same even if we dress it up with a euphemistic paraphrase: did Jesus go apart not only to pray (e.g. Mt 14:23), but also to relieve himself? (See the prophet Elijah's lavatorial satire against the Baal priests' inability to ignite fire on Mount Carmel, which he attributes to their god 'being occupied or relieving himself', 1 Kings 18:27 *LSB*; cf. Dt 23:13–4.)

Undoubtedly, it *also* concerns good manners; but if that were all that was at stake, we could bypass it just as easily as we can rephrase the vulgar to a suitable good form for any era, changing 'to shit' to 'to relieve oneself', 'to laugh' to 'a slight curl of the lips'. However, behind it lies the crucial question as far as the Incarnation goes: did he even do it? Journalist Ejvind Larsen (b. 1936) obviously wanted to be completely certain of driving his point home when he once conversed with the host in the Danish Radio programme 'Sunday Morning – About Ourselves and What We Believe In' about the opening verse of John's First Epistle. It is clearly important to John to emphasise that the appearance of the Word was not just something ethereal but highly corporeal and sensuous: 'That which was from the beginning, which we have heard, which we have seen with our eyes, which we have looked upon and our hands have touched' (*NKJ*), after which Larsen extrapolated: 'that which we sat together with on the toilet'.[329]

When we refer to this as a 'comedic' point, it is because just such a clash between the exalted nature of the Johannine and the down-to-earth nature of the Larsenian serves as a counterpart to the generic differences between tragedies and comedies which may appear superficial, yet has rich perspectives. As the literary scholar George Steiner (1926–2020) succinctly put it:

> Comedy is the art of the lesser orders of men. It tends to dramatise those material circumstances and bodily functions which are banished from the tragic stage. The comic personage does not transcend the flesh; he is engrossed in it. There are no lavatories in tragic palaces, but from its very dawn, comedy has had use for chamber pots.[330]

In light of this point, it is significant that at the same time as Oecolampadius moves to Basel, Matthias Grünewald (*c.* 1475-*c.* 1528) works on the Isenheim

---

329   In all likelihood it will not diminish the shock-effect of Larsen's punchline, but once again a historical perspective may put it in context. Where most of us react with disgust to news stories about primitive prisons or detention camps where inmates have no access to a visibly shielded toilet, because we find this tantamount to a breach of human rights, it may be quite an eye-opener to visit the archaeological excavations in Ephesus and see the public toilets, possibly dating back to when St Paul visited the city, with dozens of holes in long rows only about a foot apart.
330   Steiner 1961, 247.

Altarpiece from 1512–16, where the painting of Mary with the newborn Jesus precisely announces the fullness of the incarnation by placing a chamber pot at the Virgin's feet.

Milan Kundera (1929–2023) presented, albeit in the form of a novel, some similar reflections in *The Unbearable Lightness of Being* (1984), which he even directly connects with theological questions:

> When I was small and would leaf through the Old Testament retold for children and illustrated in engravings by Gustave Doré, I saw the Lord God standing on a cloud. He was an old man with eyes, nose, and a long beard, and I would say to myself that if He had a mouth, He had to eat. And if He ate, He had intestines. But that thought always gave me a fright, because even though I come from a family that was not particularly religious, I felt the idea of a divine intestine to be sacrilegious.
>
> Spontaneously, without any theological training, I, a child, grasped the incompatibility of God and shit and thus came to question the basic thesis of Christian anthropology, namely, that man was created in God's image. Either/or: either man was created in God's image – and God has intestines! – or God lacks intestines and man is not like Him.
>
> The ancient Gnostics felt as I did at the age of five. In the second century, the great Gnostic master Valentinus [c. 100–c. 180] resolved the damnable dilemma by claiming that Jesus 'ate and drank, but did not defecate'.
>
> Shit is a more onerous theological problem than is evil. Since God gave man freedom, we can, if need be, accept the idea that He is not responsible for man's crimes. The responsibility for shit, however, rests entirely with Him, the Creator of Man.[331]

This internationally acclaimed work by the Czech author is often cited for his famous reflections on kitsch, the most well-known being about the two tears

---

331 Kundera 1999, 243. A few years earlier, another novelist, David Lodge (b. 1935), wrote a novel about a group of Catholic students coming of age, *How Far Can You Go?* Here Lodge displays a related sensitivity to these matters by letting one of his characters, Dennis, invent a whole new concept of 'reversed transubstantiation' in order to extricate himself from his disturbing meditations when participating in communion. Dennis and his friends have been taught that Christ truly enters the bread and wine for it to become his body and blood, and to stop them from asking about when this happens or how literally it is to be understood, they have been told that this is all a mystery. But that does not stop Dennis! 'In fact, the more intently you think about the mystery, the more irreverent and disedifying your thoughts are apt to become. At what point, Dennis cannot help wondering, does the miracle of transubstantiation reverse itself, since it cannot be that Christ submits himself to the indignities of human digestion and excretion? Is it as the host begins to dissolve on the tongue, as it passes the epiglottis, or as it travels down the oesophagus that Christ jumps from His wheaten vehicle and into your soul? Such speculations are not conducive to pious recollection.' Lodge 1981, 19.

(the first one being sentimental, the second one only falls after being aware that everyone else feels the same, thus turning emotive art into kitsch). Just before that example, Kundera provides an even shorter definition: an aesthetic ideal of a world without shit is kitsch.[332] We can dismiss the author's metaphysical speculations as childishly anthropomorphic (like those of the novel's 5-year-old), but it becomes much harder to avoid the suspicion of kitsch if we apply the 'incompatibility' to the Son of God, who according to the classical doctrine about his hypostatic union was not only fully God but also fully human.[333] It is difficult to overlook the fact that the examples of paintings and sculptures depicting a Jesus with a hearty laugh in the past 52 (!) years or so are painfully kitschy when considered as art.[334] But is the idea of a Jesus who does not laugh the true theological kitsch?

---

332   Kundera 1999, 248 and 246 respectively.
333   Although Luther attributes the words to the 'Turk', he continues with his usual frankness when highlighting this theological point in all its provocative and irrational radicality: 'God alone must teach it through His Word. The Turk declares: "You will never persuade me to believe that He is God who is born of a woman, descends from heaven, lies in the Virgin Mary's womb for nine months, soils and wets his cradle [Luther's German words deserve a direct and somewhat less delicate translation: 'shits and pisses'], and later dies the wretched death of a thief and criminal on the cross! Could such a one be God?" That is the view firmly held by the Turks and also by the Jews. They reject God's Word. For their belief is based on nothing but reason, by means of which they make bold to judge the Christian faith. If they are to believe that the Christ who was crucified is the Son of God, and that no other than He who was born thus and was crucified thus is God, it is necessary for God the Heavenly Father to teach and draw them. Otherwise, without His enlightenment, all will be in vain. You must cling to His Word. They, however, would pass judgment on Scripture and say: "That is true, and that is false". In brief, you must become God's pupil. If God does not grant you the Word and faith, you will not believe it.' Luther 1530b, 157; 1959, 103.
334   This calculation of years is based on the time of writing these lines in 2024, for there is much to suggest that it was actually the Canadian Willis Wheatley (fl. 1973) who started the flood of modern attempts to depict a Jesus leaving absolutely no doubt about him laughing. In 1973 Wheatley was commissioned by the United Church of Canada to submit some new sketches of Jesus, and the one entitled 'Jesus Christ, Liberator' turned out to be a true trailblazer, later mainly known as 'The Laughing Christ' or simply 'Laughing Jesus'. Not everyone may agree that Wheatley's portrait is kitsch, nor for that matter those by the many epigones; but that judgement about its artistic value is in no way intended as a debunking of its *pastoral* value, as evidenced by the many testimonies to be found on the internet about people's reaction to these images.

To clarify the symbolic value in the discussion of whether we imagine ourselves able to hear Jesus laugh – adapting one of Hamlet's idioms – in our 'mind's ear', it can be helpful to turn our gaze towards painting (and sculpture) during a period that, purely coincidentally yet oddly enough, happens to overlap with Oecolampadius' lifetime. Here, we can closely examine a quite parallel issue: why does Michelangelo (1475–1564) omit to provide his statue, *The Risen Christ* (1514–20), with a loincloth – the loincloth that reproductions in later times carefully add, and which still today covers the genitals of the original in Santa Maria sopra Minerva in Rome? The connection between these two questions can be seen literally moulded into terracotta in Antonio Rossellino's (1427–79) statuette, *Madonna with Child* (*c.* 1465). It has become famous for depicting Jesus with a smile so broad that it is commonly referred to as *The Virgin with the Laughing Child*, which is also how the Victoria & Albert Museum labels it on their website. The laughter is so exceptional that fame attaches itself to this detail to such an extent that most people forget to lower their eyes and notice that Jesus at the same time is lifting up his blouse and exposing his penis and testicles. The motif is not uncommon, at least not during an approximately 300-year period from the mid-13th century onwards (with some of the most remarkable examples produced in the first half of the 16th century), where it is instead so frequent and demonstrative that art historian Leo Steinberg (1920–2011) has argued that iconography, in line with *ostentatio vulnerum*, should recognise an *ostentatio genitalium* as an independent artistic motif.[335]

A difficult and no doubt also challenging first task is to penetrate the veil of good taste and look the depicted image in the eye; the critical task is then to identify it as a motif and subsequently interpret it. It appears that the former task has not been the least troublesome, for when Steinberg published an updated version of his book, *The Sexuality of Christ in Renaissance Art and in Modern Oblivion* (1983) in 1996, it had swelled to almost double the number of pages in an attempt to counter the fierce reviews from colleagues and to present documentation for his observations through additional images (he eventually registered around 2,000 works). Viewed from the sidelines it appears that at least some of the attacks on Steinberg had overlooked the most important aspect in our context, namely the interpretation. For even when Steinberg, undoubtedly as the most startling and histrionic discovery, finds close to a dozen paintings from the period 1500–40 of the adult Jesus where the genitals are covered by a

---

335   Steinberg 1996, 3 and throughout (*ostentatio*), 19–21 (Michelangelo), and 22 (Rossellino).

cloth which seems to emphasise rather than conceal his erect member, it would be a gross misunderstanding to equate Steinberg with, for example, the Danish artist Jens Jørgen Thorsen's (1932–2000) project to make a movie about Jesus' sex life or even Nikos Kazantzakis' (1883–1957) novel *The Last Temptation of Christ* (1951). To be sure, not out of puritanical prudishness, but because for Steinberg it is about the unique collision between the theology of incarnation and the sovereign mastery of naturalism in art.[336] This is not only the result of newly-acquired technical skills but also because 'realism' had become an aesthetic ideal reaching a level where artists had to decide whether the Lord might have trimmed his nails – as artists were now able to let close-ups reveal them to be both too long or bitten down.[337]

Nevertheless, 'realism' should be in quotation marks because, just as the *display of wounds* was not intended as a lesson in anatomy, the intention behind the display of the genitals was also not concerned with Jesus' sexuality. According to Steinberg's interpretation, we should rather understand the exposed genitals in parallel with the well-known motif of the Virgin's exposed breast (*Madonna lactans*), which emphasises Jesus' humanity by showing us a god who does not live on ambrosia and nectar but on breast milk. The hyper-naturalistic details,

---

336   The motif of a powerless figure with an erect phallus is so strange and rare that it is indeed difficult to even acknowledge what the eyes seem to see. It is especially in connection with Ludwig Krug's (*c.* 1488–1532) *Man of Sorrows* (*c.* 1520) and Maerten van Heemskerck (1498–1574), who, over a period between *c.* 1525 and 1550, produce variations of the same motif, where it is difficult to avoid interpreting the bulge or knot on the loincloth as something other than just that, a random bulge or knot. Steinberg admits that the recognition of the motif is also hindered by the fact that he has not been able to find any contemporary written support for the painters' choice of motif. The only parallel can be found in a pre-Christian context, where Osiris, the Egyptian god of the afterlife, is depicted with a limb as stiff as a lance. On the one hand, Steinberg insists that the motif cannot possibly be intended as blasphemy, which is why we are obliged to inquire about a possible 'orthodox' interpretation. His suggestion is that the erection must be conceived as a symbolic expression of the return of the life force after burial. On the other hand, Steinberg understands well that the motif did not become a trend, as it ended up being an unsuccessful symbol: 'I do believe that Heemskerck's images of the *Man of Sorrows* were conceived with a Christian will and *de profundis*; they impress me as desperate raids on the inexpressible – the unknowable mystery of a god's unmanned body in its resurgence. Nevertheless, they remain deeply shocking, their vision of a settled Christ, alone in sterile, self-centering masculinity, seems to us – and must have seemed to most artists – a miscarried symbol.' *Ibid.*, 83–9, the quote: 89.

337   *Ibid.*, 16.

especially in Renaissance art, should not be *reduced* to descriptive naturalism, but must be understood as a figurative symbol that is as rich in symbolic effect as the stylised and non-naturalistic icons of the Eastern Church. In this sense, the efforts of the visual artists fit into an era characterised, for example, by the pictorial richness of the biblical retellings in the apocrypha, the religious plays associated with the Feast of Corpus Christi and other church holidays, and especially the emphasis on Jesus' humanity in Franciscan devotional theology.

In language, we can easily create paradoxes through duplications and negations, as when the apostle writes 'tempted [...], yet without sin' (Heb 4:15), and when the Confession allows us to say in unison 'perfect in divinity, perfect in humanity' – or with an example from the subject matter of this book: 'a silent laughter of the heart'; but how does something like that look or sound? A particularly beautiful example of the difficulty is found in the Gospel of Luke's use of the verb σκιρτάω, which means 'to leap (for joy)', for can we imagine a more outward sign of joy (and perhaps laughter) than this gymnastics of emotion, and therefore something that should be easy to make a painting of? But how does one do that, when the entire movement is wrapped up in Elizabeth's womb (Lk 1:41.44)?

Steinberg's striking consideration is that the painters of the Western Church in the early and high Renaissance did not particularly concern themselves with depicting the divinity of Jesus, as they could allow themselves to assume it to be generally believed, but instead focused all their abilities on making the miracle visible that God's Son was fully human. They may have succeeded to such a degree, writes Steinberg, that they defeated themselves in relation to a more secularised posterity, which now only had eyes for the all too human attributes and perceived them as quasi-photographic realism.[338]

In simple terms, the paradox was artistically resolved on the one hand by making the newborn Jesus as natural as possible, including normal human genitalia. The cardinal point in Steinberg's interpretation, however, is his insistence that this is neither an expression of a (classical Graeco-Roman) fascination with the naked body, nor a kind of accidental or indiscreet oversight (failing to properly cover the child). Instead, Jesus' genitalia are made visible through 'a dramatised nakedness choreographed as an active withdrawal of garments'.[339] This is evidenced by the many different hands (the Virgin's, the child's own, one of the Three Wise Men's, or the Father's in some representations of the Throne of

---

338 *Ibid.*, 6.
339 *Ibid.*, 35.

Grace) that are close to Jesus' groin, which in earlier and later periods would have covered his male organ but now draw attention to it and often seem to have the function of demonstratively pointing: look, how incarnate he was! On the other hand, Jesus' divinity is also displayed in a natural (!) way (in addition to the presence of adoring angels or halos) by making the child unnaturally (!) mature for his age. This happens both physically, as a newborn baby being able to stand or having an almost athletic body, and mentally, when, for example, he sits on his mother's lap and tellingly points to a verse in an open Bible.[340]

In an excursion on 'dogmas as pictorial objects'[341] Steinberg refers to the smile of the infant Jesus as one of these unnaturally natural signs of divinity. There are a great majority of genre paintings of Madonna with Child where the mood of both Mary and Jesus is sufficiently melancholic to signal a clear foreshadowing of the Passion. However, there are enough exceptions to indicate that likewise the smile serves a symbolic function. Mother and son are not amused by a random joke, but this child is capable of breaking Aristotle's doctrine of the 40 days, which signals his unique humanity (as with Zoroaster, cf. note 295). Does the smile also contain an augury or message? We could interpret it as a hint about what comes after the Passion, the heavenly joy and perhaps even laughter (in line with the eschatological interpretation of the Beatitudes in the Gospel of Luke, 6:21). However, Steinberg dares to suggest a combination of enjoyment both here and there:

> When a laughing Christ Child appears [...] the painter is telling us that he ([...]) imagines the nursling jubilant at his Incarnation, laughing for the very reason that the heavens rejoice. It is even conceivable that – [...] – God enjoys being man, tasting the goodness of his creation and the excellence of human milk. One thing is certain: the hilarity is projected as consonant with, better still, as indicative of the mystery.[342]

ii. Can We Even Imagine a Human Being Not Laughing?

We could put a quick stop to that question by referring to the fact, as we saw in the previous chapter, that the Earl of Chesterfield apparently had no problem imagining just that. However, the subject is still worth considering, given that the good Earl is hardly representative of a modern understanding of normal

---

340 *Ibid.*, 123 and 236.
341 'Such pictures project a new iconography that is neither iconic nor narrative, nor linked to a liturgical feast. They are historiated emblems designed to convey the central mystery of the Creed.' *Ibid.*, 122.
342 *Ibid.*, 129.

human behaviour. Already in antiquity laughter was perceived as a natural part of human nature, but in a Christian context St Paul's words provide the critical focal point with his meditation on the difficult interplay between good and evil, spirit and body (Rom 7:14–25), the point of which in this context could be translated as: indeed, laughter is natural, but not everything natural is good! This clearly applied to St Paul, as it applies to every Christian, but what about Jesus and his full humanity? In simplified terms the Church Fathers and Scholastics came up with two strategies to reconcile themselves with the idea that Jesus naturally laughed: either the prelapsarian solution or the *capax*-solution.

To lead us into the first solution, we can refer to the Madonna and Child motif, which has been prominent in the previous section, for does not every experience tell us what the proverb formulates in its anonymous wisdom: we must learn to crawl before we can walk? Think back to the 10, 100, or 1,000 paintings we might be familiar with of the Madonna and Child: the little Jesus engages in almost all natural activities (only some of them unnaturally early for his age); but has there ever been a painter who depicted Jesus crawling on all fours?! It is once again Steinberg we can thank for this curious yet extremely striking observation, and although arguably the majority of painters, intuitively and without in-depth theological studies, have refrained from such a representation, Steinberg actually succeeds in finding a plausible theological argument that a crawling Jesus is an impossible, if not necessarily explicitly forbidden, motif.

Steinberg zeroes in on certain passages in Augustine's book on the significance of infant baptism for the forgiveness of sins, where Augustine reflects on the great difference between the ability of newborn humans and animals to fend for themselves, and where the helplessness of the little child is interpreted as part of the order of the Fall. Just as Adam was immediately able to walk around and name the animals in Paradise, Adam and Eve's babies would have had the same abilities … if they had managed to procreate before the story with the Serpent. (But did they actually have sex in Paradise? This will be discussed later!) The possibly even more remarkable point made by the ancient Church Father is that he does not attribute this helplessness to the newborn Jesus, for he (Jesus) only *seems* to depend on the help of the Madonna and others (contrary to the interpretation above of the significance of the *Nursing Madonna* motif). The emphasis on 'seems' is taken from Steinberg's presentation, for as he very relevantly points out, the corresponding Greek word is δοκέω, which is recognised in the designation of the heresy that denies Jesus' full incarnation, Docetism.[343]

---

343   Ibid., 235.

The simple (!) solution to this problem is the assertion that Jesus' humanity should be understood as like Adam's ... but, NB, Adam before the Fall, in his prelapsarian state. This is truly elegant in all its simplicity, but perhaps so simple that we may feel cheated by the logic. Nevertheless, Steinberg addresses similar issues in several other contexts, where not only Augustine but also his contemporaries and theologians of the following thousand years seem to resort to precisely this solution. For example, when Hilary of Poitiers (*c.* 310-*c.* 367) somehow extends the point into Jesus' adult life in his radical distinction between the corporeality of Jesus and that of human beings by emphasising that when Jesus drank and ate he did not give in to hunger and thirst but consumed liquid and food almost out of politeness so as not to break local customs: 'when He ate and drank, it was a concession, not to His own necessities, but to our habits' (*vel cum potum et cibum accepit, non se necessitati corporis, sed consuetudini tribuit*[344]). As stated in a fantastic supplement to this line of thinking, Jesus, according to Chrysostom, does not break his fast after 40 days due to his succumbing to the demands of the body, but in order to cunningly deceive Satan into believing that he was *merely* human, as well as humbly refusing to surpass the exemplary fasts of Moses and Elijah.[345] Roughly speaking, Jesus only eats to preach; when he does so in Galilee (before Easter), it is as *demonstrative* as it is in Jerusalem after the resurrection (Lk 24:41–3).

It is no coincidence that, in addition to the 'chamber pot' mentioned by Steiner above, food, drink, sleep, and sex are included as almost constitutive elements in the comedic universe from Aristophanes (*c.* 446-*c.* 386 BCE) and Terence to Shakespeare's Falstaff, for it always elicits laughter when persons on stage are revealed to be powerless when faced with these elemental demands of nature. As the theatre critic Walter Kerr (1913–96) has so excellently put it, comedy is tragedy's secret diary that insists on not forgetting what tragedy conveniently omits in its longing for communion with the sublime, such as an itch ... no matter where on the body. When the tragic or epic hero embarks on his quest, comedy immediately notices *if* his shoelaces are untied ... or rather, *that* they are untied, because there is always something bothersome and irritating to discover if only we look closely enough with a magnifying glass with an appropriately strong (comic) zoom.[346] Over the years many have gained their claim to fame by

---

344   *De trinitate* X, 23–4; 1843, col. 361–4, the quotation is from col. 364, quoted from Steinberg 1996, 291.
345   Chrysostom's 13th Homily on Matthew (1862b, col. 209), quoted from Steinberg 1996, 291.
346   Kerr 1967, 26 f.

analysing their way to X number of (often surprisingly few) jokes, which all the millions of others are variations of; but Kerr takes the prize by essentially boiling all laugh-inducing comedy down to one joke: that *homo erectus* so easily stumbles and falls. Reformulated into a more theological-sounding version (although for Kerr, it is the definition of low comedy, farce): that a being created with freedom of will is bound by such banal impulses.[347]

The Jesus of the New Testament is neither a tragic hero nor a comic figure, so is the Apostles and Evangelists' omission of both laughter and other such human details simply a matter of propriety? It seems that neither the post-testament theologians nor the great artists have been willing to risk any uncertainty, as they – again, in all likelihood independently of each other – agree in their common endeavour to highlight the mystery of the Incarnation, while simultaneously avoiding associating Jesus with the necessities of life that otherwise define our understanding of human existence.

Even before Friedrich Nietzsche's (1844–1900) and Freud's notion of the growling dogs in the cellar (the subconscious), there was evidently a clear sense that Jesus should be kept far away from the world of dreams, and that despite well-known biblical examples of dreams as a prophetic tool (Jacob in Bethel, Gen 28:12–15, or Pilate's wife, Mt 27:19). The surest means to avoid surrendering to the potentially libidinous realm of dreams is to prevent Jesus from falling asleep. In general, the Bible seems to have little interest in sleep as a well-deserved rest, but is primarily more concerned with it as something potentially threatening that should be avoided, one extreme being the Psalmist's outcry to God (Ps 44:23–4), another being the disciples in Gethsemane (Mt 26:40), where the danger is explicitly expressed: 'Watch and pray that you may not enter into temptation. The spirit indeed is willing, but the flesh is weak' (verse 41). Sleep's other significant function in the biblical universe is to serve as an image of death.

However, there is one apparent exception where even our Lord himself is allowed to take a nap; but informed by the example of his consumption of food we can almost figure out in advance that something peculiar is happening. It is so demonstrative, indeed contrary to nature, that he would lie down to sleep and remain in slumber when heaven and earth become one during the Storm on the Sea (Mt 8:23–7), so the explanation cannot be that he was tired, but rather that it was to teach both the disciples and the (Primeval) Sea itself a lesson. The same applies in the art of painting. Is there a single example of an adult Jesus sleeping … apart from that time on the sea? And only in the early Renaissance did they

---

347   *Ibid.*, 149 and 145.

muster up courage to depict the baby lying asleep with the Madonna; even then, according to most interpreters, it is precisely as a foreshadowing of his passion and death.[348]

Although it is impossible for ordinary mortals to have full control over the life-sustaining forces, they still fall into two categories: nutrition can be regulated through fasting, and one benefit of the Divine Office in monastic life has undoubtedly been to interrupt and thereby minimise the power of sleep. However, completely foregoing food or sleep would kill a person, and it takes some exegetical contortions to avoid acknowledging that Jesus was also subject to these needs. Laughter and a sexual drive, on the other hand, seemed more promising in the sense that though they are difficult to suppress they are not direct causes of death for most people, and Jesus is not associated with them either.

Perhaps it is not life-threatening to do without laughter and sex, but is it not inhuman? Once again, we can resort to the distinction between the original and the fallen Adam and identify Jesus' humanity with the former. While the great theologians of the Western Church, from Augustine to Aquinas, acknowledged that the deeper meaning of the creation of Eve was to assist Adam in procreation even in Paradise (which was far from being taken for granted), they were keen to specify that paradisiacal procreation was the result of strict, that is to say, rational family planning under full control of the will and entirely devoid of disruptive desire. Adam's erection was a decision of the will, akin to moving the foot to take a step. However, Augustine suggests that Adam and Eve never had the chance to embrace each other before partaking of the fruit, so the lust-free intercourse never had the opportunity to be tested in practice.[349]

In passing, it is worth noting that Augustine approaches the subject with more modesty than the Puritan John Milton (1608–75), who in Book 4 of *Paradise Lost* has Adam and Eve refer to procreation ('But thou hast promis'd from us two a Race / To fill the Earth', lines 732 f.) and then consummate the union that only hypocrites and Satan himself would deny them: 'Whatever Hypocrites austerely talk / Of puritie and place and innocence, / Defaming as impure what God declares / Pure, and commands to some, leaves free to all. / Our Maker bids increase, who bids abstain / But our Destroyer, foe to God and Man?' (lines

---

348 Cf. Steinberg 1996, 293 f. Steinberg believes that in art after the Renaissance there are examples of a Jesus who 'simply' sleeps in the arms of the Madonna or under her gaze.
349 Augustine develops these thoughts in his book on a literal interpretation of Genesis, *De Genesi ad Litteram*, 1865b, col. 354–430; specifically in book 9, section 10 (col. 398–400; 1982, vol. 2, 80–2); quoted from Steinberg 1996, 232–8.

744–9). However, Milton also distinguishes, of course, between 'adulterous lust' (line 753) and '[Relations dear] Founded in Reason, Loyal, Just, and Pure' (lines 755 f.). Despite the praise of sexuality, Milton's opposition to the conventional view does not extend to humanity's other pleasure-driven activity, laughter. Milton only knows of Satan's mocking laughter and the kind of sovereign, divine laughter known to the psalmist (Ps 2:4) and to which Milton directly alludes (for example, Book 2, line 731).

The textbooks all state that there is a categorical distinction between orthodoxy and heresy, between the true doctrine of two natures and false Docetism; but it is hard not to get the impression that even the Church Fathers, when dealing with these questions, balance on a knife's edge in their interpretation of the similarities and differences between Jesus' and our humanity. For the sake of clarity it should be mentioned that there is a theologically decisive point where they do not waver, and where they do not resort to a more or less sophisticated distinction between basic human experiences and the characteristics in Adam before and after the Fall. This is also the point where pleasure (except for the sadomasochistic variant) does not come into the picture, but where only the will prevails: Jesus' willingness to take on human suffering undeservedly, but for the sake of others, and even unto death.

Death can serve as a cue for the second overarching strategy to harmonise the understanding of Jesus with something recognisably human. Just as the resurrection only makes sense if Jesus was truly mortal (and not just apparently dead when he was taken off the cross), and, as Steinberg adds, all theologians' reference to Jesus' life as virginal presupposes his sexuality in order to be a meritorious role model,[350] so, similarly, a moral point can only be derived from the New Testament's silence about Jesus' laughter if he actually could have laughed. Jesus did not suffer from a defect (either anthropologically or ontologically), but his lack of laughter should instead be assessed ethically: he managed to subject laughter to the control of the will in a kind of laughter-asceticism.

If it had been a question of an inability to laugh based solely on Jesus' divinity, control over laughter could hardly be made into something worth striving for by others. Only because Jesus could laugh (*risus capax*), could it be elevated to a virtue that he chose not to do so, and so it was established as a model and requirement in many of the various collections of monastic rules. The clearest example of how the handling of laughter fell under the domain of morality can be found in a beautiful clarifying remark in Benedict of Aniane's (*c.* 750–821)

---

350 *Ibid.*, 19.

compilation of Benedict of Nursia's rule with collections from other predecessors, *Concordia regularum* (adopted at the Synod of Aachen in 817). In a way, Benedict of Aniane's remark anticipates Immanuel Kant's (1724–1804) ethical philosophical distinction between inclination (*Neigung*) and duty (*Pflicht*): 'one ought to believe that abstinence from laughter among some pagans is born of an excess of bile or some other defect of nature rather than from virtue'.[351]

This remark is made precisely as a comment to the fact that the namesake from Nursia places laughter so high on the ladder of practising humility (see note 552), and Aniane's simple and striking logic is that the inherently and naturally sad person (i.e. the pagan!) does not earn any praise for not laughing, but only those who are inclined to laughter and can suppress their nature – and the Christians, who, by virtue of their faith and hope, have every reason to rejoice but do not show it through laughter. This interpretation of Benedict of Aniane's comment attempts to provide an alternative to the slightly more common one, where the motivation to follow Jesus' example is solely the awareness of one's own sinfulness and the thought of the impending Judgment day.[352]

If we dare to extrapolate Benedict of Aniane's logic to also apply to Jesus himself, should we then understand Jesus' lack of laughter as if he constantly carried an inner laughter that he managed to restrain? That would probably be taking the logic to absurdity, but it could challenge the one-dimensional image of Jesus as the Man of Sorrows. The remarkable thing about Benedict of Aniane is that he reflects on these considerations already at the beginning of the 9th century, which means at a time when Aristotle is still largely known in Europe only on secondhand. When the great theologians in the following centuries not only settled for a flat denial of Jesus laughing (without any sophisticated distinction between external and internal), but apparently felt compelled to nuance this detail in Christology, it is due in no small part to the conflict between the silence of the New Testament and the explicit rejections of tradition on the one hand, and on the other Aristotle's praise of cheerful eloquence (*eutrapelía*) and his description of humans as *homo ridens*.

According to Suchomski, a widespread solution among medieval theologians was to acknowledge the ability to laugh (*risibilitas*) in both Jesus and humans, but they still attempted to completely avoid questionable laughter (*risus*) in favour of

---

351 Benedict of Aniane 1864, col. 863; reference to this text and its English translation is from Resnick 1987, 99, where the author also addresses the question of Jesus' *risibilitas*.
352 *Ibid.*, 98.

legitimate joy. Even in this aspect, a distinction was constructed between joy over earthly things (*laetitia secularis*) and spiritual, heavenly joy (*gaudium spirituale*). However, even joy was not without its problems, so much so that controlling its earthly manifestation bordered closely on outright renunciation and contempt for the world (*contemptus mundi*), while the spiritual *gaudium* remained silent even in heaven.[353] Kemper, who otherwise highlights Suchomski's scholarly efforts, challenges this interpretation on the last point and argues that as the Middle Ages progressed, theologians can be found who have also *heard* the exultation and jubilation of heaven – and as an example of this, so beautiful that it is worth repeating, Dante and Beatrice are greeted with laughter as they approach heaven (see note 246).

2. Did Jesus Laugh? Maybe! (Depending on What Is Meant by 'Laughter')

The first thing that makes us wonder is that even though Clement of Alexandria and Chrysostom (to name but two), and even more so the medieval scholastics, were perfectly capable of distinguishing between different *types* of laughter, it was laughter itself that was denied to Jesus. It is even more puzzling that when it came to evaluating human laughter, to a remarkably high degree people continued to operate with such an abstract construct as 'laughter itself'. This becomes even more peculiar because in other passages a willingness and an ability to distinguish were shown.

The next thing to wonder about is that after the general cultural change in the perception of laughter during the Enlightenment and Romanticism, and particularly the ecclesiastical and theological embrace of laughter since World War Two, and after becoming aware of, conceptualising, and theorising about countless types of laughter, the laughter that is first blessed in the church and then resonates in one's inner ear in Paradise is, with very few exceptions, such an insipid and disembodied laughter that it brings to mind Leonardo da Vinci's (1452–1519) *Mona Lisa*: does that woman even smile? What can that laughter do? Is it even the laughter of sinners that one shows mercy to, or rather such a spiritualised and virtuous laughter that there is nothing to forgive, for it is worthy of a saint – and perhaps even Jesus himself?[354]

---

353   Suchomski 1975, 11–4.
354   An example could be the alluring manner in which Kranz makes use of the similarity and difference between the earthly and heavenly body to delve into an almost

It would be far beyond the scope of this book to delve into an extensive review of the explosion of theories about laughter, which are not least the result of a remarkably extensive interdisciplinary interest. As a general observation, it is difficult to avoid the impression of the involuntary comic effect when articles and monographs boldly launch yet another theory about laughter as if it were the definitive theory. It would be a good, and humorous, piece of advice to refrain from judging theories as right or wrong, and certainly not as true or false, but rather as interesting or uninteresting in relation to a particular purpose. This applies even to the 'classic' theories, and even more so to the many intermediate forms, as it quickly becomes meaningless to pit them against each other as such, because each of them can say something highly interesting and relevant in a given context.

Hyers has managed to develop a theologically based classification of types of laughter, and although we will not elaborate on it or assess its persuasiveness, it deserves to be mentioned both as a recognition of Hyers' pioneering work in the field and for the pedagogical demonstration of the benefit of not only discussing laughter in singular and definite terms. The crux of Hyers achievement is to typologise laughter as paradisiacal, fallen, and restored (alluding to Milton's *Paradise Lost* and *Paradise Regained*), into which he then distributes a long list of types of laughter, such as the pre-moral laughter of children and play in Paradise, the self-conscious and aggressive laughter among the fallen, and the sympathetic laughter of humour as a reborn laughter.[355] Apart from this, we will not delve into the individual theories here, as competent overviews are available in all major languages.[356] Most recently, Prütting has attempted to create a

---

conjurational description of laughter in heaven, which anticipates so many eventualities that it becomes a somewhat lame end product: 'Of course, this heavenly laughter will be of a different quality than earthly laughter, just as the heavenly body will be different from the earthly body. It will not be noisy, screaming, roaring; it will neither stem from pain nor illness, but only from joy and health. For the Saint in heaven is the bodily, spiritually, and soulfully complete human being. It will not be despairing, for it rejoices in the ultimate fulfillment. It cannot be a laughter of pride, contempt, mockery, but very well a laughter of humour and humility.' From earthly life, Kranz adds, we only know this laughter in glimpses, as seen in couples in love and children. Kranz 1969, 412 f.

355 Hyers 1981, 33–8.
356 Cf. N.N. Holland 1982; Morreall 1983 and 2009, and Figueroa-Dorrego & Lakin-Galiñanes 2009. The latter allows the reader to kill two birds with one stone, as besides the excellent and condensed introductions by the two editors the book also offers the possibility to read extensive excerpts from writers in their own (translated) words from Plato to Bergson.

comprehensive historical and systematic overview, but though he allows himself a couple of thousand pages to do so he too admits to not being able to cover the entire range of theories. However, with its sharp analyses and clear perspectives Prütting's *Homo ridens* remains highly recommended for those with a particular interest in the subject.

i. Different Forms of Modern Research Into Laughter

Instead, we will limit ourselves to attempting to characterise the development on a very general and simplified level. Throughout the history of philosophy competing interpretations of the nature and function of laughter have been presented. Not least the Roman textbooks on rhetoric were aware of the usefulness of adapting laughter according to purpose and context. So, variation in itself is not something new. What *is* new is that the interest in laughter has spread not only to almost all areas within the humanities and social sciences but also deep into the natural sciences, particularly the health sciences.

Gutwirth offers a useful taxonomy that provides a good sense of where some of the major fault lines and similarities exist across various disciplines, methods, and interests – and also across the common ways of distinguishing between theories of superiority, release, incongruity, etc. Gutwirth achieves this by distinguishing between functionalists, psychologists, and intellectuals. Functionalists are particularly concerned with the purpose of laughter, what it serves, such as reprimanding each other or building communities, where, especially in German research of the new millennium, the concept of *Lachgemeinschaft* frequently emerges. The functionalists' approach strives to 'integrate laughter into a larger human enterprise'. Psychologists are interested in the individual's own benefit from laughter and focus on how the emotions, perceived as central in each theory, are satisfied through laughter. Two obvious examples would be Thomas Hobbes' (1588–1679) celebrated analysis of 'Sudden Glory' (superiority in a negative, but also in a positive sense: the satisfaction of mastering a situation) or the sense of play (such as wordplay or practical jokes). Finally, intellectualists discuss the object of laughter, what makes us laugh, and here in particular attention is paid to refining considerations of the incongruities that are amusing, i.e. what makes something comic. It may indeed involve a clash between two emotions, but most often it is the element of surprise that affects cognition (my experience and understanding expected this, instead this happened or that person said this).[357]

---

357 Gutwirth 1993, 2 f.

Simon, in his dissertation on literary, philosophical, physiological, and psychological research on laughter spanning over two hundred years, provides an overlapping but even bolder simplification. Simon also highlights how the interest in laughter is extremely widespread and interdisciplinary. However, he dares to divide it into two main streams, placing the methodological differences in a historical context, where he demonstrates yet another variation of the cultural significance of the English Channel as a boundary marker. After Romanticism had almost succeeded in silencing comedy research, and consequently the interest in laughter, the study of laughter was revived from the mid-19th century onwards, but now with a significantly different foundation:

> Two scientific notions about the nature of man changed the direction of comic inquiry in the mid-nineteenth century: the physiological model of the human nervous system as a mechanism for the transformation and exchange of energy and the biological doctrine of evolution, natural selection, and survival of the fittest. Neither concept concerned comedy or laughter in any obvious way, yet each had a major effect on the development of new, uniquely modern attitudes towards laughter and comedy. Evolutionary biology and mechanistic physiology changed the ways men regarded human behaviour and the assumptions they made about its causes and effects, and one result of this was a dramatic re-evaluation of laughter as a human behaviour and of the comic sense as a human attitude, which began with biologists, psychologists, and physiologists in the second half of the 19th century and which has continued well into the 20th.[358]

This should be a fairly uncontroversial observation; however, the more daring aspect is Simon's distinction between Continental European and Anglo-Saxon research. Simon argues that to the extent that the German idealists' (and Kierkegaard's) treatment of laughter (and comedy) has survived, it has happened on the Continent (and partially in the USA), while the Anglo-American world has predominantly followed the new, more empirically oriented path. In other words, broadly speaking, there is a difference between the methods of the humanities and natural sciences, philosophical analysis vs. empirical investigations, or, as Simon summarises it in an interesting formulation: while the Germans were most interested in the *causes* of comedy and laughter, the British became increasingly focused on their *effect* (and function),[359] and '[...] if the German tradition had elevated irony, humour, the comic, laughter, and comedy to the highest achievements of man's spirit, of his art, and of his consciousness, the Anglo-American tradition reduced laughter to a basic physiological response,

---

358   Simon 1985, 178.
359   *Ibid.*, 179.

an essential part of man's biological nature.'³⁶⁰ Simon hastens to add that 'reductionist' does not mean 'simplistic', but rather that the connection between the mental and the body was pursued to such an extent that the scholar can engage with laughter without thinking about the comic, and is strictly concerned with the significance of laughter for well-being both socially and individually (for example, that laughter is healthy, a defence not only against existential but also physical pain and suffering!).³⁶¹ Believe it or not, 'laughter' can replace 'an apple' in the proverbial advice to keep the doctor away with simple means.³⁶²

Here it would be appropriate to add that already in the late Middle Ages monasteries became aware of laughter as an effective remedy against melancholy, and Oecolampadius' contemporary, Joubert, wrote medical treatises on laughter and health (see note 24). Similarly, both Erasmus' *The Praise of Folly* and the satirical diatribes and highly crude caricatures of the Reformation era demonstrate that even back then, people were fully aware of the social and political power of laughter. However, this aside gives rise to a fundamental consideration that is relevant both in relation to Simon's attempt to distinguish 'geographically' between different types of laughter research and, perhaps even more so, in relation to the historical distinction that more generally has been made use of in the context of this book.

ii. The Historical Break in the Concept of Laughter

The underlying claim so far has been that an almost categorical shift in the perception of laughter has taken place, which complicates a contemporary understanding of why Easter Laughter should even be a problem or what was at stake in the question of Jesus' laughter. In a theological and ecclesiastical context, this shift can be described as laughter transitioning from being considered devilish to heavenly. This does not make it impossible to understand the past, but it requires an effort because we must resist the answers offered by an immediate common understanding. To this end it would be tempting, for the umpteenth time, to

---

360   *Ibid.*, 187 f.
361   *Ibid.*, 188 and 209.
362   An overlapping attempt at such a bird's-eye view of the historical development of laughter and humour is provided by Jan N. Bremmer (b. 1944) and Herman Roodenburgh (b. 1951) when they observe that the dominant discourse on these subjects shifts from philosophers and rhetoricians (antiquity), to monks and theologians (Early Church and Middle Ages), and essayists (Enlightenment), to being dominated by psychologists and sociologists in modern times. 1997a, 6.

appropriate Thomas Kuhn's (1922–96) theory of paradigm shifts to 'explain' the difficulty. It is inherent to the logic of paradigms (such as a cultural self-understanding) that they function as a given discourse's presuppositions and therefore are not normally thematised *in* the discourse; but paradigms are also historical and thus changeable, replaceable. This means, among other things, that while it could easily become unfair and untimely to accuse a discourse of not accounting for its assumptions, we must be wary that relying on a given paradigm as a matter of course will cause us to lose sight of its historicity – a danger that can be countered by comparing current paradigms with those of the past.

Three methodological points should be emphasised when discussing a *natural* phenomenon as *historical*. Assuming we can rely on Crile's version of the theory of evolution (see note 321), humans laughed even before they might have been considered true humans. Therefore, we are not questioning that all humans have laughed at all times and in all places all over the world. However, what is historically interesting is that the frameworks for laughter vary geographically, culturally, epochally, and, not to be forgotten, individually. This applies even on a personal level, such as in our assessment of what makes a person laugh, that is, what kind of person does it, and what does it reveal or say about a person if he or she laughs in a certain way, at a certain time, and in a certain place. Even more so on a societal level, where, based on the principle that 'we do not have to teach our children to laugh, but when and where not to do it', we can observe that laughter both as a reaction and as an action is natural, but that there are radical changes in terms of where and when we allow it, where and when we encourage and expect it, what means we find acceptable to evoke it, and under what circumstances, etc. We can laugh at everything; indeed, nothing is perhaps more ridiculous than a prohibition against laughter, but that does not mean that as individuals, families, or societies, we can evade considering the limits of laughter, at least those that we ourselves, initially perhaps unconsciously, adhere to.

The second point emphasises that changes are not linear or irreversible, and even less can they be described as a progression (evolution!) from something lower to something higher, from something primitive to a civilisational advancement. An aspect of the non-linear is also that the changes are not synchronous and unanimous, but at any given time and in any cultural context, the occurrence of what Ernst Bloch (1885–1977) once called 'non-synchronicity' must be reckoned with: despite sharing the experience of living under the contingent factors that we may happen to incorporate into a theory to explain and describe a given historical change, in this case, the perception and use of laughter, not everyone simultaneously adopts and adheres to these conditions. In a Danish context, it is relevant to mention the newspaper Jyllands-Posten's Muhammad cartoons from

2005 as the textbook example of the collision between non-synchronous perceptions of comedy and laughter on a local and global level.

The third methodological point may seem already implied, but because we will allow ourselves to paint with a very broad brush in order to outline some of the categorical distinctions that have been alluded to above, it is still essential to mention. It is not particularly difficult to find exceptions and contradictory examples to our outline! However, the claim remains that while a bit of research undoubtedly can find this or that person before the Enlightenment who is a positive advocate for laughter, such advocates are always exceptions that confirm the rule – mere isolated voices in what we have previously referred to as an 'undercurrent' that are no match for the prevailing tradition.[363]

iii. The (Bodily) Context of Laughter

With these three methodological reservations, we wholeheartedly endorse two overlapping forms of overview according to which laughter has historically shifted its position in the body and at the same time fundamentally transitioned from an educational to a liberating function. The first theory has been explored and contributed to by many through detailed studies, but here we rely on Gilhus' *Laughing Gods, Weeping Virgins* (1997), both because she approaches the subject from a religio-historical perspective and because she is able to provide an extremely condensed and pedagogically convincing presentation.

---

363   With this recognition of examples to the contrary and 'undercurrents', an attempt is made to avoid the smarting criticism from the classical philologist, John Strong Perry Tatlock (1876–1948), when he reacts to Louis François Cazamian's (1877–1965) claim that humour is a modern phenomenon by replicating: you must master Latin to find humour in older texts! Tatlock adds the thought-provoking observation that when we study medieval texts in the vernacular languages, we should not be surprised by their sparse use of amusement. Such texts typically had an educational purpose in mind, aimed at those who were not refined enough to read French or learned enough to read Latin (where there was abundant use of jokes among peers). Tatlock 1946, 290 f. See also Olle Ferm's (b. 1947) equally terse statement about 'modernists' (i.e. those who believe that humour only arises after the Renaissance and the birth of the individual): 'The "troublesome" empiricism is limited in many modernists. Their investigations often concern a certain language area or a certain period, which normally lies after the Middle Ages. Despite this, they have definite opinions about what lies outside their actual field of knowledge.' 2002, 243, note 18. The endeavour by Tatlock and Ferm to unearth elements of humour from medieval texts is, among others, shared by How 1908 and Coxon 2008, chap. 1.

After opening with the excellent observation that laughter, despite its bad ecclesiastical press, is ideally suited as an expression of religious experiences precisely because of its ambivalent status (*pace* Rudolf Otto [1869–1937]!),[364] one of Gilhus' fundamental assumptions is that modern laughter is spiritual, or intellectual, rather than physical. This shift begins to occur with the Reformation, for example, concretely in the form of the Protestants' aversion to and work against the many church festivals such as *Corpus Christi* – and, we can add, Easter Laughter.[365] This does not mean, of course, that in 2024 we cannot make someone laugh by physically tickling them; but what Gilhus is concerned with is the meaning of laughter. Rather than laughter as a physical phenomenon, she asks about its symbolic significance ('my aim is to investigate a sign, not a sound'[366]). This distinction is further elaborated with the clarification that focus is on laughter as part of a symbolic context, and that one of these contexts is the body. This, too, must be understood correctly: '[…] we are not talking about the human body as a biological entity, but of the body as it is moulded by culture, conceived by the human mind and used as a religious symbol.'[367]

Although Gilhus emphasises that she limits herself to a Western context and only focuses on three periods, there are not many significant gaps in the historical progression when she chooses the ancient Middle East (including classical Greek), Hellenistic and Christian culture, and the modern era! The key point in this selection, however, is that these three periods encompass different perceptions of the human being and its body, and thus also three 'interpretative contexts for laughter's religious roles.'[368] In summary, this can be expressed in one lengthy sentence.

> These dominant interpretative contexts are, respectively, the cosmos in Ancient Near East and Greek religion, where laughter partakes in the creation and maintenance of the world; the body in Hellenism and Western Christianity, where laughter is mainly conceived in the context of body and spirit and in the drama of individual salvation; and the mind or psyche in the modern period, where laughter comes to be connected with the rationality of human beings and with health, happiness and knowledge.[369]

---

364 Gilhus 1997, 2.
365 *Ibid.*, 100.
366 *Ibid.*, 1.
367 *Ibid.*, 3.
368 *Ibid.*, 7.
369 *Ibid.*, 8.

In this superior perspective, Gilhus compares and distributes many of the ideas and statements that have been mentioned and quoted in the previous chapters (such as laughter as a cosmic force with direct influence on the gods, as in the case of Demeter and the Dionysian cult), while also maintaining awareness of important differences within the same parameter. Hellenism and Christianity, due to their soul-body distinction, share a complex relationship with the body, which problematises the status of laughter ('[l]aughter was related differently to the body, dependent on whether those who laughed took their stand with the spirit [as in Gnosticism], with the body [as in the carnivals of the Middle Ages], or with both [as in the English mystery plays]'). The crucial difference was that the Christians could not completely part with the body, as the body was not only seen as a burden (to which the spirit was reluctantly bound) and a challenge (which one had to practice subduing under the rule of the spirit), but also as 'a vehicle of salvation'.[370]

Indeed, Christ had not only appeared as a spiritual being but had also assumed the despicable body, and the Christian must somehow bring the body along in salvation in the form of the 'resurrection of the flesh'. In that sense, a phenomenon as closely tied to the body as laughter becomes part of a long and tension-filled history in which theologians and church communities seek a balance between subduing and, if possible, eliminating laughter through discipline and asceticism, or channelling its energies into tolerable forms (such as church plays) or even edifying forms (such as Easter Laughter).

iv. Laughter as an Educational or Liberating Force

In a somewhat more tangible and, admittedly, crude reformulation of Gilhus, we can describe the cultural history of laughter as a journey through the body, from the genitals (antiquity) to the stomach (Middle Ages) and the heart (Romanticism), and finally to the head (modernity).[371] The previous chapters

---

370   Ibid., 11.
371   Wolfgang Schmidt-Hidding (1903–67) closely aligns himself with such a historical process of change; but he supplements it with a systematic distinction based on the diverse signals of language regarding the connection between laughter and the human body. Our language about humour and related words reveal that they cannot be narrowed down to a specific bodily location; '[n]evertheless, with some justification we may say that *wit* stems from the superior brain, *fun* from the joy of life and exuberance, *humour* from the empathetic heart, and *mockery* from the moral sense, the critical awareness of values (which sometimes turns into arrogance and malice)'. Schmidt-Hidding creates a map of the many terms that we more or less associate with laughter by placing them in a coordinate system where one axis

have primarily drawn upon material from the first two periods, with much less emphasis on the latter two. Thus, it is only fitting that the second overview, which simplifies the development based on the transition from laughter's educational to its liberating function, can contribute to bringing the description up to the present day. While acknowledging that laughter is much more than just a reaction to the comic,[372] for pedagogical purposes we choose to lean on studies of comedy. By incorporating changes in the typical 'object' of laughter in drama, we get a sense of why comedy has become a serious genre in theatre during the 20th century and how it has evolved along the way.

In classical comedy people laughed at the flaws and missteps of individuals and in that sense their laughter could be described as didactic; in modern comedy laughter was revolutionary, directed at society's rigid structure and futile attempts to suppress the vibrant life within it; but in recent generations comedy took a darker turn, Here, laughter is tinged with despair because while we can still mock society and politics, the true target becomes apparent: the absurdity of the world. Laughter soon gets stuck in our throat, as we realise that while there may be hope for individual improvement (*castigat ridendo mores*[373]) or the ability to influence society through satire, there is no belief that the natural and cultural world can really be reshaped, causing laughter to rebound onto oneself. Previously, we could argue that laughter expressed hope, but lately it often reveals hopelessness. Admittedly, this latest part of the sketched development may seem more applicable to the theatre of the first decades after World War Two than to what appears on the stages in the 21st century, but perhaps today that kind of comedy has moved out of the theatres (and movies) to the ever more popular stand-up scene.

If this still appears to be painted with a brush slightly too broad, it may be helpful to combine this description with one of the oldest and in our own

---

ranges from 'forces of moral criticism' (ridicule) to 'forces of the soul' (humour), while the other axis extends from 'forces of the intellect' (wit) to 'forces of joy of life' (fun). The result is highly complex but tremendously instructive, and as Schmidt-Hidding assigns 'pun', 'nonsense', 'tease', 'practical joke', and many many others to the coordinates we are invited to contemplate agreement and disagreement with his allocations. 1963, 47–8.

372   While voicing minor disagreements with Prütting's demands for a theological contribution to the scientific explanation of laughter, Lühl, and we with him, wholeheartedly agrees with Prütting's most basic point: laughter is a much broader human phenomenon than humour and comedy. Lühl 2019, 8–12.

373   Cf. note 550.

cancel-culture most frequently used criteria to form a basic and far-reaching valorisation of the types of laughter: to operate with a categorical distinction between laughing at and laughing with someone! The articles and books, not to mention online posts, that make this distinction are countless – without many people nowadays having much regard for laughter that involves laughing at others.

In his dissertation on 'The Power of Comedy' (*Komediens kraft*, 1986), Ole Thomsen (b. 1946) traces the epoch-making shift to Friedrich Schlegel's (1772–1829) treatise 'On the Aesthetic Value of Greek Comedy' (*Vom ästhetischen Werte der griechischen Komödie*, 1794). Here, the conflict with corrective laughter breaks out and can now only be understood as uncomfortable derisive laughter, whereas laughter can also function as an important element in the playful liberation of comedy: '[…] for the Romanticist, it is inhumane to laugh at a person because they cannot cope with the norms of social reality – which is not *the* reality.'[374] The Romantic individuals understand themselves as much greater than their social role, for the Romanticists have a space deep within themselves, in utopia, where the self is either alone or where everyone is everything to each other – meaning everyone laughs genially with each other. This self-understanding manifests itself in a sensitivity that poorly tolerates the ridicule and mental (or physical) violence against the hero of comedy. In Thomsen's reconstruction, this leads to a change in the concept of genre, as we no longer accept the sharp distinction between tragedy and comedy in classicism, and instead interpret the comic hero as tragicomic (even before the Holocaust, in the early 19th century, it became difficult to be entertained by Shylock in Shakespeare's supposed comedy, *The Merchant of Venice*). Comedy was increasingly seen from the perspective of the outcast … and the spectator 'was not amused'.[375]

Using laughter to put people in their place fits perfectly with stable societies with fixed structures, and irony, sarcasm, and satire are suitable means to make individuals conform to the collective (hierarchical) order. In times of upheaval, it is the rigidity of societal structures that becomes anachronistic and ridiculous, while the adaptable comedians find new, that is to say, their own paths and can laugh with relief or triumph when they succeed.

However, it is now important to tread carefully, for are we not on the trail of considerable hypocrisy or, at best, self-deception? We may very well verbally profess an accommodating laughter, while our actual laughter practices reveal

---

374   Thomsen 1986, 74 f.
375   Cf. *ibid.*, 266.

that the louder it sounds (guffaw), the more it contains, if not as its core, certainly an element of offensive (degrading) laughter?

In the face of this inherent contradiction, Thomsen points out two interpretations that precisely avoid making laughter banal or harmless by ignoring the interplay between the dimensions of laughing-at and laughing-with. The first interpretation will only be mentioned in passing here, as Thomsen only touches briefly upon it, and because we will immediately return to it in a discussion of the English Enlightenment thinkers; but something crucial happens to laughing-at laughter when the laugher is able to include themselves as part of the object of laughter (the butt). The Romantics refer to this as laughter of humour,[376] and this is meant as a purely historical observation. On the other hand, the second interpretation is Thomsen's own attempt at a systematic theory of comic laughter, providing a thought-provoking and sharp analysis.

For seemingly without mercy, Thomsen states that 'roughly speaking comedy's view of any event is: there is nothing new in it, and of any person: there is nothing unique about him/her. What comedy sees is that everything has been *seen before*'. It is no coincidence that throughout most of theatre history, comedy has relied on a relatively narrow cast of characters, recognised in both the oldest Greek comedies and the latest episodes on Comedy Central (*senex iratus* and *miles gloriosus*, to name just two – or the constellation of pairs: Harlequin and Pierrot, Laurel and Hardy). For a Romantic era that idolised the exceptional individual, this brutal gaze at the *typical* in every individual (i.e. unique!) experience and encounter is scandalous.

The point in Thomsen's analysis, however, is that he does not remain focused solely on 'the young', that is the Romantic youths who feel their uniqueness snubbed: 'The old, on the other hand, will find that comedy acts in solidarity, for it suggests that there is a humanity: behind all differences in cross-section – that is, between people now – and in longitudinal section – that is, between now and before.'[377] In his theoretical language regarding comedy, Thomsen actually

---

376 Ibid., 266 and 297 f.
377 Ibid., 118, cf. 238 f. Thomsen seeks Belgian support in finding a strong metaphor for a laughter that can simultaneously maintain distance and be welcoming: '[…] more than 50 years ago, sociologist Dupréel showed that in addition to exclusionary laughter, there exists receptive laughter. The "most characteristic and usually most *intense* laughter", the "complete laughter", is – according to Dupréel – the "intimate union" of the malice (*malignité*) of exclusionary laughter and the joy of reunion (*joie de réunion*) of receptive laughter. The "complete" laughter is a molecule composed of two atoms: satire and sympathy, which are incompatible in all other aspects except laughter – hence, there has been a problem with laughter since ancient times, but

approaches the theological dogma of original sin, which cannot (or should not) be reduced to a pessimistic and negative view of humanity that levels everyone to the lowest common denominator. Instead, it also encompasses a dimension of solidarity – somewhat similar to when Kierkegaard, during a walk in the cemetery, reflects on death: it is not only common to all people in the sense that all have to die, but it also does away with all those differences that set people apart when they lived … or, at least, it *almost* does:

> The small families have each their little piece of about the same size. For in life it can indeed happen that a family has had to limit itself, but in death all have to do so; and in life a mighty person can indeed succeed in spreading himself, but in death they must all limit themselves. Yet there is still a little difference, like a playful reminder of the difference that was so enormously great in the world; here, if there is a difference, it is an ell or an ell-and-a-half that the one has more than the other.[378]

v. And Then There Was Humour!

When Paul Hammerich (1927–92) published his 'Chronicle of Denmark' (*Danmarks Krønike*, 1976–80) covering the period from the end of World War Two to Denmark joining the European Common Market in 1972, he began each volume with an overview of the new words that had entered the Danish language during that particular five-year period. It was remarkably effective to be able to review half a decade in such a concise manner through these lists. If we were to attempt something similar, not just for decades or centuries, but for an entire epoch, it could, in this context, suffice with a single word: humour. When Schmidt-Hidding and his team of colleagues after five years of research launched an ambitious series of books, planned to consist of 50 volumes, entitled 'European Keywords. Comparative and Historical Studies of Words', they aimed to explore, from various disciplines (etymology, philology, literature, philosophy,

---

      not with tears.' *Ibid.*, 276. Thomsen's source is Eugène Dupréel (1879–1967): 'Le problème sociologique du rire', in: *Revue philosophique de la France et de l'étranger* 106 (1928), 213–60.

378 The reflection can be found among Kierkegaard's journals, 'Paper 442, 1845 On the cemetery'. Kierkegaard would not be Kierkegaard if he did not manage to turn things upside down in the next breath: 'To have a flower on the grave is already a great difference and to have a tree on it is prosperity – alas, thus does life return in death, for indeed in childhood owning a flower was already much, and to own a tree was extraordinary. Even in the midst of the serious contemplation of death, one must smile not at the equality of all, but that there will nonetheless be difference.' 2020, 236.

etc.), the words and concepts that have shaped Western self-understanding. Their research also sought to reveal significant insights into our culture's developments, changes, and self-perception by tracing the keywords' nuanced variations across languages and shifts in meaning over time. Volume 2 would cover words such as 'morality', 'intelligence', 'enthusiasm', 'mystery', 'Lord-Lady', 'snob', 'Arbeit (work-labour, Job)', and many more. However, the opening volume from 1963, spanning almost 300 pages, was solely dedicated to 'humour' (and its most frequently associated words: 'wit', 'fun', and 'mock').[379]

While it may be unproblematic to admit being tone-deaf, poor at numbers, not appreciative of ballet or the hottest series on Netflix, it is rarely, if ever, heard that someone confesses: 'I have no sense of humour – and I also dislike people who do!' This says something about the newfound status of humour.[380] One of the more unpleasant insults about a person in the workplace or in our social circle might be that they are humourless, but why is there no word for being 'humour-free'? Shakespeare's colleague Ben Jonson (1572–1637) achieved some of his greatest successes with *Every Man in His Humour* (1598) and *Every Man out of His Humour* (1599). In both plays, the comedy arises precisely because the characters are prisoners of their 'humour', and it would clearly have been much

---

379 The series of books reached volume 3 on 'culture and civilisation' in 1967 while the remaining volumes apparently went to the grave with the editor.

380 It borders on scientific proof when and if the juiciest formulations of language lack specific statements, in this case regarding the lack of a sense of humour. It should be the definitive testimony to the new value attributed to a word and what it designates when we publicly begin to blame people for not having it – as was the case with 'sense of humour' during the 19th century. There were, of course, precedents of humourless individuals, but what is significant is that it was not generally perceived as problematic. All of this becomes evident in this insightful passage: 'It is true that elements which can be distinctly recognised as elements of the sense of humour can be traced back through Dr Johnson [Samuel Johnson, 1709–84] and Shakespeare to Chaucer and even to Piers Plowman [c. 1370–90]. Yet all the evidence indicated that the sense of humour as a separate area in the English temperament was not *generally recognised* until the last half of the nineteenth century. In all the rich and varied literature of English invective the first public figure to be accused of possessing no sense of humour was Mr. Gladstone [William Gladstone, 1809–98]; nobody accused Charles I [1600–49], or Archbishop Laud [William Laud, 1573–1645], or Milton, or even Shelley [Percy Bysshe Shelley, 1792–1822] of being deficient in this attribute; it never occurred to anybody that of the many and varied privations from which Robinson Crusoe suffered his lack of any sense of humour was the most irremediable.' Nicolson 1956, 34–5.

better, and certainly more convenient for themselves, if they could have been set free from it. This is obviously related to the fact that 'humour' at the time cannot be distinguished from 'mood' and has more to do with the ancient theory of bodily fluids than with comedy and wit.[381]

In contrast to Hammerich's lists of neologisms the mischievous aspect of 'humour' is that it is such an ancient word that at first glance we might believe that there is nothing new under the sun; the novelty lies in the fact that the word gets imbued with an entirely different meaning. In relation to what has been previously mentioned about Gregory the Great (see p. 131 f.), we could suggest that in one of 'humour's' most prominent manifestations (the British), it partially takes the place of the monastic 'laughter of the heart', as 'humour' and 'laughter' do not have a straightforward relationship with each other either. The surprising fact is how recently this transformative shift occurred, and a humorous documentation can be found in the epitome of omniscience, the *Encyclopaedia Britannica*. In its first two editions from 1771 and 1783 it only associates 'humour' with 'fluid' (and in the second edition, also with 'wit'), but in the third revision of 1797, adds 'the comic'.[382] However, humour, in this sense of the word, is after all not that young; this uncertainty about establishing its age can be attributed to the delay effect from the time when individuals, almost as an ideological project, infused new content into words until they permeate everyday language … and are eventually included in lexicon definitions.

The *Oxford English Dictionary* records the first occurrence of a word and, most importantly, the word in its various meanings. In the process of 'humour' redefinitions it carries a whole field of related words (such as 'repartee', 'pun', 'joke', and 'banter'), all of which, according to the *OED*, emerged from the mid-17th century and for about half a century thereafter.[383] The editors of a major anthology on the cultural history of laughter even dare to pinpoint the year 1682 as the moment when the concept of humour changed into its modern meaning.[384] To illustrate

---

381 Cf. Jonson's own definition in the opening of the latter play: 'As when some one peculiar quality / Doth so possesse a man, that it doth draw / All his affects, his spirits and his powers, / In their connections, all to run one way, / This may be truly said to be a Humour.' 1927, 432, l. 105–9. Cf. III,5,iii,c and Schmidt-Hidding 1963, 63.
382 *Ibid.*, 137.
383 *Ibid.*, 55–63.
384 Bremmer & Roodenburg 1997b, 1.
    It will hardly create consensus but to avoid unneccesary confusion this point deserves to be repeated. Far from all scholars accept a more or less categorical distinction between modern and pre-modern understandings of humour. Within this

the perspectives in this, we can limit ourselves to two themes: the significance of humour for the view of humanity and humour as a kind of substitute for religion.

vi. Humour and the Conception of the Human Being

As for the view of humanity shaped by humour, the entire transformation can be captured with one word: hobbyhorse! The defect (i.e. an excess of a particular humour fluid) that previously trapped a person and made them ridiculous becomes the hobbyhorse that may very well make them an eccentric, but a more or less lovable one. Laughter is not used to put the person in their place, but rather, we smile at their idiosyncrasies because the focus shifts from viewing the 'defect' as a social deviation to perceiving it as what makes the person an individual and someone unique. Writers in the new magazines and early newspapers can certainly still use humour in their strong societal engagement to reprimand and improve their fellow citizens, but the emphasis clearly lies on empathetic understanding and acceptance of diversity.[385] When humour is thus employed to look at individuals, new words must be invented to describe the 'defect', where adjectives have changed their value from negative to positive. In his treatise on tragedy, Aristotle referred to the corresponding defect in the tragic protagonist as *hamartia*, the same Greek word that in the Christian tradition took on the unequivocal colour of St Paul's use of the word to denote 'sin'. That designation becomes entirely misleading in the new era, and terms like 'whimsical' and 'odd' now emerge in English, while old words like 'quaint' and 'abnormal' change their hue.[386]

The new conception of humanity was discussed in London's coffee houses, salons, and in the era's new mass media: newspapers and magazines. However, the greatest source of inspiration, maintenance, and dissemination of this anthropology came from the authors of literature. Schmidt-Hidding addressed

---

book we quote several authors who do not bother to make such distinctions, some of whom seem to assume humour is a timeless category without giving historical change much thought (cf. notes 363 and 55). This cannot be said of Bednarz, who makes a systematic and conscious effort to broaden the concept of humour. While accepting the significance of this effort for her purposes, see for example Bednarz 2015, 3 ff. and 212 f., our interest goes in the opposite direction. We accept that it may be considered a narrowing of the concept of humour, but we find the gains in doing so outweighing the possible losses.

385 To mention just one example we can point to the founder of *The Spectator*, the influential Joseph Addison (1672–1719), Schmidt-Hidding 1963, 117.
386 *Ibid.*, 63 f.

these authors in a separate monograph, 'Seven Masters of Literary Humour in England and America' (1959),[387] where he also incorporated the German poet Jean Paul (1763–1825) and his more theoretical considerations from his philosophical aesthetics (*Vorschule der Ästhetik*, 1804).

The guiding principle in Schmidt-Hidding's analysis is to delineate the new and central concept of 'a sense of humour'. To begin with, he clarifies what he understands by literary humour, which various authors contribute to over a period of about a hundred years: 'The complex of the sense of humour combines the sense of reality and the sense of the comic, whereby, and this is striking, a distance is maintained by the humourist from oneself and from the world.'[388] Although not all authors (of fiction) nor their contemporary thinkers and publishers agree on all points, Schmidt-Hidding distils the seven characteristics that make a person a humourist. Naturally, this is an ideal type, as no actually existing (or literary) individual possesses all of them or even a majority of them in their pure form.[389] However, whether an ideal type or not, the strength of Schmidt-Hidding's list lies in the fact that the points are highly recognisable in both the art of the intervening period and everyday language: humourists have a pronounced sense of reality and its amusing contradictions, a fondness for deviations/deviants, and the ability to maintain a distance from their own preferences. They have a keen eye for contradictions within themselves and a tendency to capture and encompass the contradictions of others and themselves in ambiguous forms of language. Finally, their humour is firmly grounded in moral seriousness.[390]

---

387   The seven chosen authors consist of two 'forerunners', Chaucer and Shakespeare, as well as Henry Fielding (1707–54), Laurence Sterne (1713–68), Charles Lamb (1775–1834), Charles Dickens (1812–70), and Mark Twain (1835–1910).
388   *Ibid.*, 7.
389   *Ibid.*, 158.
390   Schmidt-Hidding 1959, 157. On pages 7–8, the author provides a more detailed overview of the list:
      '1. He [the humourist] approaches reality in a sober and precise manner, often down to its smallest peculiarities (a genius for the minutest detail, Dickens). / 2. He sees the world as full of contradictions. He smiles at the contradiction between existence and appearance, between reality and a fantastic imaginary world, thus at the usual incongruities of existence or the mistakes of the heart. / 3. The novelty in his behaviour lies precisely in his ability to love what deviates from the norm more than the normal. He loves eccentrics out of a humanitarian sense of brotherhood with all people and creatures (attachment). / 4. At the same time, he maintains a critical distance from things and people whom he loves (detachment). He understands the

vii. Humour in the Service of Critique of Religion

We do not need to make more of this conception of human nature due to its current immediate recognisability; all the more reason to dwell on the considerations of these thinkers and writers regarding the relationship of laughter and humour to religion and Christianity. Although it is recognisable from most contemporary church communities that they tolerate or encourage cheerfulness in connection with religious practice, it is still a minority who take the step fully and elevate humour to a level that may be described as a substitute religion.

The reason for interjecting the remark about it being an 'ideological project' when certain individuals developed new ideas about humour is that this new understanding of humour and laughter at the beginning of the 18th century can by and large be seen as a reaction to the endless European and civil wars of the preceding century, in which conflicts between Christian denominations had been a significant driving force. Against this general background, allegedly provoked by the arrival of a group of French refugees in London in 1707 who carried their charismatic form of Christianity with them and spread their fervent prophecies,[391] the Third Earl of Shaftesbury, Anthony Ashley Cooper (1671–1713), took up his pen and wrote an essay (which he himself calls a 'Letter') on 'enthusiasm' (1708). There is good reason to draw extra attention to the word by putting it in quotation marks, for though the Earl uses a term familiar in our days he gives it a completely different meaning. 'Enthusiasm' is simply another word

---

relativity of judgments, including his own. This knowledge strengthens his tolerance. As a free personality, he remains impartial and understanding towards the foolish world. / 5. The humourist discovers the incongruities within himself, the comical. Therefore, he prefers to make himself the target of his jokes and loves the first-person narrative. When discussing absurdities, he involves himself. Even in personal life, self-irony is the threshold to humour. / 6. Based on the paradoxical intertwining of love and distance, a stylistic preference for ambiguity emerges in the humourist. / 7. The playfulness of humour unfolds against a serious backdrop. It is a light-hearted but serious play, where the rules are dictated by the prevailing morality in society. The humourist is a smiling sage who loves the whole world with all its weaknesses and contradictions.'

A nearly identical list, but with even more details and keywords, can be found in an essay by Harold George Nicolson (1886–1968) on 'The English Sense of Humour', 1956, 33–7. A bon mot-like formulation of the important point in item 7 can be expressed as: 'The difference between Irony and Humour is often expressed as follows: in Irony, there is jest behind seriousness, in Humour, seriousness behind jest.' Høffding 1916, 68.

391   Shaftesbury 2001, vol. 1, 17.

for '(religious) fanaticism' and, according to the Earl's interpretation, it is what the 17th century had been much too full of. This all stems from the Reformation, for since then it had been preached that religious worship is closely and inseparably linked to passion and an uncontrollable desire to convert others and save souls. The Earl does emphasise that earlier times had also known the same kind of religious passions, where 'enthusiasm' ended in 'panic', as seen, for example, in the form of the Pythagoreans of antiquity.[392]

An efficient means of combating religious enthusiasm was the reinvention of the laughing-at laughter, specifically in a form where the 'at', so to speak, is decidedly directed upwards. We might be tempted to believe that Shaftesbury, on behalf of an era very confident of itself, suggested that inflated figures from the ecclesiastical hierarchy, as well as any religion and practice of worship, should undergo the 'Test of Ridicule' to prove their authenticity according to the norms of political correctness of the time.[393] Most surprisingly, however, the Earl did not take credit for inventing this brand-new litmus test but claimed that it rested, among others, on Socrates ('The divinest Man who had ever appear'd in the Heathen World') and St Paul ('our great and learned Apostle') as his key

---

392   *Ibid.*, 12. Although Shaftesbury's understanding of 'enthusiasm' and 'enthusiasts' may seem distant from common modern usage, it is not the case that he arbitrarily invented a new meaning for these terms. One predecessor can illustrate the tradition that the Earl continued. On the threshold of the English Civil War between the Puritans and the Anglicans (Royalists) the somewhat peculiar Oxford theologian and pastor, Robert Burton (1577–1640), published one of the most remarkable encyclopaedic works on what we would now call depression and stress, but which was then collectively referred to as 'melancholy'. In the final part of *The Anatomy of Melancholy* (1621, along with a series of subsequent expanded editions), where Burton examines all forms of melancholy (their symptoms, causes, and methods of healing), it is revealed that love is also a form of melancholy just as, as a special subcategory, being religious is. Those who suffer from it have been labelled with various terms in the tradition, one of which turns out to be 'enthusiasts'. To get a sense of the company, we can study this table of contents for a section in the presentation of 'Symptoms of Religious Melancholy': 'Symptoms general, love to their own sect, hate of all other religions, obstinacy, peevishness, ready to undergo any danger or cross for it; Martyrs, blind zeal, blind obedience, fastings, vows, belief of incredibilities, impossibilities: Particular of Gentiles, Mahometans, Jews, Christians; and in them, heretics old and new, schismatics, schoolmen, prophets, enthusiasts, &c.' Burton 1638, 658.

393   Shaftesbury 2001, vol. 1, 8. In addition to 'ridicule', Shaftesbury also uses the term 'raillery' interchangeably.

witnesses.[394] This is indeed the point: the Test was not meant to mock religion and church life as such but to separate the chaff from the wheat, to expose false seriousness ('gravity' and 'melancholy') so that true faith could reveal itself.[395] As Shaftesbury clarifies in a subsequent essay on 'The Freedom of Wit and Humour' (1709), the intention of *teasing* religion is deeply serious, namely to harness natural humour as a 'lenitive Remedy' against sin, superstition, and false melancholy. Regarding laughter, this entails an important distinction: 'There is a great difference between seeking how to raise a Laugh from everything; and seeing, in everything, what justly may be laugh'd at.'[396]

Thus, it is important not to misinterpret what is meant by 'ridicule' in the acclaimed 'Test of Ridicule' (or 'Raillery'), for it is far from obvious that the test was originally meant as a battering-ram for secularisation (although it has often been misunderstood or used as such by a later age[397]). However, it did assume a very specific understanding of religion where faith is not harmed but rather strengthened by and built upon humour. Shaftesbury makes this clear with this solemn declaration, which is a good candidate for an Enlightenment thinker's creed:

> Good Humour is not only the best Security against *Enthusiasm*, but the best Foundation of *Piety* and *true Religion*: For if right Thoughts and worthy Apprehensions of the Supreme Being, are fundamental to all true Worship and Adoration; 'tis more than probable, that we shall never miscarry in this respect, except thro' ill Humour only. Nothing beside ill Humour, either natural or forc'd, can bring a Man to think seriously that the World is govern'd by any devilish or malicious Power. I very much question whether any thing, besides ill Humour, can be the Cause of Atheism. For there are so many Arguments to persuade a Man in Humour, that, in the main, all things are kindly and well dispos'd, that one wou'd think it impossible for him to be so far out of conceit with Affairs, as to imagine they all ran at adventures; and that *the World*, as venerable and wise a Face as it carry'd, had neither Sense nor Meaning in it. This however I am persuaded of, that nothing beside ill Humour can give us dreadful or ill Thoughts of a Supreme Manager. Nothing can persuade us of Sullenness or Sourness in such a Being, beside the actual fore-feeling of somewhat of this kind within our-selves: and if we are afraid of bringing good Humour into Religion, or thinking with Freedom and Pleasantness on such a Subject as GOD; 'tis because we conceive the Subject so like

---

394 *Ibid.*, 19–20.
395 Cf. Schörle 2007, 197, who warns against the misuse and misunderstanding of Shaftesbury's test.
396 Shaftesbury 2001, vol. 1, 80.
397 The Victorians in particular turned Shaftesbury's 'Test of Ridicule' into a topos into which people loaded their own agendas at will, R.B. Martin 1974, 12.

our-selves, and can hardly have a Notion of *Majesty* and *Greatness*, without *Stateliness* and *Moroseness* accompanying it.[398]

Shaftesbury's essays are widely recognised as unique testimonies of the breakthrough of an era. However, to illustrate that it is not the Earl's idiosyncratic views but rather the spirit of the times that can be heard in his lines, we can simply look to Addison, the co-founder of the epoch-making journal, *The Spectator*. Here Addison expressed his views on everything under the sun several times a week, and when he finds occasion to discuss the relationship between religion, joy, and laughter, it sounds like a direct echo of Shaftesbury. For example, Addison opens an essay on 26 September 1712, clearly indicating that he himself perceives his attitudes and perspectives as universal – universal, that is, for the new era, which here distinguishes itself from the immediate past ('an Age ago'):

> About an Age ago it was the fashion in England, for every one that would be thought religious, to throw as much Sanctity as possible into his Face, and in particular to abstain from all Appearances of Mirth and Pleasantry, which were looked upon as the Marks of a Carnal Mind. The Saint was of a sorrowful Countenance, and generally eaten up with Spleen and Melancholy. [...].
>
> Notwithstanding this general Form and Outside of Religion is pretty well worn out among us, there are many Persons, who, by a natural Unchearfulness of Heart, mistaken Notions of Piety, or Weakness of Understanding, love to indulge this uncomfortable way of Life, and give up themselves a Prey to Grief and Melancholy. Superstitious Fears and groundless Scruples cut them off from the Pleasures of Conversation, and all those social Entertainments, which are not only innocent, but laudable; as if Mirth was made for Reprobates, and Chearfulness of Heart denied those who are the only Persons that have a proper Title to it.[399]

In his essay Addison invents an opponent who embodies the outdated attitudes, whom he names 'Sombrius' ('Mr. Serious'), but whom he could also have named after one of the countless Church Fathers, popes, abbots, and theologians (some of whom have been mentioned in the preceding chapters). When it comes to Sombrius' view on laughter, Addison informs us: 'He looks on a sudden fit of Laughter as a

---

398   Shaftesbury 2001, vol. 1, 15. In a subsequent essay, 'Of the Force of Humour in Religion' (1714), Shaftesbury made it clear that faith itself is light and joyful. He opens the essay with these three summarising theses: '1st, that wit and humour are corroborative of religion, and promotive of true faith. 2ly, that they are used as proper means of this kind by the holy founders of religion. 3ly, that notwithstanding the dark complexion and sour humour of some religious teachers, we may be justly said to have in the main, a witty and good-humoured Religion.' *Ibid.*, vol. 3, 98 f.
399   Addison 1891, vol. 3, No. 494.

Breach of his Baptismal Vow. An innocent Jest startles him like Blasphemy.' A crucial addition, through which Addison reveals himself as a true humourist, is when he emphasises, despite his own clear disapproval, that he will not accuse Sombrius of being a hypocrite. Partly because it is not our place to judge each other, for in such matters there is only one Judge (cf. point 4 in Schmidt-Hidding's list of characteristics of the humourist); and partly because Addison also has a sense of history: '[...] Sombrius is a religious Man, and would have behaved himself very properly, had he lived when Christianity was under a general Persecution.'

Even if neither Shaftesbury nor Addison should be seen as advocating anti-church secularism, it is at least a new form of understanding Christianity and religion that (re-)emerges here. This is evident in Addison's observation that Sombrius belongs to a time of persecution, implying that such a time is considered to be in the past. Similarly, according to Shaftesbury's analysis, 'enthusiasts' arise from a theology where the Creation is seen under the dominion of a 'devilish or malevolent power'. Only a lack of humour can lead us to believe in a 'Supreme Manager' of that kind; but how does humour manage to counter all of this? Addison provides the answer in an earlier essay with a definition of humour, or rather: he cannot define the concept directly but must use a metaphor, for humour is so fundamental and important that it is impossible to describe directly, only indirectly (it is hard not to compare this to medieval theologians' talk of *via negativa* when speaking of God!):

> [...] by supposing Humour to be a Person, deduce to him all his Qualifications, according to the following Genealogy. Truth was the Founder of the Family, and the Father of Good Sense. Good Sense was the Father of Wit, who married a Lady of a Collateral Line called Mirth, by whom he had Issue Humour.

With such a complex lineage, we should not be surprised that humour can have many faces, 'but as he has a great deal of the Mother in his Constitution, whatever Mood he is in, he never fails to make his Company laugh'.[400]

In both gentlemen it is clear that there is certainly no longer room for any speculation about a *deus absconditus*; but do we instead get the impression from their descriptions of a kind of God on vacation (cf. 1 Kings 18:27!)? This may be too polemical, given that there is hardly any support for this banter in the quotes used here; but in their elegant distancing themselves from religious fanaticism and its underlying notion of a zealous and punishing God, Addison and Shaftesbury project a God almost in their own cultivated image. It therefore comes as no surprise that Shaftesbury's 'Letter Concerning Enthusiasm' enjoyed

---

400 *Ibid.*, vol. 1, No. 35 (10 April 1711).

great popularity among the thinkers who developed and disseminated the understanding of Christianity known as Deism,[401] where a rational and benevolent God has withdrawn after completing the work of creation and has left the stage to his equally rational and loving creatures. Admittedly, the heyday of Deism is considered to be over by the mid-19th century, but there is a common thread from this 'natural religion' through Kant's famous aphorism at the end of his *Critique of Practical Reason* (1788) about 'the starry heavens above me and the moral law within me'[402] to the kind of liberal theology which the dialectical theologians confronted after World War One, and which, according to these opponents, had reduced the Trinity to a belief in a retired Creator and Jesus as a moral example, while the Holy Spirit was busy ensuring the immortality of the soul.

viii. Humour as a Substitute for Religion

If it was the new humour that acted as a midwife for a modern laughter, it was likely also the same humour's 'Christianisation' that, in the long run, opened the church's doors to a laughter that had not been heard in the sanctuary since Easter Laughter had enjoyed its popularity. However, there is a missing link to bridge the gap between the beginning of the 18th century and the period around the turn of the previous century. The humour of Addison and Shaftesbury had become part of a critical confrontation with an irrational, revealed religion and a powerful church, and could be understood (or misunderstood) as a contradiction to faith, where the sound of the 'Test of Ridicule' in its historical impact could hardly be distinguished from the derisive laughter of mockery. Therefore we need to mention the arguably most important prophet – at least in an international context[403] – who not only conveyed knowledge of the British Founding Fathers of modern humour but also

---

401   Manuel & Pailin 1999 (online edition).
402   This is taken from the first sentence in the book's conclusion: 'Two things fill the mind with ever new and increasing admiration and reverence, the more often and more steadily one reflects on them: the starry heavens above me and the moral law within me. I do not need to search for them and merely conjecture them as though they were veiled in obscurity or in the transcendent region beyond my horizon; I see them before me and connect them immediately with the consciousness of my existence.' Kant 2015, 129.
403   The reason for mentioning 'international' is that we could plausibly argue that a Dane had preceded William Makepeace Thackeray (1811–63) in elevating humour to religious heights; although initially not reaching the same wide audience (though that would certainly happen later). In *Stages on Life's Way* (1845) and *Concluding Unscientific Postscript* (1846) Kierkegaard ultimately refrained from taking that ultimate step and contented himself with allowing humour to surpass ethics and border

elevated these 'Fathers' to a level where they appeared capable of doing every day of the week what preachers in churches had done on Sundays: to propagate a special understanding of humanity and a path to salvation.

---

on religiosity as its *confinium*, cf. Schousboe 1925, 168 ff. Kierkegaard undoubtedly owes a debt to the German Romantics of the previous generation; in addition to the already mentioned Jean Paul particular mention should be made of Karl Wilhelm Ferdinand Solger (1780–1819), whom Kierkegaard repeatedly refers to in *On the Concept of Irony* (1841). According to the commentary on page 340, line 16 in the 4th Danish edition of his collected works, Kierkegaard has not directly indicated anywhere that he is familiar with Solger's main work, 'Erwin, Four Conversations about Beauty and Art' (*Erwin, vier Gespräche über das Schöne und die Kunst*, 1815). In this work, Kierkegaard could otherwise have read a conversation between two characters discussing humour and taking as their point of departure this lofty declaration: 'From this, Erwin said, one can indeed explain that reversal, whereby in humour the most timeless and sensual often attains the full power and significance of the divine.' Solger 1815, Part 1, 228.

On the other hand, Kierkegaard, Thackeray, and perhaps even the Romantics were surpassed by another Dane who saw himself as a critical heir when it comes to praising the power of humour: 'It has been my desire to carry on what Kierkegaard has hinted at in a few strokes, but also to demonstrate the unjustifiability of the limitations he imposes on the significance of this stage, in terms of scope, content, and energy, based on his assumptions.' The author succeeded with this endeavour by essentially replacing the theology in Kierkegaard's work with psychology, and since there was no God left to set the 'boundary', humour could take over the position. Not just any kind of humour (for the author identifies both 'small' and 'very small' kinds), but 'The Great Humour', which also became the title of philosophy professor Harald Høffding's (1843–1931) work. Høffding 1916, 47 (the quote) and 44 (the distinction between the sizes of humour). In all fairness, it should be added that Høffding also recognised the limitations of humour and believed that it could not be proclaimed as the highest stage of life, being surpassed by both 'the great practical endeavour' and tragic suffering, 1916, 122.

Let Hippolyte Taine's (1828–93) judgment serve as an excuse for not looking beyond the British Isles and Germany to find sources of inspiration for the Danish cultivation of humour. When he comes to the volume on 'The Contemporaries' in his *History of English Literature* (1863), Taine gives up explaining the meaning of 'humour' to his French readers while discussing Thomas Carlyle (1795–1881). Taine does so with the following resigned observation: 'This kind of mind produces humour, a word untranslatable in French, because in France they have not the idea. Humour is a species of talent which amuses Germans, Northmen; it suits their mind, as beer and brandy suit their palate. For men of another race it is disagreeable; they often find it too harsh and bitter, amongst other things, this talent embraces a taste for contrasts.' Taine 1920, vol. 4, 291.

The highly esteemed author, Thackeray, gained even greater popularity in the early 1850s by touring the East Coast of the USA and Britain with a lecture series on *The English Humourists* (published in 1853). In this series, he included renowned authors primarily from Addison's generation (whom Thackeray considered part of the literary elite), as well as a few from the following generation, starting with Jonathan Swift (1667–1745) and ending with Oliver Goldsmith (1728–74).[404] Already during these lectures, he referred to the humourists as 'Everyday Preachers', a term that played a key role when, while staying in New York during his first trip to America, he wrote a completely new lecture in support of a charitable organisation, which he titled 'Charity and Humour' (1853). This speech, supposedly dictated from bed to a secretary as one long *tour de force* (the secretary remembered it as one day, although Thackeray later mentioned in a letter that it had lasted two days[405]), became a huge success in itself. He subsequently delivered it in major American and British cities, and by the end of the decade, he had renamed it: *Week Day Preachers*.

In the opening lecture about Swift, Thackeray immediately addresses the relationship between humour and laughter: 'If Humour only meant laughter, you would scarcely feel more interest about humorous writers than about the private life of poor Harlequin [...], who possesses in common with these the power of making you laugh.' Then it is stated programmatically how much more the humourist is capable of than just eliciting laughter:

In itself, this quote provides a glimpse of a peculiar 'innocence' in the 19th-century attempt to develop a positivist humanities that readily resorted to national characters as an explanatory model. Taine makes it somewhat more digestible when Høffding, towards the end of his book, dares to conclude that '[t]he great humour has not reached its full development in German intellectual life'; and that '[i]t is characteristic that the French language uses the English form (humour) to express humour in the sense in which we take it here. The fusion or organisation that the great humour presupposes does not seem to have natural conditions on French soil'. Høffding himself gives up on providing an explanation for this but nurtures hope for the future: 'But in any case, there is a task here for further investigations, once race psychology [sic] has outgrown its infancy.' Høffding 1916, 164–5.

404 The gallery of characters, in the order Thackeray lectured on them, consists of: Swift, William Congreve (1670–1729), Addison, Richard Steele (1672–1729), Matthew Prior (1664–1721), John Gay (1685–1732), Alexander Pope (1688–1744), William Hogarth (1697–1764), Tobias Smollett (1721–71), Fielding, Sterne, and Goldsmith.
405 The editor's afterword, 'A Historical and Textual Note', Thackeray 2007, 255.

> The humorous writer professes to awaken and direct your love, your pity, your kindness – your scorn for untruth, pretension, imposture – your tenderness for the weak, the poor, the oppressed, the unhappy. To the best of his means and ability he comments on all the ordinary actions and passions of life almost. He takes upon himself to be the week-day preacher, so to speak. [...] and yesterday's preacher becomes the text for today's sermon.[406]

Although the lecture on 'Charity and Humour' was intended as a kind of meta-reflection on what the fundamentally different authors from Swift to Goldsmith had in common, especially regarding the humour they practised, the lofty declarations from the Swift lecture are closely intertwined with the opening in New York, the only difference being that it leans even more towards religious rhetoric:

> Besides contributing to our stock of happiness, to our harmless laughter and amusement, to our scorn for falsehood and pretension, to our righteous hatred of hypocrisy, to our education in the perception of truth, our love of honesty, our knowledge of life, and shrewd guidance through the world, have not our humorous writers, our gay and kind week-day preachers, done much in support of that holy cause which has assembled you in this place – and which you are all abetting, the cause of love and charity, the cause of the poor, the weak, and the unhappy; the sweet mission of love and tenderness, and peace and good-will toward men? That same theme which is urged upon you by the eloquence and example of good men to whom you are delighted listeners on Sabbath-days, is taught in his way and according to his power by the humorous writer, the commentator on every-day life and manners.[407]

Even though Thackeray heavily relies on formulations that could sound as if they were taken from a church prayer, it is equally remarkable that neither in this lecture for the charitable assembly nor in any of those about the many authors (actually, coincidentally or not, they amounted to a total of twelve), does Thackeray find occasion to mention Jesus or Christ, while God and Church only appear in colloquial phrases.[408] The humour could stand on its own! If there was no

---

406 *Ibid.*, 1–2.
407 *Ibid.*, 195.
408 However, one of the qualities that Thackeray attributes to Addison is that he was a 'true Christian', *ibid.*, 199; cf. 31: 'A better and more Christian man scarcely ever breathed than Joseph Addison.' Elsewhere, Thackeray also mentions that a reviewer had criticised his novel *Vanity Fair* (1848) for being misanthropic, and he defends himself against this accusation by stating that all authors and all readers see themselves surrounded by sinners, but then adds a faint allusion by capitalising the final word: 'so was every being who ever trod this earth, save One'. 203.

reason to invoke the usual figures of Christianity, Thackeray had the presence of mind in the new lecture to expand the circle of 'disciples' with a thirteenth writer. Quite magnanimously, as this person was his contemporary rival, but also rather prophetically, as posterity (outside the particularly Anglophile coterie) probably knows him more than the twelve others combined, his choice fell on Dickens.[409]

Interestingly, Thackeray indirectly sends his regards back to Shaftesbury (and Addison) by confessing that he himself used to believe that wit, along with love, was a constitutive part of humour. However, perhaps inspired by coming face to face with over a thousand women in New York who were dedicating their lives to raising funds for the poor, he wishes to emphasise love. Wit can affect a cool intellectual superiority in relation to people and situations, but in order to counter such a version of humour, Thackeray designates that kind of humour as the best 'which contains the most humanity, that which is flavoured throughout with tenderness and kindness'.[410] As another marker of the important difference in nuances, Thackeray formulates the bon mot-like statement about humour-infused love, that 'this kind of love is not a spasm, but a life',[411] which can be seen as a contrast rich in perspective to the blitz-like insights of wit. Indeed, perhaps the Preacher was not altogether wrong when he said about the fool, that 'his laughter is like the crackling of thorns under a pot' (Eccles 7:6), provided that we interpret his verdict as some kind of parallel to this distinction: wit may allow us quick flashes of clarity, by which we in passing can catch a glimpse of things and gain new knowledge, but these we cannot warm ourselves by and live on, as we can with the more humble yet enduring candlelight of humour.[412]

---

409   In Thackeray's praise of Dickens, he alludes to something beyond his colleague's genius. With awe and reverence, Thackeray recognises in Dickens 'a commission from that Divine Beneficence, whose blessed task we know it will one day be to wipe every tear from every eye', *ibid.*, 205.
410   *Ibid.*, 196.
411   *Ibid.*, 197.
412   Cf. Thielicke 1974, 71 f, who happens to illustrate the difference between wit and humour through their different relationship with time: the sudden vs. the enduring. In Høffding's variant, the distinction between wit and humour is transferred to a diversity of forms of humour, where a distinction is made between humour as an expression of 'momentary states (mental movements or ripples) or as more lasting states (moods) or as an expression of the real self (disposition)'. Høffding 1916, 54.

     None of these authors or Thackeray himself happens to mention Shakespeare. Although we may run the risk of being accused of Bardology a case could be made

In direct continuation of this, Thackeray also distances himself from the kind of laughter that someone like Swift can evoke (because it is 'unintelligible to thousands, who have not the wit to interpret the meaning of the visored satirist preaching from within'), in order to highlight Steele, who 'stepped off the high-heeled cothurnus, and came down into common life; he held out his great hearty arms, and embraced us all'. For Thackeray, Steele is the founder of 'sentimental writing', by which he means that laughter can also evoke tears, so our empathy is not limited to the tears of tragedy over fallen kings and widows of emperors.[413] Just as mystics could develop a theology of tears, Thackeray treats us to a hymn to 'tearful humour':

> Humour! if tears are the alms of gentle spirits, and may be counted, as sure they may, among the sweetest of life's charities, of that kindly sensibility, and sweet sudden

---

that he prophetically dramatised this precise difference between wit and humour, letting one of his characters almost didactically proclaim that it takes more than wit to gain love. *Love's Labour's Lost* (c. 1594) may not belong to the most popular of Shakespeare's plays, and in view of what we are discussing here an explanation for this could be that he ends the final act by frustrating both the four male protagonists as well as the audience's longing for marriage and 'they lived happily ever after' when he famously lets Berowne utter the surprising conclusion that in this particular comedy 'Jack hath not Jill'. A crucial dialogue happens a few moments earlier where the same Berowne is given a lesson by Rosaline, his love-interest, in how to reform his wit by taking it literally and figuratively to the hospital for a full year of learning:

'*Rosaline*: Oft have I heard of you, my Lord Berowne, / Before I saw you; and the world's large tongue / Proclaims you for a man replete with mocks, / Full of comparisons and wounding flouts, / Which you on all estates will execute / That lie within the mercy of your wit. / To weed this wormwood from your fruitful brain, / And therewithal to win me, if you please, / Without the which I am not to be won, / You shall this twelvemonth term from day to day / Visit the speechless sick, and still converse / With groaning wretches; and your task shall be, / With all the fierce endeavour of your wit / To enforce the pained impotent to smile. / *Berowne*: To move wild laughter in the throat of death? / It cannot be, it is impossible. / Mirth cannot move a soul in agony. / *Rosaline*: Why, that's the way to choke a gibing spirit, / Whose influence is begot of that loose grace / Which shallow laughing hearers give to fools. / A jest's prosperity lies in the ear / Of him that hears it, never in the tongue / Of him that makes it. Then, if sickly ears, / Deafed with the clamours of their own dear groans, / Will hear your idle scorns, continue then, / And I will have you and that fault withal; / But if they will not, throw away that spirit, / And I shall find you empty of that fault, / Right joyful of your reformation. / *Berowne*: A twelvemonth? Well, befall what will befall, / I'll jest a twelvemonth in an hospital.' Act 5, sc. 2.

413 Thackeray 2007, 200.

emotion, which exhibits itself at the eyes, I know no such provocative as humour. It is an irresistible sympathiser; it surprises you into compassion; you are laughing and disarmed, and suddenly forced into tears.[414]

ix. Do Structural Similarities Between Christianity and Humour also Imply a Causal Relationship?

Two remarks should be made in advance: it is not the intention to attribute copyright of humour to Christianity; furthermore, it can easily lead to an unfruitful dispute about words when discussing whether Christianity has historically had a decisive impact on the emergence and development of humour. To minimise that risk as much as possible, we can, for the sake of convenience, adhere to Schmidt-Hidding's aforementioned definition (see note 390), as it appears uncontroversial and reliable.

Schmidt-Hidding touches upon a strong argument for the close connection between Christianity and humour when, on the last pages of the book, he dares to draw the conclusion that if humour is indeed historical, it must have entered into history at some point. Consequently, it is legitimate to consider what had entered and what its prerequisites were. Schmidt-Hidding's plausible suggestion regarding the crucial phenomenon is to focus on the humourist's ability to keep a distance to oneself and the world, and to argue that Christianity has been able to make a contribution, if not actually the most essential, to enabling this.[415]

Simply put, Christianity achieves this through the dialectic between 'belonging elsewhere' and simultaneously 'being faithful to the world'. This could be called a kind of distanced embrace (which St Paul almost turned into a formula with the exhortation to live 'as if not', 1 Cor 7:29–31), acknowledging that distance is not necessarily an obstacle to freely engaging with one's environment, but rather can be a condition for it.[416] Despite the fact that it is almost a fixed

---

414 *Ibid.*, 201.
415 Schmidt-Hidding 1963, 287 f.
416 Schmidt-Hidding does not pursue his point beyond the fundamental observation, but his consideration can be supplemented by Campenhausen, who offers a historically more precise proposal. If we agree that humour is a historical phenomenon and also acknowledge that Christianity is its prerequisite, how can we then explain that it seemingly only emerges many centuries after the emergence of Christianity? Campenhausen points to monasticism as the decisive link: 'Here, all the prerequisites are given from which a humorous consciousness can gradually develop: the constant self-observation and self-experience, the close pastoral community, and – not least – the comical contrast between the monastery's presumably sacred "realm of its own"

repertoire in literature on these topics to refer to St Paul's juggling of 'wisdom' and 'foolishness' (1 Cor 1:18 ff.) as the main approach to the comic vision of a reversal of all values, the as-if-not passage from chapter 7 should be included as a *corrective* to a one-sided exploitation of the wisdom-foolishness model. There can hardly be much doubt that the model invites and has actually been used as a basis for a non-dialectical either-or thinking (and way of life!) that risks missing out on the distinctiveness of Christianity.

There are many philosophies of life, not least some inspired by Eastern mysticism, that manage to take a comical approach to the world. This is because their privileged insight has revealed existence as illusion and deception, and the revealed knowledge as incompatible with logic and common sense. As a result, these philosophies tend to reduce ethos to a question of willingness to renounce and resign. It is precisely here that we must bring into play the incomparable dialectic of 'as if not', which most accurately and succinctly conditions the genuinely Christian attitude: the distanced embrace of existence, which later becomes the life philosophy of the humourist. In the history of Christianity, the pilgrim myth has undoubtedly often turned into weariness of life and contempt for the world. However, from a theological perspective, the concept of creation, the historical grounding of Judaism and Christianity, and ultimately the Incarnation all make it impossible to completely abandon the world as a mere illusion. Therefore, the image of the pilgrim is essentially intended to maintain two worlds simultaneously: we are *in* the world but not *of* it; or this world is not unreal, but it is also not the ultimate reality. It is important to add that humour's characteristic distance is achieved without parting with, or despising, that from which one distances oneself. Similarly, it should be acknowledged that throughout the history of Christianity, there have certainly been forms of ecclesiastical rhetoric and

---

and the entire surrounding "world." Faced with the radical demand, the serious ascetic experiences the inevitable sense of "failure," and thus arises the melancholic humour of the human, which repeatedly attains or at least grazes the freedom of being a child of God.' Campenhausen 1963a, 326 f.

Werner Lauer (fl. 1972–97) sharpens Campenhausen's consideration with this thought-provoking reformulation: 'We only hold on to the fact that Christianity's incursion into the world of antiquity did not cause a tremendous breakthrough of humour. This raises the question: does its late appearance have special reasons? Perhaps it is not the Christian doctrine of redemption, but rather its disappointing absence, that leads to humour?' Lauer 1974, 275.

theology where it was difficult to perceive a true love of this life when described as a 'can of worms' or this world when referred to as a 'vale of tears'.[417]

It is commendable that Schmidt-Hidding does not simplify matters more than necessary but has a clear understanding of the crucial complication, namely, that, although Christianity is a prerequisite for humour (or, more cautiously expressed than Schmidt-Hidding: can be *one* of its prerequisites), humour is not found in the Bible,[418] and despite their structural similarities there is a difference between the Christian's and the humourist's attitude towards themselves and the world.:

> The difference between a Christian and a humorous relationship to the world may lie in the fact that the Christian believes in salvation from a personal God. Therefore, they do not feel the paradox too strongly that we must simultaneously keep a distance from what we love and love what we do not love. The humourist, on the other hand, smiles at the incongruity and seeks to overcome the pain of life's inadequacy through their own efforts.[419]

---

417   If not for any other reason, then because of the phrase 'having a look around in the Vale of Tears', Günther Blaicher's (b. 1938) consideration should be included, which, in a certain sense, can be said to further both Schmidt-Hidding's and Campenhausen's proposals with an even narrower designation of the source of the emergence of humour. Not Christianity in general nor monasticism as such, but rather mysticism's promotion of a new image of Christ and the relationship with God. 'This new trust in Christ as a brother displaced the notion of Christ as the Judge of the Last Day; Christ-love conquered the fear of God. The diminished fear of dreadful punishments in hell, the new, more optimistic outlook made people look around in the *vallis lacrimarium* and allowed them to enjoy the pleasures that appeared to them on the path during their earthly pilgrimage. […] Thus, mysticism liberates humans from ascetic renunciation of the world. It justified human emotions and taught that in the light of Christ's brotherly presence, a joyful spirit can be a Christian way of life. […] But we owe not only mysticism gratitude for this briefly sketched elevation of laughter, *gladness*, but also the crucial element in the new understanding smile, sympathy. Whenever the great mystics of the Middle Ages taught, in numerous meditation instructions, the immersion in the sufferings of Christ, the compassion for the child in the manger, it was essentially a guide to sympathising.' Blaicher 1970, 527 f.

418   'There is much cheerfulness and spiritual joy there, but not actually humour', Schmidt-Hidding 1964, 288. Cf.: 'Humour as we know it today is not a feature of the Bible. What the biblical books do contain is a wide range of satire and irony, bawdy and ribaldry, taunt and mockery, burlesque and lampoon, parody and denigration; but these are all quite distinct from humour. Irony is certainly not humour. Nor for that matter is the coarse language of abuse so typical of many of the harangues.' Carroll 1990, 169.

419   Schmidt-Hidding 1963, 288 f.

If for nothing else, it is worthwhile keeping Schmidt-Hidding's suggestion in mind as a heuristic thought: 'From this perspective, humour is the secularisation (humanisation) of Christianity's paradoxical mode of relating to the world.'[420]

Let it be added that regardless of how undocumented (or rather, impossible to document) we may find this idea of humour as the humanistic successor to Christianity, it is creditable that Schmidt-Hidding, while observing the striking structural similarities as far as the 'distance' is concerned, does not jump to the conclusion that the phenomena are one and the same. Instead, he offers a proposal for their historical relationship. There is all the more reason to take note of this as in the decades following Schmidt-Hidding's book, there emerged a steady stream of writers who seemingly contented themselves with the similarities without paying much attention to the underlying differences.

x. Why Does Jesus Have No Sense of Humour?

In light of the panegyric statements from the above-mentioned British writers, the question becomes urgent: is it not impossible for Jesus not to have had a sense of humour? For in the description of Enlightenment thinkers and Romantics humour has not only general religious but also clear Christian dimensions. Especially because the next section will mention authors who, as something completely new, discover Jesus' humour, it can serve as a relevant connection to consider briefly what speaks for and against it in a basic and systematic manner. For the sake of clarity, it should be specified that a verdict on Jesus' humour does not necessarily say anything about Christianity or the relationship of Christians to humour.

With the valuable insights provided by Schmidt-Hidding's clarifications, we may dare to embark on the almost suicidal project of questioning Jesus' humour. For is it not true that it is only our worst enemies (or political opponents, cf. Gladstone in note 380) we would accuse of lacking humour? If children are to

---

420   *Ibid.*, 289. Campenhausen aligns himself with this viewpoint but emphasises the point in a mischievous manner by referring to humour as a kind of byproduct of Christianity, the 'waste' left behind: 'The parables of Jesus cannot be considered tragic in their seriousness, nor should we label them as humorous in their cheerfulness. However, the sense of humour, as well as the sense of tragedy, has not arisen within the Church by chance. They can be seen as byproducts [*Abfallprodukte*], pointing to the true "centre" and the unique origin of faith, even though they may seem like deviations to the right and left. As such, they are inevitable and therefore should be tolerated […].' 1963b, 107.

be trusted, we may possibly learn something unexpected regarding this question without being distracted by the cultural and contemporary high valuation of humour. It is apparently a not uncommon experience among teachers in confirmation classes that the pupils often react very negatively to the Jesus they encounter in the Gospel of John. According to them he sounds like a self-absorbed teenager on Instagram who constantly refers to himself (we must hope their teachers can show the confirmands that Jesus also has a strong understanding of the Father and talks with and about him just as much). What the young people more or less instinctively may be onto is something that the influential Danish church historian Hal Koch (1904–63) can pinpoint for us. In his book on the origins of Christianity he distinguishes between Christianity and humanism by examining their different relationships to humour (let it be noted that Koch does not consider humour a modern invention, as we have done in this book, but treats it as an integrated, indeed, constitutive part of classical Greek culture). Humour is a way of life where the education of the individual is at the centre, and where Socrates points away from himself because he has nothing new to say and certainly does not offer any salvation. This is in distinct contrast to Christ, who must constantly point to himself, as he is the Way.[421]

Translated into the concepts used in the previous discussion, the problem for the confirmands with the Johannine Jesus is that he lacks the humourist's distance to himself and the world. Jesus cannot help but constantly commit what in the realm of humour amounts to the original sin: taking himself too seriously.[422] When Jesus, in a private conversation, speaks about the mystery of rebirth and

---

421 'A culture where humans are placed at the centre, a culture whose content is *paideia*, the shaping of humans – that is humanism. Its way of life is humour, its characteristic is ignorance, its path is conversation, the *logos* makes a bridge between people. No one has been able to express it, live it stronger than Socrates, the man who, more than anyone else, turned away from himself because he was not the possessor who could bring something new to people, let alone save them. He could only act as a midwife to bring forth what was already in their thoughts. Here, everyone is equal, with the same opportunity to approach goodness through thought. […] Christianity is not named after the man who boldly pointed to himself for no reason: come to me, all of you who suffer and are burdened, and I will give you rest [Mt 11:28].' Koch 1963, 113 f.

422 The viewpoint, only with the tone sharpened, finds support in this remarkably imposing and clear passage in Lauer's dissertation: 'The one who proclaims a "merry Jesus" undermines the absoluteness of his mission. People whose task is characterised by "singleness of mind" have no sense of humour. Jesus did not have humour. Why should he and for what purpose? There, where his relationship with the Father

responds to Nicodemus' lack of understanding of the workings of the Spirit with the remark, 'Are you a teacher of Israel and yet you do not understand these things?' (Jn 3:10), it does not necessarily have to be said aggressively and condescendingly, but it can be 'merely' teasing irony. However, the only thing that the statement definitely is *not* is a self-ironic admission like 'Oh, I don't understand it myself either' – and therefore, it is not an example of Jesus' humour.[423] It is, so to speak, the cost of being an all-knowing figure that it only has irony or sarcasm at its disposal in dealing with the less knowledgeable.

3. Did Jesus Laugh? Probably Not! (But He Began Doing So 150 Years Ago)

Such a headline invites refutation, even if we were to insert a more humble 'approximately' before the number; but let us one last time invoke a distinction between mainstream and undercurrent. In the sections on Scholasticism in chapter III it was possible to find examples of a laughing Jesus; but these were undoubtedly glimpses that we had to keep our eyes wide open so as not to miss. That is quite different with the generation after the first Enlightenment thinkers, where we meet a kind of variant of the analytical refinement that Le Goff demonstrated for the Middle Ages (cf. p. 137).

---

is at the centre, he was completely the one whose food is to do the Father's will (cf. Jn 4:34), he was complete participation, without any self-assertion, complete love. And there, where he is a friend among friends, a brother, he was compassionate and empathetic. In the revelation of God in Christ, "there is not humour, but suffering" (Reinhold Niebuhr [1892–1971]). Only where he had to assert himself, where he had to fight against the powers of darkness in his opponents as well as in his friends, could he use the weapon of the comical. And so he did: many of the Lord's words are full of irony, even biting. Evil is not in him, therefore there is no self-ironic attitude, no self-criticism that belongs to humour. But the evil outside of him is not relative, it is the terrible adversary, Satan, the murderer of humanity from the beginning (cf. Jn 8:44). To employ the attitude of humour here would be downright cynical, for humour is *also* love. But the one who is pure love is *only* love. And the one who is completely pure is only pure. The actual relativity of evil in even the "righteous" sinner is never the object of the one who has come to defeat evil. That is what the 'saved sinners' fight with, those who relativise and synthesise. "Foolish wisdom" is a characteristic of actual Christian maturity, but not a determination of the person who is without sin (cf. Jn 8:46 and Heb 4:15).' Lauer 1974, 323.

423 It is Lauer who brings this clarifying example, *ibid.*, 324.

To provide a single illustrative example, the Lutheran pastor Johann Friedrich Jacobi (1712-91) fearlessly delves into delivering 'a defence of entertainment' (which could serve as an apt short translation of his own flourishing title: 'Defense of Games, Dances, Plays, and Other Earthly Amusements, along with Instructions on How to Partake in Them Without Sinning', 1770). The approach in the book is to *differentiate* in order to provide more nuanced assessments than all-encompassing rejections of all amusements. When Jacobi thus examines individual amusements, he can indeed warn against abusing them, but he can also analyse specific examples and conclude that some of them can be harmless while others have even been put to edifying use by this or that pious prince, pastor, or other venerable person.[424] Jacobi does not shy away from theological discussions and as his most important point he holds on to the belief that God not only allows but directly bestows joys in life, that there are many amusements mentioned in the Bible without direct prohibitions against them (e.g. dance[425]); but Jacobi dares to venture into grey areas as well, where he acknowledges that an amusement can be the lesser of two evils (it is good to know, for example, that dance and theatre are less harmful than going to the tavern).[426]

As mentioned, Jacobi writes in the latter half of the 18th century; but if we fast forward a hundred years, two decisive things happen: firstly, what Jacobi could somewhat abstractly say about God is now specified and applied to his Son; secondly, such texts are no longer solitary examples but appear in flocks. A prophetic prelude could be found on the last page of Gilbert Keith Chesterton's (1874–1936) book on *Orthodoxy* (1908), where Father Brown's father takes up the old motif of Jesus' weeping and lack of laughter, but now gives it a forward-looking twist:

> The Stoics, ancient and modern, were proud of concealing their tears. [Jesus] never concealed His tears; He showed them plainly on His open face at any daily sight, such as the far sight of His native city. Yet He concealed something. Solemn supermen and imperial diplomatists are proud of restraining their anger. He never restrained His anger. He flung furniture down the front steps of the Temple, and asked men how they expected to escape the damnation of Hell. Yet He restrained something. I say it with reverence; there was in that shattering personality a thread that must be called shyness. There was something that He hid from all men when He went up a mountain to pray. There was

---

424   J.F. Jacobi 1770, 57 ff.
425   *Ibid.*, 34.
426   *Ibid.*, 20 f.

something that He covered constantly by abrupt silence or impetuous isolation. There was some one thing that was too great for God to show us when He walked upon our earth; and I have sometimes fancied that it was His mirth.[427]

By and large, Chesterton is correct in stating that up until the point he wrote his book, it had been possible to keep Jesus' mirth hidden; but that time was practically over in the same moment – without any underlying claim of a causal connection, of course – that Chesterton was born. When the American theologian Marion Daniel Shutter (1853–1936) published the book *Wit and Humor of the Bible* in 1893, he could inform his readers that according to *Poole's Index to Periodical Literature* (which was the contemporary equivalent of today's electronic databases and covered around 500 English-language journals from 1802 to 1906), an article by the same author that had been published 'some years earlier' on the same subject was 'the only extant upon the subject'.[428] Based on this information and supplemented with my own electronic searches, as well as the gathering of literature references in hundreds of articles and monographs by authors interested in this or similar topics, it can plausibly be claimed that it was *around* 1875 that things changed radically. From then on the question of laughter, humour, and comedy in the Bible and Christianity in general, specifically in relation to Jesus (and in the sermons of preachers), began to be considered so relevant and important that it needed to be lifted up into the titles of publications. Titles that connect these topics flourished in the 1950s and have exponentially increased in number with each decade since, but they made their entrance on the academic and ecclesiastical scene in the last quarter of the 19th century.[429] It can serve as a charming testimony to the groundbreaking nature of the subject

---

427 Chesterton 1912, 113. Another brilliant quote from the essay 'A Charge of Irreverence' (1906) suggests the consequences that Chesterton imagined God's 'cheerfulness' would have on human life: 'Life is serious all the time, but living cannot be. You may have all the solemnity you wish in your neckties, but in anything important (such as sex, death, and religion), you must have mirth or you will have madness.' 1958, 96.
428 Shutter 1893, 'Preface' (unpaginated).
429 Many of these titles can be found in the bibliography of this book. A particular focus has been kept on publications up until the 1980s, when research on these topics still had the character of pioneering work. The deluge of articles and monographs from the following decades is only represented by 'samples'.

Alas, only after publishing the Danish edition did I discover the books by Bednarz. Despite disagreeing with her about the best way to define the concept of 'humour' (cf. notes 384 and 54), her marvellous survey of the 'Study of Humor in the New Testament, 1863–2014' could have been a shortcut that saved me a lot of work; but

to quote the publisher's sales advertisement for Shutters' book, where, in just a few lines, several reassuring assurances (and counterattacks) are successfully incorporated:

> In this Work Dr. Shutter departs from the beaten path of theological writers in general and notes the element of humor, not only in the Bible, but what may still further appall some conventional thinkers, the sense of humor in Jesus. The treatment, however, is reverent in tone and there is no line in the work which will shock the most sincere Christian.[430]

Of course, it does not make much sense to list all the titles since they are included in the bibliography, and it would exceed our scope to go through each individual work. However, for the sake of clarity, some significant examples from the years leading up to and around Chesterton's 'sensation' (which turns out to be more of a wakeful observation than a dreamy prophecy) can be mentioned. Each of the publications mentioned below is a strong candidate for being the first in their respective fields.

Thus, a lecture from 1875 is the oldest publication I have been able to find: 'Humour and Christianity, with a special focus on Catholicism and German Protestantism. Lecture on 3 March 1875' (Meier 1876). The lecture opens with a sentence whose programmatic nature, both for Ernst Julius Meier (1828–97) himself and especially for his chronological successors, can hardly be overestimated: 'If only Christians were happier, the world would likely believe more in the gospel.'[431] (If there is a risk of bias in the current presentation due to the predominance of British writers drawn upon in the preceding sections, Meier provides a weighty counterbalance with his bold assumption that Christian humour is best preserved in German humour, indeed in Lutheran humour.[432]) Already the following year, a substantial chapter on 'Humour in the Pulpit' can be found in a book on *Deutscher Volkshumor*, which primarily provides a historical overview of humorous elements in sermons from the Middle Ages onwards, including examples from Lutheran preachers (M. Busch 1877[433]).

---

      now I content myself with the fact that on the whole we have discovered the same relevant literature and agree on identifying the timeframe for interest in this 'new' topic.
430   The advertisement, along with a list of other publications from the publisher, is placed at the back (unpaginated) of Shutter 1893.
431   Meier 1876, iv.
432   'The union of the German and Christian spirit is the pinnacle of humour, as it is the soul and character of Protestantism, especially in its Lutheran form.' Meier 1876, 12.
433   The passage about the Lutheran preachers, M. Busch 1877, 326 ff. Cf. Harrison 1888 (this reference I have second-hand, as it has not been possible to obtain a copy of the article), How 1908, and Overbeck [1919] 1963. In his dissertation, James Larohn

In the following decade, alongside articles, even monographs appear from the hands of exegetes, where it is the Old Testament scholars who believe themselves capable of finding humour, irony, and comedy in the Scriptures, as seen in the pioneering work *Humour and Irony of the Hebrew Bible* (Chotzner 1883[434]). After another decade, there is also the courage, as in the example of Shutter, to turn one's gaze towards the New Testament and Jesus. In 1893, Shutter merely mentioned that his own article had been published 'some years earlier' without giving an exact year, but with the help of *Poole's Index* it actually refers to 'The Element of Humor in the Bible' from 1885.[435] In a sense, he is overtaken at the finish line by a dual article on 'The Humor of Our Lord' (Grosart 1890–1[436]), as it not only speaks of the 'Bible' but specifically of Christ, whereas Shutter's broader title also reflects the content of his 1885 article. For here he only uses roughly a page to touch briefly on Jesus while the rest is devoted to humorous episodes, characters, and dialogue exchanges from the Old Testament (e.g. Abimelech, Samson, Nabal, and Elijah). Other authors try to disarm the sense of explosiveness that emerged from the advertisement for Shutter's book by incorporating cautious terms such as 'traces of' or 'indications of' in their titles: 'Traces of Humor in the Sayings of Jesus' (Knapp 1907) and *The Laughter of God. An Essay on the Indications of a Sense of Humor in the Son of Man* (Wordsworth 1925).

If we may trust that the bibliographic research has indeed captured all the relevant publications around the turn of the previous century, it suggests the following: after church historians, homileticians, and exegetes had paved the way the new century also brought forth systematic theologians (and historians of religion, such as Reinach mentioned in the introduction) who pondered on 'The Theology of Laughter' (Mercer 1910–1) and 'The Use of the Comic Spirit in Religion' (Smith 1911). The ultimate endorsement that these themes were not only left to mavericks and daredevils must be their inclusion in encyclopaedias, for in a way they represent the general and accepted knowledge belonging to every field of study at any given time. This happens in the two-volume work *A Dictionary of Christ and the Gospels*, which includes separate articles on humour

---

Heflin (1943–2023) cites this monograph as the first on the American market to draw attention to Jesus' use of humour: Albert Richmond Bond: *The Master Preacher. A Study of the Homiletics of Jesus* (New York: American Tract Society, 1910), Heflin 1974, 71.

434   Cf. Casanowicz 1894, Baumgartner 1896, Logan 1909, Hazard 1919, and Beet 1922.
435   Poole & Fletcher 1957, 42.
436   Cf. Paulsen 1900, Buckley 1901, Wünkhaus 1909, Jameson [1926] 1948, and Morison 1931.

(Glover 1906) and laughter (J.R. Murray 1908), both of which consider it likely that these concepts are relevant in relation to Jesus.

Among the articles and books mentioned so far, none reach the lofty heights where Dudley Zuver (fl. 1933–59) roams when he publishes a book in 1933 whose title (and content) can be considered an apotheosis scarcely matched by even the most enthusiastic authors of the last third of the 20th century. While we can polemically suspect some of these authors of subtly turning laughter into a gift of grace with soteriological power, no such investigative suspicion is necessary when it comes to Zuver, for he proclaims it boldly on the book's cover: *Salvation by Laughter*. Zuver covers a wide range of topics and not everything is profound or interesting to a reader a couple of generations later, where the subject is no longer exotic or provocative. However, it is still edifying to remember the book's concluding comic punchline, that the idea of salvation in a Christian sense is humorous in itself because there exists an unfathomable incongruity between the desirability of salvation and the means to attain it: we cannot earn it religiously, ethically, politically, economically ... but rather receive it as a gift.[437]

i. What Enabled Us to Start Hearing the Laughter of Jesus?

Without taking a stance on the virtues and shortcomings of the works mentioned in the text and notes, we venture to state that the most remarkable thing about all of them is that, like the scouts in the Book of Numbers (chapter 13), they had curiosity, will, and courage to enter into a largely *terra incognita* to investigate whether it truly was a promised land from which they could bring back untold fruits. These academics and people of the church did not have a Moses to send them out with authority, so what drove them on this expedition? If we were to offer a suggestion as to what constituted the connection between the cultural personalities of the early 18th century and the much broader, if not yet outright 'popular', breakthrough around the turn of the previous century, we could narrow it down to two 19th-century academic movements within exegesis. These movements enabled the exploration of new paths in dealing with tradition and Holy Scripture – including starting to listen for everyday laughter from the mouth of Jesus and something that was different from the mocking laughter from Him enthroned in heaven.

The main argument will, in a way, circle back to the theory of the condition of possibility for the emergence of Easter Laughter, which referred partly to

---

437   Zuver 1933, 267.

the preachers' use of the tools of everyday language and partly to the medieval immersion in the Man of Sorrows. The latter may seem counterintuitive in relation to laughter, but the preoccupation with Jesus' sufferings went hand in hand with connecting Him-who-sits-at-the-right-hand-of-God-the-Father with the carpenter's son from Nazareth. In parallel, it seems plausible to point to the offshoot of the Enlightenment's criticism of the Bible and the church's 'enthusiasts', which within biblical scholarship became historical-critical exegesis. One aspect of this new exegesis was the ambition to penetrate behind the evangelists' mythologising portrayal of Jesus Christ in order to provide a historically accurate picture of how Jesus' life and person had actually been. In this particular context, we can turn Albert Schweitzer's (1875–1965) famous criticism of the research on the Life of Jesus[438] upside down. For when Schweitzer (in some people's opinion) dealt a fatal blow to the project by demonstrating that scholars inevitably ended up reflecting more of their own time than Palestine around the year 30, that is precisely what is interesting for the present purpose, where the aim is to make them testify to when the interest in Jesus' laughter arose.

In the case of the Life of Jesus scholars, we could perhaps reuse John the Baptist's declaration of not being the man himself, but merely the one pointing to the one who is to come. For when looking through even a digitised version of David Friedrich Strauss' (1808–74) *The Life of Jesus* (1835–6), we do not find a relevant heading in the otherwise highly detailed table of contents, nor do electronic searches for (even truncated forms of) words such as 'laughter', 'smile', 'humour', or 'irony' yield any hits.[439] However, something starts to happen with Ernest Renan (1823–92) when he publishes his *Life of Jesus* (1863) thirty years later. Although Renan does not make use of the central terms either, he ventures more into speculation about Jesus' mannerisms than Strauss had had an appetite for and includes a section about the fact that the Lord speaks with a special *esprit*.[440]

While theologians of the next century, despite Schweitzer's criticism, continued to delve into the biography of Jesus, several of them referred specifically to Renan as a pioneer for drawing attention to the characteristic of Jesus that, in their English translation, showed he had wit.[441] It is possible that these individuals may be stretching the interpretation of Renan, but the crucial point is not

---

438   *The Quest of the Historical Jesus*, 1910 (German ed. 1906).
439   In vol. 2 there are three occurrences of 'ironic', but none of them are applied to Jesus.
440   Renan 1863, 90.
441   In the English edition, which was published in 1864, just a year after the French original, 'esprit' was, among other terms, translated as 'genius' (e.g. 114, corresponding

whether he implies wit, humour, and laughter with *esprit*, but rather that he and other scholars of the Life of Jesus expanded or even shifted the focus from the Creed's brutal reduction of Jesus' biographical data (he-was-born-to-die) to also consider the life he managed to live between birth and death. Once this project had been (re)legitimised, it became much easier for subsequent scholars to form ideas about the way Jesus interacted with, and spoke to, people,[442] and to elevate these investigations from incidental digressions to the main subject matter. A subject so interesting that it deserved to be announced already in the title of an article or book.

The second seminal breakthrough occurred with the assistance from colleagues in the humanities. The keyword was, incidentally, provided in the subtitle of Shutter's book, which, after 'Wit and Humor of the Bible', added: 'A Literary Study'. The intention is summarised on the last page, where the presentation concludes with this slogan: 'The [Bible] touches human nature at all points. The more we view it as "literature", the less as "dogma", the firmer its hold upon the heart of man will become.'[443] In light of the terminology in this statement, it is not surprising that Shutter declares his indebtedness to the man who, in posterity, stands as one of the fathers of what would develop into literary biblical criticism (which, to distinguish it from the use of 'literary criticism' to describe a line of research mainly interested in tracing the sources of a text, can also be called literary-critical exegesis). This refers to the English poet, philosopher of religion, and professor of literature in Oxford, Matthew Arnold (1822–88).

---

      to p. 90 in the French edition). Renan is credited, for example, in J.R. Murray 1908, 9, Vedder 1922, 37, and Hussey 1928, 331. In Terrot Reaveley Glover's (1869–1943) *The Jesus of History*, he approaches the subject by analysing Jesus' 'playfulness of speech', 1917, 48.

442   Indeed, it is true that we are referring to a much later writer, but his observation is both striking and symptomatic of this methodological starting-point: Jesus' first listeners, and even his disciples, did not relate to him based on or because of a formulated Christology; he must have attracted and influenced them solely through his personality and preaching. P. Bloch 1999, 185.

443   Shutter 1893, 218; cf. the ending of his article a few years previously: 'Viewed simply as a literary work, [the Bible] is the most interesting book in the entire realm of letters. The poetry, the dramatic portions, the oratory of the Bible, are unsurpassed; and over history, biography, drama, and most serious discussions, play the soft gleams of healthful humor, or the lightning-like bolts of sarcasm and wit. The book touches human nature at all points.' 1885, 453.

Arnold's magnum opus in this context, *Literature and Dogma* (1873), is said to have contributed decisively to the development in the Anglo-Saxon world of including the Bible as part of the curriculum in higher education, specifically no longer just in theological faculties or seminaries but in the field of English literature. The intention was to approach the Bible from a secular perspective, that is, to read it poetically. In Arnold's case, there was to some extent a critical stance towards religion, comparable to the tendencies among theologians in their demythologising liberal theology.[444] However, it also laid the fertile groundwork for the approach to the Bible that Arnold's arguably greatest 'successor' (namely Northrop Frye [1912–91]) would later formulate by borrowing an aphorism from one of William Blake's [1757–1827] graphic plates (*Laocoön, c.* 1826): 'The Old & New Testaments are the Great Code of Art.'

When teaching 'the Bible as literature', as Frye did, the aim was twofold. On the one hand, it was to explore how significant portions of world literature can be read as 'reinterpretations' of the biblical narratives. On the other hand, it was only natural to search within the Scriptures for the human element in its broadest sense, including tracing the biblical authors' use of rhetorical, dramatic, and poetic devices. If dogmas and traditions have a natural tendency to focus on what is deemed most important and to preserve it in authoritative formulations and practices, there is a risk that the reading of sources becomes narrowed. Shifting the focus to the literary qualities of the sources does not necessarily imply a contradiction to dogmatics; rather, it can invigorate it. However, it does promote an expansion of perspective when seeking out the elements – both conflicting and complementary – that the tradition may have left behind, such as the biblical authors' use of satire, irony, laughable wordplay, and humour, among others.

---

444 A sample of this could be Arnold's strategy to regain acceptance for the Bible among the enlightened people of his time, who the bishops were otherwise offering stones for bread with their metaphysics. Arnold observes that when we base the authority of the Bible and the Christian religion on miracles, it no longer convinces many people but rather leads them to perceive faith as arising from 'ignorance, deception, or mistake'. The remedy lies in a change of method, an altered perception of language that does not pit the Bible against science, but also does not compromise the idea that the Bible is about something real and important: 'To these persons we restore the use of the Bible, if, while showing them that the Bible-language is not scientific, but the language of common speech or of poetry and eloquence, approximative language thrown out at certain great objects of consciousness which it does not pretend to define fully, we convince them at the same time that this language deals with facts of experience most momentous and real.' Arnold 1874, 126 f.

ii. Will the Right Jesus be so Kind as to Step Forward?

It is certainly not uncommon to perceive a thinly veiled threat in this repeated statement by Jesus: 'he, who has ears to hear, let him hear' (e.g. Mt 11:15). This may be due to reading it in light of the prophecy in Isaiah, where the emphasis seems ominously shifted from human responsibility to the idea that God actively makes people deaf (Isa 6:9–10, quoted by Jesus in Mt 13:14–5). However, we could also interpret it as a simple observation in line with what could be the oldest hermeneutical rule in world history: what goes around comes around (perhaps better captured by the German, and Danish, idiom: 'The way we shout into the forest, the way it echoes back out'). Implicitly: if we do not shout, nothing happens, and, what is even more relevant in this context, if we shout something *else*, we get different responses. This opening reflection is meant to counter the first and most obvious objection to the various depictions of a smiling and laughing Jesus in the 20th century: he is unrecognisable!

In a historical perspective it is not only a question about the overall distinction between a radiant heavenly-enthroned Christ and a dusty wandering Jesus, but equally as much about the various artistic and mental images of the Incarnate, some of which have been particularly dominant, bordering on exclusivity. This is especially true for the Man of Sorrows in the Garden of Gethsemane on Maundy Thursday and on Golgotha on Good Friday, or the Victorious Lord on Easter Sunday. However, the images of Jesus in Galilee as a teacher (rabbi), healer, and preacher have also filled both external and internal canvases to such an extent that it can be difficult to make room for supplementary 'profiles'. The invocation of the basic rule of hermeneutics is merely intended to counter the immediate objection that a laughing Jesus lacks biblical support.

Here it certainly matters to watch our step and make use of Voltaire's (1694–1778) proverbial saying: 'God help me against my friends. I can take care of my enemies'. On the one hand, we can wholeheartedly embrace the principle that the question of biblical support depends on the eyes that see, and that throughout history both individuals and institutions have constantly found answers in the Bible to questions it simply does not immediately address – or, to put it more cautiously, at least does not provide the unequivocal answers that dogmatics have subsequently formulated (such as a specific and clear doctrine on the relationship between the Father, Son, and Holy Spirit, which could have settled a thousand years of dispute over the *filioque*). On the other hand it is hard to suppress the urge to run away screaming when, for example, Shutter launches a counterattack against those who close their eyes to the merriment of the Lord. This they do because 'they have seized upon a few of the sadder incidents of his career, and have exaggerated them into undue prominence [...]. Especially have they made much of his agony in the garden and his death upon the cross'.[445] Another writer seeks to open the eyes of the reader by comparing Leviathan in the Book of Job to Mickey Mouse in order to demonstrate how easily we find amusement in cute animals.[446]

If we only have access to the Bible by way of interpretation, this applies even more so to laughter-inducing humour, insofar as one of the most important signals to help determine if humour is at play lies in the tone of voice (and accompanying facial expressions and bodily gestures), precisely the dimensions that are lost in writing. Or rather: written language, of course, has its own means of replacing the contextual signals of being present at an event or a piece of conversation (even before emoticons!); but they often lie between the lines, so we only notice them if we are extra attentive to the 'gaps'.

Conversely, without intonation, the room for interpretation becomes even greater if and when it becomes a project to *imagine* how the language has sounded. At the same time, the metaphor 'between the lines' reinforces the suspicion that as readers we are at the mercy of pure arbitrariness. Therefore, it may be better to say that humour is often hidden in the finer nuances of language. Those nuances are indeed some of the most difficult to grasp and master in a foreign language, but it is nevertheless indicated that we are not entirely left to interpret merely according to our own mood and prejudices. If we listen to the Old Testament scholars or Jewish scholars who have focused on laughter in the Hebrew language, we are informed that the Bible quantitatively contains many diverse occurrences of formulations involving terms related to laughter.[447] We are

---

445 Shutter 1893, 82 f.
446 Rensburg 1991, 34. It must be admitted that the Book of Job (40:25–41:26) alternates between portraying the sea monster as a chaotic force of evil and, in its demonstration of God's sovereignty, treating Leviathan as if it were truly a plaything: 'Will you play with him as with a bird, or will you put him on a leash for your girls?' (41:5 *ESV*). But it is hardly meant as a cosy or amusing image. Interestingly, the motif of God's sovereignty over Leviathan points forward to the hymn by Adam of St Victor, which was cited in note 2, where this struggle is equated with Jesus' victory over death, in other words, the motif that is found in Easter Laughter, for example, in Mathesius' example.
447 Although not all humour manifests itself in laughter, reference can be made, for example, to an American dissertation where the doctoral student listed 690 examples of humour-related words appearing primarily in the Old Testament, but also in the New Testament. These words, in a contemporary English translation, are rendered as 'laughter', 'happy', 'mirth', 'joy', 'glad', 'delight', 'play', and at the other end of the spectrum, 'taunt', 'sport', 'scorn', 'mock', 'scoff', and 'folly'. Bullard 1962.

also told that for some readers of the Bible this perhaps surprisingly high number is due to the fact that in Hebrew there are not only the two best-known terms (the roots שָׂחַק [śachaq] and לָעַג [la'ag], which are often translated as 'laughing/laughter' or 'mocking/scorn'), but that the language, qualitatively, has a multitude of nuanced expressions for laughter.[448]

Although we are well advised to be sceptical when people claim to have found a brand new key to unlock texts that others have pondered over for ages, the combination of a one-sided tradition and a complex language makes it somewhat less unreasonable when Joseph Chotzner (1844–1914), twenty years after his pioneering work on humour and irony in the Bible (where we can easily imagine he must have faced intense criticism from colleagues and laypeople), concludes an article by stating that there is indeed a 'wealth of hidden meaning contained in the Bible'. His trump card is that this hidden meaning 'can only be detected by the study of the original Hebrew text, [...] which the translators, either through oversight or inability, have failed to reproduce'.[449]

Without suggesting some kind of conspiracy theory, we must acknowledge that Chotzner here touches upon a sensitive point that accentuates the hermeneutical problem. For the average Bible reader, not proficient in Hebrew or Greek, it is not enough to decide to study the Bible systematically in search of evidence for a smiling God or laughing Jesus, as they are entirely dependent on translators. Especially when grappling with a Semitic language that not only differs significantly from the Indo-European languages but is also characterised by a system where word stems can be varied in numerous ways, and where the relatively limited vocabulary therefore has a wide range of meanings, any translation is forced to make an extraordinary number of choices. It should be relatively uncontroversial to claim that the specific choices among the many possibilities inevitably reflect an era and a tradition, and that the result may deviate more or less from the original situation and culture (similar to Schweitzer's observation of the time-bound nature of the Life of Jesus research).

The purpose here is not to delve into the details and discuss possible translations of this or that particular verse but solely to present an observation and a plea on a very general level: it can be observed that once exegetes, theologians,

---

448 'Daniel Lys has meticulously compiled all expressions of God's laughter in the Old Testament, which are conveyed through no less than thirteen different Hebrew roots.' Wolff 2009, 86. Wolff is referring to Lys' [1924–2014] article 'Quand Dieu rit' from Etudes théologiques et religieuses 79/2004, 201–26.

449 Chotzner 1905, 12. Cf. note 363 for an equivalent polemic regarding required proficiency in Latin.

pastors, and others have found it legitimate and relevant to search for Jesus' smile and laughter (in or behind the given translations), they have believed themselves capable of finding not only faint echoes thereof but such loud testimonies thereto that we must almost begin to wonder about the deafness, not to say stupidity or malice, of the past. To be fair, the example from Shutter above is not representative, but it must be admitted that even a benevolent reader is often left with considerable uncertainty about how much interpreters read into, rather than out of, the biblical texts. While some, with a certain plausibility, find Jesus' speech full of 'cleaving irony, sarcasm, sulphurous invective, iconoclastic wit, comic *reductio ad absurdum*, and a touch of cynicism',[450] it looks like a misuse of syllogisms when one writer believes he can document how full not only the New Testament but also Heaven is with God's redeeming laughter with this nimble-fingered argumentation: 'The Kingdom of God' is mentioned 67 times in the New Testament; according to Jesus' beatitude, those weeping on earth shall laugh later (Lk 6:21), ergo …![451]

We could accommodate this syllogism by acknowledging that the author is on the right track by focusing on volume rather than isolated incidents or hitherto overlooked or deliberately suppressed layers of meaning in rare words. Just as we no longer may fully accept all the theological implications that tradition drew from the Evangelists' silence about Jesus' laughter, it is equally unconvincing when confronted with the often forced attempts to prove Jesus' speech filled with wit and amusement. For as Kuschel cleverly points out: if such a modern interpretation succeeds too well, we are suddenly forced to attribute a pernicious – and shared! – motive to all the New Testament authors in order to explain why they have suppressed any mention of the supposedly omnipresent laughter in and around Our Lord. In the same place, Kuschel argues a point that deserves to be fully endorsed: it must be a holistic understanding of the figure of Jesus that determines the matter. And it seems well balanced when Kuschel suggests that such a comprehensive view certainly does not portray Jesus as a jester, but

---

450 Hussey 1928, 333 f.
451 Richert 2009, 71. If we were to take such argumentation seriously, we could choose to challenge it by initially asking why the author omits to include the 32 times Matthew prefers his favourite expression 'Kingdom of Heaven' – and asking whether all occurrences of one or the other expression really do support the interpretation of a Kingdom filled with laughter. However, pursuing the topic will likely prove unfruitful and, at the very least, petty.

neither as an ascetic, and that it is strained to imagine messianic joy without any trace of smiles or laughter.[452]

In conclusion, we can on a very general level argue that just as such an image of Jesus, from an exegetical perspective, is neither better nor worse attested than the more familiar image from tradition, likewise, from a Christological and theological standpoint, it is not incompatible with the way in which Judaism and Christianity have understood Christ and God. It is perhaps inevitable for recent generations of exegetes, theologians, and people of the church to be accused of populism and political correctness if and when they seek to attribute a certain amount of humour and good-natured laughter to God and Jesus in accordance with the *Zeitgeist*. However, from a contemporary standpoint we can also reverse the question and ask on what grounds the Psalmist knew that God laughs mockingly in heaven. Who are they who allow themselves to dictate most when speaking about why and how God laughs or whether Jesus laughed or not? Is it more apt and less anthropomorphic to speak of God's anger rather than his laughter, of Jesus' suffering rather than his joy?

Our aim is certainly not to dispute that the core of Christianity is the cross, nor that it is only fair to identify words such as these from Jesus as giving our faith the strongest comfort *and* task: 'Come to me, all you who are weary and burdened, and I will give you rest. Take my yoke upon you and learn from me, for I am gentle and humble in heart, and you will find rest for your souls. For my yoke is easy and my burden is light' (Mt 11:28–30 *NIV*). However, does this imply that it is more honest and realistic to talk about seriousness ('oh, that's just how life is, we all know that!') rather than cheerfulness? Is the gospel only for bad times and not for good moments?

There are two major obstacles that threaten to hinder cheerful boldness. The paths can be daunting if we venture too far down the road that these rhetorical questions seem to point to, ending up in a kind of 'Prosperity theology' where God-with-us promises worldly success. Even if we manage to avoid that cul-de-sac, an even greater risk looms just around the corner: how to avoid becoming banal. Quite tellingly, Helmuth Friis (1944–94) opened his little gem of a

---

452 Kuschel 1994, 68 f. Even if we do not base an interpretation on a single word or piece of dialogue, a comprehensive understanding of Jesus will naturally be formed out of individual components. As early as 1908, a lexicon article provided a good starting-point for assembling a list of relevant pieces to form a supplementary image of the Lord: that Jesus distanced himself from the most strict sects within Judaism of his time (e.g. Lk 5:33 ff. regarding wedding guests, fasting, and wine in wineskins; Mt 9:10 ff. regarding table fellowship with tax collectors and sinners; Mt 9:14 ff.

book, *Joy* (1994), by stating that '[t]here can be something uncomfortable about making joy a theme, it almost inevitably becomes intrusive and shameless (like talking about eroticism)'.[453] This has probably always been the case, but yet Friis points to something particularly typical for our recent generations when he observes that '[i]f you look up the indexes in the philosophical books of this century, the word joy hardly appears. But there are so many more words like anxiety, guilt, nothingness, randomness, death, meaninglessness, and absurdity', to which he adds: 'It is symptomatic of an entire cultural epoch'.[454] The cost of this 'symptomatology' in (late) modernity has been that '[t]he refined thinking of our time makes it difficult to talk about good things, while the discourse on misery seems to absorb refinement itself. Joy is for children, scouts, fools, and primitive people. One must be foolish to be happy and naive to speak of it'.[455] Conversely, one gains something in advance by focusing on the opposites of joy, because 'it is almost impossible not to become spiritual when talking about anxiety, emptiness, and death. The unmasking of how ordinary bourgeois existence is a shield against deeper and more dangerous, therefore repressed, matters places one in the flattering position of the one who sees through it all'.[456]

Friis' mentor, professor of ethics and philosophy of religion Knud Ejler Løgstrup (1905–81), apparently had a similar intention in wanting to puncture the 'self-flattering position'. When Løgstrup famously spoke of 'sovereign expressions of life' and life as inherently good and a gift, he opened himself up to the imminent demand for a theodicy. Løgstrup countered this demand by

---

regarding the difference in fasting practices between Jesus' disciples and those of John the Baptist); that Jesus specifically made positive use of children's games (Lk 7:32 ff.) and, in general, the nature of his choice of material for making parables about the relationship with God (such as a father's joy and celebrating a returning son, Lk 15:23 ff., cf. 6:23!). Based on these and other details, the author concludes that, on the one hand, '[t]here is nothing in the Gospels to encourage the supposition that He frowned upon innocent mirth or checked its exhibition in his followers. On the contrary, on one occasion at least, He declined to interfere with a spontaneous outburst of exhilaration on their part [Lk 19:40 at the entry into Jerusalem]'; and on the other hand, that Jesus' 'chief concern was not so much to regulate the manner of their joy as to purify its motive (Lk 10:20)', J.R. Murray 1908.

453 Friis 1994, 7.
454 Ibid., 9.
455 Ibid., 8.
456 Ibid, 11. If we were to, polemically, make use of Friis' point in a pastoral-theological context, this could be a good contribution to explaining why pastors often find it more meaningful to give a speech at funerals than at weddings, and why the field of

suggesting the equal need for a *nihilodicy*: 'He who says that life and the world are created is asked from whence does all suffering and misfortune come? He who considers everything meaningless and empty, on the other hand, is never asked from whence does all joy and experience come.'[457] Why is that?

Much would be gained if we could agree, to some extent, that if we want to avoid speaking anthropomorphically about God and blasphemously about Christ, the distinction between different types of emotions and moods is not particularly relevant. It is not just the humorous talk about God that runs the risk of violating proper boundaries. All talk about him runs that risk. As Robert Edward Neale (b. 1929) has sharply pointed out: most of the time, we speak so clichéd and boringly about God that it borders on blasphemy in itself, even if all the words and formulations have been adopted at countless councils. For is not rather the real offense if the discourse about the Creator and his Son testifies to the fact that they have ceased to (be able to) surprise us?[458]

4. Did Jesus Laugh? No! (And Is That Why We Can?)

When this book nevertheless concludes with a negative response to this age-old question, it is primarily based on a historical and exegetical observation, which in turn has significant theological (and soteriological) implications. To sharpen

---

    pastoral care enjoys much greater popularity than many other disciplines. Is there not a bit more prestige in being a good pastor in a cancer ward than in being able to organise an enjoyable camp for confirmation classes?

457 Løgstrup 1995, 267.
458 Neale 1971, 36.

    Cote can complement the polemic with some factual observations when he points out that it is actually quite astonishing how anthropomorphic the Old Testament writers allow themselves to write about God. Even the most reserved among them (the Priestly texts) do not attempt to spiritualise the language by transforming it into allegories when they speak of Yahweh's hand, foot, eye, ear, mouth, face, head, and heart. God uses these body parts to listen, speak, whistle, smell, and eat, to build, shape, create, fight, punish, and write; for God can move, sit, stand, or rest, and, indeed, he can laugh, get angry, sleep, wake up, repent, regret, forget, remember, and be jealous. On the other hand, Cote notes a quite special common denominator among the parts of the human body which the authors do not dare to attribute to God: unlike the aforementioned ones, they are not relational: 'Those other human features which have no direct or obvious relational quality (bone, flesh, blood, hair, lungs, and so on), are never attributed to God.' The point of using anthropomorphic language is to emphasise 'a lively faith in a living God, a personal God, a God who remains everlastingly in touch with his people', 1986, 40 and 44 f.

the point we can employ two rough simplifications each of which touches upon a core in their respective areas, and which, of course, should be taken with more than one grain of salt.

The first (historical) observation rests on Halliwell's authoritative examination of laughter in ancient Greece. Although 'Homeric laughter' has gained a reputation, where it competes with 'sardonic laughter'[459] for the rank of being the most unpleasant, Halliwell's main concern is to document that Homer presents many different types of laughter. In this context, where the aim is not to rehabilitate the ancient Greeks, it is much more interesting that Halliwell adds a thought-provoking observation precisely about the type of laughter associated with 'the Homeric' in popular belief. This type of laughter is encountered most famously in the scene at the end of the first song of the *Iliad*, where the gods laugh unquenchably at the sight of the lame Hephaestus. This means that the laughter here is in line with the one known for centuries from marketplaces, where people paid money to stare at and be amused by cripples and freaks of nature (cf. David Lynch's [b. 1946] film *The Elephant Man* [1980] for a stirring example of this). However, Halliwell points out that this laughter has its very own domain, as the gods never laugh at humans or their situations in this way, only at each other.[460] That kind of laughter is, so to speak, horizontal.

Although Halliwell's primary subject and purpose are different, towards the end of his book, he takes a look at the New Testament, where he not only notes the silence about Jesus' laughter but also struggles to find any figures or scenes where we can imagine someone smiling or laughing good-naturedly. In relation to the concerns of the people and endeavours discussed in the preceding sections, Halliwell makes a very dry remark: 'Nor is there much trace of laughter-related states of mind in either its narratives or its doctrinal content, despite the attempts of some scholars to highlight elements of irony and wit in certain passages.'[461]

The second (exegetical) simplification can be attributed to a Dutch Christian Hebraist, Martin Gejerus (1618–87), who formulated it so epigrammatically that it could fit on a matchbox: *Deus in V.T. risisse, numquam flevisse; in N.T. flevisse, numquam risisse, legitur.*[462] It is important to immediately reiterate that it is a

---

459   Now of course not in Propp's interpretation, cf. p. 158 f.
460   Halliwell 2008, 52.
461   *Ibid.*, 475.
462   The statement can be found in Matthew Poole's (1624–79) monumental concordance of Bible commentaries. Verse by verse in every single part of the entire Bible Poole summarises, paraphrases, and quotes capturing the contributions of various exegeses (in the broadest sense) to the interpretation of almost every detail – thus serving as a

rough simplification that God in the Old Testament laughs and never cries and vice versa in the New Testament; however, it is not an idiosyncratic interpretation or stance, but a 'simple' observation (Gejerus essentially refers only to what can be read in black and white, *legitur* – and, thus, not 'between the lines'). Once we keep this in mind it still opens up far-reaching perspectives to consider who cries and who laughs in the Old and New Testaments.

In continuation of Halliwell's point about Homeric laughter, we can sensibly add that the situation is quite different for the Old Testament God. While there are a few glimpses of a divine assembly,[463] God has no one to laugh with or for that matter to laugh *at* on his own level. His laughter therefore becomes vertical – for only the downwards direction is an option. The next contrast to Homer that emerges is that the wide range of laughter forms in the *Iliad* and *Odyssey* seems to collapse, as it appears that God only has one kind of laughter left for humans: derisive laughter (most terrifying in Job 9:23 or Prov 1:26: 'I will laugh [the verb śachaq] at your calamity; I will mock [the verb la'ag] when terror strikes you' *ESV*). When God laughs, it is not an invitation but a warning that is ignored at one's peril. Laughter evidently never expresses a communion between two parties but rather serves as an important weapon in an eternal power struggle, the battle that the 'nations', 'kings of the earth', and 'rulers' have already lost in advance, as stated in Psalm 2.

In this regard we could appositely adopt the theological position that God is not necessarily someone we should have as our buddy or enjoy leisure time with. Yet it is rather depressing that the downward movement of laughter from God to humans seems to set the tone for laughter on earth as well. Job's Book is particularly intriguing in this context because it apparently provides insight into

---

Christian counterpart to the Talmud. Gejerus' conclusion regarding the distribution of weeping and laughter in the Old and New Testaments is mentioned as a commentary on Psalms 2:4 in *Synopsis criticorum aliorumque Sacræ Scripturæ interpretum et commentatorum, Summo Studio et Fide adornata, Indicibusque necessariis instructa a Matthæo Polo*. Vol. II: *Complectens Libros omnes à Jobo ad Cantici Canticorum*. Ultrajecti [Utrecht]: Cartusiæ Villenovæ, 1684, col. 513, line 40 f. I obtained the references to Gejerus and Poole from Michael Andrew Screech (1926–2018) and must mention that he immediately distances himself from the statement as misleadingly oversimplified, 1997, 43.

463   The wager between God and Satan regarding Job's endurance takes place in an assembly, likely consisting of subjects to God (Job 1:6); the convention appears to be more balanced in Psalm 82, while Yahweh is even perceived in a subordinate status in Deuteronomy 32:8.

two conflicting experiences of the nature of laughter in human-divine relationships. In one passage, we read, 'Surely God does not reject one who is blameless or strengthen the hands of evildoers. He will yet fill your mouth with laughter and your lips with shouts of joy. Your enemies will be clothed in shame, and the tents of the wicked will be no more' (8:20–2 *NIV*). It is Bildad, one of the politically and doctrinally correct interlocutors, who speaks in this manner. However, shortly thereafter, this statement clashes with Job's own experience: 'I have become a laughingstock to my friends, though I called on God and he answered, a mere laughingstock, though righteous and blameless!' (12:4 *NIV*). The prophet Jeremiah seems to support Job's perspective: 'You deceived me, LORD, and I was deceived; you overpowered me and prevailed. I am ridiculed all day long; everyone mocks me' (Jer 20:7 *NIV*).

Perhaps the most disturbing aspect of laughter in the Old Testament is that even in human interpersonal relationships it is almost exclusively used as a symbolic instrument of power – or at least as an expression of a strong sense of 'Sudden Glory'.[464] To put it bluntly, we get the impression that joy and laughter, in their other forms besides mockery, only survive in the memory of something lost, as when Job looks back to the time before Satan and remembers his interaction with his neighbours: 'I laughed with them as they could not believe it, And the light of my face they did not cast down' (29:24 *LSB*). Laughter, as something that connects rather than creates distance, is also glimpsed in Jeremiah, but again as something lost: 'I did not sit in the assembly of revellers, / I sat alone because of your hand, / for you have filled me with indignation' (15:17).[465]

---

[464] The conclusion of Flemming Friis Hvidberg's (1897–1959) groundbreaking study on *Weeping and Laughter in the Old Testament* (1938) is still worth quoting: 'It is characteristic of early Israelite humour that mostly it is not what we should call harmless. The joke told for the sake of the joke, the anecdote told only for the sake of the droll situation, – these are rarely found in the Old Testament. The humour of the ancient Israelites victimized somebody, whether the images of the neighbouring peoples, whose powerlessness before Yahweh was found ridiculous, or the neighbouring peoples themselves, whose strange names and odd appearance amused them (Gen 25:25), or enemies who got the worst of it before the popular heroes. The Old Testament "humour" – if so it may be termed – which the Israelite prophets took into the service of their case is of quite a different kind. This is not a case of the coarse joke, the comic anecdote, but rather of satire. But frequently this 'satire' is rather what a modern European would call menace, terms of abuse, or puns.' 1962, 150 f.

[465] Symptomatically both of these verses from Job and Jeremiah respectively can also be translated in such a way that the character of laughter is once again of the unpleasant kind. Compare the long list of varying English translations for each verse on biblehub.com.

On the other hand, there are plenty of examples of laughter driven by superiority, notably various forms of superiority, which is why the Book of Job even provides examples of mocking animals. Like the wild donkey that laughs at the other donkeys because they have to live as pack animals in the cities (39:5–7); or the ostrich, whom God may not have blessed with the sharpest brain, but that is so swift that it can laugh at the pursuing horseman (39:17–18).

The same ostrich can simultaneously serve as a model for the 'compensation' for the condescending laughter, that is the kind of 'restitution' known in the proverb, 'he who laughs last laughs longest'. In the introduction, it is narrated how the ostrich is ridiculed because it lacks wings like the stork and falcon (v. 13); but in the larger perspective this deficiency is turned into victory. In the case of the ostrich it is due to the power of its leg muscles; but when we hear in the Book of Judges about the Philistine lords who, 'when they were in high spirits, they said, "Call for Samson to entertain us". So they called Samson out of the prison, and he performed for them' (16:25 NRS), it is the arm muscles that have the final say. Unfortunately for the lords, they placed the supposedly enfeebled Samson between the supporting pillars of the building, and that was the last thing they came to regret. And when the young interns and chaplains from one of the competing prophetic schools (the common translation, 'little boys', is completely misleading) mocked Elisha by calling him nicknames (2 Kings 2:23), their herd mentality mistakenly led them to rely on their numerical superiority, which then, 'lastly', proved insufficient to contend with a pair of bears that came to Elisha's aid.

The model reaches its most unpleasant apotheosis far beyond the confines of the Old Testament at the end of Tertullian's *De spectaculis*, where the entire last chapter is one long vision of the ultimate 'last laughter'. Here, there is no end to amusement and laughter among the resurrected saved in heaven – not caused, we should note, by the reunion with loved ones and the eternal communion with them and the Creator, but by being able to witness the former rulers on earth and the flippant philosophers writhing in pain and shame in Hell.[466] Screech has coined an awful but apt metaphor for this wishful thinking and called it the vision of 'a celestial Belsen'. If we could have hoped that such an Early Church Father as the ascetic and legalistic Tertullian had not yet grasped the depth and scope of Jesus' lack of laughter, we sadly see the horror show repeated a thousand years later by the very Doctor Angelicus himself. As the supreme scholastic that he is, Aquinas does add distinctions and nuances, but in its essence, the logic is evidently compelling if the saved are to fully enjoy and appreciate their

---

466 Tertullian 1977, 297–301.

blessedness. For when Aquinas aligns himself with the Aristotelian principle that one fully understands something only by virtue of its opposite, then, in order for the saints to fully enjoy their joy and give even greater thanks to God for it, they must be ensured a clear view of the torments of the damned.[467]

Is that really the teaching about the joy, jubilation, and laughter, which, despite everything, are also found in the Old Testament? Amidst the otherwise one-sided portrayal of laughter, there are indeed a few, but significant, uplifting moments. Particularly in the form of the Psalms of David, where all creation and the people are encouraged to break out in jubilation and shouts of joy (e.g. Psalms 66, 81, and 95), even the entire cosmos is called to participate, as stated by the prophet Isaiah: 'Shout for joy, you heavens, for the LORD has done it! Shout joyfully, you lower parts of the earth; Break into a shout of jubilation, you mountains, Forest, and every tree in it; For the LORD has redeemed Jacob, And in Israel He shows His glory' (44:23 *NAS*; cf. 49:13). And it is claimed that laughter is included in the jubilation and shouts of joy, at least according to Psalm 126: 'When the LORD restored the fortunes of Zion, / we were like those who dream. / Then our mouth was filled with laughter, / and our tongue with shouts of joy; / then they said among the nations, / "The LORD has done great things for them". The LORD has done great things for us; / we are glad' (vv. 1–3 *ESV*). One of the few, if not the only, who is able to laugh in such a way is the 'capable woman' from the Book of Proverbs, who not only excels in managing the household but also manages to 'laugh at the days to come' (31:25; cf. the quote from Gregory the Great in note 244, where the 'woman' is interpreted typologically as 'the Holy Church').

When earlier in this book we have polemicised against the selective use of Bible verses in the past, such as omitting one half of a parallelism (e.g. 'a time to

---

467 *Summa Theologica*, III, Suppl., qu. 94, art. 1; 1906, 226; 1920 online: newadvent.org/summa/5094.htm. The reference to Aquinas is taken from Screech 1997, 18 (note 4), while the mention of Belsen can be found on p. 313. The main text is a paraphrase of Aquinas' 'I answer' section: 'Now everything is known the more for being compared with its contrary, because when contraries are placed beside one another they become more conspicuous. Wherefore in order that the happiness of the saints may be more delightful to them and that they may render more copious thanks to God for it, they are allowed to see perfectly the sufferings of the damned.' It is worth noting that Jesus indeed incorporates this line of thought when he tells the parable of the rich man and Lazarus. We must acknowledge that the parable does not contain any *apokatastasis*, but rather maintains a division between those who are damned and those who are saved. However, Jesus does not use the parable to directly assert or imply anything about Lazarus' elevated enjoyment upon witnessing the reversed order in the afterlife (Lk 16:19–31).

laugh') to only use the other half ('a time to weep'), it is only fair that we hasten to acknowledge that upon closer examination it may appear that even when it comes to these jubilant psalms, we too can easily commit a similar kind of quotation fraud. At the very least, Tertullian's and Aquinas' fantasies sharpen the focus on the fact that there is often a built-in contrast, which, depending on one's temperament, education, or tradition, we may be tempted to overlook, but which is clearly stated: 'shout for joy to God, all the earth' is followed by 'your enemies come cringing to you' (verse 1 and verse 3 respectively in Psalm 66). However, we can pin our hopes on an interpretation where the point seems to lie more in the idea of that special kind of balance where the hierarchy of the earth is reversed at some point (whether in the afterlife or in a future messianic kingdom on earth) rather than the vision of the future torment of the current rulers being a constitutive and eternal part of heavenly enjoyment.

It is unnecessary to spell out that these considerations arise solely from focusing to an extent that may seem like wearing blinders on verses and passages that involve laughter and closely related concepts. Whether we agree with the description or find the image distorted Gejerus' epigram remains. It is remarkable that despite the many (anthropomorphic) moods and emotional outbursts attributed to God – or perhaps more accurately, the many different conceptions of God that the Old Testament scriptures reveal – there is no account of God weeping. On the other hand, God often laughs, but in a manner that cannot be distinguished from mockery and scorn. Similarly, the way is prepared for a coming Messiah (for Psalm 2 begins with nations, kings, and princes rebelling not only against God, but 'against the Lord and against his anointed', verse 2): like God he will face resistance, but in the end he will be the one who laughs ... mockingly.[468]

The gospel is that it did not turn out that way because Jesus of Nazareth refrained from taking on that interpretation of the role of the anointed Christ. In the New Testament, however, the roles are reversed in a sinful mess. Admittedly, not only is there silence about Jesus' laughter, but Halliwell is right in pointing out that there is also not much laughter to be found among the other characters in the New Testament texts. Instead, the few examples of human laughter are all the more unpleasant. If we only look for the common terms for laughter,

---

468 According to Screech there have been many cases of biblical interpreters who were not familiar with Hebrew poetry's penchant for expressing itself in doubling parallelisms, and who therefore, for example, interpreted the first half of verse 4 in Psalm 2 as referring to the Father, while the second half was thought to be directed towards the Son. *Ibid.*, 50.

we will search almost in vain, as laughter is only mentioned in connection with Jesus' beatification and lamentation in the Gospel of Luke (as well as the paraphrase of the lamentation in James 4:9). It is as if laughter has now become so distorted and brutalised that the authors resort to other words to indicate an *implied* laughter.[469]

If we incorporate these terms, a clear picture emerges, and to enhance it somewhat the image resembles Psalm 2 turned upside down: there God sits in heaven and laughs downwards at humans, whereas in all three Synoptic Gospels humans stand and laugh upwards at the Lord. Already in Galilee, a foreshadowing of this occurs when Jesus' preaching and his raising of the dead girl are met with laughter (Lk 16:14 and Mt 9:24, where the word for laughter, *geláō*, is used in its intensified condescending form, *katageláō*). On the way to Jerusalem, Jesus himself predicts that he will be mocked and ridiculed (Mt 20:17; cf. Rom 15:3), and the three overlapping Greek words, *empaizō*, *ōneidizon*, and *blasfēméō*, weave in and out of the descriptions of Good Friday, as the soldiers with the crown of thorns, the council members, the crowd at Golgotha, and even one of the crucified robbers, laugh at Jesus (Mt 27:29.31.41.44, par.).[470]

What would have been more human than going on a verbal counterattack – or fleeing if the opposing force was too great? What would have been more divine than retaliating in kind? But Jesus, according to the canonical accounts, cancelled the power struggle without threats – unlike the heretical 'Apocalypse of Peter', which was quoted in the introduction of this chapter, where he mocked the foolish people who believed they had power over God's untouchable son. It can be debated exegetically and theologically whether Jesus Christ had the particular trump card hidden up his sleeve that he knew that he would have the last

---

469 Screech thoroughly examines in chapters 7 and 8 of his book all the Greek words as well as their counterparts in both the *Vulgate* and the later Latin translations from the Renaissance, particularly Erasmus'. Screech concludes that: 'So a small cluster of powerful verbs are used in the Greek Gospels for the mocking of Christ. All of them imply laughing: none specifically emphasises the act of laughing or isolates it. None tells us straightforwardly that the people simply opened their mouths and sniggered, tittered or guffawed.' *Ibid.*, 26.

470 In a similar manner, the same mocking laughter is predicted for the disciples in the conclusion of the Gospel of Matthew's version of the Beatitudes ('Blessed are you when people insult [/mock] you … because of me,' 5:11), which began on Pentecost morning when their spiritual fervour was ridiculed as mere drunkenness (Acts 2:13). Naturally, the message of resurrection had to become a target of laughter as well (Acts 17:32; in both instances, forms of a fourth term for mockery, *khleuázō*, are used).

laugh a few days later. The three Synoptic Gospels let Jesus know in advance that he will rise on the third day (Mt 20:19; Mk 10:34; Lk 18:33; cf. the subtle insider version in John's Gospel 12:23-33); but there is another possibility. Instead of looking forward to having the last laugh, Jesus chooses as *his* 'last', to surrender to the defeat of the cross; and the Father took on the Son's reinterpretation of the Messiah's dignity and allowed him to rise … though with scars.[471] Jesus did not have the last laugh, but he laid the foundation for the first.

It took us humans a long time to realise the consequences of this new relationship with God, where we can interact with each other without the power-struggle of mocking laughter. Do we laugh freely and heartily when and because we finally understand that on the eighth day, the Father and the Son together created humour and left it for the Holy Spirit to be our tutor?

---

471 After an academic career studying Luther, Marc Lienhard (b. 1935) offers a *tour de force* through several dozens of sermons where Luther talks about both God's and Jesus' laughter. Luther certainly has an ear for the condescending laughter of Psalm 2, but *thanks* to the Incarnation his sermons most often dare to refer to God's laughter as full of love and forgiveness. Lienhard 2023, 137–9.

Chapter V: Johannes Oecolampadius: *De Risu Paschali*

Wolfgang Capito's Preface, April 1518

|1| [472] Basel, 19 April 1518.[473]

Wolfgang Fabritius Capito[474] sends warm greetings to his reader.

In the last few days, I have admonished and urged Johannes Oecolampadius, perhaps more strictly than usual among friends, not to be repelled to such a degree by the completely absurd nonsense of the preachers. For some of these, as they themselves think, clever preachers claim, that as a preacher he is not serious enough because he does not with his voice or wild gestures, with made up threats like Salmonic thunder[475] make women shudder, who both by their nature and because of their superstitions are easy to frighten. But on the other hand, they declare that he is more serious than what is useful, since he

---

472 The division of the text into sections and the numbering of these is new to this edition to facilitate both reading and internal references. In the original, the twenty-five pages appear as one continuous text that only in a few places break the lines for the sake of quotations in Greek. Staehelin divides his edition into nineteen paragraphs. Our Latin text is taken from Staehelin with his ortography and various slight emendations of misprints. 1927/34, vol. 1, 44–59.

In the Latin text, [O: x] indicate page numbers in the original. When [!] occurs in the Latin text, these were inserted by Staehelin.

473 This information about location and date does not appear in the original but is inserted by Staehelin in his edition of the text from 1927. The date comes from the end of the preface and is indicated there in the somewhat special, but in the then ordinary, way: '13 days before May' – and by counting both the surrounding days, we arrive at 19 April.

474 Oecolampadius had known Capito since his student days in Heidelberg in 1514, and at the time of the letter Capito was both a cathedral preacher in Basel and affiliated to the university.

475 According to Greek mythology, Salmoneus envied the gods and pretended to be Zeus by making thunderous noises with a chariot covered in basins and torches. Among others this motif is mentioned by Vergil in *The Aeneid*, Book VI, ll. 585–91; 1907, 206.

stubbornly abstains from little stories,[476] jokes from the kitchen[477] and female abandon.[478]

|1| [Basel, 19 April 1518.]
[O: 2] V[olfangus] Fabritius Capito lectori s[alutem] d[icit].
Joannem Oecolampadium his proximis diebus admonui adhortatusque sum quam pro amicitia fortassis imperiosius, ne ab ineptissimis concionatorum ineptiis tantopere abhorreat. Nam nonnulli, ut sibi videntur, argutuli sermonum pensitatores de eo pronunciant, quod sit concionator parum serius, ut qui uocis gestusque tumultu ac fictis minis ceu Salmoneo tonitru mulierculas, quae sunt alioqui tum natura, tum superstitione, proclives ad metum, nihil territet neque in stuporem abducat, praeterea plus, quam expediat, serius, videlicet fabellis ac iocis e culina καὶ γυναικείῳ τῷ ἀνειμένῳ mutuatis, pertinaciter se abstinet.

---

476 In itself, *fabella* is a neutral term for any small narrative, both the one we associate in modern languages with 'fable' and everything from anecdotes to fairy tales to smaller plays. Particularly in the Protestants' criticism of the Catholic preachers, however, the word often became a derogatory term for rhetorical 'stuffing', that is, not only saints' legends and the like, but everything that diverted attention away from the evangelical cause. As an example in point, see Luther 1525, 208–10; 1997b, 131–3.

477 Already in antiquity, grammarians and rhetoricians drew a basic distinction between *facetiae* (lacking *gravitas*) and – the less refined – *iocus* (the opposite of *serium*). Renaissance philologists adopted this distinction but added a third category: *burla* (a kind of mild practical joke), cf. Bremmer-Roodenburgh 1997b, 4.

With regard to *iocus*, Capito highlights its low status by attaching it to *culina*. Although Luther moves the domain from the kitchen to the sitting-room, he also connects the ancient Greeks with contemporary female culture when, in the aforementioned sermon (1525, 208; 1997b, 131), he explains St Paul's *mōrología* (Eph 5:4) as follows: 'By "foolish talking" is indicated the fables and tales and other lore in which the Greeks particularly abound — a people who possess a special faculty for fiction of this sort. Similar are the tales commonly related by our women and maidens while spinning at the distaff, also those which knaves are fond of relating.' In all fairness it should be added that Luther also knows about this kind of talk among men – although he only mentions 'loafers' (*lotterbuben*). According to Curtius, 'kitchen humour' was one of the richest sources of amusement in both Roman comedy and the Christian Middle Ages, see the section on 'Kitchen humour and other *Ridicula*' in his essay on jokes and seriousness in Latin poetry, 1953, 431–35.

478 Possibly the Greek words convey a fixed expression, a cliché.

|2| He does not make his listeners burst into raucous laughter[479] when proclaiming Christ. He neither entertains with obscene[480] remarks nor behaves like an actor[481] who, by means of lewd imitations, evokes before their

---

479 Among several Latin terms for laughter, *cachinnus* (lit. 'bad sound') is the one most often used in conjunction with condemnations of it. The term not only signifies the acoustic expression of laughter itself ('loud', 'raucous'), but also that which especially arouses mistrust: the aspect of being 'uncontrolled'.

480 In view of the intense disagreement in the interpretation of the relation of laughter to sexuality, it should be emphasised that the medieval use of the word *obscenus* was not limited to the sexual ('lewd', 'vile'), but either had, especially in antiquity, the more special meaning 'ominous' or more often the broader 'ugly'. According to Moser-Rath, it was especially in the latter sense that the word was used by preachers in the Baroque period (which admittedly refers to the century after Oecolampadius), 1964, 32. However, we are sent in a different direction when Erasmus a few years later touches on the subject in his 'The Preacher or on the Art of Preaching' (*Ecclesiastae sive de ratione concionandi*). According to his description, the preachers make use of 'stories that are clearly fictional and most often even obscene' (*fabulis manifeste confictis, plerunque etiam obscænis*). It probably supports the erotic interpretation of the word when Erasmus adds that the narratives were of a kind 'which a respectable man at a banquet could not tell without shame' (*quales ne in convivio quidem vir probus sustineat absque pudore commemorare*), 1535, 126 (= 1536, 268), cf. 2015b, vol. 68, 508.

481 The word 'actor' should be taken with a grain of salt. The theatre as such was in all likelihood extinct by late antiquity and the early Middle Ages, but thanks to the humanists drama had become part of being well-educated, primarily in the form of reading the texts of antiquity and putting on 'private'(i.e. school) performances. Public entertainment theatres with professional actors in purpose-built buildings did not appear until later in the century – London's *Red Lion* from 1567 (along with James Burbage's [1531–97] much more famous *The Theatre* from 1576) is a strong candidate to being the first north of the Alps. On the other hand, in the centuries before, there had been a kind of 'amateur theatre' in connection with ecclesiastical festivals and religious plays, and 'professional' entertainment in the form of vagabond performers and travelling groups. These entertainers are especially mentioned in canon laws from the 9th century onwards with a whole series of words with overlapping meanings and, it has to be noted, where modern translations in many cases are just approximations (not to mention regional differences and changes from century to century): *histriones* (as here), *mimi* (used in the last sentence of this section of Capito's introduction: 'shameless clown'), *scurrae* ['buffoons'], *ioculatores* ['jokers'], *scenici* ['actors'], *poetae* ['poets'], *tragoedi* ['tragedians'], *comoedi* ['comedywriters'], *comici* ['comedians'], *joculares* ['jesters'], *jocistae* ['jokers'], *joculatores* ['jokers'], *corauli* ['jesters'], *cantores* ['singers'], *thymelici* ['musicians'/

eyes what spouses tend to delight themselves with in the bedroom, when they are alone and without witnesses.[482] We use this trick to defend this place, we most serious preachers, otherwise we would speak in empty churches[483] Common people are so incapable of making a judgment about anything that they prefer to listen to the loudmouth who, like some shameless clown, provokes anyone with insults, which nevertheless, as I said, are tempered by and drowned in laughter, which is unworthy of both a man and this place.

|2| *Non in cachinnum cogit auditores Christum annuncians, nec dictis obscoenis ludit, neque imitatione molli, sicut histrio, revocat ob oculos, quaecunque coniuges in conclavi, dum remotis arbitris conveniunt, caelare sunt soliti. Quo quidem artificio nunc locum tuemur, gravissimi concionatores, alioqui vacuis dicturi templis. Usque adeo vulgus est expers iudicii, quod eo potissimum clamatori det operam, qui maledictis quoslibet, ceu mimus impudens, lacessit, temperatis tamen et interstinctis interim, ut dixi, per risum viro et loco isti indignum.*

|3| But Johannes Oecolampadius, a great man, learned, spirited, and unassailable in his conduct, as befits a serious and pious priest, always exhorts all his views sincerely and modestly without, as they say, a stated theme,[484] he allows no make-up apart from the colourful and – educated as he is – innocently cheerful eloquence, and has completely avoided their nonsense, being contrary to both the evangelical faith and the authority of the gospel. But some reject this sensible distinction, namely those who are accustomed

---

'actors'], *musici* ['musicians'], *cytharistiae* ['players of string instruments'], *saltores* ['dancers'], and – in the north-western parts of Europe – *scop* ['poet']. Cf. Brockett 1999, 84 and Ogilvy 1963, 604. It is, however, perfectly possible to argue that all of these kinds of entertainers can serve as evidence for an unbroken tradition of theatre, albeit in a broader definition of 'theatre' than the traditional one, see e.g. Burningham 2017, 145 f.

482   Jacobelli claims that in the 16th century the word *mollis* not only signals 'femininity' but may have connotations to either male masturbation or female homosexuality. This meaning is implied in her translation of this passage: '... nor does he, by imitating a man masturbating, bring to mind, like a buffoon, the things that married couples are wont to do in their own room and without witnesses', 1992, 13 and 123.

483   The pragmatic argument that accepts or even advocates the introduction of extraordinary elements, such as Easter Laughter, in order to avoid empty churches, was in fact surprisingly rarely mentioned in the sources, although it is actually to this day a well-known line of reasoning when debating liturgical reforms. Cf. the section on pragmatic arguments for Easter Laughter in III,1.

484   *Themate*, a technical term from homiletics and rhetoric in general; in other words, he is blamed for 'getting straight to the point'.

to pantomime gestures in the theatre[485] and the constant cheering at every senseless action, or at least those for whom gimmicks has fallen more successfully.

|3| *Atqui Joannes Oecolampadius, vir doctrina, ingenio, vitae integritate magnus, quod gravem et pium decet sacerdotem, omnia semper ex animo et modeste suadet, absque themate, ut vocant, praeposito, nihil fuci admittens praeter eloquentiae colores et inculpatam, ut est eruditus, festivitatem, longe vitatis istorum blateramentis tanquam adversantibus evangelicae tum fidei tum autoritati. Cuiusmodi sanam distinctionem vituperant quidam, nempe assueti scaenicae gesticulationi ac perpetuis de rebus frigidis acclamationibus, aut ii certe, quibus id artificii felicius cecidit.*

|4| In his reply to my admonition,[486] our friend criticises these preachers most sharply, especially because of the inappropriate jokes with which they in every conceivable way dispel the piety and gratitude towards God that really is to be encouraged at the Easter celebration as if it was only possible to receive the risen Christ, who suffered death for us, with scurrilous joy. We confidently leave this [book] to you, honest reader, with the sole aim of using it as a grindstone to sharpen your judgment on the matter and so that you do not, without thinking, prefer a mad and noisy loudmouth to an eloquent preacher.
Best wishes, Basel 19 April 1518.

|4| *Quos hic noster, admonenti mihi respondens, acriter obiurgat, maxime ob intempestivos iocos, quibus in celebritate paschali omnibus modis augendam in Deum, pietatem et gratitudinem expugnare solent, quasi Christum pro nobis obita morte redivivum non aliter liceat quam laetitia scurrili excipere. Quam tibi, candide lector, volentes vel ob hoc impartimur, ut ea ceu cote harum rerum indicium exacuas, ne imprudens bene declamanti clamosum insanumque rabulam semper anteponas.*
Vale Basileae XIII. Cal. Maii. MDXVIII.

---

485   *Scaenicae gesticulatio*: in all likelihood the comparison testifies more to the humanist's erudition than to his own experiences in the theatre (cf. footnote 481). In his study of the Church Fathers, Capito would have been able to read about their frequent condemnations of the Roman theatre, in which there was a lively exchange between the audience and the performers; cf. Tertullian's condemnations of the gesturing of the mime actors in 'The Shows' (*De spectaculis*), ch. 17; 1977, 275–7.

486   This answer is identical to the book itself. Unfortunately Capito's original letter to Oecolampadius has not been preserved. The same applies to the allegations made by

Johannes Oecolampadius' Letter, March 1518

|5| Oecolampadius to Wolfgang Fabricius Capito ['On Easter Laughter']
Weinsberg, 18 March 1518.[487]
Dear Capito.
As I gather from your requests, dear Capito, there are three points where my critics are not quite satisfied with me. As a preacher I am too serious and yet not serious enough, indeed I am not even a preacher, because I begin my sermons without a text[488] and, as it is written, with unwashed hands [Mt 15:20].[489] Certain would-be critics unknown to me condemns these my moles, these my offences, these my beams, and enlist you – whom they know are bound to me in no ordinary friendship – to remove the beams from my watery eyes [*cf. Mt 7:3–6].

|5| [O: 3] Oekolampad an Wolfgang Fabricius Capito ['De risu paschali']
Weinsberg, d. 18. März 1518.
Oecolampadius Capitoni suo sal[utem] d[icit].

---

colleagues against Oecolampadius, if indeed they were presented in writing, which does not emerge with unequivocal certainty from the references to them by Capito and Oecolampadius.

487   As with Capito's preface, these two lines are inserted by Staehelin in his edition, which in the original printing opens with the greeting in the next line. The original has a title page that reads: *De Risv Paschali, Oecolampadii, ad V. Capitonem theologvm epistotala apologetica* ('On Easter Laughter, an apologetic letter by Oecolampadius to the theologian V. Capito').

488   According to Staehelin (note 1, p. 57), there are several examples in the surviving manuscripts that show how Oecolampadius not only left out *themate*, but also preached without a specific text. This relates to the tradition of preaching that had developed in the course of the late Middle Ages, in which a broad distinction was made between four genres: homily, text sermon, festive sermon, and thematic sermon, Staehelin 1939a, 86; cf. note 624.

489   In addition to direct quotations, Oecolampadius' text is generously seasoned with biblical allusions. Neither quotations nor allusions appear with quotation marks in the original, and with a few exceptions sources are also not given. In total Oecolampadius uses fourteen Bible quotations (of which five are contained in quotations from the Church Fathers), where six of these are from the Old Testament and seven from the New (as well as one from the Apocrypha). Allusions are of course a slightly more fluid form of reference; but we can reasonably trace upwards of sixty of these, and they are fairly evenly distributed between the two Testaments.

Tria sunt, mi Capito, quae te monitore didici, observatoribus meis admodum in me displicere. Videor enim illis nimium serius concionator, nec satis serius, sed ne concionator quidem, ut qui themate non posito χερσὶν ἀνίπτοις, quod dicitur, orationem ingrediar. Hos meos naevos, haec mea crimina, has meas trabeis censorculi nescio qui damnant et te, quem non vulgari amicitia mihi devinctum sciunt, ut e lippientibus meis oculis tigna eiicias, subornant.

|6| I wonder who these rumourmongers could have been, so cocky and so outrageous that neither shame nor common sense kept them from such foolish criticism of me, especially towards you who are no friend of this snotty way of judging things. I beg you, tell me if you were able to maintain your usual happy smile. Did not your eyes glow with inner anger when they abused your integrity by supposing you were one of theirs; when they in my, your friend's, absence had nothing to justifiably bring forward, but then accused me of just what their dignity should have made them praise? Did you consider their distorted accusations calmly, imperturbably, and serenely? Did you respond according to their 'wisdom' or according to the famous words of Demophons in Euripides: 'Who can decide a plea or judge a speech / until he has heard plainly from both sides?'[490]

|6| *Demiror, quinam rumigeruli tam perfrictae frontis, tam effrontis animi fuerint, quos ab hac insulsa censura, praesertim coram te non pituitosi iudicii amico, nullus avocaverit pudor, nulla praemonuerit ratio. Dic, oro te, cum*

Staehelin inserts quotation marks for direct quotations and adds Bible references in square brackets to both these and the allusions. This edition follows Staehelin's example but adds identification of almost twice as many allusions (indicated by a * before the reference). Both Staehelin's and the new brackets have been moved from the Latin text.

490 Euripides (480–06 BCE): *Heraclidae*, ll. 179–80; 1995, 28–9. When Oecolampadius quotes other authors, the quotations are translated from his text. If the cited texts are already available in English translations, reference will be made to them in the footnotes. Of course, there may be small deviations in the wording of the translations, just as Oecolampadius in some cases uses other sources than those on which the later English translations are based. If other quotations are given in the footnotes than those which Oecolampadius himself uses, the translation is taken from the text editions cited.

Just as Oecolampadius diligently makes use of the Bible, he demonstrates his erudition by constantly quoting and alluding to older authors. Not surprisingly, his great interest in the Church Fathers is noticeable in a dozen direct quotes together with a few allusions. The preoccupation of Humanism with antiquity in

abuterentur candore tuo, sui similem te arbitrati, cum in absente amico nihil haberent, quod merito damnarent, idque damnarent, quod honestius probassent, nihil tum demutabas ex solita vultus tui festivitate, nihil interio-[O: 4]ris turbulentiae oculorum faces offudit? Imperturbabilisne et ἀπαθὴς illorum morbos e sublimi spectabas? Respondebasne iuxta prudentiam eorum an iuxta celebrem Euripidei Demophontis sententiam: τίς ἂν δίκην κρίνοιεν ἢ γνοίη λόγον, πρὶν ἂν παρ' ἀμφοῖν μῦθον ἐκμάθῃ σαφή?

|7| Did you hesitate in your friend's absence to speak your mind because the other ear was guarded?[491] Strongly equipped with a variety of deceptions, lest they should fail to attribute what they were planning to a notable fault, they, in the meantime, as is the custom of sycophants, mixed many true and false things, which you, sparing, as I think, my tenderness, did not wish to tell me about by letter. They certainly have achieved something when they have pressured you to write to me and solemnly urge me to give up my old way of speaking and instead conform to the modern, vulgar custom.

|7| *Absenti amico, altera custodita auricula, sententiam ferre differebas? Forte illi variis instructi fraudibus, ne non insignite, quod moliebantur, vitio dandum insinuarent, plurima interim, qui mos est sycophantarum, vera falsaque commiscuerunt, quae tu parcens, ut reor, teneritudini meae per epistolam indicare noluisti. Profecto nonnihil aegere, qui extorserunt, ut literis per sacra obtestareris, exuerem priscam dicendi consuetudinem, plebeiorum et recentiorum moribus me attemperarem.*

|8| You certainly wrote to me so urgently that at first I saw no other way out or did not think that there was anything else to do than to follow your, or rather their, precepts. But a good genius whispered in my ear not to persuade myself that what you instructed me so seriously was sincere, especially since I know full well that sometimes you joke with your friend in a playful manner and thus sometimes drill my character and lead it to do battle against the crowds of enemies. For although your letter sounds

---

general is shown in Oecolampadius' ten quotations from pagan writers, as here from Euripides, as well as twice as many allusions to the Greek and Roman classics. Where Oecolampadius does not himself point this out, the sources will be identified in the footnotes. On the other hand, Oecolampadius only bothers to refer to three of his (almost) contemporaries: Erasmus, Geiler, and Poggio.

491 The interposed sentense about a guarded ear may sound a bit obscure, but Oecolampadius is clearly alluding to Demophons' wise words about hearing both parties.

different, I had to understand it that way, and I will remain of this view until you have shown by clearer means that I am wrong. In the meantime you must forgive me if I resist for a while, especially since your intention is not clear.[492]

|8| *Satis quidem imperiose scripsisti adeoque, ut sublato tergiversationis effugio nihil primo aliud cogitarem cogitandum, quam tuis, immo illorum monitis parere. At aurem mihi bonus vellicavit genius, ne a te tam serio mihi praeceptum persuadeam, praesertim cum non ignorem te nonnunquam cum amico per hilaritatem ludere, nonnunquam ingenium meum exercere et in campum contra hostium cuneos educere. Nam etsi aliud sonant literae tuae, hoc intelligere tamen debui maneboque in ea sententia, donec manifestioribus errare me docueris. Dabis interim veniam, si restitero aliquantisper maxime cum de voluntate tua non constet.*

|9| Furthermore, my critics, who with untimely jokes weaken what should be said in earnest, will not succeed in making me interpret as a joke what can be said seriously. At least I will remain serious in this one matter, so that I do not have to take what has been said in earnest differently from how it has been said. And when they accuse me of contradicting myself, I will in part accept their criticism when they quite rightly claim that I am too serious, and partly deny that I should not be serious enough. Serious, I say, not late.[493]

|9| *Porro observatores mei, qui serio dicenda intempe-[O: 5]stivis effoeminant iocis, non impetrabunt, ut et ego, quae serio dici possunt, per iocum dicta intelligam. Ero vel in hoc uno serius, ne serio dicta secus, quam dicta sint, interpreter. Et cum pugnantia obiiciant, partim in illorum sententiam concedam, ut vere nimis me serium arguant, partim recedam, ne non satis sim serius. Serius, inquam, non serus.*

---

492   It must be this passage that makes some interpreters believe that Capito belongs to, or at least agrees with, Oecolampadius' opponents. If nothing else, Capito's preface ought to be enough to put this misunderstanding to bed. It is more interesting to consider whether Oecolampadius himself may have misunderstood the letter from his friend. Let it be stated once and for all: You are not necessarily a dull person in private, just because you are not enthusiastic about Easter Laughter in the church! Yet, as far as I am aware, Oecolampadius did not have a reputation of being a jovial person, and these sentences may surely serve as an explanation why history has not handed down, as it did with Luther, a collection of his 'table talks'. At the risk of overinterpretation, we sense between the lines how Capito has tried both here and in the past to rebuke his friend with cheerful irony, which Oecolampadius, however, has found difficult to decipher with his 'common sense'.

493   In Latin, a wordplay on the similarity between *serius* and *non serus*.

|10| Now I arm myself, now I step forward, I want to face the enemy, I look forward to the infight. If indeed I feel provoked, it is not because of the insults they foolishly attempt to make against me but by which they unwittingly honour me. No, your letter provokes me, indeed, the matter itself provokes me; it should in no way be underestimated. There is something noxious at play, otherwise I do not see why you, such a friend, should find it necessary to warn me.[494] Or would you rather have kind words?

|10| *Jam accingor, iam prodeo, hostem videre desydero, iuvat conferre manum. Siquidem provocatum me credo, non equidem iniuriis meis, quas dum imprudenter intentant, gloria me nescii afficiunt. Provocant autem me literae tuae, provocat res ipsa, res neutiquam contemnenda. Subest quiddam virulentiae: alioqui non video, quid opus erat te tam classicum amicum occinere mihi classicum. An tu forte bona verba velis?*

|11| I myself detest this kind of barking slander. That's why in all innocence I want to take up the fight openly, especially since I do not know for sure who these critics are, although I certainly do not lack suspicion as to who handed me over to you, or rather who recommended me to you.[495] He has done his duty as an excellent, Christian, and devout man, who could not criticise even when that is what he most of all wanted to do. But, my dear Capito, before my defence speech you shall hear by what conjectures I have designated the man whom I dare to swear, if you had diligently inquired of him about my character, would not have refrained from weighing me on his own scale.

|11| *Et ipse a canina isthac maledicentia abhorreo. Proinde lacessam innocenter, praesertim cum certo nesciam, qui sint observatores isti, quamvis non omnino suspitione caream, quis me tibi prodiderit aut verius loquar, quis me tibi commendarit. Optimi, christiani, religiosi viri defunctus est officio, qui nec tum vituperare potuit, cum vellet longe maxime. Verum, mi Capito, quibus coniecturis virum apud me designarim, quem ausim iurare, si ex eo mores meos officiose perquisieris, non continuisse se, quin me in trutina sua suspenderit, ante apologiam accipe.*

|12| Having read your letter and not knowing what to me was praise, but to this perfect man nothing but complaints, I began to ransack the dwelling of my

---

494 Literally 'sound the war trumpet to me' thus making a word-play on the two uses and two meanings of *classicus*.
495 This opponent remains anonymous in the book, and later research has not been able to identify him.

whole conscience late into the night. I wanted to find out where this distrust of me came from, where I would have sinned in this matter, where I would have misled a brother with careless speech. And for a long time, there was nothing to disprove me, because I do not think that I deviate particularly from the general style of preachers, and I do not lack role models. I pass over the others.

|12| *Lecta epistola tua, cum laudum, ut mihi, criminum vero, ut huic perfecto viro videtur, conscius mihi non essem, occepi totam conscientiae domum [O: 6] accensa lucerna pervertere, undenam orta de me suspicio, quid in ea re peccassem, ubinam fratrem incauto sermone subvertissem. Diuque nihil me redarguebat; neque enim mihi videor tam procul a vulgari concionatorum more recedere, neque mihi desunt, quos imitor. Caeteros praetereo.*

|13| But did not you alone, how should I put it, create a whole forest of rules that I obeyed, partly when I have listened to you, partly when you found it appropriate to write to me? And would that I had imitated you as pertinently as you so pertinently have taught me! And now, in many churches on the very holy Easter Sunday itself, this pernicious custom[496] has come to mind during the sermon to deliver merry fables[497] to refresh the attention of the audience. More than once have I heard this custom criticised in the divine sermons of the most venerable Fathers, and because of my rigid and, as they say, tauromininitan nature,[498] I have never been able to approve of it.

---

496 The word 'custom' (*consuetudo*) has precisely the ambiguity between a 'practice' and a 'tradition' which is one of the hallmarks of the intense debates about the legitimacy of these and other customs. Seldom does anyone take credit for (or is being accused of) inventing this or that particular practice, but again and again those that participate in it refer to its venerable age when challenged.

497 *Fabula* was used to cover a variety of 'stories', but it is here provided with the predicate *ludicrus*, an adjective which in itself has a broad range of meaning. It is quite possible 'just' to translate it as meaning 'enjoyable' or 'entertaining'. Traditionally, however, this Latin word is used to mirror the Greek word γέλοιος (*géloios*) in Aristotle's famous definition of the characters in comedy (*Poetics*, ch. 5, 1449a34–37): 'Comedy, as we have said, is a representation of inferior people, not indeed in the full sense of the word bad, but the laughable is a species of the base or ugly. It consists in some blunder or ugliness that does not cause pain or disaster, an obvious example being the comic mask which is ugly and distorted but not painful.' 1965, 18–21.

498 Staehelin (note 5, p. 58) suggests a possible allusion to Cicero's 'Against (Gaius) Verres' (*In Verrem*); but it is not entirely clear what Oecolampadius means by this comparison. At the place in question Cicero refers to the inhabitants of Taormina

|13| *Nonne tu solus mihi, quomodo dicendum, praeceptionum sylvam suppeditasti, quas partim, cum te audirem, observabam, partim literis ad me perscribere dignatus es? Et utinam tam feliciter te imitarer, quam fideliter instituisti! Subiit tandem animum pestilens illa consuetudo, qua in multis ecclesiis, ipso sacrosancto die Paschae, inter concionandum ad recreandos auditorum animos ludicrae fabellae proferuntur. Eam ego et probatissimorum patrum oraculis reprehensam non semel audivi, et ipsas per naturam meam, ut illi aiunt, rigidam, addant et: Taurominitanam, approbare nunquam potui.*

|14| For I[499] have seen the most venerable men, otherwise not the least diligent listeners to the word of God, hiding at home at that hour, lest they should be defiled by such jokes.[500] I have also seen, and many have seen it with me, how outraged people left both the church and the preacher, though others laughed at his foolish nonsense. A certain brother who wanted to guard this custom as if it were sacred[501] – it would have suited him better if he had lamented this laughter instead of encouraging it – babbled to the applause of the uneducated crowd such ridiculous nonsense last year that

---

(Sicily) as 'calm' (*homines quietissimi*), but he also says that due to their status as allies of Rome, they dared to demolish the statue of Mithridates (135–63 BCE). This can be seen in contrast, for example, to their neighbours on the island of Rhodes, who out of respect for tradition (which had allowed a similar statue to be erected) did not pull it down despite the current war against him depicted by it. *In Verrem* 2.2.160; 1903, 281.

499   Here begins the rather long passage which Hospinian quotes almost verbatim in his book about the ecclesiastical holidays and customs (*Festa Christianorvm*, 1593), and which, much more than Oecolampadius' own book, is the source of future generations' knowledge of the phenomenon of Easter Laughter; cf. p. 76. As was the case with Oecolapadius' book Hospinian's work has never been translated; but the overwhelming majority of the contemporary or later quotations from Oecolampadius in German literature are taken from exactly the same pages that Hospinian quotes.

500   *Nugae* seems to have been used interchangeably with, among others, *ineptiae* and *ridicula* (which appear in the following sentences) about small (linguistic) jokes. However, Albrecht Classen (b. 1956) suggests that there is a kind of systematic distinction between the latter as forms of prose, while *nugae* can be considered as 'trifles in metrical verse', 2010, 19.

501   Precisely this phrase, 'this custom as if it were sacred' (*hunc morem tanquam sacrum*), formed the basis for the thesis of J.P. Schmidt and other historians of the Baroque period that Easter Laughter had (also) been a liturgical phenomenon, cf. Wendland 1980, 87 f. However, this seems to be a confusion of Easter Laughter with various other medieval religious customs, cf. above I,1.

I am ashamed to defile my writings with such jokes, so as not to offend pious ears.[502]

|14| *Vidi enim gravissimos viros, alioqui verbi divini non parum diligentes auditores, ea hora domi delituisse, ne talibus nugis contaminarentur. Vidi quoque, et viderunt mecum alii permulti, nonnullos, ridentibus aliis concionatoris ineptias, indignabundos tam auditorium quam concionatorem reliquisse. Hunc morem tanquam sacrum custoditurus frater quidam, cui plangendi quam risus excitandi officium peculiarius esse deberet, superiori anno magno satis ineruditae plebeculae plausu deblaterabat tam ridicula delira-[O: 7]menta, ut me pudeat eiusmodi nugis chartas commaculare, ne pias aures offendam.*

|15| Soon after I met that man and asked him for an explanation whence this custom had come, whether it was appropriate for the joy of Easter, whether it had originated among the Apostles and from them had flowed all the way down into our own rotten times.[503] What more can I say? I came to him at an inopportune time and then had to listen to criticism from this rude man. He lectured me on my ignorance because I did not know of this splendid and absolutely indispensable ability for a preacher to make subtle remarks,[504] that the preacher should not be too serious on Easter Sunday.

---

502 As is so often the case in history, it is a recurring irony that we only know of heresies from references to them by the orthodox and their occasional quotations from the writings of heretics. The other surviving – contemporary – informants about Easter Laughter, whether they explicitly refer to it by this expression or not, are far less noticeable. It is quite important to highlight the word 'contemporary', because posterity is teeming with descriptions which rather than deriving from their own experiences or another reliable source, are partly based on Oecolampadius (mostly *via* Hospinian), and partly combine his descriptions with other phenomena that the writer happens to be sceptical of, but which most often probably have had nothing to do with concrete examples of Easter Laughter.

503 In addition to the pragmatic arguments (e.g. to attract the attention of the congregation and keep it awake), the decisive theological argument for Easter Laughter is that there is a real and legitimate connection between joy and laughter – even though Oecolampadius would have rejected such an argument, cf. above III,5. In passing it is worth noticing: when Easter Laughter is defended as a *custom* by his opponent, then Oecolampadius' reference to the Apostles reflects the humanist as well as the Reformation principle of criticising tradition by going back to the sources, *ad fontes*.

504 In a nutshell, here is a good example of Tertullian's famous distinction between (or as some would have it: infamous seperation of) church and culture, theology

I do not want to repeat our conversation in which we debated in vain for an hour.

|15| *Eum ego hominem non multo post conveni rationem requirens, unde mos ille inolevisset, an paschalibus gaudiis dignus, an ab apostolis in has usque temporum feces profluxisset? Quid multis? Intempestiva hora hominem accessi, ab importuno male audire cogebar. Admonuit me inscitiae meae, qui pulcherrimam concionatorique imprimis necessariam τῆς εὐτραπελίας virtutem ignorarem; in paschali die non tam serium esse oportere concionatorem. Nolo dialogum nostrum inserere, quo per horam frustra inter nos disceptabamus.*

|16| The following day I presented our quarrel in a larger party, and the guests present also began to list in detail all the ridiculous nonsense that each of them had heard in different places, indeed, on the very same day.[505] One cackled like a cuckoo in a hollow willow-tree would do, after eating pieces

---

and philosophy: 'What has Athens to do with Jerusalem?', 'On Prescription against Heretics' (*De praescriptione haereticorum*, ch. 7), 1903, 246. St Paul makes it a distinguishing characteristic of the children of light that the Christian renounces the use of *eutrapelía* (Eph 5:4; the only occurrence in the New Testament; in most English Bibles translated as 'joking' combined with various descriptive adjectives such as 'crude', 'coarse', 'vulgar', 'indecent', 'obscene', and suchlike). In antiquity there are both negative and, much more often, positive statements about *eutrapelía*. In Aristotle (whom Tertullian explicitly mentions in the context referred to above) it is elevated to a hallmark of the kind of person whom it is most agreeable to be with. Such a person masters the social virtue of *eutrapelía*, having wit, and thus finds himself in the middle between him who either exaggerates (βωμόλοχος [*bōmólochos*], 'a buffoon') or understates the amusement (αγροίκος [*agroíkos*], is 'boorish', or more or less verbatim: 'a clod'), *Eth.Nic.* II.7,1108a24; 1934, 102–5; cf. 'wit [*eutrapelía*] is cultured insolence [*pepaideuméne hýbris*]', *Rh* II.12.16 1389b11; 1922, 250–1. For a condensed survey of what happened to the understanding of *eutrapelía* when it moved from the Greek philosophers into the hands of the early Christian theologians see Rahner 1965.

505 Apropos the point in note 502 about the irony of knowing about heresies through the criticisms of the Orthodox, the following series of examples can be said to have done for the special phenomenon of Easter Laughter what the famous letter from the Paris Faculty in 1445 did for the much more widespread Feast of Fools and Feast of the Ass at Christmas time. Both have been quoted endlessly and most often abbreviated to an extent that only the most titillating examples were left for the imagination to feast on; regarding the Feast of the Ass cf. M. Harris 2011 (specifically about the letter from 1445: 3–10 and 218–24) and above p. 80 f.

of bread,[506] one lay down in the middle of the cow-dung, as if he were about to give birth to a calf, while like geese he chased away with hisses those who came near; a third wrapped a layman in a robe one evening, persuaded him that he was a priest, and sent him up to the altar.[507] They described it in such a way that they could paint a picture of the matter before our eyes. There was also someone who recounted how the Apostle Peter had cheated the landlords of the bill and [the sailors of] their fare with fraud and deceit.[508] This was just a few examples; I wish to spare you the more indecent ones.

|16| *Sequenti die in convivio multorum exposui disputationem nostram, coeperuntque et sodales ridiculas gerras memoriter singuli percensere, quas alii aliis in locis audierant, eoipso die scilicet. Unus instar cuculi placentulis in cava salice devoratis cucullabat; alius fimo bubulo incubans tanquam vitulum producturus appropiantes sibilis more anserum abigebat; alius laicum una nocte cucullo indutum sacerdotem esse persuadebat et ad altare transmittebat. Ita commemorabant, ut ante oculos rem depingerent. Aderat et, qui divi Petri strophas narraret, quibus hospites symbolis et naulis defraudarit. Obscoeniores missas facio pauculis indicatis.*

---

506 The simile seems rather obscure, which is perhaps due to the fact that a straightforward translation of the sentence does not seem possible. Perhaps a slightly more meaningful, but undeniably also more free translation, could read: 'One [i.e. the priest] crowed like a cuckoo in a hollow willow tree, after he had eaten the sacramental bread.' A third attempt appears in Markus Lutz's (1772–1835) paraphrase: 'One of them had appeared like a cuckoo eating cake in a hollow willow tree, and thereby imitating the screeching of this bird.' 1814, 19. Fluck has suggested a fourth variation: 'One again and again screamed cuckoo like the bird of the same name when it ate its chicks in the hollow willow tree.' 1934, 192. Finally, Ferm also has given his take on an interpretation: 'One crowed like a cuckoo when it has eaten its small delicacies in a hollow willow tree.' 2002, 128.

507 Interestingly, a very similar incident is cited in the 1445 letter from the Paris Faculty, although there the description is elaborated with various other offensive details, cf. M. Harris 2011, 1 f.

508 There is no obvious link between this flowery example and the descriptions found in the Acts of the Apostles (or in the missionary journeys in St Paul's letters). Although the motifs with the landlord or the sailors are not to be found in Frederic C. Tubach's (b. 1930) collection of 5400 medieval religious legends, the story cited by Oecolampadius seems obviously to be based on a popular legend.

Even though Henry Mayhew (1812–87) (1864, vol. 2, 376) does not convince, when he identifies the legend with 'Brother Lustig' in the collection of the Brothers Grimm, that particular fairy tale is nevertheless a colourful example of how the

|17| I wondered how everyone suddenly was so eloquent, had such a vivid memory, and yet was both childish and crude.[509] But when I asked if they also knew the allegorical interpretation,[510] their shouting came to a stop, nobody knew what to answer.[511] Finally, there was an old man who said that he had heard from the preachers that the purpose of this was not to unravel the mysteries, but to cheer up the audience if they were not amused and merry.[512] So much for the conversation at the party.

|17| *Stupebam repente omnes tam facundos, tam felicis memoriae, alioquin infantes et rudes. Rogante autem me, nunquid et allegorias tenerent, [O: 8] subito repressus est clamor, nulli in numerato erat, quod responderet. Vix*

Apostle can use disguises and cunning in the service of a good cause. A morally more disturbing example, but one which from a formal point of view shows some similarity to St Peter's questionable behaviour, is known from a religious play in which 'in the aftermath to the Walk to Emmaus the two disciples get into a brawl with the innkeeper and give him a beating instead of money', Bergmann 1944, 189, note 1 (unfortunately Bergmann does not give his source).

509 This sentence is the only one that Hospinian omits from his long quote from Oecolampadius.

510 Oecolampadius is here alluding to the fourfold method of interpretation (*quadriga*), which in its fully developed form distinguished between the literal, allegorical (religious), tropological (moral), and anagogic (mystical) meaning. It may be useful to recall one of the main points in the long and varied tradition of basically distinguishing between the literal (*sensus literalis*) and figurative meaning (*sensus spiritualis*), because this differs significantly from the way in which allegory is often used today. When medieval theologians were looking for the 'spiritual' interpretation, they were not as interested in its 'figurative' (emotional, aesthetic) meaning as in its dogmatic or doctrinal content, for example in an image or an apparently harmless and cheerful story. In very general terms, the allegorical method of interpretation can be seen as the attempt of the early Christian theologians to compete with their pagan predecessors and, above all, to emphasise that the Bible (though authored in the simple Greek of the Septuagint's and the New Testament's *koinē*) could measure up to ancient literature and thinking.

511 It must be concluded that Oecolampadius' interlocutors are *not* representative. In the published or otherwise preserved sermons and collections of suitable narratives (*exempla*) it is exactly their allegorical (edifying) dimension that is most often pointed to in their defence. For example, Pauli makes this typical statement in *Schimpf und Ernst*: 'So what is said spiritually with the fables you should keep, and the ridiculous things you can forget', 1866, 272; but as Wendland dryly comments: if you use that as your yardstick, many of Pauli's own stories ought to be forgotten as soon as possible, 1980, 181.

512 This is where Hospinian ends his long quote from Oecolampadius.

tandem senior ait, audisse se ex concionatoribus non id tum agere eos, ut mysteria evolvant, sed ne non festivi et comes auditorium exhilarent. Haec in convivio.

|18| However, I still felt nauseous after yesterday's discussion, and I considered writing a little book on Easter Laughter,[513] into which I had decided to spew out this foolish nonsense. The book was dedicated to you. But before I could finish it, I became ill, as you know. When, by the grace of God, I had recovered, I read the pages again and discovered that I was about to teach rather than 'unteach' these foolish things.[514] So I dedicated them to Vulcan, which they suited better, and not to Wolfgang, who they feared to approach.[515]

|18| *Ego vero, ex pridiana disceptatione stomacho adhuc fervescente libellum de risu paschali condere meditabar, in quem et has ineptias invomere decreveram. Tibi dedicabatur. Antequam tamen absolverem, morbus me invasit, ut intellexisti. Ubi divina gratia convalui, repetitisque chartis cognovi, me ridicula magis docere quam dedocere. Vulcano, quo digna erant, non Volphgango, quem accedere verebantur, consecravi.*

---

513 Apart from the title of the published book (which may have been Capito's choice, cf. note to |63|) this is the first and last occurrence of those two words put together, *risus* and *paschalis* (see, however, the sentence where laughter is associated with 'Isaac' in section |64|).

There are undoubtedly independent allusions to and descriptions of the practice before and after Oecolampadius concerning the use of funny stories by preachers during the Easter season (cf. I,3). But on the basis of the available sources it is a fair assumption that it is Oecolampadius who is responsible for providing the evocative name for the practice which came to be used so abundantly over the next centuries. This holds true even if he did not actually invent the expression *risus paschalis* himself but had picked it up from somewhere else in an unknown and to this day unidentified source. If it was indeed Capito's choice to publish the letter with this title he is our first witness to the fact that Oecolampadius had come up with the definitive buzzword to catch the attention of a reader.

514 With the pun on *docere* and *dedocere* Oecolampadius proves that he himself is aware of the dangers of describing in detail what one would like to see passed over in silence. Unfortunately this limits our knowledge of the actual practice involved to the relatively short list of examples above, as well as a few, indeed very few, from other sources.

515 Yet another – amusing – pun on The God of Fire and Capito's Christian name.

|19| Notice, my dear Capito, lest I am completely mistaken, who betrayed my work to you.[516] But whoever it was, I will have to reply, so that neither will he get a cheap victory, nor will we mix up good and bad like him. The charges, if they are indeed charges, must be refuted in the same order in which they were brought forward.[517]

|19| *Vide, mi Capito, an omnino vanus augur sim, per quem tibi studia mea prodita. Verum quisquis is fuerit, ne aut incruentam sibi victoriam cedat, aut bonum malum cum eo dicamus, respondendum, diluendaque sunt crimina, si modo sunt crimina, eo videlicet, quo abiecta sunt, ordine.*

|20| First, our prankster[518] rejects a preacher who is too serious. What he wants I cannot quite figure out. I mean, one and the same person cannot be both serious and too serious at the same time, no, he cannot be too serious at all; otherwise, he would cease to be serious and become cruel, just as no one will blame the pious if they are strong by virtue of their piety. Now he will probably hold this word of wisdom against me: 'You shall not be too righteous' [Eccles 7:16]. Which I understand in this way: not that one should renounce to a certain extent the reasonable righteousness that one should always strive for, but rather that the supreme justice, as it is called, should not become the highest injustice and under the name of glorious justice be introduced as a tyranny of horrible cruelty. For if our friend thinks so of me, he turns me, with indulgence and sophistication,[519] into someone completely different.

---

516 As mentioned, this opponent was never identified.
517 Although Oecolampadius takes up the three charges one by one, what concerns him most is reflected in the fact that he only addresses the last two in sections |65| and |66| respectively.
518 As in the case of Oecolampadius' repeated use of the Latin *histrio* and *circulator*, he once more draws on the traditional terms in antiquity for the more or less professional entertainers and actors by introducing the Greek *geloiastēs*; cf. note 481.
519 The juxtaposition of the two Greek words appears to be Oecolampadius' doing, and most likely with a polemical intent. By putting them together he gives them a negative overtone, which is suggested here by a rather liberal translation of the words. This is quite different from their use by Aristotle, where they refer to two positive qualities: *eutrapelía* means both 'wit' (cf. Latin *urbanitas*) and 'liveliness' (cf. the French *esprit*), and *epieik(e)ía* is the exercise of the kind of discretion which avoids slavishly following the letter of the law, while taking a certain 'fairness' into account, cf. *Topica* VI.3,141a16 ff.; 1960, 573 ff. Unlike St Paul's negative understanding of *eutrapelía* (cf. note 504), the New Testament has two instances of *epieikeía* both with a decidedly positive meaning such as 'gentleness', Acts 24:4 and 2 Cor 10:1.

|20| *Principio reiicit γελοιαστής noster concionatorem nimis serium. Quid velit, non satis dispicio. Ego eundem puto serium et nimis serium, imo nimis serium esse non posse; alioqui serius esse desineret evaderetque crudelis, quemadmodum piis nemo vitio dederit, si pietate multum praepolleant. An ad sapientis dictum me remittet: 'Noli nimium esse iustus'? Quod ita intelligo, non ut aliquatenus a iusticiae ratione secedendum sit, quae persequenda semper, sed ne [O: 9] summum ius, quod dicitur, summa fiat iniusticia, subque excellentis justiciae titulo crudelitatis horrendae tyrannis invehatur. Quod si ita de me sentit ille noster, τῇ ἐπιεικίᾳ τε καὶ εὐτραπελίᾳ prorsum me facit alienum.*

|21| I should be criticised more openly like a Davos,[520] not like an Oedipus, for where, when, and against whom I did not act as I should. Then I could skip my defence speech, repent, and make amends for what I may have committed either out of ignorance or with intention. Anyone who accuses someone of lack of seriousness does not immediately accuse him of insensitivity. Now I think I know what he wants. He wants me to let go of some of my strictness, and he would like me to close my eyes to this abominable custom during all the solemn holidays, so that like Orpheus with his lyre I could treat the cold hearts of men with the lure of stories and the seduction of jokes.[521]

|21| *Apertius, mihi Davo, non Oedipodi oportebat opprobrare, ubi, quando, in quem inofficiosus fuerim, ut omissa apologia poenitentia diluerem, quod vel per ignorantiam vel etiam sciens deliqueram. Verum qui nec satis serium vocat, non statim crudelitatis arguit. Jam quid velit, suspicor: remittere scilicet me aliquid de severitate, et ad abominandum in tantis solenniis morem connivere desyderat, ut fabularum lenociniis et iocorum illecebris immitia hominum pectora tamquam Orphica lyra tractem.*

---

520 A slave named Davos appears in the comedy *Andria* by Terence, who in a conversation with his master Simo defends his slow-wittedness with the proverbial 'Davos sum, non Oedipus', act 1, sc. 2, l. 194; 1893, 14. This defence alludes to Oedipus' reputation for being good at solving puzzles.

521 If Orpheus could conquer not only people with his music and voice, but also nature and the underworld, a sleepy congregation should be within the realm of possibility. Cf. 'while with songs such as these, the Thracian poet is leading the woods and the natures of savage beasts, and the following rocks', Ovid, *Metamorphoses*, Book 11, ll. 1 f.; 1889, 379.

|22| He wants me to cheer up the congregation with more unbridled laughter,[522] which means that I surrender light to darkness, that I unite Christ with Belial himself,[523] indeed, that I simply do not stand before [the congregation] as a preacher, but as some vagabond juggler[524] for whom the only thing he is serious about is making insults. We are not that barbaric, that wild; we have not drunk from the udders of the Hyrcanian tigers,[525] so that we should wipe off all graciousness from our face, cut every flowery expression from the sermon, and extinguish all joy during our meetings. But our conduct is aimed at proving ourselves serious and worthy of the pulpit, if not always (God grant it could be so!), then at least during the sermon itself.

|22| *Quaerit, ut effusiore risu auditorium exhilarem, hoc est, ut lucem tenebris committam, Christum ipsi Belial associem et plane pro concionatore praestem scaenicum circulatorem, cui citra controversiam haud nimium de serio constet. Non sumus tam feroces, tam tetrici; neque enim Hircanarum tigrium ubera suximus, ut a vultu omnem detergamus gratiam, a sermone omnem decutiamus florem, a consortiis omnem excindamus laetitiam. Sed eo nostra pergit actio, ne [!], si non semper, quod utinam a Deo nobis tribueretur, vel sub ipsa dicendi hora graves adeoque concionatorio suggestu dignos praestemus viros.*

|23| It is not unknown to me that priests wear one garment when addressing people, and another during the sacred ceremonies. Therefore, when people have gone home, if these men in a manner that does not offend anyone

---

522 Oecolampadius restricts himself to the more neutral term, *risus*, but by qualifying it with the adjective *effusus* the expression acquires the same meaning as *cachinna*, i.e. the kind of laughter where the body most clearly has power over the mind.

523 One of the names for Satan which appears only once in the New Testament: 'And what concord hath Christ with Belial?', 2 Cor 6:15 (*KJV*). In the *Vulgate* the name is also used once in the Old Testament in the phrase *filii Belial*, Dt 13:13, which *KJV* translates as 'the children of Belial', whereas the *NKJ* prefers the Hebrew text and translates it as 'corrupt men'.

524 Cf. notes 518 and 481.

525 In antiquity, the tigers of Hyrcania (the area around the south coast of the Caspian Sea) were considered particularly wild; at this point Oecolampadius makes a clear allusion to Vergil's *The Aeneid*: 'But on its breast of stone / Caucasus bore thee, and the tigresses / of fell Hyrcania to thy baby lip / their udders gave', Book 4, ll. 366–9; 1908, 126.

within their own walls or in the company of honourable people can relax with innocent tales without offending the seriousness and measure of men, only to be so much more committed to the ceremonies afterwards, I would honour these men at all hours of the day.[526] I will in no way blame them; when I look at them, I rather admire the diversity of grace [1 Pet 4:10]. Because I do not want to think that a man has his cheerfulness as if by lot, as is the case with the Gentiles, but rather something that one obtains by divine gift. In my opinion wrinkles do not lack charm, nor furrowed brows their grace, nor austerity its beauty.[527]

|23| *Non me latet sacerdotes aliis, quando ad populum prodeunt, aliis inter sacrificandum indumentis uti. Quare si dimissa plebe citra scan-*[O: 10] *dalum, intra parietes suos aut in honestis conviviis inculpatis recreentur fabulis nec omnem virilis gravitatis harmoniam solvant, quo ferventiores ad sacra redeant, tanquam viros omnium horarum laudabo; tantum abest, ne taxem; admirabor in istis gratiarum ποικιλότητα. Neque enim sorte*

---

526 In early Protestantism many disapproved of the excessive liturgy of the Catholic Church where, for example, the use of chasubles and bishops' vestments was considered a theatrical sacramentalism. The protestant counterweight to this was the sermon, preferably as artless and straightforward as possible. Interestingly some of the Reformation's forerunners – prior to Oecolampadius! – are already voicing this kind of criticism, such as Gerhoh of Reichersberg (1093–1169) and John Wycliffe (1328–84); especially among the Puritans, however, it became a recurrent topic. A beautiful poetic example can be found in *Paradise Lost* when Milton significantly emphasises that Adam and Eve improvised their prayers all over again each morning (5th Song, ll. 144–152; cf. 11th Song, ll. 1–21; 1998, 289–90 and 598–9 respectively). For even the repetition of liturgically prescribed prayers with their fixed wording testified to a lack of authenticity and a theatrical superficiality, a kind of 'performed piety'; cf. Barish 1981, 76 ff. and 95 f.

Although it is not immediately clear that Oecolampadius agrees with a total rejection of liturgical vestments, his acceptance of a distinction between the sphere of worship and everyday life certainly suggests a more lenient attitude than the one found among the most radical Puritans. For them piety was a norm for life in all its aspects, and therefore they were also suspicious of laughter in the living room.

527 Oecolampadius' use of the word *sors* makes it possible to understand his argument in several ways. *Sors* can mean 'coincidence'. Thus, Oecolampadius attributes to the gentiles the opinion that either it is pure arbitrariness whether a person is cheerful or – conversely – there is something fateful about it, because *sors* is also associated with 'oracles' and 'prophecy'. Most often, however, the word has the basic meaning of 'a lot' ('drawing of lots'). If so, I must confess that this kind of lottery is not known to me as a motif in ancient texts. Perhaps Oecolampadius could be thinking of

comitatem cuipiam contingere gentilium more, sed divino munere obtineri censuerim; quo autore nec rugis sua venustas nec superciliis suae gratiae nec suus austeritati decor abest.

|24| What is cheerful wit missing, what do elegance and atticisms[528] lack that one cannot be happy without breaking out into loud laughter and smiles.[529] But in order not to go into more detail about the joy of the spirit[530] and the faithful Abraham's laughing Isaac[531] [*Gen 21:6], let such people come with their harmless pleasures, indeed, let them play on the harp of David, even if they are mocked by the foolish Michal [2 Sam 6:20]. No decent person will envy them, no wise man will not adorn them with praises. And if it pleases them, let them also bring witty speech into their teaching, of the kind, I venture to say, that no one masters as well as Isaiah.[532]

|24| *Quid festivis salibus deesset, quid in urbanitatibus et atticismis desyderaretur, quominus, quamvis citra cacchinnos et risus, oblectarent? Ut interim gaudia spiritus et fidelis Abrahae ridentem Isaac praetereamus, adferant id genus innoxias Veneres, imo ludant in citharis Davidicis, etiamsi a stulta Michol irrideantur. Nemo bonus invidebit, nemo sapiens non ornabit laudibus. Et si*

---

the 'lottery' that may be said to be implied in the distribution of human qualities and skills in the theory about the four humours (temperaments)? In any case, by emphasising a theological anthropology, Oecolampadius can object against one particular temperament being more pleasing to God than another.

528 Atticism was a movement among rhetoricians in the last century before our era, which reacted against Hellenism and its simple language (*koinē*) by advocating a return to the Attic language and style of classical orators. Not surprisingly, this ambition was revived by renaissance humanists.

529 In his polemical catalogue of less noisy forms of pleasure, Oecolampadius, in a way, ends up recommending exactly the kind of refined amusement that knows how to appreciate a stylish allusion or innuendo – which is actually quite reminiscent of Aristotle's definition of the *eutrapelía* that he criticised above, cf. |15|and |20|.

530 To prevent being misunderstood, Oecolampadius qualifies the joy as spiritual; but in general, the term *gaudium* refers to an inner joy (unlike *laetitia* that is visible – and audible). In the Middle Ages, e.g. with Gregory the Great, it was said that spiritual joy expressed itself in the 'laughter of the heart', which could not be heard but at best detected by the faintest of smiles, cf. Suchomski 1975, 16; Resnick 1987, 92, and above III,5,ii.

531 Cf. the excursus in chapter III,6.

532 What Oecolampadius has in mind may be an example of the prophet's sharp polemical wit as follows: 'Woe unto them that are mighty to drink wine, and men

lubet, lepidum dicendi genus etiam in cathedram adferant; id, inquam, in quo Esaiae principatus conceditur.

|25| You know, most learned Capito, that some of the jokes of the rhetoricians are in the words, some in the subject, others again combine the two;[533] some are concise, others infinite, and of all of these, some are scurrilous, pantomime-like and theatrical, and unworthy of decent people, much less clergy and theologians.[534] Others are cultured and refined, in which 'there is nothing incongruous, nothing coarse, nothing unpolished, nothing barbarous', as Fabius says.[535]

|25| *Scis, doctissime Capito, apud rhetores facetiarum alias verbo, alias re constare, alias ex utroque genere conflari, alias item breves perpetuasque alias, et ex iis omnibus alias scurriles, mimicas et theatricas, bono quoque viro indignas, nedum ecclesiastico et theologo, alias civiles et urbanas, in quibus 'nihil absonum, nihil agreste, nihil inconditum, nihil peregrinum' ut Fabius ait.*

|26| Which of all of these do you think our prankster will choose to squeeze laughter out of the whole congregation? Perhaps Cato's elegant jokes?[536] Perhaps those of the prophets, in which what seems more ridiculous than

---

of strength to mingle strong drink', Isa 5:22 (*KJV*). The Danish professor of Old Testament Studies, William Peter Grønbech (1873–1948), happens to refer to Isaiah as the paragon of somebody who understood how to use laughter seriously in the service of moral satire, 1951, 46.

533   In 'The Orator' (*De oratore*), Cicero reflects on ridicule and the speaker's use of it. In the introduction, he states that as far as laughter is concerned, there are 'five questions to be considered. First, what is its nature? Second, what is its source? Third, should an orator want to stir up laughter? Fourth, to what extent? Fifth, into what categories can the humorous be divided' (2.235; 2001, 186). In his remarks, Cicero also distinguishes, as mentioned by Oecolampadius, between laughter aroused either by means of thought or by language (or the object) (2.248; 2001, 190). The crucial thing about this distinction is that it opens up for an insight into the fact that laughter is not only caused by certain parts of reality but is just as often due to a certain perspective on or a way of relating to it, cf. Gilhus 1997, 45.

534   The first instance that Jacobelli (1992, 31 f.) has been able to find of warnings against clergy's use of language and narratives that can excite laughter is by Hinkmar. In his *Capitula synodica* from 852 he expressly forbids priests the use of *fabulas inanes* and *turpia ioca*, 1852, col. 776C. Cf. note 58.

535   The quote is from Quintilian and is followed by: 'whether in thought, language, voice or gesture', *Institutes of Oratory* 6.3.107; 1953, 499.

536   In the passage immediately preceding the one quoted by Oecolampadius, Quintilian refers to Cato's description of arousing laughter in an 'elegant' (*urbanus*) way,

it is is put to sleep due to the power of the maturity of the speakers? Does the exchange of letters and syllables arouse laughter, as in the case of the Holy Fathers who call Bethel Beth-Aven [Hos 10:5][537] and Gilead for Gilgal [Hos 12:12],[538] and as Isaiah, when he writes, 'And he looked for justice, but saw bloodshed; for righteousness, but heard cries of distress.' [Isa 5:7 NIV]? Perhaps by means of ambiguous expressions or contradictions or versification, which the Apostle also uses when he says, 'Cretans always lie' [Tit 1:12], or with reverse word order, figurative meaning, interpretation, exaggerations, or other kinds of which you know not a few from the Holy Scripture?[539]

|26| *Quas ex hoc numero, putas, γελοιαστής noster, ut e tota concione risum extorqueat, deliget? [O: 11] Num urbanas illas Catonianas? Num propheticas, in quibus, quod ridiculum magis videtur quam est, dicentium maturitate sopitur? Num literae aut syllabae immutatione risum captant, ut est apud sacros vates, qui* בֵּית־אֵל *vocant* בֵּית־אָוֶן, *et* גִּלְעָד גִּלְגָּל *et apud Esaiam:* וַיְקַו לְמִשְׁפָּט וְהִנֵּה מִשְׂפָּח לִצְדָקָה וְהִנֵּה צְעָקָה, *aut ambigue dictis aut antithetis aut versuum adiectione, qua et apostolus utitur, dicens:* Κρῆτες ἀεὶ ψεῦσται *aut verborum inversione, translatione, interpretamento, ὑπερβολαῖς aut aliis locis, quos tu non paucos ex sacris observas literis?*

Institutio oratoria 6.3.105; 1953, 497. This refers to Marcus Portius Cato the Elder (234–149 BCE).

537 'Beth-aven is a distortion of the name Bethel, which means House of God, while Beth-aven means House of Evil', footnote to Hos 4:15 in the Danish Bible translation of 1992.

538 'In Hebrew there is a pun on Gilgal and heaps of stones', footnote to Hos 12:12 in the Danish Bible translation of 1992. In the *KJV* it is verse 11.

539 One senses from Oecolampadius' examples of what he considers to be legitimate forms of amusement that he had both done intensive Hebrew studies under, among others, Reuchlin, and since 1515 had worked as an assistant on Erasmus' Greek-Latin version of The New Testament (first published 1 March 1516).
    Already Augustine had in the fourth book of his 'On Christian Doctrine' (*De doctrina christiana*) tried to argue that the Bible lived up to, indeed surpassed, the pagan writers in literary quality and eloquence: 'I could, however, if I had time, show those men who cry up their own form of language as superior to that of our authors (not because of its majesty, but because of its inflation), that all those powers and beauties of eloquence which they make their boast, are to be found in the sacred writings which God in His goodness has provided to mould our characters, and to guide us from this world of wickedness to the blessed world above,' ch. 6; 1865a, 577. Otherwise, we must probably go all the way forward in time to the lectures on

|27| I would argue that the uneducated people, simple-minded as they are, usually do not amuse themselves with such revelling, or immediately burst out laughing. That is why our prankster has to resort to Milesian gibberish,[540] theatre stories, and the perpetual nonsense of old women.[541] And that in itself would not even be enough, unless at the same time he imitates with his whole body the movements of the actors and adapts to their dirty language and impertinent lack of shame, forgets all about being a priest, and devotes most of his time to the one goal of portraying every abomination, indeed does not engage in anything other than playing the clown.

|27| *Eiuscemodi inquam festivitatibus indocta plebs, uti crassior, nec oblectatur plurimum, nec in risum statim prorumpet. Restat itaque, ut γελοιαστής ad Milesias nugas, ad scaenicas fabulas, ad anilia perpetuaque deliramenta se convertat. Nec satis fuerit, nisi et toto corpore histrionicos gestus imitetur, verba illota, impertinentia pudorisque nescia intermisceat, describat turpitudinem omnem bonaque horae parte in id negotii collocata, oblitus se concionatorem, nihil agat praeter circulatorem.*

Hebrew poetry (*De sacra poesi Hebraeorum* ..., 1753) by the English bishop and professor of literature, Robert Lowth (1710–87), to find a scholar with a similarly ambitious attempt. Lowth systematically tried to show how biblical Hebrew can measure itself with the Latin orators in stylistic consciousness, but of course with an independent poetics that should not be judged on the basis of non-Hebrew norms.

540   The so-called *Milesian Tales* go back to Aristides of Miletus (2nd cent. BCE), and although none of his narratives have been handed down, we will, judging by descriptions of them, be able to recognise their frivolous and erotic (and narratively incoherent) style in Petronius' (27–66) *Satyricon* and Apuleius' *The Golden Ass*. Usually they were referred to as *Milesiae fabula*, but Oecolampadius also expresses his disapproval by 'reducing' them to *nugae* (which, incidentally, no other author in all the volumes of Migne *SL* does), cf. note 500. He does refer to these stories once more, again with deep irony, but at least there he identifies them as *fabulae*, see |56|.

541   Both terms appear once in the New Testament (*Vulgate*): *deliramentum* in Lk 24:11, where the Apostles do not believe in the 'idle tales/nonsense' of the women at the tomb; but if Oecolampadius alludes to the Bible, it is more likely to the use of *anilis* in *Vulgate*'s translation of 1 Tim 4:7, where *ineptas* and *fabulas* too are included in the sentence: *Ineptas autem, et aniles fabulas devita* ('Do not waste time arguing over godless ideas and old wives' tales' *NLT*). Cf. Luther's interpretation of the same verse mentioned in note 477.

|28| Just as he wants to tell the story of Morio, who strangled one calf and then lay down in the cow-dung as if to give birth to another,[542] he will also need a frothy vocabulary. He must invent more nonsense about this fool, imitate his distorted, deformed face and lame gait, loudly extolling the dung, and every now and then sit down like his fool and with hisses scare anyone who tries to make him get up.[543] During most of the sermon he must stand up not as the evangelical rooster,[544] but as a really bad and ridiculous goose, so that no one can control the organ of his laughter anymore,[545] and so that

---

542   In Martial's (c. 40-c. 104) *Epigrams*, the figure Morio appears twice (8.13 and 14.210; 1950, vol. 2, 13 and 513), and according to Staehelin (note 12, p. 58) he became the model for the personified fool, Moria, in Erasmus' *The Praise of Folly* (*Moriae encomium*). However, the calf and the dung motifs do not appear in either of these two authors. On the other hand, Röcke finds in these motifs a kinship to the kind of Medieval theatre which, from the time shortly after Oecolampadius, has been preserved in written records, as for example in Hans Sachs' Shrovetide play *Das Kälberbrüten* (a possible translation: 'How to Hatch Calves', 1551), Röcke 2002, 337 f.
543   Cf. the similar example mentioned earlier in |16|.
544   Oecolampadius clearly alludes to the rooster in the high priest's court, Mt 26:74. Curiously, one of the much later (from 1643) but testified examples of Easter Laughter includes this oddity: the priest Abraham Widmann from Röhrmoos near Dachau had people hidden in the choir loft who were to start cackling loudly during his sermon, Niedermeyer 1972, 269. In order to prevent turning this incident into a miracle, the dating of it (which so often has been relayed in scholarly literature) may have to be adjusted a year or two, as Widmann's time at the church ended a year earlier. According to the preserved tablet with the names of the priests in Röhrmoos, Widmann served as their priest from 1636 to his death in 1642, cf. kirchenundkapellen.de/kirchenpz/roehrmoos.php (accessed May 2024).
545   Literally Oecolampadius writes 'spleen'. According to the medieval theories of organs and bodily fluids (the humoural theory), the spleen secreted the black bile associated with melancholy, that is, quite the opposite of laughter. Nevertheless, the physiologists of the time also identified the spleen as the seat of laughter. This occurs already in the very early Middle Ages with Isidore of Seville, who formulated this trendsetting catchphrase: 'For through the spleen we laugh, through the bile we get angry, through the heart we understand, through the liver we love' (*Nam splene ridemus, felle irascimur, corde sapimus, iocore amamus*), *Etymologiarum* 11,i,127; 1830, col. 413; cf. Ferm 2008, 61 f. The idea lasted well into the High Middle Ages, which can be seen in Hildegard of Bingen's medical explanation of the origin of laughter, see above III,5,iv. Interestingly this interpretation has also been taken up in the separate tradition of Jewish thinking, as the connection between laughter and spleen is mentioned once in the *Babylonian Talmud* (the 'Berakhot' tractate 61b), 1996, 418.

one would think one was in the school of Democritus[546] rather than in a church.

|28| *Velut Morionis istius fabulam, qui vitulo strangulato alterum fimo bubulino superincubans parturierat, recensiturus, spumeo verborum ambitu opus habebit, alias adfinget stulti ineptias, distorti oris vitia et claudicantem gressum notabit, stercoris laudes efferat, subsidet interdum cum suo fatuo, avocantes ab incubatu sibilis terrebit eritque inter concionandum aliquamdiu pro [O: 12] gallo evangelico male probus et ridiculus anser, adeo ut nemo splenis suae compos sit, templumque Domini Democriti putes scholas.*

|29| Because I do not condone these fooleries, I may seem too serious and utterly ridiculous, while in relation to all this levity they are very serious and deserve double honour. What proper man does not, I venture to say,[547] realise that this kind of joke should be averse to a preacher, in whose mouth jests are considered as sacrilegious, in whose eyes splinters are considered as beams [*Mt 7:5], in whose face freckles are considered as leprosy? What is allowed for shysters and infamous pantomime players is not allowed for him. For he who declares that every word uttered shall be accounted for [Mt 12:36], and who shouts that buffoonery does not befit a Christian [*Eph 5:4], why is he the first to throw rocks at them?[548]

|29| *Has ineptias quia improbo, nimis serius fortassis videor et derideculus, ii vero tanta levitate satis serii sunt duplicique honore digni. Ecquis bonus vir ignorat*

---

546 The pre-Socratic Democritus from Abdera (*c.* 460-*c.* 370 BCE) was already in antiquity referred to as The Laughing Philosopher – in contrast to Heraclitus (*c.* 535-*c.* 475 BCE) as The Weeping Philosopher (later a favourite twinned motif in the art of painting). There are no straightforward explanation for this epithet. Partly it may be due to Democritus' teaching that the soul should strive to achieve *euthymia* ('cheerfulness'), i.e. a state that is not dominated by fear and hope; partly – and as a kind of putting his theory into practice – due to his reputation for making fun of people who, conversely, let themselves be controlled by fear and hope. This reputation is mentioned, for example, by Aelian in his *Varia historia* where he also mentions the epithet *Gelasinus* ('The Laughing One'), 1665, book 4, ch. 20.

547 A very free translation of the three Greek words which form a fixed expression used to underline a point. The literal meaning is somewhat like 'twice through all', see for example Erasmus' use of it in *The Praise of Folly*, 1511, A iiij recto; 2015a, 9.

548 If we suppose this to be an allusion to the story about Moses in Numbers (20,11-2), this makes it possible to keep a 'literal' translation of Oecolampadius' figurative choice of words. In that case Jesus' proclamation in Matthew and St Paul's in Ephesians are the rocks that Oecolampadius' opponent should not have 'struck' against.

δὶς διὰ πασῶν *alienas esse huiusce generis nugas ab ecclesiastico oratore, in cuius ore nugae blasphemiae, in cuias oculis sestucae trabeis, in cuius facie lentigo lepra putatur, cui non permittitur, quod forensi rabulae, nedum quod infami ludioni? Qui enim annunciat reddendam rationem de omni verbo, qui clamat scurrilitatem indecentem christiano, cur primus in eos impingit scopulos?*

|30| As far as I can see he does not build up with one hand and tear down with the other,[549] rather, he crushes with both. He has not only the hands of Esau but also his voice [Gen 27:22], not one language or one voice but both of them. Who, nowadays, goes out into his parish to preach penance, what do these [modern preachers] accomplish with their jokes, their grins, and roars of laughter? Are we perhaps lacking incentives to do what we are naturally inclined to do? If we wash away sins with laughter,[550] then what are we to

---

549 Oecolampadius presumably draws on the pedagogical dictum: 'teaching well but living badly is like building up with one hand and breaking down with the other' (*Bene docere et male vivere, est una manu aedificare, altera destruire*) – provided that it was known in that version when he was writing! The dictum does not appear in Hans Walther's (1884–1971) enormous collection of more than 45,000 Latin proverbs and aphorisms; however, Johan Adam Weber (1611–86) includes it in his *Ars conversandi* from 1682 (p. 26, no. 16).

Without giving a specific reference J.A. Weber compares the dictum with a phrase from Chrysostom: *Bene docendo, et male vivendo, instruis Deum, quomodo te debeat condemnare*. J.A. Weber must be referring to the latter part of a passage from the so-called unfinished sermons on Matthew, which begins: *Nam bene vivendo, et bene docendo, populum instruis, quomodo debeat vivere: bene ...* (1862d, col. 876). 'For by living well and teaching well you instruct the people how they should live, but by teaching well and living badly you instruct God how he ought to condemn you' (Oden 2010, vol. 2, 343). The editors of this translation present the arguments for why Chrysostom is not considered the author – incidentally, a theory already advocated by Erasmus in his edition of the text from 1530. Although Migne includes the sermons in a volume of texts by Chrysostom, he places them under 'Spuria' and with the entry 'Incerto auctore'.

550 In his biting polemic, Oecolampadius almost creates an expression that could have gone down in history as a proverbial slogan: *peccata risibus abolemus*! It is strikingly reminiscent of what is arguably the best-known moral defence of laughter in general and comedy in particular. Although the maxim 'rebuking manners with laughter' (*castigat ridendo mores*) is attributed to the Neo-Latin poet Jean de Santeuil (1630–97), the thought threads back to Horace's (65 BCE-8 CE) 'telling the truth through laughter' (*ridendo dicere verum*), see 'Satires' (*Satyrarum Libri*): 'What hinders one being merry, while telling the truth' (*quamquam ridentem dicere verum / quid vetat?*), 1.1, ll. 24 f.; 1856, 140. Oecolampadius seems to give his firm answer to this rhetorical question in the following sentences!

do with sacks and ashes? With crying and lamentations? Foolish were the Ninevites, who at Jonah's command proclaimed a public fast [Jon 3:5 ff.; *cf. Mt 12:41]. And foolish was Hezekiah, who in bitterness pondered upon his life [2 Kings 20:1 ff.; Isa 38:1 ff.]. Also foolish was David, who wetted his bed with tears [Ps 6:7; *cf. 2 Sam 12:22]!

|30| *Videtur is mihi non una manu aedificare et altera destruere, sed utraque demoliri, nec modo manus habere Esau, sed et vocem Esau, nec linguam aut vocem unam, sed duplicem. Iam qui poenitentiae praedicandae provinciam obiit, quid illi cum iocis, risibus et cachinnis saeculi? An etiam ad quae natura propensi sumus, impulsoribus egemus? Si peccata risibus abolemus, quid opus sacco et cinere? Quid lachrymis et planctibus? Stulti Ninivitae, qui ad vocem Jonae iusticium publicum indixerunt, et stultus Ezechias qui in amaritudine recogitat dies suos. Stultus item et David lachrymis stratum suum rigans!*

|31| But now to the point! Are we messengers of the truth and the heavenly wisdom that Christ has brought us? How much does the truth differ from the joke? In addition, those who will turn to Christ, through their prayers, prepare themselves with a comprehensive effort, purify themselves, adorn their souls, put aside jokes, renounce pleasures,[551] and reject all foolish nonsense because they try to make themselves deserving of a nod from His glory.[552] And if they have come unprepared to pray without respect for His greatness, they think they have been rightly rejected.

---

551   *Voluptas* probably has a broader meaning than, for example, *concupiscentia* and can for example be translated as 'pleasure' and 'enjoyment' – both spiritually and physically; but in the latter context the two words share meanings such as 'desire', 'lust', and 'lechery'. It may seem remarkable that here a theologian on the threshold of joining the Protestant movement uses some of the terms most frequently used in Catholic moral theology. To give but one (albeit obvious!) example, the term *voluptas* – with three dozen occurrences – is included as one of the key words, when in 'The Shows' Tertullian makes a frontal attack on all forms of entertainment in Roman cultural life. In that context Tertullian also uses the verb *abdico* in several places to indicate that the Christian should 'renounce' amusements. Remarkable or not, the choice of words seems to be symptomatic of the Oecolampadius who ten years later in Basel was to contribute to the development of a strict church discipline over society.

552   Several of the medieval monastic rules have instructions about how the monks should manage laughter. One example is *The Rule of Saint Benedict* which in four instances specifies restraint and abstinence from laughter, prominently in chapter 7 which deals with the twelve steps in practising humility. On the ladder towards perfection the two penultimate steps are concerned with laughter (v. 59–61): 'The tenth step of humility is that he [i.e. the monk] is not given to ready laughter, for it is

|31| *Age, num veritatis sapientiaeque caelestis a Christo allatae praecones sumus? Veritas et ioci quanto intervallo dissident? Accedit ad haec, quod [O: 13] colloquuturi cum Christo per preculas suas permalto se studio praeparant, purificant, ornant animos suos, ponunt iocos, abdicant voluptates, repudiant ineptias, ut numinis eius nutum emereri queant, iustam se ferre repulsam rati, si contempta maiestate accesserint ad orandum imparati.*

|32| Moses took off his sandals before approaching the bush [Ex 3:1 ff.], the people were sanctified for three days before receiving the law [Ex 19:10 f.]. Well, it is no less important if He wants to announce his marvellous and hidden mysteries through us as an instrument, or when it is our turn to be the ones to experience the divine as well. Should we not then excel by not avoiding seriousness, and especially by not adding anything of our own, of the world's filth, or of diabolical spells? Why do we not agree? Why do we disagree so much? Why do we not end the discussion in a common spirit?

|32| *Moses, antequam rubum accederet, calceos solvit, populus, antequam legem acciperet, triduo sanctificatus est. Atqui non minus est, si per nos uti organum mirabilia arcanaque sua mysteria pronunciet, item, cum eos nos esse oporteat, qui et divina patiantur. An non enitendum, ne quid ex severitate relaxemus, nedum nihil addamus ex nostris, ex mundanis spurciciis, ex diabolicis incantamentis? Cur non constamus nobis? Quid tam varii? Cur non eodem spiritu peroramus?*

|33| Now, let us say with a thundering voice: 'Thus saith the Lord God of Hosts; this commandeth the Word of God, Truth himself, even so the Holy Ghost spake by the Apostles and Prophets', and at the same time we still behave like cuckoos or geese, not as worthy preachers, but as fickle mime players. Besides, we are not exactly doing a favour to those common people that are almost despised, whose simplicity is in some way mocked, whose chaste ears are offended, whose inclination to sin is given an occasion, and under whose sins, so to speak, is placed a pillow. Are we here in the company of Phaeacians and Carthaginians,[553] so it does not matter what we say?

---

written: "Only a fool raises his voice in laughter" (Sir 21:23) [i.e. v. 20]. The eleventh step of humility is that a monk speaks gently and without laughter, seriously and with becoming modesty, briefly and reasonably, but without raising his voice, as it is written: "A wise man is known by his few words" [cf. Sir 32:8].' 1981, 201.

553 In the 6th through 13th Song of the *Odyssey* Odysseus is stranded on the island of Scheria and according to the time-line makes a very short, yet narratively long stay (it takes eight songs to record it!) with its people, the Phaeacians, who are portrayed as an almost carefree ideal society, a Utopia. What makes Oecolampadius

|33| *Tonamus nunc: 'haec dicit Dominus Deus Sabaoth, ita instituit verbum Dei, veritas ipsa, ita locutus est per apostolos et prophetas spiritus sanctus', et interea simul cuculum agimus vel anserem, non tam concionatores honestos, quam leves mimos repraesentantes. Praeterea quidem haud magnopere plebi gratificamur, quae velut contemnitur, cuius quodammodo simplicitas luditur, cuius aures castae vulnerantur, cuius ad malum proclivitati ansa porrigitur, cuius sceleribus cervicalia, ut sic dicam, subduntur. An in Phaeacum Chartaginensiumve convivio sumus, ut nihil referat, quid dicamus?*

|34| Surely, we do not lack houses where we can chat and tell jokes? Or do we, like the Corinthians, count the Church of God for nothing [1 Cor 11:22]? Well, granted that these ridiculous fortune-tellers are not exactly unwelcome among people, yet is this an honourable preacher who aligns all his speech and life with the standards of the people? Will a dutiful doctor give the sick person everything he wants to eat? Why do we put obstacles in the way of the weak and the powerless? Why do we suffocate the wick where the little flame of love glows? Why do we not fan the flames instead? Do we not have enough in our own sins? It is an odd lack of judgment to want to appear deeply serious in the midst of extreme hilarity!

|34| *Num sane domus nobis desunt, in quibus nugemur et iocemur? An ecclesiam Dei [O: 14] nihil pendimus cum Corinthiis? Esto, plebi non sint ingrati ridiculi isti prophetastri; an hoc concionatoriae integritatis ad plebis trutinam, totum dicere et vivere? Aegrotone cibos omnes, quos desyderat, medicus fidelis ministrabit? Cur parvulis et invalidis offendicula ponimus? Cur linum, in quo parva charitatis flamma fumigat, extinguimus? Cur non magis sufflamus? Non sufficit nobis iniquitas nostra? Mira imprudentia in extrema levitate gravissimum videri velle!*

|35| Do we not realise that even though we have said a lot of good and beautiful things and perhaps have only missed a single syllable, we are constantly in danger of the whole sermon being maliciously criticised for its flaw? So, what are the considerations that make us stay away from the serious? I implore them, let those who are so displeased with seriousness explain what fruits and benefits jokes bring! Or are our arguments so uncomfortable that we have to dissolve them into laughter and jokes? Or will we alleviate the horror of our sins with a little jovial taunt, lest they should bother us too

---

conclude that 'it does not matter what we say'? Is it their carelessness, or rather that the Phaeacians are Gentiles? Although there are many differences between them, Homer's descriptions are clearly reflected in Vergil's *Aeneid* (1st-4th song), where Aeneas resides in Carthage after his shipwreck.

much? Or to please the audience, so that we will be called polite, refined, educated, so that we can feel ourselves refreshed by the empty breeze and milk ourselves some bits of cheese?⁵⁵⁴

|35| *Nescimus perpetuum nostrum periculum, cum multa bene praeclareque dixerimus et vel syllaba una exciderimus, totam orationem iudicii pravitate calumniari? Quae ergo tanta cura, ut a seriis cessandum? Dicant, obsecro, quibus adeo seria displicent, qui iocorum fructus, quae commoda! An tam odiosa nobis argumenta, quae necesse sit risu iocoque dissolvere? Horroremve facinorum convivali scommate elevabimus, ne nimium displiceant? An ut auditoribus placeamus, ut politi, urbani, eruditi dicamur inanique refocillemur aurula caseolosque aliquot emulgeamus?*

|36| But the apostle says, 'If I want to please men, I am not a servant of God' [Gal 1:10]. Or perhaps to thereby gain us prestige? The speakers believe that one achieves these benefits by telling jokes. But there we deceive ourselves well and truly. For one will be able to answer us, just as the philosopher answers anyone who asks when to surrender to sensuality: 'when you want to be weaker'.⁵⁵⁵ In the same way we can then make use of all this disgraceful nonsense when we wish to dissolve our reputation completely. Pay attention, I pray, to what will win you the most laughter: no elixir is as effective as the unexpected (that, which happens without expecting it).⁵⁵⁶

---

554 It is reasonable to imagine an aphorism behind this rather strange choice of words, not least because Oecolampdius uses the same phrase in his Easter sermon from 1518 (or possibly 1516/17; 1927b, 60); but according to the voluminous register in Walther 1963-69, he does not seem to have come across something comparable.

555 A statement attributed to Pythagoras in Diogenes Laertius (fl. in the 3ʳᵈ cent. CE): *Lives of Eminent Philosophers* [*Vitae philosophorum*], Book 8, ch. 1, section 9; 1925, vol. 2, 329.

556 For no obvious reason Oecolampadius resorts to the Greek word *aprosdókētos*, which indeed means 'the unexpected', but which does not appear to have been used as a literary technical term. The word appears in Aristophanes, but without relevant significance, whereas Aristotle does not use it in his reflections on the unexpected/the surprising in the context of tragedy (*Poetics*, ch. 9). On the other hand, both Cicero and Quintilian touch on the effect of the unexpected in connection with laughter, though neither of them employs any of the special expressions used in poetics (the direct Latin counterpart to *aprosdókētos* would have been *necopinatus*), but rather merely variations of the commonplace words in Oecolampadius' parentheses. Cicero seems to make an almost direct translation of the Greek *para prosdokían* into *praeter exspectationem* (*De oratore* 2,255 and 2,284; 2001, 192 and 202), while Quintilian's variants are *expectationem decipere* or *opinionem decipere* (*Institutio oratoria* 6.3.24 and 6.3.64, respectively; 1953, 451 and 473).

|36| *At apostolus inquit: 'Si hominibus placeam, Dei servus non sum.' An ut autoritatem nobis inde conciliemus? Ea enim emolumenta afferri per iocos oratores putant. Verum longe fallimur; responderi enim nobis poterit, quemadmodum philosophus cuipiam roganti, quando re venerea utendum, respondit: 'ubi infirmior fieri voles'. Et tum nobis infamibus illis gerris [O: 15] utendum, cum autoritatem interire volumus. Animo adverte, precor, quid potissimum risum conciliet: nullum tam praesens pharmacon atque τὸ ἀπροσδόκητον (id, quod praeter expectationem accidit).*

|37| But from us is expected the evangelical bread, the heavenly doctrine. Yet we fall back on the commonplace folly, so foolish and so unexpected that people are not laughing with us but at us derisively. That is why our Erasmus, the wittiest and at the same time the most learned of all mortals I have ever seen and heard,[557] so cunningly allowed his Moria to mention this error,[558] though it was not one of Moria's:[559] 'For the happy ones, laughter only deserves laughter', as Nazianzen says.[560]

---

557   Oecolampadius was recruited in 1515 by the publisher Froben to assist Erasmus with the publication of the New Testament. He served as a kind of academic proofreader in general, but in particular he had to check the Hebrew quotations in Erasmus' notes.

558   In his attempt to disqualify the use of laughter in church Oecolampadius chooses a term with quite a momentous baggage, since *vitium* has more or less the same range of meaning as the Greek *hamartía*. *Vitium* was indeed used in the Latin versions of Aristotle's *Poetics*, when the Italian humanists wanted to translate the famously enigmatic and hotly debated concept. Aristotle not only uses the word in his definition of the tragic hero in chapter 13, but *hamartía* is also included in the description of the characters of comedy quoted above in note 497: '[...] an *error* of some kind'. Whenever St Paul uses the word *hamartía*, as he does throughout his Letter to the Romans, we do not traditionally think of errors or mistakes but of the sinfulness of man, e.g. Rom 5:12 f.

559   It is, of course, a disturbing and ominous detail, which Oecolampadius' panegyrical declaration of confidence can hardly neutralise, that Erasmus puts his entire book in the mouth of the inveterate folly of Moria/Stultitia. For when Folly says almost verbatim the same thing as Oecolampadius, does it then *mean* the same – or the opposite? 'Finally, the mind of man is so constructed that it is taken far more with disguises than with realities. If anyone wants to make a convincing and easy test of this, let him go to church and listen to sermons. If something solid is being said, everybody sleeps, or yawns, or is ill at ease. But if the bawler – I made a slip, I meant to say prater – as they so often do, begins some old wives' tale [*anilem fabellam*], everybody awakens, straightens up, and gapes for it.' 1511, e iiij verso; 2015a, 63.

560   The quotation is from Gregory of Nazianzus (*c*. 329–89/ 90): ' "Carminum", Liber I: Theologica, sectio II: Poemata moralia', 1862, col. 933.

|37| *Expectatur autem a nobis evangelicus panis, caelestis disciplina; at nos in mundanas ineptias incidimus, tam ineptas, tam inexpectatas, ut non tam rideat quam derideat populus. Hinc est, quod Erasmus noster, mortalium omnium, quos ego viderim vel audierim unquam, facetissimus simul ac eruditissimus, Moriae suae quam vafre permisit, id vitii tangere, quamvis id Moriae non erat; 'γέλως γὰρ γέλωτος εὐφρονοῦσιν ἄξιος', ut Nazanzenus ait.*

|38| Truly, how could this be expressed more sharply than by entrusting to Moria herself that these extremely gracious men may be critics in appearance, but of character, that is, of words, demeanour, and in their whole attitude, are simplicity itself. He shunned envy, which no one, not even the most famous, has ever avoided, not even himself. Among other things this, too, bothered the Erasmus-faultfinders. Why not rather hate Poggio, from whom they so often fish out their wit?[561] Poggio, who, as far as I know, in the introduction to his jokes, I mean his *Facetiae*, criticises our genre in very sharp terms, and urges us not at every opportunity to jabber away with his short stories.[562] Such is our so-called reputation that Folly itself – and not undeservedly – accuses us of foolishness.

---

561 Poggio was an early Italian humanist, highly ranked in the Curia in Rome and a diligent collector of ancient manuscripts (among other things he has the honour of having rediscovered Quintilian's *Institutio oratoria*, to which Oecolampadius also refers). When he had become an elderly man, he collected 273 small stories, witty, often satirical, but also erotic and scatological. There is no system to the collection, but recurring targets are monks and clerical corruption, the sexual appetite of women, stupid peasants – and, not least, contemporary humanists whom Poggio famously engaged in scholarly feuds. The collection was first published in 1452 and in a book printed in 1470, and before Oecolampadius wrote his letter in 1518, Poggio's *Facetiae* were well on their way to being published in close to fifty reprints (though with different numbers of stories included).

562 Staehelin (note 18, p. 58) raises the question whether Oecolampadius by mentioning a *frontispicium* may refer to the front page (title page, cover) of a specific edition of Poggio. On one hand the reason for asking the question is that it is difficult to find anything that corresponds to Oecolampadius' remark in Poggio's preface; on the other hand these 'front pages' could often be quite wordy (similar to today's back cover texts with a short description of a book's content and purpose). In his preface, Poggio is much more concerned with defending both his own interest in this kind of paltry literature and the value of the genre as such. He uses the same argument that Aquinas accepts in his *Summa Theologica*, that busy and serious people need distraction and rest to recreate and be refreshed for further work (IIa.IIae, 168, a.2; 1872, vol. 4, 408; 1920 online: newadvent.org/summa/3168.htm). Moreover Poggio refers to respected predecessors who also took pleasure in the genre. Without

|38| *Verum, qui acerbius notare poterat, quam, quod suavissimos istos homines, habitu quidem criticos, moribus autem, hoc est: verbis, vultu, gestu omni μωροτάτους ipsi Moriae familiariter notos facit? Declinavit invidiam, quam clarissimorum nullus evasit unquam, nec ipse quoque. Displicuit enim et id inter caetera Ἐρασμομάστιξι. Cur non magis Pogium odere, ex quo suos lepores expiscantur persaepe, quem credo tam acriter genus nostrum prope in frontispicio nugarum, Facetiarum inquam, reprehendere obtestarique, ne suas fabellas intempestivi deblateraremus? Haec est illa autoritas nostra, ut nos stulticia ipsa, non praeter meritum, stulticiae arguat.*

|39| I had almost forgotten the reasoning of our friend of laughter:[563] to show some consideration for the sleepy. Now, before we cover our mistakes[564] with excuses, let us be careful not to insult St Paul, the preacher to the Gentiles, who struggled more than everybody else [2 Cor 11:23]. We risk accusing him of negligence because he did not keep the young Eutykos awake with some nonsense, so that he was not overwhelmed by sleep and fell from the third floor [Acts 20:9]! Oh, our sleep; so soporific, so frosty do we preach the gospel that we have to seek aid from jokes! Is there no other balm in Gilead [Jer 8:22]? Why do we not rouse them with thunder like the Sons of Thunder, who caused the entire world to wake up [Mk 3:17]? Why not with the Archangel's Doomsday trumpet [1 Thess 4:16]?

|39| *Omiseram prope, quod φιλόγελως [!] noster causatur, somniculosorum habendam rationem. Videamus [O: 16] ne dum nostris vitiis excusationes praeteximus, Paulum, praedicatorem gentium, plus omnibus laborantem, negligentiae sugillemus, qui non deliramento quodam Eutychum adolescentem*

---

mentioning them by name, Poggio could easily have Cicero and Quintilian in mind, as they both spice up their writings with countless illustrative anecdotes. The only thing that remotely resembles Oecolampadius' reference is found towards the end of the preface, where Poggio partly encourages those who find the stories stylistically inferior to improve them themselves, and partly coolly reminds 'the strictest judges of taste and the harshest critics' that they can simply refrain from reading the book. This preface is not included in Hurwood's English translation from 1968, but does appear in the German edition 1906, 3.

563 Oecolampadius probably relates only to the straightforward meaning of the Greek word. At the same time, however, the word is also the title of the oldest surviving collection (from the 4th cent. CE) of Greek 'facetiae' (ἀποφθέγματα, *apophthegmata*), with Hierocles and Philagrios (both unknown, probably after 248 CE) traditionally credited as publishers.

564 Here, too, Oecolampadius signals the gravity of these 'mistakes' by using the Latin word *vitium* with its wide range of meaning, cf. note 558.

tenuerit, ne de tertio coenaculo somno pressus rueret! *O nostrum soporem, tam oscitanter, tam frigide evangelizamus, ut fabularum nobis opus sit auxilio! Nullane alia resina in Galaad? Cur non tonitruo* בְּנֵי רַעַשׁ *excitamus, quod totum orbem evigilare fecit? Cur non tuba archangeli ad iudicium vocantis?*

|40| Once when they heard that the Romans were having fun with gladiatorial games and public spectacles, the barbarians, as we also read in Chrysostom, said, 'The Romans invented pleasures as if they had neither wives nor children'.[565] What about us? Do we also lack comfort in the Scriptures? After all, the people chase after any scam, play or lewd scene. And we, are we afraid that the earth will perish if we do not dish up indelicate delicacies[566] during the sacred acts? Let us first examine our own somnolence so that we too may awaken the brethren, for whom it is far better to sleep or be deaf than to be aroused by such virulent hisses!

|40| *Barbari olim, ut et apud Chrysostomum legimus, cum audissent Romanos theatralibus ludis et fabulis publicis oblectari, dixere: Romanos sibi excogitasse voluptates, perinde ac liberis et uxoribus careant. Et nobis solatia scripturarum desunt? Populus alioqui nullum non vanitatum, ludorum, lasciviarum genus sectatur; et nos, nisi inter sacra facetias infacetas attulerimus, periclitaturum timemus orbem? Discutiamus primum somnolentiam nostram, ut et fratres excitemus, quibus longe satius dormire vel surdos esse, quam tam virulentis sibilis excitari!*

|41| Therefore, though we may with help from elsewhere[567] take care of our own dignity and the good of the churches with greater success and honour, why

---

565 Quote from the '37th Homily on Matthew (10,7–9)', 1862b, col. 428. It is probably Oecolampadius' own translation of Chrysostom's Greek text (in the 1520s he published several translations of the Greek Church Father). Migne's translation certainly differs in various details from the one quoted here, which is also the case in an edition closer to Oecolampadius' lifetime, Chrysostomos 1543, p. 78D (there the homily, incidentally, has no. 38).

 Oecolampadius' subsequent rhetorical question is clearly an echo of Chrysostom, who devotes half of his sermon to an extensive polemic against the congregation going to the theatre; instead, they are exhorted to find pleasure in their wives, children, and friends, who are the real pleasures in life.

566 A somewhat free translation in order to reflect Oecolampadius' pun, *facetias infacetas*.

567 The reasoning seems to follow the logic of the quote from Chrysostom, who in his sermon refers to the 'wisdom of the barbarians' in order to polemically put the

then do we turn to the powers of the world [Gal 4:3.9] (not to the law, I say, but to the deranged nonsense which is more harmful than the law)? If the Gentiles, indeed, the mime writers themselves, or Cicero's freedman, the joke editor,[568] heard that this was being used in our churches, they would surely have mocked the name of God before us. According to Hesychius, the Greeks have a word for a deceitful flatterer, for a clown who does not spare the altars and robs temples. They call him a '*bōmólokhos*, one lying in wait at the altars, that is, in an ambush'.[569]

|41| *Quam ob rem, cum aliunde dignitati nostrae et ecclesiarum usui felicius atque honestius consulere possimus, quid ad elementa mundi (non ad legem dico, sed ad lege damnosiores delirantium gerras) convertimur? Quas si gentiles audirent adeoque mimographi ipsi aut Ciceronis libertus iocorum scriptor, in templis nostris tractari, nomen profecto Dei in nobis blasphemarent. [O: 17] Graeci teste Hesychio eodem nomine dolosum adulatorem, scurram nec aris parcentem et sacrilegum appellant: 'βωμολόχον παρὰ τὸ λοχεῖν εἰς τοὺς βωμούς, ὅ ἐστιν ἐνεδρεύειν.'*

|42| The disgrace is ours if our schools have to give way to the cloaks of the Greek philosophers.[570] And how much do they surpass us then, if we have

---

congregation in a bad light based on the motto: why 'cross the river for water' (Danish proverb), *in casu* for wisdom? That figure is then reversed by Oecolampadius, as 'elsewhere' will point precisely to the Bible and the church's own teachings.

568   This refers to Cicero's slave and secretary, Marcus Tullius Tiro (103–4 BCE), who after his master's death is credited, among other things, with having published Cicero's letters and authored a biography (that has not survived). However, Oecolampadius is evidently aware of the rumour that Tiro is also supposed to have published a collection of Cicero's witty statements.

569   Hesychius of Alexandria (probably 5th cent. CE) compiled a comprehensive lexicon of the Greek language, which contains an entry for *bōmólokhos*. The lexicon is a unique source for both lost words and dialects as well as antiquity's own understanding of words that were already then considered difficult. Even though, for example, Aristotle does not have much good to say about a *bōmólokhos* (cf. note 504), it would indeed have been difficult without Hesychius to guess at this very interpretation of such a character. The entry can be found in Latte's edition, 1953, vol. 1, 356.

It is remarkable and in itself a telling testimony to the 'network' of the humanists that Oecolampadius can refer to Hesychius at all, as his work is known only from a single early 15th century manuscript which only four years before, in 1514, had been printed for the first time.

570   Already in Roman times the Greek philosophers were especially associated with wearing robes, although these are not consistently referred to as a *pallium* (and

really been so careless? Seneca actually agrees with me, so much so that I am afraid that my critics will reject his statements as overly serious, as indeed they are, especially when he says: 'the serious is the true joy'.[571] Let me summon another couple of cultured gentlemen. Socrates emphasises in the third book of *The Republic* by Plato that we should not break out into overly loud laughter, because it is immediately followed by a powerful reversal;[572] here he also criticises Homer, who in his poem lets the gods laugh: 'And unquenchable laughter arose among the blessed gods, / as they saw Hephaestus puffing through the palace.[573]

|42| *Dedecus nostrum, si philosophorum palliis nostrae scholae cedant. Et quanto intervallo, si tam dissoluti fuerimus, nos praecedunt? Seneca adeo sententiae meae accedit, ut verear, ne testimonium eius observatores mei reiciant perinde ac nimium severi, praesertim cum dicat: rem severam verum gaudium. Civiles viros adferam. Socrates apud Platonem in tertio* Τῶν Πολιτειῶν *praecepit, ne in risum nimium profusi simus, effusum etenim risum vehementem mutationem sequi; ubi et Homerum carpit, qui deos ridentes finxerit canens:* '"Ἄσβεστος δ'ἄρα ἐνῶρτο γέλως μακάρεσσι θεοῖσιν / Ὡς εἶδον Ἥφαιστον διὰ δώματα ποιπνύοντα.'

|43| Nor does Xenophon let Aglaitadas give much credit to laughter when he says: 'He that makes his friends laugh seems to me to do them much less service than he who makes them weep. And fathers develop self-control

---

moreover not to be confused with the narrow woollen ribbons of the same name, which within the Roman Catholic Church are worn by popes and archbishops).

571   Seneca's statement has become an epigram in the form that Oecolampadius quotes (*res severa verum gaudium*); in the original context ('The [Moral] Epistles of Seneca [to Lucilius]', *Ad Lucilium Epistulae Morales* 23.4; 1967, vol. 1, 161), however, the words are in reverse order: *Mihi crede, verum gaudium res severa est*. Although the case clearly shows the grammar of the sentence regardless of the order of the words, it would be a not insignificant difference in nuance if we translate – and interpret! – with the subject first: 'True joy is a serious thing'.

572   More precisely in section 3.388E; 1937, vol. 1, 211.

573   *Iliad*, 1. Song, l. 599; 1924a, vol. 1, 47 (quoted by Plato in the following passage of *The Republic*, 3.389A; 1937, vol. 1, 213).

Although there are several occurrences of the word 'laughter' in the *Iliad* (and twice as many in the *Odyssey*), and although these cover a wide range of kinds of laughter, the passage with Zeus, Hera, and Hephaestus is possibly the best-known and, indeed, the cornerstone of the widespread but limited understanding of 'the Homeric laughter'. Cf. chapter 2 in Halliwell 2008, which is one extended

in their sons by making them weep, and teachers impress good lessons upon their pupils in the same way, and the laws, too, turn the citizens to justice by making them weep.'[574] Although this attitude was not accepted in the assembly of soldiers,[575] it was not rejected in the temples, perhaps just with the exception of Bacchus', although even in the midst of the rage of the Bacchantians there was room for moderation. For in Euripides, they say: 'Blessed is he, whoever being favoured, / knowing the mysteries of the gods, / keeps his life pure / and has his soul initiated / into the Bacchic revels, / dancing o'er the mountains / with holy purifications.'[576]

|43| *Nec apud Xenophontem Aglaitadas risui multum tribuit, quum ait: 'Qui amicum ad risum movet, videtur is mihi sane rem efficere minoris aestimandam, quam qui eos multis in rebus ad fletum inducit. Et parentes reddunt filios fletibus obtemperantes, et magistri pueros bene eruditos, ac leges ad iusticiam cives impellunt, quia fletibus eos instituunt.' Cuius sententia, etsi in convivio militum recepta non fuerit, e templis tamen non est explosa nisi forte Bacchi, quamvis et in mediis furoribus Baccharum modestiae locus fuerit. Aiunt enim apud Euripidem:* ῏Ω μάκαρ, ὅστις εὐδαίμων /Τελετὰς θεῶν [O: 18] εἰδὼς / Βιοτὰν ἁγιστεύει / Καὶ θιασεύεται ψυχάν / Ἐν ὄρεσσι βακχεύων / 'Οσίος καθαρμοῖσιν.'

|44| I will not quote more from the pagan writers; let this Comedian's warning suffice, even if it is known by everyone: 'Misplaced laughter is a terrible evil for mortals',[577] (so many evils does misplaced laughter bring the

---

demonstration of how differently Homer lets his various characters laugh depending on their personality and the situation.
574 *Cyropaedia* 2.2.14; 1947, vol. 1, 165. Strictly speaking, in the first sentence of the quote Oecolampadius should have written *amicos* ('friends') rather than *amicum* ('friend'), in order to have consistency between the two halves of the sentence (*eos*, 'them'), and in Xenophon (c. 425–354 BCE) the plural form φίλους is indeed used. Xenophon's 'Mirror for Princes' (lit. 'The Education of Cyrus') about the Persian king Cyrus the Great (600–530 BCE) was in antiquity, the Middle Ages, and the Renaissance a frequently quoted work – and, indeed, it is the very same Cyrus whom the prophet Isaiah even refers to as the Messiah (Isa 45:1).
575 The context in which the quote from Xenophon appears is a festive gathering between Cyrus and his officers.
576 Euripides: *Bacchae*, ll. 72–8; 1876, vol. 1, 251.
577 The 'Comedian' is Menander (342–291 BCE), and although he was considered one of the most prolific and acclaimed authors both by his contemporaries and in posterity, at the time of Oecolampadius more or less all of his plays were considered to have been lost. Nevertheless, he was, as Oecolampadius states, 'known to everyone' for

mortals). Now let our prankster rush back either to Cicero's fullery or to Demosthenes' gladiatorial school to take up arms or seek the assistance of Aristotle,[578] and he will understand how much they fight against him, how much they support us!

|44| *Non plura ex gentilibus adducam; satis monet illud Comici, vel in triviis celebre:* Γέλως ἄκαιρος τοῖς βροτοῖς δεινὸν κακόν', *quam multa mala mortalibus intempestiuus risus invehat. Recurrat nunc* γελοιαστής *noster aut in fullonariam Tullii aut gladiatoriam Demosthenis, ut arma corripiat, ab*

---

a collection of apothegms, that is 'one-line words of wisdom' (Μενάνδρου γνῶμαι μονόστιχοι, *Menandri Sententiae*). The collection had a motley history and was therefore available in several editions of divergent size and with a different wording of the individual sentences. So, too, with this one about 'untimely laughter', which is handed down in two versions. The version used by Oecolampadius corresponds to sentence no. 88 in the earlier standard edition (Meineke 1847, vol. 2, 1044). In the latest critical edition, that version is referred to a footnote, while the editor prefers (as no. 144) the alternative phrasing of this word of wisdom: 'Untimely laughter causes weeping' (Γέλως ἄκαιρος κλαυθμάτων παραίτιος), Jaekel 1964, 41.

578 Both syntactically and in terms of content, this sentence is obscure, and the meaning remains uncertain, regardless of which of the grammatical options we choose. Here the option is preferred that 'ab Aristotele suppetias petat' is a dependent clause, so that 'Aristotle' is merely a parallel to 'weapon'. It is also possible to interpret the words as a main clause, so that it corresponds instead to the whole of the preceding sentence. In both cases, however, it is something of a mystery what the meaning of the two distinctive motifs is. On the face of it Oecolampadius writes so matter-of-factly as if he were using a couple of commonly known figures of speech; but the connection between Cicero and a fullery, Demosthenes (384–22 BCE) and Gladiators, respectively, seems to lack obvious precedents. Thus, Plutarch's statement that Cicero's father, according to certain rumours, was born in a fullery must truly be too far-fetched to serve as an allusion (*Plut. Cic.* 1.1; 1967, vol. 7, 83); but possibly Plutarch's 'Parallel Lives' may still prove to hold a key to unlocking the meaning. For Plutarch does indeed compare Demosthenes with Cicero, and in the biography of the Greek orator we are far from getting the impression of him as a gladiator, rather the opposite. It is said that while Demosthenes made a strong figure in the courtroom, outside he was rather a coward who fled the battle, and when he used his great abilities as a speaker in political and military contexts, it always ended in disaster (as when he persuaded Athens to go against Alexander the Great) (*Plut. Dem.* 20.2; 1967, vol. 7, 47–9).

If this can be used as a key, Oecolampadius is being deeply ironic. A guess at the meaning could therefore be that the Prankster's attempt to summon support for his position among the ancient writers is either as misplaced as looking for weapons in a military academy led by a militarily incompetent Demosthenes, or as going to

Aristotele suppetias petat, et intelliget, quam contra se dimicent, quam nobis faveant!

|45| But our Church Fathers are a far more important testimony, and he has to trust them, whether he wants to or not. Let him come with Cicero or Macrobius,[579] and I will come with *Officia*[580] by Ambrose, a man accompanied by the Holy Ghost. Let him serve under the leadership of Aristotle or Democritus, Jerome[581] and Chrysostom shall be my standard bearers. Let the Holy Scriptures, not the Gentiles, our own, not the strangers, teach me that such misplaced, so repulsive and vulgar jokes absolutely do not belong in a Christian preacher! Therefore, I would never reject the testimonies we have received from our own.

|45| *Verum domestici nobis sunt multo gravioris testimonii antistites, quibus, velit nolit, fidem dare cogetur. Tullii verba proferat aut Macrobii, ego Ambrosii, diviniore spiritu prosequentis hominis, Officia. Sub Aristotelis aut Democriti auspiciis ille militet, mihi Hieronymus et Chrysostomus signiferi sint. Sanctae me literae, non gentiles, domesticae, non peregrinae instituant, quae christiano concionatori tam intempestivos iocos, tam putidos et obscoenos nequaquam permittent! Quare et nostrorum testimonia non repudiarim.*

|46| So let us hear, my dear Capito, what Ambrose says in his *Officia*, ch. 23: 'Men of the world give many further rules about the way to speak, which I think we may pass over; as, for instance, the way jesting should be conducted. For though at times jests may be proper and pleasant, yet they are unsuited to the clerical life. For how can we adopt those things which we do not find

---

Cicero to learn something about Aristotle (where the irony could be that Cicero was better known as an expert on Plato, whom he among other things translated into Latin). As an alternative one could choose to read the middle of the sentence as a chiasmus: the Prankster is looking for (hard) weapons in a fullery (where materials are made soft!) and searches for philosophical analysis among rough soldiers.

579 Probably a reference to the author of *Saturnalia*, whose 2nd book includes a collection of Latin and Greek *ioci* (jokes) as well as frequent references to Plato, Aristotle, and Cicero. *Saturnalia* was published as a printed book in Brescia in 1485. The identity of Macrobius is not entirely clear, but he is believed to have worked in the 4–5th century CE and, judging by his use of Greek and Latin sources, he was a learned non-Christian writer.

580 In 386 Ambrose, Archbishop of Milan (*c.* 339–97), wrote 'On the Duties of the Clergy' (*De Officiis Ministrorum*).

581 Jerome, translator of the Bible into Latin (the *Vulgate*). It is a testament to Oecolampadius' deep knowledge of this Church Father that he compiled the subject

in the holy Scriptures? We must also take care that in relating stories we do not alter the earnest purpose of the harder rule we have set before us."Woe unto you that laugh, for ye shall weep", says the Lord [Lk 6:25].[582] Do we look for something to laugh at, that laughing here we may weep hereafter? I think we ought to avoid not only broad jokes, but all kinds of jests, unless perchance it is not unfitting at the time for our conversation to be agreeable and pleasant."[583] Can it be said any clearer, can a more unambiguous rule be found?

|46| *Audiamus ergo, mi Capito, quid Ambrosius in Officiis dicat, cap. 23: 'Multa praeterea de ratione dicendi dant praecepta saeculares viri, quae nobis praetereunda arbitror, ut de iocandi disciplina. Nam licet interdum honesta sint ioca ac suavia; tamen ab ecclesiastica abhorrent regula. Quoniam, quae [O: 19] in scripturis sanctis non reperimus, ea quemadmodum usurpare possumus? Cavendum est etiam in fabulis, ne inflectant gravitatem severioris propositi. "Vae vobis, qui ridetis, quia flebitis", ait Dominus; et nos ridendi materiam requirimus, ut hic ridentes alibi fleamus? Non solum profusos, sed omnes etiam iocos declinandos arbitror.' Quid iis clarius dici, quid solidius praecipi posset?*

|47| St Chrysostom himself comes to our aid when he says: 'Then the houses were churches, but now the church has become a house. Then one might say nothing worldly in a house, now one may say nothing spiritual in a church.'[584] We will take a few short passages from his Sixth Homily on Matthew: 'Paul,' he says, 'bade us flee, foolish talking and jesting. And what is yet more grievous than these things is the subject of the laughter. For when they that act those absurd things utter any word of blasphemy or

---

and name index for Erasmus' nine-volume edition of Jerome's works, which was published by Froben in 1520.

582 If not the only, then the most important statement from Jesus and certainly by far the most frequently quoted verse from the Bible in the ecclesiastical and theological opposition to laughter, cf. p. 132.

583 'On the Duties of the Clergy' [*De officiis ministrorum*], Book 1, ch. 23, § 102 f.; 1845, col. 54; 1995, 18.

584 '32th Homily on Matthew (9:27–30)'; 1862b, col. 386; 1908, 217. Although it is undoubtedly this passage that Oecolampadius quotes, the Latin wording in Migne clearly differs: *Tunc domus ecclesiæ erant; nunc ecclesia domus facta est. Nihil tunc in domo sæculare dicebatur; nunc in ecclesia nihil spirituale dicitur.* If it is the case that Oecolampadius himself has translated from a Greek original, it is interesting that he chooses *carnale*, where Migne has *saeculare*, which is probably also the more

filthiness, then many among the more thoughtless laugh and are pleased, applauding in them what they ought to stone them for; and drawing down on their own heads by this amusement the furnace of fire.'[585] This he says against those who waste all day in the theatre for the sake of the seductive laughter. What will he say to those who even make fun of the gospel and turn the sacred buildings into a theatre?

|47| *Divus Chrysostomus et ipse nobis adest, 'domus', inquiens, 'priscis temporibus ecclesiae erant, nunc ecclesia in domum redacta; nihil in privata domo carnale loquebantur, nihil nunc in ecclesia spirituale meditantur'. Ex sexta in Matthaeum homilia paula quaedam decerpemus. 'Praecepit Paulus', ait, 'ut et stulticiam et scurrilitatem a nobis longius repellamus, ex quibus risus multo perniciosior multoque deterior. Quando enim mimi illi atque ridiculi blasphemum ac turpe quid dixerint, tunc potissimum stolidiores solvuntur in risum inde applaudentes magis, unde illos etiam lapidibus exagitare debuerant, qui fornacem sibi ignis horribilis ex huiusmodi voluptate succenderunt'. Loquitur haec contra desidentes toto die in theatris captandi risus gratia. Quid in eos dicturus, qui evangelium etiam ridiculum faciunt et ex sacratis aedibus theatrum?*

|48| The words of the Apostle certainly apply no less to churchgoers than to theatregoers, indeed, all the more so because there, in the presence of the angels, before the relics of so many saints, yea, before the holy itself, they shamelessly worship the profane. I wish our friend would read the same Chrysostom's Fifteenth Sermon on the Epistle to the Hebrews, and then let him decide whether he will not at sea or on land, as it is called, follow our point of view.[586] It is strange what an angry look the women get if they softly

---

likely translation of Chrysostom's βιωτικόν. Prevost has thus also opted for 'worldly' instead of 'carnal' in his translation.

585 '6th Homily on Matthew (2:1–2)'; 1862b, col. 71; 1908, 42. Here, too, there are notable differences between the two Latin translations.

586 '15th Homily on Hebrews (9:1–5)', 1863, col. 117–24. The last third of this sermon is about laughter and in addition to containing Chrysostom's – in this context – most famous rhetorical question ('Where do you hear Jesus laugh? Nowhere! But often that he mourned'), it is remarkable that the Church Father does *not* condemn laughter as such, but 'only' the one that is misplaced, that is, the one which is heard in the church ('When the priest of God says the common prayer, do you laugh and are without fear?').

The immediate context informs us: 'For the Church has been filled with laughter. Whatever clever thing one may say, immediately there is laughter among those present: and the marvellous thing is that many do not leave off laughing even during the very time of the prayer.'

mutter two or three words to each other, yet, when such nonsense is said from the pulpit, our friend claims that it is proper conduct.

|48| *Plane apostoli testimonium non minus in eos conpetit, qui in ecclesiis, quam qui in theatris, atque hoc magis, [O: 20] quo in conspectu angelorum praesentibus tot sanctorum reliquiis adeoque sanctis ipsis prophana impudenter meditantur. Legat homiliam, velim, eiusdem Chrysostomi, quam quintamdecimam in epistolam ad Hebraeos scripsit, et tum iudicet, an ne velis equisque, quod dicitur, nostram prosequatur sententiam. Mirum, quo supercilio mulierculae corripiantur, si duo vel tria verba submissius inter se mussitent; at e suggestu sic ineptire, probe actum contendit.*

|49| Also Chrysostom, when he had once said something that pleased the people and had been celebrated with their applause, had so attacked this that he had never in such sharp and biting terms chastised the dullness of people as he did this applause.[587] Likewise the exiled Gregory of Nazianzus who writes about himself: 'Never, even though I am the presiding officer

---

The crucial passage in relation to a broader understanding of laughter follows immediately: 'But [one says] what harm is there in laughter? There is no harm in laughter; the harm is when it is beyond measure, and out of season. Laughter has been implanted in us, that when we see our friends after a long time, we may laugh; that when we see any persons downcast and fearful, we may relieve them by our smile; not that we should burst out violently and be always laughing. Laughter has been implanted in our soul, that the soul may sometimes be refreshed, not that it may be quite relaxed. For carnal desire also is implanted in us, and yet it is not by any means necessary that because it is implanted in us, therefore we should use it, or use it immoderately: but we should hold it in subjection, and not say, Because it is implanted in us, let us use it.' 1863, col. 122; 1899, 442.

587 Without being able to determine this with certainty, Oecolampadius may have had '17th Homily on Matthew (5:27–28)' in mind (1862b, col. 255–66), which by focusing on the role of applause at least contains a fundamental consideration of the difference between an audience and a congregation: 'Did ye give praise to what has been said? Nay, I want not applause, nor tumults, nor noise. One thing only do I wish, that quietly and intelligently listening, you should do what is said. This is the applause, this the panegyric for me. But if you praise what I say, but doest not what you applaud, greater is the punishment, more aggravated the accusation: and to us it is shame and ridicule. For the things here present are no dramatic spectacle; neither do ye now sit gazing on actors, that you may merely applaud. This place is a spiritual school. Wherefore also there is but one thing aimed at, duly to perform the things that have been spoken, and to show forth our obedience by our works. For then only shall we have obtained all. Since as things are, to say the truth, we have fairly given

of shrines / neither alone nor in a larger assembly / will I speak of things that please the ear when I have cast out the Holy Ghost / as if I would be willing to use the means at my disposal to lure the large assembly.'[588] (Never, though I am a bishop of temples, either alone or in a crowded gathering, will I neglect the spiritual and say anything that amuses the ear, even though I have the means at hand to lure the crowd.)

|49| *Idem Chrysostomus, cum felicius aliquando dixisset ortusque fuisset populi congratulantis applausus, eum tulit, ut nullam unquam tam acerbe populi somnolentiam aeque atque hunc plausum acriter castigaverit, quale et exul Gregorius Nazanzenus de se scribit,* 'Οὐδὲ μὲν οὐδὲ πρόεδρος ἐὼν ἱεροῖς ἐνὶ χώροις / ἢ μοῦνος ἢ πλεόνων εἰς ἓν ἀγειρομένων, / φθέξομαι οὔασι τερπνά, τὰ πνεύματος ἔκτοθι ῥίψας / Ὥς κεν ἔοιμι πρόφρων φίλτρον ἔχων πλεόνων.' (*Numquam ego, quamvis sacrorum antistes, vel solus, vel stipante turba neglectis spiritualibus, loquar, quae aures oblectent, tanquam in promptu habeam illecebras multitudinis*).

|50| Thus Jerome also agrees with us in his commentary on the eleventh[589] chapter of the Book of Ecclesiastes. Here it is wisely said: 'The words of wise men are heard in quiet more than the cry of him that ruleth among fools.' [Eccles 9:17 KJV][590] And St Jerome comments: 'Whosoever you see in the Church declaiming and arousing applause by whatever refinery or charm, he who shakes off his laughter and incites the crowd to feigned happiness, know that this is a sign of foolishness, equally of him who speaks, and of those who listen to him. For the words of the wise are heard in peace and respectful silence. He who is foolish and is powerful speaks to fools and cannot hear himself because of either the noise of his own voice or that of the applauding crowd.'[591] Thus writes Jerome.

---

up in despair. For I have not ceased giving these admonitions either to those whom I meet in private, or in discourse with you all in common. Yet I see no advantage at all gained, but you are still clinging to the former rude beginnings, which thing is enough to fill the teacher with weariness.' 1908, 122–3.

588   '"Carminum", Liber 2: Poemata historica, sectio 1: Poemata de se ipso, Nr. 17: De diversis vitæ generibus, et adversus falsos episcopos', 1862, col. 1267.
589   Oecolampadius makes a typo, for the verse appears in chapter 9.
590   Oecolampadius uses Jerome's Latin translation in the commentary, which differs slightly from the one established in the *Vulgate*: *verba sapientium audiuntur in silentio plus quam clamor principis inter stultos*.
591   'Commentarius in Ecclesiasten', 1845a, col. 1089; 2014, no page.

|50| *Proinde et Hieronymus nobis adstipuatur, scribens super Ecclesiastis caput undecimum: ubi sapiens ait: 'Verba sapientum in quiete audiuntur, plusquam clamor potestatem habentis in stultis', adnotat divus Hier[onymus]: 'Quemcumque videtis in ecclesia,' inquit, 'declamatorem, et cum quodam lenocinio ac venustate verborum, excitare plausus ac risus excutere, au-[O: 21]dientes in affectus laeticiae concitare, scito signum esse insipientiae tam eius, qui loquitur, quam eorum, qui audiunt. Verba quippe sapientum in quiete et moderato audiuntur silentio. Qui vero insipiens est, quamvis sit potens, et clamorem sive suae vocis sive populi habeat acclamantis, inter insipientes conputabitur'. Haec apud Hier[onymum].*

|51| St Augustine, too, laments this type of sin in his third book of *Confessions* something like this: 'I dared, even while Thy solemn rites were being celebrated within the walls of Thy church, to desire, and to plan a business sufficient to procure me the fruits of death; for which Thou chastisedst me with grievous punishments, but nothing in comparison with my fault.'[592] You know as well as I do, my dear Capito, how he likewise bemoans the rhetorical huffing and puffing. For in the fourth book of *On the Christian Doctrine*, he is fully in line with our thesis when he teaches us: 'But may God avert from His Church what the prophet Jeremiah says of the synagogue of the Jews: "A wonderful and horrible thing is committed in the land: the prophets prophesy falsely, and the priests applaud them with their hands; and my people love to have it so: and what will you do in the end thereof?" [Jer 5:30 f.[593]].'[594] There is no need to go through the entire chapter; whoever wants to can examine it himself. But I will not torment you with more quotations but confine myself to these excellent testimonies. Let me just

---

592 *Confessionum Libri Tredecim*, Book 3, ch. 3; 1841, col. 685; 1886, 61. At this point in the *Confessions* Augustine talks about his pagan life, where he went to church even before his conversion. What his sinful desires and plans consisted of is not further explained, but the bold imagery probably relates to Rom 7:5: 'For when we were in the flesh, the motions of sins, which were by the law, did work in our members to bring forth fruit unto death' (*KJV*).

593 Oecolampadius quotes verbatim from Augustine's Latin verses from Jeremiah, which differs somewhat from the *Vulgate* (and most modern translations): *stupor et mirabilia facta sunt in terra / prophetae prophetabant mendacium / et sacerdotes adplaudebant manibus suis / et populus meus dilexit talia / quid igitur fiet in novissimo eius* ('A horrible and shocking thing has happened in the land: The prophets prophesy lies, the priests rule by their own authority, and my people love it this way. But what will you do in the end?' *NIV*).

594 *De doctrina Christiana libri quatuor*, Book 4, ch. 14; 1865a, col. 102; 1899, 584.

add this short quote by Philo, if it is indeed his book: 'A wise man,' he says, 'will not even laugh silently.'[595]

|51| *Deplorat et s[anctus] Augustinus in Confessionum libro tertio id genus delicti in hunc prope modum: 'Ausus sum iam in celebritate solennitatum tuarum intra parietes ecclesiae tuae concupiscere et agere negotium procurandi fructus mortis. Unde me verberasti gravibus poenis, sed nihil ad culpam meam.' Non te clam est, mi Capito, quid de rhetorico typho et tumore ibidem ingemiscat. Dixerat etiam in libro de Doctrina christiana quarto non abludentia a nostro proposito, sic docens: 'Avertat autem Deus ab ecclesia sua, quod de synagoga Judaeorum Hieremias commemorat, dicens: ["]pavor et horrenda facta sunt super terram, prophetae prophetabant iniqua, et sacerdotes plausum dederunt manibus suis, et plebs mea dilexit sic, et quid facietis in futurum["].' Non est opus, totum caput inserere; quisquis volet, requirat. Sed nec in citandis testimoniis molestus nunc ero, testibus tam insignibus contentus. Breve tamen Philonis, si modo illius est liber, dictum adpendam: 'Vir sapiens,' ait 'vix tacite ridebit.'*

|52| Let it be so: that even a wise and holy man has laughed, anyone can prove, but no one who is faithful to these worthy testimonies will seriously claim that this wise and holy man in such a serious matter has behaved like an actor to make an assembly laugh. Let our prankster mention just one of the many patriarchs, one of the many prophets, one of the many apostles, one of the many martyrs and blood witnesses who would have had time for such foolery! No one reads that Christ has laughed, but who does not know that he has wept?[596] Even though he compares his teaching to a pipe, as he says, 'we played the pipe for you, and you did not dance' [Lk 7:32]. The apostles 'walked and wept as they spread their seed' [Ps 126:6].[597]

---

595 This is the first half of verse 20 in the Book of Sirach's chapter 21, which the *Good News Translation* renders thus: 'An intelligent person will smile quietly'. The other half of the verse gives us the opposite: 'a fool roars with laughter'. Together with Lk 6:25 and Eccles 7:6 this makes up a triad of absolute key verses when critics have been searching for biblical evidence for the opposition to laughter. To name just one example, Sirach is also quoted in *The Rule of Saint Benedict* (cf. note 552). Oecolampadius is clearly aware of some of the speculations in the Early Church that the Jewish philosopher and 'scribe', Philo of Alexandria, may have been the author of parts of the apocryphal wisdom literature.

596 It can hardly be proved that Chrysostom 'invented' this observation (see notes 586 and 8); but for more than a thousand years his name is strongly associated with this trope in the ecclesiastical and theological debate on the legitimacy of laughter.

597 Countless times commentators, as here Oecolampadius, symptomatically content themselves with 'half-baked' quotes, i.e. they quote one half of a verse but omit the

|52| *Esto igitur: risisse virum sapientem et sanctum quispiam probet, nullis tamen cetibus risum movisse histrionico more in re tam seria, dignis fide testimoniis asseverabit. Pro-[O: 22]ferat γελοιαστὴς ὁ ἡμέτερος vel unum ex tot patriarchis, ex tot prophetis, ex tot apostolis, ex tot martyribus et confessoribus, qui talibus nugis vacarit! Nemo risisse Christum legit, flevisse autem nemo est, qui ignoret, etsi doctrinam suam tibiae conferat, dicens: 'tibia vobis cecinimus et non saltastis'. Apostoli 'euntes ibant et flebant mittentes semina sua'.*

|53| So multifaceted are the figures of the prophets: Isaiah walked around naked [Isa 20:2], Jeremiah smashed the jars of clay [Jer 19:1 ff.], Ezekiel dug through the wall [Ezek 8:8; 12:5 ff.], Zechariah assumed the appearance of a foolish shepherd [Zech 11:15]. But no one acts as a stage-player. These are completely serious. In their books we read 'lamentations, mourning, and woe' [Ezek 2:10 (*Vulgate* 2:9)], it is not easy to laugh. And can that come as a surprise? The righteous walked before the Lord, at once jubilant and terrified, in the glow of the midday sun they clearly saw that everything is emptiness, whatever under the sun is emptiness [*Eccles 1]; they saw traps lying ready everywhere; they saw that the judge would come upon the earth.

|53| *Tam multifariae prophetarum sunt figurae: Esaias incedit nudus, Hieremias confringit vasa figuli, Ezechiel perfodit parietem, Zacharias stulti pastoris habitum adsumit. Nullus histrionem agit. Mera seria sunt. In eorum libris legimus: 'vae planctum et carmen', risum non facile. Et quid mirum? Ambulabant iusti coram Domino exultantes pariter et tremuli, videbant sole meridiano clarius, vana esse omnia, vana quaevis sub sole; videbant laqueos undiquaque extensos, videbant orbi superventurum iudicem.*

|54| The trumpet of the Archangel sounded in their ear [*cf. 1 Thess 4:16], Satan's false accusations tormented them; and though they were not aware of any wrongdoing, they did not think themselves justified for that reason. And they did not demand, as the older son, to know why they had not received so much as a young goat [Lk 15:25 ff.], considering how frugal they had been for so many years. They never ploughed during the Sabbath

---

other; in this case: 'shall come home with shouts of joy, bringing his sheaves with him' (*ESV*). Other theologians, less blinded by an agenda, did not close their eyes to these more positive counterparts to the negative biblical statements about smiles and laughter, but typically their strategy then was – so to speak – to 'delay' the joy, to interpret it eschatologically, cf. p. 133 f.

fast [*cf. Ex 34:21], they did not boast of their tithe of cumin [*cf. Mt 23:23], and did not flash their phylacteries.[598] It was not out of superstition, as Plutarch scornfully writes,[599] that they were terrified of God, as inexorable as He is, but fearing the abyss of God's judgments, they considered laughter a fault.[600] How then could they stir the organ of laughter[601] of the wretched creatures, who they saw be torn to hell in an instant thanks to their insane laughter and foolish joy; [these wretched creatures] for whose salvation they sacrificed themselves, whom they begged to be expunged from the book of the living [*cf. Ps 69:28], whom they wished to be cursed? They lamented them that were intoxicated with the Babylonian cup [*Rev 14:8–10]; how could it be possible that they had toasted with the cup of madness?

|54| *Insonabat in auribus eorum archangeli tuba, obstrepebant sathanum calumniae; et quamvis nullius sibi criminis erant conscii, tamen non ob id iustificatos se credebant, nec cum seniore filio expostulabant, cur nec hedus quideni sibi datus, qui tot annis frugi fuerint, nec bigam ieiuniorum sabbati invehebant, non cymini decimas iactabant, non phylacteria dilatabant, nec κατὰ δεισιδαιμονῖαν ut Plutarchus irridet, Deum tanquam inexorabilem formidabant, sed abyssum iudiciorum Dei timentes, risum errorem iudicabant. Miseris autem homuncionibus, quos in momento temporis ob insanum risum fatuasque laeticias ad inferos rapi videbant, pro quorum salute se devovebant, e libro [O: 23] viventium expungi orabant, anathema esse volebant, quonam modo splenem movere poterant? Inebriatos Babylonio calice deplorabant; qui fieri posset, ut et furoris pocula propinarent?*

---

598 Jewish *tefillin*, i.e. the small boxes tied to the arm and brow during prayer, cf. Ex 13:9.
599 It is well known that Plutarch neither mentions Jesus nor the Christians, so Oecolampadius refers to his statements about worship in general and especially his book 'On Superstition' (Περὶ δεισιδαιμονίας). Oecolampadius may specifically have a passage like this in mind: 'For the superstitious fear the gods, and flee to the gods for help; they flatter them and assail them with abuse, pray to them and blame them. It is the common lot of mankind not to enjoy continual good fortune in all things.' Ch. 6; 1928, vol. 2, 471.
600 Plutarch does have a few passages about laughter but nothing that comes close to the ideas that Oecolampadius writes about here. Plutarch must therefore have been an insertion, and when Oecolampadius writes about fear, 'they' must refer back to Oecolampadius' previously mentioned biblical and Christian witnesses. The argument is therefore that when this or that theologian or clergyman has such a clear understanding of the threat to salvation posed by laughter, such a man of the church would never accept the use of laughter in the church.
601 Cf. note to |28| about the connection between spleen and laughter.

|55| Indeed, my Jeremiah, why are your lamentations so desperate and full of mourning, why are your lamentations so sad, why do you stop the music [*Lam 5:14], if pranks, roars of laughter, and dancing would have benefited your people more? Why do you, Jesus, our salvation, mourn these very people interjecting: 'If you, even you, had only known' [Lk 19:42],[602] why did you turn your cheek to the one who struck [*cf. Mt 5:39], why were you prepared to be whipped [*Mt 20:19], why did you carry the cross [*Jn 19:17], if there was another, less painful shortcut to our salvation, if it was not necessary to go through so much tribulation to enter the kingdom of God?

|55| *Eia mi Hieremia, quid eiulas tam miserabiles elegias, quid tam lactuosos threnos meditaris, quid suspendis organa, si populo tuo ineptiae, cachinni, tripudia magis profutura erant? Quid tu, Jesu, salus nostra, eandem ploras civitatem, subiiciens: 'Utinam cognovisses et tu', quid praebebas percutienti maxillam, quid in flagella paratus eras, quid crucem subibas, si aliud nostrae salutis compendium salubrius, si non oportebat per multas tribulationes ingredi in regnum Dei?*

|56| How about you, Elijah, why do you speak so hotly calling down fire from heaven [*2 Kings 1:10], burning like a torch [*Sir 48:1]? And you, John, the second Elijah [*Mt 11:11–15], why did you prepare yourself for so many years in solitude, clothe yourself in rags, live on wretched food [*cf. Mt 3:1–4]? Why did you detest life at court [*Lk 3:19]? Obviously in order to be able to bear witness worthy of Christ for whom you paved the way! You were the forerunner of the Lord, coming in humble flesh. What would you have done if you had not been the talking reed and messenger in the wilderness [*Mt 11:7], who was to proclaim the majesty of the judge, but the Archangel himself blowing his trumpet [*Mt 24:31, cf. 1 Thess 4:16]? You were way too serious! You constantly threatened with the axe, winnowing fork, and fire [*Mt 3:10.12]! You did not make the road smooth enough to hold on to your listeners [*Mk 1:3 = quote from Isa 40:3]. You should have mixed in some Milesian stories![603]

---

602 In contrast to Chrysostom, who in order to establish his effective counterpoint between laughter and weeping (cf. note 8 and the references therein) must make use of the logically and philosophically dubious *e silentio*-argument regarding laughter, the evangelists explicitly say on two occasions that he wept: here at the sight of Jerusalem (v. 41) and in the famously shortest verse in the Bible, 'Jesus wept', when meeting with Lazarus' grieving relatives (Jn 11:35).

603 Cf. note 540.

|56| *Quid tu, Elia, tam ardenter loqueris, ignem caelo devocas, ardes ut facula? Et tu alter Elia, Joannes, cur tot te annis in eremo praeparabas, impexa veste tectus, vili cibo pastus? Quid adeo abhorrebas ab aulicis moribus? Ut dignum scilicet Christo, cui viam parabas, testimonium dare posses! Eras praecursor Domini in humilitate carnis venturi. Quid facturus eras, si maiestatem iudicis annunciaturus esses non arundo vocalis deserti et angelus, sed archangelus tuba buccinans? Nimium serius eras! Securim, ventilabrum ac ignem constanter minabaris! Male conplanabas viam, ne dilaberentur auditores; Miletiae fabellae texendae erant!*

|57| Now let them come and criticise the excessive seriousness of the preachers, then the prophets, then John, then the Apostles, and then Christ himself! Let them also encourage people to lay down the cross, or if possible, do something even worse, so that we can easily shun them as heretics. For if they continue in this way to constantly declare that serious preachers only deserve criticism, then they must be careful that they have not already branded themselves with the mark of heresy!

|57| *Eant nunc et severitatem nimiam in concionatoribus post prophetas, post Joannem, post apostolos, post Christum ipsum carpant! Suadeant etiam deponendam crucem, et si quid turpius, ut plane tanquam haereticos vitare possimus. Nam si ita constanter [O: 24] adserere perseveraverint serios concionatores reprehensione dignos, viderint, ne iam haeretico cauterio signati sint.*

|58| The Pelagian[604] Doctrine dictated that a servant of God should never put a bitter word in his mouth, but always speak mildly and pleasantly. St Jerome refutes this in this way: 'It is idle to reserve smooth and pleasant speeches for the servants of God, for these are characteristic of heretics and of them who wish to deceive; as the Apostle says: "They that are such serve not our Lord Christ but their own belly, and by their smooth and fair speech they beguile the hearts of the innocent" [Rom 16:18]. Flattery is always insidious, crafty, and smooth. And the flatterer is well described by the philosophers as a pleasant enemy. Truth is bitter, of gloomy visage and wrinkled brow, and

---

604 Pelagius, British monk and theologian (fl. *c.* 390–418), who at the Synod of Carthage in 418 was convicted of heresy because of his strong defence of free will and opposition to the doctrine of predestination.

distasteful to those who are rebuked. Hence the Apostle says: "Am I become your enemy, because I tell you the truth?" [Gal 4:16].'[605]

|58| *Dogma Pelagianum praecipiebat servum Dei niliil amarum de ore suo, sed semper, quod dulce est et suave, debere proferre. Quod in hunc modum refellit divus Hiero[nymus]: 'Frustra servis Dei blanditias et dulcedines reservasti, cum hoc proprie haereticorum sit et eorum, qui decipere cupiunt audientes dicente apostolo: "huiusmodi enim Domino nostro non serviunt, sed suo ventri, et per dulces sermones et benedictiones seducunt corda innocentium"; semper insidiosa, callida, blanda adulatio; veritas amara est, rugosae frontis ac tristis offenditque correctos, unde et apostolus: "inimicus vobis factus sum veritatem vobis dicens".'*

|59| Behold, now I, too, am an overly serious preacher, at least as serious as one can be in a letter. But since I do not think that one should remove seriousness from the preacher, but that seriousness is one of the virtues that above all emphasise that any shallowness is improper, it should thus, in my opinion, be sufficiently clear that it is not at all fitting to waste time on jokes on Easter Sunday. On this day, sin is, so to speak, counted double, no, not only double, but far more seriously as this day is more holy, more exalted than all others. Indeed, it is precisely on this day that this foolish joy is utter madness for a Christian.

|59| *En iam et ego nimium serius sum concionator, et credo satis serius, quantum per epistolam licuit. Porro cum severitatem concionatori adimendam non putem, verum esse ex virtutibus, quae cum primis commendent levitatem quoque omnem dedecere, liquidum satis arbitror, minime decorum esse et in die Paschae nugis vacare. Quo die peccatum quoduis geminum est, nec modo geminum, sed tanto gravius, quo dies ille cunctis est sacratior et sublimior. Et profecto in eo die inepta laeticia christiano male sanus est furor.*

|60| But I am not that surprised if the bishops cannot uproot the immoderateness of many, when those people who claim to be role models in terms of moderation do not particularly respect the bishops and insist that they are allowed to do so. Oh, you leaders! Oh, you discoverers of the Holy Land, are these your pomegranates, your grapes, which a firmer faith provided for you for so long, when you brought us Egyptian leaders and meat pots after

---

605 'Against the Pelagians' [*Dialogus contra Pelagianos*], Book 1, ch. 26; 1845b, col. 543; 1893a, 462. The preceding sentence about Pelagius' alleged understanding of the best way for a preacher to preach is a direct quote from the introduction to chapter 26 in Jerome, col. 542.

arriving in the Holy Land [*Num 13:23 ff.]? Why do you subvert all the hardships of Lent with a brief remark?[606] You are city dwellers, indeed, but not citizens of Jerusalem. Luke and Cleopas [*Lk 24:18][607] did not discuss such matters with each other, neither did the two Marys and Salome [*Mk 16:1], nor the other apostles [*Mk 16:14].

|60| *Verum non usque adeo miror, si multorum immodestiam episcopi non extirpent, quando ii, qui primatum modestiae sibi vindicant, haud magni episcopos curant, idque sibi licere contendunt. O duces, o exploratores terrae sanctae, sunt haec malogranata vestra, hi botri, quos vobis tantorum temporum arctior [O: 25] religio ministravit, quum nobis praepones Aegyptios et ollas carnium post ingressum terrae sanctae affertis? Cur tantos Quadragesimae labores brevi dicto subvertitis? Urbani estis, sed non Hierosolymitae. Non haec inter se disputant Lucas et Cleophas, non Mariae et Salome, non caeteri apostoli.*

|61| Do you not know that one should not plant a grove next to the church [*Dt 16:21]?[608] Do you not know that honey is not to be offered in sacrifices [*Lev 2:11]? Why was it not wax but oil burning at that time in the Tabernacle, indeed pure oil [*Ex 27:20]? Not, mind you, that which is shed upon the heads of the wicked, which was exported to Egypt and which false prophets bring back [*Hos 12:1?]? Have you not read that the unleavened bread of sincerity and truth is eaten with bitterness [1 Cor 5:8]? What kind of

---

606 Cf. the section about anthropological arguments in III,4 and the quote from Kessler in note 68.

607 At this point, the historical and for Oecolampadius clearly unintentional irony becomes almost too heavy! This is not a reference to the pious exegetical detail that Oecolampadius thinks himself capable of identifying Luke as the otherwise unnamed person who, along with Cleopas, walks to Emmaus on Easter morning. Rather, it is the fact that exactly this conversation between the two wanderers (Lk 24:15) – and in particular *Vulgate*'s Latin word for it: *fabularentur* – oddly enough became one of the main arguments in the defence of telling ('fabulating') ridiculous stories on Easter Sunday. Thus, it also appears as one of the epigrams in the front of this book. Cf. p. 115 f.

608 The allusion to Deuteronomy, as well as the point of Oecolampadius using it in his polemic, is lost in many translations of the Bible (including *KJV*) but is clear in the *Vulgate*: *Non plantabis lucum, et omnem arborem juxta altare Domini Dei tui*; because the Hebrew word, which can be translated as 'grove', 'tree' or 'pole' is also part of the name of the Canaanite fertility goddess 'Ashera', cf. the *NIV*: 'Do not set up any wooden Asherah pole beside the altar you build to the LORD your God.'

honey sauce do you bring?[609] On which fire have you cooked the lamb [*cf. Isa 44:12–20]? Only after the silence of Lent to the glory of God did the Holy Fathers, in whose footsteps we should follow, speak again on this day, delivering the most glorious sermons as a witness of their learning. They praised the baptism, praised the shining light, praised the victorious Lord, and the flock, which was strengthened by fasting and fattened by the glories at the Lord's table, they did not give baby milk [*1 Cor 3:2], nor the bread of the prodigal son [*Lk 15:16[610]], nor boiled, but solid food to eat [*Heb 5:12–4].

|61| *Nescitis lucum apud templum non plantandum? Nescitis mel in sacrificiis non offerendum? Quamobrem non caera olim in tabernaculo, sed oleum adolebatur, oleumque purum, non quod impinguat caput impii, et in Aegyptum defertur et pseudoprophetae referunt. Non legistis cum amaritudine azyma synceritatis et veritatis edenda? Quae vestra illa mellita embammata? Quo igne coctus agnus? Sancti patres, quorum vestigia imitari oportebat, post silentium Quadragesimae in laudem Dei, ora sua hoc die recludebant eruditionisque suae testes exquisitissimos sermones proferebant in laudem baptismi, in laudem rutili luminis, in laudem dominici triumphi, gregi ieiuniis firmato dominicaeque mensae, delitiis saginato, non lac puerile, non furfuraceum panem filii prodigi, non elixa, sed solida proponebant.*

|62| For as Gregory of Nazianzus says: 'and not sodden, but roast, that our word may have in it nothing that is unconsidered or watery, or easily made away with; but may be entirely consistent and solid, and free from all that is impure and from all vanity'. (We translate it this way: Do not let the lamb be boiled, but roasted, just as our speech does not convey anything that does not tolerate detailed considerations, that is not flowing with the softness of water; there is nothing loose about it, not even in an appropriate way; on the contrary, it is solid through and through, tested against the fire

---

609   There is plenty of 'honey' in the Old Testament, indeed, an entire land flowing with it, but nowhere is it mentioned as an ingredient in a sauce, if that is indeed what Oecolampadius has in mind when using this quite rare Latin/Greek word, *embammata*/ ἐμβάμματα. So, this sentence remains obscure.

610   Although Luke does not let the youngest son eat bread, but beans (*siliquae*), it is obviously this parable that Oecolampadius alludes to. His polemical list consists of biblical examples of food/'equipment' of secondary (bodily) and primary (spiritual) quality. It is not at all clear, however, why Oecolampadius wants to specify that the bread was made of 'bran' (*furfuraceus*), as no such kind is mentioned in the Bible.

of purgatory, also free from any weight from this world, and without any superfluousness).[611]

|62| *Ita enim Greg[orius] Nazanze[nus] ait: 'οὐχ ἑψόμενος δὲ, ἀλλ' ὀπτώμενος, ὡς ἄν μηδὲν ἀθεώρητον μηδ' ὑδαρὲς ὁ λόγος ἡμῖν ἔχῃ, μηδ' εὐδιάλυτον, ἀλλ' ὅλος συνεστὼς ᾖ, καὶ στερρὸς καὶ τῷ καθαρτικῷ πυρὶ δεδοκιμασμένος, καὶ παντὸς ὑλώδους ἐλεύθερος καὶ ἀπέριττος.' (Quae nos sic vertimus: Non sit autem agnus elixus, sed assus, ita quod sermo noster nihil praeseferat [!] a contemplatione alienum, nihil aquea [O: 26] mollicie fluidum, nihil etiam vel decenter dissolutum: verum totus sibi constet solidus, igne purgatorio probatus, ab omni quoque materiae mole liber, atque minime supervacaneus).*

|63| Let us also add to our case this statement by Johan from Kaysersberg,[612] a person who is fondly remembered, a former pastor in Strasbourg and your close friend. In the passage about the Pilgrim's Puppy,[613] he

---

611 'Oration XLV. The Second Oration on Easter' [*Oratio XLV in sanctum Pascha*], ch. 16; 1858, col. 644 f.; 1894, 428. While the Greek quotation is almost identical to the version in Migne, there are many differences in the Latin translations. On the face of it, Oecolampadius' translation sounds rather odd when he writes that a speech can be loose in an appropriate way (which, granted, must also be avoided). One explanation could be that by 'appropriately' he means that the speech, for example, is 'just' stylistically poor or loose in thought, while 'inappropriately' could then be that the speech becomes sloppy due to scurrilous obscenities (which may arouse laughter).

612 Geiler von Kaysersberg was one of the most esteemed preachers of the late Middle Ages. His preaching contained a critique of the contemporary church, which brings him close to other so-called Reform Catholics who were active on the threshold of the Reformation movements. Despite the criticism of laughter-in-church quoted here, Geiler is otherwise known for preaching in the vernacular and for his frequent use of humour. Among other things he delivered a long series of sermons on Brant's highly popular *Das Narrenschiff* (first printed in 1494 titled *Dass Narrenschyff ad Narragoniam*), which was posthumously compiled and published as 'The Ship or Mirror of Fools' (*Navicula sive speculum fatuorum*), 1511.

613 In the book 'The Pilgrim' (*Peregrinus*) Geiler turns a puppy (referring to the dog that accompanies Tobias on his wandering, Book of Tobit 6:2 and 11:4) into a key figure in a couple of the sermons by making it an allegory of pious zeal.

How close this allegory has been to Geiler is attested by the pulpit which was erected especially for him in Strasbourg Cathedral in 1486, for it is decorated with a carved puppy still to be seen to this day. According to tradition this was not a reference to Tobit's companion but in memory of the dog that always followed Geiler and patiently lay by the pulpit throughout his sermons! Cf. Jacobelli 1992, 24.

wrote these words, which are to be repeated here: 'What is this,'[614] he says, 'has corruption grown so much during Easter, since people are provoked to laughter and levity by certain ridiculous preachers with too many excesses? Their former devotion has been completely destroyed; truly death is on the lips of such people.'[615] So much from our friend, and I could quote a lot more if this had been a book and not a letter.[616]

|63| *Adiiciamus et huic testimonio Jo[annis] Keysersbergii venerandae recordationis, olim Argentini concionatoris tibique amicissimi, calculum. Eius haec sunt verba in Catulo peregrini, quae liceat enumerare: 'Quid est hoc,' inquit, 'quod tempore paschali invaluit corruptela, ut ad risum et levitatem populus per quosdam praedicatores ridendos cum excessu nimio etiam provocatur? Plane devotionem,*

---

614   Hospinian paraphrases Oecolampadius' brief introduction and then goes on to bring the entire quote from Geiler as his final selection from *De risu paschali*.

615   Quoted verbatim from the posthumous Latin edition of *Peregrinus* from 1513. The book has no page numbers but a page header showing the chapter and roman numerals (for sections of the book), and in the margin sections of the page are identified with letters. The quote is from the sermon 'Monday after the Fifth Sunday of Lent, 6 April' ('Feria secunda post Judica. vi. Aprilis'), ch. 13,XI, section U (= scan image 195 in the online edition from the Bayerische Staats Bibliothek). The content of the book goes back to some daily sermons which Geiler gave in Augsburg in the autumn and winter of 1488–9, and which – presumably without his involvement – first appeared in print in 1494 (titled 'The Pilgrim with His Characteristics, Illustrated' [*Der bilger mit seinen eygenschaften, auch figuren*]), followed by an improved edition in 1499 ('A Helpful Little Book Called The Pilgrim which was Preached by the Honourable Dr Kaysersberg from Augsburg' [*Ein nutzlich buchlein dass man nennet / den Pilgrim das hat der würdig doctor / Keyserspert zu Augspurg gepredigt*]). Some of the material was also included in a couple of publications of his sermons in 1508 and 1510. His student, Jacob Otther (1485–1547), first published a German ('The Christian Pilgrimage to the Eternal Homeland' [*Christenlich Pilgerschaft zum ewigen Vaterland*], 1512), and the following year the Latin edition, both much expanded and edited compared to the previous ones. According to the publisher's 'preface' this was in accordance with Geiler's wishes and also with his own participation (not least regarding the new material). Cf. Dacheux 1882, xi–xvi and Bauer 1989, 494–503.

As far as the dating of the practice is concerned that Oecolampadius calls Easter Laughter, it is worth noting that Geiler's criticism does not appear in the editions published during his lifetime.

616   No letters between Capito and Oecolampadius have survived from the four weeks between the dating of the letter and the booklet respectively, so we can never be certain which of them decided that it was worthy of being published – and thus who chose its title.

quam prius conceperant, prorsus extinguentes profecto in talium labiis mors est.' Haec noster. Exaggerari possent testimonia, si volumen quam epistolam mallemus.

|64| To signal my retreat! I would prefer to be criticised along with Keysersberg rather than being praised along with them and by their deceitful lips. If it be a curse not to laugh this sardonic laughter,[617] let it come upon us, my dear Capito, and upon our children, that we may obtain the blessings of the true Isaac.[618] Let our paths be lined with thorns, lest we should go with Dina to appealing entertainments [Gen 34:1].[619] Let our tears and weeping last until the sunset of life, that at the dawn of the resurrection our lamentations may be turned to joy, and our torn sackcloth be clothed with joy [Ps 30:11]![620] Let the vanity of this world be a bitter taste in our mouths, and let hope appear to us in bitterness, joy in hope, peace in joy, Christ in peace. Christ is our only Easter Isaac and Easter Laughter,[621] he who reconciled the Father with his sacrifice, became engaged to the Church, the world's most patient spouse, and, as it was eternally destined, gave blessing to his children. Let us congratulate the conqueror, and let us rejoice in this unique salvation of ours! And may no one deprive us of this joy forever!

|64| *Ut receptui canam. Gratius mihi fuerit, cum Keysersbergio reprehendi quam cum illis et ab illis dolosis labiis laudari. Si maledictio est risum illum*

---

617 Oecolampadius can very well use both of the main meanings of this kind of laughter, i.e. both that it is mocking and that it is forced.

618 Unlike the unpleasant sardonic laughter, Oecolampadius desires the blessed laughter that Isaac symbolises, as his name in Hebrew is a pun on 'laughter', cf. Gen 21:6 and the excursus in chapter III,6.

619 At first glance it makes no sense solely on the basis of the information given in the single verse about Dina going 'out to visit the women of the land' to refer to this as participating in *curiosa spectacula*. Apparently Oecolampadius must have known about folktales that have been in line with those found in the Jewish *haggadah*. In Louis Ginzberg's (1873-1953) collection of this material, the opening of the story of Shechem and Dina reads as follows: 'While Jacob and his sons were sitting in the house of learning, occupied with the study of the Torah, Dinah went abroad to see the dancing and singing women, whom Shechem had hired to dance and play in the streets in order to entice her forth.' Ginzberg 1998, vol. 1, 395.

620 Oecolampadius uses two Latin words which in this context both ought to be translated as 'joy', though often *gaudium* signals an inner, invisible joy, as a contrast to *laetitia*, which is then translated as 'delight' – but does that English term necessarily signal a visible joy?

621 Cf. notes 618 and the excursus in chapter III,6.

Sardonium non ridere, veniat super nos, mi Capito, et, super filios nostros, ut veri Isaac benedictionibus potiamur. Sepiantur viae nostrae sentibus, ne cum Dina ad curiosa spectacula egrediamur. Ad vesperum huius vitae durent lachrymae et fletus nostri, ut in matutino resurrectionis planctus noster convertatur in gaudium, saccusque concisus circumdetur laetitia! Amara sit nobis mundi huius vanitas et in amaritudine spes, in spe gaudium, in gaudio pax, in pace Christus nobis appareat, qui solus paschalis noster Isaac et risus est, qui sacrificio suo [O: 27] patrem placavit et patientissimam sibi coniugem ecclesiam desponsavit filiisque iuxta aeternam praedestinationem impartitus est benedietionem. Cui triumphatori congratulemur inque eo unico salutari nostro gaudeamus! Et utinam gaudium eius nemo tollat a nobis in aeternum!

|65| In order not to seem too arrogant, I will respond to the other two accusations with a few brief remarks, although I am almost acquitted from the outset.

If I seem too serious, why do they call me not serious enough? I will no longer defend myself; it may be that I was gentler than my reason and my abilities required. I have never had an audience where this was necessary. And even if it should have happened, I will not behave like Salmoneus.[622] Among Christians it is enough to speak seriously if it is sufficiently weighty. Let the tyrant stay away from the pulpit: the speech of the prophets comes like raindrops,[623] not like thunderstorms or lightning.

|65| *Caeterum ad alia duo paucioribus respondebo, ne arrogantior videar, quamvis prope absolutus a priori improperatione.*

Cum nimium serius videor, cur me non satis serium vocant? Non me iam defendam; potest fieri, lenior fuerim, quam muneris mei ratio exigebat. Non contigerunt mihi hactenus auditores, quibus opus huiuscemodi. Etsi contingerent, non tamen Salmonea agere velim; apud christianos sat severe dicitur, si sat graviter. Absit tyrannis a cathedris: prophetarum eloquia stillicidia sunt, non hymbres, non fulmina.

|66| As far as the text is concerned, here, too, their complaints are mistaken. Who has fixed this canon of preaching, which contains more boasting than benefit, more traps and anguish than fertility? For my own parishioners, who already are not unaware of my ways, I usually interpret the essence of the letter to the best of my poor abilities, and thus, for me, the hope of

---

622 Cf. note 475.
623 Cf. Ps 72:6, where the version of the *Vulgate* (= 71:6) reads: *Descendet sicut pluvia in vellus, et sicut stillicidia stillantia super terram.*

spiritual edification shines stronger than if I turned and twisted every single little word for hours.⁶²⁴

|66| *De themate autem non est, quod querantur. Quis hunc concionandi posuit canonem, in quo plus ostentationis quam fructus, plus periculi et laboris quam felicitatis. Ego meis, iam morem meum non ignorantibus, nonnunquam totum caput epistolae pro tenuitate mea interpretor, in quo mihi aedificii spiritualis maior spes adfulget, quam si uno in verbulo per horam integram me torquerem.*

|67| If you have anything more convincing, explain it to me with clear arguments, just as you have so often convinced me in the most learned way. And I will bow before you, [my dear] Capito, accept it, and be eternally grateful to you.⁶²⁵

Greetings, Weinsberg, 18 March.

|67| *Tu si quid habes probatius, manifestioribus argumentis declara, uti caetera doctissime persuadere solebas. Et ego tibi capiti cedam, morem geram gratiasque habebo semper.*

Vale, Winspergi, die Marcii XVIII.

---

624   Oecolampadius seems to position himself somewhere between the previous scholarly tradition of preaching and Luther's instructions. Luther demanded that preachers should dwell on the pericope and interpret its verses one by one (which goes by the technical term: a homily) rather than immediately take a sentence from a philosopher or a theologian as the basis for a *theme*, which was then scholastically reviewed through *distinctiones* and *quaestiones*. Though Rudolf Cruel (1820–92) finds Luther's criticism excessively polemical, Luther's opinion was that these scholarly exercises were more or less irrelevant to the congregation. Cruel 1966, 658 f.

625   The first part of the sentence, as it appears in Oecolampadius' text, contains a grammatical error with both *tibi* ('you') and *capiti* ('head') in the dative (controlled by *cedam*). A correction of the text must be made. If one accepts a correction with a changed word order and another word for *tibi* so that it should have read *capiti tuo*, the greeting would be: 'I will bow to your head'. A less intrusive and more probable correction, and the one chosen here, presupposes a correction of *capiti* to the addressee '[mi] Capito' in the vocative.

Afterword and Acknowledgements

This is an abbreviated version of the book which was published in Danish and a German translation in the spring of 2019. At the same time it is also a slightly updated and emended version, as about 4,000 words have been added in order to incorporate bits and pieces from books and articles that I have managed to read since my research for the original book was finished by the summer of 2018. It is appropriate that the book was also published in German, considering that the *historical* phenomenon of Easter Laughter was exclusively part of a tradition in southern Germany. During the Covid-19 lockdown I realised that actually an English edition was perhaps even more relevant, since it appears that during the last generation or so it is particularly in the Anglo-American world that interest in Easter Laughter has seemed strongest.

I spent some of spring 2020 translating a sample for a potential publisher, but when ordinary work resumed I had to wait until I retired in the summer of 2023 before I could return to the task at hand. Thus my engagement with Easter Laughter ended as it had begun, for the books in 2019 were the fruit of close on twenty-five years of on and off interest in the topics covered, or rather more off than on, as although my interest persisted throughout those years, the actual periods available to continue research and writing came with intervals of 2–5-10 years in between.

Back in the 1990s while teaching practical theology at the University of Aarhus I was working on a project about the similarities and differences between church and theatre, such as what is the relationship between an actor and a preacher, between a performer and a priest in charge of the liturgy, and between an audience and a congregation. In particular Northrop Frye had got me interested in how to apply literary theories about tragedy and comedy to homiletics. During this research the words 'Easter Laughter' and the Latin *'risus paschalis'* kept appearing in articles and books introducing me to a concept that I had not been aware of during my theological education in the 1970s nor my studies in the 1980s as a young academic teacher and pastor. The expression in itself certainly had an appeal and raised my curiosity, so it caused all the more frustration and a nagging suspicion of name-dropping that most often it was referred to as a very old and widespread custom but without further information or any references.

Some did mention the name of Oecolampadius, for the startling thing was that there actually existed a Latin source text from 1518 written by him that described the mysterious phenomenon in detail, and in light of its apparent popularity both then and certainly now it was deeply curious that the original text had never been translated. Was that perhaps one of the explanations for the fact that mostly the references were kept brief and repetitive of the same few points? Not only had it never been translated but the original edition had never been reissued, and only 400 years later was the Latin text reprinted for the first time when Ernst Staehelin included it in his publication of 'Letters and Documents on the Life of Oecolampadius'. However, with its mere 15 pages it was easy to miss among the 1,500 pages of the two volumes.

Whether or not my suspicion was fair towards other writers, it certainly applied to me and my shaky memory of being tutored in Latin many moons ago. One of my colleagues, Eberhard Harbsmeier, suggested that his son might be able to help me, as he was a very promising young scholar of classical philology, so I contacted Martin Sander Harbsmeier in the spring of 1999. During the summer of that year he managed to make a rough draft, but when he subsequently obtained a scholarship to Humboldt University in Berlin and began work on his doctoral thesis, and as I became engaged in other projects, we never found the time to resume work on the translation before he sadly died in 2013. Without Martin's linguistic proficiency and incredible willingness to help, this book would never have come to fruition, so it is most welcome to publish it also in his memory.

Both before and after Martin's death I had received some help from his uncle, Dietrich Gottlieb Harbsmeier, in deciphering various Latin quotes from other writers related to my research, while his former teacher, Christian Gorm Tortzen, offered to proofread the Danish translation of Oecolampadius' text ahead of its publication in 2019. However, the basic task of filling out all the blanks left in Martin's rough draft as well as providing translations of most of those passages from other Latin texts that now appear in the footnotes was carried out by an old friend of mine, Søren Hindsholm. Without his help it is doubtful that I would have been able to finish the job.

At various instances in the book I marvel at the humanists' interest in not only bringing thinkers of the distant past back into European consciousness but also at their ability to connect with each other across many physical and mental, national and social borders. I would like to use this as an image of the helpfulness that has been extended to me from friends, acquaintances, and former colleagues, many of whom I had not been in contact with for years. Even more impressively I received prompt and competent replies from scholars that I had never met but had contacted out of the blue because of an article or a book of theirs that I was familiar with. For me at least this gave a vivid impression of an intact community across the humanities even in an age of electronics. Many of the pieces of advice or information have found their way into the footnotes. I would like to mention them here too with gratitude: Carsten Bach-Nielsen (Church History, University of Aarhus), Kirsten Ditlevsen (pastor and folktale aficionado), Henning Hufnagel (Romance Philology, University of Freiburg), Knud Jeppesen (Old Testament, University of Aarhus), Martin Schwarz Lausten (Church History, University of Copenhagen), Frederick J. McGinness (History, Mount Holyoke College), Erik A. Nielsen (Nordic Studies and Linguistics, University of Copenhagen), Helge Kjær Nielsen (New Testament, University of Aarhus), Erika Rummel (History, Wilfrid Laurier University), and Ueli Zahnd (Church History, University of Basel).

Fellow scholars may be puzzled by some of the literature used, and even a casual reader may wonder about the publication year of many of the referenced books. This deserves an explanation.

When dealing with topics that are, or have previously been, considered very controversial and where the debate happens to be of that fairly special kind, as it often is among theologians and people in the Church, where it is characterised by frequently referring to and incorporating authoritative texts to support opinions and statements, a somewhat embarrassing problem often arises. As has been evident throughout the book, we may harbour the criticism against a lot of the literature that has dealt with laughter in general and Easter Laughter in particular, that it treats its legitimising sources very selectively. Even in cases where all possible academic meticulousness has been shown in handling the sources, as a reader we may feel somewhat chagrined that even more from a given work has not been included, if and when our interest has been caught by a particular detail.

To address both the potential criticism and meet the academic curiosity, I strive in this book not to disappoint the reader with references like 'somewhere John Doe writes' or the even more frustrating 'someone once said'. Therefore, to the extent that it has been possible to locate viewpoints and texts, both extensive quotes and precise references have been provided, so that readers can explore the context of the references themselves, where they find it relevant.

The desire to invite the reader on a journey through familiar and possibly even more *not* so familiar texts has been decisive for the important choices made regarding editions. In almost all cases where possible, electronically available books have been chosen, even though many of them exist not only in newer, but also in text-critically improved versions. From an academic perspective this is a defensible approach, as I have not encountered cases where a given point depends on a questionable textual basis that has been changed based on newer research; and for the reader the gain is obvious, for whenever a reference catches one's interest the wider context is only a few clicks away on the computer.

The same kind of consideration is also the background for giving not only references to available English translations but also to publications with the sources in their original languages. When an English publication is referenced, the translations will be taken from it; all other translations are my own.

This brings me to my final acknowledgements as I thank the librarian at my former place of work, Annette Brøchner Lindgaard, for giving me access to its international loan service when I had to trace all my references in English-language books. A bittersweet but huge tribute is owed to the proofreader of my English manuscript, Edward Broadbridge. Having lived in English-speaking countries for almost eight years it has been a bitter pill for me to swallow finally to learn what was meant by the old aphorism about England and America being two countries divided by the same language. I thank Edward for his patience in pointing out all those differences and for his many suggestions for stylistic improvements. In that sense he has done for this English edition what my wife, Charlotte Rossel, did for the Danish. Without them the manuscripts would definitely have been written, but the books would have been a much poorer read, and what errors and weaknesses remain are totally my responsibility.

My final thanks bring both the topic and my own work full circle. One of the books that I read first and which I quote and reference most was written by Volker Wendland: 'Easter Tales and Easter Laughter'. I am happy that my editor, Adrian Stähli, agreed with me that it was only fitting for Peter Lang to publish my manuscript, considering that it was they who did the same with Wendland's back in 1980.

Benny Grey Schuster
Brøns, May 2024

Bibliography[626]

Acta Selecta Ecclesiae Augustanae: Accedit Synopsis Episcopalium Decretorum Per Eandem Ecclesiam A Tempore Concilii Tridentini Usque In Praesentem Annum Promulgatorum, Quorum Notitia Cum Historiae Ecclesiasticae Cultoribus, tum maxime Augustanae Dioecesis sacerdotibus perutilis. Collegit Joseph Anton Steiner. Augsburg: Rieger, 1785.

Adam of Saint Viktor (1880): 'Zyma vetus expurgetur', in: Migne: *SL*, vol. 196, col. 1438-9.

– (1881): *The Liturigcal Poetry of Adam of St. Victor, from the text of Gautier*, vol. 1, tr. by Digby S. Wrangham. Longon: Kegan Paul, Trench & Co.

Adams, Douglas G. (1997): *The Prostitute in the Family Tree. Discovering Humor and Irony in the Bible*. Louisville: Westminster John Knox.

Addison, Joseph (1891): ['Risu inepto res ineptior nulla est'] 'The Spectator, No. 35, Tuesday, 10 April, 1711' & ['On Cheerfulnes in Religion'] 'The Spectator, No. 494, Friday, 26 September, 1712', in: *id.*: *The Spectator, A New Edition Reproducing the Original Text both as First Issued and as Corrected by its Authors, with Introduction, Notes, and Index by Henry Morley*. London: Routledge & Sons, vol. 1, 133-6 & vol. 3, 243-6.

Adkin, Neil (1985): 'The Fathers on Laughter', in: *Orpheus: rivista di umanità classica e cristiana* n.s. 6, 149-52.

Adolf, Helen (1947): 'On Mediaeval Laughter', in: *Speculum. A Journal of Mediaeval Studies* 22, 251-3.

Aelian, Claudius (1665): *Various History*, tr. by Thomas Stanley. London: Thomas Dring.

Aichele, George, Jr. (1980): *Theology as Comedy. Critical and Theoretical Implications*. Washington: University Press of America.

---

626 Many of the books and journals in this bibliography are available online. Specific online addresses are only given for those works which have been referred to by scan images. An easy way to find out whether a given title is available online is to search for it in the Karlsruhe Virtual Catalog, but the vast majority of especially the older publications can be found at one of these services: archive.org, babel.hathitrust.org, books.google.com, gutenberg.org, jstor.org, perseus.tufts.edu, and reader.digitale-sammlungen.de.

Agobard of Lyon (1981): 'De spe et timore', in: *id.: Agobardi Lugdunensis Opera omnia* , ed. by Lieven Van Acker. Turnhout: Brepols.

Albert the Great (1894): 'Enarrationes in primam partem evang. Lucæ (I-IX)', in: *Alberti Magni Opera omnia*, vol. 23, ed. by Auguste Borgnet. Paris: Louis Vivès.

Albert, Jürgen Peter (1975): *Humor als Autonomie und Christonomie. Eine systematisch-theologische Untersuchung zum Humorbegriff*, (diss., Erlangen-Nürnberg).

Alexander of Hales (1930): *Doctoris irrefragabilis Alexandri de Hales Ordinis Minorum Summa theologica*, 'Secunda pars secundi libri', iussu et auctoritate Bernardini Klumper. Quaracchi: Ex typ. Collegii S. Bonaventurae.

Alt, Heinrich (1846): *Theater und Kirche in ihrem gegenseitigen Verhältnis historisch dargestellt*. Berlin: Plahnsche Buchhandlung.

Amandus from Graz (1695): 'Am neunten Sonntag nach Pfingsten: Dass ihrer vil lachen die billicher Ursach haben zu wainen', in: *id.: Seelen-Wayde Der Christlichen Schäfflen. 1. Dess Ersten Jahrs-Lauffs Erster Theil: Vber die Sonntäg*. Clagenfurt: Von Matthias Khleinmayr.

Ambrose (1845): 'De Officiis Ministrorum', in: Migne: *SL*, vol. 16, col. 23–184.
- 1995: 'On the Duties of the Clergy', in: *Nicene and Post-Nicene Fathers* …, Second Series, vol. 10, tr. by H. de Romestin, E. de Romestin & H.T.F. Duckworth, 1–89.

Anderson, Philip A. (1987): 'Humor as Healing and Grace', in: *Chicago Theological Seminary Register* 77, 1–10.

Anonymous [Pseudo-Chrysostomos] (1862): 'Opus Imperfectum. Eruditi commentarii in evangelium Matthæi' ['43th Homily on Matthew, ch. 23'], in: Migne: *SG*, vol. 56, col. 876. Cf. Oden 2010.

Anonymous [Jonas Conrad Schramm] (1725): *Programma De Risv Paschali Festo Resvrrectionis Domini MDCCXXV. In Academia Jvlia P.P.* Helmstedt: Schnorrius.

Anonymous (1914): 'The Spirit of Easter', in: *The Lotus Magazine* 5.7, 473–82.

Anonymous (1919): 'Religious Use of Humour', in: *Literary Digest* 63, 34.

Anonymous (1923): 'Ministerial Laughter', in: *Outlook* 51.1312, 242 ff.

Anonymous (1998): 'Humor', in: Leland Ryken; James C. Wilhoit & Tremper Longman III (eds.): *Dictionary of Biblical Imagery*. Downers Grove: InterVarsity, 407–11.

Ante-Nicene Fathers. Translations of The Writings of the Fathers down to A. D. 325, The, ed. by Alexander Roberts & James Donaldson. American reprint of the Edinburgh edition ('Ante-Nicene Christian Library', 1–24, 1870–97), revised and chronologically arranged, with brief prefaces and occasional notes by A. Cleveland Coxe, I-X. Grand Rapids: Eerdmans, 1886–1990.

'Apocalypse of Peter' (1988), tr. and introduced by James Brashler & Roger A. Bullard, in: James M. Robinson (ed.): *The Nag Hammadi Library*. San Francisco: Harper & Row, 1988³, 372–8.

- 2007: 'The Revelation of Peter', introduced and tr. by Marvin W. Meyer, in: Marvin W. Meyer (ed.): *The Nag Hammadi Scriptures, The International Edition*, the Revised and Updated Translation of Sacred Gnostic Texts, Complete in One Volume. New York: HarperCollins, 487–97.

Apuleius (1924): *The Golden Ass, Being the Metamorphoses of Lucius Apuleius*, tr. by W. Adlington [1566], revised by S. Gaselee. London: Heinemann.

Apte, Mahadev L. (1985): 'Humor in religion', in: *id.*: *Humor and Laughter. An Anthropological Approach*. Ithaca & London: Cornell University Press, 151–76.

Arbuckle, Gerald A. (2008): *Laughing with God. Humor, Culture, and Transformation*. Collegeville: Liturgical Press.

Aristotle (1883): *History of Animals* ['Historia Animalium'], tr. by Richard Cresswell. London: George Bell & Sons.

– (1912): 'De Partibus Animalium', tr. by William Ogle, in: *id.*: *The Works of Aristotle*, vol. 5. Oxford: Clarendon.

– (1922): 'Rhetoric', tr. by J.H. Freese, in: *Aristotle in 23 Volumes*, vol. 22. London: Heinemann.

– (1934): 'Nichomachean Ethics' ['Ethica Nicomachea'; 'Eth.Nic.'], new and rev. ed. tr. by H. Rackham, in: *Aristotle in 23 Volumes*, vol. 19. London: Heinemann.

– (1959): 'Politics', tr. by H. Rackham, in: *Aristotle in 23 Volumes*, vol. 21. London: Heinemann.

– (1960): *Topica*, tr. by E. S. Forster. London: Heinemann.

– (1965): 'The Poethics', tr. by W. Hamilton Fyfe, in: *Aristotle: The Poetics; 'Longinus': On the Sublime; Demetrius: On Style*. London: Heinemann.

– (1967): 'Eudemian Ethics' ['Ethica Eudemia'; 'Eth.Eud.'], tr. by H. Rackham, in: *Aristotle in 23 Volumes*, vol. 20. London: Heinemann.

– (1984): 'Tractatus Coislinianus', in: Richard Janko: *Aristotle on Comedy. Towards a Reconstruction of Poetics II*. London: Duckworth.

Arnold, Matthew (1874): *Literature & Dogma. An Essay Towards a Better Apprehension of the Bible*. London: Smith, Elder & Co.

Arpagaus, Christian (1706): *Pera Pastoralis, Oder: Geistliche Hirten-Tasch Feyrtäglicher Lob-Predigen der lieben Heiligen Gottes mit Vermischung anstehender Glaubens- und Sitten-Lehren sonderlich an das Land-Volck: Erstes Festival, sambt einem Appendix einer kräfftigen Fassnacht Predig.* Stift-Kempten: Roll.

Augusti, Johann Christian Wilhelm (1818): 'Das heilige Osterfest; oder: Die Feyer der Auferstehung Jesu Christi', in: *id.: Denkwürdigkeiten aus der christlichen Archäologie; mit beständiger Rücksicht auf die gegenwärtigen Bedürfnisse der christlichen Kirche*, vol. 2: *Die Feste der alten Christen: für Religions-Lehrer und gebildete Leser aus allen Confessionen*. Leipzig: Dykchen Buckhandlung, 220–41.

Augustine of Hippo (1841): 'Confessionum Libri Tredecim', in: Migne: *SL*, vol. 32, col. 659–868.

- 1886: 'The Confessions of St. Augustin', in: *Nicene and Post-Nicene Fathers …*, First Series, vol. 1, tr. by J.G. Pilkington, 45–207.

– (1865a): 'De doctrina Christiana Libri Quatuor', in: Migne: *SL*, vol. 34, col. 16–120.

- 1899: 'On Christian Doctrine', in: *Nicene and Post-Nicene Fathers …*, First Series, vol. 2, tr. by James Shaw, 519–97.

– (1865b): 'De Genesi ad Litteram', in: Migne: *SL*, vol. 34, col. 354–430.

- 1982: *The Literal Meaning of Genesis*, I-II, tr. and annotated by John Hammond Taylor. New York & Ramsey: Newman.

– (1948): *The City of God*, I-II, tr. & ed. by Marcus Dods. New York: Hafner.

Backus, Irena Dorota (2008): '"Lives" of Chief Swiss Reformers: Hagiographies, Historical Accounts and "Exempla": Zwingli, a Christian Hero Complete with Miracles, and Oecolampadius, a Man too Saintly for Suicide', in: *id.: Life Writing in Reformation Europe. Lives of Reformers by Friends, Disciples and Foes*. Aldershot: Ashgate, 46–95.

Bainton, Roland Herbert (1969): 'Wibrandis Rosenblatt', in: Max Geiger (ed.): *Gottesreich und Menschenreich. Ernst Staehelin zum 80. Geburtstag*. Basel: Helbing & Lichtenbahn, 71–86.

Bakhtin, Mikhail Mikhailovich (1984): *Rabelais and His World* [Russian ed. 1965], tr. by Helene Iswolsky. Bloomington: Indiana University Press.

Balthasar, Hans Urs von (1965): 'Narrentum und Herrlichkeit', in: *id.: Herrlichkeit. Eine theologische Ästhetik*, vol. 3,1: 'Im Raum der Metaphysik'. Einsiedeln: Johannes, 492–551.

Balzaretti, Claudio (2016): '"Risus paschalis". Appunti per una ricerca "in fieri"', in: *Studi e materiali di storia delle religioni* 82, 385–400.

Barash, Moshe (1997): 'De Risu: Laughter in Renaissance Psychology, Literature, and Art', in: *id.: The Language of Art. Studies in Interpretation*. New York & London: New York University Press, 172–206.

Barish, Jonas (1981): *The Antitheatrical Prejudice*. Berkeley: University of California Press.

Bärsch, Jürgen (1998): 'Risus paschalis. Der Brauch des Ostergelächters in Liturgie und Frömmigkeit', in: *Meditation. Zeitschrift für christliche Spiritualität und Lebensgestaltung* 24.2, 24–8.

Basil of Caesarea (1857): 'Regulæ fusius tractatæ', in: Migne: *SG*, vol. 31, col. 899–1079.

- 2013: *The Rule of St. Basil in Latin and English. A Revised Critical Edition*, tr. by Anna Silvas. Collegeville: Liturgical Press.

Bauer, Gerhard (1989): *Johannes Geiler von Kaysersberg. Sämtliche Werke*, Erster Teil (Die deutschen Schriften), Erste Abteilung (Die zu Geilers Lebzeiten erschienenen Schriften), vol. 1. Berlin: de Gruyter.

Baumann, Christoph Peter (2008): *Humor und Religion. Worüber man lacht – oder besser nicht*. Stuttgart: Kreuz.

Baumgartner, Antoine Jean (1896): 'L'humour dans l'Ancien Testament', in: *Revue de théologie et de philosophie* 29.6, 497–535.

Bausinger, Hermann (1958): 'Schwank und Witz', in: *Studium Generale. Zeitschrift für Interdisciplinäre Studien* 11, 699–710.

- (1992): 'Lachkultur', in: Thomas Vogel (ed.): *Vom Lachen. Einem Phänomen auf der Spur*. Tübingen: Attempto, 9–23.

Bebel, Heinrich (1907): *Heinrich Bebels Schwänke* [1508–12], I-II, zum ersten Male in vollständiger Übertragung ed. by Albert Wesselski. München: Georg Müller.

- 1931: *Heinrich Bebels Facetien, Drei Bücher*, historisch-kritische Ausg. v. Gustav Bebermeyer. Leipzig, Karl W. Hiersemann.

- 2005: *Fazetien, Drei Bücher*, tr. and with an introduction by Manfred Fuhrmann. Konstanz: Edition Isele.

Bednarz, Terri (2009): *Humor-Neutics. Analyzing Humor and Humor Functions in the Synoptic Gospels*, (diss., Brite Divinity School).

- (2015): *Humor in the Gospels. A Sourcebook for the Study of Humor in the New Testament, 1863–2014*. Lanham: Lexington Books.

Beet, William Ernest (1922): 'The Humorous Element in the Old Testament', in: *The Expositor* 8. Series, 22, 59–68.

Beil, Johann Gabriel (1847): 'De causis risus paschalis' [1746], in: Johann Ernst Volbeding (ed.): *Thesaurus commentationum selectarum et antiquiorum et recentiorum illustrandis antiquitatibus christianis inservientium*, vol. 1,2. Leipzig: Dykchen Buckhandlung, 256–9.

Benedict of Aniane (1864): 'Concordia regularum', in: Migne: *SL*, vol. 103, col. 701–1380.

Benedict of Nursia (1981): *RB 1980. The Rule of St. Benedict in Latin and English with Notes*, ed. and tr. by Timothy Fry. Collegeville: Liturgical Press.

Benson, John E. (1983): 'The Divine Sense of Humor', in: *Dialog. A Journal of Theology* 22, 190–7.

Benz, Ernst (1938): 'Heilige Narrheit', in: *Kyrios. Vierteljahresschrift für Kirchen- und Geistesgeschichte Osteuropas* 3, 1–55.

'Berakhot tractate', in: *The Talmud of Babylonia. An Academic Commentary. I Bavli Tractate Berakhot*, ed. by Jacob Neusner. Atlanta: Scholars Press, 1996.

Berger, Peter Leroy (1969): 'Christian Faith and the Social Comedy', in: *id.*: *The Precarious Vision*. New York: Doubleday & Co., 1961; repr. in: Hyers (ed.) (1969a), 123–33.

– (1997): *Redeeming Laughter. The Comic Dimension of Human Experience*. Berlin & New York: de Gruyter.

Bergmann, Lorenz (1944): *Kirkehistorie. I. Indtil Reformationen*, 6. rev.ed. Copenhagen: P. Haase & Søn.

Bernard of Clairvaux (1859): 'De consideratione', in: 'Sancti Bernardi, opera omnia, vol. 1', Migne: *SL*, vol. 182, col. 727–808.

– (1862): 'Sermo 93', in: 'Sancti Bernardi, opera omnia, vol. 2', Migne: *SL*, vol. 183, col. 715–7.

Bessiere, Gerard (1974): 'Humor – A Theological Attitude', in: Metz & Jossua (eds.) (1974), 81–95.

Betz, Otto (1981[2]): *Der Humor Jesu und die Fröhlichkeit der Christen. Vorsichtige Anfrage, ob der Christ noch etwas zu Lachen hat* [1979]. Ulm: Süddeutsche Verlagsgesellschaft.

Beuscher, Bernd (1991): 'Verstehen Sie Spass? Zur Hermeneutik des Humors in praktisch-theologischer Perspektive', in: Dietrich Zillessen (ed.): *Praktisch-theologische Hermeneutik*. Rheinbach-Merzbach: CMZ, 519–33.

Biblitèque universelle des romans, ouvrage périodique, 1er Volume. Paris: Demonville, Octobre 1786.

Biessenecker, Stefan (2012): *Das Lachen im Mittelalter. Soziokulturelle Bedingungen und sozial-kommunikative Funktionen einer Expression in den 'finsteren Jahrhunderten'*, (diss., Bamberg Universität).

– & Christian Kuhn (eds.) (2012): *Valenzen des Lachens in der Vormoderne (1250–1750)*. Bamberg: Bamberg University Press.

Billman, Carol (1980): 'Grotesque Humor in Medieval Biblical Comedy', in: *American Benedictine Review* 31, 406–17.

Blaicher, Günther (1970): 'Über das Lachen im englischen Mittelalter', in: *Deutsche Vierteljahrsschrift für Literaturwissenschaft und Geistesgeschichte* 44, 508–29.

Blanke, Fritz (1954): *Luthers Humor. Scherz und Schalk in Luthers Seelsorge.* Hamburg: Furche-Bücherei.

Bloch, Peter (1999): *Der fröhliche Jesus. Die Entdeckung seines Humors in den Evangelien.* Stuttgart: Quell.

Blumenfeld, Esther & Lynne Alpern (1986): *The Smile Connection. How to Use Humor in Dealing with People.* New York: PrenticeHall.

Boccacio, Giovanni (1903): *Decameron*, I-II, tr. by James MacMullen Rigg. London: Privately Printed.

Bokun, Branko (1997): *Humour and Pathos in Judaeo-Christianity.* London: Avon.

Bolte, Johannes (1924): 'Die späteren Bearbeitungen von Schimpf und Ernst' & 'Bibliographie und Inhaltsübersichten', in: Johannes Pauli: *Schimpf und Ernst, Zweiter Teil: Paulis Fortsetzer und Übersetzer. Erläuterungen*, ed. by Johannes Bolte. Berlin: Stubenrauch, *7-*45 & 141–221.

Bonham, Tal D. (1988): *Humor, God's Gift. The Role of Humor from Here to Hereafter*, with a Foreword by Steve Allen. Nashville: Broadman.

Boodin, John Elof (1933-4): 'Divine Laughter', in: *Hibbert Journal* 32, 572–84.

Bos, Jacob (1938): 'Heavenly Laughter', in: *Bibliotheca Sacra. A Theological Quarterly* 95, 202–18.

Bowen, Barbara C. (1986): 'Renaissance Collections of "facetiae", 1344–1528: A New Listing', in: *Renaissance Quarterly* 39, 1–15 & 263–75. Repr. in: *id.: Humour and Humanism in the Renaissance.* Aldershot & Burlington: Ashgate.

– (ed.) (1988): *One Hundred Renaissance Jokes. An Anthology.* Birmingham: Summa Publications.

Bracciolini, Gian [/Giovanni] Francesco Poggio (1968): *The Facetiae* [1452], a new translation by Bernhardt J. Hurwood. London: Tandem Books.

- 1906: *Die Facezien des Poggio Firentino*, aus dem lateinischen übers. und eingeleitet von Hanns Floerke, mit einem litteraturhistorichen Anhang von Albert Wesselski. München: Georg Müller.

Braet, Herman; Guido Latré & Werner Verbeke (eds.) (2003): *Risus Mediaevalis. Laughter in Medieval Literature and Art.* Leuven: Leuven University Press.

Brakelmann, Günter (1971): 'Glaube und Humor', in: *Wissenschaft und Praxis in Kirche und Gesellschaft* 60, 218–25.

Brandstetter, Alois (1988): 'Bibel und Humor', in: Johann Holzner & Udo Zeilinger (eds.): *Die Bibel im Verständnis der Gegenwartsliteratur*. St.Pölten & Wien: Niederösterreichishces Pressehaus, 99–108.

Branson, Roy (1973): 'The Theology of Joy', in: *Encounter* 34, 233–45.

Brant, Sebastian (1983): *The Shyp of Fooles* [1494], tr. by Alexander Barclay, 1509, ed. by Phyllis C. Robinson. Seal Harbor: High Loft.

Braun, Heinrich Suso (1940): *Vom Humor des Christen. Ein Kapitel über frohe und unfrohe Frömmigkeit*. Paderborn: Ferdinand Schöningh.

– (1960): 'Humor', in: Josef Höfer & Karl Rahner (eds.) (1957–68): *Lexikon für Theologie und Kirche*, 2nd ed. Freiburg i. Br.: Herder, vol. 5, col. 535–6.

Bremmer, Jan Nicolaas & Herman Roodenburg (eds.) (1997a): *A Cultural History of Humour – From Antiquity to the Present*. Oxford: Polity.

– (1997b): 'Introduction: Humour and History', in: *id*. (eds.) (1997), 1–10.

Bremmer, Jan Nicolaas (1997): 'Jokes, Jokers and Jokebooks in Ancient Greek Culture', in: Bremmer & Roodenburg (eds.) (1997a), 11–28.

Brenner, Athalya (1990): 'On the Semantic Field of Humour, Laughter, and the Comic in the Old Testament', in: Radday & Brenner (eds.) (1990), 39–58.

Brewer, Derek W. (1972): 'Afterword: Notes Towards a Theory of Medieval Comedy', in: Peter Rickard (ed.): *Medieval Comic Tales*, tr. by Peter Rickard, et al. Totowa: Rowman and Littlefield, 140–9. (Cambridge: Brewer, 1996².)

– (1997): 'Prose Jest-Books Mainly in the Sixteenth to Eighteenth Centuries in England', in: Bremmer & Roodenburg (eds.) (1997a), 90–111.

Brockett, Oscar Gross (1999): *History of the Theatre* [1968[1]], 8th ed. with Franklin J. Hildy. Boston: Allyn and Bacon.

Brockhaus (1816): 'Oecolampad', in: *Conversations-Lexicon oder enzyclopädisches Handwörterbuch für gebildete Stände*. Leipzig und Altenburg: Brockhaus, vol. 7, 21–2.

Bröker, Günther (1979): 'Lachen als religiöses Motiv in gnostischen Texten', in: Peter Nagel (ed.): *Studien zum Menschenbild in Gnosis und Manichäismus*. Halle (Saale): Abt. Wissenschaftspublizistik der Martin-Luther-Universität Halle-Wittenberg, 111–25.

Buchinger, Harald (2004): '"Durch des Kreuz kam Freude in die Welt". Von Sinn und Unsinn des Ostergelächters', in: *Wort auf dem Weg* 289, 38–41.

Buckard, Olof & Anders Beijbom (1990): *Humor – Guds leende på jorden*. Stockholm: Verbum.

Buckley, George Wright (1901): *The Wit and Wisdom of Jesus*. Boston: James H. West Co.

Buckner, Richard (1993): *The Joy of Jesus – Humour in the Gospels*. Norwich: Canterbury.

Budge, Ernest Alfred Wallis (ed.) (1913): 'The Book of the Resurrection of Jesus Christ, by Bartholomew the Apostle', in: *id.*: *Coptic Apocrypha in the Dialect of Upper Egypt*, ed., with English Translations by E.A.W. Budge. London: The British Museum, 179–215.

Bugenhagen, Johannes (1544): *Das leiden vnd Aufferstehung vnsers HERRN Jhesu CHristi aus den vier Euangelisten Durch D. Johan Bugenhagen Pomern vleissig zusamen gebracht. Auffs new mit vleis emendirt. Auch die verstörung Jerusalem vnd der Jüden kurtz gefasset*. Wittenberg: Georg Rhau. Online: digital.staatsbibliothek-berlin.de

- 1546: *Historia passi et glorificati Domini nostri Iesu Christi, ex Euangelistis fideliter contracta, & nunc castigatissime cum annotationibus edita*. Wittenberg: Johannes Lufft.

'Bulla de modo prædicandi', in: Labbé & Cossart (eds.): *Sacrosancta Concilia Ad Regiam Editionem Exacta: Ab Anno MCDXXXVIII. ad Annum MDIL*. Venice: Coleti & Albrizzi, 1732, vol. 19, col. 944–7.

- 'On how to preach', in: Tanner (ed.) (2000), online: 'Fifth Lateran Council', www.intratext.com

Bullard, John Moore (1962): *Biblical Humor – Its Nature and Function*, (diss., Yale).

Bunyan, John (1678): *The Pilgrim's Progress from This World to That which is to come: Delivered under the Similitude of a Dream Wherein is Discovered, The manner of his setting out, His Dangerous Journey, And safe Arrival at the Desired Countrey*. London: Ponder.

Burke, Peter (1978): *Popular Culture in Early Modern Europe*. London: Temple Smith.

– (1997): 'Frontiers of the Comic in Early Modern Italy', in: Bremmer & Roodenburg (eds.) (1997a), 61–76.

Burningham, Bruce R. (2017): 'Communities of Production', in: Jody Enders (ed.): *A Cultural History of Theatre in The Middle Ages*, vol. 2. London: Bloomsbury, 145–61.

Burton, Robert (1638): *The Anatomy of Melancholy. What it is, With all the kinds, causes, symptomes, prognostickes & serverall cures of it*. Oxford: Cripps.

Busch, Moritz (1877): 'Der Humor auf der Kanzel', in: *id.*: *Deutsher Volkshumor*. Leipzig: F.W. Grunow, 305–49.

Busch, Stefan (2004): ' "Die Welt lacht / Jesus weint. Mit einem muss mans halten in" – Zur lachfeindlichen Tradition im Christentum', in: *id.*: *Verlorenes*

Lachen. Blasphemisches Gelächter in der deutschen Literatur von der Auferklärung biz zur Gegenwart. Berlin: de Gruyter, 8–22.

Buttrick, George A. (1994): 'God and Laughter' [1959], in: Thomas G. Long & Cornelius Plantinga, Jr. (eds.): *A Chorus of Witnesses. Model Sermons for Today's Preacher*. Grand Rapids: Eerdmans, 189–97.

Bücker, Heinrich Gerhard (ed.) (2012): *Halleluja und Helau. Karnevalspredigten und Ostergelächter*. Regensburg: Pustet.

Børtnes, Jostein (1990): 'Bakhtin, Rabelais og det karnevalske', in: Ingvild Øye (ed.): *Middelalderens mentalitet*. Bergen: Bryggens museum, 123–43.

Campbell, Charles L. (2015): 'Ministry with a Laugh', in: *Interpretation* 69, 196–208.

Campenhausen, Hans von (1960): 'Die Heiterkeit der Christen' [1956], in: *id.: Tradition und Leben. Kräfte der Kirchengeschichte. Aufsätze und Vorträgen*. Tübingen: Mohr, 431–40.

– (1963a): 'Christentum und Humor' [1961], in: *id.: Aus der Frühzeit des Christentums*. Tübingen: Mohr, 308–30.

– (1963b): 'Ein Witz des Apostels Paulus und die Anfänge des christlichen Humors' [1957], in: *id.: Aus der Frühzeit des Christentums*. Tübingen: Mohr, 102–8.

– (1973): *Theologenspiess und -spass. Kaum 400 christliche und unchristliche Scherze*. Hamburg: Siebenstern Taschenbuch.

Capeller, Isaac [& Theodor Thumm] (1624): *Tractatus Historico-Theologicus, De Festis Judaeorum Et Christianorum*. Tübingen: Cellius.

Capito, Wolfgang Fabritius (1518): 'V[olfangus] Fabritius Capito lectori s[alutem] d[icit]', in: Johannes Oecolampadius: *De Risv Paschalie, Oecolampadii, ad V. Capitonem theologum epistola apologetica*. Basel: Froben, 1.

- 1927: 'Vorwort zur Druckausgabe von Oekolampads "De risu pascali"', Basel, 19 April 1518', in: Staehelin (1927/34), vol. 1, 64–5.

– (1534): 'De vita Oecolampadii', in: *In prohetam Ezechielem commentarius d[octoris] Joannis Oecolampadii per Wolfangum Capitonem aeditus*. Strassburg: Matthias Apiarius, scan-image 16–26. Online: digital.onb.ac.at

- 1536: 'Eiusdem Ioannis Oecolampadii vita per VVolfgangvm Capitonem', in: *D. D. Ioannis Oecolampadii Et Huldrichii Zvinglii Epistolarum Libri Quatuor: Praecipua Cum Religionis A Christo Nobis traditae capita, tum Ecclesiasticae administrationis officia, nostro maxime seculo, tot hactenus erroribus perturbato, convenientia, ad amussim exprimentes*. Basel: Platter & Lasius, 1536, scan-image 72–6. Online: reader.digitale-sammlungen.de

- 1555: 'La vie de Ian Ecolampade, tresdocte theologien', in: *Histoire Des Vies Et Faits De Trois Excellens personnages, premiers restaurateurs de L'Evangile, en ces derniers temps: A Scavoir De Martin Luther, par Philippe Melancthon. De Jan Ecolampade, par Vuolfgang Faber Capito, & Simon Grynee. De Huldrich Zvingle, par Osualdus Myconius. Le tout traduit nouvellement de Latin en François, & mis en lumiere*. Geneve: Poullain & Houdouyn, scan-image 91–105. Online: digital.onb.ac.at
- 1561: 'The historye of the Lyfe of Iohn Ecolampadius, set foorth by Wolfangus Faber. Capito', in: *A famous and godly history contaynyng the lyues a[nd] actes of three renowmed reformers of the Christia[n] Church, Martine Luther, Iohn Ecolampadius, and Huldericke Zuinglius. The declaracion of Martin Luthers faythe before the Emperoure Charles the fyft, and the illustre estates of the empyre of Germanye, with an oration of hys death, all set forth in Latin by Philip Melancthon, Wolfgangus Faber, Capito. Simon Grineus, [and] Oswald Miconus, newly Englished by Henry Bennet Callesian*. By Iohn Awdely, dwellyng in lytle Brittaine Streete, by great Saint Bartelmewes, 1561.
- 1934: 'Wolfgang Fabricius Capitos Lebensbeschreibung Oekolampads als Vorwort zu Oekolampads Ezechielkommentar', in: Staehelin (1927/34), vol. 2, 742–52.

Capps, Donald (2005): *A Time to Laugh. The Religion of Humor*. New York & London: Continuum.

Carroll, Robert P. (1990): 'Is Humour also among the Prophets?', in: Radday & Brenner (eds.) (1990), 169–90.

Cassian, John (1846): 'Joannis Cassiani abbatis Massiliensis collationum XXIV collection in tres partes divisa', in: Migne: *SL*, vol. 49, col. 477–1328.
- 1894: 'John Cassian: The Conferences', in: *Nicene and Post-Nicene Fathers ...,* Second Series, vol. 2, tr. by C.S. Gibson, 291–546.

Casanowicz, Immanuel Moses (1894): *Paronomasia in the Old Testament*. Boston: Cushing & Co. (Repr.: Jerusalem: Makor, 1971).

Chambers, Edmund Kerchever (1925): *The Mediaeval Stage* [1903], I-II. Oxford: Oxford University Press.

Chapman, John Jay (1910): 'The Comic', in: *Hibbert Journal* 8, 862–72.

Chaucer, Geoffrey (1907): *Chaucer's Canterbury Tales*, ed. with notes and introduction by Alfred W. Pollard. London: Macmillan & Co.

Chesterfield, Philip Dormer Stanhope, 4th Earl of (1927): *The Letters of The Earl of Chesterfield to his Son* [1774], I-II, ed. with an introduction by Charley Strachey, and with notes by Annette Calthrop. London: Methuen.

Chesterton, Gilbert Keith (1912): *Orthodoxy* [1908]. London & New York: John Lane.

– (1929): 'Humour', in: *Encyclopaedia Britannica*, 14th ed. Cambridge: Cambridge University Press, 883–5.

– (1958): *Lunacy and Letters*, ed. by Dorothy Collins. New York: Sheed and Ward.

Chevalier, Ulysse (1900–3): 'Pâques', in: *id.*: *Répertoire des sources historiques du moyen âge. Topo-bibliographie*. Montbéliard: Société anonyme d'imprimerie montbéliardaise, vol. 2, col. 2262–3.

Chotzner, Joseph (1883): *Humour and Irony of the Hebrew Bible*. Harrow: J.C. Wilbee.

– (1905): 'Humour of the Bible', in: *id.*: *Hebrew Humour and Other Essays*. London: Luzac & Co., 1–12.

Christ-von Wedel, Christine (2017): *Glaubensgewissheit und Gewissensfreiheit. Die frühe Reformationszeit in Basel*. Basel: Colmena.

Chrysostom, see: Anonymous (Pseudo-Chrysostomos)

Chrysostom, John (1543): *Divi Joannis Chrysostomi, archiepiscopi Constantinopolitani Opera*. Paris: Carolus Guillard.

– (1862a): '17. Homilia in Epistolam ad Ephesios', in: Migne: *SG*, vol. 62, col. 115–22.

– (1862b): 'Commentarius in Sanctum Matthæum Evangelistam', 'Homilia VI, Homilia XIII, Homilia XVII, Homilia XXXII & Homilia XXXVII', in: Migne: *SG*, vol. 57, col. 61–72, 207–18, 255–66, 377–88, & 419–28.

• 1908: 'Homilies on the Gospel of Saint Matthew', in: *Nicene and Post-Nicene Fathers …*, First Series, vol. 10, tr. by George Prevost, revised by M.B. Riddle, 1–534.

– (1862c): 'Contra ludos et theatra. Homilia adversus eos qui ecclesia relicta ad circenses ludus et ad theatre transfigerunt', in: Migne: *SG*, vol. 56, col. 63–270.

– (1862d): 'Homilia xliij. ex capite xxiij (In Mattheum Homil. XLIII, Opus Imperfectum)', in: Migne: *SG*, vol. 56, col. 876–80.

– (1863): '15. Homilia in Epistolam ad Hebræos (9:1–5)', in: Migne: *SG*, vol. 63, col. 117–24.

• 1889: 'Homilies on the Epistle to the Hebrews', in: *Nicene and Post-Nicene Fathers …*, First Series, vol. 14, tr. by Frederic Gardiner, 335–522.

Cicero, Marcus Tullius (1902): 'De oratore', in: *id.*: *M. Tulli Ciceronis Rhetorica*, ed. by Augustus Samuel Wilkins. Oxford: Clarendon.

• 2001: *On the Ideal Orator*, tr., with introduction, notes, appendixes, glossary, and indexes by James M. May & Jakob Wisse. Oxford: Oxford University Press.

- (1917): 'In Verrem', in: *id.: Orationes*, vol. 3: 'Divinatio in Q. Caecilivm. In C. Verrem', ed. William Peterson. Oxford: Clarendon.
- 1903: 'Against Verres', in: *The Orations of Marcus Tullius Cicero*, vol. 1, literally tr. by C.D. Yonge. London: Henry G. Bohn, 131–545.

Classen, Albrecht (2010): 'Laughter as an Expression of Human Nature in the Middle Ages and the Early Modern Period. Literary, Historical, Theological, Philosophical, and Psychological Reflections. Also an Introduction', in: *id.* (ed.) (2010): *Laughter in the Middle Ages and Early Modern Times. Epistemology of a Fundamental Human Behaviour, Its Meaning, and Consequences*. New York: de Gruyter, 1–140.

Clement, Titus Flavius, of Alexandria (1857a): 'Cohortatio ad gentes', in: Migne: *SG*, vol. 8, col. 49–246.
- 1919: *Exhortation to the Greeks*, tr. by G.W. Butterworth. Cambridge: Harvard University Press.
- (1857b): 'Paidagogos', in: Migne: *SG*, vol. 7, col. 439–55.
- 1954: *Christ the Educator*, tr. by Simon P. Wood. New York: Fathers of the Church.

Conconi, Giorgio (1998): *When Jesus Smiled* [Italian ed. 1995], tr. by Jordan Aumann. New York: Alba House.

Copenhaver, Martin B. (2007): 'Laughter at Easter. Matthew 28,1–10', in: *Journal for Preachers* 20, 15–18.

Cormier, Henri (1977): *The Humor of Christ* [French-Canadian ed. 1974]. New York: Alba House.

Cote, Richard G. (1986): *Holy Mirth. A Theology of Laughter*. Whitinsville: Affirmation Books.

Cousins, Norman (1979): *Anatomy of an Illness as Perceived by the Patient*. New York: Norton.

Cox, Harvey Gallagher (1969): *The Feast of Fools. A Theological Essay on Festivity and Fantasy*. Cambridge: Harvard University Press.

Coxon, Sebastian (2008): *Laughter and Narrative in the Later Middle Ages. German Comic Tales 1350–1525*. London: Legenda.

Crossan, John Dominic (1976): *Raid on the articulate. Comic Eschatology in Jesus and Borges*. New York: Harper and Row.

Cruel, Rudolf (1966): *Geschichte der deutschen Predigt im Mittelalter* [1879]. Hildesheim: Georg Olms.

Culpepper, R. Alan (1992): 'Humor and Wit, New Testament', in: David Noel Freedman (ed.) (1992): *The Anchor Bible Dictionary*. New York: Doubleday, vol. 3, 333.

Curtius, Ernst Robert (1939): 'Jest and Earnest in Medieval Literature', in: *id.*: 1953, 417–35.

– (1953): *European Literature and the Latin Middle Ages* [German ed. 1948], tr. by Willard R. Trask. New York: Pantheon Books.

Dacheux, Leon (1882): *Die ältesten Schriften Geilers von Kaysersberg*. Freiburg i. Br.: Herder.

Damian, Peter (1853): 'Epistola Prima, ad S.R.E. episcopos cardinales', in: 'Petri Damiani, Opera Omnia, vol. 1', Migne: *SL*, vol. 144, col. 253–9.

Danker, Frederick W. (1967): 'Laughing with God', in: *Christianity Today* 11, 16–18.

Dante, Alighieri (1980–4): *The Divine Comedy*, I-III, a verse tr. with introductions & commentary by Allen Mandelbaum. Berkeley: University of California Press.

Darden, Robert (2008): *Jesus Laughed. The Redemptive Power of Humor*. Nashville: Abingdon.

Dart, John (1988): *The Jesus of Heresy and History. The Discovery and Meaning of the Nag Hammadi Gnostic Library*. San Francisco: Harper & Row. (= A Revised and Expanded Edition of 'The Laughing Saviour. The Discovery and Significance of the Nag Hammadi Gnostic Library'. London: Harper & Row, 1977.)

Davies, John Gordon (1968): *The Secular Use of Church Buildings*. London: SCM.

– (1975): 'Worship and Humor', in: *id.* (ed.): *Research Bulletin. Institute for the Study of Worship and Religious Architecture* 5, 3–9.

Davies, Marie-Helene (ed.) (1983): 'Humor and Religion. Friends or Foes?', in: *Thalia. Studies in Literary Humor* 6.1, 3–72.

Davis, Natalie Zemon (1975): 'The Reasons of Misrule', in: *id.*: *Society and Culture in Early Modern France. Eight Essays*. Stanford: Stanford University Press, 97–123.

Defensor from Ligugé (1862): 'De risu et tristitia' [in: 'Liber scintillarum'], in: Migne: *SL*, vol. 88, col. 685–6.

Demetrius (1902): 'Libro de elocutione', in: *id.*: *Demetrius On style*, tr. by William Rhys Roberts. Cambridge: Cambridge University Press.

Demura, Akira (1964): *Church Discipline According to Johannes Oecolampadius in the Setting of His Life and Thought*, (diss., Princeton Theological Seminary).

Detweiler, Robert (1974): 'The Jesus Jokes. Religious Humour in the Age of Excess', in: *Cross Currents. A Quarterly Review to Explore the Implications of Christianity for Our Times* 24, 55–74.

Diller, Hans-Jürgen (1999): 'Lachen im geistlichen Schauspiel des englischen Mittelalters', in: Werner Röcke & Helga Neumann (eds.) (1999), 175–97.

Dober, Hans Martin (ed.) (2017a): *Religion und Humor*. Göttingen: Vandenhoeck & Ruprecht.

– (2017b): 'Hatte Luther Humor? Eine Spurensuche', in: *id.* (ed.) (2017a), 143–56.

Donnelly, Doris (1992): 'Divine Folly. Being Religious and the Exercise of Humor', in: *Theology Today* 48, 385–98.

Douglas, Mary (1975): 'Do Dogs Laugh? A Cross-Cultural Approach to Body Symbolism' & 'Jokes', in: *id.*: *Implicit Meanings. Essays in Anthropology*. London: Routledge & Kegan Paul, 83–9 & 90–114.

Downey, Patrick (2001): *Serious Comedy. The Philosophical and Theological Significance of Tragic and Comic Writing in the Western Tradition*. Lanham: Lexington Books.

Drakeford, John W. (1986): *Humor in Preaching*. Grand Rapids: Ministry Resources Library (Zondervan Publishing House).

Dreher, Bruno (1951): *Die Osterpredigt von der Reformation bis zur Gegenwart*. Freiburg i. Br.: Herder.

Dressen, Wolfgang (1986): 'Possen und Zoten. Ausflüge unter die Gürtellinie', in: Kamper & Wulf (eds.) (1986), 147–69.

Dreves, Guido Maria (1908): *Die Kirche der Lateiner in ihren Liedern*. Kempten: Kösel.

Dreyer, A. (1923): 'Ostermärchen', in: *Der Sammler. Belletristische Unterhaltungsbeilage zur München-Augsburger Abendzeitung*, Nr. 26.

Dölger, Franz (1939): 'Lachen wider den Tod', in: Theodor Klauser & Adolf Rücker (eds.): *Pisciculi. Studien zur Religion und Kultur des Altertums. Franz Joseph Dölger zum sechzigsten Geburtstage dargeboten von Freunden, Verehrern und Schülern*. Münster in Westfalen: Aschendorff, 80–5.

Dörffel, Georg Samuel (1682): *Das ärgste Seelengifft des trostlosen Pabstthums womit P. Aloysius Richardus, der Gesellschaft Jesu (wie er sich nennet) zu Prage, den Quellreichen und reinen evangelischen Trostbrunn vermittels seiner erschrecklichen Zweiffelslehre unlängst zu verunreinigen und unschuldige Hertzen hierdurch anzustecken sich unterstehen wollen: allen der evangelischen Wahrheit aufrichtigen Liebhabern und beständigen Bekennern zu christlicher Abscheu und treumeinender Warnung nach Schrifftmässiger Probe entdecket von M. Georg. Sam. Dörffelio*. Jena: Bauhofer.

Dörrer, Anton (1962): 'Ostern', in: Josef Höfer & Karl Rahner (eds.) (1957–68): *Lexikon für Theologie und Kirche*, 2nd ed. Freiburg i. Br.: Herder, vol. 7, col. 1279.

Ebach, Jürgen (1987): ' "Nein, du hast doch gelacht". Annäherung an eine biblische Wundergeschichte – zugleich: eine weitere "Ecce-homo-Variation" ', in: *Einwürfe* 4. München: Kaiser, 54–78.

Eber, Jochen (1993): 'Humor', in: Helmut Burkhardt & Uwe Swarrat (eds.) (1992-4): *Evangelisches Lexikon für Theologie und Gemeinde*. Wuppertal: Brockhaus, vol. 2, 339–40.

Eckardt, Arthur Roy (1992a): *Sitting in the Earth and Laughing. A Handbook of Humor*. New Brunswick: Transaction.

– (1992b): 'Divine Incongruity. Comedy and Tragedy in a Post-Holocaust World', in: *Theology Today* 48, 399–412.

– (1992c): 'Is There a Christian Laughter?', in: *Encounter* 53, 109–17.

– (1995): *How to Tell God from the Devil. On the Way to Comedy*. New Brunswick: Transaction.

Eckhart, Meister (1924): *Meister Eckhart*, vol. 1, ed. by Franz Pfeiffer, translation with some omissions and additions by C. de B. Evans. London: Watkins.

• 1963: *Die deutschen und lateinischen Werke*, vol. 5: 'Meister Eckharts Traktate', ed. & tr. by Josef Quint. Stuttgart: Kohlhammer.

• 2009: *The Complete Mystical Works of Meister Eckhart* [1979–87], ed. & tr. by Maurice O'C. Walshe, revised with a foreword by Bernard McGinn. New York: Herder & Herder.

Eckman, George P. (1911): 'The Humor of the Bible', in: *Methodist Review* 93, 521–31.

Eco, Umberto (1984): *The Name of the Rose* [Italian ed. 1980], tr. by William Weaver. London: Picador.

Elert, Werner (1967): 'Das Lachen in der Kirchengeschichte' [lecture from 1927], in: *id.: Ein Lehrer der Kirche. Kirchlich-theologische Aufsätze und Vorträge*, ed. by Max Keller-Huschemenger. Berlin & Hamburg: Lutherisches Verlagshaus, 184–9.

Erasmus, Desiderius (1511): *Moriae encomium*. Argentorati [Strassburg]: Schurrer.

• 2015a: *The Praise of Folly*, tr. with an Essay & Commentary by Hoyt Hopewell Hudson, with a new foreword by Anthony Grafton. Princeton: Princeton University Press.

– (1530): *De civilitate morum puerilium*. Salzburg: s.n.

• 1531: *Züchtiger Sitten zierlichen Wandels und höfflicher Geberden der Jugent: in alle weg und nach Ordnung des gantzen leibs; den Jungen sich darin* zu üben; den Alten ire Kind nach solichem ebenbild inn zücht zü erziehen. Strassbourg: Hans Preussen.

- 1695: *Galante Höfligkeit, Wodurch Fürnemlich die grünende Jugend für den politischen Augen der heutigen Welt sich also aufführen kan, dass sie allenthalben beliebt und angenehm werde. Anitzo aufs neue durch Frag- und Antwort ins Hoch-teutsche Mutter-sprache übersetzet v. M.A.S.* Leipzig: Friedrich Groschuff.
- 1985: 'On Good Manners for Boys', tr. and annotated by Brian McGregor, in: J. K. Sowards (ed.): *Collected Works of Erasmus*, vol. 25–6. Toronto: University of Toronto Press, 273–89 (vol. 25) & 562–7 (vol. 26).
- (1535): *Ecclesiastae: sive de ratione concionandi* [1523–35]. Basel: Frobenius.
- 1536: *Ecclesiastae: sive de ratione concionandi* [1523–35]. Basel: Frobenius.
- 2015b: 'Ecclesiastes 1' & 'Ecclesiastes 2–4', in: *id.*: *Collected Works of Erasmus. Spiritualia and Pastoralia*, vol. 67–8, ed. by Frederick J. McGinness, tr. by James L.P. Butrica, annotated by Frederick J. McGinness. Toronto: University of Toronto Press.

Euripides (1913): 'Bacchae', in: *id.*: *Euripidis fabulae*, ed. Gilbert Murray. Oxford: Clarendon Press.

- 1876: 'Bacchae', in: *id.*: *The Tragedies of Euripides*, I-II, tr. by T.A. Buckley. London: George Bell & Sons.
- (1995): *Children of Heracles / Heracleidae*, ed. & tr. by David Kovacs. Cambridge: Harvard University Press.

Eybl, Franz M. (1999): 'Risus paschalis', in: Walter Kasper (ed.) (1993–2001): *Lexikon für Theologie und Kirche*, 3rd ed. Freiburg i. Br.: Herder, vol. 8, col. 1201.

Fedotov, George P. (1966): 'The Holy Fools', in: *id.*: *The Russian Religious Mind*, vol. 2: 'The Middle Ages, the 13th to 15th Centuries', ed. and with a foreword by John Meyendorff. Cambridge: Harvard University Press, 316–43.

Fehrle, Eugen (1930): 'Das Lachen im Glauben der Völker', in: *Zeitschrift für Volkskunde* 40.2, 1–5.

- (1936): 'Das Wesen des Volkes', in: *Grundlagen, Aufbau und Wirtschaftsordnung des national-sozialistischen Staates*, Erster Band: 'Die weltanschaulichen, politischen und staatsrechtlichen Grundlagens des nationalsozialistischen Staates', Gruppe 2: 'Die politischen und staatsrechtlichen Grundlagen', Beitrag 11. Berlin: Industrieverlag Spaeth & Linde, 1–11.
- (1955): *Feste und Volksbräuche im Jahreslauf europäischer Völker*. Kassel: Hinnenthal.

Ferm, Olle (2002): *Abboten, bonden och hölasset. Skratt och humor under medeltiden.* Stockholm: Atlantis.

– (2008): *Det visa leendet och det narraktiga gapskrattet. Skrattet och den medeltida kyrkan.* Stockholm: Sällskapet Runica et Mediævalia och Svenska Humanistiska Förbundet.

Ferrar, Jean (1929–30): 'Laughter of the Gods', in: *Canadian Forum* 10, 443.

Figueroa-Dorrego, Jorge & Christina Lakin-Galiñanes (eds.) (2009): *A Source Book of Literary and Philosophical Writings about Humour and Laughter. The Seventy-Five Essential Texts from Antiquity to Modern Times.* Lewiston: Edwin Mellon.

Fischer, Balthasar & Johannes Wagner (eds.) (1959): *Paschatis sollemnia. Studien zu Osterfeier und Osterfrömmigkeit,* P. Josef Andreas Jungmann S. J. zur Vollendung seines 70. Lebensjahres v. Schülern und Freunden dargeboten. Freiburg i. Br.: Herder.

Fisher, Eugene J. (1977): 'Divine Comedy – Humor in the Bible', in: *Religious Education. The Journal of the Religious Education Association and the Association of Professors and Researchers in Religious Education* 72, 571–9.

Fluck, Hanns (1934): 'Der risus paschalis. Ein Beitrag zur religiösen Volkskunde', in: *Archiv für Religionswissenschaft. Vereint mit den Beiträgen zur Religionswissenschaft der Religionswissenschaftlichen Gesellschaft in Stockholm* 31, 188–212.

Flynn, Leslie B. (1960): *Serve Him with Mirth. The Place of Humor in the Christian Life.* Grand Rapids: Zondervan.

Flögel, Karl [/Carl] Friedrich (1887): 'Osterpossen', in: *id.: Geschichte des Grotesk-Komischen* [1862[1]], bearbeitet, erweitert und bis auf die neueste Zeit fortgeführt v. Friederich W. Ebeling. Leipzig: H. Barsdorf, 216–20.

Fogtmann, Laurids; Frederik Theodor Hurtigkarl & Janus Lauritz Andreas Kolderup-Rosenvinge (eds.) (1838–40): *Samling af Forordninger, Rescripter, Resolutioner og Collegialbreve, som vedkomme Geistligheden og de øvrige i Kong Christian den 5tes Danske og Norske Lovs anden Bog omhandlede Gienstande, ordnede efter Lovenes Artikler,* I-III. Copenhagen: Gyldendal.

Frank-Osterhild, Heike (2012): 'Weiterlachen – Ein Ausblick in die Neuzeit', in: Wilhelmy (ed.) (2012a), 102–7.

Francis of Assisi (1964): *The Writings of St. Francis of Assisi,* tr. by Benen Fahy and with introduction and notes by Placid Hermann. London: Burns & Oates.

- 1999: *Frans af Assisis skrifter,* indledning og oversættelse ved Marianne Powell og Hubert Hodzelsmans, OFM. Frederiksberg: Anis.

Frazer, James George (1961): *The New Golden Bough, A New Abridgment of the Classic Work*, ed. and with notes and foreword by Dr. Theodor Herzel Gaster. Garden City: Anchor.

Friis, Helmut (1994): *Glæden. Om laster og dyder.* Copenhagen: Gyldendal.

Fritsch[en], Ahasver (1689): *Der Sündliche Lacher. Das ist, Ein Tractätlein, darinnen erwiesen wird, dass das überlaute starcke Gelächter, einem Christen-Menschen übel anständig, üppig, und sündlich sey,* Auf besondere Veranlassung, kürtzlich abgefasset, von D. Ahasvero Fritschen. Jena: Oerdt.

Fudge, Thomas A. (1997): 'Icarus of Basel? Oecolampadius and the Early Swiss Reformation', in: *The Journal of Religious History* 21.3, 268–84.

Füssli[n], Johann Konrad (1753): *Beyträge zur Erläuterung der Kirchen-Reformations-Geschichten des Schweitzerlandes,* vol. 5. Zürich: Heidegger und Comp.

Gad, Emma (1918): *Takt og tone. Hvordan vi omgaas.* Copenhagen & Kristiania: Gyldendal & Nordisk Forlag.

Gash, Anthony (1986): 'Carnival against Lent. The Ambivalence of Medieval Drama', in: David Aers (ed.): *Medieval Literature. Criticism, Ideology, and History.* New York: St. Martin's, 74–98.

Gast, Johannes (1541–51): *[Convivales sermones] Convivalivm Sermonvm, Vtilibvs Ac Ivcvndis Historijs, & sententijs, omni fere de re, quae in sermonem, apud amicos dulci in conuiuiolo, incidere potest, refertus, ex optimis & probatissimis autoribus magno labore & collectus, & iam quarto recognitus & auctus,* I-III. Basel: Westheimer.

Gaster, Theodor H. (1964): *The Dead Sea Scriptures,* tr. with introduction and notes by T.H. Gaster, rev. and enlarged ed. Garden City: Doubleday.

Geier, Manfred (2006): *Worüber kluge Menchen lachen. Kleine Philosophie des Humors.* Reinbek bei Hamburg: Rowohlt.

Geiler, Johann(es), von Kaysersberg (1513): 'Feria secunda post Judica. vi. Aprilis', in: *id.: Peregrinus.* Doctissimi sacre theologie doctoris Joannis Geiler Keyserspergij Concionatoris Argentinen[sis] celebratissimi Jacobo Otthero discipulo suo congestus. Argentine [Strassburg]: Matth. Schürer, ch. 13,XI, section U.

– (1522): *Doctor keiserszbergs Postill Vber die fyer Euangelia durchs jor, sampt dem Quadragesimal vnd von ettlichen Heyligen newlich vssgangen.* Strassburg: Schott. Online: daten.digitale-sammlungen.de

Geisenhof, Georg (1963): *Bibliotheca Bugenhagiana. Bibliographie der Druckschriften des D. Joh. Bugenhagen* [1908[1]]. Nieuwkoop: E. de Graaf.

Geminianus, Monacensis (1667): *Der Weeg-Weiser gen Himmel Das ist: Catholische Predigen über alle Feyrtägliche Evangelia dess gantzen Jahrs, nach Ordnung der heiligen Catholischen Kirchen gerichtet zu Beyhülff der Prediger, Zur Auffmunderung der Layen, zur Underweisung der Irrenden, und Trost aller frommen Christen.* München: Jäcklin. Online: reader.digitale-sammlungen.de

Geraci, Anthony J. (1989): *And God Laughed. A Revival of Humor*, (diss., United Theological Seminary).

Gevirtz, Stanley (1975): 'Of Patriarchs and Puns', in: *Hebrew Union College Annual* 46, 33–54.

Geybels, Hans (2011): 'The Redemptive Power of Humour in Religion', in: *id.* & Walter van Herck (eds.): *Humour and Religion. Challenges and Ambiguities.* London: Continuum, 11–21.

Ghose, Indira (2008): *Shakespeare and Laughter. A Cultural History.* Manchester: Manchester University Press.

Giberti, Giovanni Matteo (1542): *Constitutiones.* Verona: Putelle.

Gilman, Sander L. (1974): *The Parodic Sermon in European Perspective. Aspects of Liturgical Parody from the Middle Ages to the Twentieth Century.* Wiesbaden: Franz Steiner.

Gilhus, Ingvild Sælid (1990): 'Carnival in Religion. The Festival of Fools in France', in: *Numen* 27, 24–52.

– (1991): 'Religion, Laughter, and the Ludicrous', in: *Religion. A Journal of Religion and Religions* 21, 257–77.

– (1997): *Laughing Gods, Weeping Virgins. Laughter in the History of Religion.* London: Routledge.

– (2002): 'Lachen und Weinen', in: Hans Dieter Betz, *et al.* (eds.) (1998–2007): *Die Religion in Geschichte und Gegenwart*, 4th ed. Tübingen: Mohr Siebeck, vol. 5, col. 6 f.

– (2011): 'Why Did Jesus Laugh? Laughing in Biblical-Demiurgical Texts', in: Hans Geybels & Walter van Herck (eds.): *Humour and Religion. Challenges and Ambiguities.* London: Continuum, 123–40.

Ginzberg, Louis (1998): *Legends of the Jews*, I-VII [1909–38[1]] tr. from German manuscrips by Henrietta Szold & Paul Radin, with a new foreword by James L. Kugel. Baltimore: John Hopkins University Press.

Glover, Terrot Reaveley (1906): 'Humour', in: James Hastings (ed.): *A Dictionary of Christ and the Gospels.* Edinburgh: T. & T. Clark, vol. 1, 760–1.

– (1917): *The Jesus of History*, with a foreword by the Archbishop of Canterbury. London: SCM.

Goldmann, M. D. (1952): 'Humour in the Hebrew Bible', in: *Australian Biblical Review. Official Organ of the Fellowship for Biblical Studies* 2, 2–11.

Good, Edwin Marshall (1965): *Irony in the Old Testament*. Philadelphia: Westminster. (Repr.: Sheffield: Almond, 1981.)

Goodin, William (1990): *God Laughs Too*. Lima: C.S.S. Pub. Co.

Gospel of Judas, The, from Codex Tchacos (2006), ed. by Rodolphe Kasser, Marvin W. Meyer & Gregor Wurst. Washington: National Geographic Society.

'Gospel of Philip, The' (1988[3]), introduced and tr. by Wesley W. Isenberg, in: James M. Robinson (ed.): *The Nag Hammadi Library*. San Francisco: Harper & Row, 139–60.

- 2009: in: *The Gnostic Bible*, rev.ed., ed. by Willis Barnstone & Marvin W. Meyer. Boston & London: Shamphala, 277–318.

Grant, F.C. (1960): 'Lachen und Weinen', in: Kurt Galling (ed.) (1957–62): *Die Religion in Geschichte und Gegenwart*, 3rd ed. Tübingen: Mohr, vol. 4, col. 195.

Grassi, Joseph A. (1986): *God Makes Me Laugh. A New Approach to Luke*. Wilmington: Glazier.

Grebe, Anja & Nikolaus Staubach (eds.) (2005): *Komik und Sakralität. Aspekte einer ästhetischen Paradoxie in Mittelalter und früher Neuzeit*. Frankfurt a. M.: Peter Lang.

Grebe, Anja (2005): 'Heilige Narren. Einleitende Überlegungen zur Ästhetik von Sakralität und Komik im Mittelalter', in: *id*. & Nikolaus Staubach (eds.) (2005), 9–15.

Greeley, Andrew (1974): 'Humour and Ecclesiastical Ministry', in: Metz & Jossua (eds.) (1974), 134–40.

Greenstein, Edward L. (1992): 'Humor and Wit, Old Testament', in: David Noel Freedman (ed.): *The Anchor Bible Dictionary*. New York: Doubleday, vol. 3, 330–3.

Gregory of Nazianszus (1858): 'Oratio in sanctum Pascha', in: Migne: *SG*, vol. 36, col. 623–64.

- 1894: 'Select Orations', in: *Nicene and Post-Nicene Fathers* …, Second Series, vol. 7, tr. by C.G. Browne & J.E. Swallow, 203–434.

- (1862): 'Carminum, Liber I-II. Theologica, Sectio II. Carmina Moralia', in: Migne: *SG*, vol. 37, col. 521–1600.

Gregory the Great (1862): 'Moralium libri, sive Expositio in Librum B. Job', in: Migne: *SL*, vol. 75, col. 527–1162.

- 1844: *Morals, on the Book of Job*, translated, with notes and indices in three volumes, ed. by John Henry Parker. Oxford: Parker.

Gritsch, Eric W. (1983): 'Luther's Humor. Instrument of Witness', in: *Dialog. A Journal of Theology* 22, 176–82.

Grosart, Alexander. B. (1890–1): 'The Humor of Our Lord', in: *Expository Times* 2, 36–9 & 107–9.

Grün, Anselm (2009): *Das kleine Buch der Lebenslust*. Freiburg i. Br.: Herder.

Grynäus, Simon, see: Wolfgang Capito (1555 & 1561)

Grønbech, Vilhelm (1951): *Livet er et fund. En bog om humor og tragedie*. Copenhagen: Gyldendal.

Guerike, Heinrich Ernst Ferdinand (1833): *Handbuch der allgemeinen Kirchengeschichte*. Halle: Gebauer.

- 1838: *Handbuch der allgemeinen Kirchengeschichte*, Dritte vermehrte und verbesserte Auflage. Halle: Gebauer.

Guggisberg, Hans R. (1981): 'Johannes Oekolampad', in: Martin Greschat (ed.): *Gestalten der Kirchengeschichte*. Stuttgart: Kohlhammer, vol. 1, 117–28.

Gugitz, Gustav (1949): 'Das Ostergelächter', in: *id.: Das Jahr und seine Feste im Volksbrauch Österreichs*. Wien: Brüder Hollinik, vol. 1, 180–6.

Gurevich, Aaron (1997): 'Bachtin und seine Theorie des Karnevals', in: Bremmer & Roodenburg (eds.) (1997a), 57–63.

Gutwirth, Marcel (1993): *Laughing Matter. An Essay on the Comic*. Ithaca: Cornell University Press.

Gvozdeva, Katja & Werner Röcke (eds.) (2009): *Risus sacer – sacrum risibile. Interaktionsfelder von Sakralität und Gelächter im kulturellen und historischen Wandel*. Bern & New York: Peter Lang.

Gäbler, Ulrich (1995): 'Oekolampad, Johannes', in: Müller (ed.) (1977–2010), vol. 25, 29–36.

Gössmann, Wilhelm (1976): *Ihr aber werdet lachen. Glossen für Christen*. Freiburg i. Br.: Herder.

– (1978): 'Die Lächerlichkeit des Christlichen. Ein Thema der literarischen Religionskritik', in: *Stimmen der Zeit. Katholische Monatsschrift für das Geistesleben der Gegenwart* 196, 243–52.

Götzenberger, Franz Borgia (1752): *Die In drey wichtigen Puncten Catholisch wordene Herren Lutheraner von Augsburg In einem Ostermährlein vorrgestellet*. Wien: Trattner.

H., F.J.D. (1839): 'Ueber die Ostermährlein', in: *Historisch-politische Blätter für das katholische Deutschland* 4, 372–8.

Hadorn, Wilhelm (1904): 'Oekolampad', in: Albert Hauck (ed.): *Realencyklopädie für protestantische Theologie und Kirche*, in dritter verbesserter und vermehrter Auflage. Leipzig: Hinrich, vol. 14, 286–99.

Haebler, Hans Carl von (1957–8): 'Risus Paschalis', in: *Quatember. Evangelische Jahresbriefe* 22, 65–9.

Hagenbach, Karl Rudolf (1859): *Johann Oekolampad und Oswald Myconius. Die Reformatoren Basels*. Elberfeld: R. L. Friederichs.

Halliwell, Stephen (1991): 'The Uses of Laughter in Greek Culture', in: *The Classical Quarterly* n.s. 41, 279–96.

– (2008): *Greek Laughter. A Study in Cultural Psychology from Homer to Early Christianity*. Cambridge: Cambridge University Press.

Halsall, Guy (ed.) (2002): *Humour, History and Politics in Late Antiquity and the Early Middle Ages*. Cambridge: Cambridge University Press.

Hamilton, Kenneth Morrison & Robert Thomas Haverluck (1972): 'Laughter and Vision', in: *Soundings* 55, 163–77.

Hamilton, Kenneth Morrison (1972): 'Comedy in a Theological Perspective', in: *Religion in Life* 41, 222–32.

Hammer, Karl (1992): 'Der Reformator Oekolampad (1482–1531)', in: Heiko A. Oberman, *et al.* (eds.): *Reformiertes Erbe. Festschrift für Gottfried W. Locher zu seinem 80. Geburtstag*. Zürich: Theologischer, vol. 1, 157–70.

Hantelmann, Julius [& Joachim Hildebrand] (1655): *Exercitatio Theologica De Ritibus Sacris*. Helmestadt: Müller, Abschnitt 42.

Harris, Henry F. (1908): 'The Absence of Humor in Jesus', in: *Methodist Quarterly Review* 57.3, 460–7.

Harris, Max (2011): *Sacred Folly. A New History of the Feast of Fools*. Ithaca: Cornell University Press.

Harrison, William Pope (1888): 'Humor in the Pulpit', in: *Methodist Quarterly Review* 27, 112–7.

Härtel, Klaus Dieter (ed.) (1979): *Das Lächeln in der Kirche … ist erlaubt. Gehörtes – Aufgeschnapptes – Abgeschriebens und Gesammeltes von Klaus Dieter Härtel*. Hamburg: Agentur des Rauhen Hauses.

Hartwich, Wolf-Daniel (1997): 'Die Harmonik der Erlösung. Zur Theologie und Poetik der Heiterkeit in christlicher Tradition', in: Petra Kiedaisch & Jochen A. Bär (eds.): *Heiterkeit. Konzepte in Literatur und Geistesgeschichte*. München: Wilhelm Fink, 231–60.

Haug, Walter (1989): 'Das Komische und das Heilige. Zur Komik in der religiösen Literatur des Mittelalters' [1982], in: *id.: Strukturen als Schlüssel zur Welt. Kleine Schriften zur Erzählliteratur des Mittelalters*. Tübingen: Niemeyer, 257–74.

Hauptmann, Peter (1959): 'Die "Narren um Christi Willen" in der Ostkirche', in: *Kirche im Osten. Studien zur osteuropäischen Kirchengeschichte und Kirchenkunde* 2, 27–49.

Hazard, Marshall Custiss (1919): 'Humor in the Bible', in: *Biblical World*, n.s. 53, 514–19.

Heberlin, Rudoph Wilhelm [& Christian Wildvogel] (1691): *De eo quod iustum est circa tempus quadragesimale. Vom Rechte der Fasten-Zeit.* [Jena]: Müller.

Heer, Josef (1981): 'Christlicher Humor. Oder: Umkehr zur Freude des Glaubens', in: *Bibel im Jahr 82. (Umkehr zum Leben).* Stuttgart: Katholisches Bibelwerk.

– (1991): 'Freut Euch, Ihr Armen. Herausforderung zum Glaubenshumor durch Jesus', in: Johannes Joachim Degenhardt (ed.): *Die Freude an Gott – unsere Kraft. Festschrift für Otto Bernhard Knoch zum 65. Geburtstag.* Stuttgart: Katholisches Bibelwerk, 432–8.

– (ed.) (1992): 'Nie soll er gelacht haben? Spuren des Humors Jesu', in: *Bibel heute* 28, 146–65, mit Beiträge v. Gerhard Eberts & Karl Heinz Pfeiffer (Stuttgart: Katholisches Bibelwerk).

Heerden, Willie van (2001): 'Why the Humour in the Bible Plays Hide and Seek with Us', in: *Social Identities* 7.1, 75–96.

Heffening, Willi (1927): 'Die griechische Ephraem-Paraenesis gegen das Lachen in arabischer Übersetzung, I', in: *Oriens Christianus. Hefter für die Kunde des christlichen Orients*, Ser. 3.2, 94–119.

– (1936): 'Die griechische Ephraem-Paraenesis gegen das Lachen in arabischer Übersetzung, II', in: *Oriens Christianus. Hefter für die Kunde des christlichen Orients*, Ser. 3.11, 54–79.

Heflin, James Larohn (1974): *An Evaluation of the Use of Humor in the Sermon*, (diss., Southwestern Baptist Theological Seminary).

Heinz-Mohr, Gerd (1957): *Sermon, ob der Christ etwas zu lachen habe.* Hamburg: Furche.

– (1968): *Lachen durchs Kirchenjahr.* Hamburg: Agentur des Rauhen Hauses.

– (1974): *Das vergnügte Kirchenjahr. Heitere Geschichten und schmunzelnde Wahrheiten.* Düsseldorf: Diederichs. (5. repr.: Gütersloh: Gütersloher, 1990.)

– (1988): *Der lachende Christ. Geistlicher Humor quer durch Deutschland.* Freiburg i. Br.: Herder.

– (1989^3): *Lachen macht selig. Theologenanekdoten* [1984]. München: Piper.

Hellyar, Richmond H. (1927): 'Laughter and Jollity', in: *Contemporary Review* 132, 757–63.

Heltzel, Virgil B. (1928): 'Chesterfield and the Anti-Laughter Tradition', in: *Modern Philology* 26, 73–90.

Hempelmann, Christian F. (2003): ' "99 Nuns Giggle, 1 Nun Gasps". The Not-All-That-Christian Natural Class of Christian Jokes', in: *Humor* 16.1, 1–31.

Herrick, Marvin Theodore (1950): *Comic Theory in the Sixteenth Century*. Urbana: University of Illinois Press.

Herzog, Johann Jakob (1843): 'Oekolampad, Prediger in Basel, Weinsberg und wieder in Basel. 1515 bis 1518', in: *id.: Das Leben Johannes Oekolampads und die Reformation der Kirche zu Basel*, I-II. Basel: Schweighauser'chen Buchhandlung, vol. 1, 2. Buch, 1. kap, §2, 117–32.

Hess, Salomon (1793): *Biographien berühmter schweizerscher Reformatoren*, vol. 1: *Lebensgeschichte D. Johann Oekolampads, Reformators der Kirche in Basel*. Zürich: Ziegler & Söhne.

Hesychius of Alexandria, see: Kurt Latte

Heuser (1886): 'Feste', in: Heinrich Joseph Wetzer & Benedikt Welte (eds.) (1882–1903): *Kirchenlexikon, oder Encyklopädie der katholischen Theologie und ihrer Hülfswissenschaften*, 2nd ed. Freiburg i. Br.: Herder, vol. 4, col. 1391–447.

Hierocles (1983): *The Philogelos, or, Laughter-Lover*, tr. with an introduction and commentary by Barry Baldwin. Amsterdam: J. C. Gieben.

Hieronymus (1845a): 'Commentarius in Ecclesiasten', in: Migne: *SL*, vol. 23, col. 1009–116.

- 2014: *Ancient Bible Commentaries in English. Commentary on Ecclesiastes by St. Jerome*, ed. by John Litteral, tr. by Robin MacGregor. CreateSpace Independent Publishing Platform.
- (1845b): 'Dialogus contra Pelagianos', in: Migne: *SL*, vol. 23, col. 495–588.
- 1893a: 'Against the Pelagians', in: *Nicene and Post-Nicene Fathers* ..., Second Series, vol. 6, tr. by W.H. Fremantle, G. Lewis and W.G. Martley, 447–83.
- (1845c): 'Epistola 38, Ad Marcellam', in: Migne: *SL*, vol. 22, col. 463–5.
- 1893b: 'Letter 38, To Marcella', in: *Nicene and Post-Nicene Fathers* ..., Second Series, vol. 6, tr. by W.H. Fremantle, G. Lewis and W.G. Martley, 47–9.

Hilary of Poitiers (1843): 'De trinitate', in: Migne, *SL*, vol. 10, col. 9–472.

- 1899: 'On the Trinity', in: *Nicene and Post-Nicene Fathers* ..., Second Series, vol. 9, tr. by E.W. Watson and L. Pullan, 40–233.

Hildebrand, Joachim, siehe: Julius Hantelmann (1655)

- (1701): *De Diebus Festis Libellus*. Helmestadi: Hamm.

Hildegard von Bingen (1903): *Hildegardis Causae et curae*, ed. Paulus Kaiser. Leipzig: Teubner.

- 1994: *Holistic Healing*, tr. by Manfred Pawlik (Latin text) & Patrick Madigan (German text). Collegeville: Liturgical Press.
- 2008[2]: *Causes and Cures* [2006[1]], tr. by Priscilla Throop. Charlotte: MedievalMS.

Hilgert, Earle (1971): 'Johann Froben and the Basel University Scholars, 1513–1523', in: *The Library Quarterly* 41, 141–69.

Hinkmar (1852): 'Capitula synodica', in: Migne: *SL*, vol. 125, col. 773–802.

Holland, Hyacint (1862): *Geschichte der altdeutschen Dichtkunst in Bayern*. Regensburg: Friedrich Pustet.

Holland, Norman Norwood (1982): *Laughing. A Psychology of Humor*. Ithaca: Cornell University Press.

Holmer, Paul L. (1974): 'Something about What Makes It Funny', in: *Soundings* 57, 157–74.

Holtz, Gottfried (1953): 'Der Mund voll Lachens', in: *Zeichen der Zeit. Evangelische Monatschrift für Mitarbeiter der Kirche* 7, 201–8.

– (1979): 'Volkssprache und religiöser Humor', in: Johann D. Bellmann & Heinrich Kröger (eds.): *Sprache, Dialekt und Theologie. Beiträge zur plattdeutschen Verkündigung heute*. Göttingen: Vandenhoeck & Ruprecht, 38–47.

Homborg, Johann Joachim (1683): *Historico-Ecclesiasticus De Paschate Veterum Christianorum Libellus. In quo cum varia de isthoc Festo Certamina, tum prisca illius Instituta sacrique Ritus referuntur, explicantur, censentur*. Helmstedt: Hamm.

Homer (1914): 'Hymn to Demeter', in: *The Homeric Hymns and Homerica*, tr. by Hugh G. Evelyn-White. London: Heinemann, 288–325.

– (1924a): *The Iliad*, I-II, tr. by A.D. Murray. London: Heinemann.

– (1924b): *The Odyssey*, tr. by A.T. Murray. London: Heinemann.

Horace (Quintus Horatius Flaccus) (1856): 'The Satires' ['Satyrarum Libri'], in: id.: *The Works of Horace*, tr. by Christopher Smart. London: Henry G. Bohn.

Horowitz, Jeannine & Sophia Menache (1994): *L'humour en chaire. Le rire dans l'Église médiévale*. Genève: Labor et Fides.

Horst, Pieter Willem van der (1978): 'Is Wittiness Unchristian? A Note on "eutrapelia" in Eph 5 v. 4', in: T. Baarda (ed.): *Miscellanea Neotestamentica*. Leiden: Brill, vol. 2, 163–77.

Hospinian, Rodolph (1593): *Festa Christianorvm, Hoc Est: De Origine, Progressv, Ceremoniis Et Ritibvs Festorvm Diervm Christianorum Liber vnus*. Tiguri [Zürich]: Wolphius.

How, Frederick Douglas (1908): *Clerical Humour of Olden Time, Being Sketches of Some Clerical Humourists between the Twelfth and the Eighteenth Centuries*. London: Pitman & Sons.

Hughes, Gerard (1998): *In Gottes Lachen einstimmen. Wege zur inneren Freiheit.* Würzburg: Echter.

Hugh of St Victor (1854): 'In Salomonis Ecclesiasten homiliae, Homilia 8', in: Migne: *SL*, vol. 175, col. 164–9.

Hunter, Edward Gordon (1978): *Humor in the Pulpit*, (diss., School of Theology at Claremont).

Hussey, L. M. (1928): 'The Wit of the Carpenter', in: *American Mercury* 5, 329–36.

Hübner, Kurt (1999): 'Meditation über Humor und Christentum', in: *Zeitschrift für Theologie und Kirche* 96, 508–24.

Hvidberg, Flemming Friis (1962): *Weeping and Laughter in the Old Testament. A Study of Canaanite-Israelite Religion* [Danish ed. 1938], ed. by F. Løkkegaard, tr. by Niels Haislund. Leiden: Brill.

Hyers, Merritt Conrad (ed.) (1969a): *Holy Laughter. Essays on Religion in the Comic Perspective.* New York: Seabury.

– (1969b): 'The Comic Profanation of the Sacred', in: *id.* (ed.) (1969a), 9–27.

– (1969c): 'The Dialectic of the Sacred and the Comic', in: *id.* (ed.) (1969a), 208–40.

– (1981): *The Comic Vision and the Christian Faith. A Celebration of Life and Laughter.* New York: Pilgrim. (Repr.: *The Comic Vision. Comic Heroism in a Tragic World.* Wolfeboro: Longwood Academic, 1991. 2nd ed.: *The Spirituality of Comedy. Comic Heroism in a Tragic World.* New Brunswick: Transactions Publishers, 1996.)

– (1982): 'Comedy and Creation', in: *Theology Today* 39, 17–26.

– (1983a): 'Christian Humor. Uses and Abuses of Laughter', in: *Dialog. A Journal of Theology* 22, 198–205.

– (1983b): 'The Comic Vision in a Tragic World', in: *Christian Century* 100, 363–7.

– (1987): *And God Created Laughter. The Bible as Divine Comedy.* Atlanta: John Knox.

Høffding, Harald (1916): *Den store humor. En psykologisk studie.* Copenhagen: Gyldendal.

Ice, Jackson Lee (1973): 'Notes Toward a Theology of Humor', in: *Religion in Life* 42, 388–400.

Innichenhöferus, Heinrich (1629): *Zwo christliche Predigten vom Lachen: Darin[n]en unter andern von neunzehnerley Lachen disseriret u. tractiret wird …*; colligiret durch Henricus Innichenhöferus. Wittenberg: Auerbach.

Isidore of Seville (1830): 'Etymologiarum libri XX', in: Migne: *SL*, vol. 82, col. 9–728.

– (1850): 'Regula Monochorum', in: Migne: *SL*, vol. 83, col. 865–94.

Jacobelli, Maria Caterina (1992): *Ostergelächter. Sexualität und Lust im Raum des Heiligen* [Italian ed. 1991], tr. by Fortunat Sommerfeld. Regensburg: Pustet.

Jacobi, Gerhard (1952): *Langeweile, Musse und Humor und ihre pastoraltheologische Bedeutung*. Berlin: Lettner.

Jacobi, Johann Friedrich (1770): *Vertheidigung der Spiele, Tänze, Schauspiele und anderer irdischen Lustbarkeiten, nebst einer Anweisung, wie man an selbigen ohne Versündigung Antheil nehmen könne*. S.l.: s.n.

Jacobsen, Jacob Peter (1903): *Det komiske dramas oprindelse og udvikling i Frankrig før renaissancen*. Copenhagen: Det Nordiske Forlag.

Jaekel, Siegfried, see: Menander

Jager, Okke (1956): *Die Bibel hat Humor – und wir?* [Dutch ed. 1954], tr. by Irma Silzer. Zürich: Zwingli.

Jahn, Franz (1904): 'Judentum und Christentum', in: *id.*: *Das Problem des Komischen in seiner geschichtlichen Entwicklung*. Potsdam: A. Stein, 9–10.

Jameson, John Gordon (1948): *Why Jesus Died. A Study in the Trial of Jesus and its Antecedents; also, Humour and other Features of the Style of Jesus; The ideal of the Gentleman: Its History and Origin in the Carpenter's Teaching*. Glasgow: Strickland. [1st ed.: *The Bringer of the Good News*, 1926.]

Jansen, François (1929): 'Jésus a-t-il ri?', in: *Nouvelle revue théologicque* 56, 353–72.

Jerome, see: Hieronymus

Joeckel, Samuel (2008): 'Funny as Hell. Christianity and Humor Reconsidered', in: *Humor* 21.4, 415–33.

Jonson, Ben (1927): 'Every Man out of his Humour', in: *Ben Jonson*, ed. by C.H. Herford & Percy Simpson. Oxford: Clarendon, vol. 3, 405–600.

Jonsson, Jakob (1985): *Humour and Irony in the New Testament. Illuminated by Parallels in Talmud and Midrash* [Icelandic ed. 1965]. Leiden: Brill.

Joubert, Laurent (1980): *Treatise on Laughter* ['Traitè du ris, contenant son essence, ses causes et ses merveilheus efeis, curieusement recherchés, raisonnés et observés par M. Laur. Joubert', 1579], tr. by Gregory David de Rocher. University: University of Alabama Press.

Julian of Norwich (1994): *The Shewings of Julian of Norwich* [1373], ed. by Georgia Ronan Crampton. Kalamazoo: Medieval Institute Publications. Online: d.lib.rochester.edu

Jürgens, Heiko (1972): *Pompa diaboli. Die lateinischen Kirchenväter und das antike Theater*. Stuttgart: Kohlhammer.

Jäkel, Ernst Th. (1840): *Leben und wirken Dr. Martin Luthers im Lichte unserer Zeit. Ein Denkbuck für die ganze Christenheit*, vol. 1. Chemnitz: Robert Binder.

Jäkel, Siegfried & Asko Timonen (eds.) (1994–5): *Laughter Down the Centuries*, I-II. Turku: Turun Yliopisto.

Jäkel, Siegfried; Asko Timonen, & Veli-Matti Rissanen (eds.) (1997): *Laughter Down the Centuries*, III. Turku: Turun Yliopisto.

Jørgensen, Ninna (1988): *Bauer, Narr und Pfaffe. Prototypische Figuren und ihre Funktion in der Reformationsliteratur*. Leiden: Brill.

Kant, Immanuel (2015): *Critique of Practical Reason* [German ed. 1788], tr. & ed. by Mary Gregor, with a rev. introduction by Andrews Reath. Cambridge: Cambridge University Press.

Keller, Hildegard Elisabeth (2005): 'Lachen und Lachresistenz. Noahs Söhne in der Genesisepik, der "Biblia Pauperum" und dem "Donaueschinger Passionsspiel"', in: Werner Röcke & Hans Rudolf Velten (eds.) (2005), 33–59.

Kemper, Tobias A. (2005): '"Iesus Christus risus noster". Bemerkungen zur Bewertung des Lachen im Mittelalter', in: Anja Grebe & Nikolaus Staubach (eds.) (2005), 16–31.

Kerr, Walter (1967): *Tragedy and Comedy*. New York: Simon and Schuster.

Kesselring, Ernst Friedrich [& Gottfried Wegner] (1705): *Disputatio Historico-Theologico-Homiletica, De Risu Paschali, Oratorem Sacrum, Eiusq. Auditorem Minime Decente*. Regiomonti [Königsberg]: Reusner.

Kessler, Andreas (1994): 'Tertullian und das Vergnügen in "De Spectaculis"', in: *Freiburger Zeitschrift für Philosophie und Theologie* 41, 313–53.

Kessler, Johannes (1866): *Johannes Kesslers Sabbata. Chronik der Jahre 1523–1539, Erster Theil: 1523–1525*, ed. by Ernst Götzinger. St. Gallen: Scheitlin & Zollikofer.

- 1902: *Johannes Kesslers Sabbata mit kleineren Schriften und Briefen*, unter Mitwirkung v. Emil Egli, R. Schoch; publ. by Historischen Verein des Kantons St. Gallen. St. Gallen: Fehr.

Kierkegaard, Søren Aabye (1997): 'Om Begrebet Ironi' [1841], in: Niels Jørgen Cappelørn, *et al.* (eds.): *Søren Kierkegaards Skrifter*. Copenhagen: Gads Forlag, 1997–2012, vol. 1, 1997.

– (2020): 'At the cemetery' [Paper 442, 1845], in: *Kierkegaard's Journals and Notebooks*, vol. 11, Part 2: *Loose Papers, 1843–1855*, ed. by Niels Jørgen Cappelørn, *et al*. Princeton: Princeton University Press, 236.

Kittelson, James M. (1975): *Wolfgang Capito. From Humanist to Reformer.* Leiden: E.J. Brill.

Knapp, Shepherd (1907): 'Traces of Humor in the Sayings of Jesus', in: *Biblical World*, n.s. 29, 201–7.

Knigge, Adolph Freiherr von (1936): *Über den Umgang mit Menschen* [1788]. Berlin: Deutsche Bibliothek.

Koch, Hal (1963): *Kristendommens oprindelse.* Copenhagen: Gyldendal.

Kohler, Gun-Britt (2012): 'Karneval und kultureller Raum. Überlegungen zu Bachtins Konzept des Lachens', in: Biessenecker & Kuhn (eds.) (2012), 29–52.

Kolakowski, Leszek (1962): 'The Priest and the Jester', in: *Dissent. A Quarterly of Socialist Opinion* 9, 215–35.

Kolve, Verdel Amos (1966): 'Religious Laughter' & 'The Invention of Comic Action', in: *id.: The Play Called Corpus Christi.* Stanford: Stanford University Press, 124–44 & 145–74.

Kranz, Gisbert (1969): 'Das Lachen der Heiligen', in: *Geist und Leben. Zeitschrift für Aszese und Mystik* 42, 408–14.

– (1970): *Das göttliche Lachen.* Wurzburg: Echter.

– (1978): *Schmunzelkatechismus. Eine heitere Theologie.* München: Pfeiffer.

– (1979): *Was Menschen gern tun. Essen und Trinken, Singen, Lachen, Dichten und Denken, Lieben und Erkennen.* München: Kösel.

– (1989): *Menschsein im Freude. Vom Singen, Lachen, Essen und Trinken.* Freiburg i. Br.: Herder.

Krause, Michael Ehrenfried, see: Tobias Starcke

Kremer, Karl Richard (1961): *Das Lachen in der deutschen Sprache und Literatur des Mittelalters*, (diss., Bonn: Rheinischen Friedrich Wilhelms Universität).

Kretz, Louis (1982): *Witz, Humor und Ironie bei Jesus* [1981]. Olten & Freiburg i. Br.: Walter.

Krug, Wilhelm Traugott (1833): 'Humor', 'Komische, das' & 'Lachen, lächeln, lächerlich', in: *Allgemeines Handwörterbuch der philosophischen Wissenschaften nebst ihrer Literatur und Geschichte nach dem heutigen Standpuncte der Wissenschaft.* 2. verbesserte und vermehrte Auflage. Leipzig: Brockhaus, 1832–38, vol. 2, 469–71; 628–30, & 670–3.

Kuhr, Olaf (1999): *'Die Macht des Bannes und der Busse'. Kirchenzucht und Erneuerung der Kirche bei Johannes Oekolampad (1482–1531).* Bern: Peter Lang.

Kullmann, Wolfgang (1995): 'Die Antiken Philosophen und das Lachen', in: Jäkel & Timonen (eds.) (1994–5), vol. 2, 79–98.

Kundera, Milan (1999): *The Unbearable Lightness of Being* [Czech ed. 1984], tr. by Michael Henry Heim. London: Faber & Faber.

Kuschel, Karl-Josef (1992): ' "Christus hat nie gelacht"? Überlegungen zu einer Theologie des Lachens', in: Thomas Vogel (ed.) (1992): *Vom Lachen. Einem Phänomen auf der Spur*. Tübingen: Attempto, 106–28.

– (1994): *Laughter. A Theological Reflection* [German ed. 1994], tr. by John Bowden. New York: Continuum.

Köhler, Wiebke (2000): 'Humor', in: Hans Dieter Betz, *et al.* (eds.) (1998–2007): *Die Religion in Geschichte und Gegenwart*, 4th ed. Tübingen: Mohr Siebeck, vol. 3, col. 1957.

Köhnen, Ralph N. (2012): 'Das Lachen in den Gesichtern der Litteratur – Mittelalter und Humanismus', in: Wilhelmy (ed.) (2012a), 57–67.

Labbé, Philippe & Gabriel Cossart (eds.) (1732): *Sacrosancta Concilia Ad Regiam Editionem Exacta: Ab Anno MCDXXXVIII. ad Annum MDIL*. Venice: Coleti & Albrizzi, vol. 19.

Laertius, Diogenes (1925): *Lives of Eminent Philosophers* ['Vitae philosophorum'], I-II, tr. by R.D. Hicks. Cambridge: Harvard University Press.

Lambin, Helen Reichert (1991): *In the Beginning. A Humorous Survey of the Bible*. Chicago: ACTA.

Landgraf, Artur (1940): 'Die Einschätzung der Scherzlüge in der Frühscholastik', in: *Theologisch-Praktische Quartalsschrift* 93, 128–36.

Landy, Francis (1990): 'Humour as a Tool for Biblical Exegesis' [1980], in: Radday & Brenner (eds.) (1990), 99–116.

Lang, Dov B. (1962): 'On the Biblical Comic', in: *Judaism* 11, 249–54.

Lanyon, Walter Clemow (1932): 'The Laughter of God', in: *id.*: *The Laughter of God*. London: L.N. Fowler, 9–19.

Lapide, Pinchas (1982): 'Humor in die Bibel', in: *id.*: *Mit einem Juden die Bibel lesen*. Stuttgart: Calwer, 173–87.

Lappenberg, Johann Martin (ed.) (1854): 'Von einigen späteren, dem Ulenspiegel verwandten Büchern. 1. Johannes Pauli, Schimpff und Ernst', in: *id.*: *Dr. Thomas Murners Ulenspiegel*. Leipzig: Weigel, 363–80.

Latte, Kurt (1953): *Hesychii Alexandrini Lexicon*, vol. 1. Copenhagen: Munksgaard.

Lauer, Werner (1974): 'Christliche Weltanschauung und Humor' & 'Humor und christliches Ethos', in: *id.*: *Humor als Ethos. Eine moralpsychologische Untersuchung*. Bern, Stuttgart & Wien: Hans Huber, 298–331 & 344–79.

Layman, Fred. D. (1982–3): 'Theology and Humor', in: *Asbury Seminarian* 38, 3–25.

Le Brun, Jacques (1997): ' "Jesus-Christ n'a jamais ri". Analyse d'un raisonnement theologique', in: *Homo religiosus. Autour de Jean Delumeau*. Paris: Fayard, 431–7.

Le Goff, Jacques (1984): *The Birth of Purgatory* [French ed. 1981], tr. by Arthur Goldhammer. London: Scholar Press.

– (1990): 'Le rire dans les règles monastiques du haut moyen âge', in: Michel Sot (ed.): *Haut Moyen Age. Éducation et Société. Études offertes à Pierre Riché*. Paris: Publidix, 93–103.

– (1992): 'Jésus a-t-il ri?', in: *L'historie* 158, 72–4.

– (1997): 'Laughter in the Middle Ages', in: Bremmer & Roodenburg (eds.) (1997a), 40–53.

– (2008³): *Das Lachen im Mittelalter* [2004¹], with an afterword by Rolf Michael Schneider, tr. by Jochen Grube. Stuttgart: Klett-Cotta.

Leclercq, Jean (1982): 'Humour', in: Gordon Stevens Wakefield (ed.): *A Dictionary of Christian Spirituality*. London: SCM, 201–2.

Lehmann, Paul (1922): *Die Parodie im Mittelalter*. München: Drei Masken.

Lentulus (1913): 'Brief des Lentulus an Kaiser Tiberius', in: Johannes B. Aufhauser: *Antike Jesus-Zeugnisse. Kleine Texte für Vorlesungen und Übungen*, ed. by Hans Lietzmann, vol. 126. Bonn: Marcus und Weber, 37.

- 1984: R. Joseph Hoffmann: *Jesus Outside the Gospels*. Buffolo: Prometheus Books.

Levack, John G. (1997): *Serve Him with Mirth*. Wormit: Manivelle.

Lexutt, Athina (2016): 'Humor and Wit: III. Christianity', in: Sebastian Fuhrmann & Frauke Uhlenbruch (eds.): *Encyclopedia of the Bible and Its Reception*. Berlin & Boston: de Gruyter, vol. 12, col. 575–6.

Lichtenberg, Georg Christoph (1787): 'Christliches Ostergelächter', in: *Göttinger Taschen Kalender* 1787, 151–2; repr. in: *id.*: *Vermischte Schriften*, vol. 6. Göttingen: Dieterich, 1845, 382–3.

Lichtenberger, Hermann (2017): 'Da lachen ja die Engel! Humor im Neuen Testament', in: Dober (ed.) (2017a), 95–112.

Lienhard, Fritz & Manfred Oeming (eds.) (2023): *Das Heilige und das Lachen. Humor und Spiritualität*. Leipzig: Evangelische Verlagsanstalt.

Lienhard, Fritz (2023): 'Lachen in der kirchlichen Praxis', in: *id.* & Oeming (eds.) (2023), 237–56.

Lienhard, Marc (2023): 'Die existentielle und theologische Bedeutung des Lachens bei Martin Luther', in: F. Lienhard & Oeming (eds.) (2023), 133–42.

Lindars, Frederick Chevallier (1982): 'The Irony of Jesus', in: Porter (ed.) (1982), 3–7.

Lindgren, Lauri (1995): 'Ein Beispiel des volkstümlichen Humors im Mittelalter: Der Priester in den altfranzösischen "Fabliaux"', in: Jäkel & Timonen (eds.) (1994–5), vol. 2, 185–91.

Linsenmayer, Anton (1969): *Geschichte der Predigt in Deutschland von Karl dem Grossen bis zum Ausgange des vierzehnten Jahrhunderts* [1886]. Unveränderter Nachdruck. Frankfurt a. M.: Minerva.

Lippert, Julius (1882): 'Osterzeit und Osterbräuche', in: *id.*: *Christenthum, Volksglaube und Volksgebrauch. Geschichtliche Entwicklung ihres Vorstellungsinhaltes* (vol. 1: 'Das Christenthum in seiner Verwandschaft mit den vorchristlichen Cultvorstellungen'; vol. 2: 'Unser Volksglaube und Volksbrauch. Ihr Vorstellungsinhalt und dessen Sinn und Geschichte'). Berlin: Theodor Hofmann, 601–19.

Littré, Émile (1863–72): *Dictionnaire de la langue française*. Paris: Hachette.

Lock, Charles (1991): 'Carnival and Incarnation. Bakhtin and Orthodox Theology', in: *Literature and Theology* 5, 68–82.

Lodge, David (1981): *How Far Can You Go?* [1980]. London: Penguin.

Logan, J. D. (1909): 'Comedy and Humour in the Bible', in: *Canadian Magazine of Politics, Science, Art and Literature* 34, 17–24.

Lohmeier, Georg (ed.) (1967): *Geistliches Donnerwetter. Bayerische Barockpredigten*. München: Deutscher Taschenbuch Verlag.

– (1972): *Ostergelächter und Pfingstochsen. Bayrisches für Christenmenschen*. München: Ehrenwirth.

Lot-Borodine, Myrrha (1939): 'Das Mysterium "der Tränengabe" im christlichen Osten' [1936], tr. by P. Basilius Steidle, in: *Benediktinische Monatschrift zur Pflege religiösen und geistigen Lebens* 21, 236–48.

Lotz, Johannes Baptist (1983): *Lachen ist eine Gabe Gottes. Von der Tugend des Humors*. Freiburg i. Br.: Herder.

Lowth, Robert (1753): *De sacra poesi Hebraeorum praelectionis academicae*. Oxford: Clarendon.

- 1787: *Lectures on the Sacred Poetry of the Hebrews*, I-II, tr. by G. Gregory, to which are added the principal notes of professor Michaelis, and notes by the translator and others. London: Johnson.

Luck, Georg (1958): 'Vir facetus. A Renaissance ideal', in: *Studies in Philology* 55, 107–21.
- (1994): 'Humor', in: Theodor Klauser (ed.) (1950 ff.): *Reallexikon für Antike und Christentum. Sachwörterbuch zur Auseinandersetzung des Christentums mit der antiken Welt*, in Verbindung mit Franz Joseph Dölger und Hans Lietzmann und unter besonderer Mitwirkung v. Jan Hendrik Waszink und Leopold Wenger. Stuttgart: Anton Hiersemann, vol. 16, col. 753–73.

Lühl, Max (2019): *Lachen als anthropologisches Phänomen. Theologische Perspektiven*. Berlin: de Gruyter.

Luke, Helen M. (1987): 'Laughter at the Heart of Things', in: *Parabola. Myth and the Quest for Meaning* 12.4, 6–17.

Luther, Martin (1519): 'Auslegung deutsch des Vater unser fuer dye einfeltigen leyen', in: *D. Martin Luthers Werke* (*Weimarer Ausgabe* = *WA*), vol 2, 81–130.
- 1969: 'An Exposition of the Lord's Prayer for Simple Laymen', in: *Luther's Works*, vol. 42, ed. by Martin O. Dietrich. Saint Louis: Concordia Publishing House, 15–81.
- (1523a): 'Von Ordenung Gottis Dients ynn der Gemeyne', in: *WA*, vol. 12, 35–41.
- 1997a: 'Concerning the Ordering of Divine Worship in the Congregation', in: *Works of Martin Luther*, vol. 6: *Luther's Liturgical Writings*, tr. by P.Z. Strodach. Albany: Books for the Ages, 47–50.
- (1523b): 'Taufbüchlein 1523', in: *WA*, vol. 12, 42–6.
- 1997b: 'The Order of Baptism Translated into German', in: *Works of Martin Luther*, vol. 6: *Luther's Liturgical Writings*, tr. by P.Z. Strodach. Albany: Books for the Ages, 142–6.
- (1525): 'Epistel am Sonntag Oculi. Eph. 5,1–10. Am dritten Sontage ynn der fasten Epistel. Zum Ephesern am 5.' (from: 'Fastenpostille' [1525]), in: *WA*, vol. 17.2, 205–13.
- 1997b: 'Third Sunday in Lent. Exhortation to be Imitators of God. Ephesians 5:1–9', in: *Sermons of Martin Luther*, vol. 7: *Sermons on the Epistle Texts for Epiphany, Easter & Pentecost*, ed. & tr. by John Nicholas Lenker. Albany: Books for the Ages.
- (1526): 'Taufbüchlein 1526', in: *WA*, vol. 19, 537–41.
- 1997c: 'The Order of Baptism Newly Revised', in: *Works of Martin Luther*, vol. 6: *Luther's Liturgical Writings*, tr. by P.Z. Strodach. Albany: Books for the Ages, 150–2.
- (1527): 'Vorlesung über die Briefe an Titus und Philemon', in: *WA*, vol. 25, 1–78.

- 1968: 'Lectures on Titus', in: *Luther's Works*, vol. 29, ed. and tr. by Jaroslav Pelikan. Saint Louis: Concordia Publishing House, 3–90.
- (1530a): 'Brief no. 1670, Juli? 1530 an Hieronymus Weller', in: *WA Briefe*, vol. 5, 518–19.
- 1911: *The Life and Letters of Martin Luther*, by Preserved Smith. Boston: Houghton Mifflin Co.
- (1530b): 'Reihenpredigten über Johannes 6–8 1530/32, Die zwölffte Predigtt, 1530', in: *WA*, vol. 33, 151–66.
- 1959: 'Sermons on the Gospel of St. John Chapters 6–8, The Twelfth Sermon', in: *Luther's Works*, vol. 23, ed. by Jaroslav Pelikan & Daniel E. Poellot, tr. by Martin H. Bertram. Saint Louis: Concordia Publishing House, 99–109.
- (1531-3): 'Tischreden, Veit Dietrichs Nachschriften', in:*WA TR*, vol 1, 1912, 3–308.
- 1967: 'Table Talk', in: *Luther's Works*, vol. 54, ed. and tr. by Theodore G. Tappert. Philadelphia: Fortress.

Lutz, Markus (1814): *Geschichte des Ursprungs und der Entwicklung der kirchlichen Reformation zu Basel, im Anfange des sechszehnten Jahrhunderts*. Basel: Schweighauser.

Lyons, Maurice (1990): *Encyclopedia of Biblical Humor*. New York: Shapolsky.

Lys, Daniel (2004): 'Quand dieu rit', in: *Études théologiques et religieuses* 79, 201–26.

Läuffer, Hermann (ed.) (1990): *Der Spass ist ein Meister aus Deutschland. Geschichte der guten Laune 1933–1990*. Köln: Scherrer & Schmidt.

Løgstrup, Knud Ejler (1995): 'Excerpts from "Creation and Annihilation"' [Danish ed. 1978], in: *Metaphysics*, vol. 1, tr. & with an introduction by Russell L. Dees. Milwaukee: Marquette University Press.

Macrobius, Ambrosius Aurelius Theodosius (2011): *Saturnalia*, ed. and tr. by Robert A. Kaster. Cambridge: Harvard University Press.

McKinley, Phillip B. (1976): *Guidelines for the Use of Humor by the Parish Minister*, (diss., San Francisco Theological Seminary).

McLelland, Joseph C. (1967): 'Comedy – Human and Divine', in: George Johnston & Wolfgang Roth (eds.): *The Church in the Modern World. Essays in Honor of James Sutherland Thomson*. Toronto: Ryerson, 273–87.

McNeill, John T. (1967): *The History and Character of Calvinism* [1954[1]]. Oxford: Oxford University Press.

Mallalieu, Willard Francis (1907): 'Amusements', in: *Methodist Review* 89, 869–81.

Mangoldt, Ursula von (1958): *Buddha lächelt – Maria weint. Die zwei Weisen des Heils*. München: Otto Wilhelm Barth.

Manuel, Frank Edward & David A. Palin (1999): 'Deism', in: *Encyclopædia Britannica Online*, britannica.com/topic/Deism

Martensen, Hans (1888): 'God's Kingdom and the World. Optimism und Pessimism', in: *id.*: *The Christian Ethics (General Part)* [Danish ed. 1871], tr. by C. Spence. Edinburgh: T.&T. Clark, 164–91.

Marti, Kurt (1987): 'Das Geheimnis des göttlichen Lachens', in: *id.*: *Lachen – Weinen – Lieben. Ermutigungen zum Leben* [1985]. Stuttgart: Radius, 17–24.

Martial, Marcus Valerius (1950): *Epigrams*, I-II, tr. by Walter C.A. Ker. Cambridge & London: Harvard University Press & Heinemann.

Martin, Gerhard Marcel (1996): 'Zur Idee einer Theologie des Lachens', in: Carmen Krieg, *et al.* (eds.): *Die Theologie auf dem Weg in das dritte Jahrtausend. Festschrift für Jürgen Moltmann zum 70. Geburtstag*. Gütersloh: Chr. Kaiser & Gütersloher, 376–88.

Martin, Robert Bernard (1974): *The Triumph of Wit. A Study of Victorian Comic Theory*. London: Clarendon.

Mathesius, Johannes (1566): *Historien, Von des Ehrwirdigen in Gott Seligen thewren Manns Gottes Doctoris Martini Luthers, anfang, lehr, leben und sterben. Alles ordentlich der Jarzal nach wie sich alle sachen zu jeder zeyt haben zugetragen*. Nürnberg: s.n.

- 2018: 'History of the Origins, Doctrine, Life, and Death of the Reverend, Blessed, Precious Man of God, Dr. Martin Luther (1566)', tr. by Kevin G. Walker, in: *Sixteenth-century biographies of Martin Luther* (Companion Volume to *Luther's Works*). Saint Louis: Concordia Publishing House, 103–612.

Matthiae, Gisela (2023): '"Ernst – nicht zu ernst." Humor und Glaube in der Praxis einer Clownin', in: F. Lienhard & Oeming (eds.) (2023), 275–99.

Mayhew, Henry (1864): *German Life and Manners as Seen in Saxony at the Present Day*, vol. 2. London: Wm. H. Allen.

Meier, Ernst Julius (1876): *Humor und Christentum, mit besonderen Beziehung auf den Katholizismus und den deutschen Protestantismus. Vortrag am 3. März 1875 gehalten*. Leipzig: Teubner.

Meineke, August, see: Menander

Melander, Otto (1617): *Ioco-Seria: Das ist Schimpff und Ernst: Darinn nicht allein nützliche un[d] denckwürdige sondern auch anmütige und lustige Historien erzehlet und beschrieben werden*, I-II. Darmstadt: Berner.

Mellone, Sydney Herbert (1947-8): 'The Laughter of God', in: *Hibbert Journal* 46, 37-40.

Menander: Μενάνδρου Γνῶμαι Μονόστιχοι, *Menandri Sententiae*:
- August Meineke: *Fragmenta comicorum Graecorum*, Editio minor, vol. 2. Berlin: Reimer, 1847.
- Siegfried Jaekel: *Comparatio Menandri et Philistionis*. Leipzig: Teubner, 1964.

Mercer, J. E. (1910-1): 'The Theology of Laughter', in: *Hibbert Journal* 9, 296-306.

Metz, Detlef (2013): *Das protestantische Drama. Evangelisches geistliches Theater in der Reformationszeit und im konfessionellen Zeitalter*. Köln, Weimar & Wien: Böhlau.

Metz, Johann Baptist & Jean-Pierre Jossua (eds.) (1974): *Theology of Joy*. New York: Herder and Herder.

Metz, Johann Baptist (1974): 'Editorial: Joy and Grief, Cheerfulness, Melancholy and Humour or "The Difficulty of Saying Yes"', in: Metz & Jossua (eds.) (1974), 7-12.

Meyer, Marvin W., see: 'Apocalypse of Peter'

Migne, Jacques-Paul: *Patrologiae Cursus Completus, Series Latina*, vol. 1-221. Paris, 1844-65. [*SL*]

– : *Patrologiae Cursus Completus, Series Graeca*, vol. 1-161. Paris, 1857-66. [*SG*]

Miller, Ed L. (1982): 'Oecolampadius. The Unsung Hero of the Basel Reformation', in: *Iliff Review*, 39.3, 5-25.

Miller, Henry K. (1983): 'Some Relationships between Humor and Religion in Eighteenth-Century Britain', in: M.-L. Davies (ed.) (1983), 48-59.

Milton, John (1998): *Paradise Lost*, ed. by Alastair Fowler. Harlow: Pearson Education.

Modesto, Christine (1992): *Studien zur* Cena Cypriani *und zu deren Rezeption*. Tübingen: Gunter Narr.

Mogabgab, John S. (ed.) (1994): 'Hilarity. Cheerfulness and Humor in Christian Spiritual Life', in: *Weavings* 9, 2-48.

Moltmann, Jürgen (1971): *Die ersten Freigelassenen der Schöpfung. Versuch über Freude an der Freiheit und das Wohlgefallen am Spiel*. München: Kaiser.

– (1996): *The Coming of God. Christian Eschatology* [German ed. 1995], tr. by Margaret Kohl. Minneapolis: Fortress.

Morgan, Conwy Lloyd (1914): 'Laughter', in: James Hastings (ed.) (1908-21): *Encyclopedia of Religion and Ethics*. Edinburgh: T. & T. Clark, vol. 7, 803-5.

Morison, David Niven (1931): *The Humour of Christ*. Newcastle, New South Wales: Davies & Cannington.

Morreall, John (1983): *Taking Laughter Seriously*. Albany: State University of New York Press.

– (ed.) (1987): *The Philosophy of Laughter and Humor*. Albany: State University of New York Press.

– (1989): 'The Rejection of Humor in Western Thought', in: *Philosophy East and West. A Quarterly Journal of Oriental and Comparative Thought* 39.3, 243–66.

– (1999): *Comedy, Tragedy, and Religion*. Albany: State University of New York Press.

– (2009): *Comic Relief. A Comprehensive Philosophy of Humor*. Chichester: Wiley-Blackwell.

Moser, Dietz-Rüdiger (1986): *Fastnacht – Fasching – Karneval. Das Fest der 'Verkehrten Welt'*. Graz: Edition Kaleidoskop.

– (1990): 'Lachkultur des Mittelalters? Michael Bachtin und die Folgen seiner Theorie', in: *Euphorion. Zeitschrift für Literaturgeschichte* 84, 89–111.

– (1993): *Bräuche und Feste im christlichen Jahreslauf. Brauchformen der Gegenwart in kulturgeschichtlichen Zusammenhängen*. Graz: Styria.

Moser-Rath, Elfriede (1964): *Predigtmärlein der Barockzeit. Exempel, Sage, Schwank und Fabel in geistlichen Quellen des oberdeutschen Raumes*. Berlin: de Gruyter.

– (1991): *Dem Kirchenvolk die Leviten gelesen. Alltag im Spiegel süddeutscher Barockpredigten*. Stuttgart: J. B. Metzler.

Mueller, William Randolph (1967): 'God's Fools. Biblical and Modern', in: *Theology Today* 23, 538–50.

Mullen, Thomas James (1983): *Laughing out Loud and Other Religious Experiences*. Waco: Word Books.

Mullen, Wilbur H. (1973): 'Toward a Theology of Humor', in: *Christian Scholar's Review* 3, 3–12.

Munier, Charles, see: *Statuta Ecclesiae Antiqua*

Murray, Donald (1993): 'Humour in the Bible?', in: Keith Cameron (ed.): *Humour and History*. Oxford: Intellect Books, 21–40.

Murray, James Ross (1908): 'Laughter', in: James Hastings (ed.): *A Dictionary of Christ and the Gospels*. Edinburgh: T. & T. Clark, 1908, vol. 2, 9–11.

Müller, Gerhard (ed.) (1977–2010): *Theologische Realenzyklopädie*. Berlin & New York: de Gruyter.

Müller, Monica E. (2012): ' "Das Lachen ist dem Menschen eigen …" – seine Darstellung in der Kunst des Mittelalters', in: Wilhelmy (ed.) (2012a), 68–91.

Müller-Gangloff, Erich (ed.) (1957–8): 'Fastnacht', in: *Quatember. Evangelische Jahresbriefe* 22, 65–128.

März, F. (1970): 'Humor', in: Heinrich Rombach (ed.) (1970): *Lexikon der Pädagogik, Neue Ausgabe in Vier Bänden*. Freiburg i. Br.: Herder, vol. 2, 262.

Möllendorff, Peter von (1995): *Grundlagen einer Ästhetik der Alten Komödie. Untersuchungen zu Aristophanes und Michail Bachtin*. Tübingen: Gunter Narr.

Neale, Robert Edward (1971): 'Surprise: The Horrible, the Humorous, and the Holy', in: George Divine (ed.): *New Dimensions in Religious Experience*. Staten Island: Alba House, 27–38.

Nettelbladt, Christian (1734): *Ritus ac ceremonias, quibus paschatos festum celebravere veteres Christiani*. Gryphiswaldia [Greifswald]: Höpfner.

Nicene and Post-Nicene Fathers of the Christian Church, A Select Library of the. Ed. by Philip Schaff ... in connection with a number of patristic scholars of Europe and America, vol. 1–14. New York: Scribner, 1886–90.

– Second series. Translated into English with prolegomena and explanatory notes, under the editorial supervision of Philip Schaff and Henry Wace, vol. 1–14. New York: The Christian Literature Company, 1890–1900.

Nick, Friedrich (1861): 'Osterpossen', in: *id.: Die Hof- und Volksnarren, sammt den närrischen Lustbarkeiten der verschieden Stände aller Völker und Zeiten. Aus Flögels Schriften und andern Quellen*, vol. 2: *Närrische Lustbarkeiten, weltlich und geistlich. Das Komische und Groteskkomische in Schaudarstellungen verschiedener Zeiten und Nationen, Narren- und Eselsfeste, närrische Lustbarkeiten und lustige Possen, Gecken- und Narrenorden, auch andere komische, weltliche und kirchliche Belustigungen, Curiositäten u.s.w.* Stuttgart: J. Scheible, 474–8.

Nickel, Johanna (1945): 'Das Ostergelächter', in: *id.: Österliches Brauchtum in der deutschen Barockforschung*, (diss., Berlin, 102–6).

Nicoll, Allardyce (1962): *The Theatre and Dramatic Theory*. London: George G. Harrap.

– (1963): *Masks, Mimes, and Miracles. Studies in Popular Theatre* [1931]. New York: Cooper Square.

Nicolson, Harold George (1956): 'The English Sense of Humour' [1946], in: *id.: The English Sense of Humour and other Essays*. London: Constable, 3–59.

Niebuhr, Reinhold (1946): 'Humour and Faith', in: *id.: Discerning the Signs of the Times. Sermons for To-day and To-morrow*. London: SCM, 99–115.

Niedermeier, Hans (1970): 'Wiener Volksleben im 15. Jahrhundert nach den Predigten von Johann Geus', in: *Österreichische Zeitschrift für Volkskunde* 73, 220–8.

– (1972): 'Eine altbayerische Osterpredigt [Röhrmoos, 1643]', in: *Amberland* 1, 269.

Nieting, Lorenz (1983): 'Humor in the New Testament', in: *Dialog. A Journal of Theology* 22, 168–70.

O'Connell, Michael (2002): 'Mockery, Farce, and "Risus Paschalis" in the York "Christ before Herod"', in: Wim Hüsken, Konrad Schoell, & Leif Søndergaard (eds.): *Farce and Farcical Elements*. Amsterdam: Editions Rodopi, 45–58.

Oden, Thomas C. (ed.) (2010): *Incomplete Commentary on Matthew (Opus Imperfectum)*, vol. 2, tr. by James A. Kellerman. Downers Grove: InterVarsity.

Oecolampadius, Joannes (1518): *De Risv Paschalie, Oecolampadii, ad V. Capitonem theologum epistola apologetica*. Basel: Froben.

- 1927a: '"De risu paschali", Brief an Wolfgang Fabricius Capito, 18. März 1518', in: Staehelin (1927/34), vol. 1, 44–59.

– (1927b): 'Oekolampad predigt "De vero gaudie in die Paschae", Weinsberg, Ostern 4 April 1518?' [1516/17?], in: Staehelin (1927/34), vol. 1, 59–64.

Ogilvy, Jack David Angus (1963): '"Mimi", "Scurrae", "Histriones": Entertainers of the Early Middle Ages', in: *Speculum. A Journal of Mediaeval Studies* 38, 603–19.

Oliver, Edward James (1960): *Hypocrisy and Humor*. New York: Sheed & Ward.

Overbeck, Franz (1963): 'Geistlicher Witz', in: *id.: Christentum und Kultur. Gedanken und Anmerkungen zur modernen Theologie* [1919], aus dem Nachlass ed. by Carl Albrecht Bernoulli. Darmstadt: Wissenschaftliche Buchgesellschaft, 91–4.

Ovid, Publius Naso (1889): *The Metamorphoses*, tr. by Henry T. Riley. London: George Bell & Sons.

Pachomius (1981): 'The Rules of Saint Pachomius', in: *id.: Pachomian koinonia. The Lives, Rules, and Other Writings of Saint Pachomius and His Disciples*. vol. 2: 'Pachomian Chronicles and Rules', tr. with an introduction by Arman Veilleux. Kalamazoo: Cistercian Publications, 141–95.

Palmer, Earl F. (1987): *Laughter in Heaven and Other Surprising Truths in the Parables of Jesus*. Waco: Word Books.

Palmer, Jerry (1994): *Taking Humor Seriously*. London: Routledge.

Parrott, Bob W. (1978): 'Ontology of Humor. A Basis for Biblical Exegesis', in: *Perkins Journal* 32, 14–34.

– (1982): *Ontology of Humor*. New York: Philosophical Library.

– (1983): *God's Sense of Humor – where? – when? – how?* New York: Philosophical Library.

Patrides, Constantinos Apostolos (1983-4): 'The Biblical Comic', in: *University of Toronto Quarterly* 53, 72-84.

Paul, Jean (1817): *Politische Fastenpredigten während Deutschlands Marterwoche*. Stuttgart: Cotta.

Paul VI, Pope (1976): *Gaudete in Domino. Apostolic Exhortation of His Holiness Paul VI on Christian Joy, 9 May,1975*. Online at vatican.va

Pauli, Johannes (1522): *Schimpf und Ernst: heiset das Buch mit Namen durchlaufft es der Welt handlung mit ernstlichen und kurtzweiligen Exemplen, Parabolen und Hystorien, nützlich und gut zu Besserung der Menschen*. Strassburg: Grieninger.

- 1866: *Schimpf und Ernst*, ed. by Hermann Österley. Stuttgart: Litterarischer Verein. (Repr.: Amsterdam: Rodopi, 1967.)
- 1924: *Schimpf und Ernst, Zweiter Teil: Paulis Fortsetzer und Übersetzer. Erläuterungen*, ed. by Johannes Bolte. Berlin: Stubenrauch.

Paulsen, Friedrich (1900): 'Das Ironische in Jesu Stellung und Rede', in: *id.*: *Schopenhauer. Hamlet. Mephistopheles. Drei Aufsätze zur Naturgeschichte des Pessimismus*. Berlin: Hertz, 237-59.

Perkins, William (2013): 'A Direction for the Government of the Tongue according to Gods worde' [1595], in: Nathalie Vienne-Guerrin (ed.): *The Unruly Tongue in Early Modern England. Three Treatises*. Madison & Teaneck: Fairleigh Dickinson University Press, 41-70.

Petersen, Christoph (2004): *Ritual und Theater. Messallegorese, Osterfeier und Osterspiel im Mittelalter*. Tübingen: M. Niemeyer.

Pfister, Manfred (ed.) (2002): *A History of English Laughter. Laughter from Beowulf to Beckett and Beyond*. Amsterdam: Rodopi.

- (2006): '"An Argument of Laughter". Cultures of Laughter and the Theater in Early Modern England', in: Christa Jansohn (ed.): *German Shakespeare Studies at the Turn of the Twenty-First Century*. Newark: University of Delaware Press, 42-67.

Philo of Alexandria (1960): 'On Rewards and Punishments' ['De praemiis et poenis'], in: *Philo*, tr. by F.H. Colson. Cambridge & London: Harvard University Press & Heinemann, vol. 8, 309-423.

- (1994): 'The Worse attacks the Better' ['Quod Deterius Potiori insidiari solet'], in: *Philo*, tr. by F.H. Colson & G.H. Whitaker. Cambridge & London: Harvard University Press, vol. 2, 202-319.

Phipps, William E. (1979): 'Ancient Attitudes toward Laughter', in: *Journal. Western Virginia Philosophical Society* 16, 15-16.

Pius V, Pope (1947): 'Cum primum apostolatus, 1 April 1566', in: *Codicis Iuris Canonici Fontes*, cura Empi Petri Card. Gasparri editi, vol 1. 'Concilia Generalia, Romani Pontificies usque ad annum 1745'. Romae: Typis polyglottis Vaticanis.

Plato (1937): *The Republic*, I-II, tr. by Paul Shorey. Cambridge: Harvard University Press.

Pliny the Elder (1855): *The Natural History*, tr., with copious notes and illustrations, by the late John Bostock and H.T. Riley. London: H.G. Bohn.

Pliny the Younger (1952): *Pliny. Letters*, I-II, tr. by William Memmoth. Cambridge & London: Harvard University Press & Heinemann.

Plutarch (1928): Περὶ δεισιδαιμονίας ['De superstitione'], in: *id.*: *Moralia*, vol. 2, tr. by Frank Cole Babbitt London: Heinemann.

– (1967): *Plutarch's Lives* ['Vitae parallelae'], I-XI, tr. by Bernadotte Perrin. London: Heinemann.

Poggio, see: Gian [/Giovanni] Francesco Poggio Bracciolini

Poole, William Frederick & William I. Fletcher (1957): *Poole's Index to Periodical Literature, The First Supplement from January 1 1882 to January 1 1887* [1888], with the Cooperation of the American Library Association. Gloucester: Peter Smith.

Porter, B. M. (ed.) (1982): 'Humor', in: *St. Mark's Review* 110, 1–29.

Postman, Neil (1986): *Amusing Ourselves to Death. Public Discourse in the Age of Show Business* [1985]. London: Heinemann.

Potthoff, Harvey (1980): 'Humor and Religious Faith', in: *American Theological Library Association: Proceedings* 34, 74–80.

Poythress, Diane (2011): *Reformer of Basel. The Life, Thought, and Influence of Johannes Oecolampadius*. Grand Rapids: Reformation Heritage Books.

Propp, Vladimir Jakovlevic (1984): 'Ritual Laughter in Folklore (A Propos of the Tale of the Princess Who Would Not Laugh, "Nesmejána")' [Russian ed. 1939], in: *id.*: *Theory and History of Folklore*, tr. by Ariadna Y. Martin & Richard P. Martin; ed. with an introduction and notes by Anatoly Liberman. Manchester: Manchester University Press, 124–46.

Prütting, Lenz (2013): *Homo ridens. Eine phänomenologische Studie über Wesen, Formen und Funktionen des Lachens*. Freiburg i. Br.: Karl Alber.

Quinn, Arthur (1992): 'The Mirth of God. An Essay on Biblical Humor', in: Virgil Nemoianu & Robert Royal (eds.) (1992): *Play, Literature, Religion. Essays in Cultural Intertextuality*. Albany: State University of New York Press, 41–59.

Quintilian, Marcus Fabius (1953): 'Laughter, Wit, and Humour' [= Book 6, ch. 3], in: *id.: The 'Institutio Oratoria' of Quintilian*, tr. by H. E. Butler. Cambridge: Harvard University Press, vol. 2, 439–501.

Radday, Yehuda T. (1990): 'On Missing the Humour in the Bible. An Introduction', in: Radday & Brenner (eds.) (1990), 21–38.

Radday, Yehuda T. & Athalya Brenner (eds.) (1990): *On Humour and the Comic in the Hebrew Bible*. Sheffield: Almond.

Rahner, Hugo (1965): 'Eutrapelia. A Forgotten Virtue' [German ed. 1954], in: *id.: Man at Play*, tr. by Bryan Battershaw & Edward Quinn. London: Burns & Oates (Repr. New York: Herder & Herder, 1972). Also in: Hyers (ed.) (1969a), 185–97.

Raley, A. L. (1967): 'Laughter', in: Catholic University of America (ed.) (1967): *New Catholic Encyclopedia*. Washington: McGraw-Hill, vol. 8, 532–3.

Ramondt, Marie (1962): 'Das Lachen und der Tod', in: *id.: Studien über das Lachen*. Groningen: J.B. Wolters, 7–34.

Rang, Bernhard (1957–8): 'Lob des Lachens', in: *Quatember. Evangelische Jahresbriefe* 22, 70–5.

Ratcliff, John (1970): *Humor as a Religious Experience*, (diss., Southern Baptist Theological Seminary).

Ratzinger, Joseph (1986): *Behold the Pierced One. An Approach to a Spiritual Christology* [German ed. 1984]. San Francisco: Ignatius Press.

Rauscher, Wolfgang (1690): *Oel und Wein Dess Mitleidigen Samaritans Für die Wunden der Sünder. Das ist Catholische, mit Christlichem Ernst, geistreicher Schärpffe, und Mildigkeit vermischte Predigen: zu Bekehrung und ewigen Heyl Der Verwundten Seelen angesehen, Und an denen Sonn-Tägen dess gantzen Jahrs auff der Cantzel vorgetragen*. Dillingen: Bencard.

Rehtmeyer, Philipp Julius (1707): *Antiqvitates Ecclesiasticæ Inclytæ Urbis Brunsvigæ, Oder: Der berühmten Stadt Braunschweig Kirchen-Historie: … alles aus den Archiven, raren Manuscriptis und … Historicis, sammt … Beylagen verfasset; mit Fleiss zusammen getragen …, Von Philippo Julio Rehtmeyer, Brunsvic ; vol. 2: In dem andern Theile aber Der inwendige … Zustand der Braunschweigischen Kirche … biss aufs Jahr 1521 erörtert wird*. Braunschweig, Gedruckt und Verlegt durch Christoph-Friederich Zilligers sehl. nachgel. Wittib und Erben.

Reich, Hermann (1903): 'Christologische Ethologie und Biologie, Angriff des Mimus auf das Christentum', 'Beurteilung und Verurteilung des Mimus durch die Kirchenväter', 'Vergeblichkeit des kirchlichen Angriffes gegen den Mimus; der Mimus dringt in die gottesdienstliche Handlung ein', & 'Der Mimus im Occident während des Mittelalters', in: *id.: Der Mimus*.

Ein litterar-entwicklungsgeschichtlicher Versuch. Berlin: Weidmannsche Buchhandlung, 80–109, 109–30, 130–42, & 744–859.

Reid, John (1913): 'Humour', in: James Hastings (ed.) (1908–21): *Encyclopedia of Religion and Ethics*. Edinburgh: T. & T. Clark, vol. 6, 872–3.

Reinach, Salomon (1912): 'Le Rire rituel' [1911], in: *id.: Cultes, mythes et religions*. Paris: Ernest Leroux, vol. 4, 109–29.

Reines, Chaim W. (1972): 'Laughter in Biblical and Rabbinic Literature', in: *Judaism. A Quarterly Journal of Jewish Life and Thought* 21, 176–83.

Reiser, Marius (2012): ' "Von allen Lebewesen lacht nur der Mensch" – Die griechisch-römische Lachkultur' & 'Das Lachen in der Bibel und die christliche Lachkultur', in: Wilhelmy (ed.) (2012a), 16–24 & 26–36.

Renan, Ernest (1863): *Vie de Jésus*. Paris: Lévy.

- 1864: *The Life of Jesus*, tr. by Charles Edwin Wilbour. New York: Carleton.

Rensburg, Lee van (1991): *The Sense of Humor in Scripture, Theology and Worship*. Lima: Freeway.

Rengstorf, Heinrich (1933): 'Τελάω', in: Gerhard Kittel (ed.) (1933–79): *Theologisches Wörterbuch zum Neuen Testament*. Stuttgart: Kohlhammer, vol. 1, 656–60.

Resnick, Irven Michael (1987): ' "Risus monasticus". Laughter and Medieval Monastic Culture', in: *Revue Bénédictine de critique, d'histoire et de littérature religieuses* 97, 90–100.

'Revelation of Peter, The' (2007), see: 'Apocalypse of Peter'

Richert, Friedemann (2009): *Kleine Geistesgeschichte des Lachens*. Darmstadt: Wissenschaftliche Buchgesellschaft.

Rigg, W. H. (1930–1): 'Religion and Laughter', in: *Church Quarterly Review* 111, 259–74.

Riising, Anne (1969): *Danmarks middelalderlige prædiken*. Copenhagen: Gads Forlag.

Roberts, Robert Campbell (1987): 'Smiling with God. Reflections on Christianity and the Psychology of Humor', in: *Faith and Philosophy. Journal of the Society of Christian Philosophers* 4, 168–86.

- (1988): 'Humor and the Virtues', in: *Inquiry. An Interdisciplinary Journal of Philosophy* 31, 127–49.

Rosegger, Peter (1875): *Das Volksleben in Steiermark in Charakter- und Sittenbildern dargestellt, in zwei Büchern*, vol. 2: *Das Jahr*. Graz: Leykam-Josefsthal.

Rudhardt, Jean (1992): 'Rires et sourires divins. Essai sur la sensibilité religieuse des grecs et des premiers chrétiens', in: *Revue de Théologie et de Philosophie* 124, 389–405.

Rummel, Erika (ed.) (2005): *The Correspondence of Wolfgang Capito*, vol. 1: 1507–23, ed. and tr. by Erika Rummel with the assistance of Milton Kooistra. Toronto: University of Toronto Press.

Rupp, Gordon (1982): 'Luther's Humour', in: Porter (ed.) (1982), 8–10.

– (1969): 'Johannes Oecolampadius. The Reformer as Scholar', in: *id.*: *Patterns of Reformation*. London: Epworth, 3–46.

Russ, Daniel (1984): 'The Bible as Genesis of Comedy', in: Louise Cowan (ed.) (1984): *The Terrain of Comedy*. Dallas: Dallas Institute of Humanities and Culture, 41–59.

Rzekocka, Jolanta (2011): 'Being Serious about Laughter. The Case of Early Modern Biblical Plays', in: Hans Geybels & Walter van Herck (eds.): *Humour and Religion. Challenges and Ambiguities*. London: Continuum, 156–68.

Röcke, Werner (1998): 'Inszenierungen des Lachens in Litteratur und Kultur des Mittelalters', in: *Paragrana. Internationale Zeitschrift für Historische Anthropologie* 7.1, 73–93.

– & Helga Neumann (eds.) (1999): *Komische Gegenwelten. Lachen und Literatur in Mittelalter und Früher Neuzeit*. Paderborn: Schöningh.

– (1999): 'Lizenzen des Witzes. Institutionen und Funktionsweisen der Fazetie im Spätmittelalter', in: *id.* & Neumann (eds.) (1999), 79–101.

– (2000): 'Text und Ritual. Spielformen des Performativen in der Fastnachtkultur des späten Mittelalters', in: *Das Mittelalter* 5, 85–100.

– (2002): 'Ostergelächter. Körpersprache und rituelle Komik in Inszenierungen des "risus paschalis"', in: Klaus Ridder, *et al.* (eds.): *Körperinszenierungen in mittelalterlicher Literatur*. Berlin: Weidler, 335–50.

– & Hans Rudolf Velten (eds.) (2005): *Lachgemeinschaften. Kulturelle Inszenierungen und soziale Wirkungen von Gelächter im Mittelalter und in der Frühen Neuzeit*. Berlin: de Gruyter.

Sacrosanctum Concilium Tridentinum, ed. Joannis Gallemart, *et al.* Augustæ Vindelicorum [Augsburg]: Sumtibus Matthæi Rieger P. M. Filiorum, 1781.

• 1848: *The Canons and Decrees of the Sacred and Oecumenical Council of Trent, Celebrated under the Sovereign Pontiffs, Paul III, Julius III and Pius IV*, tr. by J. Waterworth, to which are prefixed essays on the external and internal history of the council. London & New York: Burns and Oates & Catholic Publication Society Co.

Tanner, Norman P. (ed.) (1990): *Decrees of the Ecumenical Councils*, I-II, original text established by G. Alerigo, J.A. Dossetti, P.-P. Joannou, C. Leonari, and P. Prodi, in consultation with H. Jedin. London & Washington: Sheed & Ward & Georgetown University Press.

Samra, Cal (1986): *The Joyful Christ. The Healing Power of Humor* [1st ed.: 'Jesus Put on a Happy Face', 1985]. San Francisco: Harper & Row.

Sanders, Barry (1995): *Sudden Glory. Laughter as Subversive History*. Boston: Beacon.

Sandifer, D. Wayne (1991): 'The Humor of the Absurd in the Parables of Jesus', in: Eugene H. Lovering, Jr. (ed.): *Society of Biblical Literature. 1991 Seminar Papers*. Atlanta: Scholars, 287–97.

Sarrazin, Bernard (1988): 'Du rire dans la Bible? La théophanie de Job comme parodie', in: *Recherches de Science Religieuses* 76, 39–56.

– (1991): *Le rire et le sacre. Histoire de la dirision*. Paris: Desclie de Brouwer.

Sauer, Hanjo & Franz Gruber (eds.) (1999): *Lachen in Freiheit. Theologische Skizzen*. Regensburg: Friedrich Pustet.

Saward, John (1980): *Perfect Fools. Folly for Christ's sake in Catholic and Orthodox Spirituality*. Oxford: Oxford University Press.

Schäufele, Wolf-Friedrich (2013): 'Johannes Oekolampad', in: Irene Dingel & Volker Leppin (eds.): *Das Reformatorenlexikon*. Darmstadt: Lambert Schneider, vol. 1, 189–93.

Schauerte, Heinrich (1950): 'Des Volkes Scherz und Spiel mit heiligen Dingen', in: *Theologie und Glaube* 40, 534–43.

Scheidl, Joseph (1927): 'Ein Ostermärlein', in: *Zeitschrift für Kirchengeschichte* 45 (N.F. 8), 1927, 9–10.

Scherer, Georg (1603): 'Etliche Christliche Regeln für die Prediger', in: *id.: Postill Georgii Scherer über die Sontäglichen Euvangelia durch das gantze Jahr*. Bruck an der Teya: Kloster, [scan-images] 17–27. Online: reader.digitale-sammlungen.de

Schindler, Norbert (1992): 'Karneval, Kirche und die verkehrte Welt. Zur Funktion der Lachkultur im 16. Jahrhundert', in: *Jahrbuch für Volkskunde* N.F. 7, 1984, 9–57; repr. in: *id.: Widerspenstige Leute. Studien zur Volkskultur in der frühen Neuzeit*. Frankfurt a. M.: Fischer Taschenbuch, 1992, 121–74 & 343–61.

Schmidt, Johann Andreas, see: Gottfried Tentzel

Schmidt, Ioannes Petrus (1747): *De risu paschali: programma paschale = Vulgo dem Oster-Gelächter*. Rostock: Adler.

Schmidt, Thomas (1656): *Chronica Cygnea Oder Beschreibung Der sehr alten, Löblichen, und Churfürstlichen Stadt Zwickau: Von derselben Lager, Erbauung, Gebäuden, Einwohnern, Gelegenheit, von ihren Regenten, wie auch Beampten in Geist- und Weltlichen Stande, Ingleichen was sich Schrifftwürdiges, zu Kriegs und Friedenszeiten, allda und in derselben Nachtbarschaffe begeben und zugetragen*. Zwickau: Goepner.

Schmidt-Clausing, Fritz (2007): *The Humor of Huldrych Zwingli. The Lighter Side of the Protestant Reformation* [German ed. 1968], ed. and tr. by Him West, with a foreword by Matthias Freudenberg. Lewiston: Edwin Mellen.

Schmidt-Hidding, Wolfgang (1959): *Sieben Meister des literarischen Humors in England und Amerika*. Heidelberg: Quelle & Meyer.

– (ed.) (1963): *Humor und Witz*. ('Europäische Schlüsselwörter. Wortvergleichende und wortgeschichtliche Studien', ed. by Hans Moser, et al., vol. 1.) München: Max Hueber.

Schmitz, Gerhard (1980): '... quod rident homines, plorandum est. Der "Unwert" des Lachens in monastisch geprägten Vorstellungen der Spätantike und des frühen Mittelalters', in: Franz Quarthal & Wilfried Setzler (eds.): *Stadtverfassung – Verfassungsstaat – Pressepolitik. Festschrift für E. Naujoks zum 65. Geburtstag*. Sigmaringen: Thorbecke, 3–15.

– (1992): 'Ein Narr, der da lacht …. Überlegungen zu einer mittelalterlichen Verhaltensnorm', in: Thomas Vogel (ed.): *Vom Lachen. Einem Phänomen auf der Spur*. Tübingen: Attempto, 129–53.

Schmitz, Heinz-Günter (1972): *Physiologie des Scherzes. Bedeutung und Rechtfertigung der Ars Iocandi im 16. Jahrhundert*. Hildesheim: Georg Olms.

Schneemelcher, Wilhelm (ed.) (1991): *New Testament Apocrypha* [German 6th ed. 1990], rev. ed., tr. by Robert McLachlan Wilson. Cambridge: James Clarke & Co.

Schneider, Rolf Michael (2008): 'Nachwort: Plädoyer für eine Geschichte des Lachens', in: Le Goff 2008, 79–123.

Schnell, Rüdiger (2005): 'Geistliches Spiel und Lachen. Überlegungen zu einer Ästhetik der Komik im Mittelalter', in: Anja Grebe & Nikolaus Staubach (eds.) (2005), 76–93.

Schomerus, Hans (1955): 'Die Tugend der Heiterkeit', in: *id.*: *Der unbefangene Christ*. Stuttgart: Evangelisches Verlagswerk, 44–9.

Schousboe, Julius (1925): *Om begrebet humor hos Søren Kierkegaard*. Copenhagen: Arnold Busck.

Schreiner, Klaus (2002): ' "Brot der Tränen". Emotionale Ausdrucksform monastischer Spiritualität', in: Klaus Ridder, et al. (eds.): *Körperinszenierungen in mittelalterlicher Literatur*. Berlin: Weidler, 193–248.

Schroeder, Steven (1986): 'A Little Meditation on Luke and Laughter', in: Paul L. Redditt (ed.): *Proceedings, Eastern Great Lakes and Midwest Biblical Societies*, vol. 6. Grand Rapids: Eastern Great Lakes and Midwest Biblical Societies, 1986, 179–87.

Schroeter, Harald (1995): 'Osterpredigt' [including section 4.2: 'Ostergelächter'], in: Müller (ed.) (1977–2010), vol. 25, 530–3.

Schröder, Franz Rolf (1941): *Skadi und die Götter Skandinaviens*. Tübingen: Mohr.

Schröer, Henning (2002): 'Lachend ins gelobte Land. Auf dem Weg zu einer Theologie des Komischen', in: *Pastoraltheologie. Monatsschrift für Wissenschaft und Praxis in Kirche und Gesellschaft* 91, 2–11.

Schubert, Anselm (2011): 'Das Lachen der Ketzer. Zur Selbstinszenierung der frühen Reformation', in: *Zeitschrift für Theologie und Kirche* 108, 405–30.

Schütz, Karl-Otto (1963): 'Witz und Humor', in: Schmidt-Hidding (ed.) (1963), 161–244.

Schütz, Roland (1958): *Humor und Ironie bei Jesus und Paulus*. (Beihefte zur Monatsschrift 'Freies Christentum', vol. 29). Frankfurt a. M.: Deutscher Bund für freies Christentum.

Schweitzer, Albert (1906): *Von Reimarus zu Wrede – eine Geschichte der Leben-Jesu-Forschung*. Tübingen: Mohr.
- 1954: *The Quest of the Historical Jesus. A Critical Study of Its Progress from Reimarus to Wrede* [1910[1]], 3rd ed. with a new introduction by the author, tr. by W. Montgomery. London: Adam & Charles Black.

Schweizer, B., & Ott, K. H. (2016): 'Faith and laughter. Do atheists and practicing Christians have different senses of humor?', in: *Humor* 29.3, 413–38.

Schörle, Eckart (2007): *Die Verhöflichung des Lachens. Lachgeschichte im 18. Jahrhundert*. Bielefeld: Aithesis.
- (2012): 'Die Erfindung des "guten" Lachens. Lachdebatten zwischen 1650–1750', in: Biessenecker & Kuhn (eds.) (2012), 329–50.

Scott, Nathan Alexander, Jr. (1966): 'The Bias of Comedy and the Narrow Escape into Faith' [1961], in: *id.*: *The Broken Center. Studies in the Theological Horizon of Modern Literature*. New Haven: Yale University Press, 77–118.

Screech, Michael Andrew & Ruth Calder (1992): 'Some Renaissance Attitudes to Laughter' [1970], in: Michael Andrew Screech: *Some Renaissance Studies. Selected articles 1951–1991 with a Bibliography*, ed. Michael J. Heath. Geneve: Libraire Droz S.A., 216–28.

Screech, Michael Andrew (1997): *Laughter at the Foot of the Cross*. London: Allen Lane.

Scribner, Robert W. (1987): 'Reformation, Carnival and the World Turned Upside-Down', in: *id.: Popular Culture and Popular Movements in Reformation Germany*. London: Hambledon, 71–101.

Secher, Vilhelm Adolf (ed.) (1897): *Forordninger, recesser og andre kongelige breve, Danmarks lovgivning vedkommende, 1559–1660*, vol. 4, 1622–38. Selskabet for udgivelse af kilder til dansk historie. Copenhagen: Gad.

Seckendorff, Veit Ludwig von (1688): *Commentarius Historicus Et Apologeticus de Lutheranismo*. Frankfurt & Leipzig: Gleditsch.

Seneca, Lucius Annaeus (1967): *Ad Lucilium Epistulae Morales*, I-III, tr. by Richard Mott Gummere. London: Heinemann.

Sennett, Richard (1978): *The Fall of Public Man. On the Social Psychology of Capitalism* [1977]. New York: Vintage Books.

Shaftesbury, Anthony Ashley Cooper, Earl of (2001): 'A Letter concerning Enthusiasm' [1708], '"Sensus Communis": An Essay on the Freedom of Wit and Humour' [1709], & 'Of the Force of Humor in Religion' [1714] (= 'Miscellany II, Chapter III' in 'Miscellaneous Reflections on the Preceding Treaties, and other Critical Subjects'), in: *id.: Characteristicks of Men, Manners, Opinion, Times*, I-III, introduction by Douglas Den Uyl. Indianapolis: Liberty Fund, vol. 1, 3–36, 39–93, & vol. 3, 60–81.

Sharr, Roger (1982): 'Laughter and Prayer – A Meditation', in: Porter (ed.) (1982), 22–4.

Shibles, Warren (1978): *Humor. A Critical Analysis for Young People*. Whitewater: Language.

Shorthouse, Joseph Henry (1883): 'The Humorous in Literature', in: Titus Munson Coan (ed.): *Studies in Literature*. New York: G.P. Putnam's Sons, 120–58.

Shutter, Marion Daniel (1885): 'The Element of Humor in the Bible', in: *Baptist Quarterly Review* 7, 443–53.

– (1893): *Wit and Humor of the Bible. A Literary Study*. Boston: Arena Publishing Co.

Sigurdson, Ola (2021): *Gudomlige komedier. Humor, subjektivitet, transcendens*. vol. 1: *Antiken till renässansen*. Göteborg: Glänta.

Simon, Richard Keller (1985): *The Labyrinth of the Comic. Theory and Practice from Fielding to Freud*. Tallahassee: Florida State University Press.

Smith, William Austin (1911): 'The Use of the Comic Spirit in Religion', in: *Atlantic Monthly* 108, 186–91.

Snorri Sturluson (1995): 'Skaldsskaparmal' ['The Language of Poetry'], in: *Edda*, ed. & tr. by Anthony Faulkes. London: Everyman.

Solger, Karl Wilhelm Ferdinand (1815): *Erwin, Vier Gespräche über das Schöne und die Kunst*, Part 1. Berlin: Realschulbuchhandlung.

Sousa, Robert de (1987): 'When Is It Wrong to Laugh?', in: Morreall (ed.) (1987), 226–49.

Staehelin, Ernst (1927/34): *Briefe und Akten zum Leben Oekolampads. Zum vierhundertjährigen Jubiläum der Basler Reformation*, I-II. Leipzig: M. Heinsius Nachfolger Eger & Sievers.

– (1939a): *Das theologische Lebenswerk Johannes Oekolampads*. Leipzig: M. Heinsius Nachfolger. (Repr.: New York: Johnson Reprint Corp., 1971.)

– (1939b): 'Die beruflichen Stellungen Oekolampads während seiner vier Basler Aufenthalte', in: *Basler Zeitschrift für Geschichte und Altertumskunde* 16, 367–92.

– (1963): *Oekolampad-Bibliographie*. Nieuwkoop: B. de Graaf (Repr. of 'Verzeichnis der im 16. Jahrhundert erschienenen Oekolampaddrucke' & 'Bibliographische Beiträge zum Lebenswerk Oekolampads', in: *Basler Zeitschrift für Geschichte und Altertumskunde* 17/1918, 1–119 & 27/1928, 191–234).

– (1965): 'Oecolampadiana', in: *Basler Zeitschrift für Geschichte und Altertumskunde* 65, 165–94.

– (1967): 'Johannes Ökolampad als Prediger in Weinsberg und Reformator in Basel', in: Christoph Duncker: *Ausblick von der Weibertreu. Kirchen im Bezirk Weinsberg*, mit Photographien von Hermann Eisenmenger und Zeichnungen von Walter Schellenberger. Weinsberg: Wilhelm Röck, 64–72.

Starcke, Tobias [& Michael Ehrenfried Krause] (1710): *De pervigilio paschatos anastasimu von der Oster-Nacht*. Lipsia [Leipzig]: Bauch.

'Statuta Ecclesiae Antiqua' (1783), in: Georg Daniel Fuchs (ed.): *Bibliotek der Kirchenversammlungen des vierten und fünften Jahrhunderts in Uebersetzungen und Auszügen aus ihren Akten und andern dahin gehörigen Schriften, sammt dem Original der Hauptstellen und nöthigen Anmerkungen*, vol. 3. Leipzig: Hertel, 458–76.

- 1960: *Les Statuta Ecclesiae Antiqua*. Thèse pour le doctorat en théologie présentée et soutenue le 29 novembre 1958 par Charles Munier. Paris: Presses Universitaires de France.

Steadman, John Marcellus (1983): ' "Teeth Will Be Provided". Satire and Religious or Ecclesiastical Humor', in: M.-L. Davies (ed.) (1983), 23–31.

Steger, Friedrich (1871): 'Ostermärchen und Ostergelächter', in: *Europa. Chronik der gebildeten Welt*, Nr. 15, col. 457–64.

Steidle, P. Basilius (1938a): 'Das Lachen im alten Mönchtum', in: *Benediktinische Monatschrift zur Pflege religiösen und geistigen Lebens* 20, 269–80.

– (1938b): 'Die Tränen, ein mystisches Problem im alten Mönchtum', in: *Benediktinische Monatschrift zur Pflege religiösen und geistigen Lebens* 20, 181–7.

Steiger, Lothar (1986): 'Humor', in: Müller (ed.) (1977–2010), vol. 15, 696–701.

Steinberg, Leo (1996): *The Sexuality of Christ in Renaissance Art and in Modern Oblivion* [1983[1]], 2nd ed. revised & expanded. Chicago & London: University of Chicago Press.

Steiner, Joseph Anton, see: *Acta Selecta Ecclesiae Augustanae*

Steiner, George (1961): *The Death of Tragedy*. London: Faber and Faber.

Stinespring, W. F. (1962): 'Humor', in: George Arthur Buttrick, *et al.* (eds.) (1962–76): *The Interpreter's Dictionary of the Bible. An Illustrated Encyclopedia Identifying and Explaining all Proper Names and Significant Terms and Subjects in the Holy Scriptures, including the Apocrypha with Attention to Archeological Discoveries and Researches into the Life and Faith of Ancient Times*. New York: Abingdon, vol. 2, 660–2.

Stollmann, Rainer (1988): 'Lachen, Freiheit und Geschichte', in: *Jahrbuch für internationale Germanistik* 20, 25–43.

Strange, Marcian (1971): 'God and Laughter', in: *Worship. A Review Concerned with the Problems of Liturgical Renewal* 45, 2–12.

Strauss, David Friedrich (1835–6): *Das Leben Jesu, kritisch bearbeitet*, I-II. Tübingen: Osiander.

Striet, Magnus (2017): 'Kann Gott lachen? Über Humor als theologische Kategorie', in: Dober (ed.) (2017a), 70–6.

Strobl, Andreas (1694): *Ovum Paschale Novum Oder Neugefärbte Oster-Ayr, Das ist: Viertzig Geistliche Discurs, auff den H. Ostertag und Ostermontag: Worinnen Verschiedene Geschicht vnd Gedicht, oder Oster-Märl, sambt denen hierauss gezognen Sitten-Lehren, welche nicht allein denen Herren Predigern auff der Cantzel, sondern auch anderen Privat-Personen zur Conversation oder die lange Weil und Zeit zu vertreiben, sehr dienlich, vnd mit geistlichem Nutz können gebraucht werden; Auch mit einem dreyfachen Indice, sambt einem Predig-Register über die Sonn- vnnd Feyertägliche Evangelia versehen seynd*. Salzburg: Haan. [2nd ed. of Part 1: 1700; Part 2: 1698; Part 3: 1708; Collected ed.: 1710.] Online: reader.digitale-sammlungen.de

– (1698): *Noch ein Körbel voll Oster-Ayr, Das ist: Ovi Paschalis Der Anderte Theil. Oder: 32. Geistliche Discurs auff den Heil. Oster-Tag, Montag, vnd Erchtag: Worinnen Verschidene schöne Geschicht, vnd Gedicht, oder Oster-Märl, sambt denen herauss gezogenen Sitten-Lehren. Welche nicht allein denen*

Herren Predigern auff der Cantzel: sondern auch anderen Privat-Personen zur annemblichen und Ehrlichen Conversation, oder die lange Weil zu vertreiben, sehr dienlich, vnd mit Geistlichem Nutzen können gebrauchet werden; Auch mit einem dreyfachen Indice, sambt einem Predig-Register, über die Sonn- und Feyertägliche Evangelia versehen seynd. Salzburg: Haan.

Stroh, Moritz (1997): *Lachen. Interdisziplinäre und theologische Aspekte*, (Diplom-Arbeit, Wien University).

Stroumsa, Guy G. (2004): 'Christ's Laughter. Docetic Origins Reconsidered', in: *Journal of Early Christian Studies* 12.3, 267–88.

Stumpfl, Robert (1936): *Kultspiele der Germanen als Ursprung des mittelalterlichen Dramas*. Berlin: Junker und Dünnhaupt.

Sturm, Angelus (1923): 'Humor, Christentum, Mönchtum', in: *Benediktinische Monatschrift zur Pflege religiösen und geistigen Lebens* 5, 174–84.

Suchier, Walther (ed.) (1955): *Das mittellateinische Gespräch Adrian und Epictitus nebst verwandten Texten (Joca Monachorum)*. Tübingen: Max Niemeyer.

Suchomski, Joachim (1975): 'Die sittliche Beurteilung von Lachen und Scherz', in: *id.: 'Delectatio' und 'Utilitas'. Ein Beitrag zum Verständnis mittelalterlicher komischer Literatur*. Bern: Francke, 9–65 & 257–76.

Suter, Adrian (2005): 'Das Lachen der Befreiten. Der Osterfreude ganzheitlich Ausdruck verleihen', in: *Zeitschrift der Christkatholischen Kirche der Schweiz* 6, 4.

Svanberg, Jan (1994): 'Det gotiska leendet', in: Helena Edgren (ed.): *Bild och känsla från antik till nyantik*. Åbo: Åbo Akademi, 175–91.

Swain, Barbara (1932): *Fools and Folly During the Middle Ages and the Renaissance*. New York: Columbia University Press.

Swindoll, Charles R. (1991): *Laugh Again. Experience Outrageous Joy*. Dallas: Word.

Syrkin, Alexander Y. (1982): 'On the Behavior of the "Fool for Christ's Sake"', in: *History of Religions. An International Journal for Comparative Historical Studies* 22, 150–71.

Söderblom, Nathan (1919): 'Luthers humor' & 'Humorns betydelse för Luther', in: *id.: Humor och melankoli, och andra Lutherstudier*. Stockholm: Sveriges Kristliga Studentrörelses Förlag, 3–41 & 45–67.

Taine, Hippolyte (1920): *History of English Literature*, I-IV [French ed. 1863], tr. by H. van Laun. London: Chatto & Windus.

Tanner, Norman P., see: *Sacrosanctum Concilium Tridentinum*

Tatlock, John Strong Perry (1946): 'Mediaeval Laughter', in: *Speculum. A Journal of Mediaeval Studies* 21, 289–94.

Taube, Otto von (1957–8): 'Die Heiterkeit der Heiligen', in: *Quatember. Evangelische Jahresbriefe* 22, 76–84.

Tentzel, Gottfried [& Johann Andreas Schmidt] (1693): *Ovum mundanum*. Jena: Müller.

Terence (Publius Terentius Afer) (1893): 'Andria, or, The Fair Andrian', in: *The Comedies of Terence*, tr. by Henry Thomas Riley. New York: Harper and Brothers.

Tertullian, Quintus Septimus Florens (1903): 'On Prescription against Heretics', in: *Ante-Nicene Fathers …*, vol. 3, tr. by Peter Holmes, 243–64.

– (1977): *De spectaculis*, ['The Shows'] [196] tr. by Terrot Reaveley Glover. Cambridge & London: Harvard University Press & Heinemann, 230–301.

Teuber, Bernard (1988): 'Karneval als radikaler Dissens. Zur späten Übersetzung von Michail Bachtins Buch über Rabelais', in: *Merkur. Deutsche Zeitschrift für europäisches Denken* 42, 507–12.

Teuteberg, René (1979): 'Johannes Oekolampad' & 'Wibrandis Rosenblatt', in: *id.* & Rudolf Sutet (eds.): *Der Reformation verpflichtet. Gestalten und Gestalter in Stadt und Landschaft Basel aus fünf Jahrhunderten*. Basel: Christoph Merian, 21–8 & 39–42.

Thackeray, William Makepeace (2007): *The English Humourists of the Eighteenth Century* [1853], and 'Charity and Humour' [1852], ed. by Edgar F. Harden. Ann Arbor: University of Michigan Press.

Thiede, Werner (1986): *Das verheissene Lachen. Humor in theologischer Perspektive*. Göttingen: Vandenhoeck & Ruprecht.

– (1988): 'Lachen/Humor', in: Christian Schütz (ed.): *Praktisches Lexikon der Spiritualität*. Freiburg i. Br.: Herder, col. 751–3.

– (2010): 'Luthers Humor. Zur Glaubensfreude des Reformators' [2008], in: *Luther. Zeitschrift der Luther-Gesellschaft* 81, 8–18.

– (2011): 'Humor in der Kirche. Eine theologische Besinnung', in: *Geist und Leben. Zeitschrift für christliche Spiritualität* [before 2011: 'Zeitschrift für Askese und Mystik'] 84.2, 111–28.

Thielicke, Helmut (1974): *Das Lachen der Heiligen und Narren. Nachdenkliches über Witz und Humor*. Freiburg i. Br.: Herder.

Thomas (1991): 'The Infancy Story of Thomas', in: *New Testament Apocrypha*, rev. ed. ed. by Wilhelm Schneemelcher, tr. by Robert McLachlan Wilson. Cambridge: James Clarke & Co., 439–51.

Thomas, Keith Vivian (1977): 'The Place of Laughter in Tudor and Stuart England', in: *Times Literary Supplement* 21. januar, 76–83.

Thomas Aquinas (1872): 'Summa Theologica', in: *id.: Doctoris Angelici divi Thomæ Aquinatis opera omnia*, vol. 2 & 4. Paris: Louis Vivès.

– (1906): 'Summa Theologica, supplemento tertiae partis', in: *id.: Sancti Thomae Aquinatis opera omnia*, vol. 12. Rom: Typographia Polyglotta.

- 1920: *The Summa Theologiæ of St. Thomas Aquinas*, literally tr. by Fathers of the English Dominican Province, online edition by Kevin Knight 2017 at newadvent.org/summa/

Thomasius, Jacob (1693): 'De pontificiorum risu paschali' [1661], in: *id.: Dissertationes LXIII.* Halæ Magdeburgicæ: Johannis Frederici Zeitleri, 210–25.

Thomsen, Ole (1986): *Komediens kraft. En bog om en genre.* Copenhagen: Akademisk Forlag.

Thorstensen, Erik (1999): *'Og du, gamle pave, hvordan kan selv du forsvare å tilbe et esel som gud?' En lesning av dårefestens eselliturgi*, (diss., Oslo University).

Thumm, Theodor, see: Isaak Capeller

Timmerman, John H. (1987): 'Umberto Eco and Aristotle. A Dialogue on the Lost Treatise: Comedy', in: *Christian Scholar's Review* 17, 9–24.

Trokhimenko, Olga V. (2014): 'A Deeply Serious Matter. Laughter in Medieval Ecclesiastical Discourse', in: *id.: Constructing Virtue and Vice. Feminity and Laughter in Courtly Society (ca. 1150–1300).* Göttingen: V & R unipress, 63–92.

Troxell, Thomas E. (1986): 'Humor as a Preaching Tool', in: *Military Chaplains' Review* 15, 59–63.

Trueblood, David Elton (1964): *The Humor of Christ.* New York: Harper & Row.

Tubach, Frederick C. (1969): *Index Exemplorum. A Handbook of Medieval Religious Tales.* Helsinki: Suomalainen Tiedeakatemia.

Usener, Hermann (1913): 'Klagen und Lachen' [1904], in: *id.: Kleine Schriften*, vol. 4: 'Arbeiten zur Religionsgeschichte'. Berlin & Leipzig: Teubner, 469–70.

Vannorsdall, John (1983): 'Humor as Content and Device in Preaching', in: *Dialog. A Journal of Theology* 22, 187–90.

Vasey, George (1877): *The Philosophy of Laughter and Smiling* [1875[1]], 2nd ed., enl. and improved, in which the theory advanced in the 1st ed. is strengthened and corroborated by important demonstrations. London: J. Burns.

Vedder, Henry Clay (1922): *The Fundamentals of Christianity. A Study of the Teaching of Jesus and Paul.* New York: The Macmillan Co.

Veit, Ludwig Andreas (1936): *Volksfrommes Brauchtum und Kirche im deutschen Mittelalter*. Freiburg i. Br.: Herder & Co.

Verberckmoes, Johan (2003): 'What about Medieval Humour? Some Historiography', in: Herman Braet, Guido Latré & Werner Verbeke (eds.) (2003), 1–10.

Vergil, Publius Maro (1895): *Eclogues*, tr. by J.B. Greenough. Boston: Ginn & Co.

– (1908): *The Aeneid of Virgil*, tr. by Theodore C. Williams. Boston: Houghton Mifflin Co.

Via, Dan Otto (1975): *Kerygma and Comedy in the New Testament*. Philadelphia: Fortress.

Vinçon, Herbert (1997): *Osterlachen. Erzählungen und Gedichte zum Ostergeschehen*. Gütersloh: Gütersloher.

Voeltzel, René (1961): *Das Lachen des Herrn. Über die Ironie in der Bibel* [French ed. 1955], tr. by B. Marx-Schlunk. Hamburg & Bergstedt: Herbert Reich Evangelischer.

Vos, Nelvin (1967): *For God's Sake Laugh!* Richmond: John Knox.

– (1981): 'The Religious Meaning of Comedy', in: Leland Ryken (ed.) (1981): *The Christian Imagination. Essays on Literature and the Arts*. Grand Rapids: Baker, 241–53.

Walther, Hans (1963–69): *Lateinischen Sprichwörter und Sentenzen des Mittelalters in Alphabethischer Anordnung*, I-VI. Göttingen: Vandenhoeck & Ruprecht.

Ward, Hiley H. (ed.) (1968): *Ecumania. The Humor that Happens when Catholics, Jews, and Protestants Come Together*. New York: Association.

Warning, Rainer (1971): 'Ritus, Mythos und geistliches Spiel', in: Manfred Fuhrmann (ed.): *Terror und Spiel. Probleme der Mythenrezeption*. München: Wilhelm Fink. 211–39.

– (1974): 'Von der frohen Botschaft zum risus paschalis. Osterspiel und rituelles Lachen', in: *id.: Funktion und Struktur. Die Ambivalenzen des geistlichen Spiels*. München: Wilhelm Fink, 107–22.

– (1979): 'On the Alterity of Medieval Religious Drama', in: *New Literary History* 10.2, 265–92.

Webb, Joseph M. (1998): *Comedy and Preaching*. St. Louis: Chalice.

Weber, Carlo (1970): 'A God Who Laughs', in: Werner Max Mendel (ed.): *A Celebration of Laughter*. Los Angeles: Mara Books, 119–33.

Weber, Heinrich (1895): 'Ostermärchen und Ostergelächter', in: Heinrich Joseph Wetzer & Benedikt Welte (eds.) (1882–1903): *Kirchenlexikon, oder*

Encyklopädie der katholischen Theologie und ihrer Hülfswissenschaften, 2nd ed. Freiburg i. Br.: Herder, vol. 9, col. 1126-8.

Weber, Johann Adam (1682): *Ars conversandi certis regulis comprehensa*. Salzburg: J.B. Mayr.

Webster, Gary (1960): *Laughter in the Bible*. St. Louis: Bethany.

Wegner, Gottfried, see: Ernst Friedrich Kesselring

Wehrli, Max (1982): 'Christliches Lachen, christliche Komik?', in: D.H. Green; P. Johnson & Dieter Wuttke (eds.): *From Wolfram and Petrarch to Goethe and Grass. Studies in Literature in Honour of Leonard Forster*. BadenBaden: Valentin Koerner, 17-31.

– (1984): 'Komik in christlicher Kunst', in: *id.: Literatur im deutschen Mittelalter. Eine poetologische Einführung*. Stuttgart: Reclam, 163-81.

Weilner, Ignaz (1966): 'Heinrich Seuse und die Askese des Humors', in: Ephrem M. Filthaut (ed.): *Heinrich Seuse. Studien zum 600. Todestag, 1366-1966*. Köln: Albertus Magnus, 241-54.

Welliver, Dotsey (1986): *Laughing Together. The Value of Humor in Family Life*. Elgin: Brethren.

Welsh, W. A. (1967): 'Homo Ridens. Preliminary Consideration of Some Aspects of Human Laughter', in: *Lexington Theological Quarterly* 2, 95-103.

Wendland, Volker (1980): *Ostermärchen und Ostergelächter. Brauchtümliche Kanzelrhetorik und ihre kulturkritische Würdigung seit dem ausgehenden Mittelalter*. Frankfurt a. M.: Peter Lang.

Werner, Paul (2001): 'Gottes Gelächter über den Tod: der "Risus pascalis" – das Osterlachen in der Predigt', in: *Unser Bayern* 50, 29-32.

– (2005): 'Gottes Gelächter über den Tod: der "Risus pascalis" – das Osterlachen in der Ostermontagspredigt', in: *Schönere Heimat* 94, 51-4.

Wernsdorf, Johann Christian (1763): *Dies Sangvinis Et Hilaria Romanorvm Cvm Paschate Christianorvm Collata: Programma Sacro Paschali*. Helmstedt: Schnorrius.

Whedbee, J. William (1998): *The Bible and the Comic Vision*. Cambridge: Cambridge University Press.

White, Beatrice (1960): 'Medieval Mirth', in: *Anglia* 78, 284-301.

Widmaier, Jörg (2012): ' "Vultus hilaris et risus daemonum" – Die Masken von Reims als Zeichensystem des Mittealters', in: Wilhelmy (ed.) (2012a), 92-101.

Wiegmann, Hermann (2006): 'Hat Jesus nie gelacht? Ein bescheidener Beitrag zur Bibelexegese', in: *Und wieder lächelt die Thrakerin. Zur Geschichte des literarischen Humors*. Frankfurt a. M.: Peter Lang: 43-6.

Wildvogel, Christian, see: Rudoph Wilhelm Heberlin

Wilhelmy, Winfried (ed.) (2012a): *Seliges Lächeln und höllisches Gelächter. Das Lachen in Kunst und Kultur des Mittelalters*. Regensburg: Schnell & Steiner.

– (2012b): ' "Das leise Lachen" des Mittelalters – Lächeln, Lachen und Gelächter in den Schriften christlicher Gelehrter (300–1500)', in: *id.* (ed.) (2012a), 38–55.

William of Conches: *De philosophia mundi*, ed., tr., and annotated by Gregor Maurach, with the assistance of Heidemarie Telle. Pretoria: University of South Africa, 1980.

Willimon, William H. (ed.) (1986): *And the Laugh Shall Be First. A Treasury of Religious Humor*. Nashville: Abingdon.

Wimpfeling, Jacob (1506): *Apologia pro Republica Christiana*. Phorce: Anshelm.

Winkler, Klaus (1989): 'Humor', in: Erwin Fahlmusch, *et al.* (eds.) (1986–97): *Evangelische Kirchenlexikon. Internationale theologische Enzyklopädie*. Göttingen: Vandenhoeck & Ruprecht, vol. 2, col. 579–80.

– (1992): 'Lachen und Weinen', in: Erwin Fahlmusch, *et al.* (eds.) (1986–97): *Evangelische Kirchenlexikon. Internationale theologische Enzyklopädie*. Göttingen: Vandenhoeck & Ruprecht, vol. 3, col.1–3.

Winner, Julia Hull (1965): 'Some Religious Humor from the Past', in: *New York Folklore Quarterly* 21, 56–61.

Wolf, Herbert (1962): 'Predigterzählgut', in: *Der Deutschunterricht. Beiträge zu seiner Praxis und wissenschaftlichen Grundlegung* 14, 76–99.

Wolff, Stefanie (2009): *Todesverlachen. Das Lachen in der religiösen und profanen Kultur and Literatur im Frankreich des 17. Jahrhunderts*. Bern & New York: Peter Lang.

Wordsworth, William Arthur (1925): *The Laughter of God. An Essay on the Indications of a Sense of Humour in the Son of Man; with some verse*. Farnham: Martin & Sturt.

Wright, Gloria Jean (1988): *And God Laughed. Therapeutic Humor and Pastoral Counseling*, (diss., Andover Newton Theological School).

Wünkhaus, Oscar W. (1909): *Der Humor Jesu. Beitrag zur Skizzierung des historischen Christusbildes*. Heidelberg: Evangelischer.

Xenophon (1947): *Cyropaedia*, I-II, tr. by Walter Miller. London: Heinemann.

Young, Karl (1967): *The Drama of the Mediaeval Church* [1933], I-II. Oxford: Clarendon.

Zelger, Renate (1993): 'Risus paschalis. Das Ostergelächter', in: Wolfgang Kuhlmann & Helga Röhrich (eds.): *Witz, Humor und Komik im Volksmärchen*. Regensburg: Röth, 127–38.

Zeller, Johann Jacob (1771): *Das beschämte Laster Der heutigen Welt; Durch sogenannte Ostermärchen, deren jedes mit rührendem Moral begleitet ist, sammt einem Innhalt, oder Anweisung wie daraus Predigten zu machen.* Augsburg & Innsbruck: Wolff.

Zucker, Wolfgang M. (1967): 'The Clown as the Lord of Disorder', in: *Theology Today* 24, 306–17; repr. in: Hyers (ed.) (1969a), 75–88.

Zuver, Dudley (1933): *Salvation by Laughter. A Study of Religion and the Sense of Humor.* New York & London: Harper & Brothers.

Zweig, Stefan (1937): *Erasmus of Rotterdam.* Garden City: Garden City Publishing Co.

Österley, Hermann, see: Johannes Pauli (1866)

Index of Names

Numbers with a 'n' attached indicates that on that particular page the name only appears in the footnotes.

Abelard, Peter (1079-1142) 12n
Adam of St Victor (d. 1146) 12n, 160, 164, 232n
Addison, Joseph (1672-1719) 204n, 209–11, 213–5
Adelphus, Johann (Müling) (1445-1515/1522) 41n
Adolf, Helen(e) (1895-1998) 43n
Aelian, Claudius (*c.* 175–*c.* 235) 124, 273n
Agobard of Lyon (*c.* 779–840) 143
Albert the Great (*c.* 1193–1280) 142
Alexander of Hales (*c.* 1185–1245) 148, 150
Alt, Heinrich (1811-93) 95n
Amasis (d. 525 BCE) 59
Ambrose (*c.* 339–97) 287
Amman, Kaspar (*c.* 1450–1524) 72, 73n
Anaxagoras (*c.* 500–428 BCE) 124n
Anselm of Canterbury (1033-1109) 147–8
Apuleius (125-170) 162, 271n
Aquinas *see* Thomas
Arbuckle, George A. (b. 1934) 94, 95n
Aristides of Miletus (2nd cent. BCE) 271n
Aristophanes (*c.* 446–*c.* 386 BCE) 184, 278n
Aristotle (384-22 BCE) 60, 84, 124n, 126, 128, 137–41, 143, 144n, 145, 148, 158, 161n, 169n, 182, 188, 204, 257n, 260n, 264n, 268n, 278–9n, 283n, 286–7

Aristoxenus (360-300 BCE) 124n
Arnold, Matthew (1822-88) 229–30
Arsenius (350/354-445) 172n
Augusti, Johann Christian Wilhelm (1771-1841) 95n
Augustine (354-430) 59–60, 112, 160, 183–4, 186, 270n, 292–3

Bach-Nielsen, Carsten (b. 1955) 132n
Backus, Irena (1950-2019) 74n
Bakhtin, Mikhail (1895-1975) 14, 27, 30–2, 96, 98–100, 102n, 104–5, 118
Balthasar, Hans Urs von (1905-88) 15n
Balzaretti, Claudio (b. 1956) 163n, 167n
Barish, Jonas (1922-98) 112–4, 267n
Barnstone, Willis (b. 1927) 171n
Basil of Caesarea (330-79) 16n, 130–1, 132n
Bauer, Gerhard (b. 1929) 302n
Baumgartner, Antoine Jean (1859-1938) 226n
Bebel, Heinrich (1472-1518) 36, 39–43, 48, 49n, 79, 119
Bednarz, Terri (/Teresa) (b. 1962) 42n, 109n, 204n, 224n
Beet, William Ernest (1869-1954) 226n
Beil, Johann Gabriel (fl. 1746) 78n
Beleth, Johannes (fl. 1135-82) 81
Benedict of Aniane (*c.* 750–821) 187–8

Benedict of Nursia [/Benedict's Rule] (*c.* 480–547) 29n, 133n, 137, 188, 275n, 293n
Bennet, Henry (fl. 1561) 75–6
Benz, Ernst (1907-78) 15n
Bergmann, Lorenz (1875-1966) 35n, 262n
Bergson, Henri (1859-1941) 98n, 190n
Bernard of Clairvaux (1090-1153) 12n, 45n, 123
Bibliander, Theodor (1504/ 09-64) 74
Biessenecker, Stefan (b. 1978) 43n
Billman [Weiher], Carol (fl. 1975-80) 43n
Bismarck, Otto von (1815-98) 89n
Blaicher, Günther (b. 1938) 43n, 219n
Blake, William (1757-1827) 230
Bloch, Ernst (1885-1977) 194
Bloch, Peter (1935-2008) 229n
Boccaccio, Giovanni (1313-75) 36n, 45–6
Boëthius, Anicius Manlius Severinus (*c.* 480–524/525) 139n
Bolte, Johannes (fl. 1858-1937) 51n
Bond, Albert Richmond (1874-1944) 226n
Borge, Victor (1909-2000) 52
Bowen, Barbara Cherry (1937-2019) 39–41n, 119
Bracciolini, Gian Francesco Poggio (1380-1459) 36n, 39n, 254n, 280, 281n
Braet, Herman (b. 1939) 43n
Brant, Sebastian (1457-1521) 49n, 301n
Braun, Heinrich Suso (1904-1977) 19n
Bremmer, Jan N.(b. 1944) 43n, 193n, 203n, 248n

Brockett, Oscar Gross (1923-2010) 27n, 250n
Bröker, Günther (fl. 1959-79) 170n
Buckley, George Wright (b. 1850) 226n
Budge, Ernest Alfred Wallis (1857-1934) 34n
Bugenhagen, Johannes (1485-1558) 50, 53n, 69n, 70–2, 76
Bullard, John Moore (1932-2019) 232n
Bunyan, John (1628-88) 116–7
Burke, Peter (b. 1937) 52n, 90–2
Burningham, Bruce R. (b. 1964) 250n
Burton, Robert (1577-1640) 207n
Busch, Moritz (1821-99) 52n, 95n, 225

Caesarius von Heisterbach (d. *c.* 1240) 37n
Campenhausen, Hans von (1903-89) 19n, 217–20n
Capella, Martianus (fl. *c.* 410–20) 139n
Capeller, Isaac (fl. 1624) 78n
Capito, Wolfgang (1478-1541) 11, 40, 41n, 54, 64, 73–4, 75–76n, 106, 109, 111, 113, 164, 167, 247–8, 249n, 251n, 252–3, 255n, 256, 263n, 264, 269, 287–8, 292–3, 302n, 303–5
Carlyle, Thomas (1795-1881) 212n
Carroll, Robert Peter (1941-2000) 219n
Casanowicz, Immanuel Moses (1853-1927) 226n
Cassian, John (360-435) 141n
Cassiodor, Flavius Magnus Aurelius (*c.* 485–c. 585) 139n
Cato, Marcus Portius the Elder (234-149 BCE) 269–70

Cazamian, Louis François (1877-1965) 195n
Celano, Thomas (*c.* 1200–c. 1270) 29n
Chambers, Edmund Kerchever (1866-1954) 27n
Charles I (1600-49) 202n
Chaucer, Geoffrey (*c.* 1343–1400) 36n, 202n, 205n
Chesterfield, Earl of see Philip Dormer Stanhope
Chesterton, Gilbert Keith (1874-1936) 223–5
Chotzner, Joseph (1844-1914) 226, 233
Christian IV (1577-1648) 107n
Christ-von Wedel, Christine (b. 1948) 62n, 64n
Chrysostom, John (349-407) 15, 16n, 44, 59, 109, 110n, 129–30, 143, 170, 184, 189, 274n, 282, 287–91, 293n, 296n
Cicero, Marcus Tullius (106-43 BCE) 140n, 142n, 257n, 269n, 278n, 281n, 283, 286–7
Classen, Albrecht (b. 1956) 43n, 258n
Clement of Alexandria (150-215) 143, 144n, 163, 189
Congreve, William (1670-1729) 213n
Cooper, Anthony Ashley (1671-1713) 206–11, 215
Cossart, Gabriel (1615-74) 66n
Cote, Richard G. (1934-2005) 23, 237n
Cousins, Norman (1915-90) 30n
Cox, Harvey Gallagher (b. 1929) 31
Coxon, Sebastian (b. 1969) 43n, 104n, 195n
Crile, George Washington (1864-1943) 168n, 194

Cruel, Rudolf (1820-1892) 305n
Curtius, Ernst Robert (1886-1956) 43n, 98, 129, 248n
Cyrus the Great (600-530 BCE) 285n

Dacheux, Léon (1835-1903) 302n
Damian, Peter (*c.* 1006–72) 45n
Dante Alighieri (1265-1321) 45–6, 135n, 189
Davies, John Gordon (1919-90) 93n, 108n
Defensor of Ligugé (fl. 7th/8th cent.) 133n
Democritus from Abdera (*c.* 460–c.370 BCE) 273, 287
Demosthenes (384-22 BCE) 286
Demura, Akira (b. 1932) 64n
Dickens, Charles (1812-70) 205n, 215
Diller, Hans-Jürgen (b. 1934) 35n
Dober, Hans Martin (b. 1959) 106n
Dölger, Franz (1891-1968) 156n
Dörffel, Georg Samuel (1643-88) 47n
Dörrer, Anton (1886-1968) 18n
Dostoyevski, Fyodor (1821-81) 15n
Dreher, Bruno (1911-71) 154n
Dreyer, A. (fl. 1923) 96n
Dupréel, Eugène (1879-1967) 200–1n

Eber, Jochen (b. 1958) 19n
Eck, Johann (1486-1543) 62
Eckhart, Meister (*c.* 1260–c. 1328) 153, 154n
Eco, Umberto (1932-2016) 36n, 100, 105
Ephrem the Syrian (*c.* 306–73) 122–4
Erasmus, Desiderius (1466-1536) 33, 50–2, 55, 62, 63n, 64, 80, 84, 121, 125–9, 143, 167, 193,

244n, 249n, 254n, 270n, 272–4n, 279–80, 288n
Euripides (480-06 BCE) 253, 254n, 285
Eybl, Franz M. (b. 1952) 18n

Fedotov, George[/y] Petrovich (1886-1951) 15n
Fehrle, Eugen (1880-1957) 88n, 98n, 104n, 119n, 156n
Ferm, Olle (b. 1947) 43n, 104n, 122n, 143n, 195n, 261n, 272n
Fielding, Henry (1707-54) 205n, 213n
Figueroa-Dorrego, Jorge Juan (b. 1962) 139n, 190n
Flögel, Karl Friedrich (1729-88) 79, 105n
Fluck, Hanns (b. 1908, fl. 1931–4) 40–2n, 48n, 53n, 65–6n, 82n, 96–101, 102n, 103, 107, 157, 261n
Fogtmann, Laurids (1748-1821) 108n, 110n
Francis of Assisi (1182-1230) 29n
Frazer, James George (1854-1941) 14n
Freud, Sigmund (1856-1939) 118, 185
Freudenberg, Matthias (b. 1962) 106n
Friis, Helmuth (1944-94) 235–6
Froben, Johann (c. 1460–1527) 11, 73, 279n, 288n
Frye, (Herman) Northrop (1912-91) 230
Fudge, Thomas A. (b. 1962) 62n
Füssli, Johann Konrad (1704-75) 78–9

Gad, Emma (1852-1921) 128–9
Gast, Johannes (d. 1552) 38n

Gaster, Theodor Herzl (1906-92) 125n
Gay, John (1685-1732) 213n
Geiler, Johann(es) from Kaysersberg (1445-1510) 49, 54, 64, 82n, 254n, 301–2n
Geisenhof, Georg (fl. 1900-08) 70–1n
Gejerus, Martin (1618-87) 238–9, 243
Geminianus Monacensis (1606-72) 116
Gerhoh of Reichersberg (1093-1169) 267n
Gesner, Salomon (1559-1605) 71n
Geus, Johannes (c. 1370–1440) 54–5, 149
Ghose, Indira (b. 1962) 122n
Giberti, Giovanni Matteo (1495-1543) 67n
Gilhus, Ingvild Sælid (b. 1951) 18n, 94n, 164n, 165, 172n, 195–7, 269n
Gilman, Sander L. (b. 1944) 28n
Ginzberg, Louis (1873-1953) 303n
Gladstone, William (1808-98) 202n
Glover, TerrotReaveley (1869-1943) 227, 229n
Goldsmith, Oliver (1728-74) 213–4
Granger, Thomas (1578-1627) 135n
Grant, Frederick Clifton (1891-1974) 18n
Grebe, Anja (b. 1968) 15n, 43n
Gregory of Nazianzus (c. 329–389/90) 279–80, 290–1, 300–1
Gregory the Great (c. 540–604) 131, 134–6, 146, 203, 242, 268n
Gritsch, Eric Walter (1931-2012) 106n
Grosart, Alexander Balloch (1827-99) 226
Grün, Anselm (b. 1945) 104n

Grünewald, Matthias (*c.* 1475–c. 1528) 176
Grynäus, Simon (1493-1541) 74
Grønbech, Vilhelm Peter (1873-1948) 269n
Guerike, Heinrich Ernst Ferdinand (1803-78) 89–90
Gugitz, Gustav (1874-1964) 104n, 119n
Gutwirth, Marcel Marc (b. 1923) 32–3, 191
Gvozdeva, Katja (b. 1965) 43n
Götzenberger, Franz Borgia (1709-53) 118–9
Götzinger, Ernst (1837-96) 50n

Hadorn, Wilhelm (1869-1929) 18n, 63n
Haebler, Hans Carl von (1901-78) 104n
Hagenbach, Karl Rudolf (1801-74) 95n
Halliwell, Stephen (b. 1953) 104n, 124n, 139, 140n, 144n, 161–2n, 238–9, 243, 284n
Halsall, Guy (b. 1964) 43n
Hammerich, Paul (1927-92) 201, 203
Hantelmann, Julius (1633-80) 78n
Harris, Max (b. 1949) 32, 80–2, 260–1n
Harrison, William Pope (1830-95) 225n
Haug, Walter (1927-2008) 43n, 104n, 158n
Hauptmann, Peter (1928-2016) 15n
Hazard, Marshall Custiss (1839-1929) 226n
Heberlin, Rudolph Wilhelm (fl. 1691) 78n
Heemskerck, Maerten van (1498-1574) 180n

Heffening, Willi (1894-1944) 122n
Heflin, James Larohn (1943-2023) 225–6n
Heinz-Mohr, Gerd (1913-89) 104n
Helbig, Johann Lorenz (1662-1721) 80n
Heltzel, Virgil Barney (1896-1976) 127n
Hennecke, Edgar Ludwig Theodor (1865-1951) 34n
Heraclides Ponticus (*c.* 390–c. 310 BCE) 124
Heraclitus (*c.* 535–c. 475 BCE) 273n
Herzog, Johann Jacob (1805-82) 90
Hess, Salomon (1763-1837) 72n
Hesychius of Alexandria (probably 5th cent. CE) 283
Hierocles (probably after 248 CE) 281n
Hilary of Poitiers (*c.* 310–c. 367) 184
Hildebrand, Joachim (1623-91) 78n
Hildegard of Bingen (1098-1179) 151–3, 272n
Hinkmar (800/10-882) 45–6n, 65n, 269n
Hobbes, Thomas (1588-1679) 191
Hogarth, William (1697-1764) 213n
Holkot, Robert (d. 1349) 37n
Holland, Hyacinth (1827-1918) 95n, 119n
Holland, Norman Norwood (1927-2017) 190n
Homborg, Johann Joachim (fl. 1683) 78n
Homer (8th cent. BCE) 125n, 144n, 162–3, 238–9, 277n, 284, 285n
Horace, Quintus Flaccus (65 BCE-8 CE) 274n
Horst, Pieter Willem van der (b. 1946) 140n

Hospinian, Rudolph (1547-1626) 71, 76–7, 86–7, 96, 99n, 156, 258–9n, 262n, 302n
How, Frederick Douglas (1853-1936) 195n, 225n
Hugh of St Victor (*c.* 1096–1141) 124
Hurtigkarl, Frederik Theodor (1763-1829) 108n, 110n
Hussey, L.M. (fl. 1927-28) 229n, 234n
Hvidberg, Flemming Friis (1897-1959) 240n
Hyers, Merritt Conrad (1933-2013) 23, 160, 190
Høffding, Harald (1843-1931) 206n, 212–3n, 215n

Iamblichus (*c.* 245–*c.* 325) 161n
Innichenhöferus, Henrich (b. 1602, fl. 1623–42) 172n
Isidore of Seville (*c.* 560–636) 125n, 272n

Jacobelli, Maria Caterina (b. 1928) 41, 42n, 45n, 65n, 100, 102n, 103, 104n, 107, 159–60, 167, 250n, 269n, 301n
Jacobi, Johann Friedrich (1712-91) 223
Jacobsen, Jacob Peter (1869-1918) 28n
Jäkel, Ernst Th. (fl. 1840.) 95n
Jäkel, Siegfried (1929-2004) 43n
Jameson, John Gordon (fl. 1926-51) 226n
Jerome (347-420) 123n, 287, 288n, 291–2, 297–8
Johnson, Samuel (1709-84) 202n
Jonson, Ben (1572-1637) 202, 203n
Joubert, Laurent (1529-82) 30n, 193

Julian of Norwich (1342-1416) 151, 153–4

Kant, Immanuel (1724-1804) 188, 211
Karlstadt, Andreas (1486-1541) 62, 69n
Kazantzakis, Nikos (1883-1957) 180
Kemper, Tobias A. (b. 1973) 16n, 121, 135n, 144n, 189
Kerr, Walter (1913-96) 184–5
Kesselring, Ernst Friedrich (1685-1763) 78n, 156
Kessler, Johannes (*c.* 1502–74) 49, 50n, 69, 299n
Kierkegaard, Søren Aabye (1813-55) 19n, 192, 201, 211–2n
Kingo, Thomas (1634-1703) 132n
Knapp, Shepherd (1873-1946) 226
Koch, Hal (1904-63) 221
Kolderup-Rosenvinge, Janus Lauritz Andreas (1792-1850) 110n
Kolve, Verdel Amos (1934-2022) 35n
Kranz, Gisbert (1921-2009) 145n, 174, 175n, 189–90n
Krause, Michael Ehrenfried (1689-1761) 78n
Kremer, Karl Richard (b. 1927) 43n, 160n
Krug, Ludwig (*c.* 1488–1532) 180n
Kuhn, Christian (b. 1978) 43n
Kuhn, Thomas (1922-96) 194
Kuhr, Olaf (b. 1962) 63–4n
Kundera, Milan (1929-2023) 177–8
Kuschel, Karl-Josef (b. 1948) 21–2n, 104n, 105, 234, 235n
Köhler, Wiebke (b. 1963) 19n

Labbé, Philippe (1607-67) 66n
Laertius, Diogenes (fl. in the 3rd cent. CE) 124n, 278n

Lakin-Galiñanes, Christina (b. 1951) 139n, 190n
Lamb, Charles (1775-1834) 205n
Lappenberg, Johann Martin (1794-1865) 49n, 51n
Larsen, Ejvind (b. 1936) 176
Latré, Guido (b. 1954) 43n
Latte, Kurt (1891-1964) 283n
Laud, William (1573-1645) 202n
Lauer, Werner (fl. 1972-97) 218n, 221-2n
Le Goff, Jacques (1924-2014) 43n, 104n, 132-3n, 137, 143-4, 147n, 222
Lehmann, Paul (1884-1964) 36n
Lejay, Paul (1861-1920) 141n
Lentulus 174
Leodiensis, Arnoldus (d. *c.* 1309) 37n
Leonardo da Vinci (1452-1519) 189
Lichtenberg, Georg Christoph (1742-99) 79, 80n, 96n
Lienhard, Fritz (b. 1964) 45n
Lienhard, Marc (b. 1935) 245n
Lindgren, Lauri Bernhard (b. 1933) 43n
Linsenmayer, Anton (1850-1921) 35n, 95n
Lippert, Julius (1839-1909) 95n
Lodge, David (b. 1935) 177n
Logan, John Daniel (1869-1929) 226n
Løgstrup, Knud Ejler (1905-81) 236, 237n
Lohmeier, Georg (1926-2015) 104n
Lot-Borodine, Myrrha (1882-1954) 172n
Louis IX, the Holy (1220-74) 137
Lowth, Robert (1710-87) 271n
Luck, Georg (1926-2013) 19n, 158n, 162n

Lühl, Max (fl. 2019) 33n, 100n, 158n, 198n
Luscinius, Otmar (Nachtigall) (1487-1536) 41n
Luther, Martin (1483-1546) 17, 33, 48, 50, 51n, 62-3, 64n, 66, 69, 71n, 74-5, 82-5, 86-7n, 92, 93n, 106, 107n, 109, 113, 130, 178n, 245n, 248n, 255n, 271n, 305n
Lutz, Markus (1772-1835) 95n, 261n
Lynch, David (b. 1946) 238
Lys, Daniel (1924-2014) 233n

Macrobius, Ambrosius Aurelius Theodosius (4-5th cent. CE) 287
Maillard, Olivier (fl. *c.* 1500) 52n
Manuel, Frank Edward (1910-2009) 211n
Martial, Marcus Valerius (*c.* 40-*c.* 104) 272n
Martin, Robert Bernard (1918-99) 208n
Mathesius, Johann (1504-65) 34, 50-2, 53n, 55, 69, 70n, 71-2, 76, 79-80, 82-4, 89n, 118, 232n
Maximillian III (1727-77) 65n
Mayhew, Henry (1812-87) 261n
McGinness, Frederick J. (b. 1944) 51n
Meier, Ernst Julius (1828-97) 225
Melanchthon, Philipp (1497-1560) 62-3, 69n, 74
Melander, Otto (1571-1640) 38n
Menander (342-291 BCE) 285-6
Mercer, John Edward (1857-1922) 226
Metz, Detlef (b. 1964) 35n
Meyer, Marvin W. (1948-2012) 170n
Michelangelo Buonarroti (1475-1564) 179

Migne, Jacques-Paul (1800-1875) 12, 125n, 131n, 133n, 271n, 274n, 282n, 288n, 301n
Milton, John (1608-75) 186–7, 190, 202n, 267n
Mithridates (135-63 BCE) 258n
Modesto, Christine (fl. 1992) 36n
Molière, Jean-Baptiste (1622-73) 39
Möllendorff, Peter von (b. 1963) 32
Moltmann, Jürgen (1926-2024) 105, 106n
Montifontanus, Lucianus (1630-1716) 80n
Morgan, Conwy Lloyd (1852-1936) 19n
Morison, David Niven (1870-1942) 226n
Morreall, John (b. 1947) 190n
Moser, Dietz-Rüdiger (1939-2010) 31n
Moser-Rath, Elfriede (1926-93) 38–9, 41, 59, 65–6n, 77, 79–80n, 82n, 100, 101–2n, 109, 116–7n, 249n
Murray, James Ross (fl. 1886-1908) 227, 229n, 236n
Myconius, Oswald (1488-1552) 74

Neale, Robert Edward (b. 1929) 237
Nettelbladt, Christian (1696-1775) 78n
Nickel, Johanna (1916-84) 48n, 61n, 77–8, 87
Nicoll, Allardyce (1894-1976) 27n, 35–6n
Nicolson, Harold George (1886-1968) 202n, 206n
Niebuhr, Reinhold (1892-1971) 222n
Niedermeier, Hans (fl. 1963-70) 74n
Nielsen, Erik Aksel (b. 1941) 132n
Nietzsche, Friedrich (1844-1900) 185

O'Connell, Michael (b. 1943) 12n, 100n, 104n
Oden, Thomas C. (1931-2016) 274n
Oecolampadius, Johannes (1482-1531) 11–2, 17, 18n, 21, 23, 30n, 33–6, 38–44, 46n, 48–9, 51, 53–5, 62–4, 66, 69–74, 75n, 76–80, 82n, 85, 89–90, 93, 96, 98, 99n, 102, 105–6, 109, 110n, 111, 113, 117, 120–1, 125, 131n, 143, 149, 156, 160, 164, 167, 176, 179, 193, 247–295, 229–305n: *passim*
Ogilvy, Jack David Angus (1903-93) 249n
Otther, Jacob (1485-1547) 302n
Otto, Rudolf (1869-1937) 196
Overbeck, Franz (1837-1905) 225n
Ovid, PubliusNaso(43 BCE-17 CE) 265n

Pachomius (*c.* 290–345) 123–4
Pailin, David Arthur (1936-2021) 211n
Palmer, Jerry (b. 1940) 41n
Paul, the Apostle (*c.* 5 CE–c. 64 CE) 15n, 66, 83–4, 109, 116, 121n, 141, 160, 172–3n, 176n, 183, 204, 207, 217–8, 248n, 260–1n, 264n, 273n, 279n, 281, 288–9
Paul, Jean [Johann Paul Friedrich Richter] (1763-1825) 205, 212n
Pauli, Johannes (*c.* 1455–1530/33) 36–7, 39–40, 42–4, 47, 49–51, 113n, 183, 262n
Paulsen, Friedrich (1846-1908) 226n
Pelagius (fl. *c.* 390–418) 297–9n
Perkins, William (1558-1602) 130n
Petrarch, Francesco (1304-74) 40n
Petronius (27-66) 271n
Petrus Alphonsi (d. *c.* 1110) 37n
Pfister, Manfred (b. 1943) 43n, 135n

Philagrios (probably after 248
    CE) 281n
Philip of Hesse (1504-67) 63
Philo of Alexandria (*c.* 10 BCE–c.
    45 CE) 121–2n
Plato (*c.* 427–348 BCE) 124, 125n,
    127, 144n, 161n, 166, 190n,
    284, 287n
Plessner, Helmuth (1892-
    1985) 122n
Pliny the Elder (23-79) 158
Pliny the Younger (60-*c.* 113) 139
Plutarch (46-120) 162, 286n, 295
Pockh, Johann Baptist Caspar
    (*c.* 1659–1709) 59
Poggio *see* Bracciolini
Poimen (340-450) 172n
Polanus, Amandus (1561-1610) 76
Poole, Matthew (1624-79) 238–9n
Poole, William Frederick (1821-
    94) 224, 226
Pope Benedict XVI (1927-
    2022) 104n
Pope Clement X (1590-1676) 65n
Pope Innocent III (1160/
    61-1216) 81
Pope Paul VI (1897-1978) 43n
Pope Pius V (1504-72) 67
Pope, Alexander (1688-1744)
    213n
Prior, Matthew (1664-1721) 213n
Propp, Vladimir Yakovlevich (1895-
    1970) 11n, 14, 98, 100, 102n,
    156n, 157–9, 164–5, 238n
Prütting, Lenz (b. 1940) 30n, 53n,
    65n, 100n, 103, 104n, 123n, 145–
    51, 154–5, 165–8, 190–1, 198n
Pythagoras (*c.* 580–c. 500 BCE)
    59, 278n

Quintilian, Marcus Fabius (*c.* 35–
    c.98) 140n, 269, 278n, 280–1n

Rabelais, François (1494-1553) 98–9
Ratzinger, Joseph *see* Pope
    Benedict XVI
Rauscher, Wolfgang
    (1641-1709) 117
Rehtmeyer, Philipp Julius (1678-
    1742) 52–3n
Reid, John (fl. 1906-13) 19n
Reinach, Salomon (1858-1932) 14,
    41, 95–6, 98n, 99–100, 102n, 120,
    159n, 226n
Renan, Ernest (1823-92) 228, 229n
Rensburg, Lee van (fl. 1991) 232n
Resnick, Irven Michael (b. 1952)
    43n, 125n, 188n, 268n
Reuchlin, Johannes (1455-1522) 72,
    73n, 270n
Richert, Friedemann (b. 1959) 43n,
    104n, 234n
Riising, Anne (1926-2017) 58n, 81,
    111n, 154
Rissanen, Veli-Matti (b. 1969) 43n
Röcke, Werner (1944-2022) 43n,
    46n, 103–4n, 111–4, 272n
Roodenburg, Herman (b. 1951)
    43n, 193n, 203n, 248n
Rosegger, Peter (1843-1918) 79, 80n
Rossellino, Antonio (1427-79) 179

Sachs, Hans (1494-1576) 41n, 272n
Sanders, Barry (b. 1938) 141n
Santeuil, Jean de (1630-97) 274n
Savonarola, Girolamo (1452-
    98) 63n
Saward, John (b. 1947) 15n
Schaller, Johannes Damascenus
    (1620-69) 145n
Schäufele, Wolf-Friedrich (b.
    1967) 63n
Scherer, Georg (1540-1605) 67–8
Schindler, Norbert (b. 1950) 52n,
    104n

Schlegel, Friedrich (1772-1829) 199
Schleiermacher, Friedrich (1768-1834) 60n
Schmidt, Johann Andreas (1652-1726) 78n
Schmidt, Johannes Petrus (1708-90) 78n, 99
Schmidt, Tobias (d. 1659) 80n
Schmidt-Clausing, Fritz (1902-84) 106
Schmidt-Hidding, Wolfgang (1903-67) 197-8n, 201, 203n, 204-5, 210, 217, 219-20
Schmitz, Heinz-Günter (1938-2021) 44-5n, 86n, 104n, 136n, 145, 146n
Schneemelcher, Wilhelm (1914-2003) 34n
Schörle, Eckart (b. 1971) 104n, 208n
Schousboe, Julius (1886-1960) 212n
Schramm, Jonas Conrad (1675-1739) 78n
Schreiner, Klaus (1931-2015) 172n
Schröder, Franz Rolf (1893-1979) 156
Schroeter, Harald (b. 1961) 18-9n
Schweitzer, Albert (1875-1965) 228, 233
Screech, Michael Andrew (1926-2018) 104n, 239n, 241, 242-4n
Secher, Vilhelm Adolf (1851-1918) 107n
Seckendorff, Ludwig von (1626-92) 47n
Seneca, Lucius Annaeus(4 BCE-65 CE) 142n, 284
Sennett, Richard (b. 1943) 20n
Shaftesbury, Earl of *see* Anthony Ashley Cooper
Shakespeare, William (1564-1616) 15n, 39, 126, 184, 199, 202, 205n, 215-6n

Shelley, Percy Busshe (1792-1822) 202n
Shutter, Marion Daniel (1853-1936) 224-6, 229, 231, 232n, 234
Simon, Richard Keller (1945-2005) 168n, 192-3
Smith, William Austin (1872-1922) 226
Smollett, Tobias (1721-71) 213n
Snorri Sturluson (1179-1241) 156-7n
Socrates (469-399 BCE) 59, 124n, 207, 221, 284
Söderblom, Nathan (1866-1931) 106
Solger, Karl Wilhelm Ferdinand (1780-1819) 212n
Staehelin, Ernst (1889-1980) 63-4n, 66n, 72-3, 74-5n, 76, 110n, 131n, 247n, 252-3n, 257n, 272n, 280n
Stanhope, Philip Dormer (1694-1773) 127-30, 182
Starcke, Tobias (fl. 1710) 78n
Staubach, Nikolaus (b. 1946) 43n
Steele, Richard (1672-1729) 213n, 216
Steger, Friedrich (1811-94) 96n
Steidle, Basilius (1903-82) 122n, 172n
Steiger, Lothar (b. 1935) 19n
Steinberg, Leo (1920-2011) 179-84, 186n, 187
Steiner, George (1926-2020) 176, 184
Sterne, Laurence (1713-68) 205n, 213n
Strauss, David Friedrich (1808-74) 228
Strobl, Andreas(1642-1706) 58-9, 61, 64, 80n, 91n, 113
Stumpfl, Robert (1904-37) 104n, 119n

Suchier, Walther (1878-1963) 36n
Suchomski, Joachim (fl. 1975-79) 45–6n, 122n, 139–40n, 142n, 188–9, 268n
Suter, Adrian (b. 1970) 104n
Svanberg, Jan Viktor (b. 1935) 135n
Swift, Jonathan (1667-1745) 213–4, 216

Taine, Hippolyte (1828-93) 212–3n
Tatlock, John Strong Perry (1876-1948) 43n, 195n
Tentzel, Gottfried (1672-1725) 78n
Terence, PubliusAfer (c. 190–c. 60 BCE) 126, 184, 265n
Tertullian, Quintus SeptimiusFlorens (160-220) 112, 140, 143, 241, 243, 251n, 259–60n, 275n
Teuber, Bernard (b. 1954) 31n
Thackeray, William Makepeace (1811-63) 211–2n, 213–6
Thiede, Werner (b. 1955) 19n, 21n, 104n, 105, 106n
Thielicke, Helmut (1908-86) 104n, 215n
Thomas Aquinas (1225-74) 138, 140–2, 145, 148, 150, 155, 186, 241–3, 280n
Thomas, Keith Vivian (b. 1933) 33, 94n
Thomasius, Jacob (1622-84) 78n
Thomsen, Ole (b. 1946) 199–200, 201n
Thorsen, Jens Jørgen (1932-2000) 180
Thorstensen, Erik (b. 1972) 32n
Thumm, Theodor (1586-1630) 78n
Timonen, Asko (b. 1957) 43n
Tiro, Marcus Tullius (103-4 BCE) 283n
Trokhimenko, Olga (b. 1975) 43n, 153n

Tubach, Frederic C. (b. 1930) 261n
Twain, Mark (1835-1910) 205n

Usener, Hermann (1834-1905) 159n

Valentinus (c. 100-c. 180) 177
Vasey, George (1822-93) 125
Vedder, Henry Clay (1853-1935) 229n
Verbeke, Werner (b. 1944) 43n
Vergil, PubliusMaro (70-19 BCE) 158, 247n, 266n, 277n
Vetry, Jacques de (d. 1240) 37n
Vinçon, Herbert (1938-2012) 104n
Voltaire (François-Marie Arouet) (1694-1778) 231

Walther, Hans (1884-1971) 274n, 278n
Warning, Rainer (1936-2024) 100, 102n
Weber, Heinrich (1834-98) 18n, 96
Weber, Johann Adam (1611-86) 274n
Wegner, Gottfried (1644-1709) 78n
Wehrli, Max (1909-98) 35n, 104n, 153n
Weller, Hieronymus (1499-1572) 86n
Wendland, Volker (1939-2019) 13n, 15n, 35n, 38n, 41, 47–9n, 51n, 53n, 55, 56n, 58–9, 60n, 61, 66n, 70–1n, 77, 78n, 82n, 85, 87, 88n, 89, 95n, 97, 100, 101–2n, 113–4, 115n, 119n, 156, 258n, 262n
Wenzeslaus, Clemens (1739-1812) 60n
Werner, Paul (fl. 1979-2005) 104n
Wernsdorf, Johann Christian (1723-93) 78n
Wheatley, Willis (fl. 1973) 178n
White, Beatrice (1902-1986) 43n

Widmann, Abraham (d. 1642) 47n, 272n
Wildvogel, Christian (1644-1728) 78n
Wilhelm II (Friedrich Wilhelm Viktor Albert) (1859-1941) 89n
Wilhelm of Conches (*c.* 1080/1090– after 1154) 145–46, 147n, 148, 149n, 150
Wilhelmy, Winfried (b. 1962) 41n, 43n, 135n
Wimpfeling, Jakob (1450-1528) 48
Winkler, Klaus (1934-2000) 19n
Wolf, Herbert (1930-2017) 37n, 39n, 82n, 104n, 116n
Wolff, Stefanie (fl. 2009) 104n, 233n
Wordsworth, William Arthur (fl. 1925) 226

Wünkhaus, Oscar W. (fl. 1909) 226n
Wycliffe, John (1328-84) 267n

Xenophon (*c.* 425–354 BCE) 284–5

Young, Karl (1879-1943) 27n

Zeller, Johann Jacob (fl. 1767-73) 60–1, 64
Zucker, Wolfgang Max (1905-83) 32
Zuver, Dudley (fl. 1933-59) 227
Zweig, Stefan (1881-1943) 33
Zwingli, Ulrich (1484-1531) 62–3, 64n, 74, 106

Österley, Hermann (1834-91) 49n, 51n

Index of Bible Texts

Numbers with a 'n' attached indicates that on that particular page the biblical reference only appears in the footnotes.

Genesis
Gen 2:6: 147n
– **2:7**: 147n
– **9:25**: 16n
– **12:10 ff.**: 85n
– **17:17**: 160
– **18:12**: 160
– **18:12-15**: 16n
– **21:6**: 132n, 161, 268, 303n
– **21:9**: 159, 161
– **22:13**: 12n
– **25:25**: 240n
– **27:22**: 274
– **27:38**: 172n
– **28:12-15**: 185
– **34:1**: 303

Exodus
Ex 3:1 ff.: 276
– **13:9**: 295n
– **19:10 f.**: 276
– **27:20**: 299
– **34:21**: 295

Leviticus
Lev 2:11: 299

Numbers
Num 13: 227
– **13:23 ff.**: 299
– **20:11-2**: 273n

Deuteronomy
Dt 13:13: 266n
– **16:21**: 299

– **23:13-4**: 176
– **32:8**: 239

Judges
Jg 9:8-15: 117
– **16:25**: 241

1 Samuel
1 Sam 19:13 ff.: 85n

2 Samuel
2 Sam 6:20: 268
– **12:7**: 114
– **12:22**: 275

1 Kings
1 Kings 18:27: 176, 210

2 Kings
2 Kings 1:10: 296
– **2:23**: 241
– **6:19**: 85n
– **20:1 ff.**: 275

Job
Job 1:6: 239n
– **8:20-2**: 240
– **8:21**: 132n, 134
– **9:23**: 161, 239
– **12:4**: 240
– **29:24**: 240
– **39:5-7**: 241
– **39:13**: 241
– **39:17-18**: 241
– **40:25-41:26**: 232n

– **41:5**: 232n

Psalms
Ps 2: 239, 244, 245n
– **2:2**: 243
– **2:4**: 153, 154n, 161, 187, 243n
– **6:7**: 275
– **30:11**: 303
– **32:3**: 172n
– **44:23-4**: 185
– **66**: 242
– **66:1-3**: 243
– **69:28**: 295
– **72:6**: 304n
– **81**: 242
– **82**: 239n
– **89:16**: 131n
– **95**: 242
– **118:24**: 120–1
– **119:85**: 54n
– **126:1-3**: 242
– **126:6**: 293
– **140:12**: 133n

Proverbs
Prov 1:26: 239
– **10:19**: 133n
– **10:23**: 133n
– **14:6**: 133n
– **14:13**: 133n
– **15:13**: 132–3n
– **15:30**: 133n
– **17:22**: 59, 133n
– **19:29**: 133n
– **31:25**: 242

Ecclesiastes
Eccles 1: 294
– **2:2**: 132–3n
– **3:4**: 59, 132, 166
– **7:6**: 133n, 215, 293n
– **7:16**: 264
– **9:17**: 291

Isaiah
Isa 5:7: 270
– **5:22**: 269n
– **6:9-10**: 231
– **20:2**: 294
– **38:1 ff.**: 275
– **40:3**: 296
– **44:12-20**: 300
– **44:23**: 242
– **45:1**: 285n
– **49:13**: 153, 242
– **53:3**: 172n

Jeremiah
Jer 5:30 f.: 292
– **8:22**: 281
– **15:17**: 240
– **19:1 ff.**: 294
– **20:7**: 240
– **41:6**: 172n

Lamentations
Lam 5:14: 296

Ezekiel
Ezek 2:10: 294
– **8:8**: 294
– **12:5 ff.**: 294

Hosea
Hos 4:15: 270n
– **10:5**: 270
– **12:1**: 299
– **12:10**: 116n
– **12:12**: 270

Jonah
Jon 3:5 ff.: 275

Zechariah
Zech 11:15: 294

Tobit

Index of Bible Texts

Tob 6:2: 301
– **11:4**: 301

Sirach
Sir 1:13: 134
– **21:20**: 133n, 276n
– **21:23**: 133n, 276n
– **21:26**: 133n
– **32:8**: 276n
– **48:1**: 296

Matthew
Mt 3:1-4: 296
– **3:10.12**: 296
– **5:5**: 133n
– **5:11**: 244n
– **5:39**: 296
– **7:3-6**: 252
– **7:5**: 273
– **8:23-7**: 185
– **9:10ff.**: 235n
– **9:14 ff.**: 235n
– **9:24**: 244
– **11:7**: 296
– **11:11-15**: 296
– **11:15**: 231
– **11:19**: 175
– **11:28**: 221n
– **11:28-30**: 235
– **12:30**: 85, 171
– **12:36**: 85, 273
– **12:41**: 275
– **13:14-5**: 231
– **14:23**: 176
– **15:20**: 252
– **20:17**: 244
– **20:19**: 245, 296
– **23:23**: 295
– **24:31**: 296
– **26:40**: 185
– **26:41**: 185
– **26:52**: 62n
– **26:74**: 272n
– **26:75**: 172n
– **27:19**: 185
– **27:29.31.41.44**: 244

Mark
Mk 1:3: 296
– **3:17**: 281
– **9:40**: 85, 171
– **10:34**: 245
– **16:1**: 36, 299
– **16:14**: 299

Luke
Lk 1:41.44: 181
– **1:52**: 32
– **3:19**: 296
– **5:33 ff.**: 235n
– **6:21**: 43, 132, 133n, 173, 182, 234, 244
– **6:23**: 236n
– **6:25**: 132, 133n, 144n, 288, 293n, 244
– **7:32**: 142, 293
– **7:32 ff.**: 236n
– **10:20**: 236n
– **10:21**: 173
– **15:16**: 300
– **15:23 ff.**: 236n
– **15:25 ff.**: 294
– **16:14**: 244
– **16:19-31**: 242n
– **18:1**: 92n
– **18:33**: 245
– **19:40**: 236n
– **19:41**: 15n, 172, 296n
– **19:42**: 296
– **21:36**: 92
– **24:11**: 271n
– **24:15**: 115, 299
– **24:18**: 299
– **24:41-3**: 184

John
Jn 2:1-10: 175
– **3:10**: 222
– **4:34**: 222n
– **8:44**: 222n

- **8:46**: 222n
- **11:35**: 15n, 172, 296n
- **12:23-4**: 164
- **12:23-33**: 245
- **15:11**: 173
- **16:16**: 173
- **16:20**: 134n, 173
- **16:20.22**: 134
- **16:23**: 134n
- **17:13**: 173
- **19:17**: 296
- **20:3-10**: 36

Acts
Acts 2:13: 244n
- **17:32**: 244n
- **20:9**: 109, 281
- **20:19**: 172n
- **24:4**: 264n

Romans
Rom 4: 160
- **5:12 f.**: 279n
- **7:5**: 292n
- **7:14-25**: 183
- **8:3**: 169
- **15:3**: 244
- **16:18**: 297

1 Corinthians
1 Cor 1:18 ff.: 218
- **1:18-31**: 15n
- **3:2**: 300
- **5:8**: 299
- **7:29-31**: 217
- **11:22**: 277

2 Corinthians
2 Cor 5:16: 173
- **6:15**: 266n
- **10:1**: 264n
- **11:23**: 281
- **13:11**: 133n

Galatians
Gal 1:10: 278
- **4:3.9**: 283
- **4:16**: 298

Ephesians
Eph 5:4: 248, 260, 273

1 Thessalonians
1 Thess 4:16: 281, 294, 296
- **5:17**: 92

1 Timothy
1 Tim 4:7: 66, 116, 271n

2 Timothy
2 Tim 4:3: 54n
- **4:4**: 116

Titus
Tit 1:12: 270
- **2:7**: 50n

Hebrews
Heb 4:15: 169–70, 181, 222n
- **5:7**: 172
- **5:12-4**: 300

James
James 4:9: 133n, 244

1 Peter
1 Pet 4:10: 267

2 Peter
2 Pet 1:16: 116

1 John
1 Jn 1:1: 176

Revelation
Rev 14:8-10: 295

A Note on the Author[627]

Benny Grey Schuster (b. 1953) studied theology at the University of Aarhus and Christ Church in Oxford. After graduating in 1982 he first taught philosophy of religion and systematic theology in Aarhus for five years followed by another five years in practical theology. In between he served for four years as a pastor at Granly in Surrey, British Columbia, a congregation belonging to Danish Churches Abroad. From 1997 to his retirement in 2023 he was a lecturer at the Centre for Education and Research under the Evangelical Lutheran Church in Denmark.

As well as the Danish and German editions of this book on Easter Laughter he has published a lengthy theological study of Shakespeare's *Hamlet* (2004) and

---

627   The photo shows the author standing in the pulpit of the church in Weinsberg where Oecolampadius was a preacher 1510-18, and from where he arguably delivered the sermon against Easter Laughter which provoked his colleagues to complain to Capito and thus in the end made him defend himself by writing the lengthy letter condemning the custom. The photo was taken the day after attending Denmark's opening match in nearby Stuttgart at EURO 2024.

edited six other books. Apart from a single article on *Hamlet* in English the rest of his c. 100 publications are all in Danish. Together they reflect his career as a university scholar and teacher, eight articles being about Ludwig Wittgenstein and philosophy of language followed by six articles in the field of practical theology. The years spent teaching a wide variety of courses for pastors' continued education have seen thirteen articles on biblical topics approached from a literary perspective, as well as two more articles on Shakespearean themes. Other articles from the mid-1990s include two on football trying to grasp the miracle of Denmark being champions of Europe in 1992, as well as four introducing the world wide web to pastors, as Schuster was one of the first theologians in Denmark to go online. It is thus only fitting that his interest in modern church architecture and art has not only materialised into a dozen articles printed in journals and books but has also resulted in two *sites* online: www.kirkearkitektur.dk with pictures and texts about all the churches built in Denmark since 1940 (including pictures of a hundred groundbreaking European church buildings) and www.modernekirkekunst.dk, a searchable database of close to 5,000 works of art and liturgical furniture made since 1945 in Danish churches.

Printed by
CPI books GmbH, Leck